Rural
Psychology

Rural Psychology

Edited by

Alan W. Childs

Lafayette College
Easton, Pennsylvania

and

Gary B. Melton

University of Nebraska
Lincoln, Nebraska

Plenum Press • New York and London

Library of Congress Cataloging in Publication Data

Main entry under title:

Rural psychology.

Includes bibliographical references and index.
1. Sociology, Rural. 2. Rural population. 3. Rural conditions—Psychological aspects.
4. Community psychology. 5. Rural mental health services. 6. Social service, Rural. I.
Childs, Alan W. II. Melton, Gary B.
HT421.R83 1982   307.7′2′019   82-22570
ISBN 0-306-41045-1   011 0598

© 1983 Plenum Press, New York
A Division of Plenum Publishing Corporation
233 Spring Street, New York, N.Y. 10013

Printed in the United States of America

Contributors

ALAN W. CHILDS, Department of Psychology, Lafayette College, Easton, Pennsylvania

ANDREW S. DIBNER, Department of Psychology, Boston University, Boston, Massachusetts

J. WILBERT EDGERTON, Department of Psychiatry, University of North Carolina, Chapel Hill, North Carolina

NICKOLAUS R. FEIMER, Department of Psychology, Virginia Polytechnic and State University, Blacksburg, Virginia

E. SCOTT GELLER, Department of Psychology, Virginia Polytechnic and State University, Blacksburg, Virginia

EDWARD E. GOTTS, Appalachia Educational Laboratory, Charleston, West Virginia

SCOTT W. HENGGELER, Department of Psychology, Memphis State University, Memphis, Tennessee

STEVEN R. HEYMAN, Department of Psychology, University of Wyoming, Laramie, Wyoming

MARIDA HOLLOS, Department of Anthropology, Brown University, Providence, Rhode Island

RALPH W. HOOD, Department of Psychology, University of Tennessee at Chattanooga, Chattanooga, Tennessee

CHARLES D. KORTE, Division of University Studies, North Carolina State University, Raleigh, North Carolina

HERBERT M. LEFCOURT, Department of Psychology, University of Waterloo, Waterloo, Ontario

ROD A. MARTIN, Department of Psychology, University of Waterloo, Waterloo, Ontario

GARY B. MELTON, Department of Psychology, University of Nebraska, Lincoln, Nebraska

JOHN D. PHOTIADIS, Department of Sociology and Anthropology, West Virginia University, Morgantown, West Virginia

N. DICKON REPPUCCI, Department of Psychology, University of Virginia, Charlottesville, Virginia

MINDY S. ROSENBERG, Department of Psychology, University of Virginia, Charlottesville, Virginia

JOSEPH J. SIMONI, Department of Sociology and Anthropology, West Virginia University, Morgantown, West Virginia

JON R. UREY, Department of Psychology, Memphis State University, Memphis, Tennessee

WALT WOLFRAM, Department of Communication, University of the District of Columbia, and the Center for Applied Linguistics, Washington, D.C.

Contents

Chapter 3

Jon R. Urey and Scott W. Henggeler

Chapter 4

Marida Hollos

Chapter 5

ISSUES OF LINGUISTIC DEVELOPMENT IN RURAL SUBCULTURES IN THE
Walt Wolfram

Chapter 6

Andrew S. Dibner

Chapter 10

THE QUALITY OF LIFE IN RURAL AND URBAN AMERICA 199
Charles D. Korte

Chapter 11

NEEDS ASSESSMENTS IN RURAL AREAS: ISSUES AND PROBLEMS..... 217
Scott W. Henggeler

Chapter 14

Chapter 15

Chapter 16

COMMUNITY PSYCHOLOGY AND RURAL LEGAL SYSTEMS........... 359
Gary B. Melton

Chapter 17

THE ENERGY CRISIS AND BEHAVIORAL SCIENCE: A CONCEPTUAL
FRAMEWORK FOR LARGE-SCALE INTERVENTION 381
E. Scott Geller

Chapter 18

Gary B. Melton and Alan W. Childs

1

Ruralness as a Psychological Construct

Gary B. Melton

Perhaps conscious of its frontier heritage, this nation has always had a rather romantic, nostalgic view of life in the country. Even when people were migrating away from rural areas in droves, the predominant view was that the quality of life was better in nonmetropolitan areas (see Chapter 10). Life in the country was perceived as more livable; subject to natural rhythms of life rather than the rat race. The rural life was clean and simple. A person was challenged by nature, somehow a fairer challenge than the ravages of the urban, industrial marketplace in which the individual was the pawn of corporate bosses. Getting back to nature was—and often still is—perceived as a means of cleansing and testing oneself. Indeed, juvenile corrections often involved sending delinquent youth to farms in the naive belief that the "streets" were the cause of their misbehavior. Even today wilderness programs seem to be based on an assumption that a sense of one's competence and personal morals is most likely to arise from a personal confrontation with nature. Rural life, it seems, is believed to result in honesty, religiosity, and a strong sense of individualism.

Beyond this positive stereotype, there has also been a view of rural people as naive and unsophisticated, even ignorant. In addition to the "American Gothic" image of rural folks as stoically upright and self-reliant, there has also been the stereotype of "Snuffy Smith" and the "Beverly Hillbillies,"—uncultured, gullible, and prone to resolution of

GARY B. MELTON • Department of Psychology, University of Nebraska, Lincoln, Nebraska 68588.

conflicts through violence rather than verbal means. Moreover, there has been a recognition of the low levels of objective indicators of the quality of life in rural areas, such as personal income, educational opportunities, and availability of health care, social services, and cultural amenities (see Chapters 2 and 10).

Even if there was validity to the romantic view of rural America, the actual attention to rural needs and problems seems to have often been determined by these "objective" factors. People were drawn to urban areas by the promise of jobs and a better standard of living. Whether because of greater perceived economic and political importance or simply the power of numbers, there has been relatively little attention paid by scholars and politicians to rural life. The result is that what we know about the experience of living in a rural area and about patterns of behavior in rural environments is often little more than stereotype or clinical intuition. Where empirically based knowledge of rural psychology has been available, such knowledge has typically been limited to global assessments of rural-urban differences (for example, in IQ; see Chapter 4) without attention to the particular psychological demands of rural environments.

This volume is particularly timely as an initial effort to direct psychologists toward the study of rural life. For example, the recent presidential Commission on Mental Health (President's Commission, 1978) identified rural areas as underserved and a priority for future research and service programs. More generally, the last 15 years or so have seen a "great population turnaround." For the first time in the nation's history, relative population growth has been greater in rural than in urban areas (see Brown & Wardwell, 1980, for a comprehensive review of this phenomenon). Besides perhaps benefiting from a new value on "natural" things, rural areas have assumed a new economic importance, a reflection both of energy needs and of more longstanding trends toward job diversification and development of recreational projects in rural areas. Indeed, there is some evidence that the population turnaround can be explained by classical economic explanations of migration rather than by a stronger cultural value on subjective quality of life (Williams, 1981).

Despite the general timeliness of this volume, however, it is important to note that the ambivalence toward rural communities shows little sign of abating. The new attention to rural areas is likely to be lost in the Reagan Administration's general federal cutbacks. The Mental Health Systems Act, for example, which was the means of implementing the recommendations of the President's Commission on Mental Health, has been effectively gutted by block grants. Moreover, while the *relative* growth of rural areas has in fact been greater than metropolitan areas, in *absolute* terms the longtime trend toward urbanization has not been reversed. As Dillman (1981) has pointed out, the United States actually became a more urban nation in the past decade, population turnaround notwithstanding. Thus, while nonmetropolitan areas experienced almost twice as much relative growth as metropolitan areas (15.4% vs. 9.1%), nonmetropolitan areas actually did not gain nearly as much population as did metropolitan areas (8.4 million vs. 13.6 million). Thus, simply in terms of voting power, rural areas have actually continued to lose influence.

Given these conflicting cultural trends, it seems important to make certain both that what is positive and unique about rural areas is preserved and that, at the same time, rural problems are addressed in ways that are appropriate to the rural ecology. Basic to both of these goals is acquisition of a body of knowledge about life in rural communities that goes beyond supposition. Are there in fact behaviors and experiences which are characteristically rural? It is this broad, beginning question which is addressed throughout this volume. The rest of this chapter will be devoted to the analysis of some potential conceptual frameworks for understanding ruralness.

DEFINITIONS OF RURAL

A basic methodological problem of studying ruralness is establishing the parameters by which "rural" will be defined. Most typically, researchers have adopted one of two strategies, use either of intuitive idiosyncratic definitions or of United States Census standards. In the former instance, the researcher makes no attempt to define rural systematically; rather, an assertion is made that, for example, "this study was conducted in the rural Ozarks" on the basis that there is consensus that a given section of the Ozarks is indeed rural. For some purposes, such intuitive definititions are probably adequate. No one would seriously question that Manhattan is urban or that Lexington, Massachusetts, is suburban or that Cherry County, Nebraska, is mostly rural. When studies examine no more than a few communities, such subjective definitions are probably adequate; after all, the researcher can describe the specific communities studied. On the other hand, subjective definitions, at least when based solely on researcher intuition, are clearly problematic. Although a relatively isolated town of 30,000 might still be labeled as rural by some, to others it would clearly be urban. Similarly, *exurbs* quite distant from a central city and sparsely populated but still well within the influence of the central city would not be included in some concepts of rural.

Definitions of rural relying on objective, quantifiable standards avoid such confusion. Consequently, many researchers have relied on Census Bureau standards for rural (i.e., communities with fewer than 2,500 residents) or nonmetropolitan (i.e., communities not included in Standard Metropolitan Statistical Areas). Even though the Census standards offer clearly defined standards which have guided the collection of large-scale, reliable, easily accessible data, there are also conceptual problems with these standards. Specifically, the Census definitions tend to rely on single variables (i.e., community population) which may ignore other salient dimensions in ruralness (e.g., physical isolation). Flax, Wagenfeld, Ivens, and Weiss (1979) noted

> there are at least three elements that are crucial to the understanding of population dynamics: (1) population structure—for example, age and sex distribution; (2) population composition—for example, a wide range of sociodemographic characteristics including marital status, income, ethnicity, education, occupation, etc.; and (3) population distribution—or the spread and location of population over a given territory. (p. 3)

The Census definitions accordingly tell us only about population density and for the most part ignore other important population parameters.

The metropolitan/nonmetropolitan distinction does represent an effort to take into account the degree to which a community is integrated into an urbanized area. Accordingly, it may be a more sensitive correlate of ruralness than the Census definition of rural *per se*. A Standard Metropolitan Statistical Area (SMSA) is defined as including a county or group of contiguous counties that contains a central city or "twin cities" with a population of at least 50,000. Contiguous counties are included if they meet certain criteria for economic and social integration with the central city. Therefore, an urban city of 49,000 might not also be considered metropolitan under the Census definitions. In fact, in the 1970 Census, 12% of persons living inside SMSAs were considered to be rural, and 43% of residents of areas outside SMSAs were also considered to be urban. Thus, neither definition is fully satisfactory, perhaps because neither is based on a clear conceptual model of what constitutes ruralness.

Although certainly not as convenient for the researcher as Census-type definitions, there may be utility to definitions which are subjective but quantifiable. For example, rather than relying solely on the researcher's intuition, surveys might be conducted concerning whether a particular community is rural or, perhaps more sensitively, where the community fits on a Likert-type "urbanness–ruralness" dimension. Besides potentially providing a more powerful measure than unidimensional population–density measures, such a survey-based measure might help to identify the characteristics implicit in the concept of ruralness.

Population–density definitions also mask individual differences in ruralness. Presumably longtime residents and recent migrants are likely to differ in the degree to which they hold rural characteristics, however they are defined. Similarly, migrants *from* rural areas to cities may still consider themselves to be country or small-town people. The "Appalachian ghettos" of some Midwestern cities are exemplary. Thus, it would be interesting not only to ask participants whether they reside in a rural area but also whether they consider themselves rural people. Such research would be useful in learning about rural identity. Ultimately, work needs to be done to compare the predictive power of various operational definitions of ruralness. In the meantime, the field is likely to include a sometimes confusing mélange of definitions; indeed, there is considerable inconsistency in the use of the term *rural* in this book.

RURAL VALUES AND ATTITUDES

As a psychological construct, *ruralness* might of course be defined on the basis of the attitudes and values typically held by people living in rural communities, particularly as they are differentiated from urban dwellers. Rural people are said to be (relative to urban people) conservative, religious, work-oriented, intolerant of diverse ideas, familistic, individualistic, fatalistic, and so forth (Flax *et al.*, 1979). As will become clear over the course of this volume, there is some evidence to support the contention that there are real mean differences in these values between urban and rural populations. For example, there is evidence that dissemination of new knowledge tends to occur relatively slowly in rural cultures (Havelock, 1969; Rogers & Burdge, 1972; Rogers & Shoemaker, 1971). Similarly, there is empirical evidence for the notion that rural people tend to be relatively intolerant and antilibertarian (see Chapter 16). The relative political conservatism of rural areas has been frequently demonstrated in presidential elections; rural parts of Illinois tend to be more conservative than northern Illinois, for example.

There are several important difficulties with such attempts to define ruralness on the basis of rural-urban differences in values and attitudes, at least at present. First, the supportive evidence for such differences is often quite weak. In Chapter 3, for example, the evidence for familism as a persistent value in rural cultures is largely anecdotal.

Second, when differences have been noted, researchers have frequently not identified which findings could be directly attributed to ruralness, independent of correlated variables, such as region and social class. Moreover, to the extent to which such analyses have not been undertaken, some commentators have slipped into "victim-blaming" explanations (e.g., the "culture of poverty") in which there has not been a clear conceptualization of the ways in which external factors have shaped subcultural value systems. Some anecdotal reports of particular rural subcultures, such as Appalachia (cf. Weller, 1965), have been especially flawed in this regard.

Third, some stereotypical and clinical assessments of value systems have in fact been shown by more rigorous methods to be plainly wrong. For example, the popular view of a violent rural society as depicted in the book (and movie) *Deliverance* is clearly refuted by both police statistics and victim surveys (Chapter 16). Similarly, on the basis of his clinical study of 30 rural families, Coles (1967) concluded that a unifying theme among the rural poor (i.e., migrants, sharecroppers, and mountaineers) was love of the land. In fact, the available research suggests a tendency toward antienvironmentalist attitudes and behavior among rural people (Chapter 17).

Fourth, to the extent to which there are real urban-rural differences, they tend to be rather weak. The variations that do occur may often be *variations* rather than *disjunctures* in belief systems (Flax *et al.*, 1979). Moreover, where value systems do vary systematically, large proportions, indeed majorities, of the community may not adhere to the rural beliefs. Religious fundamentalism is a good example of this (Chapter 9).

Finally, without a theory to explain why rural-urban differences (independent of differences related to correlated variables) should exist, actually finding differences in values between rural and urban populations will be of little utility in understanding ruralness. What is needed at this point are attempts to develop and test such a theoretical construct.

MANNING THEORY[1]

Perhaps the most comprehensive body of theory and research in rural psychology is the "ecological psychology" of Roger Barker and his colleagues. Barker developed a method for describing everyday life in two small towns, one in Kansas and the other in England. In research carried out at the University of Kansas from 1947 to 1972, Barker and his colleagues made meticulous recordings of the "stream of behavior" of individual residents in a variety of "settings" (e.g., the grocery store, the lodge meeting, a band class) in which they were participants. In the present context, such early volumes as *One Boy's Day* (Barker & Wright, 1951) and *Midwest and Its Children* (Barker & Wright, 1955) are notewor-

---

[1]It is recognized that the term *manning theory* may have sexist connotations. However, given that this is the label for the body of knowledge which has arisen from Barker's work and that there is not currently a nonsexist synonym for "undermanning," we will use the term here. The theory obviously is not sex-linked, though, and refers generically to the deviation from homeostasis between setting and number of persons in the setting.

thy as microscopic descriptions of growing up in a small town. Even more importantly, the attempts of Barker and his associates to explain variations in behavior patterns as a function of institutional size may provide an organizing theory to explain a number of phenomena of rural life.

Barker (1960) hypothesized that each setting has an optimal number of inhabitants to fulfill the requirements of the setting. To use an analogy which Barker mentioned, on an eight-person baseball team, players will have to adjust to meet the greater demands imposed by having an insufficient number of players. Greater effort will have to be exerted, and players will have to assume more responsibility. They will also have to be more versatile and cover more territory and more positions. On the other hand, if the team is "overmanned"—if, for example, there are 12 players—some players will obviously be unable to participate fully. Moreover, their roles are more likely to be specialized than in the "undermanned" situation. With 12 players, the coach might, for example, have a left-handed pinch hitter to bring into the game when that substitution seemed to be good strategy. The more overmanned that a setting is, the more rigorous that admission standards will be and the more attention will be given to individual differences.

Perhaps the most dramatic examples of these principles came in Barker and Gump's (1964) widely cited study of the effects of school size. Consolidation of rural schools has, of course, been justified on grounds that it will be possible to offer more diverse curricula and, therefore, wider opportunities for students in large schools. Barker and Gump found this assumption to be only weakly validated. A 10% increase in school size yielded on the average only a 17% increase in class offerings. Furthermore, rather than increasing the variety of classes and extracurricular activities in which students participated, increasing size tended to result in "specialists," such as students who took advantage largely of opportunities in music. Perhaps of most consequence, a sizable proportion of students in large schools were outsiders of sorts who attended only a few settings, often only those which were required, such as assemblies. Empirically, the average large-school junior was an "operative" (i.e., an actual participant, such as a football player or cheerleader—rather than a spectator—at a game) in 3.5 settings within a three-month period; the average small-school student was an operative in 8.6 settings during the same time period.

The greater participation experienced by small-school students translated into a greater sense of responsibility for the school as well as heightened personal sense of competence and belonging. Large-school students tended to enjoy vicarious pleasures (e.g., "I enjoyed listening to the orchestra at the dance") and a sense of belonging to "something big." In short, small-school students were more likely to feel important;

large-school students were more often passive and only marginally involved.

The observations of Barker and Gump (1964) concerning the effects of school size have been replicated in studies of effects of organizational size in other institutional forms, such as churches (Wicker, 1969, 1978; Wicker & Mehler, 1971). Moreover, the predictions of manning theory have been confirmed in Darley and Latané's (1968) studies of "diffusion of responsibility" among bystanders. The basic finding of this line of research has been that, the more persons that are present, the less likely that someone is to help. As Darley and Latané understand this phenomenon, when many people are bystanders, individuals are likely to believe that there are others present who are more competent and who are responsible for taking action. Consequently, no one assumes the role of the *Good Samaritan.*

The potential importance of manning theory for rural psychology is clear. Small communities are more likely to induce participation from their members; simply put, there are many tasks to be performed by few people. The sense of satisfaction which usually accompanies life in rural communities (see the review of quality of life studies in Chapter 10) may be explained at least in part by the sense of involvement, accomplishment, and importance which accompanies such participation. Similarly, the neighborliness which is often found in rural communities (Korte, 1980) is consistent with manning theory. Undermanned settings *need* people and are unlikely to let new residents or visitors remain in anonymity or on the margins of the community. In short, many of the attractive aspects of rural life may be explained by manning theory. Accordingly, manning theory may be useful in helping to understand the nature of ruralness. Moreover, manning theory has clear implications for rural development and planning. Bigger is not necessarily better; indeed, there may be significant psychological costs derived from consolidating schools, churches, and other community institutions, particularly since the primary goal is not the production of specialists. (As economic growth and development occur, the importance of that goal should not be underestimated.) Moreover, Barker and Gump's work suggests that the efficiency gains which increasing size yields may be quite small, particularly in comparison with the human costs.

There are, however, some important limitations of manning theory as a *general* theory of ruralness. Most notably, specific settings in rural communities can obviously be overmanned, as the consolidated-school example illustrates. Second, some of the values which are supposedly typical of rural communities (e.g., traditionalism, familism) may not be easily predicted on the basis of manning theory. Nonetheless, manning theory does offer significant heuristic value in understanding many aspects of social behavior in rural communities.

Isolation

Although obviously not a theoretical construct of the sort which "undermanning" is, another concept which might be thought to contribute to an understanding of ruralness would be simply *isolation*. Certainly isolation is an apt image for many rural areas. For example, Coles (1967) vividly portrayed the children growing up in Appalachian hollows as "hidden children." Similarly, a sense of physical isolation is certainly apropos to those living on ranches in the West, where literally thousands of acres may separate individual farms.

Such physical isolation may at times translate into striking psychological and social phenomena. For example, when there are few other resources to mediate stress, individuals might come to rely heavily on their families (see Chapter 3). Moreover, isolated individuals might be so out of touch with the mainstream culture that they find it difficult to enter into it. Looff (1971), for example, observed children in Eastern Kentucky who developed a phobic response ("consolidated school syndrome") when forced to attend schools outside their immediate communities. From a less psychiatric point of view, ecological theorists have placed major emphasis on isolation as a factor in maladaptation to stress. Besides not having extensive social support, isolated families lack feedback about parenting skills and means of dealing with stress. The children themselves may not obtain diverse role-taking skills because of the dearth of models (Cochran & Brassard, 1979). Some ecological theorists (cf. Garbarino, Gaboury, Long, Grandjean, & Asp, 1982) have even suggested devaluing privacy as a means of ending destructive isolation.

In a different vein, rural individuals may be physically isolated from changes in the mainstream culture. As already noted, there is some evidence that changes in knowledge and social mores filter relatively slowly to rural areas.

However, in my view, isolation has limited value as a unifying idea in understanding rural psychology. Most basically, physical isolation does not necessarily imply social isolation, which in turn does not necessarily imply psychological isolation. Indeed, as discussed in the section on manning theory, social networks may actually be *stronger* in sparsely populated areas than in communities which are not as isolated. Moreover, the sort of isolation to which Garbarino and others have referred to as particularly destructive of family life has been conceptualized by some theorists in this group as emanating from cultural changes in twentieth-century industrialized, urbanized American life (cf. analysis of "alienation," Bronfenbrenner, 1974).

Finally, at least for highly developed societies as in the United States, even *very* physically isolated areas cannot remain too isolated from developments in metropolitan areas, thanks to the ubiquity of advances in communication and transportation. When television daily beams images of metrpolitan America, it is hard to remain isolated from changes there. Migration has similar effects, which are likely to become stronger as migration into rural areas continues to increase. Even before the trend toward reverse migration was well solidified, Coles (1967) made a similar point (see also Photiadis & Schwarzweller, 1970):

> Today Appalachia is not a stable, rural region, but a region of mixed city and farm people, with a good deal of movement—out for jobs, back in for visiting, or return from an outside found unbearable. In some areas, the people live very much like those in other American cities, but in many other areas they live under circumstances that are all their own—and with values similarly a product of a special kind of existence. It is safe to say that the region as a whole has had to face a harsh fate: difficult terrain that has not made the entry of private capital easy, progressive deforestation, land erosion, periods of affluence when "coal was king," followed by increasing automation of the mine industry (and a decreasing national demand for coal), pollution that has ruined some of its finest streams so that strip-mining can go full speed ahead. In a curious way the people of a region called "backward" face the particularly cruel burdens of an advanced, technological society. (Coles, 1967, p. 495)

The situation which Coles described has, of course, undergone additional marked changes as a result of the energy crisis. Much of the challenge in studying ruralness at this point involves taking into account these striking social changes. Not only must researchers consider the diversity of rural communities and of the residents within them, but recognition must also be given to the dynamic quality of contemporary rural life. While changes may be disseminated relatively slowly to rural areas as a general rule, it is clear that rural communities are currently undergoing striking changes in population *structure* (e.g., occupational distribution) as well as population size. Theories of ruralness which ignore these changes are likely to have little explanatory power.

THE CONTENTS OF THIS VOLUME

In contrast to the psychological orientation of this chapter, and indeed of this volume, Photiadis and Simoni, both sociologists, present in Chapter 2 an overview of the demographics and social structure of rural communities in the United States. Their survey will be particularly useful to readers unfamiliar with basic findings of rural sociology; their overview provides the context for the discussions in the remainder of the book.

Chapters 3 through 10 provide initial discussions of the experience of rural life. In Chapter 3, Urey and Henggeler review the literature, much of it anecdotal, on interaction in rural families. They suggest that many of the inferences commonly drawn must be qualified by attention to regional and social class differences. Similarly, following a thorough review of available cross-cultural research on cognitive and social development in Chapter 4, Hollos argues that studies of rural-urban differences have overemphasized gross dependent variables (e.g., IQ) without attention to the kinds of specific "highs" and "lows" in development that rural environments might foster. In reviews of linguistic development in rural subcultures (Chapter 5) and of the psychology of the religious fundamentalism common in rural areas (Chapter 9), Wolfram and Hood, respectively, conclude that scholars examining rural life have tended to reach distorted perceptions of ruralness, based on value-laden hypotheses of cultural deprivation.

In Chapter 7, Feimer undertakes a scholarly review of environmental perception and cognition in rural communities. He notes that there is a general paucity of research on processes of spatial cognition in rural environments. What, for example, are the implications for cognitive development of growing up in vast spaces? How is the cognitive representation of the environment affected? Most of what is known in this area, Feimer concludes, is based on studies of "transition experiences"—the cognitive mapping by urban persons visiting rural areas. There is a significantly larger body of research on environmental aesthetics (i.e., perceptions of scenic quality), but this literature, ironically, has also emphasized the forays of urban dwellers into rural areas. Feimer also reviews research on perception of natural hazards, an area of psychological study with particular implications for land-use planning in agricultural regions.

Even though examining quite different topics, Dibner (Chapter 6) and Lefcourt and Martin (Chapter 8) have in common a focus on whether there are clearly identifiable rural psychological phenomena. In his chapter, Dibner extrapolates from the rural sociological literature on aging and argues for more sophisticated ecological or multivariate models of ruralness which take into account the interaction between specific personal characteristics and specific environmental demands. Similarly, in their review of rural-urban differences in locus of control, Lefcourt and Martin call for examination of the ways in which particular kinds of rural settings do or do not enhance a sense of internal locus of control.

In Chapter 10, Korte provides an overview of the differences in quality of life in rural and urban communities, both objectively and subjectively. He makes a strong plea for understanding better the ingredients of the positive subjective quality of life in rural communities. Is the positive outlook in some way tied to the characteristics of people now residing in rural areas?

Chapters 11 to 13 concern general issues in service delivery in rural communities. The chapters focus on needs assessment, program development, and models of service delivery, respectively. Chapters 14 through 17 present bridges between these applied chapters and the preceding descriptions of rural psychology. In each of Chapters 14 through 17, the authors center on the ecological determinants of particular problems in rural life and of the success or failure of particular intervention strategies. Rosenberg and Reppucci (Chapter 14) provide an elegant discussion of the relationship between isolation and child abuse. Gotts (Chapter 15) describes the long-term evaluation of a preschool intervention program in Appalachia that used television and indigenous home visitors. The success of the program is linked to particular aspects of Appalachian culture. In Chapter 16, Melton draws on legal anthropology and criminology in discussing prevalent rural legal problems and modes of intervention in rural courts that are linked both to the nature of the problem and to styles of dispute resolution common in rural communities. On the largest scale, Geller (Chapter 17) notes the particular problems of energy waste in rural areas and suggests a behavioral model for dealing with this important social and economic issue.

Finally, in Chapter 18 the editors review the work presented in this volume and suggest directions for future research in rural psychology. In that chapter, we return to the question of the nature of ruralness. It is our hope that this initial volume will help to elucidate what we need to know in order to understand better the experiences of people living in rural areas, which have been chronically underserved and underresearched. Although the topics and perspectives of the contributors to this volume are quite diverse, these multiple viewpoints may lead to a more sophisticated understanding of what is special about rural environments, so that these positive attributes may be preserved as newcomers migrate there. Moreover, we believe that the attention which most of the authors give to *specific* environmental demands in rural communities may help to advance the field beyond assessment of global studies of urban-rural differences (usually focused on rural "deficits") to a better understanding of particular service needs of rural communities and of particular strategies of addressing these needs.

REFERENCES

Barker, R. G. Ecology and motivation. In M. R. Jones (Ed.), *Nebraska symposium on motivation.* Lincoln: University of Nebraska Press, 1960.

Barker, R. G., & Gump, P. V. *Big school, small school.* Stanford, Calif.: Stanford University Press, 1964.

Barker, R. G., & Wright, H. F. *One boy's day*. New York: Harper & Row, 1951.

Barker, R. G., & Wright, H. F. *Midwest and its children*. New York: Harper & Row, 1955.

Bronfenbrenner, U. The origins of alienation. *Scientific American*, 1974, *231*(2), 53–61.

Brown, D. L., & Wardwell, J. M. *New directions in urban-rural migration: The population turnaround in rural America*. New York: Academic Press, 1980.

Cochran, M. M., & Brassard, J. A. Child development and personal social networks. *Child Development*, 1979, *50*, 601–616.

Coles, R. *Migrants, sharecroppers, mountaineers. Children of crisis* (Vol. 2). Boston: Little, Brown, 1967.

Darley, J., & Latané, B. Bystander intervention into emergencies: Diffusion of responsibility. *Journal of Personality and Social Psychology*, 1968, *8*, 377–383.

Dillman, D. A. Rural sociology research: The next 10 years. *Rural Sociologist*, 1981, *1*, 209–220.

Flax, J. W., Wagenfeld, M. O., Ivens, R. E., & Weiss, R. J. *Mental health and rural America: An overview and annotated bibliography*. Washington, D.C.: National Institute of Mental Health, 1979.

Garbarino, J., Gaboury, M. T., Long, F., Grandjean, P., & Asp, E. Who owns the children?: An ecological perspective on public policy affecting children. In G. B. Melton (Ed.), *Legal reforms affecting child and youth service*. New York: Haworth, 1982.

Havelock, R. G. *Planning for innovation through dissemination and utilization of knowledge*. Ann Arbor, Mich.: Center for Research on Utilization of Knowledge, Institute for Social Research, 1969.

Korte, C. Urban-nonurban differences in social behavior and social psychological models of urban impact. *Journal of Social Issues*, 1980, *36*(3), 29–51.

Looff, D. H. *Appalachia's children: The challenge of mental health*. Lexington: University of Kentucky Press, 1971.

Photiadis, J. D., & Schwarzweller, H. K. *Change in rural Appalachia: Implications for action programs*. Philadelphia: University of Pennsylvania Press, 1970.

President's Commission on Mental Health. *Report to the President*. Washington, D.C.: Government Printing Office, 1978.

Rogers, E. M., & Burdge, R. J. *Social change in rural societies* (2nd ed.). Englewood Cliffs, N.J.: Prentice-Hall, 1972.

Rogers, E. M., & Shoemaker, F. F. *Communication of innovations* (2nd ed.). New York: Free Press, 1971.

Weller, J. E. *Yesterday's people*. Lexington: University of Kentucky Press, 1965.

Wicker, A. W. Size of church membership and members' support of church behavior settings. *Journal of Personality and Social Psychology*, 1969, *13*, 278–288.

Wicker, A. W. Importance of church size for new members. In R. G. Barker (Ed.), *Habitats, environments, and human behavior: Studies in ecological psychology and eco-behavioral science from the Midwest Psychological Field Station, 1947–1972*. San Francisco: Jossey-Bass, 1978.

Wicker, A. W., & Mehler, A. Assimilation of new members in a large and a small church. *Journal of Applied Psychology*, 1971, *55*, 151–156.

Williams, J. D. The nonchanging determinants of nonmetropolitan migration. *Rural Sociology*, 1981, *46*, 183–202.

2

Characteristics of Rural America

John D. Photiadis and Joseph J. Simoni

Demographic Characteristics

Our purpose here is to present a general demographic profile of rural America. This profile is not meant to be exhaustive; for example, a discussion of changes in demographic characteristics, or causes of such changes, is not included. However, this profile will provide the reader with basic information necessary for an adequate understanding of rural America. Questions answered will include: How many people live in rural America? What proportion of rural Americans are farmers? Geographically speaking, where do rural Americans live? How well educated are rural Americans? What kind of jobs do rural Americans have? How much money do they make? Are there any differences in educational levels, jobs, and income levels among rural whites, blacks, and Hispanics?

Definitions

Terms like *rural* and *urban* are often used in general conversation without much attention paid to specific connotations. However, if the demographic profile to be presented is to be helpful for an adequate understanding of rural America, specific connotations or meanings are necessary. Therefore, the following United States Census definitions will be used:

John D. Photiadis and Joseph J. Simoni • Department of Sociology and Anthropology, West Virginia University, Morgantown, West Virginia 26506.

Urbanized Area

An urbanized area consists of a central city (or cities with contiguous boundaries and constituting, for general social and economic purposes, a single community) of 50,000 inhabitants or more and the surrounding closely settled territory.

Urban

The urban population is defined as all persons living in urbanized areas or in places of 2,500 inhabitants or more outside urbanized areas.

Rural

The rural population is defined as all that population not classified as urban.

Farm

The rural population, for the purpose of demographic profiles, may be divided into rural farm and rural nonfarm populations. The rural farm population is defined as all rural residents living on farms. A farm is defined as 10 or more acres from which sales of farm products amounted to $50 or more in the preceding calendar year, or a place of fewer than 10 acres from which sales of farm products amounted to $250 or more in the preceding year.

Nonfarm

The nonfarm population is defined as all the rural population not classified as rural farm.

Population

According to Bureau of the Census figures, the 1970 United States total population was divided into 73.5% urban population and 26.5% rural population. The 1970 United States population picture, then, was one of approximately three-quarters urban population and one-quarter rural population, certainly a significant change from only fifty years before, when in 1920 the breakdown was approximately one-half urban and one-half rural.

The year 1920 marked the first time that the designations *farm* and *nonfarm* were used by the Bureau of the Census. In 1920, the farm population made up approximately 30% of the total United States population and approximately 60% of the rural population; this stands in marked contrast to 1970, when the farm population made up only 4.8% of the total population and only 18% of the total rural population.

In 1970, the rural nonfarm population comprised 21.7% of the total United States population and 82% of the total rural population. However, the 1980 census data recently available to us clearly indicate that while the farm population has continued to decrease over the last decade as a percentage of the total United States population, the rural nonfarm population has actually increased as a percentage of the total United States population, and more so as a percentage of the total rural population. This growth in the rural nonfarm segment of the population is generally attributed to the increase in retirement and recreational areas, the growth of colleges and universities, including branches of already established institutions, and the growth of manufacturing in nonmetropolitan areas (for a detailed discussion, see Beale, 1978).

Geographic Distribution

Where do rural Americans live? What states contain predominantly rural populations? It is our impression that most people are vague when it comes to defining specific state locations of large rural populations. For example, of all 50 states, the state with the largest percentage of rural

TABLE 1.   STATES RANKED BY PERCENTAGE OF RURAL POPULATION: 1980

Vermont	66.2	Oklahoma	32.7
West Virginia	63.8	Oregon	32.1
South Dakota	53.6	Missouri	31.9
Mississippi	52.7	Louisiana	31.4
Maine	52.5	Pennsylvania	30.7
North Carolina	52.0	Delaware	29.3
North Dakota	51.2	Michigan	29.3
Kentucky	49.2	New Mexico	27.8
Arkansas	48.4	Ohio	26.7
New Hampshire	47.8	Washington	26.4
Montana	47.1	Connecticut	21.2
Idaho	46.0	Texas	20.4
South Carolina	45.9	Maryland	19.7
Iowa	41.4	Colorado	19.4
Alabama	40.0	Illinois	17.0
Tennessee	39.6	Arizona	16.2
Georgia	37.7	Massachusetts	16.2
Nebraska	37.3	Florida	15.7
Wyoming	37.2	Utah	15.6
Indiana	35.8	New York	15.4
Wisconsin	35.8	Nevada	14.7
Alaska	35.5	Hawaii	13.5
Virginia	34.0	Rhode Island	13.0
Kansas	33.3	New Jersey	11.0
Minnesota	33.2	California	8.7

population in 1980 was Vermont, with 66.2%, and followed by West Virginia, with 63.8%. Relatively few people would know that in 1980 the populations of Alabama, Georgia, and Wyoming were all predominantely urban rather than rural. With this impression of vagueness in mind, we decided to present Table 1 (based on information found in the 1980 United States Census). Table 1 indicates the distribution of the United States rural population across all 50 states.

Education, Occupation, and Income

Educational accomplishments are very much influenced by the following three factors: (1) the availability of educational opportunity, (2) an individual's perceptions of education as a factor necessary for advancement, and (3) the perception, on the part of individuals, of real opportunity for occupational advancement and increased income resulting from greater educational preparation. Therefore, these factors should be kept in mind as the educational data presented here are examined, as urban-rural differences, and differences among whites, blacks, and Hispanics are considered.

All the educational data presented here can be found in the 1970 United States Census of Population. The first set of data, Median School Years Completed for Persons 25 Years Old and Over (Table 2) reflects more of the historical past, while the second set of educational data (Table 3) reflects more of the present situation. Both sets of data, however, emphasize the racial nature of American society, past and present, the greater availability in urban areas of educational opportunity, and differences in the perceived relevance of education for advancement among urban, rural nonfarm, and rural farm populations.

Table 4 presents occupations of employed persons by race for rural nonfarm and rural farm residence. This table describes the kinds of jobs that rural nonfarm and rural farm residents were working at as of 1970. Although a discussion of the occupational structures for rural nonfarm

TABLE 2. MEDIAN SCHOOL YEARS COMPLETED,
PERSONS 25 YEARS OLD AND OVER

	Urban				Rural nonfarm				Rural farm			
	T	W	B	H	T	W	B	H	T	W	B	H
Males	12.2	12.3	10.0	10.2	10.9	11.2	7.0	8.3	9.8	10.0	6.1	7.5
Females	12.1	12.2	10.4	9.5	11.5	11.8	8.1	8.4	11.7	11.9	7.8	8.5

Note: T = total, W = white, B = black, H = Hispanic.

TABLE 3.   MALES 16 TO 21 YEARS OLD, NOT HIGH SCHOOL GRADUATES AND NOT
ATTENDING SCHOOL, AS PERCENTAGE OF ALL MALES 16 TO 21 YEARS OLD

Urban				Rural nonfarm				Rural farm			
T	W	B	H	T	W	B	H	T	W	B	H
14.1	12.5	25.1	25.4	19.9	18.1	33.5	30.4	12.7	11.6	27.1	28.5

Note: T = total, W = white, B = black, H = Hispanic.

and rural farm residents is not our intention, we do want to indicate the
kind of information that can be gleaned from the table.

Let us consider, for example, the first six occupational categories for
rural nonfarm residents (Professional, Technical, and Kindred Workers;
Managers and Administrators, except Farm; Sales Workers; Clerical and
Kindred Workers; Craftsmen and Kindred Workers; Operatives, except
Transport) and compare for the three racial groups the percentage of
people working in all six categories taken together. For whites the
percentage was 75.1, whereas for blacks and Hispanics the percentages
were 42.2 and 52.6, respectively.

Another interesting example are the data for the three groups found
in the occupational categories Farmers and Farm Managers, Farm La-

TABLE 4.   OCCUPATION OF EMPLOYED PERSONS BY RACE
FOR RURAL RESIDENCE: 1970[a]

	Rural nonfarm				Rural farm			
	T	W	B	H	T	W	B	H
Professional, technical, and kindred workers	11.4	11.8	5.2	8.3	6.4	6.5	4.6	5.2
Managers and administrators, except farm	7.8	8.3	1.5	4.9	3.7	3.8	1.2	2.7
Sales workers	5.4	5.7	1.0	3.4	3.0	3.1	0.7	2.3
Clerical and kindred workers	12.6	13.2	4.1	8.9	7.9	8.1	2.7	5.2
Craftsmen and kindred workers	17.3	18.0	9.1	12.5	8.9	9.0	5.7	6.2
Operatives, except transport	18.3	18.1	21.3	14.6	10.8	10.7	15.5	6.2
Transport equipment operatives	4.9	4.8	6.0	4.5	3.3	3.2	4.5	2.8
Laborers, except farm	5.8	5.2	13.5	8.1	3.4	3.2	8.4	3.9
Farmers and farm managers	1.4	1.4	1.2	1.3	36.1	37.0	17.4	18.1
Farm laborers and farm foremen	2.9	2.3	10.2	19.2	9.1	8.5	21.6	40.2
Service workers, except private household	10.5	10.2	15.1	12.1	6.3	6.1	9.8	5.6
Private household workers	1.7	1.0	11.8	2.2	1.1	0.8	7.9	1.6

Note: T = total, W = white, B = black, H = Hispanic.
[a]From Table 222, Detailed Occupation of Employed Persons by Residence and Sex: 1970. 1970 Census of
Population; Volume 1, Part 1, Section 2.

borers, and Farm Foremen. The data for the first category indicate that among rural farm residents 37.0% of whites were listed as Farmers and Farm Managers, compared with only 17.4% of blacks and only 18.1% of Hispanics. The percentages for the second category, Farm Laborers and Farm Foremen, were strikingly different. Only 8.5% of rural farm whites were working as Farm Laborers or Farm Foremen in 1970, whereas the percentages for blacks and Hispanics were 21.6 and 40.2, respectively.

Data on labor force participation in 1970 indicate a gradual decline, from urban to rural nonfarm to rural farm areas, in the percentage of the population in the labor force. However, the differences between areas are relatively small and do not explain the much larger urban-rural differences in income (Table 5) and poverty (Table 6). In other words, more poverty exists in rural areas not because the rural poor do not work, but because they work for less money (low wage rates) and because they work less time and less frequently (underemployment). They work at the kinds of jobs that pay less and/or allow them less working time (For a detailed discussion, see Chadwick & Bahr, 1978.)

It should also be clear, from the educational and income data presented here, that differences in educational attainment are not the only cause for relatively large differences in income levels and resulting poverty levels. Racial and ethnic discrimination also have their place. For example, referring to the data, the relatively small difference in educational levels between rural blacks and Hispanics does not explain the relatively large differences in income and poverty levels for the two groups.

TABLE 5.   INCOME OF FAMILIES AND UNRELATED INDIVIDUALS[a]

	Mean income of families	Mean income per family member	Mean income of unrelated individuals
Urban total	11,674	3,314	4,051
Urban white	12,183	3,522	4,198
Urban black	7,549	1,889	3,055
Urban Hispanic	8,737	2,061	3,404
Rural nonfarm total	9,184	2,514	3,003
Rural nonfarm white	9,493	2,658	3,137
Rural nonfarm black	4,956	1,060	1,647
Rural nonfarm Hispanic	7,238	1,542	2,539
Rural farm total	8,677	2,389	3,280
Rural farm white	8,869	2,483	3,402
Rural farm black	4,256	868	1,484
Rural farm Hispanic	7,668	1,640	2,658

[a]From Table 94, Income in 1969 of Families, Unrelated Individuals, and Persons by Race and Urban and Rural Residence: 1970. 1970 Census of Population; Volume 1, Part 1, Section 1.

TABLE 6.   INCOMES LESS THAN POVERTY LEVEL[a]

	Percent of families	Percent of all unrelated individuals	Percent of all persons
Urban total	9.0	34.4	12.0
Urban white	6.9	32.8	9.4
Urban black	25.9	44.5	30.6
Urban Hispanic	19.2	38.6	22.0
Rural nonfarm total	15.1	50.8	18.3
Rural nonfarm white	12.6	48.7	14.7
Rural nonfarm black	49.3	72.2	54.9
Rural nonfarm Hispanic	30.6	54.7	35.2
Rural farm total	16.4	42.4	18.9
Rural farm white	14.9	40.9	16.6
Rural farm black	52.4	68.3	57.7
Rural farm Hispanic	26.6	38.3	30.6

[a]From Table 95, Poverty Status in 1969 of Families and Persons by Race and Urban and Rural Residence: 1970. 1970 Census of Population; Volume 1, Part 1, Section 1.

Summary

The demography of rural America may be briefly summarized in the following manner. First, according to 1970 United States Census definitions and data, approximately 25% of the total United States population can be classified as rural, and 18% of that rural population can be classified as farm population. Second, rural Americans do not enjoy the availability of educational and employment opportunities found in the urban sector of the country. Third, like the demographics of urban America, the demography of rural America reflects the racial nature of American society.

RURAL SOCIAL INSTITUTIONS

Rural societies for thousands of years survived as autonomous, cohesive, and highly integrated social entities. A satisfactory verification of these attributes could be secured by simply looking at the high degree of integration among the major social institutions of early societies. Such high levels of integration and autonomy can be observed even to this day in developing societies and among population units in this country which either by design (e.g., groups like the Hutterites and Amish) or because of mere isolation (e.g., certain parts of Appalachia) have remained relatively autonomous from the larger American society. However, as one moves generally from less to more industrialized societies, or from the past to the present in this country, it is clear that the dominant social processes have been increasing differentiation within certain institutions (e.g., economy, government, education), weakening of interrelationships among institutions, and, in turn, closer integration or accord between institutions of the larger society and its urban sector.

Because the themes of the larger American society emphasize a striving for material goods and a higher standard of living, the rural economy has spearheaded this process of integration of the rural into larger American society. In particular, during the earlier years of integration (1930–1960) after the "great migration," institutions such as government and education were under increased pressure to become more efficient and to contribute directly to the success of the economic institution. There were pressures for efficiency in local government and for children to receive more education so that they could contribute more efficiently to the country's economy. The contribution of the family to these processes has been both direct and indirect.

Economy

Early writers, such as Marx and Engels, and more recent writers dealing with the underdeveloped world have looked at peasantry as simplistic and uncomplicated, sometimes bordering on the subhuman. According to Loomis and Beegle (1975), peasants in medieval Europe were listed along with livestock in estate records. However, these peasants' descendants who are today living in North America are, in most cases, highly skilled and competitive and operating under constant pressure for economic survival. As a consequence, and as figures presented previously indicate, the rural farm population for years now has been declining rapidly; at the same time, organization and specialization on farms, and technical and managerial sophistication of farmers have been increasing at a rapid rate. In the last 50 years, along with rapid mechanization and adoption of recommended farm practices, the yeilds of wheat and rice per acre have doubled, and cotton and tobacco yields have tripled.

A trend toward commercialization of the farm is expected to continue. There are experts who suggest that under present available technology 300,000 farms (today close to 2.5 million exist) and 3% of the nation's labor force can produce an excess of food and fiber for the nation. But there are others who suggest that in order to preserve desirable American values and life-styles, the trend toward commercialization should be checked and the preservation of family-sized farms should be encouraged.

Another major area of rural economic development is forestry. The growing stock of sawtimber increased 25% between 1953 and 1970, the volume of products harvested grew steadily, and gross sales volumes nearly tripled. The amount of timberland during this period increased by only 1%, indicative of the more efficient utilization of available land (Ford, 1978).

Dramatic changes, similar to those in agriculture and forestry, have developed in the past 25 years in rural or nonmetropolitan industry. These changes have been facilitated by the following factors: federal policies and programs to redistribute population and industry, efforts of local communities to attract industry, and preference of industry to move into rural areas because many employers have become disenchanted with big-city conditions.

According to Bertrand (1978), industrialization has produced considerable discord in the rural society. The same is true with agricultural changes. Commenting on changes in the agricultural sector, Harshbarger and Stahl (1974) point out that while considerable progress has been made, deep scars have nonetheless been left on thousands of families who experienced great difficulty in coping with the changing economic environment. Areas, like Appalachia, which were less prepared to sustain the impact of new technology have suffered the most negative effects (Photiadis, 1974), and the general adjustment responses of these areas are discussed below in the section on rural social organization.

Government

Historically, residents of rural communities prided themselves on self-reliance, and did not demand much in the way of local government services. Today, however, rural residents expect much more from their local governments; these same governments now find themselves to be part of a rural crisis as they attempt to match limited funding to existing community needs. This experience indicates that in rural America providing necessary public services is no easy task (for a detailed discussion, see Rainey & Rainey, 1978).

Like local governments in urban areas, local governments in rural areas find themselves in a bind. Although the cost of services has risen sharply because of inflation, the amount of funding available to local rural governments for the payment of these services has risen only slightly. Local governments continue to rely on property taxes as their main source of funds. This bind is compounded by the fact that rural local governments must deal with the added reality that, on a per capita basis, it costs more to provide a service to a sparsely settled area than it does to provide that same service to a more densely populated area. Water, sewage, and road systems are just three cases in point.

Three core issues deserve special attention. One is the question of local autonomy versus involvement by state and federal entities in local community issues; a second is the question of whether local rural communities should foot the bill for long-term benefits which eventually accrue to nonrural sectors of the economy; the third has to do with the traditional conservatism of small rural communities.

Federal and state governments are becoming increasingly involved in local community issues. Many observers initially felt that such involvement carried with it a sense of salvation for small rural communities which apparently had no other funding available. Consequently, governments of rural communities welcomed the federal and state involvement with open arms. State and federal involvement, in fact, has represented a form of immediate salvation for many rural communities, but local autonomy and related initiative have been sacrificed. Local governments may become so consumed by the idea of obtaining grants from state and federal entities that they no longer give much thought to what it is they will gain by way of the grant, whether it actually serves the good of the community, or whether they can reach their goals without such outside aid. Furthermore, the goals set today by many rural local governments are dictated by the availability of state and federal aid.

Proponents of heavy state and federal involvement in local community affairs feel that local communities should receive outside grants because many of these communities are obligated to make investments that benefit the nonrural sectors of the economy. For example, local governments must provide opportunities for their residents to receive at least minimal levels of educational and health services. However, many of the healthy, educated young of these rural communities leave them for the "better life." They ultimately form part of an urban labor force that benefits urban areas and not their local home areas.

Finally, it must be realized that, with respect to social change, local rural governments have been traditionally conservative. Opportunities for the socially and economically disadvantaged of these communities very often do not exist because they are not deemed necessary by those who influence and control local government. Health and educational opportunities are not available to all residents of rural communities because in many cases local governments have not made serious efforts to provide them.

Rural residents today are more aware of the kinds of social changes occurring in communities throughout the nation. This increased awareness has encouraged them to expect more from their local governments. In response to such pressure, local governments are seeking solutions. They generally lean toward outside involvement because they believe that the state and federal governments should pay part of the bill, and because local governments are forced to work from limited tax–revenue bases. Outside involvement dictates more of a role for outsiders in local community decision-making. Observers interested in seeing increased social change in rural communities look upon this process as something positive. As social change comes to rural America and residents gain more of a voice in local community government, these same residents will become sensitive to the need for a certain degree of local community autonomy and initiative. Collective action by local citizens in rural communities is already evident; citizen groups have organized to prevent development projects which they feel are not in the best interests of their local communities.

Education

School consolidation is the major issue concerning education in rural America today. The one-rooom schoolhouse is quickly disappearing. Most rural students are now bused to school. Schools in many rural communities are no longer focal points of community life and activity, and country people no longer feel in control of the schools that their children attend (for a more detailed discussion, see Sher, 1977).

Consolidation, even for those who oppose it, symbolizes advancement, progress, the modern, the new. To many rural Americans consolidation represents an opportunity for more when they have traditionally been getting less: less teachers, less quality teaching, less equipment, etc. More of all these things, they believe, holds out the promise of a better education for their children which, in turn, should increase their childrens' chances for success. However, the empirical evidence to support such a promise does not exist. It is not yet clear whether the supposed benefits do result or whether the "bigger and better" concept of rural school consolidation outweighs the loss of local control, the loss of close relationships among parents, students and school personnel, and the loss for many students of opportunities to participate in school activities. Nor is it clear that consolidation represents a more economical, more efficient, or more equitable manner of delivering educational services to rural communities.

It is generally agreed that rural children should enjoy educational opportunity relatively equal to that enjoyed by urban children. Those people faced with the challenge of providing this opportunity to rural children have generally decided on consolidation as the solution. The rural scene presents a situation of a widely dispersed population, a situation that, in the minds of rural educators, necessitates consolidation in order to deal not only with the existing problem of distance, but also with an apparent problem of scale. Promoters of consolidation state that quality teachers, up-to-date equipment, and modern facilities for rural children are neither economical nor efficient unless those children are brought together in common educational settings large enough to legitimize the expenses.

For those rural residents and communities not already irreversibly committed to consolidation, alternatives are available. One answer to the problem of scale is regionalization: rural school districts band together on a voluntary basis and cooperate in the delivery, to all districts, of services which an individual district operating on its own budget cannot afford. Through the medium of regionalization, vocational education, special reading programs, and in-service training for teachers can be provided.

Another answer is to take the major financial responsibility for education out of the hands of local school corporations and place it in the hands of state and federal governments. There are those who fear that local communities, under such an arrangement, might lose control over their schools, and to some extent this may be true. However, this type of solution would enable rural communities to conserve their schools as focal points of community life, maintain a closeness in social relationships between parents, students, and school personnel, and allow a much higher percentage of school children to be involved in school activities than is normally possible under consolidation. Furthermore, with respect to control, teachers and school administrators truly interested in the welfare of rural communities would operate in such a way as to allow community input into the decision-making process.

Finally, a third answer or alternative to consolidation, supposedly representing modernization and advancement, is to employ advanced educational methods and modern technologies to bring specialized and varied educational opportunities to rural children. "Circuit-riding" specialists can teach particular subjects or offer special services in a number of schools. The use of telephones, radios, tape systems, and even satellite–communication systems can make it much easier to bring vital resources to rural children. There is no need to force these children from their local communities.

Family

Cross-cultural studies conducted in the post-World War II years have verified one gross empirical fact: for the first time in world history, all societies are now moving toward modernization and some form of the conjugal family system. In some parts of this country, such as rural Appalachia, the breakdown of the extended family occurred later than in other parts, but it has happened nonetheless. Even the conjugal family has changed drastically. This is more noticeable in the farm family which, in contrast to the past, now functions as two separate units, one social and the other economic.

Another noticeable change associated with modernization and industrialization is that as we analyze the family in this country from the past to the present, or all societies from the less to the more industrialized ones, the differences between rural and urban families diminish. A time lag is in evidence; attributes described for rural families today are those same attributes described for urban families a few decades earlier. For instance, in Lantz's (1968, 1973, 1975) content analyses of magazines highlighting early American urban life (for the periods 1741 to 1794, 1794 to 1825, and 1825 to 1850), the reader can see trends in process even today and attributes that are associated with today's rurality.

Some of the major trends reported in those studies are: the increasing power of women, an increasing emphasis on romantic love and personal happiness as criteria in mate selection, an increasing tolerance of premarital and extra-marital relationships, and a decreasing importance of the double standard. All these trends are associated with the development of industrialization in this country and are in many respects similar to corresponding developments in Europe, and, considering the time lag, less-developed societies. In rural areas, Burchinal (1964) points out that all empirical data indicate that these same types of changes, although parallel, take place with a certain time lag.

Changes in rural family patterns do not occur only through the diffusion of urban family patterns to the rural population. Endogenous changes in rural community organization and family patterns are associated with the continuing technological changes in American agriculture. The effects of agricultural technology are reflected in the higher levels of living and education for rural persons and in the specialization and professionalization of rural and farm occupational roles. These developments generally reinforce changes in rural family patterns induced by the diffusion of the developing urban family patterns (Burchinal, 1964). On the other hand, in spite of many similarities in trends, rural families in isolated regions with little economic potential often develop attributes considerably different from those of other rural American families. These attributes are sometimes identified with the life-styles of families living in so-called subcultures of poverty.

Now that we have examined institutions, we will take a more generalized view of rural America by considering social organization in general and rural communities in particular.

RURAL SOCIAL ORGANIZATION

Rural Communities

A *rural community*, in simple terms, is defined as the area where people meet most of their social and economic needs. In the past the center of the community was the small economic center, consisting of two or three country stores, a church, a school, an automobile service station or a milk station, and in some cases a small manufacturing concern. The large majority of these small trade centers have declined and are now identified as neighborhoods; larger trade centers have now become the centers of the community.

A rural community may be also defined as the geographic area with which most of the community members identify. A midwestern farmer may identify with his trade center community, or with the entire county. Large landowners in the South associate with families outside the local neighborhood, in contrast to their tenants or small farmers who associate with families within their neighborhoods.

> In the United States there are today approximately 35,000 trade-centered rural communities and 240,000 rural neighborhoods. Since they are products of human association, they differ widely in the degree of self-consciousness and social interaction they display. (Ensminger, 1978, p. 295)

Rural-Urban Differences

Social scientists use at least five different ways to ascertain rural-urban differences: (1) comparison of what we call the "ideal types" of communities (classification of communities in terms of typical urban and rural attributes); (2) "trait-complex" type of analysis (analysis in terms of selected traits); (3) analysis on the basis of the rural-urban continuum; (4) analysis in terms of the rural-urban dichotomy; and (5) analysis on the basis of the symbiotic interdependence between rural and urban. All these methods of analysis indicate noticeable rural-urban differences, overlappings, and increasing trends toward homogeneous life-styles.

The most common form of description of the rural-urban relationship is based on the gemeinschaft (village–family)—gesellschaft (city–business) continuum. Tonnies, the early German sociologist who dealt with this subject, saw all human social relationships existing through the will to associate:

> A group or a relationship can be willed because those involved wish to attain through it a definite end and are willing to join hands for this purpose. . . . In this case rational will, in which means and ends have been sharply differentiated . . . prevails. On the other hand, people may associate

themselves together, as friends do, because they think the relationship valuable as an end in itself. In this case natural or integral will predominates.

   There are degrees of rationality of natural will and of the communities
and groups which it forms. Thus, in order of the importance of rationality
there are the Gemeinschaft groups based on friendship, on neighborliness,
and on blood relationships. (Tonnies, 1963, pp. 4–5)

   Taylor and Jones (1964) saw distinct rural-urban differences in the
following eight areas: occupation, environment, size of community,
density of population, heterogeneity and homogeneity of population,
social differentiation and stratification, social mobility, and patterns of
interaction.

   The system of interaction constitutes one of the major forces which
created, particularly in the past, the high degree of integration and
solidarity within the rural community. Early studies of rural communities, even those carried out by the French sociologist Emile Durkheim
close to the turn of the century, showed closer integration within rural
areas than within cities. A higher degree of integration is normally associated with lower anomia. *Anomia* is a form of social alienation that refers
to the way in which the individual relates himself to society (which in
earlier years was, in large part, the community to which one belonged)
and the extent to which he feels part of it. But due to the recent rapid
technological developments, this situation has changed in recent years;
studies show that, compared to urban centers, levels of anomia are
higher in rural areas, at least in mountainous rural communities. In
order to illustrate this situation, we will use rural Appalachia as an
example because it represents a clear and intense case study of the
recent, rural, social transition processes. By studying such processes,
one can explain, at least for parts of America, some of the causes of the
higher degrees of alienation reported for certain rural, as compared to
urban, communities.

Social Discord in Rural Appalachian Communities

   In the last few decades rural communities in this country and elsewhere have been changing rapidly, at a rate unprecedented in human
history. Mechanization and commercialization on the farm, and the
availability of employment opportunities in cities, have produced a
steady stream of migration from rural to urban areas in almost all societies. This process, which led to rural depopulation, affected the organization of the community and eventually the relationship between the
individual and his entire social environment. This transition process
took place faster, within a shorter period of time, and with much more
intensity in rural Appalachia than elsewhere in the United States. Some
of the highlights of this process are discussed below.

In the past, physical isolation, because of the highly forested and extensively mountainous Appalachian terrain, the region's homogeneity of population, and the predominance of the extended family form, produced highly integrated rural community and family systems. Furthermore, due to marriage within a limited geographic area, cohesiveness was further cemented within the community, particularly the neighborhood; this, in some respects, became what some call a "kinship neighborhood." People born into these close-knit systems of relationships, due to restricted but intensive interaction (particularly on the subsistence farm, where the family functioned as both a social and economic unit), developed personalities reflective of this same social environment. This close accord between personality and community further increased integration within the community and brought relative autonomy from the larger society.

Important technological changes of later years, after the thirties and in particular during World War II years, influenced the availability of jobs in the city and, more importantly, increased interaction and communication with the outside world. Eventually the autonomy of the rural Appalachian family and community was weakened. More specifically, members of Appalachian communities and families (in the beginning, the young or more educated) became more closely integrated into the larger society, which became their primary reference group.

Therefore, under the criteria of a new reference group, the income of family members working in subsistence farming began to be perceived as insufficient. From an economic point of view, they felt relatively deprived working on the farm. This led to differentiation within the family (separation of the family's social and economic functions), to specialization on the farm (e.g., one-crop production), and to the out-migration or retraining of family members so that they could contribute more efficiently to some other aspect of the economic system. Furthermore, small farms and inefficient coal mines either became more mechanized (primarily through the acquisition of machines called "continuous miners") or were closed. As a consequence, out-migration increased and, partly because of increased interaction and communication, led to further linkages with the larger society and to its use as a reference group. This brought further out-migration by additional members of the extended family. Thus, although the migrants retained close psychological ties with the part of the family left behind, the attractiveness of the life-style of the larger society outweighed their attachment to family and community. For many of those left behind (in particular the lower - income families), newly raised but unfulfilled expectations and the breaking up of intimate relationships produced considerable psychological discords. Some of the results of such discord, for low-income families and more well-to-do families alike, were dependent personality disorders, deviation in social development, and extreme psychophysical reactions.

Rural Appalachian families gradually began using nonconventional means of adjustment to the new situation, including retreat into welfare (which happened to be available at that time), membership in sectarian churches, or return to traditional, simplistic lifestyles. These were families one could call "families in retreat" or "alienated families" (see Photiadis, 1980). Because of less isolation, more resources, and, in turn, a more gradual and moderate impact of the larger society, such nonconventional means of adjustment were more limited in other rural areas of America. But now the scene is improving rapidly in rural Appalachia. In particular, since the increased demand for coal, rapid processes of reorganization and readjustment have been taking place. They are associated with rapid increases in levels of living, education, community services, and return migration. At the sociopsychological level these changes are followed by a decline in the number of families we call "families in retreat," increased faith in the future, and also increased desires for urban conveniences.

CONCLUSIONS

Although the general focus of this chapter has been rural America, some attention has been placed on the poor and alienated segment of rural America. Although the social histories of this group of rural Americans differ in many respects from the social histories of poor and alienated urban Americans, the present social positions of the two groups, vis-à-vis mainstream U.S. society, are quite similar. Like their urban counterparts, the rural poor are faced with the enormous task of integrating themselves into a modern, industrialized social structure and economic system in order to achieve the material goods and services thought to be necessary for a desired higher standard of living. Both groups face this task in the context of a sluggish economy and an unsharing social structure characterized by both racial and class prejudice. Furthermore, both the urban and rural poor face this challenge equipped with relatively low levels of education and without the comforting social support of the extended family.

REFERENCES

Beale, C. L. People on the land. In T. R. Ford (Ed.), *Rural USA: Persistence and change.* Ames: Iowa State University Press, 1978.

Bertrand, A. L. Rural social organization: Implications of technology and industry. In T. R. Ford (Ed.), *Rural USA: Persistence and change.* Ames: Iowa State University Press, 1978.

Burchinal, L. The rural family of the future. In J. H. Copp (Ed.), *Our changing rural society.* Ames: Iowa State University Press, 1964.

Chadwick, B. A., & Bahr, H. M. Rural poverty. In T. R. Ford (Ed.), *Rural USA: Persistence and change.* Ames: Iowa State University Press, 1978.

Engsminger, D. Rural neighborhoods and communities. In R. D. Rodefeld, J. Flora, D. Voth, I. Fujimoto, & J. Converse (Eds.), *Change in rural America.* St. Louis: C. V. Mosby, 1978.

Ford, T. R. (Ed.). *Rural USA: Persistence and change.* Ames: Iowa State University Press, 1978.

Harshbarger, E. C., & Stahl, S. W. Economic concentration in agriculture: Trends and developments. *Federal Reserve Bank of Kansas City Monthly Review,* April 1974, 25–36.

Lantz, H. R., Britton, M., Schmitt, R. L., & Snyder, E. C. Pre-industrial patterns in the colonial family in America: A content analysis of colonial magazines. *American Sociological Review,* 1968, *33,* 413–426.

Lantz, H. R., Schmitt, R., & Herman, R. The pre-industrial family in America: A further examination of early magazines. *American Journal of Sociology,* 1973, *79,* 566–589.

Lantz, H. R., Keys, J., & Schultz, M. The American family in the pre-industrial period: From baseline in history to change. *American Sociological Review,* 1975, *40,* 21–36.

Loomis, C. P., & Beegle, J. A. *A strategy for rural change.* New York: Wiley, 1975.

Photiadis, J. *Community size and social attributes.* Morgantown, W. Va.: Office of Research and Development, CECE, West Virginia University, 1974.

Photiadis, J. *Community, family, and development in rural Appalachia.* Morgantown, W. Va.: Office of Research and Development, CECE, West Virginia University, 1980.

Rainey, K. K., & Rainey, K. G. Rural government and local public services. In T. R. Ford (Ed.), *Rural USA: Persistence and change.* Ames: Iowa State University Press, 1978.

Sher, J. P. (Ed.). *Education in rural America.* Boulder, Colo.: Westview Press, 1977.

Taylor, L., & Jones, A. R., Jr. *Rural life and urbanized society.* New York: Oxford University Press, 1964.

Tonnies, F. *Community and society.* (C. P. Loomis, Ed. and trans.). New York: Harper & Row, 1963.

3

Interaction in Rural Families

Jon R. Urey and Scott W. Henggeler

It has been frequently argued that the attitudes and behavior of rural families are responsible for perpetuating the relatively high levels of poverty in rural regions. These family characteristics include religious fundamentalism, fatalism, traditionalism, extreme familism, and a pervasive lack of long-range planning. Weller (1965) has suggested that the strong emotional ties of Appalachian families limit the opportunities for family members to develop socialization skills in the greater community. Similarly, Looff (1971) has reported that parents in rural families often provide inadequate child supervision and socialization training. In sum, many writers have viewed the relations of rural families from a deficit perspective. Alternatively, this chapter suggests that the family unit is one of the more positive aspects of rural life and that investigators of rural families should emphasize their strengths, rather than focus on supposedly deviant cultural values.

Despite a widespread interest in the problems of rural areas, there have been relatively few empirical investigations of rural family life. Consequently, the present review is largely based on anecdotal reports. The limitations of such a review are substantial. For example, A. M. Ford (1973) has argued that most individuals who write about rural areas do not adequately capture the viewpoints of the residents, and often fail to recognize the influence of their own values upon their subject matter. Moreover, Eller (1977) has suggested that such writings, in the absence of empirical findings, have served to perpetuate myths about rural family life.

Jon R. Urey and Scott W. Henggeler • Department of Psychology, Memphis State University, Memphis, Tennessee 38152.

This chapter reviews anecdotal reports and empirical studies which have investigated the child-rearing strategies, interaction patterns, and relations of rural families. Findings are related to the extant developmental psychology literatures in the areas of parenting, family interaction, and child psychosocial functioning. In addition, certain conclusions drawn by earlier researchers are questioned in light of the current developmental literatures. Finally, suggestions are made concerning the directions and goals of future research with rural families.

CHARACTERISTICS OF RURAL FAMILIES

Familism

Rural family members have been typically described as close-knit, loyal, supportive, and highly dependent upon one another. Based on concepts from the kinship research of Farber (1968), Heller and Quesada (1977) conducted an intensive interregional analysis and identified two forms of rural familism. The first form of familism, concentrated most heavily in the rural Southeast, was extended-kin oriented. Heller and Quesada identified several traits that were characteristic of these families. First, family members were actively involved within a network of secondary relatives who lived in close geographic proximity. Second, in order to maintain close relations with secondary kin, family members were encouraged to remain within the geographic area. Third, sentimental ties and affections were strong for both primary and secondary relatives. Fourth, these affective ties resulted in a high rate of marriages among secondary kin. Fifth, there was considerable obligation and responsibility felt toward secondary kin. Finally, the extended-kin support system served to maintain the identities of individual family members.

The second form of familism, more common in the southwestern United States, was termed primary-kin oriented. In this type, the children's identities were derived exclusively from the nuclear family unit, especially the parents. Heller and Quesada noted that these families encouraged migration to pursue economic opportunity and placed a high value on achievement in the larger society. In addition, emotional ties to nuclear family members, but not to secondary kin, were stressed. Although primary-kin oriented familism has received relatively little attention to date, it represents an intriguing and potentially useful area for further research. This type of orientation is likely dominant in regions other than the Southwest. Hence, further study of primary-kin familism might be of substantial explanatory value to other areas.

The analyses provided by Heller and Quesada illustrate the importance of considering regional variables in familism research. Throughout their paper, the authors emphasized that the identified types of familism were adaptive responses to specific socioecological conditions and problems. That is, these socioecological conditions were seen as producing two dissimilar forms of familism. Hence, familism was viewed as functional and beneficial to the adaptivity of family members. Future research should be directed toward determining the functional aspects of specific interaction patterns within these groups. For example, the emphasis on primary-kin relations observed in the rural Southwest can be seen as an adaptive response to the great geographical distances between nuclear family units. Conversely, rural southeastern families often reside in small communities in which secondary relatives are more available. These conditions would explain the intense emotional attachment to secondary kin frequently observed in the Southeast (Heller & Quesada, 1977).

Brown, Schwarzweller, and Mangalam (1963) have shown that combinations of primary-kin and extended-kin familism are common in certain regions. Their analyses were based on case study material gathered over a 20-year period. The authors examined migration patterns in eastern Kentucky and discovered that children often left their parents' household to pursue greater economic opportunities. However, the children typically migrated to areas where secondary-kin groups were already established. Furthermore, the parental household provided a place of return for those individuals who were not successful in their economic pursuits. Hence, in this system, family members were afforded the advantages of both extended-kin and primary-kin familism. Members could venture into the outside world while still maintaining a secure family base. Future research might be directed toward contrasting the strengths and weaknesses of these three types of familism across different environmental settings. For example, extended-kin familism might have greater utility in agrarian than in technological subcultures.

Analgesic Subculture Model

Ball (1970) has stated that rural cultures, especially those in Appalachia, present a number of common themes including individualism, traditionalism, fatalism, religious fundamentalism, and familism. He proposed that these characteristics reflect the institutionalization of frustration-instigated behavior (Maier, 1949). Namely, these behaviors represent a terminal response to pervasive and long-term frustration. This frustration is largely related to the family's inability to achieve their middle-class aspirations due to economic hardships. The end product of this frustration process has been labeled an "analgesic subculture" (Ball, 1970).

Although Ball's analysis of the rural culture has been accepted by some authors (A. M. Ford, 1973), others have indicated that it is not an adequate characterization (Billings, 1974; Fisher, 1977). Critics have argued that the analgesic subculture model erroneously places responsibility on rural citizens for difficulties that more likely reflect societal realities. These critics have noted, justifiably, that Ball relied very heavily on anecdotal observations from Caudill (1962) and Weller (1965) to support his argument. Furthermore, several researchers have suggested that Ball's cultural themes of individualism, traditionalism, familism, and religious fundamentalism do not pervade rural America. T. R. Ford (1962) surveyed southern Appalachia and found that the residents were not as rugged and self-reliant as previously supposed. Instead, they seemed surprisingly achievement-oriented and progressive in their ideas. Similarly, Billings (1974) examined the attitudes of families from Appalachia, from an urban-industrial region of North Carolina, and from a rural eastern-coastal plain. His findings indicated that both populations of rural families possessed a high degree of middle-class orientation. Billings argued that a situational analysis of the behavior and attitudes of rural families is the best approach for understanding such families. This viewpoint has been shared by several other authors (Valentine, 1968).

In contrast to subculture models of rural conditions, situational explanations view the behavior of rural residents as adaptations to particular socioecological circumstances and economic conditions. Consequently, this perspective has emphasized the study of rural conditions in their full context—the community (Billings, 1974). This type of analysis should lead to a more positive and less pathological view of rural inhabitants (Valentine, 1968).

There is some evidence that familism serves a highly adaptive function for the rural family. Many rural areas have suffered extreme fluctuations in their economies (Cressey, 1949; Naylor & Clotfelter, 1975). In light of such fluctuations, the maintenance of fatalistic and passive attitudes is understandable. Residents come to believe, often quite validly, that they have little control over their economic situation. During difficult times, the family unit can provide one of the few positive aspects of individuals' lives. In such cases, familism might be an appropriate and adaptive response to an environment in which family members feel powerless (Polansky, 1969). Rather than the theory that characteristics such as fatalism and traditionalism are maintained by rural family relations, a more likely explanation is that the fluctuating economy of the larger society serves to support such characteristics.

Family Dominance Patterns

The dominance patterns of rural families have been typically described as patriarchal (Berry & Davis, 1978; Sawer, 1973; Youmans, 1973). In these families, the parents, especially the father, represent the final line of authority (Cressey, 1949). Rules are stated clearly and enforced consistently (Mueller, 1974). However, in their study of eastern Kentucky families, Brown *et al.* (1963) reported that the patriarchal dominance pattern was not always stable. During times of unemployment or other economic hardship, the power structure of rural families often shifted.

Cressey (1949) has described the tremendous impact of the coal industry on the social and family dominance structure of Harlan County, Kentucky. Prior to the arrival of the coal industry, most families lived on self-contained farms. Families were independent, self-reliant, and made no class distinctions. However, with the advent of coal, the entire economic structure of this rural Appalachian community was disrupted. With increased industrialization, rural individuals became more dependent on outside sources of sustenance. The insecurity of industrial employment, coupled with the hazardous nature of the occupation of coal-mining, led the people to develop a fatalistic attitude toward life and to adopt more impulsive patterns of behavior.

Cressey indicated that a more far-reaching effect of the intrusion of the coal industry was the impact on the basic family and community structure. Families became more competitive and distrustful of one another. Due to the father's daily absence in the mines, he was not able to assume as much of the child-rearing responsibilities as he had previously. Furthermore, when the father was unemployed during periodic economic difficulties, he lost status within his family. Hence, while the father was previously considered the undisputed head of the household, his loss in status often evoked significant conflict, changes in the family power structure, and a general weakening of family ties.

Although Cressey's descriptions were written approximately 30 years ago, they still have important implications for rural families. Cressey reported that after these early economic disruptions, conditions slowly stabilized and the people adjusted to the routines of the industrial society. In a similar manner, rural communities that rely principally on agriculture have also experienced considerable change in their way of life. Naylor and Clotfelter (1975) have reported that with increased mechanization, many rural farm workers have been forced to give up their agricultural occupations and to adopt other employment. Hence, it might be expected that the dominance structures of such families experience the same changes that characterize Appalachian families. Indeed, recent research has suggested that many farm wives play a significant role in the decision-making process regarding the general management of their farms. Sawer (1973) has indicated that when wives were very involved in farm tasks, the marital partners also participated jointly in farm decision-making. This equalitarian dominance pattern was especially evident in families who operated small, less financially successful farms (Sawer, 1973).

Parenting

Willits, Bealer, and Crider (1974) examined self-report data from rural and small-town Pennsylvania high school students and found that rural parents were more likely than urban parents to hold traditional attitudes toward family life and child rearing. Some of these attitudes represent such distinctly positive characteristics as the encouragement of regular church attendance, the discouragement of "loafing" among young people, and the maintenance of control over children's behavior. Using an open-ended interview procedure, Mueller (1974) observed similar child-rearing attitudes among parents in a rural midwestern county. Mothers valued academic achievement, industry, honesty, ambition, consideration for others, high moral and religious beliefs, and ability in sports. Athletic skills were valued because they were thought to build character and to provide opportunities for the development of social relations.

Mueller further observed that the parents supervised their children quite closely. They regularly praised and rewarded appropriate academic and social performance. Inappropriate behaviors were punished through either verbal discipline or physical restriction. The parents explained the reasons behind household rules and these explanations were accepted by the children without question. The majority of the children stated that their parents attempted to understand their problems, and that they felt comfortable talking over any difficulties they had with their parents. It should also be noted that these parents took their parenting responsibilities very seriously. Typically, if both parents were employed, they worked different shifts in order to share the responsibility for child supervision.

More recently, Lawson and Slaughter (1976) interviewed 2nd through 12th graders who lived in either rural areas or in towns of the South. The children were asked to describe incidents that evoked either praise or punishment from their parents. The authors found that reported methods of reward and punishment did not differ as a function of place of residence or age of child. However, there were sex differences: Boys received more praise for sports, while girls were more likely to be praised for creative activities. The girls received more praise or punishment from the mother, and the boys received an equal amount from both parents. An important implication of these findings is that the standards which govern child-rearing patterns in rural families may be quite similar to those employed among the urban middle class. This similarity to middle-class populations has been observed by other researchers (Mueller, 1974; Roach & Gursslin, 1967). Further verification of these findings could lead to the modification of negative attitudes toward rural parenting held by previous authors (Looff, 1971; Weller, 1965).

Education

Rural families have often been described as resistant to "book learning" (Weller, 1965) and toward formal education in general (Matthews, 1965; Pearsall, 1959). Interestingly, Nelson and Frost (1971) found that rural Presbyterians in southern Appalachia placed a relatively heavy emphasis on education when compared with lower-class urban populations. Nevertheless, the rural parents evaluated their own schools more negatively, and they desired less education for their children. The authors suggested that these seemingly contradictory findings reflected the tendency of rural residents to excuse themselves for a sense of failure. Cosby, Thomas, and Falk (1976) reported a similar tendency among rural southerners. They found that the rural residents' expectations for occupational and educational attainment were unrealistically high in terms of available opportunities. Cosby et al. suggested that these expectations allow rural inhabitants to deny their present sense of failure. However, it seems that these authors might have overlooked the possibility that rural schools actually are inferior, or are so dominated by middle-class urban values that they have little relevance to the situational parameters of the rural setting. An alternative explanation might be that rural families value education, but are faced with inadequate educational opportunities.

Mueller (1974) examined family styles associated with high or low school performance among rural children. The fathers of high-achieving students worked longer hours on their jobs, had a higher mean educational level, and were more active participants in church and community life. This latter finding suggests that the fathers of high-achieving students were more socially integrated into community life. Mueller also found that almost all rural working-class families placed a heavy emphasis on education. Both low- and high-achieving students expressed a desire to continue their education beyond high school, even when their stated occupational goals did not require a college degree. This finding does not support the notion that rural families profess to value education in order to excuse their own failure.

IMPLICATIONS OF FINDINGS

On the basis of the preceding review, there are several characteristics of rural families that seem fairly well established. Again, however, it must be noted that these characteristics are based more upon anecdotal descriptions than on empirical research. This section delineates the implications of the identified family characteristics for child psychosocial development and family functioning. The discussion centers on the extended-kin family pattern since it appears to be the most frequent structure of rural families and has received the most attention in the literature.

Familism

Several authors have suggested that the extended-kin family pattern has been the primary factor in perpetuating the rural subculture of poverty (Ball, 1970; Caudill, 1962; Weller, 1965). However, the attachment to secondary relatives might also be seen in a more positive light. With the presence of several other relatives in the child's environment, the opportunity to observe appropriate role models is greatly enhanced. Grusec (1971) found that the observation of powerful and supportive models promoted altruistic behavior in children. Similarly, Mischel and Grusec (1966) found that observing such models enhanced children's ability to delay gratification. The extended-kin system can provide multiple models that are appropriate for the child's social environment.

Another benefit of the extended-kin system is that considerable support and help is available in times of crisis. Given the frequent economic adversity in rural areas (A. M. Ford, 1973; Naylor & Clotfelter, 1975), emotional and material support is extremely important. Indeed, as suggested earlier, the extended-kin pattern most likely evolved in response to periodic environmental threats. Perhaps familism could be more appropriately viewed from the perspective of the environmental factors that produced these attitudes. Such factors might include the frequent exploitation from outside forces (Cressey, 1949; Noonan, 1976), and the difficult living conditions which resulted from such exploitation. The close emotional ties of rural family members serve an extremely useful function, helping to maintain both affective and economic security.

Parenting

In general, it seems that rural parents are accepting of their children and convey considerable warmth toward them. The parents enjoy spending time with their children and provide them with appropriate attention and reinforcement. As Martin (1975) has emphasized, relatively high levels of parental affection are conducive to the positive psychosocial functioning of children.

Regarding parental control strategies, it seems that rural parents tend toward the restrictive end of the restrictive-permissive continuum (Roe, 1957; Slater, 1962). This suggests that, in rural households, parents are unlikely to yield to coercive demands from their children (Martin, 1975). It is apparent that in a culture dominated by religious beliefs and high moral standards, there should be clearly established guidelines for behavior. The nature of these rules is likely to preclude parental permissiveness. Researchers have observed that children of warm and restrictive parents tend to be more dependent upon adults and authority figures in general (Martin, 1975). Hence, rural children might be less independent and less influenced by peers than urban children.

The configuration of parental warmth and restrictiveness also encourages the interalization of traditional values in children (Maccoby, 1961; Parke, 1969; Parke & Walters, 1967). That is, rural children might be less concerned with actually being caught in a transgression than with the internal reactions associated with parental disappointment. Researchers (Baumrind, 1967; Bronfenbrenner, 1961) have shown that the interalization of values is enhanced when discipline is accompanied by an explanation of the reasons behind it, as has been reported in rural families (Mueller, 1974).

Family Dominance Patterns

In rural families the father has typically been considered the deciding force in family matters. However, as indicated previously, recent technological changes in industrial employment and increased mechanization in agriculture may have operated to alter traditional dominance patterns (Cressey, 1949; Naylor & Clotfelter, 1975; Sawer, 1973). The rural wife has taken an increasingly active role in both family matters and possible business interests. Clearly, increased maternal competency and power can have positive effects on female offspring. Daughters are afforded the opportunity to model their mothers' successful coping strategies. Consequently, the daughter might tend to become more independent and more achievement oriented. Furthermore, the shift toward an equalitarian dominance structure increases the flexibility of the family system along with its ability to adjust to societal change.

Conclusions

In overview, there are several observations that should be made. First, the present review is limited by the fact that available research has given little attention to the possible regional differences in rural family relations. Failure to consider this variable could result in inappropriate generalizations across rural populations. Typically, rurality has been conceptualized in relation to a rural-urban continuum (Bultena, 1969; Lowe & Peek, 1974). Within this frame of reference, rural areas are regarded as less populated, lower in density, less complex, and more homogeneous than urban areas. Although it is apparent that most rural areas share similar demographic characteristics, there are other factors (geographic, economic, etc.) that could influence family behavior. For example, the relative geographic isolation of nuclear family units in the rural Southwest has lead to an emphasis on primary-kin relations. Similarly, the frequent economic exploitation that has occurred in Appalachian coal-mining regions could be responsible for the development of strong familistic attitudes among the residents. Future research on such regional effects could clarify any distinctive family patterns present in rural settings, as well as highlight the adaptive qualities of these patterns. Although the present review is based largely on reports from Appalachia and rural southern regions, an attempt has been made to integrate data from other areas. However, it is clear that future studies that take a more ecological approach to rural families are necessary.

Second, based on the results of available research, the interaction patterns in rural families might not differ substantially from those of nonrural families. For example, some researchers have indicated that there is a distinctly middle-class orientation among many rural families (Billings, 1974; Mueller, 1974). It is likely that there are many more similarities between rural and nonrural families than there are differences (Fisher, 1977; Roach & Gursslin, 1967). The differences that have emerged seem to have been adaptations to specific sociological milieus.

Third, the future study of rural family patterns should be approached with the attitude that observed differences in these families are not necessarily deficits. Fisher (1977) has argued that the continued use of the deviant subculture model may eventually convince members of the subculture that they are somehow inferior. Similarly, others have argued that it is unjust to characterize rural cultural patterns as deficient or pathological versions of mainstream American culture (A. M. Ford, 1973; Valentine, 1968). As an example, familism and religious fundamentalism have often been described pejoratively in the literature. Yet it is likely that each of these characteristics has helped to optimize the psychosocial and economic functioning of rural families during times of socioeconomic hardship.

Finally, in relation to the previous two points, efforts to ameliorate the problems of rural poverty might be targeted more appropriately on the greater social system. Rather than attempting to modify individual or family values because of their supposed deviance, it would seem more advisable to capitalize on the existing strengths of rural families (Sawer, 1973). Future research should attempt to obtain an unbiased understanding of rural families as well as a more accurate identification of social needs from the perspectives of rural residents. In this manner, it should be possible to develop more effective methods for improving conditions in rural areas.

REFERENCES

Ball, R. A. Poverty case: The analgesic subculture of the Southern Appalachians. *American Sociological Review*, 1970, *33*, 885–895.

Baumrind, D. Child care practices anteceding three patterns of preschool behavior. *Genetic Psychology Monographs*, 1967, *75*, (1, Pt. 2).

Berry, B. & Davis, A. E. Community mental health ideology: A problematic model for rural areas. *American Journal of Orthopsychiatry*, 1978, *48*, 673–679.

Billings, D. E. Culture and poverty in Appalachia: A theoretical discussion and empirical analysis. *Social Forces*, 1974, *53*, 315–323.

Bronfenbrenner, U. Some familial antecedents of responsibility and leadership in adolescents. In L. Petrullo & B. M. Bass (Eds.), *Leadership and interpersonal behavior*. New York: Holt, Rinehart & Winston, 1961.

Brown, J. S., Schwarzweller, H. K., & Mangalam, J. J. Kentucky mountain migration and the stem-family: An American variation on a theme by Le Play. *Rural Sociology*, 1963, *28*, 48–69.

Bultena, G. L. Rural-urban differences in the familial interaction of the aged. *Rural Sociology*, 1969, *34*, 5–15.

Caudill, H. *Night comes to the Cumberlands*. Boston: Little, Brown, 1962.

Cosby, A. G., Thomas, J. K., & Falk, W. W. Patterns of early adult status attainment and attitudes in the nonmetropolitan South. *Sociology of Work and Occupations*, 1976, *3*, 411–428.

Cressey, P. F. Social disorganization and reorganization in Harlan County. *American Sociological Review*, 1949, *14*, 389–394.

Eller, R. D. Appalachian oral history. In J. W. Williamson (Ed.), *An Appalachian symposium*. Boone, N.C.: Appalachian State University Press, 1977.

Farber, B. *Comparative kinship systems: A method of analysis*. New York: Wiley, 1968.

Fisher, S. Folk culture or folk tale. In J. W. Williamson (Ed.), *An Appalachian symposium*. Boone, N.C.: Appalachian State University Press, 1977.

Ford, A. M. *Political economics of rural poverty in the South*. Cambridge, Mass.: Ballinger, 1973.

Ford, T. R. (Ed.). *The Southern Appalachian region: A survey*. Lexington: University of Kentucky Press, 1962.

Grusec, J. E. Power and the internalization of self-denial. *Child Development*, 1971, *42*, 93–105.

Heller, P. L. & Quesada, G. M. Rural familism: An interregional analysis. *Rural Sociology*, 1977, *42*, 220–240.

Lawson, D. E. & Slaughter, M. F. Reward and punishment patterns in rural and town schoolchildren. *Child Study Journal*, 1976, *7*, 145–158.

Looff, D. *Appalachia's children: The challenge of mental health.* Lexington: University of Kentucky Press, 1971.

Lowe, G. D. & Peek, L. W. Location and lifestyle: The comparative explanatory ability of urbanism and rurality. *Rural Sociology*, 1974, *39*, 392–420.

Maccoby, E. E. The taking of adult roles in middle childhood. *Journal of Abnormal and Social Psychology*, 1961, *63*, 493–503.

Maier, N. R. *Frustration.* New York: McGraw-Hill, 1949.

Martin, B. Parent–child relations. In F. D. Horowitz, E. M. Hetherington, S. Scarr-Salaptek, & G. M. Siegel (Eds.), *Review of child development research* (Vol. 4). Chicago: University of Chicago Press, 1975.

Matthews, E. M. *Neighbor and kin: Life in a Tennessee ridge community.* Nashville: Vanderbilt University Press, 1965.

Mischel, W. & Grusec, J. Determinants of the rehersal and transmission of neutral and aversive behaviors. *Journal of Personality and Social Psychology*, 1966, *3*, 197–205.

Mueller, B. J. Rural family life style and sons' school achievement. *Rural Sociology*, 1974, *30*, 362–372.

Naylor, T. H. & Clotfelter, J. *Strategies for change in the South.* Chapel Hill: University of North Carolina Press, 1975.

Nelson, H. M. & Frost, E. Residence, anomie, and receptivity to education among Southern Appalachia Presbyterians. *Rural Sociology*, 1971, *36*, 521–532.

Noonan, R. J. An analysis of contingencies in the Appalachian coal fields. *Community Mental Health Journal*, 1976, *12*, 99–105.

Parke, R. D. Effectiveness of punishment as an interaction of intensity, timing, agent, nurturance, and cognitive structuring. *Child Development*, 1969, *40*, 211–235.

Parke, R. D. & Walters, R. H. Some factors influencing the efficacy of punishment training for inducing response inhibition. *Monographs of the Society for Research in Child Development*, 1967, *32*, (2, Serial No. 109).

Pearsall, M. *Little Smokey Ridge.* Tuscaloosa: University of Alabama Press, 1959.

Polansky, N. A. Powerlessness among rural Appalachian youth. *Rural Sociology*, 1969, *34*, 219–222.

Roach, J. L. & Gursslin, O. R. An evaluation of the concept "culture of poverty." *Social Forces*, 1967, *45*, 383–392.

Roe, A. Early determinants of vocational choice. *Journal of Counseling Psychology*, 1957, *4*, 212–217.

Sawer, B. Predictors of the farm wives involvement in general management and adoption decisions. *Rural Sociology*, 1973, *38*, 412–426.

Slater, P. E. Parental behavior and the personality of the child. *Journal of Genetic Psychology*, 1962, *101*, 53–68.

Valentine, C. A. *Culture and poverty.* Chicago: University of Chicago Press, 1968.

Weller, J. E. *Yesterday's people.* Lexington: University of Kentucky Press, 1965.

Willits, F. K., Bealer, R. C., & Crider, D. M. The ecology of social traditionalism in a rural hinterland. *Rural Sociology*, 1974, *39*, 334–349.

Youmans, E. Age stratification and value orientations. *Aging and Human Development*, 1973, *4*, 53–65.

4

Cross-Cultural Research in Psychological Development in Rural Communities

Marida Hollos

Introduction

The last decade has witnessed an increased interest in investigating the effects of various environmental factors on cognitive development. Many of these studies measure developmental differences between rural and urban groups, either within one culture or across cultures. The findings frequently demonstrate that urban children acquire some cognitive and memory skills earlier than rural children. Instead of attempting to analyze the factors that may be responsible for the rural groups' lower performance, investigators usually resort to explanations in terms of a "lack" in the rural environment and assume that they are dealing with a "deprivation."

More recent interpretations, however, indicate that the apparent developmental lag of the rural children may be due to a biased definition of the rural environment by experimenters who have little understanding of the cognitive demands posed by that environment. This bias results in tasks being presented to rural groups that have little relevance to the skills developed in those settings. A related problem is that of the experimental situation and the presentation of the test materials: Do urban

Marida Hollos • Department of Anthropology, Brown University, Providence, Rhode Island 02912.

and rural groups interpret them similarly? Does a testing situation pose a different problem to city children than to village children?

The purpose of this paper is to evaluate some of the cross-cultural research on rural-urban differences in cognitive development and to suggest alternate strategies for future research. The first part presents a brief survey of the findings. The review will be limited to studies comparing developmental differences of rural and urban groups within the same culture. It does not pretend to be exhaustive. Rather, it intends to elucidate the pattern of differences that have been found between these groups.

The second part will present comparative studies done by the author which will demonstrate the advantages of combining ethnographic field research with psychological testing in promoting a more complete understanding of the effects of different environmental factors on child development.

CROSS-CULTURAL FINDINGS ON RURAL-URBAN DIFFERENCES IN COGNITIVE GROWTH

Rural and urban differences in the rate and style of cognitive development have been investigated in a wide variety of cultures, using different kinds of cognitive tasks. The studies include Piagetian developmental measures, classification and sorting tasks, memory tasks, and tests of verbal skills. This survey will review studies comparing developmental differences on these tasks in urban and rural groups within the same culture in several different parts of the world. Although it is recognized that making generalizations ranging across a wide variety of cultures in which *rural* and *urban* may have entirely different meanings is difficult, such an attempt might be justified if it elucidates a pattern of differences that have been found between these groups.

Piagetian Research

Peluffo (1962, 1967) compared 8- and 11-year-old Italian boys from various backgrounds on Piagetian tests of physical causality, conservation, and "combinations" and "permutations" (formal operations). Samples studied included: sons of Sardinian peasants newly moved to Genoa, sons of Sardinian immigrants who moved three years earlier, sons of native Genoans and rural Sardinians, as well as a sample of illiterate Sardinian peasants. On the test of physical causality he found that by age 11, 60% of the sons of Genoan workers and 50% of the sons of long-settled immigrants gave mechanistic (Stage 5) responses when questioned about movements of the moon, compared to only 10% of the sons of new immigrants. On the movements of the clouds, the answers were 40% mechanistic for the first two groups and 0% for the last. On the conservation task, by 11 years of age 70% and 65% of the native Genoans and long-settled immigrants conserved volume, while only 35% of the new immigrants, 30% of rural Sardinian children, and 20% of rural Sardinian adults did so. On the tests of combinations and permutations at age 11, 60% of the Genoan workers, 55% of the sons of Sardinian professionals and only 25% of the sons of Sardinian peasants and 20% of the illiterate Sardinian adults performed successfully.

Peluffo attributed these results to the "low cultural level" of rural Sardinia which "does not stimulate abstract thinking." In such an environment, relations among the elements are mainly based on perception and on the positive or negative application of the principles of identity and continguity.

Vernon (1969) constructed a large battery of tests that tapped a wide range of abilities, including Piagetian concept–development tasks, verbal and educational tests, creativity and perceptual/spatial tests. Through interviews he collected extensive material on the backgrounds of his subjects. His subjects were 10- to 12-year-old boys of different countries (Tanzania, Canadian Eskimo, Canadian Indian, Jamaica, and England). The English and West Indian samples included the comparison of rural and urban subgroups. In England he found the differences between "these subgroups unexpectedly small." The rural group, however, scored lower on most tests, but the only significant difference at the .05 level was on the test of Abstraction. He found correlations between certain environmental variables and test performance in each of the settings. Regularity of schooling affected educational attainment and the perceptual and drawing tests; socioeconomic level and linguistic background were associated with g (general intelligence factor) and with educational and verbal performance, as were "cultural stimulus" (e.g., the presence of books) in the home and planfulness.

In the West Indies, the samples included two urban groups, one from a country town and from a sugar plantation, and one from isolated rural small holdings. When compared to the English sample, the entire West Indian sample fell behind the English group, with the West Indian rural boys falling the farthest below the urban ones. In the West Indian group, the assessment of cultural stimulus in the home gave the highest correlation with the test scores. Family planfulness and rationality were particularly relevant. The most important single factors were the "cultural level" of the home, parental education and encouragement, reading facilities, and speech background (which affected all types of abilities).

Opper (1977) administered a group of seven concrete operational tasks, which fall into four categories (class inclusion, conservation, one-to-one correspondence, and seriation), to two samples of 6- to 11-year-old Thai children. One sample came from Bangkok, the other from a rural farming district. They were matched on average school performance, age, and sex. Her findings confirmed the existence of the three concrete, operational substages described by Piaget. There was a significant difference between the performance of the urban and rural children: more rural children were found to be in the lowest stage on all tasks. There was also a difference in the pattern of acquisition between the two groups. Urban children acquired the concepts gradually over a period of five years, beginning at age 6. The rural children started the acquisition at age 9, then rapidly mastered the concepts over a period of two years, indicating the importance of schooling for this group.

Like Vernon, Opper also examined a number of factors which may be responsible for producing the differences in the performance of the two groups (physical environment, nutrition, heredity, and schooling) and she found them similar in the two settings. The factors she considered important were the differences in the degree of industrialization (the pace of life is faster) and child-rearing practices (urban parents' awareness of the need for educational achievement and a less competitive rural environment).

Poole (1968) compared three groups of rural Hausa, three groups of urban Hausa, and two groups of Hausa living in large market villages on tests designed to measure "scientific concept attainment." He specifically aimed to show "how scientific concept attainment in Hausa society is affected by degree of urbanization" (p. 57). The battery of tests included tests of conservation of solids and liquids, animism, prediction of spatial relations, grasp of principles (see-saw, gears), and estimation of time between two events. The children were 10–11 years old. Poole found significant differences between rural and market village children, and between market village and urban Hausa children, with the results favoring the more urban settings. These differences were ascribed to the degree of acculturation. "The results confirm the acculturative role of urbanization" (1968, p. 62). According to Poole, scientific ideas are new ideas which rural communities resist, whereas cities have been focal points of change throughout history.

An extensive investigation of the development of conservation was carried out by Greenfield (1966) among the Wolof in Senegal. Her samples included samples of schooled and unschooled children in rural settings and an urban schooled sample. By the age of 11 to 13 years, urban and rural school children gave conservation responses. Only 50% of the nonschooled rural children achieved conservation by this age. Rural and urban children differed on the reasons for conservation and nonconservation responses. Greenfield found that the groups that showed increasing conservation with age also showed a parallel decrease in perceptual justification.

In a modified conservation experiment, Greenfield directly tested for the effect of the experimenter on the children. Nonschooled rural children who poured the water themselves gave conservation responses. Those who watched the experimenter pour did not. This procedure had no effect on urban school children. Greenfield's interpretation was that rural Wolof children believe in "action-magic"; that is, that the experimenter influenced the amount of water present in the beakers. When the children poured, this reasoning disappeared because special powers were attributed to authority figures but not to the children. To Greenfield and Bruner (1966), these results suggested that authority figures have a special role as causative agents in the thinking of the rural children, indicating a reliance on social (as opposed to physicalistic) explanations by traditional people.

Kirk (1970, 1977) compared the rate of cognitive development of 5-, 8-, and 11-year-old Ga children from rural, urban, and suburban environments. She administered three Piaget-derived tests: conservation of quantity (clay), conservation of length, and perspectives. She also made an extensive analysis of the mothers' teaching and verbal style, based on the observation and recording of a controlled teaching session between mothers and their children.

She found that children's performance on the perspectives test was highly correlated with subculture, with the rural children's performance lagging behind the other groups. Of the conservation tasks, the rural children performed better than either of the other groups on conservation of quantity (clay), whereas the suburban children showed the highest levels of performance by age 11 on the conservation of length test. On the composite of the three tests, the suburban children performed best. Kirk explained these findings on the basis of differential experiences provided by the environments to the children: suburban children have access to better schooling, there is more emphasis on concept manipulation, verbalization and intellectual achievement in their surroundings, their social milieu provides diversity, and they have been exposed to situations similar to testing. The rural children, on the other hand, have more contact with materials such as clay and mud in observing housebuilding and farming. Following Goodnow (1969), Kirk suggested that these environmental differences may produce a difference in the child's ability to perform on tasks which call for "imaged changes" or "spatial shuffling or transforming in his head," but would not affect performance where direct manipulation of the material or action was required.

When Piagetian test performance was compared with features of maternal teaching behavior, Kirk found a high correlation between these and the performance on conservation tasks, but not performance on the perspectives task. Mothers who referred to relationships by the use of specific referents, and who most frequently justified and explained, produced children with greater conservation skills, regardless of the subculture. Mothers who most frequently demonstrated this style came most frequently from the suburban group and least frequently from the rural group. Kirk concluded that "the effect of subculture on the rate of the child's cognitive development is mediated primarily through maternal behavior and that the way in which subculture affects cognitive development is almost entirely through the behavior of the mother" (1970, p. 145).

Piaget (1974), in a comment on cross-cultural research, reviewed the work of Mohseni in Iran (1966).[1] Mohseni compared Tehran school children with rural illiterate children on conservation and performance tasks (Porteus maze, graphical tests). He found a two- to three-year delay in the development of the rural children on the conservation tasks, and a four- or five-year delay on the performance tasks. According to Piaget, Mohseni attributed the lag to the lack of activity of the country children who do not go to school, have no toys, and show a constant passivity and apathy. Thus, Piaget concluded, the rural environment provides a "poor development of the coordinations of individual actions, of interpersonal actions and educational transmissions, which are reduced since these children are illiterate" (Piaget, 1974, p. 306).

Since there is little overlap between these studies in terms of tasks, it is difficult to make a direct comparison of the results. It seems, however, that on most Piagetian tasks the rural children lag behind their urban peers by some years.

Sorting and Classification

A great deal of attention has focused on the developing ability of children to sort and classify as an index of progression from concrete and context-bound to abstract and rule-governed thinking. The investigation has centered on two aspects of performance: (1) the particular attribute the subject uses as the criterion of similarity; and (2) whether or not the subject uses a single attribute consistently as the basis for grouping.

Greenfield (1966) asked Wolof subjects from three environments (bush unschooled, bush schoolchildren and Dakar schoolchildren) to sort objects depicted on cards. The cards were designed so that within

---

[1]The original study by Mohseni is not available.

each set of three, it was possible to form pairs based on the color, form, or function of the object picture on the card. She found that school-children in the village and the city performed similar to American children: their preference for color decreased with age, while form and function preferences increased. An increasing proportion of the older children justified their classification in terms of a superordinate category. Bush unschooled children, on the other hand, showed greater preference for color with increasing age and rarely justified their responses by references to a picture's category.

Greenfield attributed these results to a lack of perceptual analysis in the bush environment where children are being taught by the European-style schools. "An analysis into parts is plainly crucial to concepts based on the multi-dimensional attributes of form, whereas unitary global perception could suffice for color grouping." (Greenfield, 1966, p. 316)

Scribner (Cole & Scribner, 1974, p. 118) also had her Kpelle subjects sort into groups 25 familiar objects that "went together," with at least three items in a group. After the sorting was completed, the objects were mixed up and the subject was asked to regroup the objects exactly the same way. The subject was then asked to recall as many of the items as possible. This gave subjects the opportunity to organize material according to their preferred criteria; it also gave the experimenter the opportunity to test for the semantic categories he built into the list, as well as for the subject's own categories. The subjects were high school students, cash workers, rice farmers in a road village, and rice farmers in a village isolated in the bush. The rural isolated farmers were least likely to use taxonomic categories, which were associated with high-recall cluster scores. High schoolers almost uniformly grouped items by taxonomic category, as did cash workers and road villagers. The youngest children from any location (6 to 8 years old) ignored the categories when grouping, regardless of schooling, as did the 10- to 14-year-old non-schooled children. Their schooled counterparts, however, made groups corresponding to semantic categories.

The major difference in the performance of different groups was the ability to verbalize the results, a skill that increased with the level of education. Thus, similar to Greenfield, Scribner also attributed a major role to education in the performance of these tasks. Rural farmers who performed on the least abstract level had the least amount of schooling, a clear disadvantage on these tasks.

Maccoby and Modiano (1966, 1969) investigated the differences of cognitive style in Mexican urban and rural children by administering a sorting task and Piaget's moral-judgment test. Responses on the sorting task were classified according to the kind of reasons given: perceptible, functional, moral or affective, nominal, or reasoning by decree. These were collapsed into three types: concrete, concrete-abstract, and abstract. Urban children were more likely to give abstract criteria, while rural children were more likely to give concrete. Children who used a concrete type of reasoning in the sorting task gave more realistic and authoritarian moral judgments. Those who used abstract criteria in sorting were more likely to give more reciprocal moral judgments.

The authors found that the results reflected the skills that were needed and used in each environment; they emphasized that the differences should not be interpreted to the detriment of the rural children's intellectual skills. While abstract and theoretical thought is adaptive in an urban-industrial context, concreteness in thought may enable the peasant child to respond to subtleties and differences in his environment and help the child to maintain a deeper relatedness to his world.

After reviewing the literature on rural-urban developmental differences in Africa, Weisner (1976) set out to test the hypothesis that tasks which might be called exploratory-manipulative (requiring multiple sorts, spontaneous verbalization or reasoning and expectations to break an experimental set) would favor urban populations, whereas instruction-specific tasks (requiring compliance with direction, deference to the experimenter, and following explicit instruction) should favor rural subjects. Weisner tested a sample of rural and a sample of Nairobi children between the ages of 4 and 13 on a number of tasks which fell into the above categories. In order to eliminate the factors that usually confound direct rural-urban comparisons, the samples were matched on language, acculturation, education, age, and status of parents, but differed on urban experience.

Weisner found that on the instruction-specific tasks the younger rural children (through age 10) scored higher than the city children. Between the ages of 11 and 13 the scores were identical for boys and reversed for girls. Overall, the rural children performed somewhat better than urban children, but this advantage disappeared by age 13. The urban children, however, clearly had no advantage on this group of tasks.

On the exploratory-manipulative tasks (free sorting of cups), 35% of the rural children did not form interpretable groups at all, whereas all the urban children did. Weisner attributed this to the differential effect of the testing situation and the urban children's willingness to attempt the tasks. Rural children were more likely to produce pure, single-dimensional sorts and the urban children to give mixed sorts. All sorts, however, were based on some type of perceptible criterion, with neither group using more abstract or functional criteria for sorting.

Rural children were less talkative than urban ones and gave verbal justifications for their sorts only if they were certain of the correct criteria; otherwise they remained silent. Urban children were talkative and attempted responses even when not certain of the correct answer. This resulted in a score in which the number of wholly correct responses of city and country children was similar, with rural children proportionately somewhat better. The overall score on the exploratory-manipulative tasks was significantly higher for urban children: it showed that they were more exploratory, verbal, and manipulative than were rural children.

Weisner found close parallels in the behavior of the children in their natural settings and in the test situations and suggested that the differences may not be the result of different "modes of thought." Rather, the differences may reflect the appropriate behaviors required in the two settings which may generalize to the experimental situation. He found support for his initial hypothesis, but no support for the position that urban exposure produces general improvements in *all* tasks.

Memory Tasks

In order to examine the validity of the findings that indicate that traditional, rural, and nonschooled subjects perform less well than modern, urban, and schooled persons on memory tasks, Kagan and his associates compared recall performance in children from Guatemalan rural communities with that of children from an American city. In their first study (Kagan, Klein, Haith, & Morrison, 1973) they found that, while there were major differences in the performance of 5-year-old children on recognition memory tasks, these differences disappeared with age. They observed only minimal differences between Guatemalan rural children and American urban children by 11 years of age. This finding led Kagan to suggest that "recognition memory is a basic human process." He noted that earlier retardation seems to be partially reversible, and that cognitive development during the early years appears to be more resilient than had been supposed.

In a second study, Kagan and his associates (Kagan, Klein, Finley, Rogoff, & Nolan, 1979) compared recall performance in children from an American city with children from two Guatemalan towns which differed in size, complexity and modernity, connection to the rest of the country, concern with schooling, and levels of literacy. This study was done in response to criticisms that the findings of the earlier study were a reflection of insufficient task difficulty. The measures included two memory tasks and a series of conservation tasks. The subjects ranged from 6 to 13 years of age, with the addition of a group of young adults from the more isolated village.

The major finding was that "the slopes for rate of improvement in memory span for pictures and words occurred at different ages in the three communities: 7–8 in Cambridge, 8–9 in the more modern village and 10–11 in the more isolated village" (p. 59). There was little correlation between memory and conservation tasks. The efforts of the authors to correlate the differences in performance with specific demographic variables proved to be inconclusive. There was evidence that the cognitive functioning studied here was a direct function of "modernization" or "urbanization," but there was not a conclusive link to any of the factors associated with these conditions. Factors responsible may have been "infant deprivation, lack of variety and challenge in the lives of the preschool and school-age children, inferior schooling, poor health, or all of these factors" (p. 74).

A study assessing the development of short-term and incidental memory was carried out by Wagner (1974) in Mexico among Mayan people in Yucatan. The study was designed to assess the relative contribution of age, cultural setting, and formal education on the development of these skills. His subjects included 5 age-groups (7 to 27 years old) from the city of Merida and five age groups from a rural community. Of the rural groups, only the two youngest groups (7–9 and 10–12 years old) had an amount of schooling equal to the urban groups; the three older groups had a maximum of two years of schooling.

Wagner's findings showed that overall recall of the target items improved almost entirely as a function of number of years of education, and not as a function of age. The results of the urban subjects replicated American studies of short-term and incidental memory. The rural subjects, however, presented a different picture, which led the author to conclude that the rural subjects were "not using verbal rehearsal strategies, thereby precluding developmental increases in primacy and central task performance" (p. 395). Wagner suggested that without formal schooling, higher level mnemonic strategies in memory may not develop at all.

Sharp, Cole, and Lave (1979) conducted an extensive study, also in Yucatan. The study was designed to measure the effects of age and schooling on the development of various cognitive skills. Sharp *et al.* also conducted a sociodemographic survey to isolate the factors that determine attendance at school. Their subjects, aged 10 to 56 years, came from 37 communities on the Yucatan peninsula, ranging in size from the capital city of Merida to isolated rural farming communities. The subjects were tested on a number of experimental tasks: the categorization of objects and words, memory for objects and words, and problem solving using verbal and nonverbal materials.

The results of the experimental tasks were complex and difficult to interpret. Some tasks showed high correlations between schooling and performance, others between age and performance. For other tasks, both increasing age and educational experience were associated with increased performance. The authors concluded that "intellectual test-performance differences among our populations are best attributed to differences in education and work experience" (p. 73).

They proposed the explanation that education exerts its strongest influence on tasks where "taxonomic principles are the criterion of correct classification, where correct performance requires the subject to provide structure to the nominal stimulus array, where problems must be treated hypothetically without recourse to real-world knowledge, or where problem contexts are clearly school-related" (p. 77).

The demographic survey showed that the level of education was in a large measure determined by economic and cultural factors. Most important of these was the availability of schools in the informant's location—a factor that clearly differentiated urban from rural subjects. Second in importance were economic factors. They also found that IQ played only a minor role in the selection of children for schooling. The authors concluded that while their results were consistent with much of the recent findings of experimental cross-cultural research, this may largely be due to the bias introduced by the particular tasks used, which have little "ecological validity" outside the school context.

Another study which investigated the effects of general environmental conditions on the development of memory and cognitive skills was conducted by Stevenson, Parker, Wilkinson, Bonnevaux, and Gonzalez (1978). Their research compared the performance of a large sample of Peruvian children. Some came from the city of Lima, others from a jungle town and its neighboring villages, half of them were Mestizo and half were Quechua Indian. They were 5 and 6 years of age. Some 6-year-olds of each cultural group and in each location attended school; others did not. The children were tested on 15 different measures. The memory tasks were given to assess memory for stimuli presented in different modes of representation: verbal, pictorial, and enactive. The cognitive tasks were designed to test the child's skills in processes such as forming concepts and using categories. These were given in two forms, one in which stimuli were familiar and readily labeled, and one in which they were nonrepresentational and not easily labeled. The researchers hypothesized that since traditional societies depend on observational learning, rural children would perform as effectively or better than the urban children in pictorial and enactive memory tasks, whereas city children should perform better in tasks involving memory for verbally presented material, such as memory for words, numbers and content of story. On the cognitive tasks, they expected that the difference between schooled and nonschooled children should increase as requirements for abstraction increased.

Their results showed that school children performed better on every task than children out of school, regardless of locations or social class. Rural Quechua children performed at a much lower level than urban ones on most tasks, with the exception of single and double seriation and perceptual learning. Mestizo children in Lima performed significantly better than their rural counterparts on three tasks: serial memory for words, for numbers, and Draw-a-Person, whereas the rural Mestizos performed at high levels in perceptual learning, and single and double seriation. The influence of location was also evident in the variability in the children's performance: there was greater variability in the performance on all tasks of the rural children than those in Lima.

The researchers attributed the location effects to the different amounts and types of stimuli provided by the environments. Rural environments for the Mestizo children were ranked as offering the least amount of verbal stimulation. These same environments, however, were seen to offer special opportunities for acquiring other skills and information. Visual discrimination was well-developed among the jungle children, as was the concept of seriation. This latter ability was atributed to the rural children's experience with the *antara,* a Peruvian musical instrument consisting of graduated lengths of bamboo pipes.

Linguistic Development

Entwistle (1966) studied the linguistic development of kindergarten, first-, third-, and fifth-grade children by administering word–association tests based on Brown and Berko's (1960) study. That study showed that the appearance of certain kinds of associations is highly correlated with the use of grammatical transformations employed by a mature speaker. The shift is from a syntactic to a paradigmatic response mode. Entwistle's subjects were children of blue-collar urban workers, high-income suburban professionals, rural farmers, and Amish farmers from Pennsylvania.

Comparing the first three groups, she found no significant difference between the low and high socioeconomic urban groups. The high-IQ rural children performed similarly to the urban samples. The low-IQ rural children, however, when compared to low-IQ urban children, scored considerably lower in the first and third grades. By the fifth grade, the rural children drew close to the urban scores and lagged only in some areas. Entwistle, like many of the researchers referred to earlier, concluded that rural residence impedes language development during the preschool years. Rural children with superior endowment, however, quickly compensate. Rural residence "is apparently a modest handicap which is easily compensated for by higher intelligence." The handicap of the rural environment consists of less exposure to language, less opportunity for verbal interaction (due to the isolation of the dwellings), lack of kindergartens, and lower exposure to television and radio. The Amish group exhibited a pattern of development very similar to the rural Maryland group: the Amish children lagged behind the others in the third and fifth grades but caught up by the sixth grade.

On the basis of the above evidence, Entwistle suggested that "the well-documented IQ differences between rural and urban populations" may be due to factors other than genetic ones. She suggested that a lack of verbal stimulation at an early age may hinder the development of form-class concepts and semantics. Paradigmatic responses are determined from semantics: showing that the child knows what substitutes for what. An impoverished environment may not provide the contextual variety needed for the early development of form-class concepts.

Summary

Although analyses of the effects of location are confounded in many of these studies by such factors as schooling and acculturation to Western standards, the results do permit us to draw certain general conclusions about the nature of the findings on rural-urban differences in performance on a variety of cognitive development tasks. It is also instructive to examine the factors in the environments to which the researchers attribute the differences.

Most of the research indicates that rural children lag behind their urban counterparts on the majority of developmental measures. On the Piagetian conservation tasks, there is a difference of several years between the groups in several of the studies, with the rural children consistently giving more concrete, perceptually bound answers. On the classification and sorting tasks, the rural children also base their categories on perceptual attributes rather than on a superordinate category or taxonomic class. They are found to be more concrete, as opposed to theoretical and abstract. They also seem to be more passive and less manipulative. On the memory tasks, the rural children seem to lag behind their urban counterparts by several years, indicating a retardation in the activation of strategies to organize and structure information.

A consistent finding of the studies is the rural children's difficulty in verbalizing the results (giving verbal justifications and explanations). They are found to be less talkative in test situations and to have problems using verbal rehearsal strategies in the memory tasks.

The rural children's advantage on some of the tasks are usually explained in terms of a highly specific demand provided by their milieu. For example, when the rural Ga children perform better on the conservation of quantity, it is explained by the fact that they have had more opportunities to play with mud and clay. When the performance of Peruvian jungle children is superior on seriation tasks, this is attributed to their exposure to the Andean reed instrument, the *antara*. In neither case is there an attempt to search for other areas of performance to which these experiences may have generalized and resulted in more advanced functioning by the rural children.

The researchers attribute the developmental differences between the urban and rural samples to the opportunities provided by the urban environment. The rural environment is perceived as having a "lower cultural level" that does not stimulate abstract thinking. The pace of life is slower in rural communities; the children lack toys and other items and are seen as passive and apathetic. There is also very little verbal stimulation which is also reflected in the mothers' teaching style. Urban mothers explain well; rural ones do not. Nor do rural parents feel the need for achievement to the same extent that urban parents do; therefore, they do not push the children toward high intellectual functioning. Rural parents emphasize compliance; urban ones stimulate verbal and analytical skills. By and large, rural environments are conservative, and people tend to rely on social explanations and respect authority, whereas physical explanations and innovations are more usual in towns.

ANOTHER VIEW OF RURAL-URBAN DIFFERENCES

A number of recent studies indicate that the apparent developmental lag of rural children may be a result of the misunderstanding by experimenters of: the rural environment; the cognitive skills developed in these settings; and the lack of relevance to rural groups of the tasks presented to them. A number of these will be considered in the final discussion. In the following, an example of this difficult approach to studying rural-urban developmental differences will be given by the author's own work.

A series of studies by the author (Hollos, 1974, 1975; Hollos & Cowan, 1973) were designed to measure the effect of environmental variables on different areas of cognitive growth and to investigate in detail the components of the child's learning environment. The general strategy of the research was to select three social environments which differed primarily on one variable—the amount of verbal interaction that children have with peers and parents—and to examine performance in two kinds of cognitive tasks that might be expected to show differential effects of this variable. The children to be tested were chosen from three social settings in Norway and Hungary. These settings—a dispersed farm community, a village, and a town—varied primarily on the dimension of relative physical isolation of family dwellings, with a resultant variation in the children's amount of verbal communication with peers and adults. On a number of other important dimensions, the samples were equivalent.

Cognitive Development in Three Norwegian Subcultures

The first study was done in Norway, where the author spent 16 months doing anthropological field work in a dispersed rural community. The major focus of the research was on the cognitive development of children living in this farming community. Families here were so geographically separated that there were no peer groups with which the children could play. Prior to school age, with the exception of important holidays and family occasions, they rarely left the farm. Most of the early learning experiences of these children took place in the context of the isolated homestead, with interaction limited to family members.

The other two groups came from a rural village and a medium-sized town in the same general culture area in eastern Norway. The village was a densely settled community where peer groups were present and contact with adults outside of the family was frequent. In the town, the social structure was more complex and the children came into contact with many different kinds of adults in a much larger variety of social situations.

Eastern Norway is quite homogenous culturally. There were no systematic religious, linguistic, or ideological differences among the samples. All of the children who were tested lived in intact nuclear families (two parents and an average of three children). All families were working-class with relatively low incomes, and the type and amount of schooling received by the parents and children were virtually identical in all samples.

The fieldwork methods consisted of participant observation of community and family interaction, description and recording of verbal and nonverbal communication within and outside of the families, observation and recording of children's behavior and activities with adults and peers at home and in school, interviews with mothers, and standardized administration of Piagetian cognitive developmental measures.

The research focused on determining the channels, methods, and situations of learning that lead to concept formation. Examples of the questions asked were: How do children spend their time? With whom does a child interact and what are the forms of interaction? Assuming that young children learn a great deal from their mothers, how do mothers view their children in these communities? Are the children consciously taught certain skills or is learning mostly through experience? Does the amount of verbal interaction affect learning?

Two sets of cognitive tasks were employed. Piaget describes the child's decline in egocentrism (the growth of perspectivism) in terms of an increasing ability to coordinate one's own point of view with that of another person. This ability can be seen in nonverbal tasks such as the "three mountains" (Piaget & Inhelder, 1965), in which the child facing a three-dimensional display of mountains is asked to choose pictures representing what someone else sees from another location. It can also be seen in the child's increased ability to take the role of the other in verbal communication (Flavell, 1968). The other set of tasks concerned logical operations and such physical object concepts as classification and conservation.

The particular areas of cognitive development to be tested were identified after extended observation of the dispersed, village, and urban children's activities and environments. Kohlberg (1969) explicitly states that role-taking ability should be directly related to amount of social participation and experience in interaction. If he is correct, the dispersed farm children would be expected to perform at a lower developmental level in role-taking tasks than village children, who in turn would perform at a lower level than town children. Age and schooling effects were expected to be relatively less important than specific social interaction experience.

There were conflicting theoretical and empirical rationales concerning what could be expected of the children in terms of logical operations and physical concepts. Furth's study of deaf children (1966) indicated that spoken language experience is not necessary for the development of concrete operations, although cognitive development in deaf children is somewhat retarded. In general, cross-cultural literature on rural-urban differences suggested that the isolated farm children may not perform as well as town and village children. Bruner's hypothesis that language is a stimulant and a vehicle for development leads to the same prediction. However, other studies (e.g., Price-Williams, 1961) suggested that at least some environments provide resources and stimulation adequate to enable the child to develop as fast as urban middle-class children.

The hypothesis guiding the research was that the effects of the three social settings would be greater for role-taking tasks than for logical operations. If no differences were found among the settings in logical operations performance, or if the isolated children were found to perform better, then some of the current undifferentiated notions about social deprivation and about the types of environments supposedly favorable to cognitive development should be reexamined. One should then also be forced to take a more skeptical look at Bruner's argument concerning the role of language experience in conceptual development (Bruner, Oliver, Greenfield, *et al.*, 1967).

Settings

The farm community is a dispersed area with a population of almost 300. The total land area of the community is about 150 km^2, most of which consists of pine forest, tundra, bogs, or mountain pastures. The farms are located within the forested regions. The majority of the families reside on these farms and are thus so geographically separated that there is very little daily interaction between the homesteads. The major occupation is dairy farming, with supplementary employment in the forest or in a small local workshop. Women are not employed outside of the home, but have a major share of taking care of the animals.

Except for important holidays and family occasions, children rarely leave the farm prior to school age. Most of the early learning experiences take place in the context of the isolated homestead, with interaction limited to family members. Since the average number of children per family is three, and the average age difference between siblings is 2–3 years, interaction takes place only with older or younger individuals, almost never with contemporaries.

Children spend most of their time in solitary play or in observation of others. Since there are few commercial toys or games, solitary play involves manipulation or observation of objects that occur naturally in the environment. Siblings rarely interact directly and, when they do, interactions are most often nonverbal. Their activities consist mostly of parallel play and involve little cooperation, probably due to the age differential. Most frequent interaction takes place with the mother; the father spends much of the day away from the house. Interaction with the mother typically consists of the mother doing something for the child or performing some chore while the child observes or helps. The amount of verbal interaction between mother and child is limited. Mothers do not prompt or encourage children to talk, ask questions, or suggest activities. There are no periods of storytelling or discussion. The children are free to initiate and terminate their own activities and to come and go as they please, without directions from the mother. It is important to note, however, that the mother is almost never absent from the near vicinity of the child and is constantly available for help, companionship, and feedback to the child's activities. The feedback is most frequently a nonverbal gesture or activity, such as assistance with pouring, building, dressing, or drawing. The rest of the adults generally pay little attention to the child in the course of their daily work. The child is free to observe and imitate them but is rarely talked to or encouraged by the others. Interaction and communication between adult members of the family is limited to mealtimes and evenings. The major part of the evening is devoted to watching television or listening to news or weather forecasts. Children are allowed to be present, but no special attention is focused on them. Verbal communication on these occasions is relatively brief and restricted to statements or general observations. Sentences are short, simple, and somewhat nonspecific. This style of verbal interaction or type of communication has been called "restricted" by Bernstein (1961).

Once they begin school, farm children are bused to a neighboring community only three times a week during the first three grades. The school bus leaves the community early in the morning and returns immediately after school is out, depositing each child at the appropriate crossroad. These dispersed farm children, therefore, have no opportunity for after-school play and free interaction with the other children.

The village is a community of about 1,400 inhabitants. It is the county seat and a business, industrial, and tourist center for the region. About half of the inhabitants are engaged in dairy farming, with the other half employed in industry or by the county government. Women as a rule do not work, but are not bound to the house full-time as their isolated counterparts are; they have more time and opportunity to engage in other types of activities.

All village families live in one-family dwellings that are surrounded by yards. The houses are built closely together, along paved or gravel roads, including the main county thoroughfare. Although there are no special playing fields within the village, there are ample empty spaces where the children can play.

The number of children per family averages three, the same as in the farm community. Normally, the major part of the preschoolers' day and the schoolchildren's afternoon is spent in play with other children. From a relatively early age, children are allowed to leave the house alone and to interact freely with others. The children bicycle around the village, go down to the river, play at others' houses, ski in the winter, or play on the streets in all seasons. Interaction is not limited to peers; children encounter a number of known and unknown adults in a variety of social settings. The time spent with the mother is relatively short. In the evenings the entire family assembles, and interaction occurs, as with peers during the day, in a group.

In general, these families seem to be more verbal than the isolated farm families, perhaps because village life provides constant social interaction with others and thus fosters the development of these skills. Family members are apart during most of the day and in different settings. Since their experiences are dissimilar, attempts are made to discuss the day's activities and the children are encouraged to participate. The children are listened to politely, rather than questioned, when their accounts are unclear. The major part of the evening is spent, as on the farm, watching television. On weekends, visitors or relatives often come to the house.

In spite of the relatively higher frequency of verbal interaction among children and among adults and children, their style of communication or type of "communication code" is essentially the same as in the farm community.

The town has approximately 6,000 inhabitants. It lies at an important junction of several major highways, a factor largely responsible for the growth and regional significance of the town. The town is a county seat and a regional commercial and tourist center. It has several small industries and workshops but no major industry. It also houses the offices of the district court, which serves several counties, and the district hospital. Apart from several elementary schools, the town boasts not only a junior high school, a teacher's college and a high school, but also a free adult–education center. The presence of the educational facilities has given impetus to the broadening of the town's cultural facilities. There are several movie houses and theaters, and concerts are frequently given in the city hall. Commercially, the town also serves a large region. Residents of several counties consider it their shopping and all-purpose service center. Apart from its commercial midtown section, the residential areas consist of well-spaced, single-family houses with large green yards, connected by winding gravel roads.

The structure of the families is much like that in the village. The average number of children is again three, and there are no extended families. The only difference is that, as a result of the higher employment opportunities, some mothers work while the grandparents take care of the children during the day. Basically, there are no differences in the children's activities between the town and the village. There are large peer groups with whom children spend the majority of their time. In general, they are not required to perform any special chores, and from an early age they are free to roam around inside or outside the town without adult control or interference. The difference between village and town as social settings lies in the fact that town children meet a larger variety of adults; they are accustomed to strangers of all kinds and ages and their activities take place in more settings than those in the village. Family interaction and activity and the type of verbal communication remain essentially the same as in the village. The more complex social interaction may lead to a more complex system of communication, but the range and detail of the concepts involved appears to be characteristic of the "restricted code" found in farm and village communities.

In summary, though the communities differed in size and structure, the primary difference from the child's point of view lay in the opportunities for social-verbal interaction. The farm children spent a great deal of time with their mothers, imitating them or exploring the physical environment but with minimal verbal exchanges. The village and town children spent much of their time playing with peers and returning in the evenings to a more talkative family setting. In other major ways, the communities, and especially the samples of children chosen to be tested, were similar.

In each setting 48 children were tested, 16 at each of three age levels: preschool (7-year-olds), first graders (8-year-olds) and second graders (9-year-olds). Nine tasks were used to assess several facets of the child's ability to perform concrete operations. Six of these were primarily concerned with logical operations on objects, while three focused on the child's ability to adopt a viewpoint other than his own, an ability described as "perspectivism" by Piaget (1926) and "role taking" by Flavell (1968). The logical operations tasks included three tests of classification (class inclusion, multiplication of classes, multiplication of relations) and three tests of conservation (conservation of continuous quantity, conservation of interior volume, conservation of occupied volume). The perspectivism tasks included a test of visual perspectives (the three-mountains test), communication accuracy, and role taking.

The results showed that on the logical operations tests the dispersed farm children performed as well or better than their village and town age-mates. On the role-taking tasks, farm children did not perform as well as the other two groups. The town and village children's scores on these tasks were almost identical.

Cognitive Development in Three Hungarian Subcultures

In this study, three social settings were selected in Hungary which corresponded closely to the Norwegian settings. This similarity permitted the examination of effects attributable to a different culture. There were two questions of primary concern: first, whether the separation of logical operations and role taking found in the Norwegian study would also be found in another culture with comparable environmental settings; and second, whether the pattern displayed by the different groups of Norwegian children was a unique product of that culture, the particular environmental settings, or a result of the interaction between the setting and a particular culture.

The three samples of children came from three communities on the Hungarian plains: a dispersed farm settlement, a village, and a medium-sized town. Again, there were no systematic cultural, linguistic, religious, or ideological differences among the samples.

In each setting 45 children were tested, 15 at each of three age levels: first graders (7-year-olds), second graders (8-year-olds), and third graders (9-year-olds).

In this study 10 tasks were used, including the nine tasks used in Norway and an additional, purely verbal measure of egocentrism, based on the pronoun system of the Hungarian language.

The results closely paralleled those of the Norwegian study: farm children performed better than their village and town age-mates, especially at the earliest age levels. By age 9 the village children approached the level of the farm children, with town children lagging behind. On the role-taking tasks, the farm children performed at a lower level than the other two groups. Village children's performance was the highest of all groups at ages 7 and 8, but the 9-year-old town group surpassed their performance. The results of the two studies will be analyzed in the following section.

Discussion: Rural and Urban Patterns of Development in Norway and Hungary

In the original formulation of the above studies, the farm children were labeled in terms of their inadequacies. The fact that farm children engage in less social interaction with peers and in less verbal interaction than village and town children was emphasized.

A detailed anthropological study of the farm community in Norway indicated that in many ways the "deprivation" of the children is more apparent than real. The learning environment of these children is far from impoverished. They receive a great deal of social stimulation and support from their mothers, including countless opportunities to observe and imitate. Further, and perhaps more important, they have the freedom to engage in self-initiated play—primarily in manipulating objects and observing their interrelations. In experimental tasks emphasizing logical operations on objects, the farm children performed as well or better than their village and town age-mates. Despite the low verbal nature of their social environments, they coped well with tasks which required verbal as well as conceptual sophistication. Since the samples were equated on most social variables, the results suggest that relative social-verbal isolation in and of itself does not interfere with the development of logical operations. In fact, the data from the preschool 7-year-olds in Norway are consistent with the notion that environments that provide many opportunities for peer interaction may slow down, for a time, the development of logical operations. The data from the Hungarian study indicate that this advantage continues through a longer developmental period. Here the farm children were superior in logical operations to the other two groups at all three age levels, although their advantage diminished at successive ages.

The effects of social setting on role taking would seem to fit better with a deprivation hypothesis. Clearly, the farm children, who rarely engaged in games with their age-mates, attained lower score on role-taking tasks. An interpretation in terms of deprivation implies that somehow the children would be doing better if their circumstances were altered. It would also disregard the possibility that the role-taking skills of farm children are quite adequately developed for coping with the settings in which they live.

The studies strongly suggest that it is an oversimplification to compare the developmental scores of groups from different social milieus on only one kind of cognitive performance. Different settings may produce different patterns of "highs" and "lows." The adequacy of performance in each group should be evaluated in relation to cultural demands. The deprivation approach to the interpretation of cultural comparisons should focus in a more differentiated way on precisely what that deprivation might be.

CONCLUSIONS

Can we conclude from the cross-cultural research reviewed here on rural-urban developmental differences that, in most parts of the world, living in the country produces a form of intellectual retardation?

The research in Norway and Hungary indicates that cognitive development and social environment are closely related and that research on children's cognitive growth should proceed along with a parallel analysis of the social environmental context in which the development takes place. It has been shown that it is necessary to outline and analyze in detail the total social environment of the child in a search for correlates of cognitive growth or functioning in the environment. Some factors which seem most obvious might be misleading and produce an effect that, when in combination with other elements in the social environment, is the opposite of what might be expected. In order to learn about as many forces as possible that affect the child, one should look at his immediate context of learning, including family interaction, the physical and social space occupied by the child, and the verbal and nonverbal communication within his milieu.

A description of the social or cultural context of learning should mean more than providing a description of the child-raising practices in a group, or placing the child in particular "social class," or using variables such as "schooling" and "no-schooling," or "rural" and "urban."

Anthropologists and psychologists agree that designation of a child as from a lower- or middle-class background by itself has little meaning. In cross-cultural research this means even less. Similarly, the variables of "schooling" and "no-schooling," which seem to be in vogue in recent Piaget-type developmental studies, are used as summaries of past experience without any idea of what these experiences are. As Goodnow said,

> These terms carry their own hazards. It is very easy, for example, to think of "no schooling" as a state requiring no further specification, as a neutral state, a measure of what might have been if the organism had been left to itself. This is a dangerous assumption, likely to lead to the idea that all unschooled children are alike. (1969, p. 456)

Similarly, an enumeration of the most obvious elements of another culture without an analysis of how that culture functions adds little to our knowledge of the cultural and social forces acting on the child and the kinds of demands made on him. For example, the fact that in Senegal "socially, residentially and economically, the village is divided into fifty-nine compounds, each surrounded by a wooden palisade and inhabited by an extended family unit . . . and within each compound are several small, round thatched huts inhabited by various members of a patrilocal family" (Bruner et al., 1967, p. 227) is not a sufficient description of the rural children's social environment. Admittedly, to a Westerner, this scene's contrast to the urban sample's environment is striking, but it does not explain the demands and rewards that that type of environment makes on the child.

The actual context in which the child grows up and learns should be outlined. "Norwegian" culture or even "Norwegian rural" culture would have been misleading designations of the environmental context of our study unless certain dimensions were enumerated. All three groups of children were "Norwegian" and two of them "rural," yet their social environments and the pattern of the development were quite different. In order to understand the demands of these environments, the following questions had to be answered. What actually goes on in the everyday life on an isolated farm and what sort of stimulation do children receive from such an environment? Does spatial isolation imply psychological isolation as well? Does the level of noise in the urban environment necessarily mean stimulation? Failure to understand the combination of these factors can lead to a biased expectation and errors in the judgment of the intellectual capacities of the rural children.

These observations are affirmed by the findings of a team of researchers working in Liberia. Cole, Gay, Glick, and Sharp (1971) found that the Kpelle people performed considerably better on certain tasks than Americans did. For example, they were exceptionally good at estimating various amounts of rice. Other tasks, which at first seemed to be closely related, gave them unexpected difficulty. Finding the right task, and testing for the appropriate skills, however, was no easy matter. "Etiological questions are most properly asked after there has been considerable descriptive work tying down the processes involved in the behaviors for which we seek causes. One cannot proceed etiologically without corresponding descriptive analysis" (Glick, 1975, p. 646). This analysis then allows the researcher to search for the behaviors and abilities useful in that particular environment:

> People will be good at doing the things that are important to them and that they have occasion to do often . . . . Primitive cultures tend to make different sorts of intellectual demands than technologically advanced cultures. (Cole *et al.*, 1971, p. xi)

A similar consideration underlies some other recent research that aims at isolating particular environmental factors and experiences and attempts to determine their cognitive developmental correlates. A study by Price-Williams, Gordon, and Ramirez (1969) compared the performance of Mexican children from pottery-making families with those whose families engaged in occupations other than pottery making. "It was predicted that experience in pottery making should promote earlier conservation in substance. The question of transfer to other concepts was left open" (1969, p. 769). The children were given tasks that tested for the conservation of number, length, substance, weight, and volume. In the town of Tlaquepaque, significant differences were obtained between the groups on the conservation of substance and nonsignificant differences on the conservation of number, length, weight, and volume. On all five tasks, however, potters' sons conserved more frequently. In the village of San Marcos the differences were more dramatic: highly significant differences were obtained on all tasks between the two groups, allowing the researchers to conclude "that the role of skills in cognitive growth may be a very important factor. Manipulation may be a prior and necessary prerequisite for attainment of conservation" (1969, p. 769).

A similar attempt was made by Greenfield and Childs (1974), who investigated whether learning to weave one of the three Zinacantecan cloth patterns influenced a general ability to represent abstract linear patterns. Several tasks were specifically developed for this research and were presented to three age groups of children, each with equal numbers of boys and girls. The oldest age group of girls could weave; none of the boys could. The research demonstrated that weaving experience had little influence on a generalized facility in representing patterns. School experience had an effect similar to weaving on the pattern-generalization task. Greenfield and Childs concluded that

> practical experience develops *specific* component cognitive skills as in weavers and potters whereas other more general cultural influences, economic activity for instance, develops *generalized* cognitive performance—the representation of novel patterns by adolescent boys in our study . . . . Other studies are needed to unravel the precise nature of the environmental forces which lead to the generalization of cognitive skills. (1974, p. 146)

Cole (1975), however, proposed a different interpretation of the results of this study. He suggested that the reason for the failure to find differences between weavers and nonweavers lies in the limited number of patterns that Zinacantecan weavers learn. He proposed a study in which a sample of weavers who weave a larger number of patterns is examined in order to test for the effect of the number of patterns a person knows on the generality of pattern representation.

What has guided these studies is a belief that different cultural settings call for different skills and that testing should proceed with an array of tasks that could potentially reflect the effects of the various environmental demands. Admittedly, the results are not always clearcut; however, they are sufficient to serve as a warning against interpreting environments and their demands in simplistic or biased terms and against an assumption that the same pattern of cognitive development should be expected in all environments.

A related problem in cross-cultural work involves the experimental situation and the tests. Even if cognitive tasks are designed to reflect the skills important in a particular environment, can we assume that the behavior manifested by subjects in the experiments represents the way they process information about their world outside of the testing situation? And what evidence do we have that different cultural and subcultural groups interpret and react to these tasks in the same manner?

Psychologists and anthropologists tend to disagree on this point. Anthropologists generally claim that the experimental method is not always an applicable tool, especially in nonliterate cultures, regardless of the care with which the tasks were designed to be "culture free." In this view, it cannot be assumed that a task will tap the same cognitive skill regardless of the background of the subjects, since tests are obviously interpreted in light of the subjects' own experiences and background. It is not surprising, therefore, to find that rural, nonschooled, unacculturated subjects perform significantly more poorly than urban, schooled, and acculturated groups.

While psychologists "view experiments and tests as specially contrived occasions for the manifestation of cognitive skills" (Cole *et al.*, 1971, p. 215), this view is increasingly being questioned. For example, the recent work of Sharp, Cole, and Lave (1979) explicitly questioned the validity of their findings in Yucatan and expressed doubts about the results obtained by the experimental method from schooled and nonschooled subjects.

> The correlation between successful performance on Binet's tasks and success in school was a tautology; the items were picked because they discriminated between children at various levels of academic achievement. Might we not be witnessing the converse of that process when we observe people with educational experience excelling in experimental tasks whose form and content are like those they have learned to master in school? (1979, p. 82)

A similar argument might be made about urban-rural differences. Many observers seem to agree that the rural environment offers less verbal stimulation and probably less opportunities for social interaction. It is quite possible that the lack of verbal training and the relatively undeveloped social-interactional skills of the rural children are the factors resulting in rural children's poorer test performance.

Since in many cultural contexts the test situation remains essentially alien and artificial, a fairer assessment of cognitive capacities might be done through observation and the study of natural indicators of cognitive and other skills. Such line of inquiry was developed and promoted by the work of John and Beatrice Whiting (J. Whiting, 1966; B. Whiting, 1963) and their associates in the Six Cultures study. The method rests on the observation of natural behavior within various settings. Specifically, for the study of cognitive competency in children the technique was modified by Robert and Ruth Munroe (Nerlove, Munroe, & Munroe, 1971) and later by a group composed of Sara Nerlove and her associates who applied it in a study of the cognitive development of rural Guatemalan children (Nerlove, Roberts, Klein, Yarborough, & Hibicht, 1974). The latter study was based on spot observation of the children in natural settings, while the children were engaged in work and play. This method involves taking a "mental snapshot" the instant the subject is seen by the observer. The children were also given a number of formal developmental tasks, measuring analytic ability and language facility. The researchers found that

> the degree to which children engaged in self-managed activities entailing the following of an exacting series of sequences was associated with success at a

formal test of analytic ability; and the degree to which the children engaged in voluntary social activities was shown to be associated with success at a formal test of language ability. (1974, p. 266)

While such studies are still rare and the method needs further testing for reliance, it is a line of inquiry that should gain increasing acceptance and popularity by researchers interested in developing culture-free measures.

The task of the cross-cultural researcher is not an easy one. What has been suggested here is that in order to be able to compare groups within and across cultures, and to assess their abilities, the researcher should: first, search out and identify those features of each environment that foster the development of particular cognitive skills and second, devise tasks that accurately tap these skills. Without these efforts, however, no advances can be made in etiological studies, and certain groups (rural, lower class, nonwestern) will continue to be labeled and treated in terms of their inadequacies and deficiencies.

References

Bernstein, B. Social class and linguistic development: A theory of social learning. In A. H. Halsey, J. Florid, & C. A. Anderson (Eds.), *Education, economy, and society*. Glencoe, Ill.: Free Press, 1961.

Brown, R. W., & Berko, J. Word association and the acquisition of grammar. *Child Development*, 1960, *31*, 1–14.

Bruner, J. S., Oliver, R. S., Greenfield, P. M., *et al. Studies in cognitive growth*. New York: Wiley, 1967.

Cole, M. An ethnographic psychology of cognition. In R. W. Brislin, S. Bochner, & W. Lonner (Eds.), *Cross-cultural perspectives on learning*. Beverly Hills, Sage, 1975.

Cole, M., & Scribner, S. *Culture and thought*. New York: Wiley, 1974.

Cole, M., Gay, J., Glick, J., & Sharp, D. *The cultural context of learning and thinking*. New York: Basic Books, 1971.

Entwistle, D. R. Developmental sociolinguistics: A comparative study of four sub-cultural settings. *Sociometry*, 1966, *29*, 67–84.

Flavell, J. F. *The development of role-taking and communication skills in children*. New York: Wiley, 1968.

Furth, H. *Thinking without language: Psychological implications of deafness*. New York: Free Press, 1966.

Glick, J. Cognitive development in cross-cultural perspective. In F. D. Horowitz (Ed.), *Review of child development research* (Vol. 4). Chicago: University of Chicago Press, 1975.

Goodnow, J. Problems in research on culture and thought. In D. Elkind & J. H. Flavell (Eds.), *Studies in cognitive development*. New York: Oxford University Press, 1969.

Greenfield, P. On culture and conservation. In J. Bruner, R. Oliver, & P. M. Greenfield (Eds.), *Studies in cognitive growth*. New York: Wiley, 1967.

Greenfield, P., & Bruner, J. Culture and cognitive growth. *International Journal of Psychology*, 1966, *1*, 89–107.

Greenfield, P., & Childs, L. C. Weaving, color terms, and pattern representation cultural influences and cognitive development among the Zinacantacos of Southern Mexico. In J. Dawson & W. Lonner (Eds.), *Readings in cross-cultural psychology: Proceedings of the First International Conference of the International Association for Cross-Cultural Psychology*. Hong Kong: University of Hong Kong Press, 1974.

Hollos, M. *Growing up in Flathill: Social environment and cognitive development*. Oslo and Bergen: Scandinavian Universities Press, 1974.

Hollos, M. Logical operations and role-taking abilities in two cultures: Norway and Hungary. *Child Development*, 1975, *46*, 639–649.

Hollos, M., & Cowan, P. Social isolation and cognitive development: Logical operations and role-taking abilities in three Norwegian social settings. *Child Development*, 1973, *44*, 630–641.

Kagan, J., Klein, R. E., Haith, M. M., & Morrison, F. J. Memory and meaning in two cultures. *Child Development*, 1973, *44*, 221–223.

Kagan, J., Klein, R. E., Finley, G., Rogoff, B., & Nolan, E. A cross-cultural study of cognitive development. *Monographs of the Society for Research in Child Development*, 1979, *44*(5).

Kirk (Fitzgerald), L. *Cognitive development among Ga children: Environmental correlates of cognitive growth rate within the Ga tribe*. Unpublished doctoral dissertation, University of California, Berkeley, 1970.

Kirk (Fitzgerald), L. Maternal and sub-cultural correlates of cognitive growth rate, the Ga pattern. In P. R. Dasen (Ed.), *Piagetian psychology: Cross-cultural contributions*. New York: Gardner Press, 1977.

Kohlberg, L. Stage and sequence: The cognitive-developmental approach to socialization. In D. A. Goslin (Ed.), *Handbook of socialization theory in research*. Chicago: Rand McNally, 1969.

Maccoby, M., & Modiano, N. On culture and equvalence II. In J. Bruner, R. Oliver, & P. M. Greenfield (Eds.), *Studies in cognitive growth*. New York: Wiley, 1966.

Maccoby, M., & Modiano, N. Cognitive style in rural and urban Mexico. *Human Development*, 1969, *12*, 22–33.

Munroe, R. H., & Munroe, R. L. Household density and infant care in East African society. *Journal of Social Psychology*, 1971, *83*, 3–13. (a)

Munroe, R. H., & Munroe, R. L. Effect of environmental experience on spatial ability in an East African society. *Journal of Social Psychology*, 1971, *83*, 15–22. (b)

Nerlove, S. B., Munroe, R. H., & Munroe, R. I. Effects of environmental experience on spatial ability. *Journal of Social Psychology*, 1971, *84*, 3–10.

Nerlove, S. B., Roberts, J. M., Klein, R. E., Yarborough, C., & Hibicht, J. Natural indicators on cognitive development: An observational study of rural Guatemalan children. *Ethos*, 1974, *3*, 265–295.

Opper, S. Concept development in Thai urban and rural children. In R. P. Dasen (Ed.), *Piagetian psychology: Cross-cultural contributions*. New York: Gardner Press, 1977.

Peluffo, N. Les notions de conservation et de causalite chez les enfants provenat de differents milieux physiques et socio-cultureles. *Archives de Psychologie* (Geneva), 1962, *38*, 275–291.

Peluffo, N. Culture and cognitive problems. *International Journal of Psychology*, 1967, *2*, 187–198.

Piaget, J. *The language and thought of the child*. Meridian: New York, 1955. (Originally published, 1926).

Piaget, J. Need and significance of cross-cultural studies in genetic psychology. In J. W. Berry & P. R. Dasen (Eds.), *Culture and cognition*. London: Metheun, 1974.

Piaget, J., & Inhelder, B. *The child's conception of space.* Routledge & Kegan Paul, London: 1956.

Poole, H. E. The effect of urbanization upon scientific concept attainment among Hausa children. *British Journal of Educational Psychology,* 1968, *37,* 57–63.

Price-Williams, D. R. A study concerning concepts of conservation of quantity amongs primitive children. *Acta Psychologica,* 1961, *18,* 297–305.

Price-Williams, D. R., Gordon, V., & Ramirez, M. Skill and conservation: A study of pottery-making children. *Development Psychology,* 1969, *1,* 769.

Sharp, D., Cole, M., & Lave, C. Education and cognitive development: The evidence from experimental research. *Monographs of the Society for Research in Child Development,* 1979, *44*(1–2).

Stevenson, H. W., Parker, T., Wilkinson, A., Bonnevaux, B., & Gonzalez, M. Schooling, environment and cognitive development: A cross-cultural study. *Monographs of the Society for Research in Child Development,* 1978, *43*(3).

Vernon, P. E. *Intelligence and cultural environment.* London: Metheun, 1969.

Wagner, D. The development of short-term and incidental memory: A cross-cultural study. *Child Development,* 1974, *45,* 389–396.

Weisner, T. S. Urban-rural differences in African children's performance on cognitive and memory tasks. *Ethos,* 1976, *4,* 223–250.

Whiting, B. (Ed.). *Six cultures: Studies of child rearing.* New York: Wiley, 1963.

Whiting, J. W. M. *Field guide for the study of socialization in five societies* (Vol. 1). Six culture series. New York: Wiley, 1966.

5

Issues of Linguistic Development in Rural Subcultures in the United States

Walt Wolfram

Introduction

Although language may be viewed as a type of code for the transmission of information, it is certainly much more than that. Language is also an integral aspect of human behavior, and, as such, is a vehicle for the manifestation of cultural and social identity. From this latter perspective, it is hardly surprising that a distinction between "urban" and "rural" subcultures might be manifested in language differences. As early industrial metropolitan centers in the United States were set apart from outlying agricultural areas, a corresponding variation in the language patterns developed. While the resulting language differences might have been viewed as simple regional variations, they were certainly tied in with the developing sociocultural distinction between urban and rural lifestyles.

By the time that professional students of dialects in the United States began initiating a formal, large-scale survey of the dialects of English in the United States in the early 1930s, it was common knowledge that "there are clear urban and rural dialects" (Kurath, 1930, p. 70). Thus, we find the following observation in one of the earliest modern

WALT WOLFRAM • Department of Communication, University of the District of Columbia, Washington, D.C. 20001, and the Center for Applied Linguistics, Washington, D.C. 20007.

descriptions of a dialect area in the United States (New England) by
dialectologists:

> Regional differences within New England, as elsewhere, are greater in
> the homely vocabulary of the family and the farm than in the vocabulary of
> "society" and of urban areas. Hence most of the illustrations given are hum-
> ble words. Such words reflect most clearly the regional pattern of pre-indus-
> trial New England, which must be reconstructed as well as possible if we
> would understand fully the present speech areas and trace the sources of
> New England speech. (Kurath, 1939, p. 1)

This observation must, of course, be placed in historical perspective, in that the population had now had ample time to distribute itself,
and to develop and maintain distinct cultural subgroups. Naturally, this
was not an instantaneous process, but one that had developed progressively with the demarcation of different regional and social groups.
In fact, many of the earliest travelers to the Colonies were impressed
more with the lack of clear-cut dialect differentiation than the presence
of clearly defined dialects (cf. Marckwardt, 1958). But by the time the
industrial revolution had taken its toll on the population, dialect areas
were becoming much more definable and readily acknowledged by both
lay people and students of language. So by the time the large-scale
survey of *The Linguistic Atlas of the United States* was undertaken in the
1930s, the distinction between urban and rural dialect areas was a major
variable to be considered.

In itself, the association of linguistic diversity with rural subcultures
is neither good nor bad—it is simply one of the many variables that can
be correlated with language variation. Unfortunately, the social scientist's isolation of variables does not exist in an objective vacuum in real
life. People hearing language differences make value judgments about
those differences that are inextricably tied to their judgments about the
people exhibiting the language variety. Assessments of character, morality, and intellectual capability may all derive from the perception of
language differences. In this context, then, it becomes crucial to have an
accurate understanding of the basis of language differences in rural
subcultures.

As mentioned above, the existence of an urban and rural parameter
in the dialects of American English should not be taken to mean that this
dimension operates in isolation from other variables. Regional differences invariably intersect with other parameters such as status, eth-
nicity, sex, age, and so forth. The intersecting dimensions of rural language differences must be recognized in any realistic discussion of this
topic; the failure to recognize the multifaceted nature of the social and
cultural dimension can only lead to a simplistic and distorted picture of
the language situation.

In considering issues of language development in American society, the rural-nonrural distinction has been considered most frequently in connection with socioeconomic class. Clearly, the recent focus on rural language has concentrated on lower socioeconomic class rural lifestyles. Accordingly, issues of language development in these populations typically have been restricted to a particular class rather than the rural population *per se*. That the notion "rural language" should be used so frequently to mean low socioeconomic class rural is, in itself, a commentary on how "rural subculture" has come to be viewed in American society, but the development of such an association will not concern us here. Instead, we shall deal with the issues of language development as they have arisen in American society, and these issues have largely concerned the rural lower-socioeconomic classes.

The Basis of Difference

The way in which rural varieties of English developed does not involve any great mystery. Various settlement patterns, migratory movements within the population, and particular social organization patterns resulted in the emergence of English dialects associated with the rural subcultures within the United States. These are the natural factors that provide the course for languages to divide themselves into dialects, and are certainly not unique to the situation that exists with respect to the rural varieties of English. Regional and social distance can invariably be expected to result in dialect differences. Language variation is a fact of society, linked to the traditions of a people and the social factors that distinguish different social, cultural, and ethnic groups from each other.

The facts of language change and variation are fairly straightforward and are, in themselves, quite neutral. Unfortunately, however, a popular American mythology has grown around language differences, without an understanding of the real nature of language and how it is used in society. It thus becomes essential to expose some of these myths as a starting point. One of the most popular myths in American society concerns the systematic nature of linguistic diversity. It has become a well-established tradition in our schools and public places to view non-mainstream varieties of English as haphazard, unworthy approximations of what is commonly termed "standard English." Thus, Dial makes the following observation after surveying current opinion of so-called Appalachian English, one of the prominent representatives of a "rural" dialect of English:

> The dialect spoken by Appalachian people has been given a variety of
> names, the majority of them somewhat less than complimentary. Educated
> people who look with disfavor on this particular form of speech are perfectly
> honest in their belief that something called the English Language, which they
> see as a completed work—unchanging and fixed for all time—has been taken
> and, through ignorance shamefully distorted by the mountain folk. (Dial,
> 1970, p. 16)

In reality, of course, rural dialects are *not* simply imperfect and distorted renditions of the standard variety—they are varieties that are governed by a different set of rules. It is fairly simple to demonstrate the systematic and rule-governed nature of a rural variety such as Appalachian English, though its rules naturally differ somewhat from other varieties of English.

Consider, for example, the case of the prefix *a-* that can be attached to particular forms ending in *-ing*, giving sentences such as *All of a sudden a bear came a-runnin' and it comes a-runnin' toward him and he shot it between the eyes.* Although we might think that this *a*-prefix can be added to any *-ing* form, there are actually some quite rigorous conditions governing where it may and may not be added. Thus, it can be added to verbs or adverbs, but it is not added to nouns or adjectives. Accordingly, we hear sentences such as *She woke up a-screamin'* or *He was a-chasin' the bear,* but not *The movie was a-interestin'* or *A-sailin' is fun.* Any genuine speaker of this rural variety would use it according to these rules, since these rules are something organized within a speaker's mental capacity. Many examples of this type could be cited to illustrate how rules of pronunciation and grammar are an internalized set of organizational principles and that rural varieties are just as rule-governed and systematic as the standard, mainstream variety, albeit different.

Another myth concerning the language variations associated with some rural subcultures concerns their status in relation to other varieties. They are often described as the language of the "ignorant" or "simple folk," as if there were some inherent relationship between language deprivation and belonging to a nonmainstream subculture within American society. History, of course, tells us that our current version of standard English was yesterday's socially stigmatized variety of English, and that some of the nonstandard English of today will develop into tomorrow's standard variety of English. Thus, there was a period of English in which multiple negation (*He didn't do nothing*) was the standard form of negation. Such forms were common in Early Middle English (e.g., *He taketh nothing to hold of no men ne of no women*). Even the shibboleth of nonstandard speech, the use of *ain't*, had its day, as there is evidence indicating that it was used freely by many upper middle-class, educated speakers in the southern part of England as late as the turn of the century (J. M. Williams, 1975). Language standardization is a matter of social status, not a matter of language organization. There is no inherent relationship between language deprivation and belonging to a nonmainstream group.

It seems fairly obvious that language stigmatization goes hand in hand with social stigmatization. It is hardly surprising that a rural Appalachian subculture described by the distinguished historian Arnold Toynbee in the following way would be considered to possess an impoverished linguistic system:

> The Appalachian has relapsed into illiteracy and into all the superstitions for which illiteracy opens the door. . . . The Appalachian mountain people are the American counterparts of the latter-day white barbarians of the Old World: The Rifis and Kabyles and Tuareg, the Albanians and Caucasians, the Kurds and the Pathans and the Hairy Ainu . . . [They] are *ci-devant* heirs of the Western Civilization who have relapsed into barbarism under the depressing effects of a challenge which has been inordinately severe. . . . [Their] nearest social analogues . . . are certain "fossils" of extinct civilizations which have survived in fastnesses and have likewise relapsed into barbarism there. (Quoted in Mencken, 1962, p. 116)

Given such a description of an isolated rural culture, we can expect a corresponding view of the language. The view of language, after all, is highly conditioned by the view of the people who use it.

Although not all the caricatures of rural speech are as negative as those represented above, misrepresentation of language in isolated rural settings still persists. For example, it is commonly noted that these areas often retain older "relic" or "archaic" forms of English, and this observation has led to the conclusion that these areas may have retained intact an older, fifteenth- or sixteenth-century version of English. For example, the following type of observation is not atypical:

> Southern Mountain dialect (as the Appalchian folk speech is called by linguists) is certainly archaic, but the general historical period it represents can be narrowed down to the days of the first Queen Elizabeth and can be further particularized by saying that what is heard today is actually a sort of Scottish flavored Elizabethan English. (Dial, 1978, p. 49)

Marckwardt warns against such a simplistic interpretation of language variation:

> Unfortunately, the proponents of the notion of archaism in American English are often vague and superficial in their expositions of it. On an average of once every five years some well-meaning amateur in the field of folklore or cultural history "discovers" that either the Kentucky or the Virginian or the Ozark mountaineers or members of some relatively isolated group speak the undefiled English of Chaucer or Shakespeare. The evidence adduced usually runs to such stereotyped examples as *ax* for *ask*, *hit* for *it*,

mought for *might*, *bigged* for *"to get with child."* . . . it is quite wrong to suppose that any form of American English regional or otherwise, has preserved the language of the fourteenth or the sixteenth century without any change whatsoever. (1958, p. 60–61)

Certainly, the existence of particular archaisms is fairly easy to establish in many rural varieties. Thus, an historical investigation reveals that the *a*-prefix cited above was well represented in an earlier version of English. Or, the use of an *h* preceding *it* (*hit*) or *ain't* (*hain't*) as found in some rural varieties can be traced to an earlier stage in the development of English. And, in both of these cases, the form is retained in some rural areas while disappearing in nonrural dialects of English. To claim that these cases lead to the conclusion that an undefiled version of "Elizabethan English" is retained in such isolated rural enclaves, however, is certainly not justified. Such a claim has a certain amount of romantic charm, but it is too simplistic and categorical to be meaningful. More importantly, it denies the fundamental fact that all language systems are constantly undergoing change.

At the same time some rural varieties retain features representing genuine archaisms, other structures have changed in ways different from other varieties. Thus, the "regularization" of irregular verb usage, such as *knowed* and *blowed* (e.g., *He knowed he was right, He blowed the candle out*), probably anticipates changes yet to come to other varieties of the English language, as language systems tend to change toward the regularization of historical irregular forms. Similarly, the lack of distinction between past and present forms for items such as *come* and *run* (e.g., *Yesterday he come to school, Yesterday he run all the way to school*) by analogy with current forms in English such as *put* (e.g., *Yesterday he put the feed in the barn*) are the types of changes we might expect through time. In essence then, it is the particular combinations of something old with something new that makes a rural variety different from other varieties of English. Language systems are dynamic rather than static systems, building from, but not confined to, their past history. Rural varieties thus show characteristics of both retention and change.

LANGUAGE LEARNING AND RURAL SUBCULTURES

The controversy about language differences comes to a head over the issue of language learning. Generally speaking, middle-class, non-rural children are viewed as acquiring a linguistic system that is suprioer to their rural, lower-class counterparts in its explicitness, grammatical correctness, and capacity for cognitive development. This observation has been reified in the distinction between what the British sociologist

Basil Bernstein (1967) has called "elaborated" and "restricted" communicative codes. In an elaborated code, a speaker makes extensive use of the structural possibilities of the linguistic material, utilizing more complex and less predictable lexical and syntactic structures. Restricted code, on the other hand, is typified by more predictable lexical and syntactic options, as a speaker uses only a part of the structural possibilities in the linguistic material. According to the Bernstein hypothesis, the lower-class speaker uses only the restricted code while the middle-class speaker has additional access to the elaborated code.

Linguistic Structure

A number of linguistic characteristics have been cited to substantiate the distinction between restricted and elaborated code. These include the structure of sentences (restricted code is grammatically more "simple," with more unfinished sentences, whereas elaborated code reveals more complex sentences, with more completed sentences), the use of adjectives and adverbs (restricted code shows a wider range of adjective and adverb selection), and pronoun selection (elaborated code reveals a higher incidence of the personal pronoun *I* whereas restricted code uses more impersonal pronouns such as *they* and *you*), among other linguistic differences.

Assuming the validity of such measured differences between groups (and there is ample evidence to dispute the significance of some of the differences based on the way the supportive data have been collected and the groups manipulated (cf. Dittmar, 1976), we must raise several issues over the interpretation of these differences. Common to these concerns are the normative middle-class value judgments that underlie the interpreted significance of results. For example, it is assumed that diversity in the use of structural types and lexical choices leads to more efficient communication. While such diversity may be valued by the middle classes, there is no empirical base for concluding that a particular quantitative difference will lead to more communicative efficiency. Does the use of "unusual" adjectives lead to greater communicative adequacy? Does more grammatical subordination lead to more efficient communication strategy? The assumption that quantitative diversity is related to "efficient" communication in real life contexts is a correlation unwarranted by current evidence.

In essence, a strong bias in favor of the middle-class values placed on verbosity, qualification, and complexity in structure is revealed as the basis for determining that the lower-class person has limited expressive ability. Labov (1970), however, in contrasting a middle-class and lower-class argumentative discourse, has shown that verbosity, qualification, and complexity in structure do not necessarily lead to greater lucidity or logical argumentation in any rigorous sense, even though the subjective assessment they are accorded in our society might lead to that conclusion. In fact, some of the stylistic cues that give the impression of more developed argumentation might have the opposite effect, leading to a less logically coherent argumentative discourse.

It must also be noted that such a tabulation of linguistic forms focuses on some of the very superficial aspects of language, again biased in the direction of middle-class norms. Thus, the greater use of the passive voice favored by the middle classes is interpreted as a more elaborated form than the active voice, when in reality the passive may reflect nothing more than a stylistic alternative to the same underlying meaning expressed in an active form. Similarly, the tabulation of overt forms of conjunctions or prepositions, which Bernstein does, overlooks how such underlying relations between units can be manifested in other ways. A child who utters a sentence such as *You take my toy and I'ma hit you upside the head* has certainly communicated a conditional relationship, but done so without the superficial manifestation of *if* and *then*. There are few children who would fail to understand the conditional nature of the statement, yet it has been done so without the traditional standard English construction *If you take my toy, then I'll hit you in the head*. The notion that the surface manifestation of particular forms is a significant aspect of elaborated language usage can only come from the most superficial and naive understanding of the nature of language structure and its relation to communication.

The characterization of lower-class speech as linguistically restricted is particularly ironic when applied to some lower-class rural subcultures. These are subcultures that have developed and maintained a strong oral tradition—and one that highly values the imaginative, creative and "colorful" use of language. Thus, Cratis Williams, a lifelong student of folklore in the Appalachian mountain range, describes their use of language in the following way:

> The speech of the Southern Mountaineers bristles with strong language, pungent metaphors, vivid similes, and vigorous personifications. . . . Like the aphorisms, the neat rejoinders, the sharp retorts that have impressed outsiders who have taken time to converse with mountaineers, they are but part of the folk heritage of the region, stereotypical tricks of language that have in many instances served the highlander and his ancestors since before Chaucer. (1962, p. 9)

How is it that today's user of a "linguistically impoverished" code can turn out to be tomorrow's manipulative and crafty user of language? Or is it that the facts of real life language use have been obscured by the external norms inappropriately imposed on a different language system?

Can the assessment of "communicative efficiency" be restricted to the quantitative measurement of superficial linguistic forms?

Language Socialization

If the evidence for the alleged linguistic limitations of the lower-class world were simply based on the facts of language structure, it would be easy to disregard. The underlying assumptions about language structure and communication are naive, and the results superficial and dubious. However, the Bernstein hypothesis about language codes goes much further than that, including the process of socialization and the psychological correlates of the speech code. The impact of such an hypothesis, then, is much more interdisciplinary in its appeal, and has far-reaching implications. As it turns out, the quantitative measurement of linguistic structures is only one dimension of the distinction between restricted and elaborated codes.

The significance of social structure on the range of communicative codes can be observed in the following:

> If a social group, by virtue of its class relation—that is, as a result of its common occupational function and social status—has developed strong communal bonds; if the work relations of this group offers little variety; little exercise in decision-making; if assertion to be successful must be a collective rather than an individual act; if the work task requires physical manipulation and control rather than symbolic organization and control; if the diminished authority of the man at work is transformed into an authority of power at home; if the home is over-crowded and limits the variety of situations it can offer; if the children socialise each other in an environment offering little intellectual stimuli—if all these attributes are found in one setting, then it is plausible to assume that such a social setting will generate a particular form of communication which will shape the intellectual, social, and affective orientation of the children. (Bernstein, 1970, pp. 28–29)

From this perspective, the constellation of the family structure is of particular importance, and it is hypothesized that there is a causal relationship between family structure and linguistic interaction. Two types of families are distinguished, the "status-oriented" and the "person-oriented" family. In the status-oriented family, status is determined by the positional role in the family, and is not a matter for negotiation. On the other hand, in the person-oriented family, parents are more sensitive to the uniqueness of each child, and child-rearing methods take into account individual differences. Roughly speaking, there is an important difference in the way authority is established and its susceptibility to negotiation.

Given the particular social structure, a form of language practice emerges that is consonant with the distinction between restricted and elaborated code. According to Bernstein, a middle-class child in a person-oriented family discovers early about the advantages of the elaborated code. It is a medium that affords a conscious means of arbitration and negotiation, explanation, and other coping skills that are a necessary part of the socialization process. In a status-oriented family, however, socialization is more likely to take place through the means of a few short, rigid linguistic utterances related to authoritarian roles. Thus, commands predominate, and explanation is founded in the authority status rather than in "reasoned negotiation." Naturally, it is concluded that lower-class families are typically status-oriented, and hence predisposed to the restricted code, while middle-class families are person-oriented, and hence predisposed to the elaborated code.

In terms of the linguistic socialization process, the parent–child role, particularly that of the mother, is focused upon as the key to linguistic development. As Olim (1970) puts it:

> The behavior which leads to social, educational, and economic poverty is learned; it is socialized in early childhood. This socialization takes place in large measure by way of language. Since the mother is the primary socializing agent in most instances, the learning takes place in the context of the mother–child communication system. (Olim 1970, p. 212)

Several aspects of the mother–child relationships that predispose children are highlighted in contrastive studies of middle-class and lower-class families. First, it is maintained that middle-class mothers elaborate speech more than lower-class mothers when they interact with their children. For example, middle-class mothers engage in more expansion of the child's telegraphic utterances (e.g., When the child says, *This ring*, the parent expands it as, *This is a round ring*). The lower-class mother also appeals more to her status relationship as the basis for instruction as opposed to the middle-class parent, who appeals more to reason. Thus, more direct imperatives related to status (e.g., *Do this because I say so*) are used by the lower-class mother, whereas the middle-class mother may appeal to personal reasoning (e.g. *If you do this, here's what can happen*).

Finally, the middle-class child gets more stimulation for rationale and cognitive development than the lower-class child. Presuppositions and the consequences of actions are more likely to be made conscious or explicit in mother–child relationships, so that the child can develop strategies for logical arguments and evaluation of particular actions.

The types of caricatures presented above for lower-class families in general seem to be the kinds typically found in the descriptions of the isolated rural non-middle-class child. For example, consider the following types of conclusions reached in the study of language learning in Rosepoint, a rural lower-class community in Louisiana (Ward, 1971).

> Any theory of language learning would have to explain Rosepoint in which the children appear to receive little formal instruction and even less practice in their emerging skills. (p. 57)

> In Rosepoint imperatives are the primary focus of verbal manipulation. Simple, direct, and unambiguous commands may be the only verbal contact between mother and child for hours on end. (p. 64)

> Two styles of language used in the control of children have been contrasted. The style found in Rosepoint is called apodictic. Like the Ten Commandments, it is incontestable and categorical. . . . Thus, the children are unable to negotiate or bargain about their position vis-à-vis this authority.
> An alternative form, illustrated by the personalized family of Bernstein, . . . or the examples from the American middle class, is the practice of "casuistry," the application of general ethical principles to specific cases. The past, the future, and the nature and personality of the individuals involved are taken into consideration. In the process of socialization, language becomes the major element of control. The constant justifications and bargainings become more and more sophisticated.
> Casuistry is not the order of life in Rosepoint where there's "no such thing as doesn't and won't." (p. 74)

Such a characterization of the language-learning process in the lower-class rural subculture is certainly not uncommon; in fact, it seems to be the predominant viewpoint of the language-learning process in such a context. For this reason, it seems essential to consider in this connection: (1) the validity of the research findings that have led to such conclusions and (2) the significance of observed differences between groups in language socialization. To a large extent, our previous discussion focused on some of the inadequacies of the research basis for the distinction between restricted and elaborated code, so we will add little here. Dittmar (1976) concludes the following, based on the specific review of studies that have supported the Bernstein hypothesis:

> No investigation was able to prove conclusively that lower-class children have an intellectual or linguistic deficit. Such a conclusion is dubious not only because of the type of tests and the way they are carried out but also because the methods used to analyse linguistic and cognitive differences was shown to be largely inadequate. (Dittmar, 1976, p. 78)

To say that there are flaws in the research carried out to support the Bernstein hypothesis is not to say that there are no differences in language socialization as it may be found in nonrural middle-class settings and rural lower-class environments. Notwithstanding individual differences, there do appear to be differences in language socialization that relate to different subculture patterns. Various ethnographic descriptions of language socialization in different cultural settings support this observation (e.g., Slobin, 1967; Ward, 1971). Thus, cross-cultural ethnographic descriptions of language-socialization patterns support different roles for interlocutors in relation to language learning and different kinds of interaction with children acquiring language. While the mother may be the major input of language stimulus in the American middle-class nuclear family, other cultures utilize other sources in a major way, including other adults within the extended family, older siblings and peers (cf. Slobin, 1967). Thus, it is not surprising that in the rural community of Rosepoint described above, a range of members within the extended family share more responsibility for language development (Ward, 1971). This, in itself, is neither good nor bad; in fact, according to Slobin (1967) these extended models for language acquisition are more commonly found among representative cultures of the world than is the American middle-class pattern of vested responsibility in the mother.

Even though differing models for language socialization are, in themselves, neutral, they take on significance when one particular type of relationship is assured *prima facie* as the primary or exclusive model for developing language. Inherently, there is no advantage for language learning in a mother–child relationship *vis-à-vis* some other primary model, although popular research views on language development appear to assume such an advantage (e.g., Olim, 1970). Ultimately, the examination of language socialization must be viewed in an ethnographic context, and the available ethnographic studies of language development in rural subcultures do not justify the simplistic measurement of the quality and quantity of language interchange in an exclusive relationship such as that between mother and child. Accordingly, value interpretations from research findings based on such a culture-specific, single-dimension socialization model must be viewed with great suspicion.

Cultural differences may also exist with relation to the mode of language instruction that takes place with children. Some ethnographic observation tends to support the conclusion that middle-class mothers engage in more formal teaching than their working-class rural counterparts (cf. Ward, 1971) but this cannot be taken to mean that less language is acquired, or that it is acquired less efficiently. Here again, middle-class American culture may be in a minority in terms of the emphasis placed on formal instruction in language for children. Many other cultures simply rely upon the human capacity of language acquisition through exposure to language in the context of the immediate environment. From all available evidence (cf. Lenneberg, 1966; Chomsky, 1965), the exposure is perfectly adequate for the normal development of language. Language appears to be primarily self-taught, and the formal instructions by parents in language seem to have, at best, an incidental effect. In fact, viewed from one perspective, the availability of a range of informal sources for language development offers a certain advantage not found in limited formal instruction by a mother. Ward notes:

At any rate, the children spend most of every day within earshot of every type of speech event the community has to offer. This might be called an eavesdropping theory of language learning. Language learning in Rosepoint differs in this respect from that of a community in which a child receives more formal language training in the home but has less chance to observe a wide range of adult behavior. (1971, p. 56)

Although the advantage of a variety of informal models might be disputed, it seems indisputable that formal instruction is unnecessary for the normal child to acquire adequate language facility. After all, this is the process utilized in the majority of cultures; if it is found that this is the case in rural subcultures, then it is simply another example of a cultural alternative for language socialization.

Finally, there may certainly exist cultural differences in standards for language usage. All cultures maintain certain types of standards for language usage, but the emphasis may vary between groups. Thus, one group may emphasize standards of language concerning the particular forms of usage, while another may emphasize the particular uses of language that reflect what is considered appropriate behavior within the culture. From this viewpoint, it is not surprising to find differences between middle-class nonrural communities and isolated rural communities. The middle-class suburban socialization process is well known for its emphasis on using the "correct" grammatical forms as represented by standard English. In this context, a rural child who uses a nonmainstream variety would certainly not conform to this standard. But by the same token, a rural child may be socialized concerning behaviorally appropriate ways to use language. Thus, the use of respect forms (e.g., *ma'm* and *sir*) might be emphasized as the "right way to act," and children might be conditioned not to initiate conversation when adults are talking to each other. The value that "children should be seen, not heard" may thus be an important cultural component to be learned. In this context, the suburban middle-class child who assumes a turn in an adult conversation and who does not address adults by the proper respect terms would be the one who has not learned how to use language properly. Learning language inevitably involves socialization with respect to standards, but these standards certainly may take different foci depending on the values within a culture.

On the basis of the preceding discussion, it is reasonable to conclude that differences in language socialization correlate with rural subcultures. To the extent that there exist different family structures, different kinds of social interaction, and different cultural values concerning language behavior, there will be different types of social environments for language learning. To deny the potential of such a difference would be unrealistic with our understanding of some of the subcultural differences that distinguish rural from nonrural communities in American society. But by the same token, our examination of current research forces us to conclude that there is no evidence that the cultural differences in any way predispose children to a linguistic handicap. Linguistic differences simply cannot be equated with linguistic deficit.

INSTITUTIONALIZED DISCONTINUITY

If various communities in American society simply operated as independent, isolated entities, the language and language socialization of the rural child would be of little concern. This, however, is not the case and the rural child is invariably subjected to standards of language that are not indigenous to the community. For most of these children, the

TABLE 1. ITPA GRAMMATICAL CLOSURE SUBTEST WITH COMPARISON OF "CORRECT" RESPONSES AND APPALACHIAN ENGLISH ALTERNATE FORMS[a]

Stimulus with "Correct" item according to	
Test manual	AE alternate
1. Here is a dog. Here are two *dogs/doggies*.	
2. This cat is under the chair. Where is the cat? She is on/ (any preposition—other than *under*—indicating location).	
3. Each child has a ball. This is hers; and this is *his*.	*his'n*
4. This dog likes to bark. Here he is *barking*.	
5. Here is a dress. Here are *two dresses*.	
6. The boy is opening the gate. Here the gate has been *opened*.	
7. There is milk in this glass. It is a glass *of/with/for/o'/lots of milk*.	No preposition
8. This bicycle belongs to John. Whose bicycle is it? It is *John's.*	
9. This boy is writing something. This is what he *wrote/has written/did write*.	*writed/writ, has wrote*
10. This is the man's home, and this is where he works. Here he is going to work, and here he is going *home/back home/to his home*.	*at home*
11. Here it is night, and here it is morning. He goes to work first thing in the morning, and he goes home first thing at *night*.	*of the night*
12. This man is painting. He is a *painter/fence painter*.	*a-paintin'*
13. The boy is going to eat all the cookies. Now all the cookies have been *eaten*.	*eat, ate, eated, et*

(*continued*)

Table 1 (*Continued*)

Stimulus with "Correct" item according to	
Test manual	AE alternate

14. He wanted another cookie; but there weren't *any/any more*.	*none/no more*
15. This horse is not big. This horse is big. This horse is even *bigger*.	*more bigger*
16. And this horse is the very *biggest*.	*most biggest*
17. Here is a man. Here are *two men/gentlemen*.	*mans/mens*
18. This man is planting a tree. Here the tree has been *planted*.	
19. This is soap and these are *soap/bars of soap/more soap*.	*soaps*
20. This child has lots of blocks. This child has even *more*.	
21. And this child has the *most*.	*mostest*
22. Here is a foot. Here are two *feet*.	*foots/feets*
23. Here is a sheep. Here are lots of *sheep*.	*sheeps*
24. This cookie is not very good. This cookie is good. This cookie is even *better*.	*gooder*
25. And this cookie is the very *best*.	*bestest*
26. This man is hanging the picture. Here the picture has been *hung*.	*hanged*
27. The thief is stealing the jewels. These are the jewels that he *stole*.	*stoled/stealed*
28. Here is a woman. Here are *two women*.	*womans/womens*
29. The boy had two bananas. He gave one away; and he kept one for *himself*.	*hisself*
30. Here is a leaf. Here are two *leaves*.	*leafs*
31. Here is a child. Here are three *children*.	*childrens*
32. Here is a mouse. Here are two *mice*.	*mouses*
33. These children all fell down. He hurt himself; and she hurt herself. They all hurt *themselves*.	*theirselves/theirself*

*a*Wolfram, 1977, pp. 233–234.

discontinuity of their local rural language variety and the external standard comes into focus when the children are introduced in the formal educational process, whether it be Head Start, some comparable preschool program, or the elementary school classroom. As the children enter the classroom, the different language patterns can be expected to clash with the language standards of the dominant mainstream culture. Different norms, standards, and underlying values about language meet head on.

The conflict starts with standards and norms set forth in the initial screening of a child's speech. Norms of "correctness" are inevitably set forth in terms of the mainstream standard English variety. Consider, for example, how a standardized test of language development may affect the view of a child's language acquisition. For illustrative purposes here, we will examine specifically the "grammatic closure" subtest of the Illinois Test of Psycholinguistic Abilities (Kirk, McCarthy, & Kirk, 1968), a test commonly used to determine a child's level of language development. This test, like many of its parallels, is dialect restricted, in that only forms given in "standard American English" are considered correct responses. In many respects, this variety is quite different from the variety spoken in many rural Southern communities, where the linguistic forms differ systematically from their standard English counterparts. In Table 1, we indicate the items that are considered correct responses according to the examiner's manual, and contrast those with corresponding forms in what has been described as Appalachian English (Wolfram & Christian, 1976). All of the different forms, which must be considered normative for the Appalachian variety, follow particular rules that have been described for the variety, albeit different from standard English.

Of the 33 items in the test, 25 of them have legitimately different forms in Appalachian English—forms that are normative within the variety but different from standard English. The significance of the discrepancy becomes more apparent when we examine the score in terms of a correlation table that matches the raw score with a "psycholinguistic age level." For example, if a 10-year-old Appalachian child gives all correct responses according to the different Appalachian English norm, then this child correlates with a psycholinguistic age level of a child less than five years of age. Is it any wonder, then, that these children are viewed as retarded in their language acquisition? Is it any wonder that they are viewed as linguistically deficient? The interpretation, however, may be a product of the inappropriate and discriminatory use of standardize tests that have been applied to a different language system. When these simple differences in linguistic form are placed in the context of the culture differences of which they are a part, including values concerning language standards, appropriate and inappropriate language usage, and the language-socialization processes, there can emerge a picture of serious discontinuity in language.

The educational response to the distorted picture of linguistic deficiency derived from the application of inappropriate norms has been to set up programs of remediation—programs of "compensatory education" that can be used to bring these children up to the standards of middle-class children. Such programs have now made their way into many preschool and elementary school programs, with the hope that these children can be brought up to the external norm. Unfortunately, in many cases, the underlying premises of these programs share the same ethnocentric biases about language differences found in the standard-ized testing instruments. Thus, it is declared that these children show "a total lack of ability to use language as a device for acquiring and process-ing information. Language for them is unwieldy and not very useful" (Bereiter & Engelmann, 1966, p. 39). In essence, the answer to their lin-guistic ills is speaking standard English as middle-class suburban chil-dren speak it.

Although there may certainly exist some advantages in using a standard variety with respect to social mobility (and, in speaking, there are varieties—not one variety—of standard English), these must clearly be separated from basic issues of language development and adequacy. Certainly, detailed discussions of hunting, fishing, and various indige-nous crafts can be communicated in a rural context that would leave the middle-class suburbanite dumbfounded and uncomprehending by com-parison. Certainly, some of today's rural children will develop the art of story-telling in a way that would make their middle-class counterparts seem dull, colorless, unexpressive, and illogical. Certainly, some of the respect forms and politeness in deference to adults found in rural areas would make the middle-class child seem disrespectful and impolite by contrast. And certainly, some of today's "bad English" that serves as the basis for unfounded speculation about linguistic ability was once em-ployed by the highest-ranking citizens of England and Scotland.

CONCLUSION

So where does all this leave us? Our intention is not to denigrate the speech of middle-class suburbanites, for surely it differs from that of the lower-class rural community, just as the speech of the rural community is different from standard English. The point simply is to show that middle-class ethnocentrism about language has led to many unjustifia-ble conclusions about language forms and uses. In many cases, linguistic depravity may be ultimately in the mind of the beholder, not in the reality of the community.

These are not conclusions that are of simple philosophical interest to scholars who argue such issues at scholarly conferences and in aca-demic journals. For better or for worse, they affect the way children are viewed, the way they are categorized intellectually, the programs in which they are enrolled educationally, and the opportunities these chil-dren may be provided in life. These are serious issues that have to be faced by both researchers and educators, for the stakes are indeed high.

Eliot Wigginton and the *Foxfire* materials (1972) should have taught us that there is certainly hope for the development of language arts skills in isolated rural settings, and that the key is the utilization of the community as a resource of strength rather than weakness. The rich cultural and linguistic heritage must be built upon rather than disregarded. But such cases of success will certainly remain isolated and restricted until the language of the community is genuinely accepted as part of the culture, and the legitimate differences are understood practically in the educational process. And this extends from the assumptions about language differences by researchers to the testing and assessment of children's language capabilities in a classroom setting.

REFERENCES

Bereiter, C., & Engelmann, S. *Teaching disadvantaged children in the preschool.* Englewood Cliffs, N.J.: Prentice-Hall, 1966.

Bernstein, B. Elaborated and restricted code: An outline. In S. Lieberson (Ed.), Explorations in sociolinguistics, Part 2 of *International Journal of American Linguistics.* Bloomington: Indiana University, 1967.

Bernstein, B. A sociolinguistic approach to socialization: With some reference to educability. In F. Williams (Ed.), *Language and poverty: Perspectives on a theme.* New York: Markham, 1970.

Chomsky, N. *Aspects of the theory of syntax.* Cambridge: M.I.T. Press, 1965.

Dial, W. P. Folk speech is English, too. *Mountain Life & Work,* February 1970, 16–18.

Dial, W. P. The dialect of the Appalachian people. In D. N. Mielke (Ed.), *Teaching mountain children: Towards a foundation of understanding.* Boone, N.C.: Appalachian Consortium Press, 1978.

Dittmar, N. *A critical survey of sociolinguistics: Theory and application.* New York: St. Martin's Press, 1976.

Kirk, S., McCarthy, J., & Kirk, W. *The Illinois test of psycholinguistic abilities.* Urbana: University of Illinois Press, 1968.

Kurath, H. Plans for a survey of dialects of New England. *Dialect Notes,* 1930, 6(2), 65–72.

Kurath, H. *Handbook of the linguistic geography of New England.* Providence: American Council of Learned Societies, 1939.

Labov, W. The logic of nonstandard English. In J. A. Alatis (Ed.), *Georgetown Monograph Series on Languages and Linguistics No. 22.* Washington, D.C.: Georgetown University Press, 1970.

Lenneberg, E. (Ed.). *New directions in the study of language.* Cambridge: M.I.T. Press, 1966.

Marckwardt, A. H. *American English.* New York: Oxford University Press, 1958.

Mencken, H. L. *The American language: The fourth edition and the two supplements,* R. I. McDavid (Ed.), New York: Knopf, 1962.

Olim, E. G. Maternal language styles and cognitive development of children. In F. Williams (Ed.), *Language and poverty: Perspectives on a theme.* Chicago: Markham, 1970.

Slobin, D. I. *A field manual for cross-cultural study of the acquisition of communicative competence.* Berkeley: University of California, 1967.

Ward, M. C. *Them children: A study in language learning.* New York: Holt, Rinehart & Winston, 1971.

Williams, C. D. Metaphor in mountain speech, Part 7. *Mountain Life & Work,* 1962, 38(9), 11–12.

Williams, J. M. *Origins of the English language: A social and linguistic history.* New York: Free Press, 1975.

Wigginton, E. *The foxfire book.* Garden City, N.Y.: Anchor Books, 1972.

Wolfram, W. Language assessment in Appalachia: A sociolinguistic perspective. *Appalachian Journal*, 1977, *4*, 224–235.

Wolfram, W., & Christian, D. *Appalachian speech.* Arlington, Va.: Center for Applied Linguistics, 1976.

6

Is There a Psychology of the Rural Aged?

Andrew S. Dibner

Among other things, this century is witnessing "the graying of America." Whereas in 1910 only 2% of the population of the United States was over 65 years of age, by 1970, 11% had reached this age, and by 2030, 25% will be considered elderly.

This population change is of considerable concern because chronological age is tied in innumerable ways to the way our society functions and how people behave toward one another. Since ancient times stages of human agehood have been used to designate roles and responsibilities, rights, privileges, and expectations (Fischer, 1978).

Of great practical concern in the graying of America is how to insure a vital, productive society if its members are increasingly tending to become retired, to suffer the major and minor behavioral inefficiencies due to normal biological changes accompanying old age, and to develop chronic, debilitating medical conditions. It is true, most aged are healthy, but 60% of our medical expenditures today are for persons over 65, and medical costs are an alarmingly increasing segment of our gross national expenditures. With the anticipated growth of the older population, future medical costs could rise astronomically.

Improved planning and allocation of health and supportive services, as well as more effective prevention programs, are required. However, better planning and strategies will depend on the state of our information about the aged, and the theoretical tools with which to

---

ANDREW S. DIBNER • Department of Psychology, Boston University, Boston, Massachusetts 02215.

analyze the problems they pose. Unfortunately, most studies of aging are descriptive in regard to some demographic variables and employ univariate designs using chronological age as the independent variable. The results of such studies are of limited use in understanding behavior and in planning for the future. Several sociological variables have been known to have powerful influences on older persons' behavior, and studies which ignore such factors as cultural background, education, marital status, and economic status can be misleading. Is "rurality" also an important variable? Are the rural aged a special group requiring special understanding? Is there a psychology of rural aging?

I searched for psychological studies of the rural aged conducted in the past 20 years to see if there is a rural psychology of the aged. My search revealed an almost nonexistent psychological literature but a substantial sociological one that gives some insights into the psychology of aging in a rural environment. This chapter will point out some of the more salient issues.

WHAT IS RURAL? WHO ARE THE RURAL AGED?

It is difficult today to define the concept *rural*. Traditionally, rural has been defined either quantitatively or qualitatively. Quantitative definitions use population density criteria, such as towns of less than 2,500 population, or density of population in the open country. Qualitative definitions emphasize agriculture and social patterns that are more personal and informal, such as simplicity of life style, slow social change, and little social differentiation.

But it is no longer sufficient to describe rural in terms of agriculture or density of population. Our rural environments have been changing and are becoming so infiltrated by industrial and commercial enterprises, and mass communications which spread the national culture, that they are no longer the idyllic, isolated, natural environs they once were. Not only has the topography changed, but the gemeinschaft society which had typified the concept of rural has also been in the process of change. Younger persons growing up in rural America today will not, when they become old, be the same as their grandparents are today.

As the population in the United States has grown by almost 100 million persons since 1900, practically all the growth *seems* to have taken place in urban areas and in their suburbs. Proportionately, nonmetropolitan populations appear to have declined. In actual numbers, the United States Census shows little change in the rural (farm and nonfarm) population, with 52 million in 1920 and 54 million in 1970, but this apparent constancy is due to shifting definitions by the Census

Bureau. In 1900, the Census definition of rural was all places of less than 4,000 population density. By 1910, this had been changed to 2,500. In 1930, the concept of rural nonfarm was added, and in 1960 the category of metropolitan rural areas was added. Areas that were previously considered rural (e.g., farms) but that were located within the county boundaries of a Standard Metropolitan Statistical Area were not considered rural any longer (Adams, 1975). Thus the statistical definition of rural has become more restricted. The very concept of rural as we have known it may have a limited future because of the continual growth of urban and suburban areas.

The rural population also appears to have "aged" more rapidly than the urban. Youth have moved from rural to urban areas, and though there is evidence of a recent reversal of the trend toward greater urban growth, it appears to be retired people, not youth, who have been settling back to the country (Ahearn, 1979). The farms being left by the rural aged are not being taken over by younger generations but are passing into the conglomerates of agribusiness (Adams, 1975).

Over one-third of the nation's total older population lives in rural areas. They are concentrated in the north central and southern regions of the United States. Actually, over half of the older people living on farms reside in only 10 states (Harbert & Wilkinson, 1979). Vermont has the highest proportion (64.8%) of older people who are rural (Atchley, 1975).

More men than women are among the aged in rural farm areas, but the most rapidly growing rural elderly category is the nonfarm, and these are mostly women. Migration of the elderly from farms seems to be mostly to rural nonfarm or to small towns rather than to cities.

Deficiencies in Definitions of Rural Aged

Several inadequate assumptions underlie demographic definitions of the rural aged. As Adams (1975) points out, it is as if the person suddenly came into existence at the age of 65 at the location at which she or he is found. But, of course, this is not the case. Some old people remained and grew old on the farms and the small towns in which they were raised; many old people now in small towns retired there from the cities. These retirees have developmental histories vastly different from the country-raised elderly. They may have different values, different expectations, and less deeply rooted support systems (Coward, 1979).

Most gerontological research, especially "theories of aging," can be criticized for ignoring past histories of persons and explaining behavior simply in terms of a person's current environmental and social situation

(Adams, 1975). Adams suggests instead the "life course" frame of reference of Youmans (1969), which requires that the cultural expectations and abilities associated with older age be compared with those of earlier stages of life.

Since they represent dozens of national and cultural backgrounds, we must consider the rural elderly as a nonhomogeneous group of persons. For a theoretical understanding, can we really consider the following rural aged as the same—the southern blacks, Hispanics, Native Americans, Appalachian subsistence farmers, Wyoming cowboys, Alabama patriarchs, coal miners in rural Pennsylvania and Kentucky, and Wisconsin dairy farmers (Youmans, 1973)?

Thus, as we think of the rural aged today, we are thinking of persons of diverse cultural backgrounds, some of whom were raised in the country, and others who were not, and most of whom are living in a rural environment which has changed over the recent past. Adams (1975) calls the present-day aged, "strangers in a strange land." Pihlblad (1975) calls them "a disappearing generation" to be replaced by generations raised in the mass culture.

Differences between Rural and Nonrural Aged

Early in this century sociologists pointed out distinct differences between the relatively stable rural life and the fast-paced urban life, and many of the present old people in the country are products of those times. Studies of residents of small towns in Missouri pointed out the differences between the social and moral climate of the small town and that of the metropolitan area during the early decades of the century.

> There was an intimacy of close personal knowledge of one's neighbors, and widespread familiarity with the family backgrounds of most acquaintances . . . The anonymity and impersonality of the city were unknown . . . in general the world of the villager was limited to his own local community. (Pihlblad, 1975, p. 51)

The virtues of the simple country life, belief in God, hard work, honesty, prudence, frugality, abstinence, personal responsibility, courage, and modesty and the core of the Protestant ethic were contrasted with the artificiality, sin, and corruption of city life. There was a belief in social equality in a classless society.

In Plainville in 1938 the prevailing individualistic ideology of small town people was composed of the principles of independence and individual responsibility for one's fate. One was expected to take care of oneself in one's old age, to remain in one's home after retirement if possible, and to bear hardship and poverty without complaining (West, 1945). This independence did not necessarily mean loneliness or isolation, however, for old friends would gather to gossip, and there was much individual visiting.

Many changes occurred between early in the century and the present day. Small towns which saw the penetration of mass media and the increased use of highways were absorbed into the mass culture. For the young in the small towns, socialized in this national culture, there would be little difference between urban and rural roles, expectations, and values. Some sociologists believe the differences between ruralism and urbanism will disappear (Adams, 1975; Dewey, 1960).

However, the elderly in the small towns in the 1960s and 1970s maintained the values of the social system in which they were socialized early in the century. "They continued to rely on themselves as much as possible, to look on 'the welfare' as something to be avoided at all costs, even to reject the aid offered by their children and to rely on agemates for friendship and association" (Pihlblad, 1975, p. 58).

A large survey by Schooler (1975) reported differences between rural and urban elderly on such variables as mobility, income, education, housing, employment, health, self-image, and availability of services. The sample was drawn by area–probability procedures, with 4,000 interviews of persons 65 years of age or older. The two-hour interviews contained questions pertaining to residential environment, health, social relationships, and morale. In addition, there were conventional demographic items and questions concerning the knowledge and use of social services. Some of the findings most pertinent to this chapter are:

1. Older women, especially widows, tended to move to more urban areas, while older men remained on the farm longer.
2. Rural elderly had lower income than urban elderly: 53% of urban elderly had incomes below the $2,000 mark; 64% of the rural elderly fell into that category.
3. Proportionately more rural elderly were poorly educated. Twice as many urban elderly as rural had some college education.
4. Compared to urban, more rural elderly lived in their own homes (77%). Only 10% (or less) of the rural elderly rented their homes. Twice this number of urban elderly rented homes.
5. There were no differences between the two groups in paid employment. Slightly less than 12% of both urban and rural elderly claimed to be employed.
6. There was no difference in age of retirement between rural and urban.

7. Overall, differences in social relationships of urban and rural elderly were slight.
8. Schooler found the rural elderly more "alienated" than the urban, and their self-image seemed to be less positive.
9. Urban elderly reported their health to be better, but rural elderly scored higher on questions relating to functional performance on a variety of personal tasks.
10. There were practically no differences in perception of housing between urban and rural elderly.
11. There were strong differences in "distance to services." Actually, this is perception of distance to services, and the rural tended to perceive themselves as more distant. However, in perception of convenience of services, friends, and relatives, rural elderly were more likely to see themselves as situated conveniently, compared to urban elderly.

In summary, Schooler found remarkable similarities between urban and rural elderly, and by studying changes with repeated data collection over a three-year period, he found a substantial relation between changes in morale and health among the urban elderly, but not among the rural. Schooler suggests that a rural experience might have some "buffers" in social relationships that preserve health in the face of the insult of deteriorating morale.

Independence, Dependence, and Isolation

Social relationships have been among the most frequently studied variables in research on rural-urban aging. With whom do the aged live and interact? To whom do they turn for help? Unfortunately, most studies report only on frequency rather than quality of contacts.

For most aged, being able to maintain independence is a source of considerable satisfaction, and the threatened loss of independence from financial difficulties or health problems can be a major source of worry. In studies of rural communities in Iowa and Pennsylvania, the elderly showed considerable resistance to the idea of living with relatives, since that would be visible proof of increasing dependence (Powers, Keith, & Goudy, 1975). In general, the rural aged lived with a spouse or lived alone, but if they lived with someone other than a spouse, it was most likely with their children. The young of the rural are highly mobile. Only 19% of the children of the rural aged in Iowa lived in the same community as their parents, compared to 34% of the children of urban aged in Iowa (Bultena & Oyler, 1971).

Are the rural elderly more isolated? Counting face-to-face contacts alone, one would conclude that they are more isolated than urban elderly, but not if one counts phone and mail contacts. Probably as a result of distance, there is more direct visiting between urban elderly and their children. More than half of the contacts of rural elderly with their children is by telephone; only one third is face-to-face. However, considering all sources of interaction (phone, face-to-face, and mail), 94% of rural elderly had at least one child-contact a week and 63% had two or more child-contacts a week. Despite the high out-migration of children, most rural elderly have at least one child who is readily accessible by phone. Powers *et al.* (1975) conclude, "there is little suggestion that the rural aged are isolated." However there is regional variation in values of dependence on family. In Appalachia, Youmans found surprisingly strong dependence values in the rural elderly, compared to those in the metropolitan center. The rural aged were significantly more dependent on their families and relatives and on the government (Youmans, 1973).

Although a higher percentage of urban elderly than rural elderly live alone, the fact is urban aged persons are more likely to have their children living nearby, allowing the urban elderly to visit with their children more often than rural elderly. However, rural-urban differences appear to be minimal in friendship and neighboring patterns and in the help they provide for the elderly (Bultena, 1969; Powers *et al.*, 1975).

The effects of widowhood are also not much different for the elderly in the city or the country. One study found that almost 40% of the rural aged are widowed, and it seems to be an especially isolating experience for males. Widows are twice as likely and widowers four times as likely as married persons to be isolated. Most men and women continue to live alone after widowhood, maintaining independence but keeping contact with children and other relatives. Rural-urban differences in social isolation were insignificant for widowed individuals. Some studies have shown no relationship between widowhood and morale or outlook on life (Montgomery, 1965).

Need for and Availability of Services

There are no studies of percentages of rural or urban elderly who are in nursing homes, homes for the aged, and other types of institutions. If a rural farm resident enters a rural nursing home or home for the aged, that person is then listed in the census as living in a nonfarm environment. Similarly, a rural resident who enters an urban institution for the elderly becomes an urban resident. The census data have been useless in determining differential effects on the incidence of the institutionalization of the elderly (Taietz, 1978).

More helpful data are available for the noninstitutional elderly. The percentage of elderly who are unable to carry out their major activities increases from 14.4% for the ages 65–74 to 32.9% for those aged 85 and over (National Center for Health Statistics, 1978). Since 60% of the elderly live with a spouse or other relatives, the proportion of disabled elderly living without family assistance who may be in need of home care is estimated to be 14% of the remaining 40%, or 5.6% of the total elderly (Taietz, 1977).

The disabled older person's ability to maintain noninstitutional living arrangements (whether urban or rural) depends upon (1) the availability of organized community services, (2) the availability of family members and supportive services provided by them, (3) the interaction with and help received from friends and neighbors, (4) the quality of housing, (5) transportation, and (6) income. Rural environments are relatively weak in all these resources.

Although community based services have become more established in rural areas, they are still not accessible to many persons because of a lack of mass transportation. The rural elderly are almost totally dependent upon the automobile for transportation. They often do not own or cannot drive a car themselves and are dependent upon relatives and neighbors. Lack of transportation has been cited as a major obstacle to obtaining medical care as well as being detrimental to maintaining a social life.

Housing

According to the United States Census, the rural elderly are more deprived in terms of housing than the urban elderly. The housing of the rural elderly is older, of lower value, and more likely to be substandard. One-quarter of the rural elderly is reported to live in inadequate housing, lacking central heat, plumbing facilities, or a telephone. Of persons aged 60 and over living in rural dwellings, 20% lack a bathroom, 17% lack a telephone, 16% lack hot and cold piped water, and 15% lack a flush toilet (Lohmann, 1978).

The rural aged have a disadvantage both in attempting to maintain their private homes and in attempting to move into public housing. They have less assistance from younger family members to help repair their homes, and there is little access to public housing, which has been extensively used for urban areas (Lipman, 1978).

Income

Rural elderly have a considerably lower median income than the urban elderly. The average income of an elderly couple living in rural America is 20% less than that of a comparable couple living in a metropolitan area; finding employment to supplement income is more difficult because of the limited supply of jobs available in rural areas (New York Senate Research Service, 1980).

How They See It

Thus, with inadequate income, poor housing, lack of transportation, and inconsistency of services, is the historical "integrated rural community" a congenial place to maintain disabled elderly in their own homes? Although the logical answer is no, the rural elderly do not perceive themselves as relatively deprived as one would imagine. Lipman (1978) calls this "needs inconsistency."

> We find evidence that in the socio-emotional realm the rural setting appears to be a far more satisfying one for the aged person than does the urban environment. The older rural individual appears not to perceive himself as relatively deprived compared to the older urban individual. (Lipman, 1978)

Data from a 1973 national probability sample survey yielded the conclusion that "the rural elderly were found to be more satisfied with their community, expressed greater general happiness, and had less fear than the urban elderly" (Hynson, 1975).

Thus, urban elderly may have more social contacts, but the rural elderly may have more satisfying, though less frequent, contacts with other perons. This raises the general issue of the difference between quantitative and qualitative findings in these areas. Using a quantitative index is really perhaps a measure of the complexity of life of the urban area. The rural life is a simpler one (less frequent contact), but from a phenomenological point of view the rural life may be sufficiently rich to the aged person. This matching of expectations with experience may be seen as "congruence" of person–environment interaction (Kahana, 1975), or achieving a "preference for simplicity" (Dibner, 1972), or "social disengagement" (Cumming & Henry, 1961).

More sophisticated research is needed on feelings of satisfaction in rural and urban aged. Using the same National Opinion Research Center (NORC) data, but subjecting it to multivariate analysis, Sauer, Sheehan, and Boymel (1976) found that the rural-urban differences in life satisfaction reported by Hynson (1975) were not upheld. They found other factors to be much more salient in affecting life satisfaction, including health, marital status, race, income, and work status. Controlling for these variables reduced completely the importance of the urban-rural variable.

However, other national studies show that a person's sense of well being increases consistently as he or she moves from larger cities to rural areas, even after income variables are controlled. Fear of crime, which has repeatedly been shown to be a serious problem for a large percentage of persons over 65, seems to be primarily an urban fear. The rural aged person not only is faced with a lower objective crime rate, but he also perceives his environment as safer and is less afraid than his city counterpart (Lipman, 1978).

Another example of "needs inconsistency" occurs in the area of housing. Lohmann (1978) points out that older persons' perceptions of their needs for housing are not the same as that of service providers. Despite the conclusions of the United States Census that housing conditions among the rural aged are poor, most older rural persons perceive their housing as highly adequate.

Studies of urban-rural differences in adjustment to public housing for the elderly have emphasized that residence in different parts of the country leads to different expectations and preferences for physical layout, privacy, social interaction, etc. (Nahemow & Lawton, 1978). Rural residents of public housing, compared to urban, were found to be more satisfied with their housing and with the development of friendships in the site. There was a linear relationship between community size and tenant well-being. The larger the community, the more dissatisfied the tenant, and the fewer friends he or she made. In contrast, participation in activity followed a different pattern. In the middle-sized cities, people were more likely to attend formal activities. The limited participation in rural areas was explained by the absence of available activities in which to participate (Nahemow & Lawton, 1978). One of the difficulties encountered by this type of research is the fact that the types of housing vary from region to region, affecting the findings. For example, high-rise housing is built in cities, not in rural sites; and in "Middle America," housing is usually age segregated and often racially segregated.

LONELINESS

Loneliness and isolation are commonly thought to be significant factors in the lives of older people. Butler (1975) pointed out that loneliness may be a frequent reaction to the major crises of old age, such as widowhood, late-life marital and sexual problems, retirement, sensory loss, aging, disease, pain, institutionalization, and death. A Harris survey (1975) found that loneliness was considered a "serious problem," preceded only by the fear of crime, poor health, and inadequate income. Many older persons express feelings of loneliness despite substantial contacts with others, although some persons who have only minimal contacts may not perceive themselves as lonely or isolated at all.

The rural aged, especially, are thought of as potentially lonely. Kivett (1979) studied loneliness in rural elderly, with her sample consisting of 418 adults, 65–99 years of age living in a rural county in North Carolina. Good sampling procedures were used to get a representative sample of the county. A multiple step-wise discriminant analysis was used which incorporated 13 physical and social variables to determine the best linear combinations for classifying adults according to levels of loneliness (quite often lonely, sometimes, and almost never lonely). The dependent variable, feelings of loneliness, was measured by the responses to the question, "Do you find yourself feeling lonely quite often, sometimes, or almost never?"

Fifteen and one-half percent of the adults described themselves as quite often lonely, 41.8% as sometimes lonely, and 42.6% as never lonely. The most important variables in terms of relative discriminating power of loneliness were adequacy of transportation, widow versus married contrast, self-rated health, adequacy of vision, organizational activity, frequency of telephoning, and single versus married contrast.

Of note is Kivett's finding that 15.5% of his rural subjects were often lonely, not much different from the 12% found in the Harris survey. Also, except possibly for transportation, the dominant variables for loneliness are not positively related to rurality. One can hardly conclude that rurality leads to loneliness.

Is Rurality an Important Variable?

There is little convincing evidence at the time that rurality is a fruitful variable in considering the rural aging. Those aged living in the country are not a homogeneous group but one with a great number of cultural and experiential backgrounds. The very concept of rural as we have known it has been disappearing both quantitatively and qualitatively.

The country is being urbanized. The social-moral climate typifying rural life early in the century is yielding to a mass culture. The children of today, when they become aged, will not be like the aged of today.

It is true that certain differences between urban and rural do still prevail—distances, transportation, and housing. The health of rural elderly is poorer, and there is less availability of services. But despite these differences, the perceptions of the rural elderly, of their needs and life satisfactions, are not to any great extent different from their urban counterparts.

The social relationships of rural and urban aged show few differences if availability of family and friend support is viewed in terms of face-to-face, phone, and mail contacts. Also, there are no generalized differences in reactions to widowhood or dependence on family and no rural differences in perceived loneliness.

ENVIRONMENTS AND ADAPTATIONS

Although rurality as a global construct may not be a practical approach in our concern about rural aged, some salient characteristics of rurality (as described in contrast to urbanness) may enable us to consider the environmental factors that influence the aging. There have been some promising starts in theories of environment and aging (Windley, Byerts, & Ernst, 1975), though most work thus far on environment and the aged has dealt with housing, institutional settings, and urban issues, and not with the rural aged.

Of the several nascent theories of man–environment relations, Lawton and Nahemow's Ecological Theory of Aging is probably the most developed (Lawton & Nahemow, 1973; Lawton, 1975). It uses the $B = f(P:E)$ paradigm, viewing behavior as a resultant of interaction of characteristics of the Person (P) and his contemporary Environment (E). Behavioral efficiency (B) is seen as the result of an interaction of personal competencies (e.g., biological health), environmental presses (e.g., ambient temperature), and interactive ($P \times E$) terms (e.g., social activities). Figure 1 illustrates the relationship among the variables.

In theory, given a situation of inadequate performance and negative affect, the theory will guide an analysis of the P, E, and $P \times E$ components of the situation. Then one may develop procedures to promote a more effective adaptation, perhaps by increasing P's competence (through therapy, education, or prosthetics), or by reducing the environmental press (perhaps through simplification or decreased stimulation), thus creating conditions for more optimal performance and positive affect. As an example, consider the relocation of an individual to a nursing home. The proper setting for a very competent person would be a home with a stimulating program of activities, but that same setting would be overwhelming to an individual who has sensory or motor dysfunctions and who is thus less able to cope. Highly competent per-

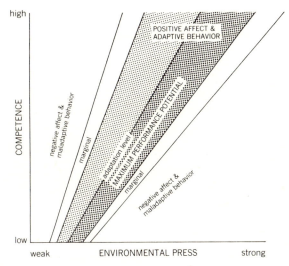

FIGURE 1. Diagrammatic representation of the behavioral and affective outcomes of person–environment transactions. (From "Ecology and the Aging Process" by M. P. Lawton and L. Nahemow, in C. Eisdorfer and M. P. Lawton (Eds.), *The Psychology of Adult Development and Aging.* Copyright 1973 by the American Psychological Association. Reprinted by permission.)

sons can tolerate a wider variety of environmental press and still maintain good adaptation, but the less competent person is less able to adapt to environmental changes (Lawton's "environmental docility" hypothesis, 1975).

Adapting the ecological theory to the problems of the rural aged might prove helpful, although Lawton acknowledges the prematurity of measuring the critical variables, especially environmental ones. One of the most difficult issues is that of conceptualizing *P* or *E* concepts *independently,* for people *are* in environments and environments can affect people through their perceptions (and therefore interpretations). Ecological theory, then, needs to be expanded to include cognitive components.

The obvious rural environmental presses of distances to resources, limited support services, inadequate transportation, or inadequate income are not simply measurable in terms of miles or dollars but are subject to interpretation by the individual elderly person. The "beta" press, or environmental stress as perceived by the individual, is important; it includes cognitive components, the result of cultural influences and personal life experiences. An illustration is the "needs inconsistency" data referred to above in which rural elderly were found to be no more dissatisfied with their housing than urban residents, despite the lack of plumbing, etc. Adding cognitive components to the ecological theory allows us to include factors in the individual's developmental history which bear on his interpretations of the present and his expectations of the future, and thereby affect his behavior.

I would like to try to illustrate the complexity of predicting behavior in three hypothetical older persons living in the country and the effects of life events upon them. The illustration utilizes ecological theory but also includes cognitive variables not yet included in the theory.

First, consider Tom Road ("traditional rural aged") who grew up and grew old in a rural setting that has changed relatively little. Second, Connie Rupert ("conflicted aged") is a woman native to the country but surrounded by social change. As she grew older, her community became more modernized. The third person is Niles Winter ("nouveau rural aged"), a man who grew up in the city but moved to the country upon retirement.

Based upon research findings, we may hypothesize how these rural persons, each with a different background, each living in a different rural setting, would adapt to a succession of expectable life changes. Our thesis is that the rural aged person (no differently than the urban aged person) is one whose adaptation is dependent upon the interaction between three variables: (1) personality as developmentally shaped, (2) age-related events, and (3) current environment, which is both stressful and supportive.

For simplicity and for reasons of space, we must consider the three hypothetical examples as if there were no differences of sex, race, or ethnic background, which, of course, there are—and very striking ones.

Tom Road ("traditional rural aged") grew up on a small farm. His family was close-knit, and he developed values of independence, self-reliance, hard work, integrity, honesty, and a sense of responsibility. His relationships among family, church, friends, and neighbors were strong and of long standing. But life had been far from easy, considering the stresses of little money, little education, poor housing, great physical distances (both between people and to shopping and other resources), and minimal health services. Now Tom Road is in his 70s. Most of his children have left the area, but one remains, not too far away, and they are in touch with one another. There are still old friends and neighbors who, though they may not be close in distance, can visit by phone or by car.

Now consider Tom Road in respect to four expectable events of later life: retirement, sensory and behavioral slowing, widowhood, and a severe medical problem.

How will retirement affect him? Research indicates he probably will not completely retire. It is within his control to continue his type of farm-related work activities at a reduced level if he wishes. To some extent he can manipulate the press of his work environment.

What will happen as his competence changes, as he slows with age, a result of sensory, perceptual, psychomotor, and neurological changes—changes not due to illness but rather to natural aging processes? He may not be too severely affected, because his rural environment (unless he lives in deep snow country) is not so demanding that he must press himself beyond his limits.

A role change owing to the death of his spouse would be more traumatic; adaptation to this sudden role change to widowhood will depend on the stability of his social network, and on his ability to make new alliances to replace the old (Abrahams & Patterson, 1978; Lowenthal, Thurmber, & Chiriboga, 1975). As a traditional rural aged, Tom Road has developed a strong social network over his lifetime. He is likely to adapt to widowhood in time.

The occurrence of a traumatic disability like blindness or a stroke-related hemiplegia might provide the greatest stress for Tom Road. Such an event would be disorienting, interfering with his mobility and making him vulnerable to environmental dangers; at the same time, it would be socially stigmatizing (and thus isolating). There would be chronic conflict between his old values of insularity, independence, and self-sufficiency, and new requirements for dependency on others—for transportation, cooking, and perhaps personal care. Tom Road would have to deal with strangers, agencies, and government red tape.

To summarize, a rural aged person who grew old in a setting which did not undergo significant change may have a relatively high level of adaptation in his rural environment unless severe disability brings on a dependency role conflict.

A second hypothetical example is Connie Rupert (a "conflicted rural aged"). Connie Rupert grew up in a small town and remained there into old age, when a busy highway brought modernization to her town. These changes left her with rural values in a faster-paced environment, in conflict with the younger generation's more urban values (a greater rejection of tradition, weaker ties to kin, and a faster pace of change). As a result of this clash in values, Connie Rupert, at 75, often felt harried, rejected, lonely, and out of touch with the contemporary life around her.

After her children grew up and left home, Connie Rupert faced conflict as a "retired person." She saw herself as "devalued" and felt that life had lost meaning. So long as she maintained her competencies, she had to seek some means of making her life challenging, through work, volunteer activities, or socializing. However, her competencies were reduced through normal psychological slowing. She adapted by disengaging, comfortably reducing the breadth of her activities, and accepting her life with less conflict.

Widowhood was a severe stress for Connie Rupert because the changes in her town had created a more disjointed social network, making it difficult to replace her lost relationship. The possible events of blindness or stroke would be extremely stressful for Connie Rupert because conflicts regarding dependence on others would be compounded by her weak social network. To sum up, the urbanizing of the rural setting has made adaptation to the crisis of aging a more difficult one for the conflicted rural aged.

Now consider Niles Winter (a "nouveau rural aged"), who moved from the city to the country to retire. He found the pace slower, and a smaller number of resources from which to choose. If the new pace is much discrepant from his expected pace, he may find country retirement a disappointment. However, if it coincides with his slowing because of age, he will be satisfied.

Niles Winter's adaptation to the shock of widowhood will be made more difficult by his lack of a local family support network; only if he is able to make new contacts, more likely in a small town than in the country, will he be able to have a positive adjustment.

The stress of a severe disability might be less traumatic for Niles Winter than for the other two persons used as examples, since he might find the sick and dependent role not discrepant with his sophisticated, urban values, where one is accustomed to use other's services.

In summary, there is no one rural aged, and there can be no one pattern which typifies adaptation of the rural aged. Understanding adaptation requires viewing each person in terms of the background from which he or she comes, the life events which occur as he or she ages, and the interaction with the type of rural errvironment in which he or she now lives.

UNDERSTANDING THE RURAL AGING

Two questions were posed at the start of this chapter. Is rurality an important psychological variable? Are the rural aged a special group requiring special understanding? Rurality as a general concept is fading in clarity, the rural aged are too heterogeneous to be considered as a group, and their life, as perceived, is not that much different from the urban aged. The behavior and the problems of the rural aged can probably be understood best by using general concepts of aging and man-environment relations applicable to people who are old in many different settings. These concepts and developing theory must include a cognitive and "life course" orientation which reflects the situation of the uniquely developing and perceiving individual adapting to his physical and social environment.

ACKNOWLEDGMENTS

The able assistance of Eileen Eisenberg in the literature search is acknowledged.

References

Abrahams, R. B., & Patterson, R. D. Psychological distress among the community elderly: Prevalence, characteristics and implications for service. *International Journal of Aging and Human Development*, 1978–79, *9*, 1–18.

Adams, L. Who are the rural aged? In R. C. Atchley (Ed.), *Rural environments and aging*. Washington, D.C.: Gerontological Society, 1975.

Ahearn, M. C. *Health care in rural America*. U.S. Dept. of Agriculture, Economics, Statistics and Cooperative Services. Agriculture Information Bulletin No. 428. Washington, D.C., July 1979.

Atchley, R. C. (Ed.). *Rural environments and aging*. Washington, D.C.: Gerontological Society, 1975.

Bultena, G. L. Rural-urban differences in the familial interaction of the aged. *Rural Sociology*, 1969, *34*, 5–15.

Bultena, G. L. Health and disengagement vs. morale. *Aging and Human Development*, 1971, *2*, 142–148.

Cumming, E., & Henry, W. E. *Growing old*. New York: Basic Books, 1961.

Coward, T. Planning community services for the rural elderly: Implications from research. *Gerontologist*, 1979, *19*, 275–282.

Dewey, R. The rural-urban continuum: Real but relatively unimportant. *American Journal of Sociology*, 1960, *66*, 60–66.

Dibner, A. S. *Psychological aging as preference for simplicity*. Paper presented at the Annual Meeting of the Gerontological Society, Houston, October 1972.

Fischer, D. H. *Growing old in America*. New York: Oxford, 1978.

Harbert, A. S., & Wilkinson, C. W. Growing old in rural America. *Aging*, Jan.–Feb. 1979, pp. 36–40.

Harris, L., & Associates. *The myth and reality of aging in America*. Washington, D.C.: The National Council on Aging, Inc., 1975.

Hynson, M. Rural-urban differences in satisfaction among the elderly. *Rural Sociology*, 1975, *40*, 64–66.

Kahana, E. A congruence model of person–environment interaction. In P. G. Windley, T. O. Byerts, & F. G. Ernst, (Eds.), *Theory development in environment and aging*. Washington, D.C.: Gerontological Society, 1975.

Kivett, V. R. Discriminators of loneliness among the rural elderly: Implications for intervention. *The Gerontologist*, 1979, *19*(1), 108–115.

Lawton, M. P. Competence, environmental press, and the adaptation of older people. In P. G. Windley, T. O. Byerts, & F. G. Ernst (Eds.), *Theory development in environment and aging*. Washington, D.C.: Gerontological Society, 1975.

Lawton, M. P., & Nahemow, L. Ecology and the aging process. In C. Eisdorfer & M. P. Lawton (Eds.), *The psychology of adult development and aging*. Washington, D.C.: American Psychological Association, 1973.

Lipman, A. Needs inconsistency of the rural aged. *Proceedings of the Workshop on Rural Gerontology Research in the Northeast*, May 24–27, 1977. Northeast Regional Center for Rural Development, Cornell University, Ithaca, New York, July 1978.

Lohmann, Nancy. *Research on the rural aged: Implications for social work practice.* Third National Conference on Rural Social Work, August 1978.

Lopata, H. Z. Loneliness: Forms and components. *Social Problems*, 1979, *17*, 248–261.

Lowenthal, M. F., Thurmber, M., & Chiriboga, D. *Four stages of life.* San Francisco: Jossey-Bass, 1975.

Montgomery, J. *Social characteristics of the aged in a small Pennsylvania community.* University Park, Pa.: College of Home Economics, Research Publication 233, 1965.

Nahemow, L., & Lawton, M. P. *Urban-rural differences in adjustment to housing for the elderly.* Paper presented at the Annual Scientific Meeting of the Gerontological Society, Dallas, November 16–20, 1978.

National Center for Health Statistics. *Current estimates from the health interview survey: United States, 1977.* Vital and Health Statistics, Series 10, No. 126. DHEW Publication No. (PHS) 78-1554.

Neugarten, B. (Ed.). *Middle age and aging: A reader in social psychology.* Chicago: University of Chicago Press, 1968.

New York Senate Research Service. *Old age and ruralism . . . A case of double jeopardy.* Albany, New York, May 1980.

Pihlblad, C. T. Culture, life style and social environment of the small town. In R. C. Atchley (Ed.), *Rural environments and aging.* Washington, D.C.: Gerontological Society, 1975.

Powers, E. A., Keith, P., & Goudy, W. Family relationships and friendships. In R. C. Atchley (Ed.), *Rural environments and aging.* Washington, D.C.: Gerontological Society, 1975.

Sauer, J., Sheehan, C., & Boymel, C. Rural-urban differences in satisfaction among the elderly: A reconsideration. *Rural Sociology*, 1976, *41*, 269–275.

Schooler, K. A comparison of rural and non-rural elderly on selected variables. In R. C. Atchley (Ed.), *Rural environments and aging.* Washington, D.C.: Gerontological Society, 1975.

Taietz, P. The needs of the elderly: Rural-urban comparisons. *Proceedings of the Workshop on Rural Gerontology Research in the Northeast*, May 24–27, 1977. Northeast Regional Center for Rural Development, Cornell University, Ithaca, New York, July 1978.

West, J. *Plainville U.S.A.* New York: Columbia University Press, 1945.

Windley, P. G., Byerts, T. O., & Ernst, F. G. (Eds.). *Theory development in environment and aging.* Washington, D.C.: Gerontological Society, 1975.

Youmans, E. G. Some perspectives on disengagement theory. *Gerontologist*, 1969, *9*, 254–258.

Youmans, E. G. Perspectives on the older American in a rural setting. In J. G. Cull & R. E. Hardy (Eds.), *The neglected older American.* Springfield, Ill.: Charles C Thomas, 1973.

Youmans, E. G. The rural aged. *Annals of the American Academy of Political and Social Sciences*, 1977, *429*, 81–90.

7

Environmental Perception and Cognition in Rural Contexts

Nickolaus R. Feimer

Introduction

The emergence of environmental psychology over the last fifteen years has revitalized an interest in the analysis of the larger ecological context in connection with human behavior. In that time many avenues have been explored, but none has been more fervently pursued than that of environmental perception and cognition. The popularity, and perhaps centrality, of this substantive domain is easily explained. As Ittelson (1973b) has observed, the study of perceptual-cognitive processes has been considered central to an understanding of behavior since psychology's inception, for it is through those processes that we come to know and comprehend our surroundings. Furthermore, it is upon that comprehension that behavioral adaptation is predicated. Inasmuch as a rural psychology is concerned with a comprehensive understanding of behavior in a specific environmental context, an examination of the manner in which individuals respond to it via their cognitive-perceptual capacities is of clear interest.

At the outset, it is important to distinguish the treatment of perception and cognition in environmental psychology from its more familiar treatment in traditional psychological circles. Although drawing sub-

Nickolaus R. Feimer • Department of Psychology, Virginia Polytechnic Institute and State University, Blacksburg, Virginia 24061. An early version of this chapter was presented at a symposium on rural psychology at the 26th Annual Meeting of the Southeastern Psychological Association, Washington, D.C., March 27, 1980.

stantially from the theoretical and empirical reservoirs of perception and cognition in mainstream psychology, the study of environmental perception and cognition has diverged rather clearly in several respects. Three major differences are discernible and characterize the principal divergence of the two disciplines.

First, in environmental perception and cognition, as indeed in environmental psychology as a whole, the external stimulus of interest is the *molar* sociophysical environment (Craik, 1970, 1973; Ittelson, 1973b; Stokols, 1978). The term molar connotes whole or unitary and thus implies that the entire ecological context that envelops and impinges upon the individual is the appropriate unit of analysis. Traditional theory and research in perception and cognition has focused upon stimuli that are abstracted from the larger environmental context such as objects, lights, figures, and the like.

Second, unlike traditional views on perception and cognition, the distinction between those two components of the information-processing system is confused if not absent in the balance of the literature on environmental perception and cognition (Downs & Stea, 1973a; Ittelson, 1973b; Leff, Gordon, & Ferguson, 1974; Moore & Golledge, 1976a; Proshansky, Ittelson, & Rivlin, 1976; Stokols, 1978). Of course, it must be noted that most current theories of perceptual and cognitive processes outside the confines of environmental psychology obscure that distinction as well. Current views generally opt for a model integrating the component processes of sensation, perception, and memory as an interactive system (Lindsay & Norman, 1977; Neisser, 1967, 1976; Newell & Simon, 1972; Norman, 1976). Nonetheless, where environmental perception and cognition are concerned, the distinction between those component processes is even more undifferentiated; virtually anything within the individual's sphere of awareness concerning the sociophysical environment, including sensation, memory, attitudes, and beliefs may be (and has been) subsumed under the rubric of either perception or cognition.

Third, a difference in the relative emphasis placed on the process versus the content of perception and cognition is evident (Downs & Stea, 1973a; Ittelson, 1973b; Proshansky *et al.*, 1976). As Ittelson (1973b) and Proshansky, Ittelson, and Rivlin (1976) point out, mainstream psychology has emphasized the former, whereas environmental psychology has focused on the latter. Thus, theory and research in mainstream psychology have centered on a specification of the structural and operational properties of perception and cognition. Conceptual and empirical efforts in environmental perception and cognition, on the other hand, have been primarily concerned with specification of the features of environmental contexts that are represented *in* perception and cognition.

Another salient feature of conceptual and empirical efforts in environmental perception and cognition is the high degree of interdisciplinary involvement. In fact, it is to some degree presumptuous and chauvinistic to characterize the field as a substantive domain within environmental psychology. Many significant contributions, and in some cases dominant ones, have come from anthropologists, architects, city planners, engineers, geographers, and sociologists. The diverse viewpoints brought to bear on the issues within the field by these interdisciplinary contributions have broadened and enriched the base of knowledge considerably.

It should be apparent that the substantive boundaries encompassing environmental perception and cognition are broadly defined, focusing largely upon the individual's experience and knowledge of the surrounding environment. The sheer diversity of the field makes an in-depth programmatic review within current space limitations impractical, to say the least. For example, several volumes have been devoted to *selected topics* under the rubric of environmental perception and cognition (e.g., Craik & Zube, 1976; Downs & Stea, 1973b; Ittelson, 1973a; Lynch, 1960; Moore & Golledge, 1976b; Zube, 1980; Zube, Brush, & Fabos, 1975). Thus, rather than attempting a discussion of all facets of environmental perception and cognition as they might apply to rural contexts, this paper will focus on three substrates of research that constitute important focal points in the field, and where there are reasonable empirical developments in rural environments. These topics are spatial cognition, the perception of natural hazards, and scenic quality analysis.

Before delving into these substantive issues, it should be noted that a relatively unconstrained interpretation of the term *rural* was employed in selecting representative research. This position was taken for two reasons. First, as a perusal of the other contributions to this volume will reveal, there is far from unanimous agreement on the precise demarcation of rural from nonrural contexts. Although it may be of some solace to know that after many years of considering the issue, our diligent counterparts in sociology still seem reasonably removed from consensus (see Falk & Pinhey, 1978), it instills one with little confidence concerning the establishment of rigid delimitations. Second, much of the research in environmental perception and cognition is not organized around the rural-urban distinction. A near facsimile is the urban-natural distinction; however, the term *natural* has been used in a more inclusive manner than what may be implied by connotations of *rural*. According to standard English usage (*Funk and Wagnalls New Standard Dictionary of the English Language*, 1963; *The Oxford English Dictionary*, 1970), rural connotes a nonurban, pastoral, agricultural context. This implies humanity's pervasive influence in the form of an established resident society with significant modification of the environment via agricultural practices, albeit in a manner that does not emphasize buildings and their appurtenances. The term *natural,* on the other hand, as well as encompassing rural areas, has also been used to encompass wilderness, semi-wilderness, and recreational environments, where there is relatively little evidence of human influence and no resident society (e.g., Canter & Stringer, 1975; Heimstra & McFarling, 1978; Ittelson, Proshansky, Rivlin, & Winkel, 1974; Kameron, 1973). With these considerations in mind, the literature to be discussed in this paper was selected to be largely nonurban and nonwilderness in its focus. However, due to their relevance with regard to the issues under consideration, selected conceptual and empirical contributions concerning clearly nonrural environments will also be discussed.

SPATIAL COGNITION

Spatial cognition consists of the processes whereby individuals acquire, code, store, recall, and decode information concerning environmental attributes and their relative location (Downs & Stea, 1973a). The product of these processes is a mental representation of the spatial configuration of the geophysical environment, which can be considered to be the cognitive analog of the cartographic map. In fact, as Downs and Stea point out, the production of cartographic maps and cognitive representations of the spatial environment require similar transformations of information. These operations consist of (1) scale reduction; (2) rotation of perspective; and (3) schematization. Because of the functional similarity between cartographic and cognitive spatial representations, the terms *cognitive mapping* and *cognitive map* are widely used to refer to the respective processes and product of spatial cognition.

From a utilitarian perspective the function of spatial cognition is quite clear: it is central to orientation and navigation, or more simply, way-finding. In modern society the implications of way-finding are much less dramatic than they might have been several thousand years ago when, as S. Kaplan (1973, 1976) suggests, a person's survival as a hunter and gatherer depended upon it. Although there are circumstances in today's world where misdirection can be life-threatening (e.g., being lost in the wilderness, or inadvertently wandering into the crime-laden district of a city), satisfaction, convenience, and frustration with the experience of going places and finding desirable locations while avoiding undesirable ones are the primary consequences of spatial knowledge.

The great majority of research on spatial cognition has focused on urban, or built environments. Based upon this general body of research some generalizations concerning significant facets of spatial cognition may be advanced.

Structural Elements of Cognitive Maps

The structural elements of cognitive maps may be represented by five constructs specified by Kevin Lynch (1960) in his classic study of citizens' images of three American cities (Boston, Los Angeles, Jersey City). These constructs are *paths, edges, districts, nodes* and *landmarks. Paths* consist of channels of movement, whether by automobile, foot, water, rail, or any other means; they may be formally constructed, as is a paved roadway, or they may arise merely by usage, as trails in natural areas frequently do. *Edges* are linear elements that form discontinuities in the individual's conception of the environment; they are boundaries that define the extent of areas within the larger environment, often forming barriers to traversal by ordinary travel. Examples include rivers, freeways, and mountain ranges. *Districts* are subsections of the larger environmental context that are distinguishable from one another. According to Lynch (1960, p. 47), they are "recognizable as having some common, identifying character." Examples of these identifying characteristics include land-use patterns, economic activities, and ethnic or sociocultural dominance of an area. The critical feature of districts is that the identifying attributes provide discriminant cues, implying that there is uniformity or homogeneity within districts and clear divergence among districts. *Nodes* are strategic places, limited in areal extent (i.e., smaller than districts) which serve as focal points for travel; they are frequently endpoints or junctions of pathways, but may also be spots where there is a concentration or predominance of a given social or economic activity. Examples include marketplaces, the intersections of highways or major roads, and rail or subway stations. *Landmarks* are visually distinct entities that serve as important reference points for judging relative location and distance. According to Lynch (1960, p. 48), "they are usually a rather simply defined physical object: building, sign, store, or mountain."

Subsequent research using Lynch's scheme (e.g., Appleyard, 1970, 1976; de Jonge, 1962; Devlin, 1976; Francescato & Mebane, 1973; Gulick, 1963; Ladd, 1970; Orleans, 1973) underlines its utility in representing components of cognitive maps. Furthermore, an empirical analysis aimed at classifying environmental elements according to their natural cognitive association supports Lynch's taxonomy (Magana, 1978).

Variations in Cognitive Maps

The organization of structural elements and the amount of information (detail) represented in cognitive maps varies as a function of several factors. Three of the most prominent will be briefly discussed: environmental features, intensity of experience, and ontogenetic differences.

Environmental Features

The physical features of environments have been implicated in the representation of structural elements of cognitive maps (de Jonge, 1962; Francescato & Mebane, 1973; Lynch, 1960). Based upon his analysis, Lynch (1960) suggested that the relative salience of structural elements in cognitive maps is a function of their salience in the actual environment. Moreover, he argued that the more distinct and differentiable the elements are in the environment, the clearer and more prominent will be their mental representation; as an end result, the more comprehensible the environment will be. The available empirical evidence indicates that comprehension is facilitated by clear, systematic path networks (de Jonge, 1962; Francescato & Mebane, 1973) and visually and functionally distinct landmarks (Acredolo, Pick, & Olsen, 1975; Allen, Siegel, & Rosinski, 1978; Devlin, 1976; Heft, 1979; R. Kaplan, 1976; Siegel & Schadler, 1977).

Path networks in particular seem to play an important role in promoting cognitive map development (Appleyard, 1970, 1976; Lynch, 1960). The critical feature of path networks, insofar as the promotion of clear and accurate cognitive maps is concerned, seems to be their regularity. Two patterns have been identified that display a high degree of regularity and promote environmental comprehension: one is the rectilinear-grid path pattern (Appleyard, 1970; Lynch, 1960; de Jonge, 1962), and the other is the concentric-grid path pattern (de Jonge, 1962; Francescato & Mebane, 1973). Ideally, the former consists of series of parallel linear path elements crossed to form perpendicular intersections, and the latter consists of a series of circular paths nested within one another with radial paths emanating from the innermost element and intersecting the circular paths at perpendicular tangents (see Figure 1). It is unclear, however, whether either of these two dominant path patterns is inherently more superior, and an obvious next step is a comparative analysis that evaluates the relative effectiveness of the two path patterns in promoting environmental comprehension.

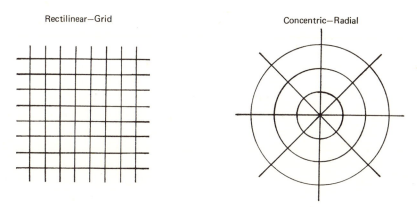

FIGURE 1.   Path patterns for optimal spatial comprehension.

Intensity of Experience

The structure and content of cognitive maps vary as a function of the individual's experience with a given environment. Two dimensions of experience relevant to cognitive map development are discernible at present. One dimension is *temporal,* and simply represents the amount of time an individual is exposed to a given environmental context. This variable has also been referred to as *familiarity* (Evans, 1980; Moore, 1979). The other dimension reflects the individual's degree of *sensorimotor involvement* during the time he or she is in the environment, and is generally referred to as a dimension of *activity–passivity* (Hart & Moore, 1973; Lee, 1973; Moore, 1979; Stea, 1976). This latter dimension represents the individual's relative allocation of perceptual-cognitive capacities for spatial information processing along with coordinated motor activity directed at movement through the environment.

Evidence concerning the effects of temporal exposure may be adduced from studies relating cognitive mapping to length of residence in a city, and relative proximity to places where daily activities are carried out. Length of residence is, of course, a fairly direct indication of relative temporal exposure. Relative proximity, however, serves as an indication of temporal exposure by inference: places where daily activities are carried out are places where a relatively large proportion of one's time is spent. Studies focusing on length of residence indicate that over time cognitive maps progressively change from being path-oriented to being landmark-district oriented (Appleyard, 1970, 1976; Devlin, 1976) and exhibit greater detail and elaboration of both path and landmark structures (Devlin, 1976; Evans, Marrero, & Butler, 1981). Similarly, detail and articulation in cognitive maps increases as a function of proximity to locations that serve as focal points for the individual's daily activity patterns, particularly the home, school, and workplace (Devlin, 1976; Evans, 1980; Horton & Reynolds, 1971; Milgram & Jodelet, 1976; Milgram, Greenwald, Kessler, McKenna, & Waters, 1972).

The effects of sensorimotor involvement in cognitive mapping are evidenced largely by Appleyard's (1970, 1976) study of spatial cognition in Ciudad Guyana. Appleyard found that the coherence and detail of cognitive maps were related to the individual's predominant mode of transportation. Bus riders had relatively fragmented cognitive maps, while those using automobiles "presented a coherent and continuous system," (Appleyard, 1970, p. 11). Bus riders can take a casual approach to organizing the environment, since navigation is not their responsibility. Moreover, their motor activities are minimal; they must merely board the bus, sit quietly, and exit. Automobile travelers, on the other hand, are largely responsible for navigation. This is particularly true for drivers, who compose a large proportion of automobile travelers; they need to attend carefully to spatial cues to reach their destination, and must engage their motor capacities in guiding their movement through the environment.

Ontogenetic Differences

Several years ago, Hart and Moore (1973) provided an incisive integration of the organismic-structural-developmental perspectives of Heinz Werner (see Langer, 1969; Wapner & Werner, 1957; Werner, 1957) and Jean Piaget (see Flavell, 1963; Langer, 1969) along with the voluminous empirical work on the concept of space in children by Piaget and his followers (reviewed in Hart & Moore, 1973; Laurendeau & Pinard, 1970; Piaget & Inhelder, 1967; Piaget, Inhelder, & Szeminska, 1960) to provide a comprehensive theoretical framework for explaining the development of spatial cognition of large-scale environments. Specifically, three hierarchial stages in the development of large-scale spatial cognition were postulated (Hart & Moore, 1973; Moore, 1976, 1979): *egocentric orientation, fixed reference systems,* and *coordinated reference systems.*

In egocentric orientation, comprehension of spatial relations is governed by the child's own position and movement through the physical environment. This leads to a conception of the spatial environment as consisting largely of routes of locomotion. Landmarks as points of reference are not identified apart from their association with a particular route (Hart & Moore, 1973), but they appear to be prominent in the learning of routes because of their salience in connecting points and providing directional cues (Siegel & White, 1975; Siegel, Kirasic, & Kail, 1978). Between the ages of 4 and 7 the child begins to make the transition from an egocentric system of orientation to a fixed reference system.

During this second stage of development, the child is able to make use of fixed objects in the environment (i.e., landmarks) as frames of reference for orientation, but there is still an incomplete integration of topographic information. Children using fixed reference systems "cannot appreciate the totality of relations between landmarks which occur in the environment because the landmarks are fixed in partially coordinated subgroups, each based on an independent vantage point or on a particular journey" (Hart & Moore, 1973, p. 279). At roughly 9 to 12 years of age, fully coordinated systems of reference evolve. The child is now able to abstract and interrelate elements and components of the environment independent of his or her position and prior paths of locomotion. Thus, a formal reference system is adopted where the environment is understood as an abstract euclidean space (Hart & Moore, 1973).

Subsequent research on the development of spatial cognition has generally supported the sequence specified by Hart and Moore (Acredolo, 1976; Evans, 1980; Moore, 1979). However, as Evans (1980) has pointed out, considerable disagreement remains regarding both age delimitations for stage transition and the degree to which the developmental sequence represents qualitative versus quantitative change.

Spatial Cognition in Nonurban Settings

An obvious and salient difference between urban and rural environments is the relative presence of built or man-made features. As a result, the emphasis on urban and small-scale built environments in spatial cognition research raises a number of questions regarding the generality of the derivative constructs and relationships to spatial cognition in rural environments. For example, are the structural elements of cognitive maps the same in rural and urban environments? If so, is their relative importance in orientation the same? What environmental features define them? Are functional, man-made elements more or less important in rural environments? Does the vastness of the natural component of the environment, with its seeming lack of clear boundaries, lead to a less-differentiated cognitive representation of the environment? And what are the ontogenetic implications of differences in spatial cognition between rural and urban settings? Unfortunately, the paucity of research on spatial cognition in rural contexts does not allow a clear response to any of these questions. However, a few pertinent studies in nonurban contexts have begun to break ground. These efforts have focused largely on two issues: (1) the microgenetic development and promotion of spatial comprehension in novel settings; and (2) ontogenetic differences in spatial cognition in urban versus rural populations. Following the terminology of R. Kaplan (1976, p. 47), the former may be considered cognitive mapping in *transition experiences*.

Cognitive Mapping in Transition Experiences

Research on the microgenetic development and promotion of spatial comprehension in nonurban environments has emphasized recreational settings and transitions to small towns. The most comprehensive
of these is a series of studies on way-finding in the natural environment
reported by R. Kaplan (1976). She and her associates were interested in
finding ways to make experiences in natural settings more pleasurable
for those with predominantly urban environmental experience. It was
hypothesized that a clear spatial understanding of an area reduces anxiety by reducing fearful uncertainties associated with orientation. The
first study was directed at delineating the most important elements of
cognitive maps of natural areas so that they could be highlighted in
orientation exercises prior to experience with a given environment. College students were taken on a guided tour of a natural park area, and
were subsequently asked to sketch a map of the area. The majority of
maps consisted of a series of landmarks connected by paths, and a large
minority depicted the area as a series of regions which differed in flora
and topography. This finding seems to reaffirm the central role of landmarks and paths in early environmental learning, and points to what
appears to be the natural environment analog of the urban district (i.e.,
subregions defined by floral and topographic variation).

Next, Kaplan and her associates carried out a series of three studies
designed to assess the effects of learning through active experience with
graphic representations accompanied by some verbal description. The
subjects in all of these studies were junior-high school students aged
12–15. The primary learning experience consisted of board games in
which the board was comprimsed of either a schematic-graphic or a
pictorial-panoramic representation communicating the relative eleva-
tions, pathways, and landmarks of a natural environment. The goal of
the game always entailed orientation and movement through the environment, and was always accompanied by some form of supplementary verbal information concerning features of the area which could be
acquired "en route" during the game. Among the most notable findings
were: (1) prior experience with a schematic representation of an environment does tend to aid in orientation; (2) if there are discrepancies between the environment and the information conveyed by the schematic
representation, the experience will not be as positive as it will for a
group with generic orientation information but no specific information
on the environment to be experienced; and (3) learning with a schematic
representation of the environment results in greater cognitive mapping
accuracy and better orientation than does learning with a pictoral representation, but learning with a pictoral representation results in a more

positive outlook toward the outing than does learning with a schematic map. The last of these findings is quite intriguing. Why should schematic maps result in a better orientation and a greater spatial comprehension but a less positive attitude toward an outing than a pictoral presentation? R. Kaplan forwards a plausible explanation: schematic contour maps are more effective in focusing attention on features that are important to orientation, but pictorial representations convey a more natural spatial feeling that heightens the sense of familiarity with the area.

Knopf's (1979) study of spatial and historical comprehension at Gettysburg National Park also supports the role of schematic representations in facilitating learning in novel situations. He assessed the degree to which various combinations of visitor-aid facilities promoted an understanding of spatial and historical aspects of the famous Civil War battle. The visitor aids included: (1) a visitor center with Civil War artifacts but no information integrating spatial and historic features; (2) an electronic map consisting of a three-dimensional representation of the battleground integrating significant aspects of the battle with spatial and landform features and accompanied by narration as well as audio and visual special effects; (3) a 360-degree painting (cyclorama) depicting the battle and landscape with an emphasis on spatial and historic features and accompanied by narration as well as audio and visual special effects; and (4) a 12-mile self-guided auto tour. Analysis of questionnaires of first-time park visitors indicated that the individual's perceived gain in knowledge was highest when the elecronic map (schematic representation) was visited first and then followed by visitation of the cyclorama and auto tour.

Devlin's (1976) study of the microgenetic development of spatial cognition is also pertinent in the current context. She focused on cognitive map formation in individuals who were making a transition to a small town that was "fairly rural in character" (Devlin, 1976, p. 60). She had women complete a map sketch of the town two to three weeks after their arrival, and once again after three months. Devlin found that both the initial and follow-up maps were comprised predominantly of path structures, with landmarks playing an important but less prominent role. Landmarks were largely man-made and were both functionally and perceptually prominent. Moreover, both paths and landmarks in the initial maps exhibited wide individual variations that, in part, reflected an emphasis on home territory and other areas that were personally meaningful. The follow-up maps were less idiosyncratic and reflected a substantial elaboration of both paths and landmarks. Interestingly, natural aspects of the environment played a minor role in the cognitive maps.

In contrast to the findings of R. Kaplan (1976) and Knopf (1979),

Devlin reported that cognitive maps were not enhanced by the use of reference maps. However, in Devlin's study the effect of reference map use on cognitive mapping was based on a correlation between map-sketch accuracy and self-reported frequency of reference map consultation. The reference maps used by subjects presumably were independently acquired and were therefore likely to vary in content and quality. It seems plausible that unreliability in memory recall for reference map consultation, and variability in the information accurately conveyed by reference maps, could account for the apparent lack of a relationship between reference map utilization and map-sketch accuracy.

Taken as a whole, the research on spatial cognition in transition experiences gives rise to several inferences. First, path networks and functionally and perceptually distinct landmarks appear to be the most salient features in cognitive maps. Second, there is in some cognitive maps a structural element that represents a subsection of a larger area in much the same way that a district in the urban environment does. Third, when both natural and man-made elements are present in the environment, the latter appear to be more prominent in cognitive maps. This is most likely due to their centrality as focal points for human activities. Fourth, prior environmental learning with a schematic representation or a model of the test area tends to enhance orientation and comprehension.

Rural-Urban Ontogenetic Differences

A small number of studies have assessed differences in the development of spatial concepts among rural and urban populations. The results of these studies are stimulating but inconsistent.

Stea and Blaut (1973) tested Puerto Rican school children on their ability to interpret aerial photographs and found that urban middle-class children emitted more correct and fewer incorrect responses in identifying features of the photographs than did urban lower-class and rural children of the same grade level. However, a comparison of children through 6th grade indicated that by the 2nd grade, performance among all groups tended to equalize. Stea and Blaut suggested that this trend toward equalization might be a function of socialization and learning in a formal setting. Data reported by Page (1973) support that position. He tested Zulu youths ranging from 11 to 20 years of age on a series of length- and distance-judgment tasks adopted from Piaget, Inhelder and Szeminska (1960). The results indicated that rural youths displayed a relatively egocentric, topological conception of space, whereas the conception of space in urban youths tended to be more elucidean. However, formal education enhanced spatial abilities in both urban and rural individuals.

In sharp contrast to the findings of Stea and Blaut (1973) and Page (1973) are data reported by Stoltman (1972) and Norman (1980). Stoltman (1972) assessed the comprehension of geographical territorial relationships in 1st- through 6th-grade children from northern Georgia and found no differences that could be ascribed to rural-urban residence. Norman (1980), on the other hand, found rural children to be more advanced in spatial reasoning. He had 10-year-old children from rural Appalachian and suburban and rural New England draw a map of a model representing a miniature landscape containing "houses, roads, trees, a hill, a lake, and a bridge" (Norman, 1980, p. 288). The maps were scored for level of development on four content dimensions drawn from Piaget's theory of spatial conceptualization: perspective, symbolization, arrangement, and proportion. Rural children scored higher than suburban children on proportion, perspective, and symbolization, and higher than urban children on proportion and perspective. Urban and suburban children did not differ significantly on any dimension.

The apparent inconsistencies in the foregoing studies are difficult to reconcile. It may be the case that experience with detached, reduced scale, multiperspective views of geographical areas has an impact on the emergence of higher-order spatial abilities. If so, the discrepant results of the studies reviewed could yield no interpretation. Preschool or uneducated rural and lower-class urban children outside of the United States might have little access to the media that make detached, reduced scale, multiperspective views of geographical areas possible (i.e., books, magazines, photographs, television), and as a result their spatial abilities lag behind those of urban preschool children. However, through formal educational systems, the media that facilitate advanced spatial conceptualization become available; eventually, the disadvantage of rural and lower-class urban children disappears. In the United States, media that impart the appropriate spatial experience are presumably more widely accessible, and hence rural children are not at a developmental disadvantage. However, such an explanation is speculative at this point, and does not account for the superior performance of rural children in Norman's (1980) study. It is equally likely that any one of a number of situational factors could account for the observed discrepancies. Indeed, educational systems, culture, geographical-environmental features, and measures of spatial abilities all varied substantially among the studies cited.

Research Directions

Research on spatial cognition in rural environments is fragmentary at this point, and virtually any direction could be fruitfully explored. A first step would be a more intensive investigation of the structural elements that constitute the basic building blocks of cognitive maps. Evidence to date suggests that paths, landmarks, and a unit akin to a city district are the most prominent components of nonurban cognitive maps. Moreover, man-made elements, where present, seem to play a central role. However, the research to date has focused on a narrow range of contexts that are representative of neither rural environments nor rural populations. Studies focusing on environments that manifest variation in landform features and levels of development could contribute significantly to our understanding of spatial cognition. Above all, studies in rural contexts need to focus on resident populations. Studies of urban to rural transition experiences may tell us a great deal about the manner in which urbanites adjust to the nonurban physical environment cognitively, but they reveal little about the effects on spatial cognition of long-term experience and learning in rural environments.

Research concerning urban-rural developmental differences is inconclusive at this point, largely due to uncontrolled variation in certain critical determinants of environmental learning. Studies controlling for variation in formal educational systems, the availability of incidental environmental learning aids, and geographical or landform features need to be carried out before the locus of rural-urban differences in the development of spatial cognition can be specified.

Perception of Natural Hazards

Natural hazards are those environmental events of geophysical and meteorological origin that pose significant threats to property, economic and social activities, and both mental and physical well being. Although directly affecting only a small proportion of the United States and world populations in any given year, the impact of natural hazards upon a significant number of individuals is unquestioned. The scope of the problem has been aptly characterized by Burton, Kates, and White:

> In a time of extraordinary human effort to control the natural world, the global toll from extreme events of nature is increasing. Loss in property from natural hazards is rising in most regions of the earth, and high loss of life is continuing or increasing. . . . Each year the population equivalent of a city of about 250,000 dies in disaster, and the material loss exceeds the per capita gains of many nations. (1978, pp. 1–4)

Natural hazards vary widely in the physical parameters that determine the nature of their impact on human populations. A dimension which characterizes hazards according to those physical parameters most important in determining their impact on individuals and society has been presented by Burton *et al.* (1978) and Kates (1976). At one end of the continuum, hazards are defined as *intensive,* and are characterized as "small in areal extent, intensive in impact, of brief duration, sudden onset and poor predictability" (Kates, 1976, p. 139). Examples of these hazards include earthquakes, volcanic eruptions, tornadoes, and avalanches (Burton *et al.,* 1978; Kates, 1976). The force and magnitude of intensive hazards coupled with their poor predictability render preventative and mitigating measures largely ineffective, and can lead to substantial loss of life and destruction of property. Fortunately, the restricted areal impact of intensive hazards reduces both the amount of population at risk and the likelihood of destruction.

Pervasive hazards define the other end of the hazard continuum. They can be characterized as widespread in areal extent, diffuse in impact, of long duration, gradual in onset, and predictable with a reasonable degree of accuracy (Kates, 1976). Examples of pervasive natural hazards include drought, excessive heat or precipitation, and snow (Burton *et al.,* 1978; Kates, 1976). Because of their greater predictability and more gradual onset, pervasive hazards allow a wider range of preventive and mitigating responses that generally allow individuals in affected areas to escape serious injury. However, because their impact is spatially and temporally diffuse, the economic, social, and psychological effects of pervasive hazards can accrue to a relatively large proportion of the population in a given region.

Other classes of hazards, such as floods, wind, tidal waves, and hurricanes are closer to the center of the pervasive-intensive continuum. They may display characteristics of intensive and/or pervasive hazards, depending on their geophysical and meteorological properties, as well as on the geomorphology of the area affected (Burton *et al.,* 1978; Kates, 1976).

Although any segment of society may be affected by natural hazards, rural populations appear to be particularly susceptible. This vulnerability stems largely from the centrality of agriculture as an economic mainstay and a determinant of land-use patterns. Both economic and health risks are implicated. Economic risks result from potential crop damage that can be inflicted by recurrent extremes in temperature and precipitation, such as rain, hail, frost, heat waves, flood, and drought. Health risks result from residence in floodplains, which are desirable as agricultural lands because of their rich topsoil. The periodic flooding that created those rich farmlands is likely to recur, and in severe instances can result in injury or death to members of the resident community.

An understanding of the factors associated with perceptual-cognitive responses to natural hazards plays an important role in minimizing the economic, social, and psychological losses that may accompany the occurrence of a hazardous event. The comprehension of salient hazard dimensions and the appropriate choice of preventive and mitigating measures determine the nature and magnitude of damage sustained. Over the past two decades a significant body of research has evolved concerning these issues, largely fostered by researchers in geography. The strong conceptual and empirical tradition established by Burton, Kates, and White, and their associates (e.g., Burton, 1972; Burton & Kates, 1964a, 1964b; Burton, Kates, & Snead, 1969; Burton, Kates, & White, 1968; Golant & Burton, 1969; Hewitt & Burton, 1971; Kates, 1962, 1963, 1967, 1976; White, 1964, 1974; White & Haas, 1975) has been particularly influential in elucidating aspects of perception and choice in connection with natural hazards.

From a psychological perspective, hazard–perception research can be divided into two portions. One of these focuses on the recognition of hazards and the perceived probability of their occurrence or recurrence. The other portion of the research focuses upon choices of coping responses.

Perception of Risk

There is ample evidence to indicate that perceptions of the likelihood of natural hazard occurrence vary substantially among individuals (Baker & Patton, 1974; Burton et al., 1968, 1969, 1978; Dupree & Roder, 1974; Heathcote, 1974; Islam, 1974; Kates, 1962, 1963, 1976). At the same time, it is clear that most inhabitants of areas subject to threats from natural hazards recognize the existence of personal risks (Burton et al., 1978; Kates, 1976); in relative terms, these perceptions of the likelihood of hazardous events appears to be reasonably veridical. Research comparing objective and subjective estimates of the occurrence, recurrence, or prevalence of natural hazards, including blizzard (Burton et al., 1978), drought (Heijnen & Kates, 1974; Kirkby, 1974; Saarinen, 1966), flood (Burton et al., 1978; Kates, 1962, 1963), hurricane (Baker & Patton, 1974; Burton et al., 1978), frost (Jackson, 1974; Ward, 1974), and tornado (Burton et al., 1978) indicate that the probability of past hazard occurrence does have an impact upon subjective estimates of future hazard occurrence. In areas where objective evidence indicates that hazards are more likely to occur, individuals tend to give higher likelihood estimates of hazard occurrence than do individuals in areas where the objective likelihood of hazard occurrence is lower. However, in absolute terms, likelihood estimates of hazard occurrence generally fall short of the true probabilities (Burton et al., 1978; Kates, 1962, 1976; Jackson, 1974;

Saarinen, 1976). Thus, the likelihood of hazardous events is underestimated by the average hazard-zone occupant.

The wide variation in likelihood estimation concerning natural hazards, as well as the tendency for an underestimation of hazard likelihood, may be the result of two common cognitive heuristics that bias judgments and lead to errors in decision making under uncertain conditions. One of these is the *availability heuristic* and the other is the *representativeness heuristic* (Slovic, Fischoff, & Lichtenstein, 1977; Slovic, Kunreuther, & White, 1974; Tversky & Kahneman, 1974).

In the availability heuristic, events which are more accessible in memory tend to be judged as more probable. Factors which make events more accessible, thus leading to higher probability estimates, are those that are: (1) experienced on a more regular basis, (2) emotionally charged, and (3) more recently experienced. The latter two are normally unrelated to actual probability (Slovic *et al.*, 1974, 1977; Tversky & Kahneman, 1974). Support for the operation of the availability heuristic may be adduced from a study reported by Kates (1962). He found that estimates of flood likelihood were more accurate when: (1) floods had been experienced with relatively high frequency; (2) when floods had been experienced relatively recently; and (3) when floods were relativley high in magnitude. Individuals with less frequent and less recent flood experience would be more likely to underestimate the likelihood of floods, since representative instances of floods would be more difficult to retrieve from memory. Similarly, unless the magnitude of an experienced flood was relatively large, it would be unlikely to be readily accessible in memory, and consequently would result in a low likelihood estimate. Because hazard events of a large magnitude are relatively infrequent and are unlikely to have been experienced recently by most individuals, the availability heuristic and its attendant cognitive biases could account for the general underestimation of the likelihood of natural hazards.

The representativeness heuristic reflects a general tendency for individuals to base probabilistic inferences upon small samples of events drawn from a parent population. Since small samples are often unrepresentative of the parent population, inferences based upon those samples frequently result in judgmental errors. Where natural hazards are concerned, many years of experience within an environmental setting are clearly required to accumulate representative instances of extreme events. Consequently, it is unlikely that most individuals possess the repertoire of experience required to arrive at accurate likelihood estimates. As a result, likelihood estimates may either underestimate or overestimate true hazard probabilities, depending upon the sample of events the individual has undergone. Furthermore, since extremely hazardous events are generally of low frequency, they will often not be in the individual's repertoire of experience and should generally result in an underestimation of hazard likelihood. However, as individuals increasingly experience the environment and the extreme events of nature it holds in store for them, their sample of events should become more representative and their judgments more accurate. Saarinen's (1966) study of drought perception provides supportive evidence for this proposition. He found that accuracy in perception of drought by midwestern farmers increases with age until roughly midlife, when it becomes asymptotic. Thus, it appears that, up to a point, increased experience with hazards increases the sample of events available to an individual and consequently improves the accuracy of likelihood estimates. Subsequent experience is largely redundant and leads to little increased judgment accuracy.

In situations where the likelihood of natural hazards is not systematically underestimated, aspects of the judgment task and cognitive biases other than those already discussed may be responsible for inaccuracies in likelihood estimates. For example, Ward (1974) has presented data that may be consistent with a judgment bias known as *conservatism*. Conservatism (Edwards, 1968) is a tendency to moderate extreme probability estimates by adjusting them toward the median of the probability range. Ward compared subjective and objective estimates of frost likelihood and found that orange growers tend to underestimate the frequency of mild frosts, which damage fruit, but overestimate severe frosts, which damage tree wood. The actual probability of frosts that damage fruit is high (.30) relative to the probability of frosts that damage wood (.05). Consistent with the conservatism bias, underestimation of the former and overestimation of the latter represent a regression toward the median of the frost–probability range.

Others (Burton *et al.*, 1978; Kates, 1976) have also reported data that show both underestimation and overestimation of hazard likelihood, but they suggest a quite different source to account for those variations. They compared subjective and objective probability estimates for the occurrence of five natural hazards: blizzard, flood, hurricane, ice storm, and torando. Data on objective estimates were obtained from a study by Hewitt and Burton (1971) and subjective estimates from a related study by Moon (1971). They found that for three of the five hazards (blizzard, flood, and hurricane) the median subjective probability was lower than the actual probability, but for the other two (ice storm and tornado, the discrepancy between subjective and objective estimates was inconsequential (.0195) and can be considered as a case where perception is largely veridical. The estimation of ice storm likelihood, on the other hand, was more disparate. Subjective probabilities of ice storm occurrence were characterized by a bimodal distribution, with a large number of extreme high and low judgments. For blizzards, where the median subjective estimate was lower than the objective probability level, a similar subjective probability distribution was observed. Burton *et al.* (1978) suggested that the bimodal subjective probability distributions reflected a discrepancy in the implicit meaning of hazards for individuals. Thus, individuals may not differ as much in their recognition of the salient features of snow and ice accumulation as in their establishment of a criterion for defining a specific level of intensity of those factors as hazardous. This point is an important one, for it reflects a general inadequacy of hazard research. In most studies, terms referring to natural hazards and their magnitude are imprecisely defined, if defined at all. As a result, the wide range of variation in judgments concerning hazard likelihood may in part be a function of individual variations in both the implicit meaning of hazard terms and the implicit standards for magnitude estimation.

Urban-rural differences in perception of threat from natural hazards have also been noted, and appear to be tied to dominant resource use (Burton *et al.*, 1978; Burton & Kates, 1964b; Kates, 1967, 1976; Saarinen, 1976). Rural residents engaged in agricultural pursuits tend to be more sensitive to the likelihood of natural hazards. This sensitivity is largely due to the economic dependence on agriculture that characterizes rural populations. As noted previously, agricultural activities are particularly susceptible to a wide range of natural hazards; as a result, rural populations are particularly attentive to their occurrence. In urban areas, the effects of many natural hazards is less acute. Burton *et al.* (1978) and Kates (1976) suggest that for the urbanite, social and technological hazards are more relevant. They also point out that the higher residential mobility of urban populations results in a more limited range of experience to use in assessing the likelihood of natural hazards for any given locale, causing hazard estimates to be more variable and inaccurate.

To this point, errors in judgment concerning the occurrence of natural hazards have been discussed in terms of probabilistic estimates. In fact, the occurrence of hazardous events can be represented as being of random but determinable probability. Most hazard-zone occupants recognize the probabilistic quality of natural hazards, though a small minority does not. Kates (1976) reports that, from a worldwide study of hazard perception, 74% of hazard-zone occupants recognize the probabilistic but random nature of hazard occurrence. Among individuals who fail to perceive natural hazards as random and probabilistic, a variety of alternate attitudes prevail. The most common are: (1) a belief that hazards are of a predictably cyclical nature (Burton *et al.*, 1969; Heathcote, 1974; Kates, 1962; Kirkby, 1974; Moline, 1974; Saarinen, 1966), and (2) a belief that hazards are unpredictable but in the hands of higher authority, such as God (Burton *et al.*, 1969; Dupree & Roder, 1974; Islam, 1974; Kates, 1962; Saarinen, 1966).

Overall, the perception of threat from natural hazards can be considered to be relatively veridical, but quite variable. Within the current context, variations in perception of risk from natural hazards are seen as largely a function of four principal factors: (1) imprecision in research techniques, (2) patterns of land use, (3) beliefs in nonrandom and nonprobabilistic causes of natural hazards, and (4) a series of cognitive decision-making biases. A number of cognitive heuristics and biases other than those discussed may also be relevant but could not be included due to space limitations. An excellent discussion of the full range of cognitive heuristics and biases as they relate to hazard perception is given by Slovic *et al.* (1974).

Choices in Response to Natural Hazards

Choices concerning purposeful actions, or adjustments, in response to natural hazards fall into three general categories (Burton *et al.*, 1978; Kates, 1976). One is simply the absorption of the consequence of the hazard. In this case, losses are either borne by the individual or are distributed to some segment of society. Distribution normally entails government action at local, regional, or national levels; in some cases programs in the private sector are involved, like disaster insurance. A second option is a reduction of the consequences of the hazard through preventive measures. These measures may entail modification of the environment and behavioral adaptation (Burton *et al.*, 1978; Kates, 1976; Baumann & Sims, 1974). Environmental modifications are intended to reduce or circumvent entirely the destructive impact of the event, and include such actions as the building of dams, flood channels, irrigation systems, and structural changes in buildings. Behavioral adaptation normally entails an attempt to reduce personal injury and economic loss through directed action, and includes such activities as the development and deployment of prediction and warning systems, and evacuation, sheltering, and rescue programs. A third option is an avoidance of the consequences of the hazard through changes in location or land use. Changes in location simply involve migration, whether local, regional, national, or international. Changes in land use entail a reorganization of existing resource–utilization patterns in order to eliminate activities that would be hazardous under certain environmental circumstances. A clear example of land-use change is the conversion of residential beach strips on hurricane coasts to recreational areas (Burton *et al.*, 1969, 1978; Baumann & Sims, 1974).

Obviously, the foregoing choices concerning adjustments need not be mutually exclusive, and in many cases more than one is selected. By far the most frequently chosen is loss absorption or distribution (Baumann & Sims, 1974; Burton et al., 1969, 1978; Dupree & Roder, 1974; Kates, 1976; Moline, 1974; Ramachandran & Thakur, 1974; Saarinen, 1966), although in many instances a limited range of preventive measures are used in conjunction (Burton et al., 1978; Kates, 1976; Saarinen, 1966). Preventive and mitigating actions are most often taken where the likelihood of potential loss from natural hazards is high (Harding & Parker, 1974; Kates, 1962; Miller, Brinkmann, & Barry, 1974; Rowntree, 1974; Ward, 1974), and where sociocultural values stress self-determination of fate (Baumann & Sims, 1974; Saarinen, 1966; Sims & Baumann, 1972; Sims & Saarinen, 1969). The most drastic action, a change in either location (migration) or land use, is not viewed as a viable alternative by most individuals (Burton et al., 1969, Heathcote, 1974; Islam, 1974; Moline, 1974; Ramachandran & Thakur, 1974), since both of these options entail considerable economic and familial disruption.

Research Directions

Additional research is needed to clarify many aspects of the processes surrounding the perception of natural hazards. A further investigation of judgment heuristics and biases in the context of risk assessment would be particularly fruitful, since current evidence suggests that a number of those processes and biases may be relevant. At present, however, little direct evidence is available concerning judgment processes and biases as they affect the appraisal of hazard likelihoods; thus, further substantiation is needed. Once the judgment inaccuracies that affect hazard evaluations are more clearly understood, it may be possible to develop educational programs aimed at sensitizing individuals to, and guiding them toward, more adaptive judgment strategies.

Future investigations also need to emphasize precision in the definition of the hazard terms and magnitude criteria used by study respondents. Methodological imprecision concerning these factors could account for much of the observed variation in the perception of hazard likelihood and could be readily eliminated.

At present, the process underlying the choice of adjustment to natural hazards is poorly understood. Past research has focused upon the degree to which various options for response to hazards are adopted or are seen as viable. Psychological models of the decision-making process have been discussed in connection with adjustments to hazards (see Burton et al., 1978; Slovic et al., 1974) but have not been systematically investigated. Future research needs to focus more directly on the process of choice itself, as it is exercised in the context of natural hazards.

SCENIC QUALITY ANALYSIS

In an era of shrinking resources and environmental degradation, public attention has focused on the need for policy directed at environmental preservation and resource management. Prominent in the list of resources in need of stewardship is the aesthetic quality of the landscape. During the last two decades, a spate of legislation has been spawned that explicitly or implicitly requires the inclusion of aesthetic values in environmental quality and resource–management programs at federal, state and local levels. Among the most significant of these legislative mandates are the Multiple Use-Sustained Yield Act of 1960, Highway Beautification Act of 1965, National Wild and Scenic Rivers Systems Act of 1968, National Environmental Policy Act of 1969, Coastal Zone Management Act of 1972, National Forest Management Act of 1976, and the Surface Mining and Reclamation Act of 1977 (Craik & Feimer, 1979; Zube, 1976).

Decision-makers faced with the task of evaluating land-use alternatives that are based, at least in part, on their aesthetic impact, have actively encouraged and supported research aimed at the vacuum of knowledge concerning aesthetic responses to the environment. As a consequence, a broad empirical literature concerning aspects of environmental aesthetics of particular significance to resource management has begun to evolve. Four general features define much of this research. First, it has been decidedly problem oriented, focusing upon specific geographical localities and the restricted range of land-use problems faced by individual resource–management agencies. Representative examples of land-use activities confronted by resource–management agencies on the basis of management objectives and geographical contexts include mineral mining (e.g., coal, limestone), oil exploration and extraction, power plant and utility corridor siting, road construction, and silvicultural practices (e.g., timber harvesting, brush removal). Second, the vast majority of the research has centered upon the visual or the scenic aspects of aesthetic experience. This emphasis derives largely from a general conviction among research scientists and resource managers that the visual-sensory modality is the most salient in aesthetic appreciation, as well as from the emphasis on visual-aesthetic factors represented in much of the pertinent public policy. Third, a substantial portion of the research has focused on natural and recreational environments, reflecting a recognition that many land uses are particularly threatening in areas not already dominated by human-related artifacts. And fourth, a desire to ease decision-making difficulties that arise from the use of imprecise and unsystematic information has led to an increasing emphasis on quantitative assessment systems. (Zube, 1976, and

Arthur, Daniel, & Boster, 1975, have variously pointed to similar emphases in the landscape–perception literature.)

The ensuing discussion will focus on some of the significant aspects of research on scenic quality and the analytic strategies which have been enlisted in the development of scenic quality appraisal and impact–assessment methods. Unfortunately, space limitations proclude a detailed discussion of scenic quality research in the wide range of pertinent landscape and land-use contexts; thus, the emphasis will be on aspects of scenic quality research that seem to be of generic value and emobdy reasonable generality across landscape–land-use conditions.

Scenic Quality Criterion Measures

The specification of a criterion measure is central to the investigation of any construct. Derivative observations are of scientific or practical merit only when the criterion accurately reflects the phenomenon of interest. In the context of scenic quality analysis, the phenomenon of interest is the aesthetic response of individuals to visually perceived features of the landscape. Although the nature of aesthetic responses is far from being understood or agreed upon by researchers, they can generally be considered to be affective or evaluative responses (Wohlwill, 1976) that reflect pleasure or displeasure (Berlyne, 1974). Defined in this manner, aesthetic responses may be assessed through verbal, psychophysiological, and behavioral measures (Berlyne, 1974; Wohlwill, 1976).

Verbal measures have been the dominant response criteria to a virtually exclusive degree in scenic quality research. Two related but distinct self-report criterion measures characterize most of the research. One is simply a measure of stated preference for an array of discrete landscape–land-use stimuli, and has taken primarily three forms: (1) a ranking of stimuli from the most to least preferred (e.g., Carls, 1974; Jackson, Hudman, & England, 1978; Shafer, Hamilton, & Schmidt, 1969; Shafer & Tooby, 1973); (2) a rating of relative preference for stimuli on a numerical scale (e.g., Hammitt, 1979; R. Kaplan, 1977; S. Kaplan, R. Kaplan, & Wendt, 1972; Probst & Buhyoff, 1980; Wohlwill, 1968); and (3) a paired comparison paradigm where preference is given to one of a pair of stimuli presented simultaneously, usually involving the comparison of each stimulus with every other one (e.g., Bernaldez & Parra, 1979; Buhyoff & Leuschner, 1978; Buhyoff, Leuschner, & Arndt, 1980; Buhyoff, Leuschner, & Wellman, 1979; Buhyoff & Riesenman, 1979; Buhyoff & Wellman, 1979, 1980; Buhyoff, Wellman, Harvey, & Fraser, 1978; Macia, 1979; Wellman & Buhyoff, 1980). The other dominant criterion measure is a global dimension intended to directly embody the visual-aesthetic construct; it is generally referred to as scenic or visual quality (e.g., Briggs & France, 1980; Brush & Palmer, 1979; Jones, Jones, Gray, Parker, Coe, Burnham, & Geitner, 1975), or as scenic beauty (e.g., Arthur, 1977; Daniel & Boster, 1976; Feimer, Smardon, & Craik, 1981; Patey & Evans, 1979; Schomaker, 1978; Schroeder & Daniel, 1980), and is normally assessed by having individuals rate an array of landscape - land-use stimuli on a numerical scale. A notable alternative to the direct rating of scenic quality is the application of Q-sort methodology (Stephenson, 1953), which in this case entails a sorting of stimuli into discrete categories along the scenic quality continuum (see Craik, 1968, 1971; and Pitt & Zube, 1979, for a discussion of pertinent applications of the Q-Sort method). Normally, numerical values are assigned to those categories, yielding an end result similar to that attained through rating scales. The most significant divergence of the Q-sort from most rating systems occurs when, as is frequently the case, a forced distribution specifying the numbers of stimuli to be placed in each category is employed. The use of a forced distribution prevents those nondiscriminating judgments that may occur in free-rating situations.

Since both preference and global scenic quality judgments purport to represent visual-aesthetic response, it is important to consider their degree of convergence. Preference judgments have been criticized on the grounds that they may embody personal tastes and inclinations other than those pertaining to the visual-aesthetic value of the landscape, particularly those concerning commercial, recreational, and residential land use (Arthur, Daniel, & Boster, 1977; Brush, 1976; Craik, 1972b; Zube, 1973; Zube, Pitt, & Anderson, 1975). Scales that are labeled as *scenic quality, visual quality,* or *scenic beauty,* on the other hand, seem explicitly to evoke the visual-aesthetic construct.

Research concerning the convergence of preference and global scenic quality judgments has been largely lacking, but two sets of studies reporting pertinent data indicate that these two types of measures tend to be highly related. Zube, Pitt, and Anderson (1975) compared semantic differential preference and scenic quality ratings completed by the same subjects and found a high correspondence ($r = .80$) between them. The lack of independence of the two measures could, however, have resulted in an inflation of the magnitude of the relationship. Daniel and Boster (1976), on the other hand, also reported a substantial convergence between entirely independent preference and scenic quality measures. They found that composite preference and scenic beauty judgments by two independent sets of subjects resulted in an identical rank ordering of four study areas. Although the use of composite indices and a small number of rankings increases the likelihood of such significant relationships, the findings are encouraging nevertheless. It is also noteworthy that in the Daniel and Boster study, subjects were specifically directed to base their preference judgments upon scenic quality. Thus, it may be as Arthur *et al.* (1977) suggest: instructional sets play an important role in the degree to which aesthetic responses reflect variations in visual-aesthetic responses to landscapes and land uses. Instructions directing subjects to focus upon visual-aesthetic factors may well elminate the personal biases that might otherwise be expressed by preference judgments.

Since the available evidence suggests a reasonable degree of convergence between preference and global scenic quality judgments, they will both be subsumed under the rubric of scenic quality for the balance of this discussion.

Predictors of Scenic Quality

A profusion of variables aimed at predicting scenic quality have appeared in the research literature in recent years. Common to all these methods is their focus upon descriptive assessments of physical properties of the environment; they differ principally in the degree to which they may be represented by direct measurement of those physical features. In general, two classes of predictors may be delineated: (1) *physical variables* and (2) *transactional variables*. (Somewhat similar distinctions have been made by Arthur *et al.*, 1977, and Wohlwill, 1976.)

Physical Variables

Many physical properties of the environment that are relevant to visual-aesthetic responses may be assessed directly and objectively. Mechanical measurement techniques are often enlisted in the assessment of physical variables, minimizing the judgmental role of the individual who performs the assessment. Even where purely judgmental estimates are obtained, their environmental referents are so clear and distinct that a high degree of consensus is typically attained. Consequently, the accuracy and reliability of physical variables is likely to be quite high, although in most cases reliability estimates have not been reported in the research literature.

A vast number of physical dimensions have been used in the assessment and prediction of scenic quality. From among these, a small number stand out as particularly salient predictors across a number of landscape settings and studies. The presence of *water* clearly increases the scenic quality of the landscape, and evidence to date suggests that scenic quality increases as a function of the proportion of a landscape scene covered by water (Briggs & France, 1980; Brush & Palmer, 1979; Carls,

1974; Nassauer, 1979; Shafer *et al.*, 1969; Zube, Pitt, & Anderson, 1975). It seems apparent, however, that once exceedingly large proportions of the scene become dominated by water, scenic quality begins to decrease, suggesting that the relationships is nonlinear (Brush & Shafer, 1975; Shafer *et al.*, 1969). *Topographic relief* (Briggs & France, 1980; Buhyoff & Wellman, 1980; Leopold, 1969; Zube, Pitt, & Anderson, 1975) and *slope* (Zube, Pitt, & Anderson, 1975) are also related to scenic quality as increasing functions, although evidence presented by Buhyoff and Wellman (1980) suggests that the relationship between scenic quality and relative presence of sharp mountainous terrain in a landscape scene is monotonic but nonlinear. The presence of *man-made elements* in a landscape scene generally detracts from scenic quality (S. Kaplan *et al.*, 1972; R. Kaplan, 1975) in proportion to the area obscured (Briggs & France, 1980; Brush & Palmer, 1979; Buhyoff & Wellman, 1980; Carls, 1974; Crystal & Brush, 1978). However, evidence presented by Buhyoff and Wellman (1980) again suggests that the relationship may be nonlinear but monotonic. Finally, the presence of *vegetation* has a clear impact on scenic quality judgments. Vegetative density is positively related to scenic quality (Arthur, 1977; Briggs & France, 1980; Brush & Palmer, 1979; Crystal & Brush, 1978; Daniel & Boster, 1976; Schroeder & Daniel, 1980), but it seems that some dispersion to allow unobstructed viewing is desirable. Evidence from a number of studies (Brush, 1979; Echelberger, 1979; Patey & Evans, 1979; Shafer & Rutherford, 1969) suggests that thinning out dense shrubbery and forest stands to a modest degree results in increased scenic quality.

Transactional Variables

Landscape perception arises from an interaction of the individual with the physical environment (Craik, 1969; 1972b; Craik & Feimer, 1979). The physical properties of the environment constitute a complex net of stimuli that the individual must organize in a meaningful way. Transactional variables in scenic quality analysis reflect that interaction: they characterize physical properties of the environment in terms of their human significance. Thus, they may best be understood as combinations of physical dimensions that are interpreted in a way defined by the human information-processing system.

The range of transactional variables that might be considered in the context of scenic quality analysis and impact assessment is almost limitless. Among these is virtually any descriptive dimension which requires human judgment and cannot be fully evaluated by purely physical measures. However, a small number of variables have emerged which are appealing on both empirical and theoretical grounds: complexity, congruity, mystery, and spatial enclosure. *Complexity* refers primarily to diversity in the number of perceptually distinct elements of a given landscape scene (Arthur *et al.*, 1977; Wohlwill, 1976); the greater in number and more varied the elements of the landscape scene are, the more complex it is. *Congruity* reflects the degree of harmony evident in the interrelation of the elements of a given landscape scene; it embraces the concepts of *fittingness* and *compatibility*, which refer to the congruity of man-made and natural components of the landscape (Wohlwill, 1976; Wohlwill & Harris, 1980). *Mystery* conveys a sense of alluring uncertainty, created by the promise of additional information upon further exploration. *Spatial enclosure* refers to the extent of surrounding enclosure, or conversely, a openness created by vertical topographic and vegetative elements.

Based upon the available evidence, it appears that congruity (Feimer *et al.*, 1981; Wohlwill & Harris, 1980) and mystery (R. Kaplan, 1973, 1975) are related to scenic quality as positive linear functions. Complexity is related to scenic quality in a positive linear fashion for natural landscapes (S. Kaplan *et al.*, 1972; Wohlwill, 1976), but as man-made influences increasingly dominate, the relationship begins to reverse at the high extreme of the complexity continuum, approximating an inverted U-shaped function (Wohlwill, 1976, pp. 46–48). The relationship between spatial enclosure and scenic quality seems on the surface to be nonlinear, but there is no direct evidence to support that view. From the extant research, including the research on silvicultural practices cited previously, it seems reasonably clear that a moderate to moderately high degree of spatial enclosure is most desirable (with extreme high and low amounts less desirable). Individuals respond favorably to small, open spaces surrounded by enclosing landform and vegetative features (e.g., small valleys and forest glades or meadows).

Related Issues

A number of concerns have been raised about the influence of factors other than those reflecting environmental variation on judgments of scenic quality or related variables. Among the most notable of these concern (1) the adequacy of photographic simulations in representing landscapes, and (2) the extent to which systematic individual differences in personality and background affect perceptions of scenic quality. Briefly,[1] neither of these factors has been found to overshadow the relationship between scenic quality and environmental attributes. Research con-

---

[1] Space limitations preclude a detailed discussion of these and other factors which influence scenic quality and environmental evaluations. For more detailed discussions the reader is referred to Arthur *et al.* (1977), Brush (1976), Craik (1971), Zube (1976), and Wohlwill (1976).

cerning the effects of photographic simulations indicates that photographic prints or photo–slide projections elicit responses highly similar to those obtained *in situ* (Daniel & Boster, 1976; Jackson *et al.*, 1978; Shafer & Richards, 1974; Zube, Pitt, & Anderson, 1975). Research concerning the effects of individual differences has focused on personality variables (e.g., Craik, 1975; Feimer, 1980; Macia, 1979), socioeconomic variables (e.g., Craik, 1975; Feimer, 1980; Jackson *et al.*, 1978; Zube, Pitt, & Anderson, 1975), environmental familiarity (e.g., Hammitt, 1979; R. Kaplan, 1977; Pedersen, 1978; Wellman & Buhyoff, 1980), and professional versus nonprofessional status in design disciplines (e.g., Arthur, 1977; Buhyoff *et al.*, 1978; Craik, 1972a; Daniel & Boster, 1976; Zube, 1973, 1974; Zube, Pitt, & Anderson, 1975). In general, each of those factors accounts for some variation in scenic quality judgments, but the effects tend not to be exceedingly large even when cumulated.

Research Directions

Over the last decade, substantial gains have been made in the elucidation of factors relevant to the perception and assessment of scenic quality. A number of salient physical and transactional variables related to scenic quality have emerged, and a number of prediction systems have been developed to serve public needs in decision-making contexts. However, the level of understanding concerning the manner in which physical properties of the landscape elicit aesthetic responses is still in the early stages. There is an evident need for additional research in many areas, but there are three that seem particularly noteworthy.

First, there is a clear need for research that interrelates physical and transactional variables. Since transactional variables emphasize the organization and abstraction of physical environmental elements, a greater understanding of the manner in which physical properties are combined to produce those abstractions would lead to a better understanding of the nature of aesthetic responses.

Second, future research must address more fully the construct validity of both preference and global scenic quality judgments. By and large, both are considered face valid, with much of the attention centering around their degree of convergence. Future research needs to incorporate a wider range of criterion measures, particularly nonverbal ones.

Finally, the effects of individual differences need to be more fully explored. It is evident that a variety of personality and background variables affect scenic quality judgments, but the magnitude of those relationships is still in question. Furthermore, little is currently known concerning the *manner* in which personality and background variables affect perceptions and judgments of scenic quality. A greater emphasis on experimental studies aimed at specifying the effects of personality and background variables on environmental information processing and judgment could be beneficial in that regard.

Concluding Remarks

The foregoing discussion has focused on three significant substrata within the domain of environmental perception and cognition. The emphasis has been on rural environments, although most of the issues raised are equally significant for other contexts. In retrospect, it seems quite clear that inasmuch as theory and research on environmental perception and cognition are in very early stages of development, all the more so is such a study of rural environments. Research is lacking in many aspects of environmental perception and cognition in rural contexts, particularly where rural populations are concerned. Ironically, much of the focus has been urban oriented, emphasizing the experiences of urbanites on recreational forays. Although it is not at all clear that it is necessary or beneficial for research in environmental perception and cognition to focus on rural environments and populations as a separate course, it is apparent that a greater emphasis on both is necessary for research in environmental perception and cognition to be fully representative.

References

Acredolo, L. P. Frames of reference used by children for orientation in unfamiliar spaces. In G. T. Moore & R. G. Golledge (Eds.), *Environmental knowing: Theories, research, and methods.* Stroudsburg, Pa.: Dowden, Hutchinson, & Ross, 1974.

Acredolo, L. P., Pick, H. L., & Olsen, M. Environmental differentiation and familiarity as determinants of children's memory for spatial location. *Developmental Psychology,* 1975, *11,* 495–501.

Allen, G., Siegel, A., & Rosinski, R. The role of perceptual context in structuring spatial knowledge. *Journal of Experimental Psychology: Human Learning and Memory,* 1978, *4,* 617–630.

Appleyard, D. A. Styles and methods of structuring city. *Environment and Behavior,* 1970, *2,* 100–116.

Appleyard, D. A. *Planning a pluralistic city.* Cambridge, Mass.: M.I.T. Press, 1976.

Arthur, L. M. Predicting scenic beauty of forest environments: Some empirical tests. *Forest Science,* 1977, *23,* 151–160.

Arthur, L. M., Daniel, T. C., & Boster, R. S. Scenic assessment: An overview. *Landscape Planning,* 1977, *4,* 109–129.

Baker, E. J., & Patton, D. J. Attitudes toward hurricane hazard on the Gulf Coast. In G. F. White (Ed.), *Natural hazards: Local, national, global.* New York: Oxford University Press, 1974.

Baumann, D. D., & Sims, J. H. Human response to the hurricane. In G. F. White (Ed.), *Natural hazards: Local, national, global*. New York: Oxford University Press, 1974.

Berlyne, D. E. The new experimental aesthetics. In D. E. Berlyne (Ed.), *Studies in the new experimental aesthetics: Steps toward an objective psychology of aesthetic appreciation*. New York: Wiley, 1974.

Bernaldez, F. G., & Parra, F. Dimensions of landscape preferences from pair-wise comparisons. *Proceedings of Our National Landscape: A Conference on Applied Techniques for Analysis and Management of The Visual Resource*. Berkeley, Calif.: USDA Pacific Southwest Forest and Range Experiment Station, General Technical Report PSW-35, 1979, 256–262.

Briggs, D. J., & France, J. Landscape evaluation: A comparative study. *Journal of Environmental Management*, 1980, *10*, 263–275.

Brush, R. O. Perceived quality of scenic and recreational environments: Some methodological issues. In K. H. Craik & E. H. Zube (Eds.), *Perceiving environmental quality: Research and applications*. New York: Plenum Press, 1976.

Brush, R. O. The attractiveness of Woodlands: Perceptions of forest landowners in Massachusetts. *Forest Science*, 1979, *25*, 495–506.

Brush, R. O., & Palmer, J. F. Measuring the impact of urbanization on scenic quality: Land use change in the northeast. *Proceedings of Our National Landscape: A Conference on Applied Techniques for Analysis and Management of The Visual Resource*. Berkeley, Calif.: USDA Pacific Southwest Forest and Range Experiment Station, General Technical Report PSW-35, 1979, 358–364.

Brush, R. O., & Shafer, E. L., Jr. Application of a landscape-preference model to land management. In E. H. Zube, R. O. Brush, & J. G. Fabos (Eds.), *Landscape assessment: Values, perceptions, and resources*. Stroudsburg, Pa.: Dowden, Hutchinson, & Ross, 1975.

Buhyoff, G. J., & Leuschner, W. A. Estimating psychological disutility from damaged forest stands. *Forest Science*, 1978, *24*, 424–432.

Buhyoff, G. J., & Riesenman, M. F. Manipulation of dimensionality in landscape preference judgments: A quantitative validation. *Leisure Sciences*, 1979, *2*, 221–238.

Buhyoff, G. J., & Wellman, J. D. Seasonality bias in landscape preference research. *Leisure Sciences*, 1979, *2*, 181–190.

Buhyoff, G. J., & Wellman, J. D. The specification of a non-linear psychophysical function for visual landscape dimensions. *Journal of Leisure Research*, 1980, *12*, 257–272.

Buhyoff, G. J., Wellman, J. D., Harvey, H., & Fraser, R. A. Landscape architects' interpretations of people's landscape preferences. *Journal of Environmental Management*, 1978, *6*, 255–262.

Buhyoff, G. J., Leuschner, W. A., & Wellman, J. D. Aesthetic impacts of southern pine beetle damage. *Journal of Environmental Management*, 1979, *8*, 261–267.

Buhyoff, G. J., Leuschner, W. A., & Arndt, L. K. The replication of a scenic preference function. *Forest Science*, 1980, *26*, 227–230.

Burton, I. Cultural and personality variables in the perception of natural hazards. In J. F. Wohlwill & D. H. Carson (Eds.), *Environment and the Social sciences: Perspectives and applications*. Washington, D.C.: American Psychological Association, 1972.

Burton, I., & Kates, R. W. The floodplain and the seashore. *Geographical Review*, 1964, *54*, 366–385. (a)

Burton, I., & Kates, R. W. The perception of natural hazards in resource management. *Natural Resources Journal*, 1964, *3*, 412–441. (b)

Burton, I., Kates, R. W., & White, G. F. *The human ecology of extreme geophysical events*. Toronto: University of Toronto, Department of Geography, Working Research Paper No. 1, 1968.

Burton, I., Kates, R. W., & Snead, R. E. *The human ecology of coastal flood hazard in mega-lopolis.* Chicago: University of Chicago, Department of Geography, Research Paper No. 115, 1969.

Burton, I., Kates, R. W., & White, G. F. *The environment as hazard.* New York: Oxford University Press, 1978.

Canter, D., & Stringer, P. *Environmental interaction.* New York: International Universities Press, 1975.

Carls, E. G. The effects of people and man-induced conditions on preferences for outdoor recreation landscapes. *Journal of Leisure Research,* 1974, *6,* 113–124.

Craik, K. H. The comprehension of the everyday physical environment. *Journal of the American Institute of Planners,* 1968, *34,* 29–37.

Craik, K. H. Human responsiveness to landscape: An environmental psychological perspective. In K. Coates & K. Moffett (Eds.), *Response to environment.* (Student Publication of the School of Design 18). Raleigh: North Carolina University Press, 1969.

Craik, K. H. Environmental psychology. In K. H. Craik, B. Kleinmuntz, R. L. Rosnow, R. Rosenthal, J. A. Cheyne, & R. H. Walters, *New directions in psychology* (Vol. 4). New York: Holt, Rinehart & Winston, 1970.

Craik, K. H. The assessment of places. In P. McReynolds (Ed.), *Advances in psychological assessment* (Vol. 2). Palo Alto, Calif.: Science and Behavior Books, 1971.

Craik, K. H. Appraising the objectivity of landscape dimensions. In J. V. Krutilla (Ed.), *Natural environments: Studies in theoretical and applied analysis.* Baltimore: Johns Hopkins University Press, 1972. (a)

Craik, K. H. Psychological factors in landscape appraisal. *Environment and Behavior,* 1972, *4,* 255–266. (b)

Craik, K. H. Environmental psychology. *Annual Review of Psychology,* 1973, *24,* 403–422.

Craik, K. H. Individual variations in landscape description. In E. H. Zube, R. O. Brush, & J. G. Fabos (Eds.), *Landscape assessment: Values, perceptions, and resources.* Stroudsburg, Pa.: Dowden, Hutchinson, & Ross, 1975.

Craik, K. H., & Feimer, N. R. Setting technical standards for visual assessment procedures. *Proceedings of Our National Landscape: A Conference on Applied Techniques for Analysis and Management of The Visual Resource.* Berkeley, Calif.: USDA Pacific Southwest Forest and Range Experiment Station, General Technical Report PSW-35, 1979, 93–100.

Craik, K. H., & Zube, E. H. (Eds.). *Perceiving environmental quality: Research and applications.* New York: Plenum Press, 1976.

Crystal, J. H., & Brush, R. O. Measuring scenic quality of the urban fringe. *Landscape Research,* 1978, *3,* 9–11; 14.

Daniel, T. C., & Boster, R. S. *Measuring landscape esthetics: The scenic beauty estimation method.* Forest Service Research Paper RM-167, Ft. Collins, Colo.: USDA Rocky Mountain Forest and Range Experiment Station, 1976.

de Jonge, D. Images of urban areas: Their structure and psychological foundations. *Journal of the American Institute of Planners,* 1962, *28,* 266–276.

Devlin, A. S. The "small town" cognitive map: Adjusting to a new environment. In G. T. Moore & R. G. Golledge (Eds.), *Environmental knowing: Theories, research, and methods.* Stroudsburg, Pa.: Dowden, Hutchinson, & Ross, 1976.

Downs, R. M., & Stea, D. Cognitive maps and spatial behavior: Process and products. In R. M. Downs & D. Stea (Eds.), *Image and environment: Cognitive mapping and spatial behavior.* Chicago: Aldine, 1973. (a)

Downs, R. M., & Stea, D. (Eds.). *Image and environment: Cognitive mapping and spatial behavior.* Chicago: Aldine, 1973. (b)

Dupree, H., & Roder, W. Coping with drought in a preindustrial, preliterate farming society. In G. F. White (Ed.), *Natural hazards: Local, national, global*. New York: Oxford University Press, 1974.

Echelberger, H. E. The semantic differential in landscape research. *Proceedings of Our National Landscape: A Conference on Applied Techniques for Analysis and Management of The Visual Resource*. Berkeley, Calif.: USDA Pacific Southwest Forest and Range Experiment Station, General Technical Report PSW-35, 1979, 524–531.

Edwards, W. Conservatism in human information processing. In B. Kleinmuntz (Ed.), *Formal representation of human judgment*. New York: Wiley, 1968.

Evans, G. W. Environmental cognition. *Psychological Bulletin*, 1980, *88*, 259–287.

Evans, G. W., Marrero, D., & Butler, P. Environmental learning and cognitive mapping. *Environment and Behavior*, 1981, *13*, 83–104.

Falk, W. W., & Pinhey, T. K. Making sense of the concept rural and doing rural sociology: An interpretive perspective. *Rural Sociology*, 1978, *43*, 547–558.

Feimer, N. R. Personality and environmental perception: Alternative predictive systems and implications for evaluative judgments (Doctoral dissertation, University of California, Berkeley, 1979). *Dissertation Abstracts International*, 1980, *41*. (University Microfilms No. 8014673)

Feimer, N. R., Smardon, R. C., & Craik, K. H. Evaluating the effectiveness of observer based visual resource and impact assessment methods. *Landscape Research*, 1981, *6*, 12–16.

Flavell, J. H. *The developmental psychology of Jean Piaget*. Princeton, N.J.: Van Nostrand, 1963.

Francescato, D., & Mebane, W. How citizens view two great cities: Milan and Rome. In R. M. Downs & D. Stea (Eds.), *Image and environment: Cognitive mapping and spatial behavior*. Chicago: Aldine, 1973.

Funk & Wagnalls New Standard Dictionary of the English Language. New York: Funk & Wagnalls, 1963.

Golant, S., & Burton, I. *The meaning of a hazard-application of the semantic differential*. Toronto: University of Toronto, Department of Geography, Working Research Paper No. 7, 1969.

Gulick, J. Images of an Arab city. *Journal of the American Institute of Planners*, 1963, *29*, 179–197.

Hammitt, W. E. Measuring familiarity for natural environments through visual images. *Proceedings of Our National Landscape: A Conference on Applied Techniques for Analysis and Management of The Visual Resource*. Berkeley, Calif.: USDA Pacific Southwest Forest and Range Experiment Station, General Technical Report PSW-35, 1979, 217–226.

Harding, D. M., & Parker, D. J. Flood hazard at Shrewsbury, United Kingdom. In G. F. White (Ed.), *Natural hazards: Local, national, global*. New York: Oxford University Press, 1974.

Hart, R. A., & Moore, G. T. The development of spatial cognition: A review. In R. M. Downs & D. Stea (Eds.), *Image and environment: Cognitive mapping and spatial behavior*. Chicago: Aldine, 1973.

Heathcote, R. L. Drought in South Australia. In G. F. White (Ed.), *Natural hazards: Local, national, global*. New York: Oxford University Press, 1974.

Heft, H. The role of environmental features in route learning: Two exploratory studies of way-finding. *Environmental Psychology and Nonverbal Behavior*, 1979, *3*, 172–185.

Heijnen, J., & Kates, R. W. Northeast Tanzania: Comparative observations along a moisture gradient. In G. F. White (Ed.), *Natural hazards: Local, national, global*. New York: Oxford University Press, 1974.

Heimstra, N. W., & McFarling, L. H. *Environmental psychology* (2nd ed.). Monterey, Calif.: Brooks/Cole, 1978.

Hewitt, K., & Burton, I. *The hazardousness of a place: A regional ecology of damaging events.* Toronto: University of Toronto, Department of Geography, Research Paper No. 6, 1971.

Horton, F., & Reynolds, D. Effects of urban spatial structure on individual behavior. *Economic Geography,* 1971, *47,* 36–48.

Islam, M. A. Tropical cyclones: Coastal Bangladesh. In G. F. White (Ed.), *Natural hazards: Local, national, global.* New York: Oxford University Press, 1974.

Ittelson, W. H. (Ed.). *Environment and cognition.* New York: Seminar Press, 1973. (a)

Ittelson, W. H. Environment perception and contemporary perceptual theory. In W. H. Ittelson (Ed.), *Environment and cognition.* New York: Seminar Press, 1973. (b)

Ittelson, W. H., Proshansky, H. M., Rivlin, L. G., & Winkel, G. H. *An introduction to environmental psychology.* New York: Holt, Rinehart & Winston, 1974.

Jackson, R. H. Frost hazard to tree crops in the Wasatch Front: Perception and adjustments. In G. F. White (Ed.), *Natural hazards: Local, national, global.* New York: Oxford University Press, 1974.

Jackson, R. H., Hudman, L. E., & England, J. L. Assessment of the environmental impact of high voltage power transmission lines. *Journal of Environmental Management,* 1978, *6,* 153–170.

Jones, G., Jones, I., Gray, B. A., Parker, B., Coe, J. C., Burnham, J. B., & Geitner, N. M. A method for the quantification of aesthetic values for environmental decison making. *Nuclear Technology,* 1975, *25,* 682–713.

Kameron, J. Experimental studies of environment perception. In W. H. Ittelson (Ed.), *Environment and cognition.* New York: Seminar Press, 1973.

Kaplan, R. Predictors of environmental preference: Designers and clients. In W. F. E. Preiser (Ed.), *Environmental design research.* Stroudsburg, Pa.: Dowden, Hutchinson, & Ross, 1973.

Kaplan, R. Some methods and strategies in the prediction of preference. In E. H. Zube, R. O. Brush, & J. G. Fabos (Eds.), *Landscape assessment: Values, perceptions, and resources.* Stroudsburg, Pa.: Dowden, Hutchinson, & Ross, 1975.

Kaplan, R. Way-finding in the natural environment. In G. T. Moore & R. G. Golledge (Eds.), *Environmental knowing: Theories, research, and methods.* Stroudsburg, Pa.: Dowden, Hutchinson, & Ross, 1976.

Kaplan, R. Preference and everyday nature: Method and application. In D. Stokols (Ed.), *Perspectives on environment and behavior: Theory, research, and applications.* New York: Plenum Press, 1977.

Kaplan, S. Cognitive maps in perception and thought. In R. M. Downs & D. Stea (Eds.), *Image and environment: Cognitive mapping and spatial behavior.* Chicago: Aldine, 1973.

Kaplan, S. Adaptation, structure, and knowledge. In G. T. Moore & R. G. Golledge (Eds.), *Environmental knowing: Theories, research, and methods.* Stroudsburg, Pa.: Dowden, Hutchinson, & Ross, 1976.

Kaplan, S., Kaplan, R., & Wendt, J. S. Rated preference and urban visual material. *Perception and Psychophysics,* 1972, *12,* 354–356.

Kates, R. W. *Hazard and choice perception in flood plain management.* Chicago: University of Chicago, Department of Geography, Research Paper No. 78, 1962.

Kates, R. W. Perceptual regions and regional perception in flood plain management. *Papers and Proceedings of the Regional Science Association,* 1963, *11,* 217–228.

Kates, R. W. The perception of storm hazard on the shores of megalopolis. In D. Lowenthal (Ed.), *Environmental perception and behavior.* Chicago: University of Chicago, Department of Geography, Research Paper No. 109, 1967.

Kates, R. W. Experiencing the environment as hazard. In S. Wapner, S. B. Cohen, & B. Kaplan (Eds.), *Experiencing the environment.* New York: Plenum Press, 1976.

Kirkby, A. V. Individual and community response to rainfall variability in Oaxaca, Mexico. In G. F. White (Ed.), *Natural hazards: Local, national, global.* New York: Oxford University Press, 1974.

Knopf, R. C. *Cognitive map formation as a tool for facilitating information transfer in interpretive programming.* Paper presented at The Second Conference on Scientific Research in the National Parks, San Francisco, November 1979.

Ladd, F. Black youths view their environment: Neighborhood maps. *Environment and Behavior,* 1970, *2,* 74–99.

Langer, J. *Theories of development.* New York: Holt, Rinehart & Winston, 1969.

Laurendeau, M., & Pinard, A. *The development of the concept of space in the child.* New York: International Universities Press, 1970.

Lee, T. R. Psychology and living space. In R. M. Downs & D. Stea (Eds.), *Image and environment: Cognitive mapping and spatial behavior.* Chicago: Aldine, 1973.

Leff, H. L., Gordon, L. R., & Ferguson, J. G. Cognitive set and environmental awareness. *Environment and Behavior,* 1974, *6,* 395–447.

Leopold, L. B. *Quantitative comparison of some aesthetic factors among rivers.* Geological Survey Circular 620, U.S. Geological Survey, Washington, D.C., 1969.

Lindsay, P. H., & Norman, D. A. *Human information processing: An introduction to psychology* (2nd ed.). New York: Academic Press, 1977.

Lynch, K. *The image of the city.* Cambridge, Mass.: M.I.T. Press, 1960.

Macia, A. Visual perception of landscape: Sex and personality differences. *Proceedings of Our National Landscape: A Conference on Applied Techniques for Analysis and Management of The Visual Resource.* Berkeley, Calif.: USDA Pacific Southwest Forest and Range Experiment Station, General Technical Report PSW-35, 1979, 279–285.

Magana, J. R. An empirical and interdisciplinary test of a theory of urban perception (Doctoral Dissertation, University of California, Irvine, 1978). *Dissertation Abstracts International,* 1978, *39,* 1460B. (University Microfilms No. 78-15, 840)

Milgram, S., Greenwald, J., Kessler, S., McKenna, W., & Waters, J. A psychological map of New York City. *American Scientist,* 1972, *60,* 194–200.

Milgram, S., & Jodelet, D. Psychological maps of Paris. In H. M. Proshansky, W. H. Ittelson, & L. G. Rivlin (Eds.), *Environmental psychology: People and their physical settings* (2nd ed.). New York: Holt, Rinehart & Winston, 1976.

Miller, D. J., Brinkmann, W. A. R., & Barry, R. G. Windstorms: A case study of wind hazard for Boulder, Colorado. In G. F. White (Ed.), *Natural hazards: Local, national, global.* New York: Oxford University Press, 1974.

Moline, N. T. Perception research and local planning: Floods on the Rock River, Illinois. In G. F. White (Ed.), *Natural hazards: Local, national, global.* New York: Oxford University Press, 1974.

Moon, K. D. *The perception of the hazardousness of a place: A comparative study of five natural hazards in London, Ontario.* Toronto: University of Toronto, Unpublished master's research paper, 1971.

Moore, G. T. Theory and research on the development of environmental knowing. In G. T. Moore & R. G. Golledge (Eds.), *Environmental knowing: Theories, research, and methods.* Stroudsburg, Pa.: Dowden, Hutchinson, & Ross, 1976.

Moore, G. T. Knowing about environmental knowing: The current state of theory and research on environmental cognition. *Environment and Behavior,* 1979, *11,* 33–70.

Moore, G. T., & Golledge, R. G. Environmental knowing: Concepts and theories. In G. T. Moore & R. G. Golledge (Eds.), *Environmental knowing: Theories, research, and methods.* Stroudsburg, Pa.: Dowden, Hutchinson, & Ross, 1976. (a)

Moore, G. T., & Golledge, R. G. (Eds.). *Environmental knowing: Theories, research, and methods.* Stroudsburg, Pa.: Dowden, Hutchinston, & Ross, 1976. (b)

Nassauer, J. Managing for naturalness in wildland agricultural landscapes. *Proceedings of Our National Landscape: A Conference on Applied Techniques for Analysis and Management of The Visual Resource.* Berkeley, Calif.: USDA Pacific Southwest Forest and Range Experiment Station, General Technical Report PSW-35, 1979, 447–453.

Neisser, U. *Cognitive psychology.* New York: Appleton-Century-Crofts, 1967.

Neisser, U. *Cognition and reality: Principles and implications of cognitive psychology.* San Francisco: W. H. Freeman, 1976.

Newell, A., & Simon, H. A. *Human problem solving.* New Jersey: Prentice-Hall, 1972.

Norman, D. A. *Memory and attention: An introduction to human information processing* (2nd ed.). New York: Wiley, 1976.

Norman, D. K. A comparison of children's spatial reasoning: Rural Appalachia, suburban and urban New England. *Child Development,* 1980, *51,* 288–291.

Orleans, P. Differential cognition of urban residents: Effects of social scale on mapping. In R. M. Downs & D. Stea (Eds.), *Image and environment: Cognitive mapping and spatial behavior.* Chicago: Aldine, 1973.

Page, H. W. Concepts of length and distance in a study of Zulu youths. *Journal of Social Psychology,* 1973, *90,* 9–16.

The Oxford English Dictionary (Vol. 8). London: Oxford University Press, 1970 (1933).

Patey, R. C., & Evans, R. M. Identification of scenically preferred forest landscapes. *Proceedings of Our National Landscape: A Conference on Applied Techniques for Analysis and Management of The Visual Resource.* Berkeley, Calif.: USDA Pacific Southwest Forest and Range Experiment Station, General Technical Report PSW-35, 1979, 532–538.

Pedersen, D. M. Relationship between environmental familiarity and environmental preference. *Perceptual and Motor Skills,* 1978, *47,* 739–743.

Piaget, J., & Inhelder, B. *The child's conception of space.* New York: Norton, 1967.

Piaget, J., Inhelder, B., & Szeminska, A. *The child's conception of geometry.* New York: Basic Books, 1960.

Pitt, D. G., & Zube, E. H. The Q-Sort method: Use in landscape assessment research and landscape planning. *Proceedings of Our National Landscape: A Conference on Applied Techniques for Analysis and Management of The Visual Resource.* Berkeley, Calif.: USDA Pacific Southwest Forest and Range Experiment Station, General Technical Report PSW-35, 1979, 227–234.

Probst, D. B., & Buhyoff, G. J. Policy capturing and landscape preference quantification: A methodological study. *Journal of Environmental Management,* 1980, *11,* 45–59.

Proshansky, H. M., Ittelson, W. H., & Rivlin, L. G. Environment perception and cognition. In H. M. Proshansky, W. H. Ittelson, & L. G. Rivlin (Eds.), *Environmental psychology: People and their physical settings* (2nd ed.). Holt, Rinehart & Winston, 1976.

Ramachandran, R., & Thakur, S. C. India and the Ganga flood plains. In G. F. White (Ed.), *Natural hazards: Local, national, global.* New York: Oxford University Press, 1974.

Rowntree, R. A. Coastal erosion: The meaning of a natural hazard in the cultural and ecological context. In G. F. White (Ed.), *Natural hazards: Local, national, global.* New York: Oxford University Press, 1974.

Saarinen, T. F. *Perceptions of the drought hazard on the great plains.* Chicago: University of Chicago, Department of Geography, Research Paper No. 106, 1966.

Saarinen, T. F. *Environmental planning: Perception and behavior.* Atlanta: Houghton Mifflin, 1976.

Schomaker, J. H. Measurement of preferences for proposed landscape modifications. *Landscape Research,* 1978, *3,* 5–8.

Schroeder, H. W., & Daniel, T. C. Predicting scenic quality of forest road corridors. *Environment and Behavior,* 1980, *12,* 349–366.

Shafer, E. L., Jr., & Richards, T. A. *A comparison of viewer reactions to outdoor scenes and photographs of those scenes.* USDA Forest Service Research Paper NE-302, Northeast Forest Experiment Station, Upper Darby, Pa., 1974.

Shafer, E. L., Jr., & Rutherford, W. Selection cuts increased natural beauty in two Adirondack forest stands. *Journal of Forestry,* 1969, *67,* 415–419.

Shafer, E. L., Jr., & Tooby, M. Landscape preference: An international replication. *Journal of Leisure Research,* 1973, *5,* 60–65.

Shafer, E. L., Jr., Hamilton, J. F., Jr., & Schmidt, E. A. Natural landscape preferences: A predictive model. *Journal of Leisure Research,* 1969, *1,* 1–19.

Siegel, A. W., & Schadler, M. Young children's cognitive maps of their classroom. *Child Development,* 1977, *48,* 388–394.

Siegel, A. W., & White, S. H. The development of spatial representations of large-scale environments. In H. W. Reese (Ed.), *Advances in child development and behavior* (Vol. 10). New York: Academic Press, 1975.

Siegel, A. W., Kirasic, K. C., & Kail, R. V., Jr. The development of children's representations of geographic space. In I. Altman & J. F. Wohlwill (Eds.), *Human behavior and environment: Advances in theory and research* (Vol. 3). New York: Plenum Press, 1978.

Sims, J. H., & Baumann, D. D. The tornado threat: Coping styles of the north and south. *Science,* 1972, *176,* 1386–1392.

Sims, J. H., & Saarinen, T. F. Coping with environmental threat: Great Plains farmers and the sudden storm. *American Association of Geographers Annals,* 1969, *59,* 677–686.

Slovic, P., Kunreuther, H., & White, G. F. Decision processes, rationality, and adjustment to natural hazards. In G. F. White (Ed.), *Natural hazards: Local, national, global.* New York: Oxford University Press, 1974.

Slovic, P., Fischoff, B., & Lichtenstein, S. Behavioral decision theory. *Annual Review of Psychology,* 1977, *28,* 1–39.

Stea, D. Program notes on a spatial fugue. In G. T. Moore & R. G. Golledge (Eds.), *Environmental knowing: Theories, research, and methods.* Stroudsburg, Pa.: Dowden, Hutchinson, & Ross, 1976.

Stea, D., & Blaut, J. M. Notes toward a developmental theory of spatial learning. In R. M. Downs & D. Stea (Eds.), *Image and environment: Cognitive mapping and spatial behavior,* Chicago: Aldine, 1973.

Stephenson, W. *The study of behavior: Q-technique and its methodology.* Chicago: University of Chicago Press, 1953.

Stokols, D. Environmental psychology. *Annual Review of Psychology,* 1978, *29,* 253–295.

Stoltman, J. P. *Children's conception of territory: A study of Piaget's spatial stages* (Doctoral dissertation, University of Georgia, 1971). *Dissertation Abstracts International,* 1972, *32,* 5623A. (University Microfilms No. 72-11, 047)

Tversky, A., & Kahneman, D. Judgment under uncertainty: Heuristics and biases. *Science,* 1974, *185,* 1124–1131.

Wapner, S., & Werner, H. *Perceptual development.* Worcester, Mass.: Clark University Press, 1957.

Ward, R. M. Decisions by Florida citrus growers and adjustments to freeze hazards. In G. F. White (Ed.), *Natural hazards: Local, national, global.* New York: Oxford University Press, 1974.

Wellman, J. D., & Buhyoff, G. J. Effects of regional familiarity on landscape preferences. *Journal of Environmental Management,* 1980, *11,* 105–110.

Werner, H. The concept of development from a comparative and organismic point of view. In D. B. Harris (Ed.), *The concept of development.* Minneapolis: University of Minnesota Press, 1957.

White, G. F. *Choice of adjustment to floods.* Chicago: University of Chicago, Department of Geography, Research Paper No. 93, 1964.

White, G. F. (Ed.). *Natural hazards: Local, national, global.* New York: Oxford University Press, 1974.

White, G. F., & Haas, J. E. *Assessment of research on natural hazards.* Cambridge, Mass.: M.I.T. Press, 1975.

Wohlwill, J. F. Amount of stimulus exploration and preference as differential functions of stimulus complexity. *Perception and Psychophysics*, 1968, *4*, 307–312.

Wohlwill, J. F. Environmental aesthetics: The environment as a source of affect. In I. Altman & J. F. Wohlwill (Eds.), *Human behavior and environment: Advances in theory and research* (Vol. 1). New York: Plenum Press, 1976.

Wohlwill, J. F., & Harris, G. Response to congruity or contrast for man-made features in natural-recreation settings. *Leisure Sciences*, 1980, *3*, 349–365.

Zube, E. H. Rating everyday rural landscapes of the northeastern U.S. *Landscape Architecture*, 1973, *63*, 370–375.

Zube, E. H. Cross disciplinary and intermode agreement on the description and evaluation of landscape resources. *Environment and Behavior*, 1974, *6*, 69–89.

Zube, E. H. Perception of landscape and land use. In I. Altman & J. F. Wohlwill (Eds.), *Human behavior and environment: Advances in theory and research* (Vol. 1). New York: Plenum Press, 1976.

Zube, E. H. *Environmental evaluation: Perception and public policy.* Monterey, Calif.: Brooks/Cole, 1980.

Zube, E. H., Brush, R. O., & Fabos, J. G. (Eds.). *Landscape assessment: Values, perceptions, and resources.* Stroudsburg, Pa.: Dowden, Hutchinson, & Ross, 1975.

Zube, E. H., Pitt, D. G., & Anderson, T. W. Perception and prediction of scenic resource values of the Northeast. In E. H. Zube, R. O. Brush, & J. G. Fabos (Eds.), *Landscape assessment: Values, perceptions, and resources.* Stroudsburg, Pa.: Dowden, Hutchinson, & Ross, 1975.

8

Locus of Control and the Rural Experience

Herbert M. Lefcourt and Rod A. Martin

Introduction

For several decades it has been commonplace to read about the discomfort and anguish that is the lot of the urban dweller. Newspapers continually report the violence and tragedies that seem to characterize city living. In contrast, rural existence has often been portrayed as stable, quiet, and friendly, a true respite from the burdensome tempo of the unfriendly, anonymous city.

However, those who write about rural experience also speak of the isolation, the lack of places to go, and the oppressive impact of social criticism in small town milieus. More recently, it has been asserted that there is an inordinately high incidence of battered wives in rural regions.

What can be gleaned from such descriptions? For one, there is no idyllic setting where the problems of living can be universally eliminated. Both urban and rural living offer problems and challenges to which some persons will succumb and others will strive with success.

It is our purpose in this chapter to describe a set of personality constructs that are at least partially shaped by particular sorts of milieus and that in turn can affect the manner in which persons adapt to those milieus. Rather than dwelling upon the "goodness" or "badness" of urban vs. rural life, our concern will be with the ways in which particular settings help to shape their inhabitants' beliefs regarding their own

Herbert M. Lefcourt and Rod A. Martin • Department of Psychology, University of Waterloo, Waterloo, Ontario, Canada N2L 3G1.

effectiveness and competence, as well as their feelings of futility and fatalism. It will be our contention that persons in urban and rural settings learn to be effective in some realms of their existence while feeling helpless about other aspects of their lives; each setting affords experiences that may facilitate the growth of perceived competence in certain realms of experience and not in others.

To introduce our subject matter we will begin with a description of the personality constructs that will serve to guide our discussion.

The Locus of Control Construct and its Cognates

In laymen's language there are many words that can be used to describe a person's sense of effectiveness. While *canness* is the term used by Heider (1958) to describe an individual's belief about his ability to affect life events, in social learning theory (Rotter, Chance, & Phares, 1972) the personality construct *locus of control* has been used to describe such beliefs. Briefly, locus of control refers to the ways in which causation is attributed. An internal locus of control refers to a belief that the outcomes of interactions between persons and the events that befall them are, at least in part, determinable by the acts of those persons. An external locus of control refers to the belief that events occur for reasons that are irrelevant to a person's actions, and thus are beyond attempts at controlling them. A more complete description of this construct and related research can be found elsewhere (Lefcourt, 1976; Phares, 1976).

The locus of control construct has proven to be highly useful in the prediction of a range of behaviors that have serious consequences for persons (such as the manner in which they cope with various stressors, respond to attempts at influencing them, and think about the conditions within which they have to function). Generally speaking, persons who maintain a more internal locus of control orientation—who believe that they are to some degree responsible for the kinds of experiences they undergo—tend to be more active in their attempts to understand and cope with their circumstances. In addition, they seem to be less easily molded by immediate social influence.

Other constructs that share some similarities with locus of control in the prediction of criteria such as the above are (1) powerlessness, a facet of alienation (Seeman, 1959), (2) personal causation (de Charms, 1968), (3) hope (Stotland, 1969), and (4) helplessness (Seligman, 1975). What has concerned each of these investigators are the ways in which individuals conceive of their own competence or *effectance*—their ability to affect the events that occur in their lives (R. White, 1959). Most importantly for the purposes of this chapter, the ramifications of causal beliefs have been found to have importance for the ways in which people come to terms with those aspects of their milieus that characterize urban, as opposed to rural, environments. Not less important have been those findings that indicate how one's sense of effectance or locus of control is shaped by the characteristics of one's surroundings.

In the following section certain research will be described that suggests how causal beliefs are shaped by the immediate milieu and how they in turn affect the manner in which the milieu is experienced.

THE SHAPING OF CAUSAL EXPECTANCIES AND THEIR RAMIFICATIONS

In some of the earliest research literature pertaining to locus of control, it was found that blacks, Spanish Americans, Native Americans, and other minority groups that do not enjoy as easy an access to opportunity as do the predominant Caucasian groups in North America are likely to hold fatalistic, external control beliefs. In general, it was concluded that perceived control is positively associated with access to opportunities, a point well demonstrated by a correlation of .50 ($p < .001$, $N = 221$) obtained between measures of objective access to opportunity and perceived control in a compelling field study by Jessor, Graves, Hanson, and Jessor (1968).

More recently, there have been several studies published that concern the shaping of causal beliefs in *total institutions* (such as nursing homes). Langer and Rodin (1976) described one such investigation in which elderly residents were induced to have a greater sense of control within their nursing home. That is, certain residents were encouraged to believe that they could affect their surroundings in order to maximize their satisfactions. Others were offered the same satisfactions but without any sense of active decision making, participation, or control.

Subsequent assessments of the residents' morale revealed that those who believed that available satisfactions could be attained by their own behaviors rated themselves, and were judged by others to be, more active, happier, and, as found in a follow-up investigation (Rodin & Langer, 1978), lived longer than did those residents who were offered the same amenities through the largesse of the institution staff.

Similar findings were obtained by Shulz (1976), who reported that elderly residents of a nursing home were happier when they themselves could schedule when they would be visited by youthful volunteers, than when those visits occurred in a less controllable fashion. The visits were less pleasurable and more upsetting when they were unpredictable and uncontrollable events.

In each of these studies among the elderly, the satisfactions offered were valued by the recipients. In both instances, however, the means to attain those satisfactions were varied so that some subjects felt they had to enact roles to attain their pleasures, whereas others were simply given their pleasures passively. Because this is not the place to present a large summary of studies, let it suffice to note that these findings have been sufficiently replicated with varying methods that our confidence in these results is not exaggerated.

What can be concluded from such data? While opportunity for satisfaction is necessary if one is to develop an internal locus of control, there must also be opportunity to participate in the obtaining of satisfactions. The "gift" of pleasure may be no equal to those pleasures earned by one's efforts or obtained by actively making choices.

In a similar way, the annoyances and aversive events thought to characterize urban life have the greatest impact when suffered passively. Glass and Singer (1972), for example, found that loud noises that occurred unpredictably had deleterious consequences for their subjects' ability to concentrate upon given tasks and to withstand the frustrations of failing to accomplish them. However, when those subjects knew that they *could* extricate themselves from the noise (although in actuality they did not exercise this privilege), the noise did not have the same impact on their performance of those tasks. Given that noise is one feature of an urban setting, it may be possible to conclude that characteristics of urban settings may not produce inevitable results upon inhabitants (since people vary in the ways in which they can cope with those characteristics). The belief that one *can* find relief if one needs it may alter dramatically the impact of potentially aversive stimuli.

Findings similar to those of Glass and Singer have been reported by Sherrod (Sherrod, 1974; Sherrod, Hage, & Halpern, 1977; Sherrod & Cohen, 1978) regarding crowding, another urban difficulty. While Sherrod found that crowding has adverse effects upon cognitive functioning, he also found that those effects were modified when subjects believed that they *could* leave the crowded setting if it became too aversive. This belief alone is apparently sufficient to lessen the negative impact of crowding, since subjects rarely took advantage of their options.

These empirical findings appeal to common sense. Panic would not ensue in a crowded theater if persons in the crowd learned that there were many exits and that departure was always possible. The possibility of fire and a dearth of exits, however, would create the feeling that one may not be able to leave if necessary, a feeling of entrapment that could help to create a surge toward panic.

The fact under consideration here is that the conditions of one's environment affect one's state of well-being. Also, the beliefs we entertain, which can likewise result from the structure of our milieu, can serve to modify those environmental conditions, allowing us to survive certain aversive conditions with minimal effects. In the studies discussed thus far, perceptions of causality or locus of control have been created through descriptions of subjects' options. That is, the participants in each study became aware of choices and options; this knowledge caused them to be more active in the pursuit of satisfaction and more tolerant of aversive stimuli in situations where performance deterioration could have been expected.

Studies concerned with density and noise have obvious relevance for urban dwellers. What, on the other hand, can be said for rural persons? As noted earlier, isolation, loneliness, and social coercion may be more important negative influences for these individuals. Though we have little data to offer in a discussion of these factors, it would seem highly plausible that a rural person's belief that he or she could terminate isolation or coercion (through visiting or participating in other locales) would have an effect similar to the urban subject's belief that he or she could avoid crowding or noise if it were too burdensome. Likewise, the pleasures of rural life would prove to be of greater import if they were attainable through actions and choices of the rural dweller.

At this point it may prove valuable to contrast the urban and rural environments as a means of learning whether these contrasting settings offer varied opportunities for satisfying or aversive circumstances, and seeing whether a sense of control, efficacy, or competence is apt to be found more in one setting than in another.

RURAL AND URBAN SETTINGS

Milgram (1970) defined the basic "facts of city life" in terms of "large numbers, density, and heterogeneity," which were said to be experienced as "overloads" at the level of "roles, norms, cognitive functions, and facilities." In turn, overloaded social environments were said to require an adaptation characterized by a disregard of the needs, interests, and demands of those who are less relevant to one's own need satisfactions; this accounts for the familiar absence of eye contact and verbal interaction between strangers in urban centers. As Milgram notes, "A rule of urban life is respect for other people's emotional and social privacy, perhaps because physical privacy is so hard to achieve" (p. 1462).

Summarized in Milgram's (1970) paper were a number of findings, updated by other investigators. For example, in contrast to urban dwellers, residents of small towns have been found to be more willing to help strangers, admitting them into their homes at least twice as frequently as have urban dwellers, and small-town residents are found to be better acquainted with their fellow residents, a situation offering security and familiarity at the possible cost of feeling stifled. Urban conditions that promote anonymity, on the other hand, provide freedom from repetitive social ties at the possible cost of alienation, uncertainty, and detachment.

The first author, having been reared and having lived most of his life in urban settings, had occasion to reside in a cottage in a rural village on the island of Tobago for a two-week period immediately preceding the writing of this chapter. It was an isolated fishing–cocoa bean plantation village on a very remote, completely rural Caribbean island. The descriptions offered by Milgram of the city versus village life are consequently rather vivid to this writer. The friendliness of the villagers and their curiosity concerning foreigners were readily apparent both in the mountains and on the village streets and paths. The ready inclusion of strangers into certain aspects of village life made for the creation of friendships that seemed unlikely to dissipate at the end of two weeks. While few villagers were aggressively friendly, their readiness to engage with strangers was easily observable. Along with sensations of warmth and friendliness, this urban dweller experienced the decline of what is perhaps the most omnipresent of an urbanite's feelings, that of vulnerability. One could feel secure that one's self and possessions were not likely to be abused; consequently, one felt less apt to fall into the urban attitude of "me first."

Despite this near idyllic experience, one anecdote comes to mind that may reveal something about urban versus rural existence. One local fisherman, who often would take cottage residents out on night fishing expeditions, had on several occasions sat and chatted away an evening on the author's cottage veranda. His life was revealed as consisting of rearing his family of four daughters, working for the government, fishing, tending to a tract of farmland (on which he raised cocoa, bananas, plantain, papayas, etc.), and spending an evening at the local equivalent of a pub. His day began rather early—Tobagans rise with the sun at 5 A.M.—and his "government work" was usually completed by 9 or 10 A.M. This work consisted of sweeping, cleaning, and scooping up refuse and garbage in the village streets, a chore requiring much attention since garbage cans were nonexistent and garbage trucks unknown, and because the almost 35-degree angles of the streets prevented the creation of dump sites.

Following this two-hour stint, the fisherman was free to decide how to spend his day—fishing for tuna, working on his farm, lazing about, swimming, socializing, etc. The fisherman was asked whether he had any preferences if he were limited to only one of his occupations for the whole day. Without a second's delay he answered "government work," much to the writer's surprise. That he would prefer the most routinized, least demanding of his possible occupations seemed disparate from the common conception of man as working for indepencence and desiring opportunity for skillful behavior. As a fisherman, the villager was patient and talented, netting squids as they emerged from the ocean surface with rarely a miss, coping with the excitement of pulling in sharks with hand-held fishing lines. He was obviously competent, able to rise to the challenges of deep-sea fishing that lure so many urban dwellers to the ocean shores. But this demanding occupation was not the preference of this fisherman, who would rather work with a crew of men cleaning the village streets.

When the writer questioned the fisherman about his choice, his reasons became clear. Sometimes, he said, there are no fish when he is out fishing. The government, on the other hand, was always there with its checks. Certainly, the noncontingent largesse of the government (the street cleaners were hardly to be found overworking) seemed preferable to the competence-demanding task. It occurred to the writer that some assessment of the fisherman's feelings, made while he performed his respective duties, might have contradicted these statements; he may have had more positive feelings while fishing than while sweeping the streets.

What does this encounter suggest? First, the ability to choose one's daily course of actions that is more prevalent in a rural setting is not necessarily a preferred state. Second, the exercise of competence—sensing that one determines one's own outcomes—may be outweighed by a need for security that may be better served by the regularities associated with organizations and urban settings. The uncertainties of nature on land and water limit the degree to which the villager on Tobago can feel secure of his livelihood, regardless of his perceived competence. Given these limitations, the draw of the city to the rural person becomes as understandable as the attraction of rural life to the urbanite.

Farmers are often noted to be suspicious of governments, cities, and those forces that shape the nation's economy. The sense of being the victim of injustice and of being helpless before such inexorable forces seems to be the lot of rural dwellers. Whereas competence is experienced in daily action, whether in farming, fishing, or the like, helplessness seems to be experienced with regard to the larger world outside. Whereas the urban dweller may feel competent at completing forms and wending his way through red tape and bureaucracy, but helpless at the tasks of maintaining his plumbing, the rural person would seem more likely to feel competent at his management of the things that surround him. When encountering the "outside" world, however, with the management of formalities and the contact with strangers that this entails, he may experience a helplessness equivalent to that of the city dweller facing the failure of his appliances.

The Tobagan fisherman, as competent as he was in fishing and farming, lacked confidence in his ability to earn dollars, the token of trade with which he could participate in the wider economy of his island home. Faced with economic uncertainties, his choice was the secure if unchallenging means, the choice of a fatalistic person. As we noted earlier, persons in urban and rural settings will probably be found to differ in their sense of effectiveness with regard to different realms of their experience. We may have caught a glimpse of just such differences in this interaction with the Tobagan fisherman.

In the next section we will review the available empirical data concerning locus of control, alienation, anomie, etc., in relation to rural life.

RESEARCH ON LOCUS OF CONTROL AND RURAL LIFE

As noted above, the psychological construct *locus of control* is closely related to the sociological concepts of *alienation* and *anomie*. Seeman (1959), for example, in his definitive article on alienation, included "powerlessness" (which he identified with the locus of control construct) as one aspect of alienation, along with meaninglessness, normlessness, isolation, and self-estrangement. Dean's (1961) Alienation Scale, which is widely used in sociological research, includes subscales for powerlessness, normlessness, and social isolation. These three subscales have been found to be intercorrelated, suggesting a generalized alienation concept, but they are distinctive enough to be taken separately as well. The nine-item powerlessness subscale contains such items as "There is little or nothing I can do towards preventing a major 'shooting' war," and "We are just so many cogs in the machinery of life."

Another frequently used questionnaire, Srole's (1956) Anomie Scale, measures a generalized sense of despair, distrust, and alienation from the total social context. It contains five items including "Nowadays a person has to live pretty much for today and let tomorrow take care of itself," and "It's hardly fair to bring children into the world with the way things look for the future." Although less directly related to locus of control, this scale has been found to correlate with measures of powerlessness (e.g., Crader & Belcher, 1975).

The concept of alienation has a prominent place in modern sociological theory. Following the writings of Marx, Durkheim, Wirth, and others, conventional sociological theory has associated widespread feelings of alienation, anomie, disillusionment, and helplessness with the rise of urbanization and industrialization in contemporary society. According to this view, rural dwellers should experience less alienation, including less feelings of powerlessness, than their urban counterparts. However, recent empirical research has cast considerable doubt on these "intellectual folk-myths" concerning the alienation of urban life (cf. Seeman, 1971).

In one survey (Killian & Grigg, 1962), Srole's scale was administered to representative samples of whites and blacks from two southeastern communities, one of 300,000 and the other of 3,000 population. The initial results showed a significantly higher degree of anomie in the urban environment for the white sample only; when education level was controlled this difference disappeared entirely. A similar study, using Srole's scale, failed to find clear evidence for reduced anomie among rural dwellers, prompting one writer to conclude that "the differences between dwellers of large urban areas and those of less urbanized communities have often been exaggerated" (Mizruchi, 1960). One study that did report rural-urban differences, although they were in the direction opposite that predicted by sociological theory, was that by Nelson and Frost (1971). They found rural southern Appalachian residents to be more anomic than their urban counterparts. This finding may be explained by the poverty and limited access to means of success in the rural areas of this region, rather than by increased alienation brought about by the vagaries of urban existence.

Other studies using measures more directly related to locus of control have also failed to find generalized differences between people in urban and rural environments. In the original validational research with Dean's scale, using a sample of 384 residents of Columbus, Ohio (Dean, 1961), a negligible, although statistically significant, point-biserial correlation of $-.10$ was found between the powerlessness subscale and rural background (i.e., people who had migrated from the country reported feeling slightly less powerless than did those who were born in the city). In other studies using Dean's scale, no differences in powerlessness were found between residents of high and low density areas of New York and Vermont (Ducharme, 1975), nor between businessmen in Minnesota communities ranging in population size from 300 to 312,000 (Photiadis, 1967). Fischer (1973a), who also reports a failure to find any rural-urban differences in powerlessness, concludes that "this fundamental dimension of personality, in all its names—sense of efficacy, internal locus of control, fate control—seems unaffected by urbanism" and that "the attribution of alienation to 'urbanism as a way of life' seems incorrect" (p. 326).

It seems safe to coincide, then, that no generalized differences in alienation (including locus of control orientation) exist between inhabitants of urban and rural environments. It may be argued that the modern means of transportation and communication have had a certain leveling effect, and that the apparent freedom from noise, crowding, and the rat race enjoyed by rural dwellers is offset by the conflict over rural and urban values and the discrepancy between ideals and means of attainment that is brought about by exposure to the mass media. In keeping with these conclusions, recent studies have found little or no rural-urban differences in mental health (Webb, 1978), suicide rates (Niskanen, Koskinen, Lepola, & Venalainen, 1975), or general malaise (Fischer, 1973b).

Any attempt to find rural-urban differences in locus of control must turn, then, from generalized, global expectancies of control to more specific areas of endeavor. For example, rural-urban differences continue to exist regarding receptivity to education, and some research findings suggest that locus of control may play a role in these differences. Olsen and Carter (1974) found that rural, disadvantaged grade school children from southeastern Ohio scored significantly lower on a "self-concept-of-academic ability" scale than did disadvantaged children from a large city in western New York. "Self-concept-of-academic ability" in this study is defined as "the evaluation one makes of oneself with respect to the ability to achieve in academic tasks in general as compared with others" (p. 84), and as such appears very similar to the concept of locus of control for academic achievement. These researchers concluded that their findings support the notion that "rural inhabitants resist 'book learning' because education does not have an immediate and specific application to their lives" (p. 90). They argue that an awareness of the inferior quality of rural school facilities and personnel may be reflected in the reduced feelings of academic efficacy among rural children. Yancey (1973) reports similar results using the same scale with rural and urban southern sixth-grade elementary school children.

Olsen and Carter's conclusions are similar to those drawn by Nelson and Frost (1971), who report curious findings in the southern Appalachian region. They found that rural residents of this area appear to value education, as indicated by a higher percentage who stressed education as necessary for success, in comparison with urban respondents who more often emphasized hard work. Paradoxically, these same rural dwellers also expressed less desire for higher education for their sons than did urbanites. The authors attribute this apparent discrepancy to the tendency on the part of these rural residents to blame the opportunity system rather than themselves for their lack of economic success. In locus of control terms, they tend to see economic success and failure as contingent upon "external" rather than "internal" factors.

In contrast to the above studies, however, Entwisle and Green-berger (1972) failed to support the notion of rural-urban differences in academic locus of control. These researchers compared rural and urban ninth graders from in and around Baltimore, Maryland, on the Crandall Intellectual Achievement Responsibility Scale (Crandall, Katkovsky, & Crandall, 1965), which is designed to reveal the respondents beliefs concerning their control over their own academic successes and failures. No clear rural-urban differences were found, although various interactions with sex, race, socioeconomic status, and IQ were revealed. The authors conclude that "social class or residential locus cannot be considered apart from IQ" (p. 218).

We now turn to an investigation of some of the factors that influence feelings of personal efficacy and the consequences of such feelings within the rural environment.

One of the trends in modern rural society which has been welcomed by some and denounced by others, is the movement away from the traditional family farm to large corporate farms or *agribusinesses*. Several studies have investigated the effects of this trend on individuals' feelings of personal efficacy.

Heffernan (1972) divides American farms into three types: (1) the family farm, in which the work is provided by the family, which also generates and controls the capital invested in the production unit; (2) the corporate-integratee structure, where a large corporation provides the variable inputs (feed, fertilizers, livestock, pharmaceuticals, etc.), while the worker supplies his land, labor and facilities; and (3) the corporate-farmhand structure, in which a corporation owns everything and hires farmhands to provide the labor. It was hypothesized that these three structures represent a decreasing amount of control and decision making, and an increasing potential for feelings of powerlessness and alienation on the part of the respective workers. In addition, the owners and/or managers of corporate-farmhand structures were predicted to be least characterized by such feelings.

In order to test these hypotheses, Heffernan administered Dean's alienation scale to 85 workers representing all three of these farm structures and to 28 owner-managers of "corporate-farmhand" farms. The study focused on one midwestern county that had the largest number of contract poultry producers (representing the corporate-integratee structure) in the state, and that also had only one major town. Only whites were included as subjects, in order to control for possible racial differences. The results of this study generally supported the hypotheses. Although no significant differences were found in scores on the social isolation subscale, the powerlessness and normlessness scores were different across groups. Owner-managers of corporate-farmhand structures had the lowest scores in powerlessness and normlessness, followed by family-farm workers, with workers from corporate-farmhand and corporate-integratee structures reporting greatest feelings of alienation on these two subscales. Contrary to expectations, the corporate-farmhand workers reported slightly less feelings of powerlessness than did the corporate-integratee workers, although their normlessness scores differed in the predicted way. A similar pattern of differences was found in measures of informal social interaction, community integration, involvement in formal voluntary organizations, and political involvement. Thus, it would appear that the trend toward large-scale agricultural enterprises is exerting a deleterious impact on the quality of life of rural workers.

Similar findings were reported by Martinson, Wilkening, and Rodefeld (1976). They found that a sample of hired workers on large-scale farms in Wisconsin reported significantly greater feelings of powerlessness than did the owners and managers of the farms. This powerlessness difference was found to remain after controlling for age, education, income, church attendance, farm size, and a number of other variables, but it disappeared when number of magazine and newspaper subscriptions was controlled. This last variable may be an index of the individual's general interest and involvement in external events, and provides an indication of the ways in which adverse effects on personal efficacy may be minimized in any situation through various behavioral or cognitive styles. Another interesting finding was a negative correlation between farm size (measured in annual sales) and workers' feelings of powerlessness. Despite the general loss of control felt by workers on large corporate farms, they nevertheless appear to acquire a vicarious sense of efficacy proportionate to the size of the farm on which they work.

Apart from individual coping styles, feelings of loss of personal efficacy brought about by the intrusion of big business into the agricultural process may also be minimized by economic-political organization of the workers (cf. Neal & Seeman, 1964). This hypothesis finds support in research carried out by Hoffman (1978). Hoffman used a variation of Rotter's (1966) I–E scale to assess the locus of control orientation of 102 male Chicano seasonal farm workers in California who were differentially related to the United Farm Workers Union (UFW), a nonviolent, empowerment-oriented movement. He found that union members were significantly more "internal" in locus of control orientation than nonunion members. In addition, those who had been members for four years or more were more internal than members of less than four years, and those whose commitment to the union extended to organizing a boycott were even more internal than other members of four years or more. The fact that no significant difference in locus of control was found between nonmembers and members of less than four years lends support to the argument that involvement in the union has an ameliorating effect on locus of control. Further support for this line of reasoning is found in self-reports of the UFW workers, many of whom reported important personal gains in the direction of greater control, mastery, competence, and confidence as a result of increasing involvement with the union. Hoffman concludes that "participation by the poor in self-help, social-change-oriented organizations can significantly reduce debilitating feelings of powerlessness, as a contribution to the enhancement of psychological well-being" (p. 220).

This picture is somewhat complicated, however, by another study (Rushing, 1970) that indicates that feelings of perceived power are not always directly related to actual "position" power, and that they may be modifed by peer group reference. In a survey carried out in the state of Washington, Rushing failed to find differences in personal efficacy between 240 affluent farmers who were members of a farmers' union and 1,031 unorganized, poverty-level farm workers. In fact, when age and income were controlled, it was found that the farmers felt *more* powerless than the farm workers. A clue to these surprising results was provided by responses to a number of open-ended questions. When asked about their fears and worries for the future, 17% of the farmers mentioned government control, interference, or oppression, and 10% cited fear of losing personal freedoms or control over their farming operations. In contrast, not one of the farm workers voiced such fears. Thus, fears of growing bureaucratic power appeared to have a deleterious effect on farmers' feelings of personal power (despite their apparently greater "position" power), whereas workers may have seen themselves as benefiting from increased government control of agriculture. Incidentally, Rushing observes that farmers appeared to be of two minds concerning government controls: although voicing fears concerning loss of control to the government, they also appreciated the fact that government controls do reduce the risks of farming. (This observation brings to mind the first author's conversation with the Tobagan fisherman described earlier.)

Rushing further suggests that reference group processes may also be involved in influencing perceptions of efficacy. The farmers' power, which is largely collective, may not provide the individual farmer with a sense of *personal* power. Indeed, much of the propaganda generated by the farm organization is that farmers are powerless and therefore need the organization. Individual farmers may internalize much of this publicity, and interaction with other farmers may reinforce such concerns. Thus, although the farm union provides farmers with some means of controlling their collective fate, this control is still perceived as being external to themselves individually. In contrast, one might conjecture that the farm workers, who have no strong economic-political organization to represent them, may perceive their life chances as being primarily a result of their own effort. Thus, the "norm-sending process may be an important intervening variable to the hypothesis that organizations serve as a bulwark against powerlessness" (Rushing, 1970, p. 175).

At this point we will look at one way in which locus of control may have a differential effect on individuals' responses to the rural environment, namely in the area of innovation-proneness and adoption practices. One might reason that a farmer who has a sense of personal efficacy will be more apt to adopt innovative agricultural techniques in order to achieve the greatest efficiency in his farm management; conversely, the farmer who perceives his farming success to be controlled by external forces (e.g., fate) will have a tendency to "stick with the old ways of doing things." A few studies provide some evidence to support this line of reasoning.

Chattopadhyay and Pareek (1967) interviewed 173 farmers in a village near Delhi in northern India. Among the variables of interest were: (1) a behavioral measure of the farmers' *adoption quotient*—propensity to adopt improved farm practices (improved strains of wheat, fertilizers, plows, threshers, and artificial insemination); (2) a questionnaire measure of *fatalism*—the belief that human situations and acts are predetermined and cannot be influenced by individual volition (in contrast to the belief that human situations are the result of natural and/or social forces which can be understood and changed by human volition or action); (3) *level-of-aspiration*—measured by a semistructured projective technique; and (4) *change-proneness*—the disposition of a person to accept or reject change. The analysis of data yielded significant correlations between adoption quotient and: fatalism ($-.585$, $p < .01$), change-proneness ($.629$, $p < .01$), and level-of-aspiration ($.217$, $p < .01$), as well as correlation of $-.583$ ($p < .01$) between fatalism and change-proneness. The authors note that

> the results show that the magnitude of level-of-aspiration is not as important for adoption behavior as awareness of the ways of approaching the problems, sense of efficacy to control one's future and influence agricultural results, and responsiveness to new ideas. (p. 331)

Barban, Sandage, Kassarjian, and Kassarjian (1970) reported similar findings in a study of 828 commercial farmers in Illinois. These researchers made use of a scale of "Inner–Other Social Preference" based on Reisman's theory of social character. The "inner-directed" individual in this conceptualization is the one who "believes that he has control over his own life and sees himself as an individual with a career to make," a description comparable to "internal" in locus of control terms. "Innovation-proneness," the "propensity to be the first to try out a new farm practice or idea," (Barban, *et al.*, 1970, p. 233) was also measured using a three-item self-rating scale. The results showed a significant difference in mean innovation-proneness scores for subjects in the highest and lowest quartiles of I-O scores ($p < .02$), with the inner-directed respondents exhibiting the highest degree of innovation-proneness. Thus, a farmer's tendency to adopt new agricultural methods appears to be related to his sense of efficacy or personal control over the environment.

What may we conclude from these research findings about locus of control as it relates to rural life? First, these data support the argument that the rural as opposed to the urban environment does not necessarily provide people with either a greater or lesser sense of personal efficacy. The secret of survival for the human species has been, at least in part, its remarkable resilience and adaptability to new environments. The noise and crowding of the modern megalopolis do not necessarily and automatically promote greater feelings of alienation and powerlessness, any more than do the isolation and social pressures of the country. Second, within each of these environments different positions in the social power structure and different levels of access to means of success will produce a wide range of individual differences in feelings of powerlessness or efficacy. This point is exemplified by the differences in locus of control orientation found in people at different levels in the hierarchy of large corporate farms, as well as by the limited differences observed in academic locus of control. Third, some of the data cited suggest that the impact of such environmental influences on locus of control may be moderated both by various behavioral and cognitive coping styles and by collective political and economic action. Finally, the research relating locus of control to innovation-proneness and adoptive practices illustrates the well-documented observation that an individual's locus of control orientation will have a determinative effect on his adaptive responses to the environment, whether urban or rural, in which he finds himself.

CONCLUSION

The prevalent anti-urban sentiment in our society has an ancient, time-honored tradition, dating as far back as the Old Testament and ancient Oriental and Greek literature, and finding continuing support in medieval writings, early American thought, and, most recently, the "rural renaissance" in America (cf. Ericksen, 1954; White & White, 1962; Morrison & Wheeler, 1976). As Webb (1978) points out, this tradition is undoubtedly rooted in fact:

> The noxious conditions attributed to city life may well have characterized cities of earlier, preindustrial times. Then, anti-urbanism was not only a realistic outlook but also a consequence of a rural dominated society. (p. 42)

Modern society, in contrast, is dominated by the city; very few rural areas exist that remain unaffected by urban values and life-styles.

We do not, of course, seek to minimize the very real ills of modern city life, nor do we wish to imply that there is no need for urban renewal and revitalization. Rather, we have attempted to point out that, in comparison with rural environments, the modern city does not appear to have a more deleterious effect on human functioning. More specifically, in terms of locus of control and related constructs, both rural and urban milieus exert various kinds of pressures that may cause feelings of powerlessness and alienation in some individuals; other persons rise to the challenges of their environment and, gaining a sense of personal control over it, find ways of effectively shaping it and creatively adapting to it.

REFERENCES

Barban, A. M., Sandage, C. H., Kassarjian, W. M., & Kassarjian, H. H. A study of Reisman's inner–other directedness among farmers. *Rural Sociology*, 1970, *35*, 232–243.

Chattopadhyay, S. N., & Pareek, U. Prediction of multipractice adoption behavior from some psychological variables. *Rural Sociology*, 1967, *32*, 324–333.

Crader, K. W., & Belcher, J. C. Fatalism and fertility in rural Puerto Rico. *Rural Sociology*, 1975, *40*, 268–283.

Crandall, V. C., Katkovsky, W., & Crandall, V. J. Children's beliefs in their control of reinforcements in intellectual academic achievement behaviors. *Child Development*, 1965, *36*, 91–109.

Dean, D. G. Alienation: Its meaning and measurement. *American Sociological Review*, 1961, *26*, 753–758.

deCharms, R. *Personal causation: The internal affective determinants of behavior.* New York: Academic Press, 1968.

Ducharme, S. H. *The relationship of alienation to age, population density, and self-concept.* Unpublished doctoral dissertation, United States International University, 1975.

Entwisle, D. R., & Greenberger, E. Questions about social class, internality-externality, and test anxiety. *Developmental Psychology*, 1972, *7*, 218.

Ericksen, E. G. *Urban behavior.* New York: Macmillan, 1954.

Fischer, C. S. On urban alienations and anomie: Powerlessness and social isolation. *American Sociological Review*, 1973, *38*, 311–326. (a)

Fischer, C. S. Urban malaise. *Social Forces*, 1973, *52*, 221–235. (b)

Glass, D. C., & Singer, J. E. *Urban stress*. New York: Academic Press, 1972.

Heffernan, W. D. Sociological dimensions of agricultural structures in the United States. *Sociologia Ruralis*, 1972, *12*, 481–499.

Heider, F. *The psychology of interpersonal relations*. New York: Wiley, 1958.

Hoffman, C. Empowerment movements and mental health: Locus of control and commitment to the United Farm Workers. *Journal of Community Psychology*, 1978, *6*, 216–221.

Jessor, R., Graves, T. D., Hanson, R. C., & Jessor, S. *Society, personality, and deviant behavior*. New York: Holt, Rinehart & Winston, 1968.

Killian, L. M., & Grigg, C. M. Urbanism, race, and anomia. *American Journal of Sociology*, 1962, *67*, 661–665.

Langer, E. J., & Rodin, J. The effects of choice and enhanced personal responsibility for the aged: A field experiment in an institutional setting. *Journal of Personality and Social Psychology*, 1976, *34*, 191–198.

Lefcourt, H. M. *Locus of control: Current trends in theory and research*. Hillsdale, N.J.: Lawrence Erlbaum, 1976.

Martinson, O. B., Wilkening, E. A., & Rodefeld, R. D. Feelings of powerlessness and social isolation among "large-scale" farm personnel. *Rural Sociology*, 1976, *41*, 452–472.

Milgram, S. The experience of living in cities. *Science*, 1970, *167*, 1461–1468.

Mizruchi, E. H. Social structure and anomia in a small city. *American Sociological Review*, 1960, *25*, 645–654.

Morrison, P. A., & Wheeler, J. P. Rural renaissance in America? The revival of population growth in remote areas. *Population Bulletin*, 1976, *31* (Whole No. 3).

Neal, A. G., & Seeman, M. Organizations and powerlessness: A test of the mediation hypothesis. *American Sociological Review*, 1964, *29*, 216–226.

Nelson, H. M., & Frost, E. Residence, anomie, and receptivity to education among southern Appalachian Presbyterians. *Rural Sociology*, 1971, *36*, 521–532.

Niskanen, P., Koskinen, T., Lepola, U., & Venalainen, E. A study of attempted suicides in urban versus rural areas, with a follow-up. *Acta Psychiatrica Scandinavica*, 1975, *52*, 283–291.

Olsen, H. D., & Carter, D. E. Social psychological impact of geographical location among disadvantaged rural and urban intermediate grade children. *Child Study Journal*, 1974, *4*, 81–92.

Phares, E. J. *Locus of control in personality*. Morristown, N.J.: General Learning Press, 1976.

Photiadis, J. D. Social integration of businessmen in varied size communities. *Social Forces*, 1967, *46*, 229–236.

Rodin, J., & Langer, E. J. Long term effects of a control-relevant intervention with the institutionalized aged. *Journal of Personality and Social Psychology*, 1978, *35*, 897–902.

Rotter, J. B. Generalized expectancies for internal versus external control of reinforcement. *Psychological Monographs*, 1966, *80* (Whole No. 609).

Rotter, J. B., Chance, J. E., & Phares, E. J. *Applications of a social learning theory of personality*. New York: Holt, Rinehart & Winston, 1972.

Rushing, W. A. Class, power, and alienation: Rural differences. *Sociometry*, 1970, *33*, 166–177.

Shulz, R. Effects of control and predictability on the physical and psychological well-being of the institutionalized aged. *Journal of Personality and Social Psychology*, 1976, *33*, 563–573.

Seeman, M. On the meaning of alienation. *American Sociological Review*, 1959, *24*, 783–791.

Seeman, M. The urban alienations: Some dubious theses from Marx to Marcuse. *Journal of Personality and Social Psychology*, 1971, *19*, 135–143.

Seligman, M. E. P. *Helplessness: On depression, development, and death*. San Francisco: W. H. Freeman, 1975.

Sherrod, D. R. Crowding, perceived control, and behavioral aftereffects. *Journal of Applied Social Psychology*, 1974, *4*, 171–186.

Sherrod, D. R., & Cohen, S. Density, perceived control, and design. In J. R. Aiello, & A. Baum (Eds.), *Residential crowding and design*. New York: Plenum Press, 1978.

Sherrod, D. R., Hage, J. N., Halpern, P. L., & Moore, B. S. Effects of personal causation and perceived control on responses to an aversive environment: The more control, the better. *Journal of Experimental Social Psychology*, 1977, *13*, 14–27.

Srole, L. Social integration and certain corollaries: An exploratory study. *American Sociological Review*, 1956, *21*, 709–716.

Stotland, E. *The psychology of hope: An integration of experimental, clinical, and social approaches.* San Francisco: Jossey-Bass, 1969.

Webb, S. D. Mental health in rural and urban environments. *Ekistics*, 1978, *45*, 37–42.

White, M., & White, L. *The intellectual versus the city: From Thomas Jefferson to Frank Lloyd Wright*. Cambridge: Harvard University Press, 1962.

White, R. Motivation reconsidered: The concept of competence. *Psychological Review*, 1959, *66*, 297–323.

Yancey, L. H. *The self-concept of academic ability and significant others of rural and urban southern sixth grade elementary school children.* Unpublished doctoral dissertation, Ohio University, 1973.

9

Social Psychology and Religious Fundamentalism

RALPH W. HOOD, JR.

Religion is obviously shaped by the social context within which it exists. Hence, one might expect some legitimacy to the concept of rural religion. Furthermore, if there is even partial truth to the claims that, relative to more cosmopolitan cultures, rural cultures are less heterogeneous, less tolerant of divergencies in belief and action, and less abstract in their conceptualizations, then these claims should hold true to the same extent for rural religion as they do for rural culture in general. In this sense, religious fundamentalism is not unanticipated in rural areas. Yet, as we shall see, it is more than just a curiosity that the persistence of the faith of the rural Roman (the *paganus*) became an English word for unbeliever (pagan) and the religious conservatism of the English heath dwellers became another word for unbeliever, heathen (Smith & Zopf, 1970). Yet these terms conceal a bias that also characterizes the scientific study of religion in general and of religious fundamentalism in particular. The problem of bias, noted through many chapters of this text, is even more apparent when investigators confront not only a rural culture unlikely to be their own, but also a religious fundamentalism dominant in that culture and to which they are unlikely to subscribe.

Within psychology's sister science, the scientific study of religion has always been of importance, so much so that at least one eminent sociologist (Freidrichs, 1971) has found developmental parallels in the

RALPH W. HOOD, JR. • Department of Psychology, University of Tennessee at Chattanooga, Chattanooga, Tennessee 37402.

recent decades of sociological theory with the theological, apocalyptic, and prophetic theological paradigms of Cox (1967). Yet it is an odd fact that within the field of psychology interest in religion has never been great, despite the fact that at least one quarter of past APA presidents have themselves indicated keen interest in religion at some point in their careers (Dittes, 1969). Furthermore, though one could point to the recent emergence of a new division in the APA concerned with religious issues (Division 36) as perhaps indicating an increased concern with religion among contemporary psychologists, a 5% random sampling of members of 17 divisions in the APA indicated that only a little over 1% of psychologists across all these divisions were even interested in religion as an area of psychological concern (Malony, 1977). Hence, it is apparent that while religion may not necessarily be a "taboo" topic of investigation, as Douglas (1966) claims, it clearly is neither a topic of major interest to psychologists, nor a particularly "mentionable item" in current introductory psychology textbooks (Comp & Spilka, 1979). Not surprisingly, then, we have little firm psychological knowledge concerning religion in general, much less fundamentalism in particular. As one recent assessment of empirical studies on the psychology of religion has noted that, with only a very few exceptions, "an analysis of the empirical studies within the decades of the 1960's in the psychology of religion would have to be negative" (Warren, 1977, p. 98). This conclusion is given added weight in that it echoes Dittes's (1969) earlier assessment that the psychology of religion as a whole has been characterized by lack of methodological sophistication and a poverty of empirical findings.

If this is the state of the field of psychology of religion in general, what then of the social psychology of religious fundamentalism? It is here that we begin with a serious theoretical problem regarding the appropriate methodological stance of what must, in some sense at least, be viewed as competing explanatory systems (Tremmel, 1971). When the social psychologist confronts religious fundamentalism, the troublesome centrality of the supernatural to such beliefs emerges. As Hodges (1974) has recently noted, "Although social scientists rarely say so explicitly, most of them believe it is scientifically illegitimate to include as propositions any statements about the supernatural in theories which attempt to explain or predict religious behavior" (p. 393). Although Hodges's statement is perhaps a bit exaggerated given Berger's (1967) insistence upon a methodological atheism as the appropriate stance for scientists interested in religion, it clearly converges nicely with Garrett's (1974) discussion of the persistence of what he so nicely terms the "troublesome transcendence" that is central to scientific studies of religion. Yet Garrett's own plea for a "methodological agnosticism" as a solution cannot effectively confront the perhaps insolvable problem that occurs when one system of explanation claims to explain another, which is inevitably debunked in the process. As Sartre (1968) has noted:

> The sociologist is not situated; or if he is, concrete precautions will suffice to desituate him. It may be that he tries to integrate himself into the group, but this integration is temporary; he knows that he will disengage himself, that he will review his observations objectively. In short, he resembles those detectives whom the movies often present to us as models, who win the confidence of the gang so as to be better able to trap it. Even if the sociologist and the detective participate in a collective action, it is evident that they put their act between parentheses, that they make these gestures for the benefit of a "higher interest." (p. 70)

Sartre's point is well taken, since the issue of "cops" and "gangs" is central to the scientific study of religion, especially in terms of appropriate methodological procedures. As Desroche (1973) has commented with respect to this same Sartrian point:

> Since the field of religion is situated precisely on this level of "higher concerns," it follows that when its concerns and the concerns of those studying it are at variance there will be a sharp conflict of the kind described by Sartre. This is why the sociology of the field is, in a special way, torn between two poles: if it remains objectively removed from the subject and without authentic participation it becomes a "sociology for cops"; if it participates in the life of its subject, but without any real objective distance, it remains a "sociology for the gang." (p. 6)

This question of "higher interest" is particularly relevant when one considers recent efforts to provide more sympathetic accounts of religious movements than those usually proferred by mere scientific reductionism, however thinly disguised. For instance, Richardson, Stewart, and Simmonds (1978) have commented upon difficulties in conducting participant–observation research among fundamentalists who pressure toward conversion to their faith perspective, a phenomenon also noted by Robbins and Anthony (1972) in their study of the Meher Baba sect. Likewise, Bellah's (1970) symbolic realism perspective, which explicitly extols the existential validity of religious symbolism, nevertheless has difficulty treating fundamentalist religions. For instance, Robbins, Anthony, and Curtis (1973) have argued that symbolic realism may be an appropriate perspective when dealing with liberal, mainline religious denominations, but it suffers severely with more fundamentalist religious perspectives whose orientations are likely to challenge the pluralism and relativity inherent in the symbolic realism perspective. Hence, it would appear that fundamentalism is a particularly difficult topic of investigation, not even amenable to what must be considered a most sympathetic perspective to religion as more liberally conceived. That this is indeed the case will become even more evident as we proceed. For if, as Hill (1972) claims, fundamentalists are "prototypical existentialists," then we ought not to be too surprised if they continually present us with the "cops" and "gangs" dilemma so nicely noted by Sartre.

THE GROUNDING OF FUNDAMENTALISM

Only a few decades back a popular fundamentalist preacher bemoaned what he perceived as the "liberal" stereotype of those who would call themselves fundamentalists:

> I have found that there is an idea abroad among certain religious liberals that if a person believes what is usually called "old-time religion," he must, so to speak, have a greasy nose, dirty fingernails, baggy pants, and he musn't shine his shoes or comb his hair. (Quoted in Gasper, 1963, p. 13)

Lest one discount these words too quickly, one must take note of the very recent claim in a major sociological journal that sociologists have contributed very little to our understanding of fundamental and evangelical religions due to biases rooted in social class differentials, differing belief perspectives, and general political ideological differences (Warner, 1979). Similarly, as Ethridge and Feagin (1979) have recently noted:

> As currently used, "fundamentalism" is a catch-all label for reactionary religiosity. It lacks conceptual clarity, and there is little consensus regarding its measurement as a sociological variable. In some cases it is synonymous with and in other cases it is distinguished from orthodoxy, conservatism, religious dogmatism, revivalism, sectarianism, Biblical literalism, supernaturalism and millenarianism. In addition, current usage suffers from an American Protestant bias. (p. 37)

Likewise, such a sympathetic spokesperson for religion as Bellah (1976), who admittedly explicitly fears that American fundamentalism might provide the orthodoxy for a possible imminent right wing relapse into "traditional authoritarianism," nevertheless is forced to admit that, "Fundamentalism in America is not simply an expression of backward yokels" (p. 337). What then can be said of the content of fundamentalism, since it is evidently so susceptible to stereotyping from so many sources, including the social sciences that claim to investigate it?

Ethridge and Feagin (1979) have recently reminded us that the social scientists who study fundamentalism have generally ignored its history and have tended to utilize rather ad hoc measures of fundamentalism that do violence to its very nature. Yet their own proposed solution, rooted in a Parsonian (Parsons, 1966) treatment of fundamentalism in terms of "boundary maintenance," perpetuates an error that can only be attributed to ignorance of the history of fundamentalism, a characteristic they have themselves bemoaned. By their own admission, such a Parsonian perspective ignores the content of belief in terms of the process by which the beliefs function, so that even "the reaction of some of the officers in the military to the new diversity of men's hair styles can be viewed as a *kind of* fundamentalism" (Ethridge & Feagin, 1979, p. 39, emphasis added). This "kind of" approach erroneously equates widely differing beliefs on the basis of their function, when in fact such beliefs radically vary in terms of both the content and source. We readily admit that such an approach simplifies social scientific investigation, allowing one to "bracket" the content or source of beliefs. Yet this approach remains only a proximate solution, since ultimately both the content and source of beliefs must at some point be confronted (Mannheim, 1936). The irony of all this is that the attempt to sidestep the content of beliefs, or to minimize them in terms of an apparently accepting liberal functionalism, is precisely one aspect of "modernism" that the fundamentalists oppose; in fact, it provides much of the grounding for their existence, if one simply notes the history of the concept. Furthermore, the "fundamentalist–modernist" debate is not over, as Moberg (1962) reminds us, nor is the history of this debate irrelevant to contemporary empirical assessments of fundamentalism, as Ethridge and Feagin (1979) have emphasized.

HISTORICAL CONSIDERATIONS

The stereotype of the fundamentalist is often one of a backward, hardly literate, and even less cultured person. Yet the origin of the American movement itself is usually traced to a series of twelve pamphlets published in 1910 by two successful Los Angeles *businessmen,* Lyon and Milton Stewart. Their pamphlets, entitled *The Fundamentals: A Testimony to the Truth,* were widely distributed, free of charge, to churches, prayer groups, Sunday schools, business and civic organizations, and to almost any other group who would accept them. The purpose of these pamphlets was to react to various "modernist" tendencies, particularly the belief that scientific advancements denied the validity of a literal interpretation of scripture and required the *reassessment* and *reinterpretation* of scripture in a manner congruent with the claims of modern science. Thus, the crux of fundamentalism was the *reaffirmation* of the literal interpretation of scripture, perceived as the verbally inspired and inerrant word of the fundamentalists' god. It is this affirmation of the literal truth of the revelatory word of the fundamentalists' god that is the one essential defining characteristic of fundamentalism, in both its historical and contemporary contexts (Cole, 1963; Furniss, 1963; Gasper, 1963; Sandeen, 1970). To ignore this conceptually central aspect of fundamentalism is to risk, at best, only tangentially touching base with the phenomenon of concern.

Yet despite the appeal to an absolute scriptural source, specific beliefs vary widely among fundamentalists; it would be at best a short-sightedness, quickly corrected by appropriate data, to try to identify fundamentalism by only a few specific beliefs. Although to identify such a core of beliefs would be easy, it would do little to illuminate the tremendous diversity among fundamentalists. For instance, many fundamentalists assent to such specific beliefs as the Virgin Birth, the atonement and bodily resurrection of Jesus, the imminent second coming of Christ, the natural depravity of man, and the bodily resurrection of faithful Christians. Indeed, these beliefs have been identified historically as the essence, with varying degrees of centrality, of the original fundamentalist pamphlets (Gasper, 1963), and probably account for the coining of the phrase "fundamentalist" by America's popular press just after the turn of the century. Yet given the complexity of the source to which fundamentalists appeal for their beliefs, it is not surprising that infinite variations in beliefs emerge. Indeed, as Photiadis (1978) has reminded us, part of the problem with the popular stereotyping of "fundamentalists" is that the term itself masks the great diversity that exists within their ranks. Furthermore, Ethridge and Feagin (1979) have factorially identified three forms of fundamentalism, even within such closely historically related denominations as the Disciples of Christ and the Church of Christ.

Hence, it is apparent that we ought not to expect a single, simple picture of fundamentalism to emerge. To expect so is perhaps to be trapped within biases that arise when the social distance between investigators and their subject matter is great (Drucker, 1971). Furthermore, the fundamentalist rooting of beliefs and actions within individual subjectivities provides for a radical foundation of individualism, with the extreme emphasis upon being "born again" or what historically was identified as the "New Birth" (Mathews, 1977). Perhaps the most correct though often overlooked parallel is the existential rooting of fundamentalism, which denys efforts at systematization so central to scientific efforts. This existential basis has been noted by historians who have attempted to illuminate the paradoxical role of a religion rooted in absolutes that nevertheless maximizes individualism (Gasper, 1963; Hill, 1972; Mathews, 1977) and by at least one contemporary social scientist who reminds us that existentialism is also a dominant influence in the "lost world" theology of Billy Graham, a most popular fundamental evangelist not likely to be linked to existentialism by most liberal intelligentsia (Apel, 1979).

WHERE ARE THE FUNDAMENTALISTS?

If we now turn to the social scientific data regarding fundamentalists, it is logical to start by attempting to locate American fundamentalists within a broad sociological context. Here the data are not surprising, for though it is true that fundamentalists can be found across all social classes and within a wide variety of geographical contexts, they tend to be situated in such a manner that Cox's (1977) rather condescending assessment of the Protestant nostalgia for a fundamentalism of "an allegedly more godly small-town Currier and Ives America" is not totally inappropriate or inaccurate after all.

As a general statement, social class and fundamentalism tend to be inversely related. In addition, the obvious fact that rural areas are assessed in general lower-class terms (almost inevitably confounding these two measures) means that rural areas also tend to be characterized by fundamentalism as one predominant religious ideology. Glock and Stark (1965) found in a nationwide survey that as a general rule religious conservatism, including fundamentalist beliefs, tended to characterize smaller communities. Nelson, Yokley, and Madron (1971) have more recently provided survey data reaffirming increased religious orthodoxy in more rural areas, a finding consistent with the more general conservative attitudes and behavior noted in rural areas (Glenn & Alston, 1967). Studies of southern Appalachia, an area containing some of America's most rural areas, continually affirm the importance of fundamentalist beliefs in rural Appalachia (DeJong & Ford, 1965; Ford, 1961; Jackson, 1961; Photiadis, 1978; Photiadis & Schnabel, 1977). In fact, Kerr (1978) has recently characterized the theological stance of the majority of churchpersons in Appalachia as being typified by five dominant beliefs that have long characterized fundamentalism in general: the virgin birth of Christ, literal interpretation of scripture, adult believer baptism, total salvation, and the second coming of Christ.

However, the fact that rural areas tend to be fundamentalistic does not imply that these areas do not exhibit wide diversities in religious beliefs. In addition, the general phenomena of social class and geographical region both complement and confound the problem of rural-urban differences. The fact that lower-class persons tend to be more fundamentalistic is so well established in the literature that recently Warner (1979) pointed out that such a class bias has emerged in the field that the existence of fundamental beliefs within other social classes has been ignored by researchers. Likewise, the general relationship between rural area, social class, and fundamentalism is tempered by concerns with geography. For instance, the predominance of fundamentalism in the South, considered purely as a geographical region, has long been noted (Broughton, 1975; Hill, 1967; Reed, 1972; Shortridge, 1977). Investigators are quick to note the predominance of Southern Baptists among the most conservative and fundamental of the major Protestant denominations. This group, in terms of Marty's (1970) "two Protestantism" thesis, has sided with and indeed often taken the leadership of the fundamentalist side in the "fundamentalist-modernist" debate. Hence, it is not surprising that recent studies of the popularity of Billy Graham indicate that while his popularity is increasing most rapidly in the North, it remains greatest in the South and heaviest in rural areas (Alston, 1973). These findings mesh nicely with a recent study indicating that those who attend a Billy Graham crusade tend to hold more conservative religious beliefs than appropriate control samples (Clelland, Hood, Lipsey, & Wimberly, 1974). However, these same data indicated that Graham crusade participants were definitely not lower-class, nor were they infrequent church attenders. These findings may at first glance appear incongruous with assumptions regarding lower-class, rural religiosity but in fact they concur with relevant empirical data. In particular, we refer to data concerning the relationship between church attendance and social class.

CHURCH ATTENDANCE AND RELIGIOSITY

It has been well established in research on religion and social class that religiosity as measured by frequency of church attendance varies *directly* with social class. In the past, the debates in the literature have centered not so much on the validity of this finding, but rather on the possibility that confounding variables may attenuate the relationship. For instance, Lenski (1961) provided the purely conceptual claim that lower-class persons are less involved in all types of formal social relationships and hence their lack of church participation is due more to this general fact than to less religiosity *per se*. However, Lenski's assertion had not until recently been empirically tested. Goode (1966) employed a sophisticated, multivariate procedure to test Lenski's assertion and to contest an earlier empirical study by Stark (1964) in a non-American population. Stark argued that even when controls are provided for general associational activity, the direct relationship between social class and church attendance still holds. Indeed, Stark suggests that the lower classes were less religious overall, based upon their lower rates of church attendance.

Goode's study is important not only for its methodological sophistication, but also because its samples were widely drawn from both rural and metropolitan areas, including southern Appalachia. The findings not only indicate that social class and church attendance are directly related precisely because the higher social classes participate more frequently in all forms of formal associational activity, but they also show that when appropriate statistical controls are applied, the direct relationship is greatly attenuated. Although Goode's data still suggest a weak but statistically significant direct relationship between social class and church participation, the data suggest that such participation has distinctively different meanings for differeing social classes. For the upper classes, church participation is merely part of a larger associational network, devoid of any unique meaning. For the lower classes, church participation remains uniquely religious, unrelated to other associational activities. Goode's findings mesh nicely with data indicating that as Southern Baptists migrate North, they tend to become more church oriented if they are upwardly mobile socially (Boling, 1967, 1972) or if they move into more urban areas (Jitodi, 1964). However, these data must be cautiously noted, in light of at least one study indicating that they are valid for whites but not blacks (Boling, 1975). Furthermore, as Van Roy, Bean, and Wood (1973) have shown, social mobility has very little effect on predicing orthodoxy beyond what can be accounted for by status of origin and distinction.

Overall it would appear that church participation primarily relates to a general associational factor, devoid of any particular religious significance. Hence, church attendance is not appropriately an indicator of religiosity and certainly not of religious fundamentalism. Still, the particular meaning of religious church participation among lower-class and rural persons must be confronted, since the apparent paradox remains that rural, lower-class persons tend to be more fundamentalistic in terms of uniquely religious beliefs and actions, yet less active in terms of church participation. However, before we confront this issue we must consider the additional confounding variable of education.

EDUCATION AND RELIGIOSITY

A rather persistent research tradition exists linking education with rejection of religion. For instance, Hoge and Petrillo (1978) have noted that despite wide denominational differences, as Protestant tenth-grade children became more abstract in their thinking they had an increased tendency to reject their church and its doctrines. This finding is particularly intriguing in light of Broughton's (1975) finding that concrete imagery is associated with traditional religiosity in American Protestantism and is confounded with general cognitive sophistication. Nelson (1973) has shown that, across denominations and controlling for social class, increased intellectualism is associated with increased *church attendance,* which in light of what we have noted previously, is not inconsistent with *decreased religiosity*, especially of a fundamental variety. Furthermore, Nelson's data suggest that across generations, intellectualism leads to increased church attendance while low intellectualism leads to decreased church attendance.

Several investigators have considered the particular importance of college education to religiosity, including church attendance. Feldman (1969, 1970) has concluded that religion is generally not very important to entering college students, and is even less important to seniors. Similarly, Wuthnow and Mellinger (1978) have compared religious defection in the Berkeley, California, area and concluded that generally disatisfaction with religion now occurs even prior to college but then tends to stabilize. Wuthnow and Glock (1973) indicate that entering college students who proclaim a conservative Protestant commitment are most likely to retain their commitment; if they change, they are likely to move in a liberal Protestant direction. The latter phenomenon attributed by Wuthnow and Glock to "increased cognitive sophistication." Yet these studies of defection from religion as a function of college attendance must be cautiously interpreted, in light of the general claim that the period from 18 to 30 years of age represents the greatest rejection of religion, regardless of education (Argyle & Beit-Hallahmi, 1975). Furthermore, at least one study (Dudley, 1978) has shown that defection from fundamentalist religion by adolescents at equivalent educational levels may be more a function of the quality of interpersonal relationships between their parents and religious authorities. However, overall data suggest that general notions of intellectualism are clearly associated to some degree with rejection of the more concrete, literal religious beliefs likely to characterize fundamentalism, even though intellectualism may also be associated with increased church attendance.

These conclusions must be tempered a bit in light of studies of the effects of education within particular religious orientations. For instance, studies of Mennonites have shown that they do not tend to liberalize their fundamental religious orientations as a function of college attendance (Hunsberger, 1976, 1978). Furthermore, general religious orthodoxy among Mennonites is more positively correlated with rural residence than with educational level (Kauffman, 1979), even though increased education apparently predicts increased church participation among Mennonites with equal belief commitments (Gaede, 1977). Also relevant is a study by Christensen and Cannon (1978) indicating that at Brigham Young University the general atmosphere has recently become more conservative, a change more evident in attitudes than in behavior. Finally, Berg (1971) found that self-identified fundamentalism tended to decrease as a function of Protestant seminary education, with early identifying fundamentalists tending to have high attrition rates regardless of denomination.

Nevertheless, the overall effects of education upon fundamentalism would appear to be negative, if we can make such a conclusion from the available data (which is at best suggestive). Because rural and lower social class persons tend to have less education, a rather congruent picture emerges that locates fundamentalism among the poor and disadvantaged, the dumb and downtrodden. Our phrasing is deliberate, for it smacks of stereotyping, and indeed this may be the case.

Blessed are the Poor?

One of the dominant explanatory theories used to explain the religion of the poor is deprivation theory. Dittes (1971) reminds us that this is an explanation at least as old as the Old Testament, where religion is rooted among nomads and exiles. This conception of religion continues in the New Testament, in which religion is existentially rooted in the poor, the sick, and the alienated. In fact, as Dittes (1971) correctly notes, "Among modern social scientists, one would be hard pressed to find any major theorists who did *not* formulate his understanding of religion as a compensation for deprivation" (p. 394). To illustrate Dittes's point, one need but confront examples from two pivotal theorists. First, Freud on one hand (1964) treats obviously fundamentalist beliefs as *illusional*, implying psychological deprivation (wish fulfillment) but no assertion with respect to the truth or falsity of such beliefs; on the other hand (1961) he treats religions as a *delusion*, implying not only more serious psychological deprivation (pathology) but tending to negate the truth claims of such beliefs in a move clearly unwarranted by purely methodological procedures. Second, Marx's (1964) treatment of religion as the "spirit of a spiritless situation" implies both its truth value with respect to expressions of suffering and distress and its alienating nature as "ideology." Importantly, what unites both Freud, Marx, and many less eminent deprivation theorists is their rejection of the truth value of religion. Marx does his more sophisticatedly than Freud. However, Mannheim (1936) reminds us that the move to explain the existence of beliefs purely in terms of existentially rooted factors is but part of the social scientific effort to avoid the ultimately crucial problem of the truth of falsity of the content of beliefs. Accordingly, we ought to suspect that current empirical treatments attempting to "test" deprivation theses are likely to be shortsighted concerning possible positive benefits of fundamentalist religious beliefs and practices, since the researchers are very likely socially and intellectually distant from their subjects. Since many excellent reviews of deprivation theory and the empirical research it has generated are available (Argyle & Beit-Hallahmi, 1975, pp. 191–207; Bibby, 1976; Bibby & Brinkerhoff, 1974; Hine, 1976; McNamara & George, 1978; Richardson, 1976), we shall restrict our own comments to those issues in deprivation theory most germane to fundamentalism, which is likely to be less favorably received even by those investigators most sympathetic to religion.

Glock (1964), whose work initiated the empirical tradition in deprivation research, initially defined deprivation as including any manner in which either a person or group felt lower by comparison to other persons or groups. Obviously, such a broad definition must be operationalized in some fashion. Much of the empirical research has attempted to solve this problem by using objective indicators of presumably obvious face validity as indicators of deprivation. Argyle and Beit-Hallahmi (1975) have noted that the kinds of deprivation that social scientists are likely to perceive have been numerous, and their own gross categorizations have been based on economic, social, organismic, ethical, and psychic characteristics. At the other end of the continuum is perhaps the use of such simple indicators of deprivation as a person's sex (Christopher, Fearon, McCoy, & Nobbe, 1971). The latter example is indicative of what Dittes (1971) has appropriately called "promiscuous empiricism" in response to the statistically sophisticated yet conceptually impoverished nature of many studies of deprivation.

The crucial question raised by simple attributions of deprivation based upon such presumably "objective indicators" as social class, status, education, or sex is: "By whose criteria are they objective?" This is particulary crucial with respect to fundamentalism, since the assumption that the lower class, the less educated, the rural—the fundamentalists—are "deprived" may in fact be unfairly stereotypical at several levels, not only in terms of who the fundamentalists are but what the *experience* of their life must be like (Campbell, Converse, & Rodgers, 1976; Warner, 1979; Lefever, 1977). Researchers in deprivation theory are becoming sensitive to this issue. For instance, both Hoge and Carroll (1978) and Bibby and Brinkerhoff (1974) have emphasized that measures of self-perceived deprivation are necessary in order to adequately test deprivation theories. However, when such efforts have been made, deprivation theory appears to be less than obviously valid. For instance, McNamara and George (1978) have recently utilized the data of Campbell *et al.* (1976) (collected in their massive "Quality of Life" study) in order to incorporate *felt deprivation* as a variable in testing deprivation theory. The results of their study generally indicate support for the thesis that the objectively deprived would be more religious than the objectively nondeprived. The study also found support for the thesis that the status disadvantaged, again as assessed by common objective indicators, would be more discontented with their lives. Overall, however, the data *do not* support deprivation theory if the crucial variable of felt deprivation is included. In particular, it was not found that religion made one's objectively hard life either easier to endure or personally happier. Furthermore, Hadawy and Roof (1978), analyzing data from the Campbell *et al.* (1976) study, emphasize that no combination of variables predicts much of the variance of felt psychological well-being. Thus, it appears that one must accept the view of McNamara and George (1978) that the issue is more effectively addressed by examining the *ways* in which religion is rooted in one's existential life situation and how it is "used"—regardless of one's objective social fate—than by seeking to find whether religion is merely a cushion against an otherwise harsh existence. This is particularly the case since both the content and the perceived source of fundamentalist beliefs are likely to contradict social scientific assessments of how religion *should* function, especially when confronting the deprived. For instance, Lefever (1977) has noted, "The poor, because of the daily existential crises they face, have an understanding of tragedy and suffering that is frequently lacking from the sensibilities of the nonpoor" (p. 232). So it is perhaps no accident that, as Apel (1979) has noted, Billy Graham in an address to Harvard University not only quoted the existentialist Sartre, but built his sermon upon the phrase for which Sartre is perhaps best known, "There is no exit from the human dilemma." Likewise, both Herberg (1960) and Marty (1959) have critiqued those religious orientations that attempt to minimize the tragic dimension of human existence. Lasch (1978) has recently provided a major critique of what he perceives as the effort to escape into a "culture of narcissism" in a fashion not unrelated to the attempt to avoid more tragic aspects of existence.

If, as fundamentalists often do, one existentially acknowledges a tragic sense of life, then conceptual reconsiderations of much of the social scientific literature about fundamentalism must be made. For instance, it would be absurd, as Lee and Clyde (1974) have noted, to assume that the religions of the poor are characterized by *anomie*, as many studies in the Durkheimian tradition claim. Clearly, an adherence to fundamentalist religious beliefs is itself a form of normatively guided behavior that ipso facto negates the simple claim that those beliefs are characterized by *"normlessness."* Hence, one need not be surprised by Hauser's (1976) failure to find a relationship between anomie and church attendance. Lefever (1977) emphasizes that what may appear as social disorganization from one perspective is in fact simply another form of social organization that is certainly not indicative of anomie, as many might want to claim.

In a related sense, the assumption that the fundamentally religious are psychopathological is conceptually absurd if the very religious beliefs and practices of these persons redundantly are used as indicators of their pathology. As Stark (1971) has noted, there is no firm empirical evidence to indicate a positive relationship between religiosity and psychopathology. He argues that it is logically absurd to assume that psychopathological states account for the existence of stable social groups. The more reasonable assumption is that psychopathology impedes religiosity as it does other phenomena, an assumption more consistent with available empirical evidence. For instance, psychopathology not only negatively correlates with normative forms of institutional religious behavior (Lindenthal, Myers, Pepper, & Stern, 1970); among the hospitalized mentally ill, personal dimensions of religiosity parallel declines in psychological well-being (Lowe, 1966). Furthermore, some investigators apparently expect a positive correlation between religion and mental health and they react negatively when they find little evidence to support this claim (Sanua, 1969).

Stark (1971), however, makes a distinction between conventional and pathological forms of religious commitment and clearly implies that what are likely to be associated with more fundamentalist beliefs and activities may in fact be pathologically rooted. This claim is so pervasive within the literature concerning religious fundamentalism that we shall use it, rather tangentially, as the basis for integrating the contents of the rest of this chapter. This claim too, appears to be but another stereotype that itself must be corrected before any significant social scientific illumination of fundamentalism can proceed.

A variety of methodological and conceptual studies have begun to suggest that the criteria by which social scientists evaluate the contemporary varieties of fundamentalism are hopelessly and perplexedly biased. This is particularly the case with the intense religious experiences common to fundamentalists. For instance, the tendency to evaluate negatively almost any form of intense personal experience is likely to lead scientists to seek pathological explanations for such experiences rather than more normal socially rooted explanations. Many of the instruments used to assess the presumed psychopathology of such experiences are themselves explicitly contaminated with anti-fundamentalist biases. For instance, the MMPI contains items with content specifically rooted in fundamentalist religious beliefs and scored such that agreement is reflective of psychopathology. It is not surprising that persons with more fundamental religious beliefs are likely to appear "pathological," especially when using subscales heavily loaded with these particular items from the MMPI (Hood, 1974).

Within the context of field research, it is readily apparent that "extreme" religious behaviors among certain southern Appalachia fundamentalistic sects are nevertheless normatively sanctioned and legitimated by particular fundamentalistic sects; they cannot be labeled "pathological" except by researchers with social scientific prejudices. For instance, the phenomenon of serpent handling (practiced by some southern Appalachia sects), which might appear irrational to an outsider, is likely to be quickly legitimated by participants with appeal to specific scriptural reference (Mark 16: 17, 18). Likewise, fire handling has scriptural legitimacy for some southern Appalachia fundamentalistic sects (Isaiah 43:2; Daniel 3:20–27). Field studies of such phenomena indicate normative patterns and practices within these sects, belying any simple *a priori* conceptual claim to the psychopathology of the participants (Daugherty, 1978; Kane, 1978; La Barre, 1962). Contrary to some expectations, one might note that not only is serpent handling perhaps a genuine theological innovation of southern Appalachia, but sensitive observers have noted that such "extremist" activities as fire handling, drinking poisonous substances ("Hallelujah cocktails"), and serpent handling are legitimate sacramental activities within the confines of these sects (Daugherty, 1978; Kane, 1978). Likewise, Simmonds, Richardson, and Harder (1976) have noted that even though converts to a Jesus commune indicated "maladjustment" on an objective personality test, such persons were obviously not maladjusted within their own social group.

Appropriate consideration of intense religious experiences cannot ignore the fact that such experiences are clearly rooted in the history of evangelical and fundamentalist religion in America. For instance, Mathews (1977) has emphasized that intense emotional experiences generated within fundamental and evangelical sects are often the intended target of preaching activity, especially in the lower classes and rural areas. Mathews (1977) notes that however "irrational" such experiences might appear to outsiders, they in fact are normatively governed and serve the psychological function of equating all persons in terms of a common experiential relationship to their god. Similarly, Lefever (1977) and Schwartz (1970) have emphasized the role of such experiences in offering an alternative to normally sanctioned status differential between persons within a purely "worldly" oriented ideology. This latter point has also been described in historical terms as a radical rejection of the social system by evangelical and fundamental religious groups whose apparent acceptance of the social structure (in terms of their presumed conservatism) in fact makes a more radical rejection of the hierarchical structure of society (Gasper, 1963; Mathews, 1977).

LIBERALIZING FACTORS

The rejection of the hierarchical ordering of society, historically rooted in fundamentalism and evangelicalism, is not unrelated to contemporary research regarding what Hadden (1969), in an aptly titled work, has called *The Gathering Storm in the Churches*. Relevant to our discussion here is the evidently increasing disparity between laity and clergy in terms of political and religious liberalism, indicated by increasingly liberal clergy heavily concerned with social activism (Hadden, 1969; Hoge, 1976). This phenomenon, however, apparently is at least partly related to organizational principles, with social activism and religious liberalism associated with churches that are characterized by more hierarchical organizations (Woodrum, 1978). Furthermore, Takayama and Sachs (1976) demonstrated that, even when controlled for social class, Baptist churches with hierarchical structures maintained a more liberal stance than other Baptist churches when faced with court-ordered Memphis integration.

Related to organizational factors predisposing more liberal theological stances is research suggesting that the more liberal theologies are likely to be rooted in social scientific metahpors rather than in more fundamental orthodoxies. For instance, Klausner (1964) has noted that what he terms "the religio-psychiatric" movement is an affair between liberal Protestantism and the social sciences. Stark and Glock (1968) note that a largely social scientifically rooted ethicalism replaces orthodoxy for those church members demanding social activism. Similarly, Smith (1972) has shown that clergy wives tend to adopt a more social scientific perspective within urban environments, while rural clergy wives tend to maintain religious orthodoxy. Among Catholic samples it has been shown that dissident protests in a southern town tended to be characterized by a "psychotherapeutic ethic" rather than by a commitment to church authority (Schneider & Zurcher, 1970). Likewise, among Catholic laity, Dixon and Hoge (1979) have shown that the more fundamentally oriented tend to stress evangelicalism rather than the social action favored by those with more ethical orientations. The fact that these findings parallel earlier research with Protestants demonstrates that the more fundamentally orthodox laity stress evangelicalism over social activism (Hoge, Perry, & Klever, 1978).

The distinctions between more fundamentally, "other worldly" oriented orthodoxies and more ethically, "worldly" oriented ideologies not only are a contemporary reflection of the continuing "fundamentalist-modernist" controversy, but they have also served to foster new conceptualizations of religion that are important in guiding future empirical research. One important contribution is Davidson's (1972) clarification of vertical and horizontal dimensions of religiosity.

Davidson has argued that religions can serve either as havens for the oppressed and downtrodden, the sick and alienated, and all that the deprivation thesis implies *or* as centers for protest and political activism for the radically socially concerned. One need go no further than the title of recently quite popular books on religion to illustrate each side of Davidson's claim: Benton's (1965) *The Comfortable Pew* for the former and Berger's (1961) *The Noise of Solemn Assemblies* for the latter. Davidson's conceptual contribution is to identify a vertical religious dimension primarily concerned with personal "other worldly" concerns and a horizontal religious dimension primarily concerned with social or "this worldly" concerns. Not surprisingly, Davidson places fundamentalism primarily on the vertical dimension by the very nature of the items used to assess this dimension (1972, p. 68). This is a correct placement considering fundamentalism in its historical and theological context. However, it makes empirical assessments of certain consequences of fundamentalism rather tenuous at best, since it would be difficult to make an *independent* "vertical" assessment of fundamentalism as on such variables as social activism. Furthermore, the failure to appreciate the theological stance of fundamentalism as a vertically oriented theology has led to serious conceptual problems with otherwise sophisticated methodological studies. Once again the danger is in stereotyping fundamentalism, especially in the face of impoverished conceptual appreciations of the content of its diverse theologies.

COMPASSION AND PREJUDICE

Rokeach (1969a, 1969b) has tried to demonstrate that religiously oriented persons are in fact quite "incompassionate" as measured by a variety of value-oriented measures of social activism. Furthermore, he claims that even within Protestant denominations among the more likely fundamentalist denominations such as Baptists, values such as "salvation" tend to negatively correlate with social activist compassion measures. Yet even assuming these data to be adequate, one need not except Rokeach's (1969a) "hypocrisy" explanation. Obviously, by the very nature of their theological commitment, fundamentalists are likely to rate salvation *relatively* more important than social activism of any kind; from their perspective, to do so is neither hypocritical nor incompassionate. Within the vertical orientation of a fundamentalist, social activism, however important, is but an effort to ameliorate conditions within time that must not override the fundamentalist's more pressing concern—the eternal salvation of his or her soul. Hence, Rokeach's study is not a test of religious social compassion, but a rather weak empirical reflection of a theological commitment—a commitment that can be judged only on terms other than the more empirical relative ranking of values. Indeed, it is not surprising that Rokeach's data suggest that a fundamentalism-modernism dimension within Protestantism corresponds rather nicely with the relative ordering of denominations on the salvation/compassion relationship. This is but another way of indicating fundamentalism's possibly unique position among modern faiths, a point not inconsistent with Sandeen's (1967) claim that fundamentalism is historically a genuine theological innovation. Similarly, it corresponds with factor analytic studies indicating that fundamentalism-liberalism is either a dimension of modern faith commitment (Broen, 1957) or a distinct factor in and of itself (Gorsuch & McFarland, 1974).

Furthermore, studies relating social activism and fundamentalism must consider the specific content of fundamentalist beliefs in terms of the broader methodological issue of the paradoxical effects of belief saliency upon any orthodoxy-consequence claims. In particular, it is apparent that only when the content of belief orthodoxy is relevant to a particular social consequence and the saliency of that belief is high can one expect empirical relationships to emerge (Bord & Faulkner, 1975; Gibbs, Mueller, & Wood, 1973; Roof & Perkins, 1975). It again is apparent that the *relative* merit of personal salvation versus social compassion is expectedly different for various groups along the "fundamentalist-modernist" continuum not only in terms of general theological orientation, but also in terms of specific beliefs.

Not surprisingly, empirical studies that have attempted to replicate Rokeach's findings among such specific religious groups as the Mennonites have generally found them to be "incompassionate," especially when the social conventionality of beliefs is considered (Kauffman, 1979; Rusby & Thrush, 1973). Much conceptual work needs to be done before empirical tests of social compassion among fundamentalist religious groups can be more fruitfully conducted. The empirical data available at present are of minimal value and as unexpected as would be the failure to find Christian Scientists in medical school.

As an aside, one might note that research suggesting that religiosity is more relevant to "victimless" crimes (such as drug addiction and alcoholism) than to presumably more serious crimes directed toward others needs to be meaningfully incorporated into a perspective that considers the particular content and meaning of "the personal" in fundamentalist theologies (Albrecht, Chadwick, & Alcorn, 1977; Burkett & White, 1974; Peek, Chalfant, & Milton, 1979). Again, while one is free to impose a particular perspective upon a set of data, the very imposition of that perspective suggests, in an existential sense, an alternative. It must be recognized that, in fact, fundamentalists have such an alternative whose content cannot simply be ignored if a more adequate scientific understanding is to be forthcoming.

Closely related to the claim that the religious, especially the fundamentally religious, are socially incompassionate, is the claim that the religious are prejudiced. Gorsuch and Aleshire (1974) have recently provided an exhaustive review of the mass of literature concerning this claim. Although their claim of a curvilinear relationship between church attendance and prejudice is a fair conclusion from the relevant literature, their claim that the intrinsically, nonfundamentalist, and theologically discriminating are the least prejudiced must be qualified. What is of concern here is not that a particular type of religious person has been empirically found to be more tolerant, but rather the implication that another type is the culprit: the fundamentalist.

Gorsuch and Aleshire (1974, pp. 295–296) cite at least fifteen studies that test the relationship between prejudice, variously measured, and religious fundamentalism. All fifteen of these studies essentially find a positive relationship between prejudice and fundamentalism. Such empirical infallibility is rare in the social sciences and suggest either a bedrock of firm fact upon which to build a theoretical edifice or a pervasive bias to be reassessed. We suggest that the latter is the case, not only in terms of various theological interpretations that must be considered in assessing the meaning of apparent prejudice as measured by general attitude or social distance scales, but also in terms of authoritarian and dogmatic measures.

Many investigators who find a relationship between fundamentalism and prejudice explain the relationship in terms of authoritarianism. For instance, several researchers have reported that, at least within America, orthodoxy and ethnocentrism are related (Gregory, 1957; Keedy, 1958; Siegman, 1962). Similarly, Photiadis and Biggar (1962) and Photiadis and Johnson (1963) argue that fundamentalism (orthodoxy) is related to the social distance of minorities because the orthodox are more authoritarian. Photiadis and Schweiker (1970) have argued that more authoritarian persons tend to join more authoritarian religious organizations, presumably including fundamentalist groups.

However, Hoge and Carroll (1973) have indicated that it is dogmatism and not the theological content of beliefs that determines prejudice, and Gilmore (1969) has shown that even among persons with similar fundamentalist beliefs, the dogmatism with which such beliefs are held varies. Stark (1971, pp. 171–175) indicates no empirical support for a relationship between authoritarianism and conventional religiosity and warns of the tendency to repeat claims only widely assumed to be empirically well-substantiated. In fact he concludes:

> The widespread belief that there is a strong relationship between religious orthodoxy and authoritarianism appears to be a prominent instance of this tendency to transform suspicions and speculations into certainties. (Stark, 1971, p. 172)

It appears that a critical reassessment of the literature relating prejudice to fundamentalism is needed, both in terms of what mediating role variables such as authoritarianism might play and in terms of how indices to assess such variables might themselves prejudice fundamentalists in terms of the theological content of their beliefs. It is ironic that the relevant empirical literature is so consistent on a purely empirical level and yet apparently finds no compassion or tolerance among a religious group whose religious practices have historically fostered an equality among races both in the content of their theology and in the unique nature of their religious experience (Mathews, 1977). Indeed, it is particularly ironic that the rich influence of nonwhite, non-American cultural factors upon fundamentalism and evangelicalism is apparently unnoticed by persons conducting purely empirically oriented research without guidance from theological and historical considerations (Hudson, 1972; Mathews, 1977).

ASSOCIATION PATTERNS

If the issue of social compassion and prejudice is in need of reassessment, especially in terms of historically and theologically influenced conceptualizations that may, at a minimum, shed a different light upon the meaning of empirical findings, a final area of research regarding patterns of relationships among fundamentalists cannot go unnoticed. This research is ultimately rooted in Toennies' (1957) concepts of gemeinshaft and gesellschaft, more typically expressed in terms of the concepts of community and association. For our purposes the most suggestive area of this research are empirical claims, congruent with its historical reality (Mathews, 1977), that fundamentalism is related to communal rather than associational organizational patterns. For instance, Anderson (1969) found not only that matched cities differing in proportion of Protestant/Catholic majorities varied along a communal-associational dimension with the Protestant-dominated city more communal, but that within denominations, more conservative bodies were more communally oriented. Similarly, Moberg (1970) has provided data suggesting that within Protestant churches in Milwaukee, those more fundamentally oriented were more communal. Nelson (1971) has argued that as society becomes more differentiated, churches tend to be more associational, a finding one suspects for purely social considerations also characterizes rural-urban church patterns. Furthermore, in terms of a fundamentalist–modernist debate, Hiller (1971) argues that more communally and conservatively organized churches avoid ecumenicalism precisely because they wish to protect a community of shared values and commitments. Hence, what appears as reaction against liberalization and social progress may in fact be interpreted as serving other positive functions from a more fundamentalist perspective. These data are not unrelated to the issues of hierarchical organization discussed previously and they suggest that even attitudinal studies along a "local-cosmopolitan" dimension should indeed prove to be powerful predictors of religiosity, as recent research is beginning to suggest (Roof, 1972).

However, one must again be cautious in interpreting the meaning of these data, especially in light of the negative connotation likely to be attributed to the more "restricted" view of locally oriented believers committed to their church in a pattern of communality while nevertheless oriented to a vertical dimension of religiosity likely to be seen as less relevant by their more liberal, cosmopolitan, and "worldly" brethren. Otherwise excellent treatments of the conservative dimension of fundamentalism have suffered from this shortsightedness (Gabennesch, 1972; Wuthnow, 1973).

FUNDAMENTALISM: OLD OR NEW?

We cannot come full circle in this discussion of fundamentalism and social psychology due to the nature of the field itself. We simply have no social psychology of fundamentalism. The literature is historically uninformed, fragmented, methodologically weak, and conceptually biased. Yet the future holds promise. The recent work by Ethridge and Feagin (1979) perhaps marks the application of more sophisticated statistical techniques to differentiations within wide varieties of fundamentalism, and general religious fervor threatens a concern with a "new fundamentalism" that should make researchers more sophisticated with respect to the "old." Let us conclude by briefly noting two examples.

With respect to the "old fundamentalism," Kelley's (1972) popular book, *Why Conservative Churches Are Growing*, has stimulated research helpful to the study of fundamentalism for at least two reasons. First, Kelley (1978) has more recently emphasized that more relevant to his thesis is the fact that passionately believing, biblically rooted, and ultimately demanding churches are growing while more liberally oriented, ecumenical, and compromising churches are declining. The overriding variable appears to be nothing other than *seriousness*. In Kelley's (1978) own words:

> If ecumenical churches feel that they are as serious about what they believe as fundamentalists are, then it behooves them to find appropriate ways to exercise that seriousness. Why should the devil have all the good tunes? (p. 171)

Second, empirically oriented research regarding the growth of more "conservative" denominations suggest that there are operating many of the variables that we have suggested are associated with fundamentalism. For instance, Bibby and Brinkerhoff (1973) investigated the membership additions to 20 evangelical congregations over a five-year period and found that only 10% were converts from outside the evangelical community, and even many of these were converted by such factors as intermarriage. What appeared to account for growth was the ability to retain children (20% of growth) as congregation members and the reaffiliation or migrant affiliation of previous church members (70% of growth). These findings are congruent with research indicating that more conservative churches maintain high levels of overall active participation, including the continued participation of younger members (Bibby, 1978; Bouma, 1979). While the data are far from conclusive, they do appear to indicate that more conservative churches are at least resistant to declines in membership and hence provide a stable base within which specific varieties of fundamentalism are likely to persist, regardless of other trends.

Finally, with respect to the "new fundamentalism," one must note that the widely acknowledged emergence of the "new religions" (Needleman & Baker, 1978) not only has stimulated and revitalized the entire field of the social scientific study of religion, but promises to be important for the study of religious fundamentalism in particular. As Robbins, Anthony, and Richardson (1978) have noted:

> Although there is clearly room for substantial debate about the significance of new patterns of religiosity . . . it seems apparent that some sort of cultural re-orientation is taking place and that rational humanistic religiosity as embodied in liberal denominational Christianity is being repudiated. (p. 113)

Already the patterns are immense and varied, suggesting a grouping for appropriate forms. Yet clearly many of these patterns are characterized by a "new fundamentalism" in which Durkheimian notions of the sacred, not perceived to be grounded in any social determinants, absolute, and utterly not profane, are clearly present. Such views, especially when expressed in literal biblical terms, mesh nicely with the "old fun-

damentalism" that Glock and Stark (1965) had predicted was an innocence that could not long maintain itself. Yet maintain itself it has, and
for social scientists still prophetically inclined, the task of predicting
"the return of the sacred"—to use a phrase already stimulating much
debate (Wilson, 1979)—is well underway. And while predictions vary,
the reemergence of evangelical, fundamental Christianity as a major
religious option is well noted (Bell, 1977; Bellah, 1976). Yet, although
this return to the sacred, if it is that, may be dialectically encountered in
new forms and become a "second innocence" for some, one must not
forget that it continues as an uninterrupted "innocence" for many others. If one accepts these claims, then it is apparent that research conceptually influenced by something other than precepts regarding "modernist" religious perspectives or scientific reductionism is badly needed. For
not only do we not have a body of scientific knowledge about the "old
fundamentalism," we also do not have the conceptual tools to confront
the "new fundamentalism." It is not surprising that much debate regarding the appropriate scientific study of religion has centered upon
appropriate methodological procedures and conceptual orientations,
both of which continually call for "new" sciences of religion (Lemert,
1975).

Thus, we might anticipate that future research will focus upon more
sympathetic, yet objective, investigations of more fundamentally oriented religious practices, if for no other reason than that the "new
fundamentalisms" are likely to be located with a population that shares
a closer social distance to those who will likely investigate them. Not
only should this help produce a body of empirical findings more meaningfully reflective of the existentially rooted claim of these new religions
(Stone, 1978), but they should suggest meaningful parallels to the "old
fundamentalism," which has been rather casually dismissed by even the
most sensitive of scientists who study religion.

This dismissal is most unfortunate, precisely because simplistic
views of fundamentalists as ignorant, deprived, and having nothing to
offer their more intelligent, sophisticated brethren feed into stereotypical modes of thought that may be more characteristic of the scientific
study of fundamentalism than of fundamentalism itself. It would appear
that fundamentalism is more appropriately empirically confronted with
a sympathetic consideration of existential concerns. Certainly fundamentalism represents a refusal to accept many tendencies within modern cultures that themselves are becoming more and more problematic.
Yet this refusal also has its vicissitudes. This refusal remains relatively
nonproblematic for many rural persons, given an environment that is
congenial to a more communal situation in which families remain intact
and churches that serve more localized and less heterogeneous groups;

it also is becoming a socially controversial alternative for those in more cosmopolitan environments in which the values and life-styles mandated by fundamentalism are perhaps becoming more attractive, yet problematically realizable, alternatives.

What we have in this chapter, then, is not a social psychology *of* fundamentalism but a mere social psychology *and* fundamentalism. On the more social side, we can at least locate some of the fundamentlists, while on the psychological side we can say little that is meaningfully rooted in scientific fact. Much remains to be done, since fundamentalism in its numerous varieites, both old and new, cannot be without scientific importance. If much of the tone in this chapter appears apologetic, so must it be, for despite the immense gulf between our own views and those of the fundamentalists, it is evident that their treatment at the altar of science has been less than fair. Yet this is not to impugn the integrity of any efforts so far but only to suggest the more pervasive problem noted by Argyle and Beit-Hallahmi (1975) in the broader context of social psychology and religion in general: "If and when psychologists develop an extended view of human nature and the research methods to go with it, the relation between psychology and religion may be very different" (p. 207). What this might mean for fundamentalism in particular, old or new, remains to be seen.

ACKNOWLEDGMENTS

Appreciation is expressed to Ms. Debbie Edgemon, who kindly typed the manuscript and to Ms. Rebecca Stern, who edited the original draft.

REFERENCES

Albrecht, S. L., Chadwick, B. A., & Alcorn, D. S. Religiosity and deviance: Applications of an attitude-behavior contingent consistency model. *Journal for the Scientific Study of Religion*, 1977, *16*, 263–274.

Alston, J. P. Review of the polls: The popularity of Billy Graham, 1963–1969. *Journal for the Scientific Study of Religion*, 1973, *12*, 227–230.

Anderson, C. H. Denominational differences in a white Protestant community. *Review of Religious Research*, 1969, *2*, 66–72.

Apel, W. D. The lost world of Billy Graham. *Review of Religious Research*, 1979, *20*, 138–149.

Argyle, M., & Beit-Hallahmi, B. *The social psychology of religion*. London: Routledge & Kegan Paul, 1975.

Bell, D. The return of the sacred? *British Journal of Sociology*, 1977, *28*, 419–449.

Bellah, R. Christianity and symbolic realism. *Journal for the Scientific Study of Religion*, 1970, *9*, 89–96.

Bellah, R. N. New religious consciousness and the crisis in modernity. In C. Glock & R. N. Bellah (Eds.), *The new religious consciousness*. Berkeley: University of California Press, 1976.

Benton, P. *The comfortable pew*. New York: J. P. Lippincott, 1965.

Berg, P. L. Self-identified fundamentalism among Protestant Seminarians: A study of persistence and change in value orientations. *Review of Religious Research*, 1971, 88–94.

Berger, P. L. *The noise of solemn assembles*. New York: Doubleday, 1961.

Berger, P. L. *The precarious vision*. New York: Doubleday, 1967.

Bibbey, R. W. Reply to Richardson's critique. *Review of Religious Research*, 1976, 17, 160–161.

Bibby, R. W. Why conservative churches really are growing: Kelley revisited. *Journal for the Scientific Study of Religion*, 1978, 17, 129–137.

Bibby, R. W., & Brinkerhoff, M. B. The circulation of the saints: A study of people who join conservative churches. *Journal for the Scientific Study of Religion*, 1973, 12, 273–283.

Bibby, R. W., & Brinkerhoff, M. B. Sources for religious involvement: Issues for future empirical investigations. *Review of Religious Research*, 1974, 15, 71–79.

Boling, T. E. Southern Baptists in the North. *Review of Religious Research* 1967, 8, 95–100.

Boling, T. E. Southern Baptist migrants and converts: A study of Southern religion in the urban North. *Sociological Analysis*, 1972, 33, 188–195.

Boling, T. E. Black and white religion: A comparison in the lower class. *Sociological Analysis*, 1975, 1, 73–80.

Bord, R. J., & Faulkner, J. E. Religiosity and secular attitudes: The case of Catholic Pentecostals. *Journal for the Scientific Study of Religion*, 1975, 14, 257–270.

Bouma, G. D. The real reason one conservative church grew. *Review of Religious Research*, 1979, 20, 127–137.

Broen, W. F. A factor-analytic study of religious attitudes. *Journal of Abnormal and Social Psychology*, 1957, 54, 176–179.

Broughton, W. Theistic conceptions in American Protestantism. *Journal for the Scientific Study of Religion*, 1975, 14, 331–344.

Burkett, S. R., & White, M. Hellfire and delinquency. *Journal for the Scientific Study of Religion*, 1974, 13, 455–462.

Campbell, A., Converse, P. E., & Rodgers, W. L. *The quality of American life: Perceptions, evaluations, and satisfactions*. New York: Russell Sage Foundation, 1976.

Christensen, H. T., & Cannon, K. L. The fundamentalist emphasis at Brigham Young University: 1935–1973. *Journal for the Scientific Study of Religion*, 1978, 17, 53–57.

Christopher, S., Fearon, J., McCoy, J., & Nobbe, C. Social deprivation and religiosity. *Journal for the Scientific Study of Religion*, 1971, 10, 385–392.

Clelland, D. A., Hood, T. C., Lipsey, C. M., & Wimberley, R. In the company of the converted: Characteristics of a Billy Graham Crusade audience. *Sociological Analysis*, 1974, 35, 45–56.

Cole, S. G. *The history of fundamentalism*. Hamden, Conn.: Archon Books, 1963.

Comp, G., & Spilka, B. *Faith and behavior: Religion in introductory psychology texts of the 1950's and 1970's*. Paper presented at the Annual Meeting of the Society for the Scientific Study of Religion, San Antonio, Texas, October 1979.

Cox, H. *On not leaving it to the snake*. New York: MacMillan, 1967.

Cox, H. *Turning East*. New York: Simon & Schuster, 1977.

Daugherty, M. L. Serpent-handling as sacrament. In J. D. Photiadis (Ed.), *Religion in Appalachia*. Morgantown: West Virginia University Press, 1978.

Davidson, J. D. Belief as an independent variable. *Journal for the Scientific Study of Religion*, 1972, 11, 65–75.

De Jong, G. F., & Ford, T. R. Religious fundamentalism and denominational preference in the Southern Appalachia region. *Journal for the Scientific Study of Religion*, 1965, 5, 24–33.

Desroche, H. *Jacob and the angel*. Amherst: University of Massachusetts Press, 1973.

Dittes, J. The psychology of religion. In G. Lindzey & E. Aronson (Eds.), *The handbook of social psychology* (Vol. 5). Reading, Mass.: Addison-Wesley, 1969.

Dittes, J. Conceptual deprivation and statistical rigour. *Journal for the Scientific Study of Religion*, 1971, *10*, 393–395.

Dixon, R. C., & Hoge, D. R. Models and priorities of the Catholic Church as held by surburban laity. *Review of Religious Research*, 1979, *20*, 150–167.

Douglas, W. Religion. In N. L. Farberow (Ed.), *Taboo topics*. New York: Atherton Press, 1966.

Drucker, E. Cognitive styles and class stereotypes. In Eleanor B. Leacock (Ed.), *The culture of poverty*. New York: Simon & Schuster, 1971.

Dudley, R. L. Alienation from religion in adolescents from fundamentalist religious homes. *Journal for the Scientific Study of Religion*, 1978, *17*, 389–398.

Ethridge, F. M., & Feagin, J. R. Varieties of "fundamentalism": A conceptual and empirical analysis of two Protestant denominations. *Sociological Quarterly*, 1979, *20*, 37–48.

Feldman, K. A. Change and stability of religious orientations during college (Part I). *Review of Religious Research*, 1969, *2*, 40–60.

Feldman, K. A. Chance and stability of religious orientations during college (Part II). *Review of Religious Research*, 1970, *2*, 103–128.

Ford, T. R. Religious thought and beliefs in the Southern Appalachians as revealed by an attitude survey. *Review of Religious Research*, 1961, *3*, 2–21.

Freud, S. *Civilization and its discontent*. New York: W. W. Norton, 1961.

Freud, S. *The future of an illusion*. New York: Anchor, 1964.

Friedrichs, R. W. Sociological paradigms: Analysis of theology, apocalypsy, and prophecy. *Sociological Analysis*, 1971, *32*, 1–6.

Furniss, N. F. *The fundamentalist controversy, 1918–1931*. Hamden, Conn.: Archon Books, 1963.

Gabennesch, H. Authoritarianism as world view. *American Journal of Sociology*, 1972, *77*, 857–875.

Gaede, S. Religious participation, socioeconomic status, and belief-orthodoxy. *Journal for the Scientific Study of Religion*, 1977, *16*, 245–253.

Garrett, W. R. Troublesome transcendence: The supernatural in the scientific study of religion. *Sociological Analysis*, 1974, *35*, 167–180.

Gasper, L. *The fundamentalist movement*. Paris: Mouton, 1963.

Gibbs, D. G., Mueller, S. A., & Wood, J. R. Doctrinal orthodoxy, salience, and the consequential dimension. *Journal for the Scientific Study of Religion*, 1973, *12*, 33–52.

Gilmore, S. K. Personality differences between high and low dogmatism groups of pentecostal believers. *Journal for the Scientific Study of Religion*, 1969, *8*, 161–164.

Glenn, N. D., & Alston, J. P. Rural-urban differences in reported attitude and behavior. *The Southwest Social Science Quarterly*, 1967, *47*, 381–400.

Glock, C. Y. The role of deprivation in the origin and evolution of social groups. In R. Lee & M. E. Marty (Eds.), *Religion and social conflict*. New York: Oxford University Press, 1964.

Glock, C. Y., & Stark, R. *Religion and society in tension*. Chicago: Rand McNally, 1965.

Goode, E. Social class and church participation. *American Journal of Sociology*, 1966, *72*, 102–111.

Gorsuch, R. L., & Aleshire, D. Christian faith and prejudice: Review of research. *Journal for the Scientific Study of Religion*, 1974, *13*, 281–307.

Gorsuch, R. L., & McFarland, S. Single vs. multiple-item scales for measuring religious values. *Journal for the Scientific Study of Religion*, 1974, *11*, 53–65.

Gregory, W. E. The orthodoxy of the authoritarian personality. *Journal of Social Psychology*, 1957, *92*, 153–154.

Hadaway, C. K., & Roof, W. C. Religious commitment and the quality of life in American society. *Review of Religious Research*, 1978, *19*, 295–307.

Hadden, J. K. *The gathering storm in the churches*. Garden City, N.Y.: Doubleday, 1969.

Hauser, W. J. Anomie and religiosity: An empirical re-examination. *Journal for the Scientific Study of Religion*, 1976, *15*, 69–74.

Herberg, W. *Protestant-Catholic-Jew*. New York: Doubleday, 1960.

Hill, S. S., Jr. *Southern churches in crisis*. New York: Holt, Rinehart & Winston, 1967.

Hill, S. S., Jr. Toward a chapter for a Southern theology. In S. S. Hill, Jr. (Ed.), *Religion and the solid South*. Nashville, Tenn.: Abingdon Press, 1972.

Hiller, H. Community as a dimension of ecumenical negativism. *Review of Religious Research*, 1971, 11–114.

Hine, V. H. The deprivation and disorganization theories of social movements. In I. I. Zaretsky & M. P. Leone (Eds.), *Religious movements in contemporary America*. Princeton: Princeton University Press, 1976.

Hodges, D. L. Breaking a scientific taboo: Putting assumptions about the supernatural into scientific theories of religion. *Journal for the Scientific Study of Religion*. 1974, *13*, 393–408.

Hoge, D. R. *Division in the Protestant house*. Philadelphia: Westminster, 1976.

Hoge, D. R., & Carroll, J. W. Religiosity and prejudice in Northern and Southern churches. *Journal for the Scientific Study of Religion*, 1973, *12*, 181–197.

Hoge, D. R., & Carroll, J. W. Determinants of commitment and participation in surburban Protestant churches. *Journal for the Scientific Study of Religion*, 1978, *17*, 107–127.

Hoge, D. R., & Petrillo, G. H. Development of religious thinking in adolescents: A test of Goldman's theories. *Journal for the Scientific Study of Religion*, 1978, *17*, 139–154.

Hoge, D. R., Perry, E. L., & Klever, G. L. Theology as a source of disagreement about Protestant church goals and priorities. *Review of Religious Research*, 1978, *19*, 116–138.

Hood, R. W., Jr. Psychological strength and the report of intense religious experience. *Journal for the Scientific Study of Religion*, 1974, *13*, 65–71.

Hood, R. W., Jr. Conceptual criticisms of regressive explanations of mysticism. *Review of Religious Research*, 1976, *17*, 179–188.

Hudson, C. The structure of a fundamentalist Christian belief-system. In S. S. Hill, Jr. (Ed.), *Religion and the solid South*. Nashville, Tenn.: Abingdon Press, 1972.

Hunsberger, B. Background religious denomination, parental emphasis, and the religious orientation of university students. *Journal for the Scientific Study of Religion*, 1976, *15*, 251–255.

Hunsberger, B. The religiosity of college students: Stability and change over years at the university *Journal for the Scientific Study of Religion*, 1978, *17*, 159–164.

Jackson, A. K. Religious beliefs and expressions of the Southern highlander. *Review of Religious Research*, 1961, *3*, 21–39.

Jitodi, T. T. Migrant status and church attendance. *Social Forces*, 1964, *43*, 241–248.

Kane, S. M. Holiness fire handling in Southern Appalachia: A psychophysical analysis. In J. D. Photiadis (Ed.), *Religion in Appalachia*. Morgantown: West Virginia University Press, 1978.

Kauffman, J. H. Social correlates of spiritual maturity among North American Mennonites. *Sociological Analysis*, 1979, *40*, 27–42.

Keedy, T. C. Anomie and religious orthodoxy. *Sociology and Social Research*, 1958, *43*, 34–37.

Kelley, D. M. *Why conservative churches are growing*. New York: Harper & Row, 1972.

Kelley, D. M. Comment: Why conservative churches are still growing. *Journal for the Scientific Study of Religion*, 1978, *17*, 165–172.

Kerr, J. M. A pastor's view of religion in Appalachia. In J. D. Photiadis (Ed.), *Religion in Appalachia*. Morgantown: West Virginia University, 1978.

Klausner, S. V. The religo-psychiatric movement. *Review of Religious Research*, 1964, *5*, 63–74.

La Barre, W. *They shall take up serpents*. New York: Schocken Books, 1962.

Lasch, C. *The culture of narcissism*. New York: W. W. Norton, 1978.

Lee, G. R., & Clyde, R. W. Religion, socioeconomic status, and anomie. *Journal for the Scientific Study of Religion*, 1974, *13*, 35–47.

Lefever, H. G. The religion of the poor: Escape or creative force? *Journal for the Scientific Study of Religion*, 1977, *16*, 225–236.

Lemert, C. C. Social structure and the absent center: An alternative to new sociologies of religion. *Sociological Analysis*, 1975, *36*, 95–107.

Lenski, G. *The religious factor*. Garden City, N.Y.: Doubleday, 1961.

Lindenthal, J. J., Myers, J. K., Pepper, M. P., & Stern, M. S. Mental status and religious behavior. *Journal for the Scientific Study of Religion*, 1970, *9*, 143–149.

Lowe, C. M. Differences in religious attitudes in mental illness. *Journal for the Scientific Study of Religion*, 1966, *5*, 435–445.

Malony, H. N. The psychologist-Christian. In H. N. Malony (Ed.), *Current perspectives in the psychology of religion*. Grand Rapids, Mich.: Wm. B. Eerdmans, 1977.

Mannheim, K. *Ideology and utopia*. New York: Harcourt, Brace, & World, 1936.

Marty, M. *The new shape of American religion*. New York: Harper, 1959.

Marty, M. *Religious empire: The Protestant experience in America*. New York: Dial Press, 1970.

Marx, K. Contribution to the critique of Hegel's philosophy of right. In R. Niebuhr (Ed.), *Marx and Engels on religion*. New York: Schocken Books, 1964.

Mathews, D. G. *Religion in the old south*. Chicago: University of Chicago Press, 1977.

McNamara, P. H., & George, A. S. Blessed are the downtrodden? An empirical test. *Sociological Analysis*, 1978, *39*, 303–320.

Moberg, D. O. *The church as a social institution*. Englewood Cliffs, N.J.: Prentice-Hall, 1962.

Moberg, D. O. Theological position and institutional characteristics of Protestant congregations: An exploratory study. *Journal for the Scientific Study of Religion*, 1970, *9*, 53–58.

Needleman, J., & Baker, G. *Understanding the new religions*. New York: Seabury Press, 1978.

Nelson, G. K. Communal and associational churches. *Review of Religious Research*, 1971, 102–110.

Nelson, H. M., Yokley, R. L., & Madron, T. W. Rural-urban differences in religiosity. *Rural Sociology*, 1971, *36*, 389–396.

Nelson, H. M. Intellectualism and religious attendance in metropolitan residents. *Journal for the Scientific Study of Religion*, 1973, *12*, 285–296.

Parsons, T. *Societies: Evolutionary and comparative perspectives*. Englewood Cliffs, N.J.: Prentice-Hall, 1966.

Peek, C. W., Chalfant, H. P., & Milton, E. V. Sinners in the hands of an angry God; Fundamentalist fears about drunken driving. *Journal for the Scientific Study of Religion*, 1979, *18*, 29–39.

Photiadis, J. D. (Ed.). *Religion in Appalachia*. Morgantown: West Virginia University, 1978.

Photiadis, J. D., & Biggar, J. Religiosity, education, and ethnic distance. *American Journal of Sociology*, 1962, *67*, 666–672.

Photiadis, J. D., & Johnson, A. L. Orthodoxy, church participation, and authoritarianism. *American Journal of Sociology*, 1963, *69*, 244–248.

Photiadis, J. D., & Schnabel, J. F. Religion: A persistent institution in a changing Appalachia. *Review of Religious Research*, 1977, *19*, 32–42.

Photiadis, J. D., & Schweiker, W. Attitudes toward joining authoritarian organizations and sectarian churches. *Journal for the Scientific Study of Religion,* 1970, *9,* 227–234.

Quebedeaux, R. *The young evangelicals.* New York: Harper & Row, 1974.

Quebedeaux, R. *The worldly evangelicals.* New York: Harper & Row, 1978.

Reed, J. S. *The enduring South.* Lexington, Mass.: D. C. Heath, 1972.

Richardson, J. T. Critique of Bibby and Brinkerhoff's "Sources of religious involvement." *Review of Religious Research,* 1976, *17,* 158–160.

Richardson, J. T., Stewart, M. W., & Simmonds, R. B. Researching a fundamentalist commune. In J. Needleman & G. Baker (Eds.), *Understanding the new religions.* New York: Seabury Press, 1978.

Robbins, T., & Anthony, D. Getting straight with Meher Baba. *Journal for the Scientific Study of Religion,* 1972, *11,* 122–140.

Robbins, T., Anthony, D., & Curtis, T. E. The limits of symbolic realism. *Journal for the Scientific Study of Religion,* 1973, *12,* 259–271.

Robbins, T., Anthony, D., & Richardson, J. Theory and research on today's "New Religions." *Sociological Analysis,* 1978, *39,* 95–122.

Rokeach, M. Religious values and social compassion. *Review of Religious Research,* 1969, *11,* 3–23. (a)

Rokeach, M. Value systems in religion. *Review of Religious Research,* 1969, *11,* 24–39. (b)

Roof, W. C. The local-cosmopolitan orientation and traditional religious commitment. *Sociological Analysis,* 1972, *33,* 1–15.

Roof, W. C., & Perkins, R. B. on conceptualizing saliency in religious commitment. *Journal for the Scientific Study of Religion,* 1975, *14,* 111–128.

Rushby, W. F., & Thrush, J. C. Mennonites and social compassion: The Rokeach hypothesis reconsidered. *Journal for the Scientific Study of Religion,* 1973, 16–28.

Sandeen, E. R. Toward a historical interpretation of fundamentalism. *Church History,* 1967, *36,* 66–83.

Sandeen, E. R. *The roots of fundamentalism.* Chicago: The University of Chicago Press, 1970.

Sanua, V. C. Religion, mental health, and personality: A review of empirical studies. *American Journal of Psychiatry,* 1969, *125,* 1203–1213.

Sartre, J. P. *Search for a method.* (H. E. Barnes, trans.) New York: Vintage Books, 1968.

Schneider, L., & Zurcher, L. Toward understanding the Catholic crisis: Observations on dissident protests in Texas. *Journal for the Scientific Study of Religion,* 1970, *9,* 197–207.

Schwartz, G. *Sect idologies and social status.* Chicago: University of Chicago Press, 1970.

Shortridge, J. R. A new regionalization of American religion. *Journal for the Scientific Study of Religion,* 1977, *16,* 143–153.

Siegman, A. W. A cross-cultural investigation of the relationship between religiosity, ethnic prejudice, and authoritarianism. *Psychological Reports,* 1962, *11,* 419–424.

Simmonds, R. B., Richardson, J. T., & Harder, M. W. A Jesus movement group: An adjective check list assessment. *Journal for the Scientific Study of Religion,* 1976, *15,* 323–333.

Smith, H. W. Urbanization, secularization, and the role of the professional's wife. *Review of Religious Resarch,* 1972, 134–139.

Smith, T. L., & Zopf, P. E., Jr. *Principles of inductive rural sociology.* Philadelphia: F. A. Davis, 1970.

Stark, R. Class, radicalism, and religious involvement in Great Britain. *American Sociological Review,* 1964, *29,* 698–706.

Stark, R. Psychopathology and religious commitment. *Review of Religious Research,* 1971 (Spring), pp. 165–176.

Stark, R., & Glock, C. Y. *American piety: The nature of religious commitment*. Berkeley: University of California Press, 1968.

Stone, D. New religious consciousness and personal religious experience. *Sociological Analysis*, 1978, *39*, 123–134.

Takayama, K. P., & Sachs, D. G. Polity and decision premises: The church and the private school. *Journal for the Scientific Study of Religion*, 1976, *15*, 269–278.

Toennies, F. *Community and society*. (C. P. Loomis, trans.) East Lansing: Michigan State University Press, 1957.

Tremmel, W. C. The converting choice. *Journal for the Scientific Study of Religion*, 1971, *10*, 17–25.

Van Roy, R. F., Bean, F. D., & Wood, J. R. Social mobility and doctrinal orthodoxy. *Journal for the Scientific Study of Religion*, 1973, *12*, 427–439.

Warner, R. S. Theoretical barriers to the understanding of evangelical Christianity. *Sociological Analysis*, 1979, *40*, 1–9.

Warren, N. C. Empirical studies in the psychology of religion: An assessment of the period 1960–1970. In H. N. Malony (Ed.), *Current perspectives in the psychology of religion*. New York: Wm. B. Eerdmans, 1977.

Wilson, B. The return of the sacred. *Journal for the Scientific Study of Religion*, 1979, *18*, 268–280.

Woodrum, E. Towards a theory of tension in American Protestantism. *Sociological Analysis*, 1978, *39*, 219–227.

Wuthnow, R. Religious commitment and conservatism: In search of an elusive relationship. In C. Y. Glock (Ed.), *Religion in sociological perspective*. Belmont, Calif.: Wadsworth, 1973.

Wuthnow, R., & Glock, C. Y. Religious loyalty, defection, and experimentation among college youth. *Journal for the Scientific Study of Religion*, 1973, *12*, 157–180.

Wuthnow, R., & Mellinger, G. Religious loyalty, defection, and experimentation: A longitudinal analysis of university men. *Review of Religious Research*, 1978, *19*, 234–245.

10

The Quality of Life in Rural and Urban America

Charles D. Korte

Considerable uncertainty exists about the quality of life to be found at present in rural America. In 1957, Max Lerner wrote movingly of the demise of the small town in rural America, observing that this form of settlement had been eclipsed by the forces of urbanization and mechanization. According to Lerner, it was no longer possible to restore the American small town to its previous state of strength and vitality (Lerner, 1957). This is not an uncommon view of rural and small-town America, which depicts the conditions and resources of these areas as seriously deficient relative to the rest of our society. Yet, this gloomy diagnosis and prognosis seem much diminished in more recent accounts of rural America. Bradshaw and Blakely (1979) speak of a "new rurality," where the countryside is blossoming with resources and opportunities made possible by new transportaion and communication technologies and where new rural residents, part of the urban to rural "reverse migration," bring new talents and energies to the small towns of America. One might ask whether it is only the experts and social analysts who are ambivalent about the present state of rural America. Consider, then, the contradiction expressed in the *attitude* of the American public toward rural living versus their *actions* with regard to actual residential location. On the one hand, Americans show a longstanding and continuing preference to live in small towns and rural areas—65% of a national survey sample indicated this preference in 1948, 49% in 1966,

CHARLES D. KORTE • Division of University Studies, North Carolina State University, Raleigh, North Carolina 27650.

55% in 1970, and 58% in 1976 (Elgin, Thomas, Logothetti, & Cox, 1974; Gallup, 1978). On the other hand, the actual movement of Americans has been, until very recently, largely from the small towns and the countryside into metropolitan areas. This suggests that Americans do hold a positive image of rural and small-town living, but that this pull is not sufficiently strong to overcome the attractions that the larger population centers offer.

The concern of this chapter is to examine the quality of life in rural America, particularly to see how it measures up with what is found in urban, or metropolitan, America. The quality of life concept offers a useful means of exploring the strengths and weaknesses of rural America, allowing us to go beyond the myths and stereotypes that guide much of our thinking on this topic. Yet the concept itself requires some examination and its usage has occasioned some controversy. Before turning to this, we must first clarify the term rural America as used in this paper. The term rural America will be used to refer to the non-metropolitan areas of this country, including open countryside, small towns, and larger towns as well. The metropolitan-nonmetropolitan distinction is currently recognized as the most meaningful one between rural and urban areas. In any case, the only appropriate geographical breakdown in much of the quality of life data is between metropolitan and nonmetropolitan areas, where *metropolitan* is defined as a Bureau of the Census Standard Metropolitan Statistical Area (SMSA): counties containing at least one city with a minimum population of 50,000 as well as adjacent counties that are economically and socially integrated to this city (Bollens & Schmandt, 1970). It is worth noting that using this definition, about one-third of the American population lives in nonmetropolitan areas.

The term *quality of life* is generally used to refer to an overall evaluation of the conditions of life as experienced by an individual or a set of individuals. It has arisen out of the growing research on social indicators (see Campbell, Converse, & Rodgers, 1976; Andrews & Withey, 1976) and for the most part the measurement of quality of life is made by using a variety of indicators. Two types of indicators can generally be distinguished, objective and subjective. *Objective* measures are relatively straightforward descriptions of quantitative characteristics of places or people, such as crime rate, park acres, number of hospitals, etc. *Subjective* measures tap individuals' perceptions of their own living conditions and their satisfaction with these conditions. Arguments have been made for the preference of one of these types of measures and even for the elimination of the objective-subjective distinction (Andrews & Withey, 1976). It would seem that the role of both types of measures is necessary as long as it is possible that people will differ in their subjective evaluation of the adequacy or importance of a particular set of conditions. If there were total agreement concerning the importance and salience of certain conditions for an individual's well-being, then the objective measurement of these conditions would accurately portray the quality of life in any given locale. Yet this assumption can rarely be true. For example, certain conditions attain a greater value as the possession of those conditions becomes less certain. An area's low unemployment rate is far more meaningful to an unskilled factory worker than it is to a dentist. Likewise, our personal values and life-style determine which conditions are to be prized and which deplored; a stock car racetrack may have exactly opposite effects on the sense of personal well-being of the factory worker and the dentist. It would seem imperative in any large-scale, pluralistic society to consider quality of life through the filter of individual needs, values, and preferences. Viewed this way, the quality of life in rural America depends very much on how well the rural environment is meeting the needs of the people that live there; their needs may differ from those of urban Americans. Accordingly, the subjective indicators of quality of life must figure prominently in any comparison of rural and urban areas.

The importance of the subjective indicators, however, does not render the objective indicators inconsequential. Certainly, particular conditions are essential to the well-being of all of us. Freedom from the threat of crime would seem to be a near universal concern of Americans at this time; the objective measures of this threat should obviously be a key element in assessing quality of life. In any event, the objective measures give us baselines to identify certain relevant urban-rural comparisons and to shed light on the meaning and significance of some of the subjective indicators.

In this review, I shall turn first to the subjective indicators and examine two in particular—residential preference and community satisfaction—to see what they tell us about the quality of life in rural America. Next the evidence pertaining to objective indicators will be reviewed, with a focus on four categories of indicators: economic conditions, services and facilities, environmental quality, and social indicators. Finally, an effort will be made to integrate the findings from the subjective and objective measures of quality of life in order to reach some conclusions about the present state of life in rural America.

Subjective Indicators of Rural and Urban Quality of Life

One indication of the quality of life in rural America is whether people have any inclination to live there. As has already been indicated, Americans have often expressed a favorable evaluation of rural America when asked where they would most prefer to live. National surveys dating back thirty years characteristically show that a majority of Americans prefers to live in either small towns or the countryside, as opposed to metropolitan areas (Elgin *et al.*, 1974). Quite naturally this is the preference of people who already live in rural America but, strikingly, it is also the preference of the majority of urban Americans. A recent Gallup poll (Gallup, 1978) showed that 51% of the inhabitants of cities with a population over 50,000 would ideally prefer to live in either small towns or rural areas.

Given the fact that a subjective indicator like residential preference reflects individual perspectives and circumstances, we might ask which individuals in particular prefer a rural residential location over an urban one. Interestingly, the only characteristic that has been identified as showing a correlation with rural versus urban residential preference (apart from the obvious characteristic of *present* rural vs. urban residence) is race: whites are much more in favor of living in rural America than blacks are—54% versus 33% of a national sample in 1972 (Mazie & Rawlings, 1972). There are many factors that might explain why blacks take a dimmer view of living in rural America (e.g., expectations of greater prejudice and lower economic opportunities). There is no definitive research on black attitudes toward rural life and it is worth noting that the correlation between race and residential preference may simply reflect the influence of *present* location (i.e., since blacks are far more likely than whites to live in metroplitan areas, they are thus prone to prefer this location).

One problem with asking people where they would like to live is that we do not know whether their response is conditioned by certain unspoken assumptions. When people say they would like to live in a small town or city, do they perhaps have *particular* small towns or *particular* cities in mind, which may not be very representative of small towns or cities in general? Several studies suggest that this may be the case for many rural and small town enthusiasts. Fuguitt and Zuiches (1975) found that the preference for small-town living was very much conditional on the town's proximity to a large city. In their study, describing the small town as located more than 30 miles from a large city reduced the preference for such a place from 75% to 19%. Likewise, if living in a small town means a reduction in personal income (which is often the case), the enthusiasm for small towns is diminished further (Carpenter, 1977). These studies help explain the attitude of many Americans that small towns are not really self-sufficient locales for living but are rather attractive places as long as one does not have to forfeit the attractions of a large city.

As a subjective measure of rural quality of life, preferences about residential location are an uncertain mix of experience and stereotype. In light of this, a more meaningful subjective indicator would seem to be the degree of satisfaction that people express toward their present community. The residential preference data would lead us to expect that rural inhabitants are more satisfied with their communities than urban inhabitants. This is in fact the case. The most comprehensive study to confirm this rural-urban difference in community satisfaction was a 1971 national survey carried out by Campbell, Converse, and Rodgers (1976) and analyzed in further detail by Rodgers (1979). In this study, respondents were asked how satisfied they were with their home community as a place to live; the results showed significantly higher levels of satisfaction as community size decreased. For example, 48% of rural respondents were *completely* satisfied with their place of residence, a level of satisfaction higher than any other group surveyed (e.g., 19% for the central city inhabitants of our largest cities). Similar conclusions have been reported by Dillman and Tremblay (1977) as well as by Elgin *et al.* (1974). In addition, a Harris poll result (Harris, 1970) showed that city residents felt that the quality of life in their communities had declined over the past few years. Rural residents, on the other hand, felt that their communities had changed for the better.

The superior satisfaction of rural residents with their home communities is important evidence that the quality of life in rural America is in a healthy state. Nevertheless, it would be helpful to know which particular features of nonmetropolitan communities are responsible for the high satisfaction ratings given by rural residents. There is only a small amount of evidence on this question, but the results are fairly consistent in pointing to the importance of the social atmosphere in small towns as a basis for the high level of community satisfaction. This is evident in research by Goudy (1977) and Rodgers (1979). Goudy carried out a factor analysis of satisfaction ratings of various community features in small towns and examined the correlation of these factors with the rating of overall community satisfaction. The highest correlation was with a social atmosphere factor, which included items on how well residents knew one another, how similar they were to each other, and how active residents were in community affairs. Similar results were obtained by Rodgers (1979), who found that satisfaction with neighbors was one of the important explanations for the higher overall community satisfaction in smaller-sized communities. Rodgers also found that this increase in satisfaction was mediated by an increase in satisfaction with the "standard of living" (i.e., the satisfaction of rural residents with their communities reflects in part their satisfaction with their present "standard of living"). As we shall see below, this latter finding is paradoxical since, objectively, the standard of living is actually *lower* in rural areas.

The picture that emerges from these two subjective measures of quality of life (residential preference and community satisfaction) is that a rural residence is perceived quite widely as a preferred location (though this assumes that a large city is not too far away) and that in fact those people living in rural areas are more satisfied with their communities, a satisfaction that reflects, in part, a favorable response to the social aspects of small towns. There are of course areas in which rural residents are less satisfied with their communities than are urban residents; for example, rural residents are less satisfied with the public transportation services in their communities (Campbell, Converse, & Rodgers, 1976). From the perspective of subjective evaluations, the *overall* picture of rural America is clearly quite a positive one. With this in mind, we shall now examine whether the objective indicators of rural life produce a similar picture of rural America. Such expectations could be ill-founded if, for example, rural residents evaluate in a positive light conditions that are objectively deficient according to particular scales of reference.

Objective Indicators of Rural and Urban Quality of Life

There are many conditions that affect the quality of life of people in any particular locale. As was seen with the subjective measures, the social atmosphere of a place is a very important factor in people's sense of satisfaction. On the other hand, the long-standing flow of people from rural to metropolitan areas is widely attributed to the poor economic conditions of rural America, while the more recent flow toward small towns (Beale, 1975) is viewed as reflecting a renewed appreciation of the environmental and recreational qualities of our rural areas. From the wide diversity of conditions that are relevant to quality of life, four of the most salient ones will be reviewed here in order to determine the reality of rural-urban differences. These four are economic indicators, services and facilities, environmental quality, and social indicators.

Economic Indicators

A considerable number of reviews have compared the economic conditions of rural and urban America (e.g., Brinkman, 1974; Dillman & Tremblay, 1977; Elgin *et al.*, 1974; Hines, Brown, & Zimmer, 1975; Hoch, 1972; Ross, Bluestone, & Hines, 1979; U.S. Department of Agriculture, 1978). The conclusions uniformly show consistent and pervasive economic weaknesses in rural America. Compared to metropolitan areas, our rural areas show lower levels of mean income, higher levels of underemployment, and higher proportions of people living below the federally defined poverty line. Nearly all the economic indicators that allow for these comparisons have been derived from the 1970 census, so it is possible that data from the 1980 census will alter the nature of the rural-urban differences reported here. For instance, data from 1976 (U.S. Department of Agriculture, 1978) suggest that the economic gap between rural and urban America is closing. We will see that this is the case for a number of other objective indicators.

The median income of urban families is nearly $3,000 greater than that of rural families (Hines *et al.,* 1975). In addition, the level of income for families living in nonmetropolitan areas decreases monotonically as the area becomes more rural (i.e., fewer and smaller population centers) and more distant from a metropolitan area. This inequity in income levels is partially offset by two factors. One is the cost of living, which is clearly lower in rural areas. This rural economic advantage, though, only makes up about half of the difference in the income differential suffered by rural residents (Dillman & Tremblay, 1977; see also Hoch, 1972). The second factor is the rate of income increase, which is presently higher in rural areas, resulting in a lessening of the rural-urban gap. Calculated as a percentage of the mean income level of *urban* families, the income level of rural families was 69% in 1960, 73% in 1970 and 80% in 1976 (Brinkman, 1974; U.S. Department of Agriculture, 1978). Correspondingly, the growth rate in rural family income between 1960 and 1970 was 78%, versus 67% for urban families.

Another indicator of the economic quality of life is the unemployment rate, which is calculated in federal statistics as the total number of unemployed persons, 16 years old and over, actively seeking work as a percentage of the civilian, noninstitutional labor force 16 years old and over. Measured this way, unemployment rates have not differed substantially between rural and urban areas during the 1970s (Nilsen, 1979). Nevertheless, the federal definition of unemployment has been criticized as being a method of measurement that obscures a genuine employment disadvantage in our rural areas. Nilsen (1979) has pointed out that there are significant rural-urban differences in a variety of employment-related indicators. First, rural workers have a higher rate of "involuntary" part-time employment, such as part-time employment in lieu of preferred full-time employment. Second, among the unemployed, there is in rural areas a higher proportion of workers who want work but are no longer actively seeking employment because they believe no jobs are available. Finally, a fully employed rural worker earns much less than a fully employed urban workers. If the unemployment rate were measured to include some of these factors, it would show a clear disadvantage for rural America. As Nilsen points out, this would have the beneficial effect of giving rural areas a more favorable proportion of federal funds for economic development ($16 billion in 1976), which are allocated to areas on the basis of the federally defined unemployment rate.

A third indicator of the poor economic condition of rural America is the proportion of people living below the poverty line. Families are categorized as below the poverty line on the basis of their income (adjusted for cost of living), number of children, sex of family head, and farm–nonfarm residence. By this definition, poverty is far more prevalent in rural areas, although the rural-urban gap is closing. In 1970, 17% of rural residents were living below the poverty line, compared with a rate 10.2% for urban residents (Brinkman, 1974). This is a considerable reduction from 1959, when the rates of poverty were 33.2% and 15.3%, respectively. Not surprisingly, rural poverty is particularly high within certain minority groups (e.g. blacks, Native Americans, and Hispanic migrant farm workers). Among rural blacks, for example, the rate of poverty was 51.6% in 1970 (when the poverty line for a farm family with two children was $3385).

Overall, the economic indicators are very consistent in pointing to a disadvantage in economic conditions in rural America. The explanation for this undoubtedly lies in the employment opportunities, the wage scales, and the labor force characteristics of rural America; this is an issue beyond the scope of this paper and has been well covered in other sources (see Hines *et al.*, 1975; Hoch, 1972; Nilsen, 1979). In terms of rural versus urban quality of life, the conclusion to be drawn is that rural America suffers a relatively lower quality of life in terms of employment opportunities and standards of living. Yet it must be remembered that two important points modify the strength of this conclusion. First, economic disadvantage is not evenly spread throughout rural America. There are important differences between regions (Ross, Bluestone, & Hines, 1979) and between population groups (Brinkman, 1974); thus, overall rural-urban differences disguise considerable variation within the rural sector. Second, there is the paradoxical observation that rural residents express *higher* levels of satisfaction with their standard of living (Rodgers, 1979). This brings into question the meaningfulness of the objective economic standard of living as a quality of life indicator: rural residents are less well-off economically, but more *satisfied* with their economic situation. This discrepancy is probably best explained by the relativity of judgments about economic well-being. The economic aspiration and standards of comparison of the urban residents may cause them to judge even fairly high standards of living to be disappointing and unsatisfactory. As we will see below, there is often an inconsistent relationship between objective conditions and level of satisfaction with those conditions. The occurrence of such a discrepancy in the case of economic indicators illustrates the importance of evaluating quality of life by means of both objective and subjective indicators.

Services and Facilities

Quality of life depends not only on economic well-being but also on the availability of facilities and services for meeting everyday needs (e.g., medical, educational, cultural, recreational, and shopping). It is an obvious fact that the presence of many types of services and facilities depends upon an adequate population base to support these services. This is clearly illustrated in a series of computations reported by Keyes (1958), which showed how large a place needed to be before it was virtually certain (95%) to have different types of facilities. For example, a book store, hospital, and Elk's Club were only guaranteed to be features of communities with a population of at least 100,000. In terms of the availability of these different features, rural America is clearly at a disadvantage. This is particularly clear in the case of two types of facilities with an undisputed relevance to quality of life—medical and educational.

Medical services in rural America are weak from the standpoint of the number of health professionals, the quality of the medical facilities, and the level of usage of these facilities. In 1970, there were twice as many physicians per capita in urban America than in rural America (Dillman & Tremblay, 1977). In particularly short supply in rural areas are medical specialists (e.g., dentists, cardiologists, and surgeons). Rural hospitals generally provide a numerical capacity (beds per capita) equal to that of metropolitan areas; however, the rural hospitals are often inadequatly staffed, nonaccredited, and lacking in advanced medical technology (Brinkman, 1974). The utilization of medical facilities—specifically contacts with physicians—is less in rural than in urban areas. Rural residents make fewer trips to the doctor each year and have a frequency of contact with specialists that is less than half of the urban rate (Fischer, 1976). These figures are especially striking in light of the higher incidence of serious health problems in rural America (Brinkman, 1974).

Compulsory education guarantees the presence of a certain minimum of educational facilities throughout the United States. Nevertheless, the standards of these facilities appear to be lower in rural America. For example, in 1968 the average expenditure per child in rural public school systems was three-fourths the amount spent in urban schools (U.S. Department of Agriculture, 1971). In addition, rural education shows deficiencies in both the rate of school enrollment of age groups outside the compulsory years and the overall level of educational attainment. The proportion of preschool children in cities who are enrolled in some sort of educational program is double that found in rural areas, while the length of education attained is 12.2 years for urban residents versus 11.2 years for rural residents (Hines *et al.*, 1975). This one year difference in educational level nevertheless represents a substantial closing of the gap from what it had been 10 years earlier.

These figures confirm that, besides weaknesses in conditions of employment and the economic standard of living, rural America also falls short in its medical and educational facilities, to name only two types of important facilities. It is worth considering whether the state of these conditions has parallels in the level of satisfaction of urban and rural residents with this aspect of their communities. The evidence does not clearly support a consistent correspondence between objective conditions and levels of subjective satisfaction. The small amount of evidence on this point is, in fact, contradictory. Campbell and his associates (1976) found that satisfaction with local schools actually *increases* with decreasing community size; as a group, small town residents are the most pleased with their schools, with 47% rating them as "very good" (versus 17% for residents of our twelve largest cities). This study also showed rural residents to be more satisfied with other services and facilities as well (e.g., garbage collection and police protection). Johnson and Knop (1970) and Warner and Burdge (1979), on the other hand, found rural residents generally *less* satisfied with various services and facilities. On one education-related item (teacher ability) rural residents were found to be *less* satisfied; this was true also for their evaluation of medical facilities, shopping, and entertainment opportunities (Johnson & Knop, 1970). Likewise, Warner and Burdge (1979) found a perfect correspondence for five community services between the urban-rural differences in objective standards (higher for urban) and level of satisfaction (higher for urban). The discrepancy between these two studies and the fact that the Campbell *et al.* figures showed higher satisfaction for rural residents is hard to reconcile and leaves this point unresolved. The discrepancy may of course reflect the different samples used in these studies, so further clarification will require more data beyond the little that have been collected. In any case, we have seen once again the divergence of subjective evaluations of community features from the objective indicators of those features.

Environmental Quality

One factor that has risen dramatically in its importance for quality of life assessments is environmental quality. To many, quality of life is synonymous with quiet settings, clean air and water, and unexploited natural environments. One of the strongest stereotypes of rural and urban America is the vastly superior environmental qualities of rural America; this is an important part of the appeal that rural living has for many Americans. There is now a considerable amount of data to support the validity of these impressions: our small towns are indeed quieter, they have cleaner air, and they feature more pleasant climates, to name three of the more important environmental features relevant to quality of life.

The average level of outdoor noise has been found to increase steadily with community size (Dillman & Tremblay, 1977; Elgin et al., 1974; Environmental Protection Agency, 1972; Fischer, 1976; Hoch, 1972). A sample of noise readings from a variety of locales by the Environmental Protection Agency in 1971 showed that the quietest moments for inner-city apartments in a sample of major metropolitan areas were invariably noisier than the noisiest moments experienced by small town residential areas. It also seems likely, though the evidence related to this is fragmentary, that levels of "unacceptable" noise are more frequently encountered in cities. Prolonged exposure to noise above the level of 90 dBA can result in permanent loss of hearing; this level is readily surpassed in the case of subway trains, construction noise, and low-flying aircraft. Cohen, Glass, and Singer (1973) carried out a study of urban children living near a highway and found that with increasing proximity to the highway, the children showed increased hearing losses and lower reading scores. We are at present less informed about the particular psychological and social consequences of high noise levels, but it appears clear that whatever those consequences might be, they are more likely to be manifest in an urban environment.

Air pollution is another environmental factor that affects quality of life. A very detailed analysis of air pollution levels in rural and urban areas has been presented by Hoch (1972), who concludes that there is a relationship between city size and levels of air pollution. Another study found that air pollution was 15 times greater in urban areas than in rural ones (Fischer, 1976). Serious episodes of air pollution, such as the Los Angeles smog, are uniquely urban phenomena and may be linked to several lung and respiratory diseases such as lung cancer, which occurs much more frequently in urban than in rural areas.

Climate also shows a systematic variation between cities and towns, with major differences in sunshine (rural areas have more), rain (urban areas have more), temperature (it is hotter in urban areas), and wind (more in rural areas). These differences are largely due to air pollution, the density of buildings in cities, and the higher levels of heat generation and absorption in urban environments (Elgin et al., 1974; Hoch, 1972). Given the widespread consensus concerning what constitutes "pleasant" weather, we conclude from this that climatic conditions are more favorable in rural areas.

There are many other environmental features that can also be related to quality of life (e.g., esthetic qualities, recreational facilities, and unspoiled outdoor environments), but it is not necessary to review them all to see that these indicators clearly point toward a definite environmental advantage for rural America. For once there is no uncertainty in the link between these objective environmental conditions and levels of satisfaction: rural residents do express higher levels of satisfaction with their climate, their parks and playgrounds, and their geographical milieu (Campbell, et al., 1976; Johnson & Knop, 1970). In addition, the positive environmental qualities of rural America appear to play an important role in the attractiveness of rural areas and in people's reasons for locating there (Beale, 1975; Schwarzweller, 1979). It is interesting to reflect that if environmental quality continues to increase as a valued component of quality of life, this will have very favorable implications for the future of our sentiments and attraction toward rural America. Whether such sentiments and attractions will be beneficial for rural America is, of course, another matter.

Social Indicators

Earlier in the paper, we saw that the social atmosphere of smaller communities is one of the primary explanations of the high level of satisfaction of rural residents with their home areas. We turn finally to the data that will indicate whether some aspects of local conditions are in fact more favorable in rural America. This is undoubtedly the most difficult aspect of quality of life in terms of finding valid indicators. Nevertheless, some guidance is afforded by the stereotype of small-town living, which stresses features that can be evaluated to various degrees by reliable data. Above all, small towns are seen as characterized by satisfying human relationships: friendly neighbors, intact families embedded in extensive contact with relatives, and civil and helpful relations between the unacquainted. The stereotype of rural America also depicts rural life as being relatively free of the distressing social disturbances of the city: crime, psychopathology, and alienation. Let us now turn to the social indicators that relate to these variables.

A previous review by the author (Korte, 1980) examined the reality of urban-rural differences in the nature of social contact between relatives, friends, neighbors, and strangers. The studies in this area partially confirm the rural stereotype: the only indicator that shows improvement in rural areas over cities is contact between neighbors and strangers. Familiarity and social involvement between neighbors has been shown to increase with decreasing community size (Fava, 1958; Fischer, 1973; Key, 1968), while a fairly large number of studies show that the level of civility and helpfulness between strangers is consistently higher in small towns than cities (see Korte & Kerr, 1975; Korte & Ayvalioglu, 1981; Milgram, 1970; Rushton, 1978). Comparisons between city and town on (1) frequency of contact between friends and between relatives, (2) the number and intimacy of friendship ties, and (3) the support that is derived from friends and relatives, give little confirmation of urban-rural differences in this realm. In addition, apart from features like marital status and family size, urban and rural families are not different in ways that have a potential relation to the well-being of family members, such as whether a husband and wife live together and whether children live with either one or with neither of their parents (Fischer, 1976; Hines *et al.*, 1975; Ross *et al.*, 1979). Hence, the reality of a presumed superiority in the realm of human relationships in rural America is restricted to the relationships between neighbors and strangers. This is of course not an insignificant benefit from a quality of life perspective.

Crime statistics very dramatically bear out the relative safety from crime in rural areas (Dillman & Tremblay, 1977; Fischer, 1976; Hoch, 1972). In all categories of crime—crimes against persons, crimes against property, and vice—the rate of occurrence in the United States rises with increasing community size. The murder rate in rural areas is three-fourths of the urban rate, with even greater differences occurring for aggravated assault (one-half the urban rate) and robbery (one-thirteenth the urban rate). These striking rural-urban differences partly reflect the uneven distribution of minority groups that show particularly high rates of crime; in fact, it is important to consider whether urban-rural crime differences are actually anything more than a reflection of population differences. Hoch (1972) carried out an analysis of the relationship between crime rate and community size, with controls entered to eliminate the effect of the proportion of minority members in the population, and found that the relationship, though weakened, was still significant. On the other hand, the lack of reliability in crime rate data means that the relationship is only roughly approximated by any of these methods. For example, if crimes are more likely to go undetected or unreported in urban areas, as is suspected, then urban-rural differences may actually be greater than current figures suggest.

The final component of social atmosphere to be considered here—psychological distress and alienation—turns out to be one part of the urban stereotype with very little factual support. Suicide and alcholism show no variation in rate between rural and urban areas (Fischer, 1976; Ross *et al.*, 1979). Community surveys designed to assess the levels of personal adjustment and psychological distress (e.g., nervous break-downs) indicate no conclusive advantage in favor of either the rural or urban population. Similarly, indications of personal alienation (e.g., powerlessness, normlessness, and social isolation) were reviewed carefully by Fischer (1976), who concluded that the research evidence on these phenomena gives no support to the existence of urban-rural differences. The one exception to this is interpersonal trust, which does show a decline from rural to urban areas, both in terms of trusting attitudes (Fischer, 1973) and trusting actions toward strangers (Korte, 1978, 1981).

To summarize, then, we can conclude that the social atmosphere of rural America shows some advantage over the conditions found in our metropolitan areas, though the differences are not as extensive as the stereotype would have us believe. What we find is that in rural America there is more social contact between neighbors, more civility and help-fulness between strangers, less crime, and more trusting attitudes and behavior. Of course, these features are probably interrelated to a considerable degree; for example, the reduced threat of crime in rural areas may greatly facilitate the favorable manner of interaction observed to occur between strangers. Nevertheless, the indicators cited in this last section may be the least reliable of those that have been reviewed in this paper, so considerable caution needs to be attached to conclusions drawn about urban-rural differences in social atmosphere. This concern should in no way diminish the regard for the importance of the social atmosphere dimension in quality of life assessments. It is worth noting that the social indicators, as previously pointed out, do show a close correspondence to the levels of satisfaction expressed by urban and rural residents toward this aspect of their community (Goudy, 1977; Miller & Crader, 1979).

CONCLUSIONS

A concluding judgment about the quality of life in rural America involves considerable interpretation of the variety of indicators that have been reviewed in this paper. At the very least, we can say that an extreme judgment on rural living is not in order: Rural America is not in as bad a condition as some of its critics would have us believe, nor is the picture as rosy as the opposite viewpoint would suggest. Across the four areas of objective indicators, rural American fares well in comparison with our urban areas, while on the subjective indicators, rural America looks very good indeed on nearly all counts. Objectively, rural America is weak in employment opportunities, standard of living, and the adequacy of a variety of services and facilities. On the other hand, rural America is superior in its environmental qualities (clean air, lower noise levels, pleasant climate), its low crime rate, its favorable social atmosphere in the realm of neighbors and strangers, and its general level of interpersonal trust. The subjective indicators tell a somewhat different story, one that is clearly favorable to our rural areas. There is first of all the residential preference data, which show a widespread inclination to favor smaller-sized communities as places to live. This data is somewhat hard to interpret, as it reflects an uncertain mixture of experience, stereotype, and implicit assumptions about hypothetical communities (e.g., that they will be near cities). Nevertheless, the more meaningful subjective indicator—residents' satisfaction with their communities—conveys an equally positive impression of rural America. Rural residents show a higher level of satisfaction with their standard of living, their environmental quality, and the social atmosphere of their communities. The results are mixed on the services and facilities component, with some studies showing that rural residents are less satisfied with these features of their communities, while other studies show they are more satisfied.

To make a judgment about the overall quality of life in rural versus urban America requires an evaluation of the essential *importance* of each of the features discussed here, an exercise of dubious validity. Of course, it is an exercise that each individual presumably undergoes to some degree in making various life decisions; it would be very illuminating to have a form of indicator that reflects this type of overall individual judgment. One such indicator might be the overall level of community satisfaction or satisfaction with life in general (Campbell *et al.*, 1976). As we have seen, rural residents do express higher levels of such general satisfaction (see Rodgers, 1977). Yet the meaning of such overall satisfaction still remains questionable, since the phenomenon of rural satisfaction has been continually contradicted historically by the phenomenon of rural-to-urban migration (DeJong & Sell, 1977). It would then seem best, at present, to retain a multidimensional concept of quality of life, especially maintaining the distinction between objective and subjective indicators. This is important particularly in relation to social policy. The *needs* of rural America can certainly not be assessed from objective indicators alone, as the objective-subjective discrepancies identified in this paper have made clear. Even the subjective satisfaction data are not sufficient guides, since they give little indication of the perceived *priority* of needs from the perspective of the rural resident; police protection, for example, could be judged as very unsatisfactory while at the same time it might be a very low priority for rural residents. Social policy will require a particular form of data, linked to the quality of life measures described here; the tradition of user–needs analysis is certainly a useful model for this approach.

Finally, it is appropriate to consider some concerns that relate to the future. One concern is the possibility of misunderstanding the essential nature of the favorable quality of life in rural America. We do not yet know whether this attractiveness depends on the characteristics of the particular people who presently inhabit rural America or whether it is a quality inherent to rural areas, there to be enjoyed by all who might chose to move to smaller-sized communities in order to reap the particular benefits of rural America. Considerable frustration will be in store for the new urban-to-rural migrants if the pleasures of rural America presume a certain type of personality or social background. This leads to a second concern, that of the possibility of *changes* in the quality of life of rural America. Presently, rural America is more than just a place where people *say* they would like to live: People are actually moving to rural America in sufficient numbers that an urban-to-rural migratory trend is now an important feature of our present, and presumably future, demographic situation. Will this threaten that very quality of life that is seen by many as a principal magnet for the new migrants? It is certainly a credible fear that growth and development in many rural areas of our country might seriously weaken the environmental and social features of those areas. Useful defenses against these fears are a greater awareness of the quality of life indicators that are important to a particular locality and an identification of the policies and practices that foster these qualities.

REFERENCES

Andrews, F. M., & Withey, S. B. *Social indicators of well being: Americans' perceptions of life quality.* New York: Plenum Press, 1976.

Beale, C. Renewed growth in rural communities. *Futurist*, 1975, 9, 196–202.

Bollens, J., & Schmandt, H. *The metropolis.* New York: Harper & Row, 1970.

Bradshaw, T., & Blakely, E. *Rural communities in advanced industrial society.* New York: Praeger, 1979.

Brinkman, G. The conditions and problems of nonmetropolitan America. In G. Brinkman (Ed.), *The development of rural America.* Lawrence: University of Kansas Press, 1974.

Campbell, A., Converse, P. E., & Rodgers, W. L. *The quality of American life: Perceptions, evaluations, and satisfactions.* New York: Russell Sage Foundation, 1976.

Carpenter, E. The potential for population dispersal: a closer look at residential locational preferences. *Rural Sociology*, 1977, 42, 352–370.

Cohen, S., Glass, D., & Singer, J. Apartment noise, auditory discrimination, and reading ability in children. *Journal of Experimental Social Psychology*, 1973, 9, 407–422.

DeJong, G., & Sell, R. Population redistribution, migration, and residential preferences. *Annals of the American Academy of Political and Social Sciences, 1977, 429,* 130–144.

Dillman, D., & Tremblay, K., Jr. The quality of life in rural America. *Annals of the American Academy of Political and Social Sciences, 1977, 429,* 115–129.

Elgin, D., Thomas, T., Logothetti, T., & Cox, S. *City size and the quality of life.* Washington, D.C.: National Science Foundation, 1974.

Environmental Protection Agency. *Report to the President and Congress on noise.* Washington, D.C.: U.S. Government Printing Office, 1972.

Fava, S. Contrasts in neighboring: New York City and a suburban community. In W. H. Dobriner (Ed.), *The suburban community.* New York: Putnam, 1958.

Fischer, C. On urban alienation and anomie. *American Sociological Review, 1973, 38,* 311–326.

Fischer, C. *The urban experience.* New York: Harcourt Brace Jovanovich, 1976.

Fuguitt, G., & Zuiches, J. Residential preferences and population distribution. *Demography, 1975, 12,* 491–507.

Gallup, G. *The Gallup poll.* Wilmington, Del.: Scholarly Resources, 1978.

Goudy, W. Evaluations of local attributes and community satisfaction in small towns. *Rural Sociology, 1977, 42,* 371–382.

Harris, L. *A survey of public attitudes toward urban problems and toward the impact of scientific and technical developments.* New York: Corporation for Public Broadcasting, 1970.

Hines, F., Brown, D., & Zimmer, J. *Social and economic characteristics of the population in metro and nonmetro counties, 1970.* Washington, D.C.: USDA, Agricultural Economic Report No. 272, 1975.

Hoch, I. Urban scale and environmental quality. In R. Ridker (Ed.), *Population, resources, and the environment* (Vol. 3). Washington, D.C.: Government Printing Office, 1972.

Johnson, R., & Knop, E. Rural-urban differentials in community satisfaction. *Rural Sociology, 1970, 35,* 544–548.

Key, W. Rural-urban social participation. In S. Fava (Ed.), *Urbanism in world perspective.* New York: Thomas Crowell, 1968.

Keyes, F. The correlation of social phenomena with community size. *Social Forces, 1958, 36,* 311–315.

Korte, C. Helpfulness in the urban environment. In A. Baum, J. Singer, & S. Valins (Eds.), *Advances in environmental psychology* (Vol. 1). Hillsdale, N.J.: Lawrence Erlbaum, 1978.

Korte, C. Urban-nonurban differences in social behavior and social psychological models of urban impact. *Journal of Social Issues, 1980, 36,* 29–51.

Korte, C. Constraints on helping behavior in an urban environment. In J. Rushton & R. Sorrentino (Eds.), *Altruism and helping behavior.* Hillsdale, N.J.: Lawrence Erlbaum, 1981.

Korte, C., & Ayvalioglu, N. Helpfulness in Turkey: Cities, towns and urban villages. *Journal of Cross-Cultural Psychology, 1981, 12,* 123–141.

Korte, C., & Kerr, N. Response to altruistic opportunities under urban and rural conditions. *Journal of Social Psychology, 1975, 95,* 183–184.

Lerner, M. *America as a civilization.* New York: Simon & Schuster, 1957.

Mazie, S., & Rawlings, S. Public attitude toward population distribution issues. In *The Commission of Population Growth and the American Future* (Vol. 5). Washington, D.C.: U.S. Government Printing Office, 1972.

Milgram, S. The experience of living in cities. *Science, 1970, 167,* 1461–1468.

Miller, M., & Crader, K. Rural-urban differences in two dimensions of community satisfaction. *Rural Sociology, 1979, 44,* 489–504.

Nilsen, S. *Assessment of employment and unemployment statistics for non-metropolitan areas.* Washington, D.C.: U.S. Department of Agriculture, 1979.

Rodgers, W. *Size of place and the subjective quality of life.* Paper presented at the American Psychological Association Convention, San Francisco, 1977.

Rodgers, W. *Residential satisfaction in relationship to size of place.* Ann Arbor, Mich.: Institute for Social Research, 1979.

Ross, P., Bluestone, H., & Hines, F. *Indicators of social well-being in U.S. counties.* Washington, D.C.: U.S. Department of Agriculture, 1979.

Rushton, P. Urban density and altruism: Helping strangers in a Canadian city, suburb, and small town. *Psychological Reports,* 1978, *43,* 987–990.

Schwarzweller, H. Migration and the changing rural scene. *Rural Sociology,* 1977, *44,* 7–23.

U.S. Department of Agriculture. *The economic and social condition of rural America.* Washington, D.C.: U.S. Government Printing Office, 1971.

U.S. Department of Agriculture. *Rural development perspectives.* Washington, D.C.: U.S. Government Printing Office, 1978.

Warner, P., & Burdge, R. Perceived adequacy of community services: A metro-nonmetro comparison. *Rural Sociology,* 1979, *44,* 392–400.

11

Needs Assessments in Rural Areas

Issues and Problems

Scott W. Henggeler

Rural areas are popularly characterized as quiet and tranquil places where individuals can void the psychonoxious aspects of modern living. However, epidemiological studies have demonstrated that significant mental health problems exist in rural communities (Bentz, Hollister, & Edgerton, 1971; Leighton, Leighton, & Armstrong, 1964; Llewellyn-Thomas, 1960). In fact, Husaini, Neff, and Stone (1979) have suggested that a variety of physical and interpersonal problems have higher incidence rates in rural than in urban areas. Despite the apparent need for mental health services, rural communities do not have many of the services that are readily available to urban dwellers (Willie, 1972). This relative absence of mental health services is not a simple reflection of the increased poverty in rural areas. Hoagland (1978) observed that 49% of urban poverty areas had adequate mental health services, yet, only 17.5% of rural poverty areas had such services. Hence, it seems that rural residents present significant mental health needs but receive fewer services (Falcone, 1979).

The primary aim of this review is to describe and critique the ways in which community mental health need priorities are determined, especially in rural areas. Although, unfortunately, many community men-

Scott W. Henggeler • Department of Psychology, Memphis State University, Memphis, Tennessee 38152.

tal health centers (CMHCs) perform needs assessments in a perfunctory manner, valid assessments are of extreme social import (Sallis & Henggeler, 1980b). Since CMHCs operate on limited budgets, the mental health priorities established through needs assessments are instrumental in determining which segments of the community will be serviced and which segments will not be serviced. Consequently, it is imperative that needs assessments accurately reflect community mental health needs.

Federally funded CMHCs are mandated by Public Law 94-63 to assess the mental health needs of their catchment area, and based on these needs, design, implement, and evaluate ameliorative programs (Sallis & Henggeler, 1980b). Stewart (1979) has noted that a comprehensive needs assessment should identify community problems from several perspectives and describe the community resources that exist to meet such problems. Then, priorities can be set for developing new programs or modifying existing services to satisfy unmet needs. Similarly, Siegel, Attkisson, and Carson (1978) have concluded that needs assessments should be utilized to maintain a dialogue between the CMHC and a broad range of community residents. This dialogue helps to assure that community mental health needs are being met and that existing services are relevant.

Several authors have emphasized that needs assessments are a component of the process of service planning, delivery, and evaluation (Pharis, 1976; Raeburn & Seymour, 1979; Turner, Kimbrough, & Traynham, 1977). As such, needs assessments are meaningless unless CMHCs are both monetarily and ideologically committed to utilization of the results (Sallis & Henggeler, 1980b). Likewise, the planning and delivery of mental health services without prior assessment of needs is absurd. As a consequence of this relationship, several of the problems encountered when conducting needs assessments in rural areas are similar to those observed for the delivery, planning, and evaluation of rural services. Before these problems are discussed, the hypothesized strengths and weaknesses of existing needs assessment techniques are described.

NEEDS–ASSESSMENT TECHNIQUES

Researchers and CMHC personnel have developed numerous techniques in attempting to assess and set priorities for community mental health needs. Reviewers of these techniques have typically classified them into two or three broad categories. For example, Sallis and Henggeler (1980b) differentiated hard data from impressionistic strategies.

However, in examining the various classification schemes, it seems that Stewart's (1979) scheme is the most descriptive. He has noted that a comprehensive needs assessment included an evaluation of "problem," "desire," and "solution." *Problem* includes descriptions of the size and nature of the particular problems in a particular community as well as a consideration of the services that are available to meet these problems. *Desire* is an assessment of diverse community members' attitudes concerning both the problems and the existing services. *Solution* is a joint decision-making process and is based on an analysis of the problems and the desires. Stewart's scheme is used to classify each of the needs–assessment techniques that are currently in use. The impressions of several reviewers (Aponte, 1978; Bell, Nguyen, Warheit, & Buhl, 1978; Sallis & Henggeler, 1980b; Siegel, Attkisson, & Carson, 1978) are integrated to briefly delineate and describe the general usefulness of each technique.

Problem

Social and Health Indicators Analysis

The underlying assumption of this approach is that certain descriptive social and demographic statistics (e.g., number of single-parent families) relate to the number of residents who need specific mental health services. This technique is widely used and is strongly supported by the federal government. Since the pertinent statistics are readily available in public records, social and health indicators analysis is an easy, inexpensive way to meet funding requirements. However, there are serious limitations to the use of this approach. Foremost is that its global nature does not permit an analysis of the most needed mental health services. For example, the fact that there exists a certain percentage of single-parent families in a catchment area can be used to justify a wide variety of intervention programs (e.g., day care, parent training, big brothers and big sisters, adult education, psychopharmacology, individual psychotherapy, and recreational centers). Consequently, CMHC staff often use this needs–assessment technique to justify the development of preconceived treatment services.

Rates under Treatment

Users of this technique typically assume that client demands for service accurately reflect community needs. Hence, community service agencies are surveyed to determine the numbers and characteristics of their respective clients. This is a relatively easy and inexpensive procedure because it capitalizes on existing data. However, the exclusive use of the rates-under-treatment approach fails to consider that demands for service are influenced by factors other than mental health need (e.g., availability of service, publicity, consumer attitudes toward mental health in general and the CMHC in particular). Furthermore, residents who have needs that are not addressed by current services are ignored. As such, the use of this approach typically supports the status quo.

Epidemiology

Epidemiological surveys attempt to assess the distribution of mental disorder in the population. This is accomplished by administering a mental status questionnaire to a random sample of community residents. Such direct procedures can provide valuable hypotheses about the emotional and interpersonal characteristics of different community segments. However, the epidemiological approach is very expensive. In addition, several researchers have questioned the validity of the instruments that are commonly employed within this approach.

Desire

Survey of Community Residents

Random samples of community residents are asked to give their perceptions of the community's mental health needs. Surveys can be conducted on a door-to-door basis, by telephone, or through the mail. Residents' knowledge and evaluations of existing services can also be solicited. Surveys of community residents serve several valuable functions. First, since CMHCs are mandated to service the community, an assessment of community-perceived needs seems essential. Second, such an evaluation is an excellent public relations device for the CMHC, presenting an image of flexible responsivity. Finally, such surveys lay the groundwork for more active consumer participation and input. Although surveys of community residents can be expensive, the potential advantages are certainly worth the additional cost.

Survey of Key Informants

This approach assesses the perceptions of various professionals (e.g., clergy, police, mental health, medical, and educational) who are directly or indirectly involved in the delivery of social services. Since these people are both knowledgeable about and in close contact with community residents, it is assumed that they have a good understanding of the extant mental health problems. Such surveys can promote positive relations between the CMHC and other agencies, identify pockets of resistance in the community, and determine what services are readily available. A disadvantage of this approach is that the professionals might tend to report need priorities that are self-serving.

Community Forum

Diverse community residents, especially those who represent special interest groups, are invited to a meeting. The purpose of the meeting is to ascertain opinions about possible community mental health problems. This approach is inexpensive and allows for the expression of a wide range of ideas. Such meetings can also promote interagency contacts and serve as catalysts for change. However, it is important that all points of view are heard and that the session is not dominated by a select few.

Solution

Nominal Group Process

After the problems are identified and ranked, a group of individuals meet to decide which problems require program development. This group typically includes community representatives, key administrators, civic leaders, and mental health professionals. It is essential that each participant has a chance for substantial input. An opportunity to question and clarify ideas from several diverse perspectives is thereby facilitated. Additional advantages include the possibility of increased interagency harmony and wide-range support for subsequent program decisions.

Needs Assessments in Rural Areas

The mental health need-priorities identified in rural communities differ substantially from those in urban communities. Christenson (1974) surveyed 3,115 heads of households across the state of North Carolina. Each respondent completed a questionnaire that assessed his or her perception of the seriousness of a wide variety of social, health, environmental, and political problems. Rural residents tended to perceive more problems as serious than did urban residents. Rural residents were especially concerned about such issues as: employment opportunities; recreational facilities; cultural opportunities; and social services to children, the elderly, and handicapped citizens. On the other hand, urban residents were more concerned about water and air pollution, the use of illegal drugs, the adequacy of law enforcement, public transportation, and race relations. Similar differences between rural and urban perceptions were identified by Willie (1972) in New York State. Rural residents reported that the development of ambulatory health care facilities, outpatient mental health services, and programs for the elderly were high need priorities. Urban residents, who already had such services, were more concerned with upgrading them.

Researchers have also used epidemiological surveys to assess mental health needs in rural communities. Edgerton, Bentz, and Hollister (1970) administered the Health Opinion Survey (HOS) to 1,405 adults who lived in rural North Carolina. The HOS primarily assesses psychoneurotic and psychophysiological symptoms. Overall, the responses of 10% of the respondents reflected psychiatric impairment and the responses of an additional 14% reflected probable impairment. Especially high rates of disorder were evidenced among individuals who were nonwhite, older, not married, and of lower socioeconomic status. Similar findings were reported by Husaini, Neff, and Stone (1979) who administered three psychiatric impairment inventories, including the HOS, to 713 adults residing in rural Tennessee. Results indicated that approximately 12% of the respondents evidenced psychiatric impairment. High rates of impairment were observed for adults who were female, not married, and of lower socioeconomic status.

Problems in Rural Needs Assessment

Although there are certain problems in conducting any needs assessment, there are some difficulties that are special to needs assessments conducted in rural areas. In general, these problems relate to either (1) the reliability and validity of needs–assessment techniques, or (2) the attitudes and interpersonal behaviors of the evaluators and the community residents. Within each of these domains there are numerous factors that can complicate and distort the evaluation of need priorities.

Reliability and Validity of Techniques

Despite the social and economic importance of needs assessments, the reliability and validity of needs–assessment techniques have received little attention in the scientific community. Minimally, different needs–assessment techniques should yield similar priority rankings when conducted on the same population. Furthermore, the outcomes of needs assessments should suggest specific intervention programs that are needed by the community.

Comparisons of Techniques

Several researchers have found that when different community groups are surveyed, they report widely divergent community mental health need-priorities. Henggeler, Sallis, and Cooper (1980) administered a questionnaire to a random sample of university students and to professionals who met the mental health needs of students and their families. The questionnaire assessed the respondents' perceptions of the seriousness of various mental health problems among university students and their families. The need priorities established by the students differed considerably from those established by the professionals. For example, the students rated problems of substance abuse as most serious, whereas the professionals rated problems of an academic/career or neurotic nature as most serious. Since the professionals had a vested interest in treating academic/career and neurotic problems, the authors concluded that they might have been biased toward presenting more socially acceptable and personally advantageous views of university mental health needs. At any rate, the fact that the groups identified very different need priorities suggests that the isolated use of either survey technique would lead to the establishment of intervention programs that may or may not reflect actual community needs.

The conclusions of Henggeler *et al.* (1980) are supported by survey research conducted in nonacademic settings. Burdick (1980) reported that residents in an Indiana catchment area indicated that substance abuse was the community's most serious problem. However, CMHC staff reported that family problems and neuroses were most serious. Weiss (1975) assessed the perspectives of five community groups regarding several community mental health problems. Of these groups, the mental health professionals perceived the greatest need for additional mental health services. Similarly, Neigher and Baker (1976) observed that surveys of community residents and CMHC staff yielded many discrepancies in the priorities set by each group. Finally, Sallis and Henggeler (1980a) reported that findings from an epidemiological survey did not relate to priorities established by community residents. However, there was some indication that the need priorities established by the community mental health professionals did relate to those of the epidemiological survey.

Need priorities established by the rates-under-treatment technique do not relate to priorities established by either epidemiological surveys or by social and health indicator analyses. Schwab, Warheit, and Fennell (1975) interviewed a representative sample of residents in Alachua County, Florida, regarding their mental health status and their service utilization. Although 18.4% of the respondents were classified as probable needers of mental health care, only 4.6% utilized mental health services. Furthermore, their degree of mental health need did *not* relate to their service utilization; well-adjusted individuals were as likely to use mental health services as were poorly adjusted individuals. Similarly, in a rural study described earlier, Husaini *et al.* (1979) observed that indices of psychiatric difficulties did not predict service utilization. In another study, Husaini and Mathis (1978) examined the relations between the social indicators of the Mental Health Demographic Profile System and the utilization of mental health services in an urban black community. The Overall Index of the social indicators was not significantly correlated with rates of service utilization.

Two general conclusions can be drawn from these findings. First, the need priorities established by different needs–assessment techniques do not relate to those established by other techniques. Second, the responses of the community mental health professionals tend to serve their own interests.

Utility of Techniques

The overriding purpose of conducting needs assessments is to help decide whether new services are needed and whether existing services should continue at their present level. Most reviewers (e.g., Bell *et al.*, 1978; Siegel *et al.*, 1978) have reported that various needs–assessment techniques are very useful toward this end. However, such conclusions reject the complex nature of psychosocial difficulties. Unless the disease model of mental illness is accurate, the etiology of psychosocial difficulties and the factors that maintain such difficulties vary greatly from individual to individual. Typically, ameliorative interventions should focus on either these etiological or maintaining variables. Most needs assessments give little information toward this end. Two examples are given to clarify this point.

The social and health indicators analysis is a widely accepted needs–assessment technique. Yet, what is the significance of finding that 5% or 25% of community residents live below the poverty level? What mental health interventions are suggested by this statistic? Do residents require improved child–management skills, psychoanalysis, Gestalt group training, medication, biofeedback, learning disabilities classrooms, day hopsitals, or any other of the many treatment strategies available? Findings from social and health indicators analysis can be and have been used to justify a wide and diverse range of intervention programs. Nevertheless, the technique does little to specify the mental health priorities of the community.

Epidemiological surveys are also highly touted. Yet, what are the clinical implications of a finding that 1% or 10% of community residents are depressed? Many depressions are normal, nonpathological reactions to loss (e.g., Kübler-Ross, 1969). The etiological and maintaining factors associated with other depressions vary widely. Such factors might include unemployment; poor living conditions; financial difficulties; problems with spouse, parents, or children; poor nutrition; learned helplessness; unrealistic attitudes and expectations; high neighborhood crime rates; low levels of norepinephrine or serotonin; the list could continue. For each person, the same symptomatology might require very different treatment. Hence, ameliorative programs could range from having new industry locate in the community to dispensing tricyclics and monoamine oxidase inhibitors. Again, the use of the needs–assessment technique does little to identiy which intervention programs are most needed by the community.

Relation between Community Residents and Mental Health Professionals

Needs assessments are components of program development and service delivery. Consequently, it is important to consider the interpersonal relationships between the assessors of need and the community members. It is likely that assessors who possess contrasting interpersonal styles will obtain different perspectives from respondents. Some individuals are capable of facilitating open and clear communications, but others are not. When assessment strategies require extensive interpersonal contact, the potential influence that this contact has on outcome data must not be ignored.

This section considers the influence that residents' attitudes toward both mental illness and mental health professionals might have on the evaluation of community mental health needs. The actions of the mental health professional during this phase of program development is critical since first impressions are often quite durable. Furthermore, the necessity of working within the existing power structure and attending to the web of social interrelationships is emphasized.

Attitudes toward Mental Illness and Mental Health Professionals

Bentz, Hollister, and Edgerton (1971) have reported that rural residents attach greater stigma to mental illness than urban residents. Yet, rural community leaders, teachers, and residents agree that mental illness is a serious problem that varies in form and severity (Bentz, Hollister, Edgerton, Miller, & Aponte, 1973). These authors observed that, compared to leaders and teachers, community residents tended to believe that heredity, moral weakness, and physical injury are primary factors in the etiology of mental illness. Thus, rural residents felt that deviant behavior should be dealt with punitively. However, Michaux, Dasinger, Foster, and Pruim (1974) have noted that the families of rural patients have a greater appreciation for the sources of stress experienced by the patient.

Investigations of the attitudes of rural residents toward mental health professionals have provided contradictory results. For example, Bentz *et al.* (1973) found that the vast majority of community leaders, teachers, and residents reported that they would seek psychiatric help when faced with a problem and would encourage a friend to do likewise. A high percentage of the residents felt that psychiatric treatment would benefit the client; community leaders and teachers, however, were less optimistic.

In contrast to the above findings, Turner *et al.* (1977) observed that for a variety of mental health problems the local CMHC was not an attractive source of help. Members of several community organizations ranked eight referral sources (e.g., friends, pastor, state mental hospital) in regard to their preference for ameliorating nine mental health problems (e.g., drug abuse, persecution thoughts, mental retardation). Results showed that the CMHC was ranked above fifth for only two mental health problems. The center was never viewed as the primary help source for a particular problem. These findings are consistent with Falcone's (1979) conclusion that clinicians in rural areas often perceive a lack of community support for their services (Boris, 1971; Gertz, Meider, & Pluckham, 1975). Such clinicians have reported that community residents are skeptical regarding the efficacy of their treatment (Suchman, 1965).

In overview, it seems that rural residents hold several beliefs concerning the etiology of mental illness and several attitudes toward the mental health profession that are not likely to facilitate the acquisition of accurate needs–assessment data. Remedies for this problem are described in the following pages. For the most part, solutions require mental health professionals to (1) communicate clearly and without condescension with residents, (2) recognize the many inherent weaknesses of clinical interventions, and (3) emit those behaviors that are conducive to positive reciprocity with highly divergent individuals.

Assessing Needs in Unserved Areas

Two groups of authors have described their attempts at evaluating the mental health needs of unserved rural areas. As outsiders, these authors have recognized the importance of proceeding slowly and cautiously. Their different methods provide useful models for other professionals faced with such a task.

Naftulin, Donnelly, and O'Halloran (1974) developed a strategy that allowed community leaders to determine for themselves the community's needs and to begin programs designed to meet those needs.

Three physicians from Coalinga, California, requested the authors' assistance in determining more effective ways of resolving the community's mental health problems. The group decided to conduct a course in mental health counseling at the local community college for the community's care givers. The course was run flexibly and all who attended were actively encouraged to participate. Upon completion, the participants were able to concretely and realistically specify the nature of the community's problems. They felt that many of these problems could be resolved without outside funding if pertinent individuals and agencies would interact and coordinate their services. The participants also published a 41-page directory of community services and distributed it to community residents.

Kahn, McWilliams, Balch, Chang, and Ireland (1976) developed mental health services for Marana, Arizona, in order to provide relevant training for doctoral students in clinical-community psychology. To determine the community's mental health needs, teams of graduate students surveyed community leaders, a clergyman, the police, a social worker, and several teachers. The students and faculty supervisors decided that the identified problems could best be met through consultation in the schools and the establishment of a small mental health clinic. At first, very few residents sought services. However, as contacts with indigenous community workers were cultivated, referrals increased. The authors reported that the political perspectives of the residents differed greatly from those of the students (i.e., conservative vs. liberal). Hence, it was important for the students to understand the others' perspectives and not unilaterally advocate their personal biases. Finally, the authors noted the importance of strengthening the traditional community lines of communication to facilitate cooperation.

Interpersonal and Systems Issues

In a very interesting and pragmatic article, Jeffrey and Reeve (1978) have discussed the dynamic nature of the interface between the new rural mental health center and the existing social and professional community. The authors noted that in an urban area the emergence of a new agency may pass unnoticed. However, in a rural area the new agency evokes a shift in the equilibrium of the existing system so that the agency is either isolated or integrated. The existing equilibrium has developed over many years and is highly relevant to the participants. Competent or not, the professionals know each other and have a history of interaction. Consequently, the newcomer must assess the system patiently and cautiously. Attempts to bypass the assessment phase (by implementing innovative services) can evoke difficulties. A flurry of activity will be perceived by the local professionals as threatening. They might fear that the mental health workers do not appreciate the complexity of local problems or that their own services will not compare favorably to the innovative ones. Consequently, the mental health worker must accept that the local professionals possess significant knowledge about the community and have valuable insight to its problems. In rural settings, personal trust is more important than professional expertise. Without trust, expertise will be ignored. Thus, workers should cultivate interpersonal relationships before innovative programs. Jeffrey and Reeve suggested that a joint fishing trip might be more productive than displays of esoteric prowess.

Similar recommendations for needs assessment, the initial stage of program development, have been advocated by other authors (Berken & Eisdorfer, 1970; Halpern & Love, 1971; Hladky, 1968; Hurder, 1968; Jones, 1972; Macgregor, 1966; Wedel, 1969). Macgregor (1966) has argued that health professionals must understand the values of the community as well as its social structure. For example, self-reliance is highly valued in rural New England. Therefore, to assure the success of a local immunization clinic, it was necessary to avoid its appearance as a welfare activity for the poor. This was accomplished by upper middle-class women inviting low income families to accompany them and their children to the clinic. Other health programs encouraged self-testing (e.g., diabetes).

Macgregor (1966) and the other authors noted above have discussed several additional guidelines that are relevant to the assessment of rural mental health needs and the establishment of ameliorative services: (1) Legal authority alone is not sufficient. The entire network of existing agencies must be involved in the process. (2) The community must believe that a problem exists before it will accept a new program. (3) Assessments of need and initiation of services are best achieved by individuals who are regarded highly by the community. Alliances with individuals who are outside the community's mainstream may be counterproductive. (4) Contradicting or ignoring traditional beliefs regarding the etiology of problems may lead to the rejection of programs. (5) Any leadership by outside professionals must be preceded by extensive involvement with the social network. The professionals should go through proper channels and avoid any existing political conflicts between or within community agencies.

CONCLUSION

The two main issues in conducting rural needs assessments center on (1) the lack of established reliability/validity of needs–assessment techniques, and (2) attitudinal and interpersonal problems encountered during the assessment. These difficulties can be attenuated by following certain suggestions. First, the exclusive reliance on the social and health indicators analysis, rates-under-treatment, or epidemiological approaches will provide little clarification of specific community mental health needs and will not promote the CMHC in the community. Second, the most productive approach would be for the CMHC staff to survey cautiously community residents, professionals, and key informants regarding their perceptions of mental health needs as well as their attitudes toward mental illness and the mental health profession. A covert purpose of these surveys is to establish interpersonal contact and to begin the development of trusting and respectful relations. Third, when the surveys are completed, representatives of the survey groups should meet to discuss differences in perceptions and jointly determine need and service priorities. A CMHC staff member should act as a consultant and moderator, not as the chairperson. His or her role is to provide information regarding what is and what is not practically feasible. Finally, pertinent community individuals and agencies should be involved, in whatever way is appropriate, in the development of any services.

REFERENCES

Aponte, J. F. A need in search of a theory and an approach. *Journal of Community Psychology*, 1978, *6*, 42–44.

Bell, R. A., Nguyen, T. D., Warheit, G. J., & Buhl, J. M. Service utilization, social indicator, and citizen survey approaches to human service need assessment. In C. C. Attkisson, W. A. Hargreaves, M. J. Horowitz, & J. E. Sorenson (Eds.), *Evaluation of human services programs*. New York: Academic Press, 1978.

Bentz, W. K., Hollister, W. G., & Edgerton, J. W. Assessing the stigma of mental illness. *The Psychiatric Forum*, 1971, Winter, 17–22.

Bentz, W. K., Hollister, W. G., Edgerton, J. W., Miller, F. T., & Aponte, J. F. *Experiences in rural mental health*. Chapel Hill: University of North Carolina, 1973.

Berken, T. E., & Eisdorfer, C. Closed ranks in microcosm: Pitfalls of a training experience in community consultation. *Community Mental Health Journal*, 1970, *6*, 101–109.

Boris, H. N. The Seelsorger in rural Vermont. *International Journal of Group Psychotherapy*, 1971, *21*, 159–173.

Burdick, J. A. Personal communication, April 1, 1980.

Christenson, J. A. *North Carolina, today and tomorrow, Vol. 5: Rural-urban problems in North Carolina*. Raleigh: North Carolina Agricultural Extension Service, Misc. Ext. Publication 113, 1974.

Edgerton, J. W., Bentz, W. K., & Hollister, W. G. Epidemiological data for mental health center planning: Demographic factors and responses to stress among rural people. *American Journal of Public Health*, 1970, *60*, 1065–1071.

Falcone, A. M. *The delivery of rural mental health services: A review and assessment of the literature*. Unpublished manuscript, 1979. (Available from A. M. Falcone, Department of Psychology, Memphis State University, Memphis, Tennessee).

Gertz, B., Meider, J., & Pluckham, M. L. A survey of rural community mental health needs and resources. *Hospital and Community Psychiatry*, 1975, *26*, 816–819.

Halpern, H., & Love, R. W. Initiating community consultation in rural areas. *Hospital and Community Psychiatry*, 1971, *22*, 274–277.

Henggeler, S. W., Sallis, J. F., & Cooper, P. F. Comparison of university mental health needs priorities identified by professionals and students. *Journal of Counseling Psychology*, 1980, *27*, 217–219.

Hladky, F. A psychiatric program in a rural mental health plan. In L. J. Duhl & R. L. Leopold (Eds.), *Mental health and urban social policy: A casebook of community actions.* San Francisco: Jossey-Bass, 1968.

Hoagland, M. A new day in rural mental services. *New dimensions in mental health: Report from the Director, National Institute of Mental Health.* Washington, D.C.: U.S. Government Printing Office, 1978.

Hurder, W. P. Maximum service–minimum manpower. In L. J. Duhl & R. L. Leopold (Eds.), *Mental health and urban social policy: A casebook of community actions.* San Francisco: Jossey-Bass, 1968.

Husaini, B. A., & Mathis, A. Mental health needs and service utilization in a predominantly black community. *Journal of Community Psychology*, 1978, *6*, 303–308.

Husaini, B. A., Neff, J. A., & Stone, R. H. Psychiatric impairment in rural communities. *Journal of Community Psychology*, 1979, *7*, 137–146.

Jeffrey, M. J., & Reeve, R. E. Community mental health services in rural areas: Some practical issues. *Community Mental Health Journal*, 1978, *14*, 54–62.

Jones, M. Community involvement in the planning of a rural mental health center. In A. Beigel & A. D. Levenson (Eds.), *The community mental health center: Strategies and programs.* New York: Basic Books, 1972.

Kahn, M. W., McWilliams, S. A., Balch, P., Chang, A. F., & Ireland, J. Developing a rural mental health service from a base in an academic clinical psychology program. *American Journal of Community Psychology*, 1976, *4*, 113–127.

Kübler-Ross, E. *On death and dying.* New York: Macmillan, 1969.

Leighton, D. C., Leighton, A. H., & Armstrong, R. A. Community psychiatry in a rural area: A social psychiatric approach. In L. Bellak (Ed.), *Handbook of community psychiatry.* New York: Grune & Stratton, 1964.

Llewellyn-Thomas, E. The prevalence of psychiatric symptoms within an island fishing village. *Canadian Medical Association Journal*, 1960, *83*, 197–204.

Macgregor, G. The development of rural community health services. *Human Organization*, 1966, *25*, 16–19.

Michaux, M. H., Dasinger, E. M., Foster, S. A., & Pruim, R. J. Treatment outcome in an urban and a rural day hospital. *Social Psychiatry*, 1974, *9*, 31–38.

Naftulin, D. H., Donnelly, F. A., & O'Halloran, P. B. Mental health courses as a facilitator for change in a rural community. *Community Mental Health Journal*, 1974, *10*, 359–365.

Neigher, W. D., & Baker, D. P. Approaches to community mental health needs assessment: The community residents' survey. In W. Neigher, R. J. Hammer, & G. Landsberg (Eds.), *Emerging developments in mental health program evaluation.* New York: Argold Press, 1976.

Pharis, D. B. The use of needs assessment techniques in mental health planning: A review of the literature. *Community Mental Health Review*, 1976, *1*, 1–10.

Raeburn, J. M., & Seymour, F. W. A simple systems model for community programs. *Journal of Community Psychology*, 1979, *7*, 290–297.

Sallis, J. F., & Henggeler, S. W. *Mental health needs assessments in relation to incidence of problems.* Paper presented at the meeting of the Southeastern Psychological Association, Washington, D.C., March 1980. (a)

Sallis, J., & Henggeler, S. W. Needs assessment: A critical review. *Administration in Mental Health*, 1980, *7*, 200–209. (b)

Schwab, J. J., Warheit, G. J., & Fennell, E. B. An epidemiologic assessment of needs and utilization of services. *Evaluation*, 1975, *2*, 65–67.

Siegel, L. M., Attkisson, C. C., & Carson, L. G. Need identification and program planning in the community context. In C. C. Attkisson, W. A. Hargreaves, M. J. Horowitz, & J. E. Sorensen (Eds.), *Evaluation of human service programs*. New York: Academic Press, 1978.

Stewart, R. The nature of needs assessment in community mental health. *Community Mental Health Journal*, 1979, *15*, 287–295.

Suchman, E. A. Social patterns of illness and medical care. *Journal of Health and Human Behavior*, 1965, *6*, 2–16.

Turner, J. T., Kimbrough, W. W., & Traynham, R. N. A survey of community perceptions of critical life situations and community helping sources as a tool for mental health program development. *Journal of Community Psychology*, 1977, *5*, 225–230.

Wedel, H. L. Characteristics of community mental health center operations in small communities. *Community Mental Health Journal*, 1969, *5*, 437–444.

Weiss, A. T. The consumer model of assessing community mental health needs. *Evaluation*, 1975, *2*, 71–73.

Willie, C. V. Health care needs of the disadvantaged in a rural-urban area. *HSMHA Health Reports*, 1972, *87*, 81–86.

12

Problems in Program Development and the Development of Alternatives

Steven R. Heyman

Overview

Until very recently, only a few articles in community psychology have addressed the particular problems, needs, and alternatives confronting the *rural* community psychologist. This chapter addresses the unique difficulties inherent in the development, implementation, and evaluation of traditional and alternative services in rural areas. The key assumption is that the basic problems are not founded in the more obvious hindrances to rural programs (such as fewer professionals or larger geographic areas requiring service) but in the patterns and processes of rural life that professionals, often trained in urban areas or at large universities, are not aware of on initial entrance into rural areas. Programs, models, and original research are described to illustrate the alternatives available to the rural community psychologist.

If rural community psychology were to select a symbolic representative, I would propose the Roman deity Janus. Unique among these deities, Janus's two faces allow him to see past and future, and to see multiple situations simultaneously. Certainly rural life is a part of America's past, and yet remains a part of the future. Moreover, rural commu-

STEVEN R. HEYMAN • Department of Psychology, University of Wyoming, Laramie, Wyoming 82071.

nity psychology must look not only to the past for programs and models that have been utilized, in order to learn what has and has not worked, but to the future as well, so that new models and methods can be developed.

The problems and advantages that are obvious and inherent in rural psychological research, and those that are subtle and complex, need recognition. In learning from the experiences of others, researchers must not ignore the unique, individual aspects of each rural area. It is necessary to look beyond the stereotypes and generalizations about rural life to the very real and diverse situations that encompass America's rural communities. For these multiple requirements, the unusual abilities of Janus would be of great help, even if only symbolically.

BACKGROUND

The problems in program development for rural community psychology have their sources in the preparation (or, more accurately, the lack of preparation) for the rural experience of the professional psychologist and mental health worker. A review of the *American Journal of Community Psychology* reveals only four articles that are clearly based on a rural experience or a rural population (Johnson, 1975; Kahn, McWilliams, Balch, Chang, & Ireland, 1976; Kahn, Williams, Galvez, Lejero, Conrad, & Goldstein, 1975; Tyler & Dreyer, 1975). A sampling of several recent community psychology texts (Heller & Monahan, 1977; Iscoe, Bloom, & Spielberger, 1977; Mann, 1978; Nietzel, Winnett, MacDonald, & Davidson, 1977; Rappaport, 1977; Zax & Specter, 1974) finds no pages identified specifically as dealing with rural problems, although there are some references to programs done in "rural" areas. Each text more directly addresses the problems of the urban community psychologist.

In a survey of the content of graduate training programs and internships with a community psychology/community mental health component, Barton, Andrulis, Grove, and Aponte (1976) report that urban-based action programs were ranked 5th in percentage of time devoted to the topic out of 36 areas addressed by graduate programs, and sixth for internship programs. Rural community action programs were 31st in university programs and 35th for internship programs. Many of the graduate programs and internship settings are located in urban areas and are concerned with urban programs (Perlmutter, 1979). Even when located in what would otherwise be rural areas, the presence of a large university indelibly changes the community into something quite different, and typically the school's programs do not focus on rural problems (Heyman, 1979).

The consideration of rural areas conjures stereotypes and generalizations, even for professionals. While most no longer consider rural populations to be made up of numbers of "Ma and Pa Kettles" sitting on a decaying porch with a jug of moonshine hidden in the bushes, other, less obviously inaccurate characterizations are drawn.

Informal discussions with urban psychologists often produce the assumption that rural community members and community leaders are less aware of, or less sympathetic toward, the psychological needs and problems of community members. This may have been true in the past (Gurin, Veroff, & Feld, 1960), although the research was not clear or definitive. More recent research suggests that the understanding and sympathies of urban and rural residents are far more similar than they are different (Bentz & Edgerton, 1970).

Often, problem-oriented urban models or programs filter gradually into less urban areas, and some assume a lack of awareness in rural areas (Buxton, 1973). The electronic media transmit information instantaneously to rural and urban areas alike. The slower response by community mental health workers, as seen by those working in rural areas, is more related to the absence of personnel or facilities with which to respond (Buxton, 1973; Daniels, 1967).

There are problems, both obvious and subtle, that confront the rural community psychologist. This slag, however, is as much a part of the ore as is the gold—the opportunities for unique, challenging, and meaningful opportunities that await the rural psychologist (Daniels, 1967; Heyman, 1979; Huessy, 1972).

The most obvious problems confronting the development of programs in rural areas are: large and sparsely populated geographic areas to be served; fewer available trained professionals; difficulties in recruiting personnel to work in these areas; logistics in obtaining and maintaining funding for rural services. These are cited in many of the articles dealing with rural issues (Eisdorfer, Altrocci, & Young, 1968; Flax, Ivens, Wagenfeld, & Weiss, 1978; Gertz, Meider, & Pluckhan, 1975; Huessy, 1972a,b; Jeffrey & Reeve, 1978; Jones, Wagenfeld, & Robin, 1976). These obstacles perpetuate other difficulties:

> When number relative to population is considered, psychologists are concentrated in affluent urban states and in university towns. The same pattern was obtained for all the groups providing mental health services. No evidence was obtained that any of these groups is distributed in a way offering special advantages for serving groups such as poor, black, or rural people, who need better access to mental health services. (Richards & Gottfredson, 1978, p. 1)

Based on another nationwide survey, McPheeters and Harding (1978) report similar findings.

One urban psychologist suggested, cavalierly, "All these problems can be solved by buckets of bucks." This assumed that the provision and placement of services guarantees their appropriate and successful use. The literature suggests this does not occur automatically in urban areas (Zax & Specter, 1974), and may be less true in rural areas, where the more direct view of a service and its personnel can contribute to success or failure (Buxton, 1973; Libo & Griffith, 1966).

A recurring theme in the literature on rural mental health describes the problems faced by personnel and services until they are accepted, and the possibility of the rejection of personnel by that amorphous being, "the community." (Buxton, 1973; Heyman, 1979; Libo & Griffith, 1966). There are two problems of definition further complicating the consideration of these issues: the definitions of *rural* and of *community psychology*, topics central to this paper.

One could define rural quite easily, based on objective federal standards, and locate all rural mental health centers based on these criteria (Flax *et al.*, 1978; Gertz *et al.*, 1975; Jones, Robin, & Wagenfeld, 1974). When Jones *et al.* (1976) state that "rural America is characterized, in part, by widespread proverty, physical isolation, and a paucity of human services resources" (p. 178), a powerful image of Appalachian poverty can be conveyed that obscures the key words *in part*. Clarifying the overgeneralizations about ruralness, we find:

> A poor southern county with a preponderantly black population is very different from an affluent Iowa farm community. Rural areas in New England, in turn, are very different from ranch areas in the Rocky Mountains. In short, even among rural areas there are great differences with regard to such factors as affluence, distance, and social organization. (Huessy, 1972a, p. 200)

An urban worker would expect problems and resources to vary from city to city, and within a city. As Biegel and Naparstek (1979) state, "People don't live in cities; they live in neighborhoods."

Rural areas are not identical, simplistic, stereotyped units. Each needs to be understood in its own context. Programs designed similarly and implemented in close geographic proximity may be well received and work beautifully in some areas, and not in others (Libo & Griffith, 1966).

The definition of "community psychology" presents an even more difficult problem, as there are no objective guidelines that can be used, let alone any clear consensual agreements. The terms *mental health services* and *community mental health* are often, though not necessarily, tied to the provision of more standard therapeutic services, while *community psychology* often refers to supplemental, alternative, or prevention-oriented programs (Daniels, 1967; Hodges & Mahoney, 1970; Rappaport, 1977; Sarason, 1973; Zax & Specter, 1974).

The Problem in the Process

Regardless of the definition of rural community psychology, the critical aspects are not simply the programs that are developed, nor the geographic areas of the professionals involved, but the *process* that unfolds. To examine only one aspect of the process, such as the setting or the program, obscures the overall patterns and the overall process. The professional enters into a system that existed prior to his or her presence, and that will continue whether the professional becomes a part of the process or leaves the system. How the rural community psychologist enters into the system, interacts with it, and the resulting programs, reactions, and outgrowths are visible aspects of the process.

In considering the problems of program development, and the development of alternatives in rural areas, it is possible to isolate artificially some of these facets to allow for a more systematic examination. In reality, however, the professional, the situation encountered, and the interactive processes are interrelated and simultaneous.

THE PERSON

The Rural Community Psychologist

Who is the person coming to the rural area, and what does she or he bring? Is the person someone who has gone to a university for specialized training, and returns to a home area? Is this someone who, looking for a paying position after graduate school, takes a position in a rural area, without caring, or, reluctantly because it is in a rural area? Is the person someone who, for personal reasons, wishes to locate in a rural area? If so, does the person have a familiarity with the psychology of rural areas?

Any professional, working in any setting, will have an impact on those with whom he or she works, as well as on the community. The rural psychologist, however, not only will have a more obvious and (positively or negatively) significant impact on the surrounding community and agencies (Herbert, Chevalier, & Meyers, 1974; Huessy, 1972a,b; Jeffrey & Reeve, 1978; Witt, 1977), but will himself or herself be affected by the interactions. At a basic level, education, dress, grooming, and manners may set the "outside" worker apart from the community (Buxton, 1973).

The professional who comes to a rural area must learn to understand the area for itself, in a phenomenal way. As Buxton (1973) notes, an area considered rural by a city dweller may seem quite large to someone from a village or farm. It is not uncommon for more rural residents to prefer spending as little time as possible in the neighboring "big" city of 5,000 or 50,000 people. The rural life-style, set against a smaller backdrop, should not be prejudged as "simpler." The sociopsychological complexities of personal and business relationships will share a number of similarities with urban and suburban dwellers. The rural life-style may be more complex in certain ways because of the overlapping relationships, close proximity, and lack of anonymity.

There has been some suggestion that a female psychologist may face more problems in entering a rural community than a male would (Riggs & Kugel, 1976). This should not be an automatic assumption, and should be recognized as a stereotype. In many rural areas, the farm or ranch wife has been an equal partner in the responsibilities and privileges of life. It was Wyoming that first enfranchised women, and in the 1920s it elected a female governor, the first state to elect a woman to that position in the history of the United States. The rural woman is given to expect tough work, and can develop the ability to express herself. In many ways such women can be far more androgynous than urban women. Where one finds instability among lower socioeconomic groups, women have been the unifying family members. There is no reason to expect the rural female professional to have any greater, or any fewer problems, than the urban professional woman.

It is desirable for the person entering into a rural area to have both an understanding of rural areas in general and a knowledge of the specific area in which he or she is to work. This is true, of course, for everyone working in a relatively closed system, in which their movements will be noticed clearly and have almost immediate impact. In a closed urban ghetto, with low transiency and strong, informal communication patterns, the same would hold true.

The Service Provider

There is a difference between the situation of the professional entering a rural area for the purpose of supplying traditional mental health services, and that of the person desiring a greater involvement with the community, particularly toward developing newer, innovative programs.

Several writers have described the experience of coming to rural areas to provide, in essence, more traditional services (Boris, 1971; Gurian, 1971; Mazer, 1976; Thomas, 1973). Mental health practitioners, entering into a system in which they are highly visible, will need to have members of the community develop feelings of trust and confidence in them (Cardoza, Ackerly, & Leighton, 1975; Hodges & Mahoney, 1970; Jeffrey & Reeve, 1978; Jones, 1972; Libertoff, 1979). While professionals may at first be granted acceptance based on status or position, over time much of the reaction they elicit will be due to their personal qualities (Wedel, 1969). Libertoff (1979) reports being told by an indigenous caretaker, "not to let those psychologists and social workers and government people come in and mess up and ruin something . . . really important" (p. 1).

If one were to summarize the characteristics of the successful rural mental health worker (Boris, 1971; Gurian, 1971; Mazer, 1976; Thomas, 1973; Wedel, 1969), included would be: a sensitivity and responsiveness to the community; a willingness and ability to work with other agencies; the ability to be a visible, contributing member of the community; and a skill at maintaining good, informal contacts within the community, including "sidewalk consultations." These are general guidelines for any mental health worker, but deviations will be more visible and, like a reverberatory circuit, will have a greater impact upon the rural community and the rural professional.

There are special concerns for the rural mental health worker.

Loss of Client–Therapist Incognito. In a rural setting, the client and therapist are likely to meet socially, professionally, or by accident outside of the office. The therapist may hear about the client in other contexts, from people who know the client but may not know that he or she is the therapist's client. Office staff or co-workers who have been in the community longer than the therapist may be sources of information and gossip about a client (Gertz *et al.*, 1975; Jones *et al.*, 1976).

The therapist, too, will be visible. As one social worker remarked, "I've had a number of clients tell me they'd checked me out before coming in for therapy, not with any agency, organization, or even other professionals, but with people around town." Similar experiences are reported by others (Boris, 1971; Mazer, 1976).

Isolation. The therapist may be the only trained mental health professional in the area. This minimizes the opportunities for case conferences, professional feedback, referral, and comradery.

Multiple Roles. The therapist may be known in the community by role. In many other situations he or she may be addressed in this role, and not as simply another person or community member.

Unrealistic Treatment Expectations. If a therapist is establishing a new service in a community, there may be unrealistic expectations about what can be done. As the planning for a new center or service develops, other agencies or individuals may begin to earmark clients for the mental health worker; when the service begins, they may be disappointed, angry, or frustrated when all cannot be seen or "cured" (Jeffrey & Reeve, 1978). The therapist must be aware of his/her own treatment expectations

> When coming into a new area, one experiences a natural desire to develop programs and services as quickly as possible . . . [the worker] may try to cut short the assessment stage . . . a flurry of new programs, innovative techniques, and charismatic leaderships are likely to be seen not as stimulating but as threatening. (Jeffrey & Reeve, 1978, p. 56)

Albert Schweitzer Syndrome.   Like one of history's truly great men, some workers assume that in going to a rural community they are going to barbaric, uncivilized areas, bringing light, truth, and healing. If the worker comes into the community in a solicitous, pitying, or patronizing way, with a stance of *noblesse oblige*, the community likely will reject the worker *and* his or her services.

Threat to Others.   Generally, there will be an overt welcoming of mental health services. Some individuals within the community, however, may feel threatened by this new person. Family physicians, social service workers, school personnel, ministers, or "just plain folk" may have been the natural caregivers within the system. They may be less willing to share this role with a professional, or may be unsure whether the professional will, in fact, do a better job (Thompson & Bell, 1969; Libertoff, 1979).

In a small community, the mental health worker is not an island, nor could he or she be. Even if the professional were to wish to do no outreach, no consultation, and no prevention-oriented programs, the person's presence alone would have an impact and would elicit a response from the community. Agencies and groups will need to be contacted, and will request services. Inquiries and referrals (direct and indirect) will come from agencies, schools, civic groups, and curious or concerned citizens.

Let us consider the following example in order to illustrate the important role that personalities play in determining the success or failure of community programs:

> *Jack*, a master's level psychologist, worked four days a week at a center in a community of about 12,000 people. Jack is hard-driving, aggressive, and a somewhat insecure man, who might appear "pushy" at first. *Frank*, a doctoral psychologist, has a cool, easy manner, and a good sense of humor. Both engaged primarily in outpatient therapy. Based on a thumbnail sketch, one might assume Jack would be the less successful, but the opposite was true.
>
> Jack spent a great deal of his free time circulating among the different agencies in town, often "dropping in" to chat. He would arrange to meet others for coffee. He was very open to requests for conferences and consultations with other agencies, and was involved as a community member in

several civic groups. His caring, concern, and participation within the community opened many doors for him. He received referrals and requests from all segments of the community.

Frank would appear before community groups, but in a hesitant way. He did little to build good informal relationships with others, and had no real involvement as a community member. When he and his wife had personal problems in their marriage, varieties of rumors were generated in response to the publicly vicious things they said about each other. There were no direct confrontations between Frank and the community members, but his service became less trusted and valued. Various physicians advised clients to seek help elsewhere, and one social service agency stopped making any referrals to the agency, even though no other therapists were available. It was "Frank's service" and a boycott of him generalized to a boycott of "his" agency.

It is unlikely, however, that a professional will come to a rural agency expecting to do only traditional therapy with outpatients, and not expect to develop consultations or indirect prevention programs. It is likely that the community will expect these services, and most state or federal programs require such activities. Additionally, the worker is likely to need to generate as much local funding as possible for his or her service. Often, such funding is generated through consultation and program development with welfare, criminal justice, Head Start, or school programs.

The Community Psychologist

The more involved with the community the worker is, the greater the impact she or he can have. The double edge is that the greater the involvement with the community, the greater the possibility for errors.

There are conceptions of the personal qualities and related professional abilities that the rural community psychologist, in particular, should have in order to maximize effectiveness and minimize problems in working with, and within, the community. Table 1 summarizes points that recur most often, although only some of the articles are cited in which such ideas are discussed.

It would be artificial to try to subdivide the list into "personal" and "professional" skills. In reality the two are fused together, much like the elements in a chemical compound. Hollister and Miller (1977) suggest that consultants have been guilty of attempting to provide consultation without studying the consultee's framework, mission, values, and working patterns or without setting goals.

The worker will need to draw on his or her personal abilities to identify the crosscurrents of needs, desires, expectations, and groups within a community. Cardoza and associates (1975) describe the work-

TABLE 1. FACILITATIVE PERSONAL QUALITIES
OF THE RURAL COMMUNITY PSYCHOLOGIST

---

1. Ability to be a process observer, a process consultant (Cardoza *et al.*, 1975; Heyman, 1979)
2. Understanding of the social and political networks in the community (Buxton, 1973; Jones, 1972; Witt, 1977)
3. Knowledge of community needs as seen by individuals, groups, and agenices within the community (Jeffrey & Reeve, 1978; Jones, 1972)
4. Integration of efforts with other agencies and professionals (Jeffrey & Reeve, 1978; Robin & Wagenfeld, 1977; Thomas, 1973)
5. Skill at assisting others in community development and organization (Huessy, 1972a,b)
6. Willingness to utilize and work with advisory councils and community groups (Gertz *et al.*, 1975)
7. Ability to maintain communication with all segments of the community, keeping them informed (Daniels, 1967)
8. Good communication skills (Stai & Atkinson, 1972)
9. Realistic, genuine, nonpatronizing concern for the community (Boris, 1971; Mazer, 1976)
10. Willingness to be a generalist in therapy with clients and in community involvement (Ginsberg, 1966)
11. Motivation to encourage and assist staff to be flexible and innovative (Jones *et al.*, 1976; Kinzie, Shore, & Pattison, 1972)
12. Commitment to and involvement with community outside of work (Jones *et al.*, 1974)
13. Initiative to locate and develop programs that utilize indigenous workers (Daniels, 1967; Herbert *et al.*, 1974; Lee, Gianturco, & Eisdorfer, 1974; Raft, Coley, & Miller, 1976)

---

er's need to understand the community's process, and to identify individuals who play key roles, while ascertaining their motivations, capabilities, and their interactions within the community. "The total process of bringing together felt needs and resources . . . often means a working through and reformulations of the felt needs in terms of specific goals and plans for action" (p. 219). Similar patterns are described by Halpern and Love (1971).

In their comparisons of urban and rural mental health workers, Jones *et al.* (1976) found that rural workers spent about twice as much time as urban workers in community planning and development. The workers saw themsevles as more active in the community, and having a greater interest in "community mental health" ideology. Without such an orientation, in a rural area, a worker may be in conflict with local norms and tacit expectations. Rural workers are described as more innovative—avoiding of the traditional medical model—and more stable in their jobs, with comparatively less role conflict. These workers are oriented toward *and* more able to be involved with community programs and process. This is, however, a generalization, and some studies that report the opposite situation exist (Perlmutter, 1979).

The psychologist in the community faces particular problems. In developing consultation or educational programs, or other services to the community, the psychologist is likely to discover that within the community there are disagreements about what *exactly* should be provided. What eventually develops may be quite different from what the varying groups and the professional envisioned initially. The burden is on the worker to understand clearly what is wanted. In commenting on the "idiosyncratic expectations" confronting workers, Hodges and Mahoney (1970) describe the worker's "shaping such diverse aspirations into a realistic program of service" as "a hazard and a strength" of the community movement. They, as others (Thompson & Bell, 1969; Wedel, 1969) caution that the worker must introduce and develop realistic expectations in terms of what can be accomplished, in ways that the community can understand, or else face frustration and disillusionment.

Ongoing contact and communication between the worker, the community, and community members can be critical. This includes feedback on problems, cases that are referred, and programs that are being proposed or developed. This mutual involvement keeps a positive feeling of involvement and concern alive.

One might assume that the successful rural community psychologist is an activist, a politically astute and powerful individual. This assumption, however, is not likely in most cases. It is here that the urban model, which focuses often on social activism in a direct way (Perlmutter & Silverman, 1973), and the rural model diverge sharply. This does not mean the rural community psychologist will not be active within the community. In cases where immediate advocacy is required, the model of the activist may be adopted. In many instances, however, subtle and fragile relationships exist between agencies, individuals, and communities. The activist model, in such a process, might produce fewer gains than would other roles or patterns.

The worker with an active community orientation inevitably becomes an active part of the community process. The more personal and political he or she becomes, however, the more personal and political will be the response. In some cases the rural community psychologist may be in a position like that of Julius Caesar, being offered the crown of authority or power by the community. This can be unhealthy, if accepted, for the professional and his or her services, particularly if the implications of this role are not accurately assessed (Huessy, 1972a,b; Perlman & Hartman, 1980).

Jones (1972) advises that the community psychologist be patient, meeting the community where it is, and moving as softly and slowly as necessary. Newer plans should be developed only as the community members are "educated" in language and terms compatible with the community's views of the problems. The professional should be aware of his or her own needs, beliefs, plans, and prejudices, so that they do not become a weapon or wedge within the community.

Rather than utilizing a stance as expert or teacher, Cardoza *et al.* (1975) describe how the staff at a center worked collaboratively with the community. They caution the worker to be "always the bridesmaid, and never the bride." The worker may be a catalytic agent, but is advised not to take the executive position or major responsibility for programs developed within the community. Halpern and Love (1971) describe the potential problems of becoming overly involved or overly identified with any single agency or group.

The role opposite that of activist—that of a passive, invisible worker—is not suggested as *THE* role for the rural community psychologist. The process observer and the process consultant, persons able to work with and within the community, to satisfy in reasonable, realistic ways felt needs within the community, and to help develop awareness and services for other programs will likely be most successful. Such a role is described by Hollister and Miller (1976).

Jones *et al.* (1976) describe the willingness of rural workers to initiate community change, even when confronted by resistance. The manner, method, and community relationships involved will be important parts of the process.

> Occasionally, the mental health center will purposely associate itself with a "maverick," but it should be done knowingly, rather than because of incomplete knowledge of the system. (Jeffrey & Reeve, 1978, p. 57)

At the least, the person in rural programs needs to develop a number of qualities and skills, along with an awareness of the rural environment. Most often, although training for rural workers is suggested (Buxton, 1973; Clark & Moore, 1979), few such programs exist (Clark & Moore, 1979; Kahn *et al.*, 1976).

The task confronting the rural community psychologist who wants a clear involvement with the community is a difficult one. In some ways graduate experience in urban areas (or large university communities) will not prepare the person for rural areas, and may provide negative transfer. Trained in larger urban or university areas, students may be accustomed to more impersonal, structured situations, in which roles are clearly defined and a differentiation exists between personal and professional identities (Jeffrey & Reeve, 1979). The students may not be prepared for the sociocultural differences that can create tensions, feelings of isolation, and even exclusion (Kahn *et al.*, 1976). Graduate training in urban areas, or in large university communities, may neglect those special process needs cited by rural workers as important. Indeed, learning to function within nonrural areas may prepare the students to work with such a different process that when they enter a rural area there will be a negative transfer of experience. The rural worker needs education and training experiences that foster an awareness of the critical importance of working with *and* within the community, and contribute to the worker's understanding the structure and functioning of the community and his or her place in it (Barton *et al.*, 1976; Daniels, 1967; Halpern & Love, 1971; Hodges & Mahoney, 1970; Jeffrey & Reeve, 1978; Jones, 1972; Wedel, 1969).

The preparation, the situation, and the development of these personal skills and qualities are the critical variables. The many rewards available are, in essence, parallel to the problems, pitfalls, and frustrations. An understanding of oneself, of the systems active in a particular rural situation, and of the interactive process is of paramount importance.

THE SITUATION

There are generalizations, over-generalizations, and stereotypes about rural areas that the worker will need to clarify. Useful information should be gleaned from the situations and experiences of others, but should not become blinders that prevent the rural worker from viewing each situation on its own terms.

For example, ask colleagues which states have the largest rural populations. They are not southern or western states, but New York and Pennsylvania (Ginsberg, 1966). The situation presented by the rural areas in these states are overshadowed, no doubt, by the metropolitan areas, but are quite different from the situations of Montana, Wyoming, or Mississippi.

There are the very real problems in rural areas of lesser manpower, greater difficulty in obtaining and sustaining funding, and greater geographic expanses to serve (Gertz *et al.*, 1975). Mazer (1976) notes that from 1960 to 1970, rural population in four New England states grew *faster* than urban population. This growth phenomenon is being experienced by "sunbelt" and western states, and is expected to continue, altering the communities and the situations that confront the rural worker.

Many communities will expect rural psychologists to be treatment generalists, able to solve a multitude of problems (Jeffrey & Reeve, 1978). Workers may have difficulty in developing an awareness of the needs for programs with greater emphasis on consultation, education, or prevention (Huessy, 1972a,b), but this will not be the case in every community. Some will actively solicit these programs, being aware of them through media presentations and other modalities (Heyman, 1979).

There is a multitude of specific situational variables that may create problems in program development for rural areas. The literature suggests four basic categories: community resistance; the absence of knowledge or information in the community about nonmedical models; the needs of special, often ethnic groups; and negative transfer from previous workers.

In most areas the community leaders are likely to want (and welcome) clinical services, particularly if the financial costs are low. Although the attitudes in the community may be quite progressive (Bentz & Edgerton, 1970), their expectations may be tied to a medical model (Perlmutter, 1979).

Some novices assume that mental health services will be resisted by religious groups, but that seems unlikely. Some sects may see psychological problems as religious or demonic in origin (this can be a factor in some unusual areas) but these groups are relatively few. Many rural workers, however, have achieved progress with the help of ministers and church groups (Dworkin, 1974; Heyman, 1979; Thomson, 1968). Many times the most concerned and sensitive citizens will be found within these groups.

If the worker should carelessly attack religious beliefs, problems could develop. The only instance I have seen of a near conflict occurred when a social worker described his views of psychological problems as "humanistic." Among some fundamentalist groups, "humanistic" has become a buzzword for an "atheistic religion," that claims man to be supreme and inherently denies the existence of God. The situation was resolved when a Methodist minister explained to the group that "humanistic" did not mean a denial of God, but could represent a very Christian caring and concern for others.

Many more difficulties confront a new worker who inherits a service from someone who has antagonized the community and has left. A protracted period of testing can begin, and the shadows of the previous worker may not be exorcised easily. In the year after Frank left the situation described previously, few referrals were made to what was still thought of as "his" agency.

The most challenging and perplexing situations will likely confront the worker who serves a special population, usually an ethnic or racial group, or extremely poor, isolated populations. In such situations the worker is clearly an "outsider" from several perspectives. In addition, he or she may be working for the very agencies associated with repression or discrimination. One school counselor working with Native American students was reminded, from the time of his arrival until his very personal acceptance by that community, that the school, its administrators, and personnel had tried to crush Native American culture by forbidding the expression of language, dance, and beliefs into the 1950s.

In rural areas where there are different minority groups, as in urban areas, one may find suspicion and hostility dividing these groups, and dividing the community agencies and its workers. In one Kansas town of about 50,000, one social services center was seen as favorable to and trusted by blacks, while another agency was the Indian and Chicano agency. It was impossible to trace the causes of the division, or to find examples of discrimination by the staff, but there was little ethnic crossover between the centers. In areas with different Indian tribes, it is not uncommon to find workers trusted by some tribes but not by others (Kinzie, Shore, & Pattison, 1972).

Working with these special groups requires a special type of understanding and attention to their patterns, norms, and cultural traditions that takes time to acquire. Much of the literature in rural community mental health has focused on programs with particular groups, including Native Americans (Attneave, 1974; Bloom & Richards, 1974, 1976; Kahn & Delk, 1974; Kahn et al., 1975; Kinzie et al., 1972; Ostendorf & Hammerschlag, 1977; Robertson & Bayerman, 1969; Torrey, 1970); Chicanos (Barrera, 1978; Kiev, 1968; Padilla & Arando, 1974); rural blacks (Coles, 1969; Reul, 1974); rural whites (Lee, Gianturco, & Eisdorfer, 1974); and the poor in general (Coles, 1969; Copp, 1976; Looff, 1971; Reul, 1974; Rogers & Burdge, 1972). A greater examination of the problems presented in working with special populations will not be attempted here. Some general concepts will be presented in a later section dealing with the development of alternatives.

THE INTERACTIVE PROCESS

As suggested in the last section, improving the situation encountered remains the critical work of the rural community psychologist. The situation and the person come together in an active, dynamic way, to form the *process* of program development.

The situation the worker finds will have important pattern or process implications. A community that is paralyzed by socioeconomic strife, divided by ethnic or racial issues, or lacking effective organization and leadership presents problems difficult to change. The well-organized community, however, can also present problems. In a survey of community agencies, organizations, and leadership, Heyman (1979) found that a relatively few individuals, usually representing the most influential segments of the community, were responsible for most of the leadership in political, social, and service organizations, including paraprofessional services. Individuals from the poorer segments of the population (or from racial and ethnic minority groups) who were active and visible within their subgroups were sought out by different community representatives. Often, however, there was little real involvement with many of the groups or causes in which membership was offered or invited. The community members and organizations did not pursue effectively the development of involvement by other, less well-known ethnic or racial group members, nor did the subgroup representatives help develop such community involvement. At times, the subgroup representatives appeared to overidentify with the major group and to bask in their new prominence. These factors seriously inhibited their effectiveness.

A program involving the powerful or influential may achieve much goodwill, obtain local funding, and nevertheless fail (or put more charitably, may not be the success for which the workers had hoped). Lee *et al.* (1974) describe the chasm that exists between the community mental clinic and the poorer people in a rural area despite attempts to publicize services and create involvements. It may be that these efforts reach only some segments of the community: the more affluent and involved. Far more planning, outreach, personal involvements, and active inclusion of members of the other segments of the community may be required for a more complete community involvement (Attneave, 1974; Beier, Robinson, & Micheletti, 1971; Bethel, 1976; Bloom & Richards, 1976; Herbert *et al.*, 1974; Huessy, 1972; Lee *et al.*, 1974).

In a program described by Kahn *et al.* (1976), graduate students were placed in an impoverished, rural, multiethnic area, whose representatives had sought volunteer mental health services. The service, when established, was not widely used by clients, nor were there many referrals to the service, despite strong verbal support. No doubt there were a number of problems common to the beginning of any new part-time volunteer service in a community where the volunteers are themselves foreign to the community's ethnic and cultural heritage. A more critical *process* obstacle, however, may have been subtle and unrecognized. What follows is an introductory sentence from the report, with emphasis added:

> The development of a Community Mental Health Service for a multiethnic rural area by an academic psychology department clinical program was *carried out for the purpose of providing relevant training for graduate students* through realistic service functions. (p. 113)

While other motivations doubtless were involved, including service to the community, one might wonder whether the departmental motivations and needs, as situations entering the process, did not create obstacles in the community. Did the community come to view the service as something for the department's benefit?

Mazer (1976) describes the frustrating bind that presents process problems to many rural workers, as it does to urban workers:

> Mental health clinics do not offer easy entry for the very segments of the population which are most in need of their services—the poor, racial, and ethnic groups, the otherwise disenfranchised, and those whose illnesses involve passivity or a deficiency in the social skills required to enter institutionalized system. . . . [They] may not perceive their difficulties as falling within the category of psychiatric disorder. The simple struggle for survival, the constant anxiety of keeping one's job or giving one's children a better chance, the fear of aging in a manual worker . . . may relegate to a low priority . . . those distressing feelings that others recognize as psychological in origin. Yet these very . . . symptoms further impair the . . . processes involved in earning a living, conducting a marriage, being an adequate parent, and living with a modicum of joy. (p. 174)

Simply placing a service in a community, therefore, does not guarantee its usage, as the reports of Lee et al. (1974) and Kahn et al. (1976) indicate. Getting the service into the system, however, remains an initial process problem.

Upon entering into a system, the professional will meet community members who are active or influential by virtue of employment, political office, social connections, or informal community networks. These people may have little direct involvement with services or plans, yet without their positive reception others in the community may not become involved (Buxton, 1973). It is likely that the perception of the need for psychological programs will not be harsh or provincial (Bentz & Edgerton, 1970), but problems can still develop. Community members may fear involvement either with a program (as clients), or with the professional, for fear of being classified as a "problem" within the community. One report, however, found no significant loss of clients from a rural center to a neighboring urban center (Murphy, 1973).

A process problem related to understanding the needs and reactions of a community is the difficulty one encounters in obtaining honest feedback about efforts. In small communities, where little change of members occurs, a system is likely to develop that encourages direct cooperation, at the expense of emotional honesty. In the Midwest and South there is the concept of the "good ol' boy." Public accommodation may mask hidden feelings, or feelings not openly discussed that can become unseen obstacles (Kahn et al., 1976; Mazer, 1976). Taylor (1975) reported how pejorative rumors that were affecting the community's response to a center were tracked to their sources; this allowed misunderstandings, distortions, and even hostility to be dissipated, and a greater community consensus developed.

The placement of a center and its services may create a recognition of problems that leads to tension or discomfort in a community. Rural areas, like urban areas, will subscribe to some of the bucolic myths about rural life. Vidich and Bensman (1968) have described how shared illusions can come to affect and direct life in small communities.

> The school superintendent in a rural Oklahoma community of about 10,000 refused to allow any alcohol, drug, or sexual abuse prevention programs within the school system. His reason was "Such problems don't exist here." When confronted by evidence that such problems did exist, he declared, "If these programs go on, the problems will get worse." Although others in the community, including influential citizens, were concerned about these problems, they would not directly confront the superintendent. Nor did it matter to the superintendent that a neighboring community with these programs had fewer of these problems. (Heyman, 1979)

Another rural leader declared in a conversation about local problems, "You know, a problem doesn't exist until someone finds it." Although members of a community may want all of the services available in an urban area, the recognition that a problem exists can create ambivalence or anxiety, due to the blow to the community's sense of pride, security, and shared illusion. An urban area enjoys a diffusion of responsibility for problems, an "out there" awareness. In a small community, the identification of problems means the identification of friends, relatives, and neighbors. It is "in here," one paraprofessional worker stated, pointing to her heart.

With regard to more traditional services, the removal of problem persons to the state hospital, or to aftercare programs in nursing homes, may be quite comfortable and safe (Murphy, 1973). Developing aftercare services within the community can create stress for the families and for the community. Some centers, usually serving larger catchment areas, may seek to establish treatment centers such as day hospitals, or alcohol or drug treatment programs. The reception of these programs in rural areas is not likely to be any warmer than it would be in an urban neighborhood. Not unlike the psychotherapist, the community psychologist will need to be sensitive to the client community's readiness, willingness, and ability to recognize and deal with problems.

One last process problem that should be dealt with is *funding*. In urban areas funding is often an impersonal process, channeled through faceless federal, state, and city bureaucrats. Rural areas present far more difficult problems. When local funding is required in truly rural areas, no one community is large enough to sustain the services. The lower population density and broader geographic area often mean that no one community sees the center as its responsibility. The community in which the center is located, or from which the satellites are coordinated, may be seen as the most responsible by other communities, yet the central community may wish to contribute only a proportional share, if that much.

When a service is developed using decreasing federal or state funds, it may be very difficult, and require a great amount of time, for workers to negotiate contributions. Even where such funding is obtained, there are few guarantees that the funding will be increased in proportion to inflation or other factors (Wedel, 1969). It is not uncommon, in rural areas, for other valuable service providers (e.g., teachers) to be underpaid. They serve everyone. The mental health worker, serving a smaller segment of the population, may be paid equally poorly.

Some recommend that rural workers have "grantsmanship" skills. The experience of this writer, like that of Wedel (1969), is that the community ethos may denigrate the use of federal funds since this leads to a dependency on outside sources, as well as the need to satisfy demands of anonymous bureaucrats.

The more cynical reader might wonder if a rural area—or any area—would turn down federal funds. The *situation* of funding would be only a part of the process. Such a program might be accepted reluctantly by the community, and in *process* ignored. The personnel from that program may be rigorously tested before being accepted by the community, if in fact they ever are accepted.

THE DEVELOPMENT OF ALTERNATIVES

Perhaps the image most closely associated with America's consciousness of its rural history is in the characterization of the pioneer. The older literature in rural mental health envisions the worker as a pioneer, bringing traditional services to isolated areas. This is not really a pioneering effort, but, in an apolitical sense, a reactionary one. Services and systems that are applicable to urban areas should not be transposed automatically to a rural area. Rather, such services need to be integrated within the community (Cardoza et al., 1975; Daniels, 1967; Robin & Wagenfeld, 1977). The pioneering spirit will be needed to bring vital services to communities in vital ways. This does not mean traditional services are of no importance in rural areas, but that they should be a part of a greater system of efforts.

When such inherent problems as the shortages of manpower, the larger geographic areas to be served, funding problems, and differences in background between the professionals and the community are considered, it becomes clear that rural community psychology and rural mental health will need to look to the development of alternative services. The placement of traditional services and satellite clinics is only a first step.

A major goal, if approaches in rural areas are to be successful, will involve a multiplicative approach to services. Rather than providing treatment alone, the rural worker should be able to develop educational and consultation programs within the community, mobilize ideas and motivations, and synergize with the efforts of others. The development of constructive paraprofessional programs also holds great promise.

As might be expected, the emphasis of this section will be a process-oriented one. The development of alternatives is not simply the development of programs. Such an approach can provide a crazy quilt of services with a diminishing return to the system. The city of Lawrence, Kansas, for example, is technically in a rural area, although it is the home of a major university and is located only 30 miles from a metropolis. In 1976 there were well over 100 professional and paraprofessional agencies in that community, including social service agencies, mental health agencies, specialized services, numerous paraprofessional services (e.g., patients' rights groups), and "counter-culture" services. All of the programs were motivated by care and concern, as well as by needs in the community, and all had client populations. There was, however, considerable ignorance in the community and within agencies about the services provided by the different agencies, as well as notable hostility, suspicion, and competition between agencies.

Paraprofessional and Volunteer Programs in Rural Areas

Much has been written in general about the potential uses of paraprofessionals (Alley & Blanton, 1978), and some of the literature is devoted to the issue of rural workers (Dworkin, 1974; Herbert et al., 1974; Raft, Coley, & Miller, 1976; Snyder, 1971). A program using paraprofessionals needs to be developed and justified within the community, staffed, and evaluated. It will have to develop a relationship with the community and with its creators, even if they, as professionals, gradually withdraw. The programs may involve any needs and reflect the concerns of all mental health workers: sexual assault (Matthews, Mufson, Gottlieb, Bishop, & Matz, 1979); aftercare programs (Mitchell, 1966); youth problems (Carman, 1973; Denison, 1971); and suicide/crisis intervention services (Greene & Mullen, 1973; Heyman, 1979; Thomson, 1968).

The communication patterns in rural areas, and the responsiveness of community members, allows for the possibility of readily available workers for paraprofessional programs. None of the programs described above reported any difficulty in obtaining workers, and, it should be noted, most did not use college students. A new worker, or a worker not tapping the right needs or sources, may have problems in developing alternative programs. If the pattern and process of the community are accurately gauged, these problems should be considerably lessened. The rapid success of a program, however, may also become a problem: too many of the "same old people," or the "leaders, the big *machers*" can become so involved as to close out new people.

Some studies have reported exceptionally positive responses to the use of indigenous community members in the running of the community mental health centers and its programs (Herbert *et al.*, 1974; Raft *et al.*, 1976). The paraprofessional may be able to penetrate segments of the community that the professional cannot. Often it is not the subcommunity's leaders who are sought for active involvement, although as a rule their good auspices are likely to be necessary (Buxton, 1973). Gatekeepers, "natural helpers," and *potential* natural helpers may be involved through recruitment, or through the suggestions of neighbors. The qualities of concern, perceptiveness, and energy will have been recognized by friends and neighbors long before the professional entered the system (Biegel & Naparstek, 1979; Libertoff, 1979).

If the training of the paraprofessionals includes a definition of goals that can be shared by the workers; if their participation is truly valued in word *and* deed, such as involvement in goal setting and decision making; and if they are allowed the flexibility to utilize their natural talent and perceptions of needs, one might develop, as did Herbert *et al.* (1974), "an unabashedly successful program (p. 308)." The paraprofessional can provide services that a professional could not or would not, such as transporting clients, making home visits, and in many ways being seen by the clients as an ally (Halpern & Love, 1971; Herbert, *et al.*, 1974; Raft *et al.*, 1976). The program may be so successful that, as Raft *et al.* (1976) report, should the paraprofessional leave, clients, particularly from the lower socioeconomic and minority groups, may decrease their use of the service.

Various programs have reported successes in locating non-psychological professionals in the community, who may be functioning as crisis–intervention workers and nonprofessional therapists (Huessy, 1972a,b; Snyder, 1971). Several programs have actively sought out some of these professionals (including ministers, physicians, and pharmacists) for specialized training in counseling and crisis–intervention skills (Dworkin, 1974; Huessy, 1972a,b).

Other programs have located and worked with natural caregivers

within the community's psychological ecology. At times this has involved *very* nontraditional allies, including shaman (Torrey, 1970), spir-
itualists, and folk healers (Barrera, 1978; Ruiz & Langrod, 1976). The
professional who might gasp at the suggestion of using these groups
will, on reflection, recognize the cultural value—and sanity—of this approach. As natural caregivers, they have been sanctioned by the community and are seen as important, understanding segments of the community. They may be turned to long before a professional is consulted.
There is likely to be far *less* stigma attached to their consultation than to
professional therapy (Biegel & Naparstek, 1979). The papers reporting
this unorthodox approach also report good results (Barrera, 1978; Ruiz &
Langrod, 1976; Torrey, 1970).

More commonly, paraprofessionals are recruited from the general
community's population for specific programs. I would like to describe
two successful programs, and one that did not work. The first program,
called *Helpline*, was a process long in its initial research and development, and yet brought a quick response from the community.

Helpline

In rural western Oklahoma there are only a few, limited mental
health services. Typically, each county has an aftercare worker and an
alcohol abuse counselor. Some areas have small Child Guidance Centers, with one master's level and one doctoral psychologist, engaging
primarily in direct treatment services.

In one area the county Mental Health Association had been resur-
rected after years of hibernation, through the efforts of two influential
women and two ministers. Recognizing the problems with funding and
obtaining new, qualified staff, the association asked several professionals about the possibility of developing some community-based and
staffed paraprofessional programs. What follows is a description of the
events set in motion by that request.

Initial Poll.   Different community agencies and individuals were
asked what service(s) they thought would be of most help to the community, and would not involve or require new professionals or funds.
Of the feasible suggestions, the one cited most frequently (62%) was a
"crisis line," a place people in crisis or with problems could call for
counseling or referral to appropriate agencies.

One such program had existed about 10 years before, but had not
had professional involvement and had never attracted wide community
support.

Proposed Plan.   Before we, the professionals, could proceed, one
minister suggested a "Christian Ministry Hotline" to the Mental Health

Association. They warmly responded to the idea, while the professionals were cold, at first. As we investigated the service, however, we discovered that it was a crisis–intervention service, done from a spirit of "Christian concern and caring," but *was not* the religious, evangelistic, or proselytizing service that we had expected. In fact such approaches were clearly not its goals. As we met with a regional representative of the group, reviewed the purposes and materials, and included community members in this process, we found a growing sense of community support. Local ministers were quite favorable, as were church groups and other concerned community sectors. It became clear that this would help attract volunteers and community funding. Would there be problems? Of course; we expected some.

A Second Survey. Volunteers for the service would be obtained through publicity on local radio stations, in newspapers, and in church bulletins, as well as from talks given to civic and social groups. A second survey was designed to gather new information in order to assess (1) the kinds of problems of which people in the community were aware; and (2) who "they" thought would be good listeners, that is, natural helpers. Based on 1970 census information, questionnaires were mailed out to randomly selected addresses reflecting low income ($8,000) middle income ($13–25,000), and upper income groups ($30,000 and above). The questionnaire asked, "What are the types of mental or psychological problems from which you think people in this community suffer?" The questionnaire then defined the planned service and asked, "Who do you know that you could recommend as someone who would be a good listener or helper? Please do *not* list doctors or ministers, but rather people like yourself."

An initial mailing of 150 went out, 50 to each socioeconomic group (SEG), but it took a total of 236 questionnaires before 50 were obtained for each group. Almost all of the respondents were female, although more males in the upper income group responded (15%) than in the lowest group (8%).

In calculating problems described, a tally was made of each different problem, with duplications being counted only once. To the first question, the mean number of problems raised by each group was: lowest SEG: 6.2; middle SEG: 9.3; upper SEG: 14.1. All groups mentioned specific problems such as alcohol, drugs, sexual deviations, and divorce, but the middle and upper groups were more specific, and could define and subgroup terms such as "neurotic" or "psychotic." Terms such as "weak nerves," "nervous breakdown," and "crazy" were used by all groups, but were most common among the lower SEG. Although not determined, the education level of the respondents was probably a factor in the obtained differences.

Of the persons nominated as potential helpers or listeners by 5 or more of the respondents, 4 were named by the lower SEG, 12 by the middle SEG, and 16 by the upper SEG. There was considerable overlap between the middle and upper groups, likely reflecting the meeting and working together of these individuals, as well as their greater visibility within the community. Only one of the lower SEG nominees occurred among both the middle and upper SEG.

The Planning Process. It took a year from the initial discussions until our initial program implementation. A steering committee had been developed that consisted of an interested Episcopal minister, a social worker, and myself. We found that a local Methodist minister had in his seminary years worked for a local "Helpline" and he agreed to join with us. We gradually planned our training program and drives for funding and recruitment of volunteers.

Expected Process Problems. Certain problems that we anticipated were: getting people to work actively on the planning committees, particularly for publicity, recruiting, and training; finding facilities and equipment; dealing with the rivalry between the two large cities (each with approximately 10,000 population) vying to have the service located in its facilities; dealing with people who might want to use the phone to preach or evangelize.

Unexpected Process Problems. It took longer to implement the service than expected and there was a lack of real manpower support from the Mental Health Association.

Implementation. In December, 1978, we were ready to recruit our first training group. We expected 10–12 volunteers from those nominated in our original poll, and hoped to obtain at least 10 others from the community. Two community members (active, respected women) agreed to take charge of recruiting. When we returned from Christmas break we found a group of 53 volunteers!

Training. We met weekly, for 16 weeks, and had 4 long Saturday sessions to permit special programs and more intensive role-play exercises. During the course of training there were theory inputs on crisis counseling and topical problems, as well as discussions of controversial topics and role plays. Most of the people who were less suited for phone work because of dogmatic, judgmental attitudes, or because of needs for religious witnessing, dropped out voluntarily, often after other volunteers questioned or confronted them. Others decided to work only on committees and not on the phones. For most volunteers the training was a growth-enhancing experience, in which they came to understand themselves more clearly and fully.

Certification. 35 members finished the training, and 28 agreed to work on the phones, allowing us to develop an evening and night service.

Resources. Very quickly, members in each of the cities located settings in which we could place the phones at no cost. Funds for the purchase of the phone lines and related equipment were readily obtained from churches, civic groups, social groups, and charitable groups. Because of the distance between the two cities, a center was located in each city, with two tie lines so that a worker in one city could answer phones serving both towns. This was expensive, with an average bill of $150 per month, but within the first few weeks of operation we had raised over $4000.

Interface with Other Agencies. As a part of the compilation of a service directory for use by phone workers, all local and regional services were contacted for information and asked how "Helpline" could help them. Most agencies welcomed the service and its interest. Ministers were asked if they wished to be included on a list of pastoral counselors, should callers ask for such assistance.

Implementation Problems. Scheduling was an immediate problem. It took several weeks to work out a system by which volunteers could select their own shifts and, in the event of a needed change, could locate an alternate worker.

Follow-up. A year later, three training classes had been processed, and a third city began to develop its adjunct to the service. The number of calls to the service varied, from a low of 17 one month to a high of 43. During the slower months, the volunteers expressed some discontent; this was ameliorated by increasing the number of training and social "get-togethers."

Comparisons with other reported crisis services in rural areas (Greene & Mullen, 1973; Thompson, 1968) reveals processes that are similar in concept and execution, although these other programs served more concentrated areas. The Helpline program was a vivid experience of the potential for such programs in rural areas that are ostensibly void of services. It was developed by interaction within the community and between the community and its professionals. Red tape was sliced away easily, and cooperation consistently forthcoming. The service became a source of pride within the community. It was not the specific program that was a success, but the process.

The data collected as a part of the early stages of the Helpline program supported the expected social class differences in response to psychological awareness (Zax & Specter, 1974). The peer–nomination process holds promise as a method of identifying natural helpers.

Follow-up research on the use of paraprofessionals in mental health centers finds that they are used in a wide variety of ways, including outreach work and basic counseling situations (Alley & Blanton, 1976). One rural mental health center, to which I was a consultant, had an excellent program. It is called the "Two Chiefs" program, and is described below.

Two Chiefs

The "Two Chiefs" Mental Health Center served a tri-county area in the rural South. The center was typical in its initial stages, with a full-time psychologist, social worker, and psychiatric nurse, and a visiting psychiatric consultant. When an additional $19,000 in funding became available, the original plan was to hire another professional. After some deliberation, however, the staff decided to recruit community members and train them as paraprofessionals. Volunteers were solicited from the community, through organizations and informal communications. Of the volunteers, six were selected for part-time, paid positions while six others agreed to work without pay. All of the volunteers were women, none had attended college, and about half had never finished high school. The average age was 36. This was, to say the least, quite a different group from that used by Rioch (1967) in the often mislabeled "housewife" study (Magoon & Golann, 1966; Rioch, Elkes, Flint, Usannsky, Newman, & Sibler, 1963), which had used a group of highly educated, sophisticated women.

In the Two Chiefs program, after 8 weeks of short theory courses, discussions of the community and its needs, visits to different community agencies and with key people within the communities, and training that included role plays, the paraprofessional workers went through an initial period of cotherapy. When this was completed, they were allowed to work by themselves, with supervision. They did intakes and basic counseling. They went to community agencies and organizations on an informal basis, to speak with and to meet people. They were able to keep staellite centers in surrounding towns open daily. Each received regular supervision, and there was a weekly conference for which all the workers assembled at the main center.

The caseloads grew, reflecting the socioeconomic makeup of the community. All community agencies made referrals. The only friction with the community occurred when some of the "better citizens" decided that they, too, wanted to be involved with the program, and could not be included. They were placed on a waiting list, which provided some relief. Within the service, there was no tension between the professionals and paraprofessionals. The professionals had their own caseloads, but were always available for consultation and referrals. Typically, they were given the more disturbed clients.

Some tension existed between the salaried and nonsalaried workers. The nonsalaried workers were somewhat less reliable. One of the salaried workers did less than any of the other workers, and was more likely to take days off. This became the center of resentment and subtle hostility, but there was no willingness to confront the worker, which is not unexpected (Buxton, 1973). She was planning to move within a few months and the paraprofessionals wanted the situation to resolve itself in this way. The professionals recognized that forcing a direct confrontation would have disrupted the patterns the paraprofessionals chose, and in essence would have accomplished little.

With the likely availability of interested, willing workers, and an ease of recruitment in a rural system where formal and informal communication works quickly, it is easy for the professional to lean more toward paraprofessional programs. In fact, it is too easy. Paraprofessionals can provide important services, and be critical links to the community. This presumes, however, that the program is well designed and implemented in a way that enhances and is compatible with the community process. The program must meet the community members at a level meaningful for them. A paraprofessional program is not an automatic, guaranteed success. What follows is the description of a program that carried the seeds of its own failure.

The Peer Program

Peter, a doctoral student in clinical psychology, was to have primary responsibility for establishing a peer counseling program in a rural high school. He had the clear support of the school and its personnel. Plans were developed to solicit and screen volunteers.

The program should have been a great success. Peter, however, had a monolithic approach in all his clinical work, and had no real experience with any group other than college students. He was completely oriented toward Gestalt therapy, and had worked in a number of Gestalt sensitivity groups with college students. He planned to use the same model with the high school volunteers, utilizing highly unstructured personal growth exercises. He had no plans to explain their purpose to the students, nor how these exercises would relate to their later functioning as peer counselors.

Nothing could persuade Peter to utilize a more structured training model, nor to interact meaningfully with the ninth, tenth, and eleventh graders in order to find out how they saw themselves and what they would be doing.

Although I was supposed to work with Peter, I withdrew from the program. I was more concerned about the threatening situation that would be created for the students (one which they had not been advised of, nor prepared for) and I doubted the program could work. The potential impact on each volunteer was great, and could have been quite negative.

After a few weeks, the program was disbanded as a training disaster. All of the students had resigned or withdrawn psychologically. Accounts of confusing meetings, strange demands, and general confusion caused other students and the staff at the high school to question the program. It was dissolved.

Consultation and Education

A recurring theme in much of the rural community psychology literature is the need to develop consultation programs with primary caregivers in the community (Kinzie et al., 1972). This can help the caregivers deal more adequately with psychological problems that may be brought to them in other guises (Halpern & Love, 1971; Snyder, 1971). Although Daniels (1967) attacks the traditional mental health center model as inappropriate to the need for indirect services and consultations within rural areas, Mahoney & Hodges (1969) and Kinzie et al. (1972) suggest that the center can develop alternative programs if it is committed to the community, flexible, resourceful, and creative in its response to problems.

The rural worker can be quite effective in helping other agencies plan and develop services (Libo & Griffith, 1966). The worker can play a role in conducting the educational or training aspects of these programs. This will help to establish important bridges while enhancing existing service capabilities, and does not require additional funding or staff (Cardoza et al., 1975).

Some programs may be needed to help others deal with newly developed problem awarenesses. For example, it has been only a decade since a clear awareness of the problems of the rape victim has developed. Many police, social service, ministerial, and other professional groups have had no training in this area. Matthews et al. (1979) describe a program designed to provide sexual assault education to potential caregivers of sexual assault victims in rural areas. In a rural school system plagued with alienation, visible vandalism, mischief, and student–authority conflicts, Carman (1973) was able to help develop an effective interactive process. This was done in spite of poor relations between the school and other community agencies. In general, the school had used agencies as punishments for "last resort" students. Very likely those referrals did not solve problems to the satisfaction of the school's personnel, and additionally alienated the students. As a consultant to both the students and the school, Carman helped develop an awareness of the sources of conflict and communication blockage. These were addressed, and more positive patterns replaced them; significant positive responses followed from the students, school personnel, the community, and law enforcement agencies.

The patterns or procedures of consultation and education in rural areas might seem, on the surface, quite similar to those of urban areas. In rural areas, however, there are fewer trained professionals offering these services. The needs for some of these services may be more clearly visible in rural areas. As mentioned, the utilization of consultation and educational programs can depend not only on the needs present, but also on the evaluation of the professional by the community, and its response to him or her.

The Development of Alternatives

The possibilities for alternative services are as endless as the flexibility and creativity of the rural worker (Kinzie et al., 1972; Mahoney & Hodges, 1969). The appraisals of the needs and patterns of the community are necessary first steps. The development of alternative services, whether they utilize paraprofessionals or provide consultation or educational programs, requires the professional to become integrally involved with the community, and the community with the professional. If rural communities are typified by the gemeinschaft sociopsychological pattern (Nisbet, 1966), the community will expect and respond to such programs.

The development of alternatives, however, will depend on a clearer, more exact understanding of rural America and the psychological values and needs of the different rural communities. It is likely that there will be the need to transcend the traditional mental health center model, or models more applicable to urban areas (Daniels, 1967). Some proposals are made in the next section for directions that this developmental stage can take.

IMPLICATIONS FOR FUTURE DIRECTIONS

This chapter has shown that the literature of community psychology and community mental health has largely neglected rural problems as a special issue. There is little emphasis on rural issues in doctoral psychology programs (Barton et al., 1976). Few articles have been published in the American Journal of Community Psychology, and no substantive references about rural issues are made in major texts (Heller &

Monahan, 1977; Iscoe *et al.*, 1977; Mann, 1978; Nietzel *et al.*, 1977; Rappaport, 1977; Zax & Specter, 1974). This vacuum is in contrast with other developments. The federal government has given rural mental health a funding priority (NIMH, 1978). Calls have been made for the development of specialized training programs for rural workers (Buxton, 1973; Clark & Moore, 1979; Daniels, 1967; Kahn *et al.*, 1976) and important reviews of the literature have been published (Flax *et al.*, 1978; Flax *et al.*, 1979; Heussy, 1972a, 1972b).

The funding priority given to rural mental health, the attention to training needs, and the appearance of major literature reviews reflect, or perhaps portend, the increasing attention that rural mental health issues will receive in coming years. The publication of the book in which this chapter appears should be a major step in that direction. At this time, however, there are no models for rural community psychology or rural mental health delivery programs, nor have clear questions or research issues been generated. It may be best that the formulation of questions and research issues precede the development of rural models, and, later, continue interfacing with them.

The Rural Worker

A number of articles reviewed in this chapter have made valuable comments about the personal functioning and impact of the rural mental health worker (Boris, 1971; Buxton, 1973; Carman, 1973; Daniels, 1967; Eisdorfer *et al.*, 1968; Gertz *et al.*, 1975; Gurian, 1971; Jeffrey & Reeve, 1978; Jones *et al.*, 1974; Lee *et al.*, 1974; Mahoney & Hodges, 1969; Mazer, 1976; Perlmutter, 1979; Riggs & Kugel, 1976). Except for some very general issues (Jones *et al.*, 1974; Robin & Wagenfeld, 1977) no research on the rural worker exists. If the personal characteristics of the worker are as important as theorized, and the potential impact of the person so closely related to these characteristics, then the rural worker needs careful examination.

As beginning points, an examinition of who selects rural areas in which to work, and the motivation for this choice, emerge as possible questions. Peer or supervisor ratings may be utilized to relate these factors to effectiveness. This is not meant to imply a unidimensional model, such as a simple comparison of "successful" and "unsuccessful" workers. The characteristics of the rural worker need to be viewed within a more complex model, including such variables as the situations encountered, client population, community structure and needs, service goals, and related situational factors. Such a model would not be unlike the contingency model of leadership described by Fiedler (1971) in terms of how variables may be specified and investigated. The systems analysis model of Lewin (1948, 1964) also could be of use. These models allow for the specification of the strength and importance of critical factors, and the variation of these factors over time and with different situations.

The literature on the rural worker cites the unique frustrations and obstacles faced. There are implications worth examining concerning the longevity and effectiveness of workers: how and why do some continue to function effectively within the rural setting while the effectiveness of others diminishes, and still others leave? The loss of interest, and staff, in mental health settings is a topic receiving increasing attention, and is generally known as the *burn-out syndrome* (Kahn, 1978; Maslach, 1978; Pines & Maslach, 1978). Freudenberger (1975) has described the burn-out syndrome in alternative institutions, and has indicated some preventive measures that can be taken. If burn-out is a particular problem facing the rural worker, as experience and the literature indicate, research can be of tremendous assistance in understanding the contributing factors of this syndrome. In addition, studies of individuals and their personal and professional styles, the settings in which they work, the programs on which they work, and the worker–program–community interaction may indicate ways of coping with the inherent difficulties in rural settings, preventing burn-out, and developing potential preventive resources.

Social-Communication Ecology

The research described in this chapter in connection with the Helpline programs is an illustration of some basic aspects of the community that are particularly important in rural areas. The rural community presents the opportunity for conducting field research in an exciting, visible social system. It is likely, however, that the concept of the *participant-observer* will be needed. The rural field researcher will not have the luxury of the anonymity of a laboratory researcher, or even that of a field researcher in a larger social setting. The researcher's very presence may directly affect the social system.

Within the Division of Community Psychology (Division 27) of the American Psychological Association, a social-ecology interest group has developed. This group examines and shares interests in several major streams of social ecology, including (but not limited to) natural support systems, environmental psychology, behavioral community psychology, self-help, and volunteerism (Jeger, 1980). The rural area presents an excellent opportunity for individuals with interests in rural issues and social-communication ecology to develop research projects and address program issues and service delivery.

The work reported by Biegel and Naparstek (1979) and Libertoff

(1979) suggest the importance of the indigenous social-communication ecology for the psychological supports in a community, Beier *et al.* (1971) indicate an example of how these patterns can lead to the effective development and usage of more formal agency structures. Beiser (1971) presents an initial study of personal characteristics that are likely to be assets in a rural area. The beliefs about the resources in rural systems, and their usage, have been discussed in different reports (Attneave, 1974; Barrera, 1978; Bentz & Edgerton, 1970; Bethel, 1976; Carman, 1973; Herbert *et al.*, 1974; Hodges & Mahoney, 1970; Huessy, 1972b; Lee *et al.*, 1974; Libo & Griffith, 1966). It may be hypothesized that the success of a rural program will be related to, and dependent upon, the network of involved community members. The broader, more involved, and influential this network (in terms appropriate to the community being studied), the more successful the program will be.

Where problems occur in the development, implementation, or usage of services, as described, for example, by Denison (1971), Herbert *et al.* (1974), Kahn *et al.* (1976), Lee *et al.* (1974), and Libo and Griffith (1966), an analysis of the social-communication ecology of the person–program–community interaction would be useful. Such an analysis could not only point to blockages, omissions, and other needs, but could also serve as a control to determine if changes in patterns follow whatever actions are taken.

These are but some suggestions. In rural communities, as in any community, the knowledge gained from an analysis of the social-communication ecology will be of great help to the mental health worker and the psychological planner. It may be easier to develop an understanding of these patterns, and to act upon them, in rural areas. Previous reports indicate the use of natural relationship systems in the prevention and treatment of problems is most compatible with rural values (Libertoff, 1979; Pattison, 1975), and one particularly excellent model has been described (Cutler & Madore, 1980).

Utilization of Rural Geography

The rural environment, physically, can provide opportunities for unique therapeutic programs. The rural landscape is a part of the heritage, mythology, and values that are distinctly American. Rural America is associated closely with the "Pioneering Spirit," the challenges to be overcome by effort; from such effort comes growth. There have been reports indicating that physically and psychologically demanding outdoor survival experiences may be highly beneficial in helping juvenile delinquents develop psychological attitudes and skills conducive to improved life patterns (Baer, Jacobs, & Carr, 1975; Kelly &

Baer, 1968, 1971; Kole & Busse, 1969). These studies suggest that a decrease in anxiety, an increase in self-concept, and a more internal orientation in locus of control accompany active participation in these programs, with lower recidivism rates for the active participants.

It should be stressed that these are survival experiences, not innocuous recreational camp-outs; they are challenging, demanding, and physically rigorous activities, supervised by expert outdoor guides. Such programs should not be expected to perform quick cures. They usually last several weeks or longer. It seems very possible, however, to incorporate such programs into other treatment approaches. There is the possibility, for research purposes, of comparing recidivism rates for individuals involved in such programs with control groups. It would be worth determining what the critical factors are where recidivism is reduced, even if only in part, by participation in such programs. If such programs were useful in reducing recidivism, they may have preventive possibilities with "at risk" populations.

Other types of survival programs may be of benefit to other client populations, including the emotionally disturbed (Bernstein, 1972; LaTour, 1979). LaTour (1979) describes a long-term therapeutic camping program that includes group sessions and, increasingly, family therapy as a part of an overall emphasis. These therapeutic outdoor programs are innovative, and require flexibility and expert guides. Their utilization of the rural environment holds significant enough promise to warrant additional examination.

Training: Developing Alternatives

The development of programs for rural community psychology and rural mental health services requires an alternative to currently available training in psychology. The review by Barton et al. (1976) illustrates the low priority given rural issues in doctoral psychology programs. Although calls have been made for specialized training programs (Buxton, 1973; Kahn et al., 1976; Richards & Gottfredson, 1978), few such programs exist, and has been little communication about these programs. In an extensive review of material relating to rural issues in clinical and community psychology, only one article (Howe, 1980) and two programs could be located that explicitly indicate an emphasis on training for rural applications and involvements. One such program is a master's program at Mansfield State College, Mansfield, Pennsylvania (Keller, 1979), and the other is a doctoral program in clinical psychology at the University of Nebraska-Lincoln (Howe, 1980). No doubt other programs exist; however, little communication, and no real forums for this communication, exist at the time of the writing of this chapter.

The personnel problems in rural mental health can be dealt with only by increasing the number of training programs that prepare workers for the special situations presented by rural areas. Increasing the attention to rural issues in training programs would likely carry with it increasing research on rural problems. It is a general reality that mental health centers tend to do little research and concentrate on treatment. This is particularly true of smaller, more rural centers. Often, what research is done will relate to funding requests or documentation of service needs. Academic researchers can bring a coordination of efforts and an integrative perspective that an individual center might not have.

It may be difficult for larger universities to work directly with mental health centers, in training professionals or paraprofessionals, or in placing students for practice. This suggestion is advanced only tentatively, as a warning. Programs sponsored by larger universities may be viewed as intrusive, and run by outsiders for the benefit of the distant, large university rather than for the community or the center. The smaller regional colleges and universities, however, may have an advantage by being more involved with the rural communities. The Helpline program was successful because the university is seen by the rural areas served as a community resource, and because personal working relationships exist between faculty, professionals in the community, and the citizens.

It is easy, in word, to take the next step, and propose that, with the federal priority for rural mental health, funding be sought to assist with the training and research issues raised. Unfortunately, mental health administrators are caught between the Scylla of the ever-changing political winds in Washington, D.C., and the Charybdis of the antipathy found in rural areas for federal programs and regulations. It will be worth examining ways in which constructive programs can be built while steering through these dangers.

The Rural Network: A Proposal

One of the problems faced by rural workers at personal and professional levels is isolation (Boris, 1971; Buxton, 1973; Gertz *et al.*, 1975; Jones *et al.*, 1976). This is seen, usually, at an individual level, and is related to morale, longevity, and effectiveness within the community. As a *process issue*, however, isolation is critical in the consideration of the problems in program development and the development of alternatives. To deal effectively with rural problems, more than an individual effort will be required. There needs to be a sharing of knowledge, experience, research, and training activities. There must be a cross-pollination of ideas and approaches, and the development of a communication network with the potential to become a meaningful, valuable resource.

At this time, several different networks are forming. The Rural Mental Health Association (Hargrove, 1980) publishes a newsletter, and each year has a communication and training meeting. At the meeting of the American Psychological Association in September of 1980, I coordinated a Contact Hour on Rural Issues for the Division of Community Psychology. This meeting led to the development of a recognized rural interest group. (A summary of the results of this meeting, and subsequent developments are available from the author.)

A major goal of these networks should be to develop regional groupings of interested mental health workers, since it is not possible for many workers to attend distant national meetings. Regional groupings may be able to help combine efforts to work on similar programs, and develop resources within geographic areas.

Although articles on rural problems appear in the *Community Mental Health Journal*, and less frequently the *American Journal of Community Psychology*, several new publications are focusing directly on rural issues. *Rural Connections* (Webb, 1980) is a newsletter, sharing information and ideas. The *Journal of Rural Community Psychology* (the initial issue of which appeared in July, 1980) will be a valuable vehicle for longer reports and research (Kenkel, 1980).

These reporting and communication possibilities must begin to fill a vacuum for the rural community worker and the academician. Far too often organizations and journals have become the province of the academician, and have excluded the worker. In other instances, there have been tensions between workers, who face very real problems daily, and the academician or researcher, who may deal incompletely or artificially with these problems.

As a process issue, the development of a meaningful network becomes a key consideration of alternatives. Such a network will achieve more than simply the amelioration of isolation. There can be a sharing of program models and modifications, experiences, program evaluations, and additional research. Such a communication network can help students and professionals locate settings in which they might like to work. The development of such a network is just now beginning. If initial contacts are accurate, it is safe to say that this will be of major importance for rural mental health and rural community psychology.

SOME CONCLUDING THOUGHTS

As the awareness of the needs of rural America increases over the coming years, there will be parallel efforts to take remedial actions for the absences of services and programs that have existed. These steps will be taken partly because rural America will be seen as a "new" needy minority group. There will be a tendency by some, particularly in the initial stages of this effort, to view rural America as an anachronism in the last part of the twentieth century. The glaring needs of rural areas, and the reclaiming of rural areas by population trends, will create a more serious attitude. Although at the writing of this chapter only brief reports about the 1980 census have been issued, rural populations are increasing, as Mazer (1966) noted. This seems due to two factors, both of which are in sharp contrast to the trends of the first half of this century. Rural children are not deserting their home areas for urban areas, and urban dwellers and businesses are moving to rural areas.

The creation of programs and services for rural areas, and the placement of professionals in these areas, need to take into account the social system patterns that they enter. There have been unique problems and frustrations for program development and placement in rural areas. The literature clearly reflects, however, the failure of rural programs in addressing the system's process (Kahn et al., 1976; Libo & Griffith, 1966). Certainly this happens in urban areas as well, but in rural areas these failures, and the resulting problems, are far more visible.

When services, programs, and professionals are placed in rural areas, and this seems inevitable (NIMH, 1978), highly meaningful programs can be *developed*, and not just erected (Daniels, 1967), if the workers are trained to understand and work with the special factors in rural situations, and if they are given freedom and flexibility. The little research done on rural workers suggests they have been more community-oriented and have shown a greater preference for working with the client-community than urban workers (Jones et al., 1974, 1976). If this is allowed to continue, and is encouraged, the increased resources that become available (NIMH, 1978) will redress at least some of the problems in program development that have existed; more significantly, it will facilitate the development of meaningful alternatives.

REFERENCES

Alley, S., & Blanton, J. A study of paraprofessionals in mental health. *Community Mental Health Journal*, 1976, 12, 151–160.

Alley, S., & Blanton, J. (Eds.). *Paraprofessionals in mental health: An annotated bibliography from 1966 to 1977*. Berkeley, Calif.: Social Action Research Center, 1978.

Attneave, C. L. Medicine men and psychiatrists in the Indian Health Service. *Psychiatric Annals*, 1974, 4, 49–55.

Baer, D. J., Jacobs, P. J., & Carr, F. E. Instructors' ratings of delinquents after Outward Bound survival training and their subsequent recidivism. *Psychological Reports*, 1975, 36, 545–553.

Barrera, M. Mexican-American mental health service utilization: A critical examination of some proposed variables. *Community Mental Health Journal,* 1978, *14,* 35–45.

Barton, A. K., Andrulis, D. P., Grove, W. P., & Aponte, J. F. A look at community psychology training programs in the seventies. *American Journal of Community Psychology,* 1976, *4,* 1–11.

Beier, E. G., Robinson, P., & Micheletti, G. Susanville: A community helps itself in mobilization of community resources for self-help in mental health. *Journal of Consulting and Clinical Psychology,* 1971, *36,* 142–150.

Beiser, M. A study of personality assets in a rural community. *Archives of General Psychiatry,* 1971, *24,* 244–254.

Bentz, W. K., & Edgerton, J. W. Consensus on attitudes toward mental illness between leaders and the general public in a rural community. *Archives of General Psychiatry,* 1970, *22,* 468–473.

Bernstein, A. Wilderness as a therapeutic behavior setting. *Therapeutic Recreation Journal,* 1972, *6,* 160–161; 185.

Bethel, L. Rural man discovers mental health. *MH(Mental Hygiene),* 1976, *60,* 13.

Bible, B. L. Health care delivery in rural areas. *Journal of the American Medical Association,* 1971, *216,* 1635–1637.

Biegel, D., & Naparstek, A. *The natural helper's role in help seeking and receiving.* Paper presented at the 87th annual meeting of the American Psychological Association, New York City, September 1979.

Bloom, J. D., & Richards, W. W. Mental health program developments in rural Alaska. *Alaska Medicine,* 1976, *18,* 25–28.

Bloom, J. D., & Richards, W. W. Alaska native regional corporations in community mental health. *Psychiatri Annals,* 1974, *4,* 67–75.

Boris, H. N. The *Seelsorger* in rural Vermont. *International Journal of Group Psychotherapy,* 1971, *21,* 159–173.

Buxton, E. B. Delivering services in rural areas. *Public Welfare,* 1973, *31,* 15–20.

Cardoza, V. G., Ackerly, W. C., & Leighton, A. H. Improving mental health through community action. *Community Mental Health Journal,* 1975, *11,* 215–217.

Carman, R. S. Ameliorating alienation in a rural school system: Community mental health–school counseling collaboration. *Psychology,* 1973, *10,* 7–11.

Clark, R. D., & Moore, V. *Problems and solutions in training school psychologists for rural settings.* Paper presented at the 87th annual meeting of the American Psychological Association, New York City, September 1979.

Coles, R. *Migrants, sharecroppers, mountaineers. Children of crisis* (Vol. 2). New York: Little, Brown, 1969.

Copp, J. H. Diversity of rural society and health needs. In E. Hassinger & L. Whiting (Eds.), *Rural health services: Organization, delivery, and use.* Ames: Iowa State University Press, 1976.

Cutler, D. L., & Madore, E. Community–family network therapy in a rural setting. *Community Mental Health Journal,* 1980, *162,* 144–155.

Daniels, D. N. The community mental health center in the rural area: Is the present model appropriate? *American Journal of Psychiatry,* 1967, *124*(Oct. supplement), 32–37.

Denison, M. J. An unusual social experiment to help youth in crisis. *Canadian Medical Association Journal,* 1971, *104,* 15–19.

Dworkin, E. P. Implementation and evaluation of a clergy in-service training program in personal counseling. *Journal of Community Psychology,* 1974, *2,* 232–237.

Eisdorfer, C., Altrocci, J., & Young, R. F. Principles of community mental health in a rural setting: The Halifax County program. *Community Mental Health Journal,* 1968, *4,* 211–220.

Fiedler, F. E. *Leadership.* New York: General Learning Press, 1971.

Flax, J. W., Ivens, R. E., Wagenfeld, M. O., & Weiss, R. J. Mental health and rural America: An overview. *Community Mental Health Review,* 1978, *3,* 1; 3–15.

Flax, J. W., Wagenfeld, M. O., Ivens, R. E., & Weiss, R. J. *Mental health and rural America: An overview and annotated bibliography.* Washington, D.C.: U.S. Government Printing Office, 1979.

Freudenberger, H. J. The staff burn-out in alternative institutions. *Psychotherapy: Theory, Research & Practice,* 1975, *12,* 73–82.

Gertz, B., Meider, J., & Pluckhan, M. L. A survey of rural community mental health center needs and resources. *Hospital and Community Psychiatry,* 1975, *26,* 816–819.

Ginsberg, L. H. (Ed.). *Social work in rural America: A book of readings.* New York: Council on Social Work Education, 1966.

Greene, R. J., & Mullen, F. G. A crisis telephone service in a nonmetropolitan area. *Hospital and Community Psychiatry,* 1973, *24,* 94–97.

Gurian, H. A decade in rural psychiatry. *Hospital and Community Psychiatry,* 1971, *21,* 40–42.

Gurin, G., Veroff, J., & Feld, S. *Americans view their mental health.* New York: Basic Books, 1960.

Haley, J. A quiz for young therapists. *Psychotherapy: Theory, Research & Practice,* 1977, *14,* 165–168.

Halpern, H., & Love, R. W. Initiating community consultation in rural areas. *Hospital and Community Psychiatry,* 1971, *22,* 30–33.

Hargrove, D. S. Personal communication, May 19, 1980.

Heller, K., & Monahan, J. *Psychology and community change.* Homewood, Ill.: Dorsey Press, 1977.

Herbert, G. K., Chevalier, M. C., & Meyers, C. L. Factors contributing to the successful use of indigenous mental health workers. *Hospital and Community Psychiatry,* 1974, *25,* 308–310.

Heyman, S. R. *Community psychology in rural areas: Problems, advantages, and program development.* Paper presented at the 87th annual meeting of the American Psychological Association, New York City, September 1979.

Hodges, A., & Mahoney, S. C. Expectations for the comprehensive mental health center: The community. *Community Mental Health Journal,* 1970, *6,* 75–77.

Hollister, W. H., & Miller, F. T. Problem-solving strategies in consultation. *American Journal of Orthopsychiatry,* 1977, *47,* 445–450.

Howe, H. E. Specialty training in rural mental health delivery: University of Nebraska-Lincoln. *Rural Connections,* 1980, *1*(1), 4–6.

Huessy, H. R. Rural models. In H. H. Barten & L. Bellak (Eds.), *Progress in community mental health: Volume II.* New York: Grune & Stratton, 1972. (a)

Huessy, H. R. Tactics and targets in the rural setting. In S. E. Golann & C. Eisdorfer (Eds.), *Handbook of community mental health.* New York: Appleton-Century-Crofts, 1972. (b)

Iscoe, I., Bloom, B. L., & Spielberger, C. D. (Eds.). *Community psychology in transition.* Washington, D.C.: Hemisphere, 1977.

Jeffrey, M. J., & Reeve, R. E. Community mental health services in rural areas: Some practical issue. *Community Mental Health Journal,* 1978, *14,* 54–62.

Jeger, A. M. Personal communication, June 18, 1980.

Johnson, D. M. Community satisfaction of black return migrants to a Southern metropolis. *American Journal of Community Psychology,* 1975, *3,* 251–260.

Jones, J. D., Robin, S. S., & Wagenfeld, M. O. Rural mental health centers: Are they different? *International Journal of Mental Health,* 1974, *3,* 77–92.

Jones, J. D., Wagenfeld, M. O., & Robin, S. S. A profile of the rural community mental health center. *Community Mental Health Journal,* 1976, *12,* 176–182.

Jones, M. Community involvement in the planning of a rural mental health center. In A. Beigel & A. I. Levenson (Eds.), *The community mental health center: Strategies and programs*. New York: Basic Books, 1972.

Kahn, M. W., & Delk, J. Developing a community mental health clinic on an Indian reservation. *International Journal of Social Psychiatry*, 1974, *19*, 299–306.

Kahn, M. W., Williams, C., Galvez, E., Lejero, L., Conrad, R., & Goldstein, G. The Papago Psychology Service: A community mental health program on an American Indian reservation. *American Journal of Community Psychology*, 1975, *3*, 81–98.

Kahn, M. W., McWilliams, S. A., Balch, P., Chang, A. F., & Ireland, J. Developing a rural mental health service from a base in an academic clinical psychology program. *American Journal of Community Psychology*, 1976, *4*, 113–117.

Kahn, R. Job burnout: Prevention and remedies. *Public Welfare*, 1978, *36*(2), 61–63.

Keller, P. A. Personal communication, September, 1979.

Kelly, F. J., & Baer, D. J. *Outward Bound Schools as an alternative to institutionalization for adolescent delinquent boys*. Denver: Colorado Outward Bound School, 1968.

Kelly, F. J., & Baer, D. J. Physical challenge as a treatment for delinquency. *Crime and Delinquency*, 1971, *17*, 437–445.

Kenkel, M. B. Editorial statement. *Journal of Rural Community Psychology*, 1980, *1*, 60.

Kiev, A. *Curanderismo*. New York: Free Press, 1968.

Kinzie, J. D., Shore, J. H., & Pattison, E. M. Anatomy of a psychiatric consultation to rural Indians. *Community Mental Health Journal*, 1972, *8*, 196–207.

Kole, D. M., & Busse, H. Trail camping for delinquents. *Hospital and Community Psychiatry*, 1969, *20*, 150–153.

LaTour, K. A camp that leads kids out of the woods. *American Way*, 1979, *11*(Sept.), 106–109.

Lee, S. H., Gianturco, D. T., & Eisdorfer, C. Community mental health accessibility: A survey of the rural poor. *Archives of General Psychiatry*, 1974, *31*, 335–339.

Lewin, K. *Resolving social conflicts: Selected papers on group dynamics*. (G. W. Lewin, Ed.) New York: Harper, 1948.

Lewin, K. *Field theory in social science: Selected theoretical papers*. (C. D. Cartwright, Ed.) New York: Haper & Row, 1964.

Libertoff, K. *Natural helping networks in rural youth and family services*. Paper presented at the 87th annual meeting of the American Psychological Association, New York City, September 1979.

Libo, L. M., & Griffith, C. R. Developing mental health programs in areas lacking professional facilities: The community consultant approach in New Mexico. *Community Mental Health Journal*, 1966, *2*, 163–169.

Looff, D. H. *Appalachia's children*. Lexington: University of Kentucky Press, 1971.

Lopes, G. A. Development and delivery of mental health services to 7 rural counties in North Dakota. In A. Biegel & A. I. Levenson (Eds.), *The community mental health center: Strategies and programs*. New York: Basic Books, 1972.

Magoon, T. M., & Golann, S. Nontraditionally trained women as mental health counselors/psychotherapists. *Personnel and Guidance Journal*, 1966, *44*, 788–793.

Mahoney, S. C., & Hodges, A. Community mental health centers in rural areas: Variations on a theme. *Mental Hygiene*, 1969, *53*, 484–487.

Mann, P. A. *Community psychology: Concepts and applications*. New York: Free Press, 1978.

Maslach, C. Job burnout: How people cope. *Public Welfare*, 1978, *36*(2), 56–58.

Matthews, N., Mufson, D., Gottlieb, J., Bishop, B., & Matz, B. *Sexual assault education for rural caregivers*. Paper presented at the 87th annual meeting of the American Psychological Association, New York City, September 1979.

Mazer, M. *People and predicaments*. Cambridge: Harvard University Press, 1976.

McLaughlin, B. E. Recognition and treatment of youthful depression in a rural area. *Psychosomatics,* 1970, *9,* 420–421.

McPheeters, H. L., & Harding, J. R. *Distribution of mental health professionals.* Atlanta: Southern Regional Education Board, 1978.

Mitchell, W. E. Amicatherapy: Theoretical perspectives and an example of practice. *Community Mental Health Journal,* 1966, *2,* 307–312.

Murphy, H. B. M. Results from evaluation of a Canadian regional mental health program. *Hospital and Community Psychiatry,* 1973, *24,* 533–539.

National Institute of Mental Health. *New dimensions in mental health: A new day in rural mental health services.* Washington, D.C.: National Institute of Mental Health, 1978 (DHEW Publication No. ADM 78–690).

Nietzel, M. T., Winett, R. A., MacDonald, M. L., & Davidson, W. S. *Behavioral approaches to community psychology.* New York: Pergamon Press, 1977.

Nisbet, R. A. *The sociological tradition.* New York: Basic Books, 1966.

Ostendorf, D., & Hammerschlag, C. A. An Indian controlled mental health program. *Hospital and Community Psychiatry,* 1977, *28,* 682–685.

Padilla, A. M., & Arando, P. *Latino mental health: Bibliography and abstracts.* Rockville, Md.: National Institute of Mental Health, 1974.

Pattison, E. M. A psychosocial kinship model for family therapy. *American Journal of Psychitry,* 1975, *132,* 1246–1250.

Perlman, B., & Hartman, E. A. *Characteristics and problems of rural administrators.* NIMH Manpower Research and Demonstration Grant, Number IT24 MH1590701. Department of Psychology, University of Wisconsin, Oshkosh, Wisconsin, 1980.

Perlmutter, F. D. Consultation and education in rural community mental health centers. *Community Mental Health Journal,* 1979, *15,* 58–68.

Perlmutter, F., & Silverman, H. A. Conflict in consultation-education. *Community Mental Health Journal,* 1973, *9,* 116–122.

Pines, A., & Maslach, C. Characteristics of staff burn-out in mental health settings. *Hospital and Community Psychiatry,* 1978, *29,* 233–237.

Raft, D. D., Coley, S. B., & Miller, F. T. Using a service guide to provide comprehensive care in a rural mental health clinic. *Hospital and Community Psychiatry,* 1976, *27,* 553–559.

Rappaport, J. *Community psychology: Values, research, action.* New York: Holt, Rinehart & Winston, 1977.

Reul, M. R. *Traditional boundaries of rural poverty: Profiles of exploitation.* Center for Rural Manpower and Public Affairs: Michigan State University Cooperative Extension Service, 1974.

Richards, J. M., & Gottfredson, G. D. Geographic distribution of U.S. psychologists: A human ecological analysis. *American Psychologist,* 1978, *33,* 1–9.

Riggs, R. T., & Kugel, L. F. Transition from urban to rural mental health practice. *Social Casework,* 1976, *57,* 562–567.

Rioch, M. J. Pilot projects in training mental health counselors. In E. L. Cowen, E. A. Gardner, & M. Zax (Eds.), *Emergent approaches to mental health problems.* New York: Appleton-Century-Crofts, 1967.

Rioch, M. J., Elkes, C., Flint, A. A., Usdansky, B. S., Newman, R. G., & Sibler, E. NIMH pilot study in training of mental health counselors. *American Journal of Orthopsychiatry,* 1963, *33,* 678–679.

Robertson, C. G., & Bayerman, M. Psychiatric consultation on 2 Indian reservations. *Hospital and Community Psychiatry,* 1969, *20,* 186.

Robin, S. S., & Wagenfeld, M. O. The community mental health worker: Organizational and personal sources of role discrepancy. *Journal of Health and Social Behavior,* 1977, *18,* 16–27.

Rogers, E. M., & Burdge, R. J. *Social change in rural societies* (2nd ed.). Englewood Cliffs, N.J.: Prentice-Hall, 1972.

Ruiz, P., & Langrod, J. The role of folk healers in community mental health services. *Community Mental Health Journal*, 1976, *12*, 392–398.

Sarason, I. G. The evolution of community psychology. *American Journal of Community Psychology*, 1973, *1*, 91–97.

Schein, E. H. *Process consultation: Its role in organizational development*. Menlo Park, Calif.: Addison-Wesley, 1969.

Snyder, J. A. The use of gatekeepers in crisis management. *Bulletin of Suicidology*, 1971, *18*, 39–44.

Stai, R., & Atkinson, T. M. Decentralized services in a rural setting. In A. Biegel & A. I. Levenson (Eds.), *The community mental health center: Strategies and programs*. New York: Basic Books, 1972.

Taylor, C. B. Using rumors for therapeutic purposes. *Community Mental Health Journal*, 1975, *11*, 267–270.

Thomas, G. C. G. Breaking from tradition in a small mental health center. *Hospital and Community Psychiatry*, 1973, *7*, 472–473.

Thomson, C. P., & Bell, N. W. Evaluation of a rural community mental health program. *Archives of General Psychiatry*, 1969, *20*, 448–456.

Thompson, C. P. Suicide prevention in a rural area. *Bulletin of Suicidology*, 1968, *15*, 49–52.

Torrey, E. F. Mental health services for American Indians and Eskimos. *Community Mental Health Journal*, 1970, *6*, 455–463.

Tyler, J. D., & Dreyer, S. F. Planning primary prevention strategy: A survey of the effects of business location on Indian reservation life. *American Journal of Community Psychology*, 1975, *3*, 69–76.

Vidich, A. J., & Bensman, J. *Small town in mass society*. Princeton, N.J.: Princeton University Press, 1968.

Wagenfeld, M. O. *Cultural barriers to the delivery of mental health services in rural areas: A conceptual overview*. NIMH: Conference on Rural Mental Health, 1977.

Webb, P. Resource center notes. *Rural Connections*, 1980, *1*(1), 1.

Wedel, H. L. Characteristics of community mental health center operations in small communities. *Community Mental Health Journal*, 1969, *15*, 437–444.

White, R. P. The development of an emergency listening post manned by ministers. In A. Biegel & A. T. Levenson (Eds.), *The community mental health center: Strategies and programs*. New York: Basic Books, 1972.

Wilson, V. E. Rural health care systems. *Journal of the American Medical Association*, 1971, *216*, 1623–1626.

Witt, J. Beyond the cities. *MH(Mental Hygiene)*, 1977, *60*(4), 4–6.

Zax, M., & Specter, G. A. *An introduction to community psychology*. New York: Wiley, 1974.

13

Models of Service Delivery

J. Wilbert Edgerton

In order for an account of models of service delivery in rural areas to have meaning, it is necessary to know something of the rural context and the issues involved that have given rise to those particular models. Rural people, and those professionals authorized to serve them, have of necessity invented a number of ingenious methods for providing the services that have been needed. It has not always been easy, and problems remain, but there have been some innovative models developed especially for rural mental health services. Because psychologists have been extensively involved in mental health services (in contrast to the other human services) and because much experience has been amassed by federal, state, and local government officials in attempting to meet rural mental health needs, this chapter will proceed from the perspective of mental health services. This is not to say, however, that many, if not most, of the same issues and problems would not also apply to the provision of other human services in rural areas.

ISSUES IN RURAL SERVICE DELIVERY

There are at least six issues which have a bearing on rural mental health services delivery:

1. *Low tax base for support of services.* Rural property taxes that customarily support services are relatively low in comparison with urban places. There are also fewer people to pay them. Additionally, rural

J. WILBERT EDGERTON • Department of Psychiatry, University of North Carolina, Chapel Hill, North Carolina 27514.

people have lower incomes, with approximately twice the percentage of their numbers falling under the federally defined poverty level (Segal, 1973).

2. *Fewer professionals.* Qualified mental health professionals are generally clustered in urban places where there are more consumers, more facilities, and more income. There is also less professional isolation and there are more cultural advantages for themselves and their families. Rural places have difficulty matching the salaries of urban professional personnel, even under uniform personnel merit systems; rural facilities all too often end up with a cadre of lesser trained, less costly staff, who may be charged with responsibilities beyond their experience and professional training.

Similar problems attend the recruitment of professionals who are members of various ethnic minorities. Those who are qualified often locate in urban centers where the cultural advantages are greater, leaving rural centers without minority professionals who can communicate effectively with the various rural minorities that are a part of their constituency.

3. *Making effective use of existing professionals and services.* Although not usually blessed with the relative abundance of services found in urban places, practically every rural community has schools, a social services agency, a health service, law-enforcement services, churches and clergymen, and some access to dentists, physicians, and attorneys. A special resource of rural areas is the Agricultural Extension Service, which makes available farm agents, home agents, and various child and family life specialists. Mental health professionals in this setting have to be generalists, doing planning, program development, and administrative work in addition to the usual clinical services of intake, diagnosis, and treatment. The most effective plan for mental health services includes contributions from all available helping professionals who have a stake in the mental health enterprise. All the public and private agency personnel need each other in order to maximize each agency's mandate, so a very important issue is how to utilize effectively the existing resident professionals.

4. *Rural culture and belief systems.* Rural people in some parts of the country traditionally have exhibited a "frontier" interdependence, stressing the fact that "We can take care of our own." They are willing to help each other, but are not interested in institutionalized helping services (Tranel, 1970). In Appalachia the term "fiercely proud" is a characterization frequently applied to independence and an expectation that people wil solve their own problems. These attitudes carry with them special meanings for illness and the sick role, in which there is great tolerance by the community for the minor illnesses, and even for some

"strangeness," as long as a family member or neighbor can continue to work (and in some cases when he or she cannot). These same people are content with symptom relief, rather than the prolonged processes involved in reconstructive psychotherapy (Tranel, 1970). The rural culture then, frequently as impoverished as its economy may be, perceives mental health services and their utilization differently. This is particularly true of those middle-class, urban, programs that often focus on self-realization and self-improvement (Wagenfeld, 1977; Flax, Wagenfeld, Ivens, & Weiss, 1979). Resisting these programs that they perceive as inappropriate, rural people delay availing themselves of services and frequently are more seriously ill when they do come. This factor influences the form that mental health services must take.

5. *Geographical distance and transportation problems.* The issue in rural areas is getting services to the people or getting the people to services. Of the more than 50 million Americans who live in nonmetropolitan areas, some live in relatively densely populated areas and others in areas that are very sparsely populated. They live in 2,100 mostly rural counties, encompassing 90% of the land area of the United States (Segal, 1973). The rural service areas established under the federal mental health centers program (Public Law 88-164) average 17,000 square miles, with most containing over 5000 square miles (Flax, Wagenfeld, Ivens, & Weiss, 1979). One catchment area in Montana is comparable in size to the state of Pennsylvania, and one in Arizona covers 60,000 square miles. These extremes serve to emphasize the difficulty in time, distance, and money of providing services within convenient reach of rural people.

6. *Local government by personal dynamics.* More often than not, county government in rural areas and small rural towns operates by personal relationships rather than by professional and formal order. Leaders come to be known by almost everyone and the procedures are carried out through personal politics, with no anonymity. Everybody seems to know everybody else's business. This can be facilitative in supporting and implementing services, but it can also be a handicap if a powerful local leader is opposed to expenditures for services.

THE MODELS

In this writer's view, the comprehensive community mental health center, with its array of clinical and non-clinical services, and the planning, coordinating, and community organizational functions that it performs for a specified geographical and demographic community, remains the single best service–delivery model. As the community's mental health authority, the mental health center can either deliver services, contract for their delivery, or make compacts with any or all other public or private helping agencies or individuals. This requires the generation of a plan through which it is mutually determined who has the responsibility for a given element of the total mental health program. For example, some appropriate part of the program could be delivered by or through the schools, another by or through the social services department, and another by or through the organized health agency. Ideally, all participants develop the plan, all "own" it, and all carry it out without the destructive rivalries that sometimes interfere with harmonious interagency collaboration.

This community mental health center model is equally suitable for both rural and urban communities, but because of the special issues previously cited, its application to the rural community must be modified. The 12 services[1] previously required (Public Law 94-63) in federally funded mental health centers can be provided, but only with special ingenuity and adaptations. Fortunately, many adaptations have occurred; information about them is available through a burgeoning literature and the activities of a number of organizations that focus on the rural scene.

The following sections of this chapter will describe models that are essentially adaptations of the conventional service delivery models and are devised to deal with the issues of distance, cost, shortage of mental health workers and other professionals, and cultural differences.

Outpatient Clinical Services

The average professional and rural citizen alike, when queried as to the most likely needed mental health service, will respond with some concept of outpatient services. The service in question will be provided either by a public agency professional or by a private practitioner (physician, psychologist, social worker, nurse, marriage counselor) in his or her office. It is around the delivery of outpatient services that so many models have evolved over the years, models designed either to take the services to where the people are or to provide the services in a place to which the people can come.

---

[1]These services are: (1) inpatient care; (2) outpatient care; (3) partial hospitalization; (4) emergency services; (5) consultation and education; (6) services for the elderly; (7) services for children; (8) screening services for courts and other referring agencies; (9) follow-up care for patients discharged from mental hospitals; (10) transitional services that help formerly hospitalized patients adjust to community life; (11) alcoholism and alcohol-abuse services; and (12) drug addiction and drug-abuse services.

The Traveling Clinic

Among the solutions to the problem of geographic distance is the traveling clinic. The constituent clinic staff (traditionally a psychiatrist, a psychologist, a social worker, and sometimes a nurse) appears regularly at an appointed time and place. This can be one or two days a week, a day every two weeks or one day a month. Scheduling and intake may be done by a local health or welfare worker or secretary, or by the team itself. For several reasons this model has not proved to be satisfactory (Stai & Atkinson, 1972). One reason is that the team members almost never become a part of the fabric of the visited community and may remain unfamiliar with its structure and problems. Also, the logistical problems of traveling together conveniently are difficult to manage, particularly if team members are not personally compatible. Yet another reason is that traveling in uncertain and inclement weather, particularly in mountainous terrain, frequently proves to be an insurmountable obstacle. Such services are hardly cost-effective, since salaries and travel are expensive in relation to the amount of services actually delivered.

The Mental Health Worker

Another solution to the problem of rural service delivery is the posting of a mental health worker in an outlying area. This person provides some direct services and makes referrals to more centrally located services. The worker, usually a psychologist, a social worker, or a specially trained person, can become known in the community and can come to represent a point of entry into service. He or she can provide consultation to other helping agency personnel and assist in the organization and development of more extensive services. New Mexico pioneered the use of such a person (McCarty & Rosen, 1965; Griffin & Libo, 1968), and both Florida and North Carolina used this method in the days before the development of comprehensive mental health centers.

Itinerant Psychological Services

For some 40 years the North Carolina Department of Social Services has operated an intinerant psychological services (Kilburn, 1980). A cadre of psychologists is posted, one to a district, and each one travels a regular circuit of county Social Services departments. They perform evaluations for adoptions and make referrals to mental health services and they provide consultation to Social Services personnel, parents, and other agency staff. They also provide in-service training for the staffs of the Department of Social Services and other community agencies on methods of intervention, child and spouse abuse, parenting the foster child, and other pertinent psychological topics. These itinerant psychologists also supervise interventions by Social Services staff. Thorough awareness of the guidelines, policies, constraints, and programs is required in order to assist in minimizing adverse effects on the movement of children into or out of foster families or child-care institutions. There is much contact with the courts concerning adoption, foster care, termination of parental rights, and guardianship. These psychologists become rather specialized in these knowledges and skills, including their applicability to the rural and minority cultures from which so many clients come.

These specialized services have undoubtedly contributed to the survival of the Psychological Services Branch of the North Carolina Department of Social Services. From time to time the proposal is made that the branch be abolished and its activities absorbed by local mental health centers. Each time, however, the usefulness of the services within the Social Services structure has been reiterated forcefully and strategically, and the activities continue. These activities have been especially crucial in the many rural counties of North Carolina.

Psychological Consultants

Individual psychological consultants continue to provide clinical service one or two days a week in many rural facilities. These may be psychologists in private practice who travel by automobile or airplane on a day or overnight basis, or they may come from university training centers. Although most psychologists in private clinical practice are clustered in urban areas, more of them are beginning to live in the small towns that service rural communities.

The Satellite Center

The development of satellite centers has probably been the most effective means of providing outpatient services over large rural areas. This model entails the operation of smaller outpatient services for particular small towns and their environs. These services are usually under the administrative direction of a central program director for the whole catchment area. Some professional mental health staff (psychologists, social workers, or counselors) and support staff live in the community and may serve full-time in the satellite center. Citizens in the vicinity may receive services there, or through the satellite center may have access to the whole range of programs available from the central facility. These can include inpatient services or day care, for example, which might not be cost-effective for the satellite. Certain staff from the central site are usually available to the satellite center on a part-time basis, and usually serve other satellites. Psychiatrists or other specialized personnel are examples of such staff.

In-school Satellite Centers

An attractive rural adaptation for satellite outpatient services is the establishment of programs within the schools. An example of this is the Smoky Mountain Area Mental Health Center of North Carolina, which works together with the school systems in the seven-county mountain catchment area (Coffey, 1979). Through a contractual realtionship, the Mental Health Center places within the schools a psychologist for each 1,900 students. The same services are provided to the children as are available in the local office of the Center. The psychologist functions as a combination school-clinical psychologist and must have completed at least a master's degree and either two year's experience with children and youth, or an internship in the Center's program.

There are many advantages to such a program. It saves travel time for students, parents, and psychologists because the distance to the school is probably less than to the mental health center in the county seat. Students do not have to lose a half day of school. Referral for services is easier and may even be verbal. Referrals also are made earlier than if the psychologist were not so conveniently near. Rapport and trust are easier to establish. Follow-through is facilitated, and if someone misses an appointment another child or youth or teacher may be seen. Children become accustomed to seeing the psychologist and are less apprehensive in an appointment than they would be when visiting the mental health center. Children and youth refer themselves. "Rap" sessions and psychology courses at school facilitate self-referral (as opposed to being "sent" by someone else to the mental health center). Parents see the school as a safer place, without the stigma that some may attach to the mental health center. The parents may themselves have attended the same school and thus feel more at ease with appointments there. Teachers may refer themselves for personal problems because of the easy availability of help, and this may provide secondary gains for the children in their classroom. Finally, the psychologists bring their talents to bear on academic learning problems, along with their assistance on personal adjustment and behavior problems. Workshops for teachers are available through which they can earn teaching certificate renewal credit. The main benefits of this in-school satellite arrangement, besides the benefits of effective intersystem collaboration, are a higher quality of services delivered in a more cost-effective manner than the usual satellite outpatient service.

Van or Bus Service

As another means of getting people to service, many mental health centers operate vans or minibuses that make regular runs to bring people to central facilities. These may bring people to regular outpatient appointments but are used even more extensively to bring rural people to day care. Agencies may collaborate in the use of van transportation because transportation is one of the major problems for all of them in the delivery of services in rural areas. Community action agencies and agencies organized to serve older Americans commonly provide this kind of transportation service.

Multicounty Catchment Area Programs

A further elaboration of the central unit–satellite unit model is represented by the multicounty mental health catchment area or district programs of rural America. This is essentially a centralized-decentralized set of program services with an area or district director and various county unit directors. Central office program specialists not affordable by all county units are available to all outlying rural units on a regular basis. These may be substance abuse, mental retardation, children's services, or consultation and education specialists, in all of whom is vested the substantive program leadership. The structure lends itself nicely to governance by an area or district management team consisting of line administrators (central and county unit directors), program specialists, and appropriate central office support staff. The management group can effect program planning and coordination based on needs assessment and priority setting, and programs can be modified on the basis of program evaluation data. Key advantages of such a decentralized arrangement are that the staff members identify with the communities they live in and serve, the program is "owned" by the county in which it is located and thus is more readily supported financially, the unit is visible and can be integrated permanently with the usual other helping agencies, and it is accessible to local residents with a minimum of travel. For rural areas the maximum acceptable travel time has sometimes been set at 90 minutes. This model seems to be the best arrangement yet developed for the delivery of comprehensive services.

Emergency Services and Crisis Intervention

In 1977 a national survey of crisis–emergency services in federally funded mental health centers was completed (Miller, Mazade, Muller, & Andrulis, 1978). Miller later (1982) compiled the data from only those mental health centers serving populations comprised of at least 50% rural people.

He found that more than 80% of the rural centers offered the following services:

1. Disposition consultation for persons potentially dangerous to themselves or others
2. Consultation to and/or direct intervention into emergencies and crises arising in jails, schools, and nursing homes
3. Emergency walk-in service at the center
4. Formal referral for community residents inquiring about mental health services
5. Counseling with victims of child abuse
6. Counseling with rape victims
7. Consultation available in the emergency rooms of local hospitals

Several ingenious models for providing emergency-crisis intervention services have been developed in rural communities. Attention will now be given to four of these that incorporate several of the services listed in the Miller (1980) study.

Mental Health Agency Staff on Call

A common arrangement is for the mental health program staff to be on call to the local hospital emergency room, to the local constabulary, or to general practitioners or other professionals who may need dispositional assistance. In multicounty catchment areas where distances and terrain are formidable barriers and where resources are limited, special communication arrangements by telephone or law–enforcement radio networks, or a combination of these, are frequent.

One special example is the operation in the catchment area of the seven westernmost counties of North Carolina (Monroe, 1980). The seven mountain counties are divided into three zones with face-to-face contact provided by residential mental health center staff at the emergency room of the contractual local hospital in each zone.

A telephone coordinator, or a staff member of the inpatient unit at the central facility, receives all crisis calls and judges if and when the caller is to be seen. Three options are open:

1. The telephone coordinator can decide that the crisis may be handled more appropriately by another agency or individual, such as Social Services, Vocational Rehabilitation, or a clergyman. If so, the caller is referred, and in two days the coordinator must check with the agency to whom the referral is made to see if there is follow-through.

2. The crisis situation may be alleviated over the telephone. In this case the telephone coordinator uses the same techniques as he or she would use if the caller was in his or her office. After the crisis is stabilized, referral to the zone mental health center may be appropriate.

3. Face-to-face contact may be necessary to help solve the problem.

This is indicated when the caller or subject of the call is suicidal, psychotic, violent, or extremely anxious. The person in need is directed to go to the emergency room of the hospital in his or her zone; if needed, assistance with transportation to the hospital is provided. This may come from the law–enforcement agency in the caller's zone.

The telephone coordinator alerts the mental health staff person on call in the caller's zone through law–enforcement agency personnel, who have access to each other through the Back Bone Communication System (a series of transmitters located on various mountain ridges to permit intercounty communication). This system is a mutual aid agreement between law–enforcement agencies and the mental health center. After being alerted, the clinician is given the crisis information and proceeds to meet the caller at the emergency room of the contract hospital in his or her zone.

The Service Guide

The Service Guide represents a new role in rural mental health services, developed and utilized in a rural feasibility study in North Carolina (Hollister, 1970; Hollister, Edgerton, Bentz, Miller, & Aponte, 1973). The role was modeled after the English welfare worker and the American public health investigator, and was to be an "ombudsman on wheels" to be an advocate for patients and help them get the services they needed. As the role developed, the Service Guide became a crucial person in the provision of emergency services and crisis interventions in the rural study.

The Service Guide was available by telephone at all times during the week and on weekends. Emergencies were handled in callers' homes or at the local hospital emergency-room, with physician-on-call back-up. The Guide might transport the patient to the hospital, or from the hospital or the jail to the state mental hospital. This person also served to reassure patients and their families in emergencies and was a vital link in the state hospital–rural community relationship.

Other important services provided by the Service Guide included case-finding, aftercare services, and educational services. He or she would bring patients and their families to services at the outpatient clinic and the local and state hospitals, or take services to patients in the form of medications (or public health nurses to administer medications), without which rehospitalization would have been necessary.

It is rather surprising that the use of such a person has not been more widely adopted in rural areas. The Service Guide does not require formal professional mental health education in order to be effective. It is more important to have a helping disposition, a willingness to learn, and to be adaptive and creative in serving clients' needs. Being indigenous to the rural area served is also an advantage to the Service Guide, because it facilitates entry and acceptance to the community's culture and processes. A further advantage to establishing the service guide function is that the cost is considerably less than would be required for a degreed mental health professional to provide similar services.

The CARE Team

The CARE Team was an invention of the Suicide Crisis Intervention Service that was established in Gainesville, Florida, in 1969 (McGee, 1974). Care is an acronym for *contact* with clients, *assessment* of the situation, *relief* or *rescue*, and *engaging* the client in the intervention process. It evolved from the original concept of the *Trouble Team* that responded to anyone in trouble, as promulgated by Lifeline in Australia and CONTACT Teleministry, Inc., in the United States. Numerous mental health centers and/or their communities have active CONTACT programs to take care of some of the emergency services and crisis interventions in their catchment areas. The Service Guide is a one-person service provided by a nonprofessional who is trained on the job. CARE Teams are two-person units, both members of which are experienced crisis workers. Teams are mobile and have access to two-way radio communication. Team members are telephone volunteers who have demonstrated satisfactory performance in crisis intervention procedure, as measured by objective ratings of their effectiveness. CARE Teams operate around the clock outside the regular hours of the crisis service center.

While the CARE Team activity is not conceived as a health-related service, nor necessarily as a mental health service, and usually is not a service of the mental health center, the concept is applicable to rural areas. The original CARE Team contracted with the mental health center to provide emergency services to a 10-county, mostly rural area.

The CARE Team philosophy is to participate in the solution of any human problem whenever and wherever it is asked to do so. It is broader than a mental health service in that respect. Its progenitors have conceived it as a demonstration of applied community psychology, in which psychologists can function as a care givers and consultants to volunteers in the community helping systems.

In other places persons employed as expediters or case managers perform roles similar to some of those taken by the CARE Team and the Service Guide. The role of the Service Guide, or its variants, is particularly useful in rural areas, to help clients with transportation problems and to help coordinate client contacts with appropriate services from a multiplicity of agencies.

Emergency Service/Institutional Intervention Program

This service, located in Chesapeake, Virginia, and subtitled "Alternatives to Commitment," is a court-related but independent mental health service, the goal of which is the reduction of commitments to the state mental institutions (LeCompte, 1978). The services are provided through an around-the-clock court intervention activity provided by crisis-trained mental health personnel upon the initiation of a commitment petition.

More specifically, the service goals are:

1. To reduce the number of inappropriate commitments to state mental hospitals
2. To seek alternatives to commitment through referral and use of community-based facilities
3. To secure assessment information about persons for whom commitment is sought in order to facilitate judicial decisions and to expedite community-based or institutional treatment
4. To provide follow-up services for a maximum of 60 days to individuals and families who have experienced needs for institutional placements, in order to determine if these needs are dealt with satisfactorily and to assure receipt of services that may prevent or decrease recurrences of need for commitment
5. To provide specific liaison personnel for local human service agencies and state hospitals around commitment and admission procedures, and preadmission and release planning for committed persons
6. To provide data that would help to identify mental health and related services needed in the community to prevent inappropriate institutionalization and to facilitate the effective transition of patients from the state hospital to the community

The effectiveness of the service is shown by a decrease in the rate of commitments from 88% to 12% of petitions in the six-month pilot phase of its operation. In 1978–79, largely rural Chesapeake reported the second lowest admission rate to the state hospitals in all of Virginia. The rate was 103.6 per 100,000 population, including readmissions, and this compared with very much higher admission rates in the adjacent urban places of Norfolk (191.83/100,000), Portsmouth (203.49/100,000), and Hampton-Newport News (271.94/100,000), which did not have a similar service. The adjoining rural area of Suffolk, which also did not have the intervention service, had an admission rate of 228.85/100,000.

In the following year, 1979–80, the Chesapeake admissions rate to the state hospital rose to 118.74/100,000, against a state average of

193/100,000. Other rural rates in Virginia without the emergency intervention service ranged from 143.26 to 331.27/100,000. In Chesapeake 68% of the referrals for commitment received alternative care. Half of those actually committed were sent to the state hospital, and half were sent to local facilities (LeCompte, 1980). Not only is this a cost-effective service, but it provides a better organized and more humane way of dealing with commitment emergencies. It has fulfilled its goals very well and has added short-term treatment and client-tracking services which help to assure continuity of care and appropriateness of services.

Like the CARE Team in Florida, the Chesapeake Emergency/Intervention Service elected to have its own administrative and programmatic identity. The purpose of this was, in both cases, to assure their equal standing among the other agencies and to highlight their different mode of functioning from that of the usual outpatient mental health clinic. Both wanted to be perceived as symbols of aggressive outreach and a broadened scope for problem solving, in contrast to the relatively passive stance of the outpatient service.

Transitional Care

Many rural mental health centers administer halfway houses or other forms of transitional care between the mental hospital's most restrictive care and the least restrictive mode of independent living in the community. They may also facilitate the establishment of an independently administered home and contract for services there for their clients. They may also service clients directly from the community who need these services without having been hospitalized. Clients may be adults, youths, or children with mental or emotional disorders; they may also be adult or youthful alcoholics. These programs and facilities may operate in a fairly conventional form, but exist in the small town or rural place.

An innovative rural adaptation of a program of transitional care exists at the Smoky Mountain Area Mental Health Center previously cited (Monroe, 1979). Called *The Therapeutic Home Program,* each unit is a private home which serves one or two adult clients or one or two young clients. Couples who wish to provide the service in their homes must be intelligent and caring and have space for up to two clients, and one member must not be employed outside the home. The home must meet fire safety and health standards.

Therapeutic Home Providers are trained by the mental health center staff to understand behavioral disturbances, to exercise skills in communication, to set goals and to exercise skills in making behavior changes occur, and they practice the development of these skills.

Clients are admitted on their therapist's recommendation. The therapist devises a treatment plan which is implemented by the home providers, with weekly supportive contact by the therapist. Clients attend the day hospital program and see their therapists weekly. The stay in a therapeutic home is not longer than three months and participation in the usual family activities is required. When children and adolescents are involved, the therapist keeps in contact with the primary parents in order to facilitate the clients' return to their own homes as soon as feasible, which might be before the three months limit.

Financial support is paid both by the client (on a sliding scale based on ability to pay) and by third-party payers. Some advantages of this program are that it supplies a needed service easily accessible in a rural area, as close to the home community as possible, and at a cost that favorably outstrips all other transitional care in money and staff/client ratio. Therapeutic Home Providers are reimbursed only for the period of time that clients are assigned to them.

A variant of these homes has been proposed as *Sobriety Homes,* to be a part of the spectrum of services available to alcoholics. Clients would be in the Sobriety Home for two to seven days for social detoxification. This is a type of transitional care that has features of crisis intervention (Monroe, 1979).

Consultation

Consultation as a model of service delivery is as old as the first time one professional asked the opinion of another concerning a problem of a client or a patient. Case consultation as practiced in medicine has a long history. Referral to other agencies has been advocated as a part of the community mental health program from the inception of the National Mental Health Act of 1946. In 1963, with the enactment by Congress of the Community Mental Health Centers Act, consultation became a mandated service for federally funded centers (Public Law 88-164, 1963).

The rationale for consultation is that the psychological or mental health problems exhibited by the clientele of the helping agencies in the community can be managed more economically by agency professionals, with the consultative assistance of the mental health program staff. This is a way to extend the talents of the relatively scarce mental health staff, and at the same time to provide their services to persons referred directly to the mental health agency, persons whose disorders may be more acute and require direct service from mental health specialists. It is also a way to strengthen helping-agency personnel, who in turn will alter their interventions with their clients towards promoting healthier growth, in line with the mental health principles of problem solving, appropriate self-sufficiency, and effective interaction.

The focus is on the work concerns of the consultees (the agency personnel) and is educational in character, rather than clinical treatment-oriented. Client change is achieved through assistance from the consultee, (who is expected to be more effective through the consultation method). This consultation concept of strengthening the helping professionals found in every community is particularly relevant to rural communities, with their scarcity of both professional personnel and specialized services. It helps to assure the maximum use of all the resources available in the community. Perhaps the greatest demand is for case consultation, which is but a step away from the administrative or organizational consultation that frequently develops once fruitful working relationships have been established.

Psychologists and other mental health professionals are heavily involved in consultation programs in rural areas. They may operate from the mental health agency base, from university settings, or from a private practice arrangement, all through formal contracts that may or may not involve the exchange of money. From the impetus of the federal mandate and also from sheer necessity, the service delivery model of consultation activities and programs has become a very important part of the organized helping enterprises in rural communities.

Psychologists have been in the forefront of efforts to understand consultation processes, both in consultant–consultee relationships, and those processes involved in developing consultation programs. They have been very active in teaching consultation skills and consultation programming. Psychologists have contributed extensively to the science of organization development, and there are numerous firms of psychologists who are consultants to management and to organizations. Rural agencies make use of these consultation services, though not as extensively, perhaps, as is the case in urban settings.

In the evaluation of consultation programs, the strategies have been to assess change in consultees, change in their clients, and change in systems, all as a result of the consultation. Although there is much literature on evaluation, little of it reports a causative relationship of changes in all three. Nevertheless, research with appropriate controls shows that consultation does produce effective change in consultees. Other valid research shows changes in consultees and clients, while still other studies have shown significant system change (Mannino & Shore, 1979). It is apparent that consultation–program evaluation is complex and that more efforts should be made to determine outcomes as a routine activity of rural program services.

Aftercare-Community Support Programs

The rapid and almost precipitous movement of chronic mental patients from large state mental hospitals in the past 25 years has produced what perhaps should be known as the new "shame of the states." All too often such patients are moved to nursing homes, boarding homes, hostels, and other local facilities, where treatment or needed support services are essentially lacking. Where there are organized community support plans, too many times the agency personnel charged with administering them are overwhelmed by the volume of need and the complexity of implementing the plans.

The chronically ill from rural communities have been in double jeopardy—they are underserved as ill people and as rural people (President's Commission, 1978c). The plight of these people has given rise to a new model for service delivery, which may be administered within the mental health center program or another appropriate agency. Referred to as a *Community Support Program,* this model provides not only for the expected medical or psychiatric care, but also aggressively fosters access to such other necessities as housing, work, and social support. In these elements it goes beyond previous formally organized programs, with their responsibility for only the mental health of individual clients, as a model for service delivery in the community.

Although the simplicities of rural living have been emphasized, it may well be that the rural citizen who is chronically mentally ill is subjected to even greater disabling stressors than is his urban counterpart. He may be more isolated and inaccessible geographically. Access to friends or family supports may be more of a problem. Social and recreational supports may be more limited. Access to gainful employment may also be more difficult. The lack of self-confidence and the vulnerability of the rural mental patient are certainly no less.

There is a growing mandate for rural community support programs, and some structure in which case management can be operative. Case management will require the capacity to mobilize resources across agency boundaries on an as-needed basis, to procure work at the level it can be performed, and to provide access to training in community awareness, independent living skills, and remotivation. The case manager will have to program access to leisure-time activities, recreation, education, and self-help groups. Housing that meets the need and level of independence of the client must also be accessible.

The Federal Government is reinforcing this comprehensive model of community support through special grants to states and through housing subsidies to the chronically mentally ill via the Department of Housing and Urban Development. Loans are available for the development of community-based housing, as are grants for rental subsidies to the prospective residents.

So far, very little of the housing funds have been utilized in rural areas. There has not been enough organized leadership for developing plans and applying for grants. The chronically mentally ill in rural communities thus suffer from the unique problems of rurality outlined earlier. In one way, however, they may be less handicapped, since the attitudes of families and communities are more disposed to providing for their needs in the absence of an organized community support program.

Mental Health Services in Primary Health Care

A rapidly developing model of rural services delivery is one that links mental health services and primary community health care. Besides the fact that the services need each other, impetus for these linkages in rural services has come from several actions by the federal government.

In 1975 the Rural Health Intiative and Health Underserved Rural Areas programs were instituted for the establishment of ambulatory health-care systems in medically underserved rural areas. A requirement for these health services is that they be coordinated or linked with other health services, including mental health facilities (Public Law 95–626, 1978). Also in 1975, the amendments to the national community mental health centers legislation require federally funded rural mental health centers to provide consultation to health services agencies and to coordinate mental health services with the services of health agencies (Public Law 94-63, 1975).

Before these two events took place, the 1974 health-planning legislation passed by the Congress (Public Law 93-641, 1974) had already specified that the primary activities of the health systems agencies created by the legislation must include mental health needs assessment. It further stated that mental health must be included in the health plan that is developed on a specified periodic basis.

In 1978 the President's Commission on Mental Health recommended that a "working alliance" between the health and mental health systems be strengthened by requiring community mental health programs to establish cooperative working arrangements with health-care settings (President's Commission on Mental Health, 1978a). The rationale for this recommendation is that since mental and physical disorders frequently coexist, and since the majority of persons with some level of mental or emotional disorder will be cared for in general health-care settings, it is only sensible that mental health services be readily available in those settings.

Prior to these developments at the federal level, a number of practitioners had become vocal advocates for some form of integration of mental health services with other health services. Morrill (1972, 1975), in describing mental health services through a neighborhood health center in Boston, emphasized several advantages. Among these are: (1) earlier, more personal and less traumatic referrals because of less stigma, and easier physical and psychological accessibility; (2) increased effectiveness of primary, secondary, and tertiary prevention through access to health services clientele; (3) increased communication among health and mental health staff regarding patients and referrals; (4) appreciation among health and mental health staff of each others' capabilities and contributions to each others' missions, including opportunities to work together in joint psychosomatic programs; and (5) movement of mental health staff toward a family-oriented practice that utilizes increased information about family events. Borus and associates, also drawing on experience in neighborhood health centers in Boston, added that providing health and mental health services in the same location can both improve the efficiency of the primary health-care system and make community members more sensitive to mental health problems (Borus, Burns, Jacobson, Morrill, & Wilson, 1978).

Borus, Janowitch, and Kieffer (1975) and Morrill (1975) have delineated four types of linkages between the health agency and the mental health agency. The first of these is the *Consultation Model,* in which health center patients are referred to the separate mental health center that is also separately financed. The second type of linkage is the *Community Mental Health Center Outpost Model,* in which a pseudopod of the mental health center extends into the health center. It is funded and staffed by the mental health center, but exists in the health center. The third type is the *Joint Endeavor Model,* in which funds and staff for the mental health program in the health center are provided by both agencies, with perhaps the most highly trained mental health staff contributed by the mental health center. The fourth type of linkage is the *Autonomous Neighborhood Health Center Model.* In this model the health center has its own funds and operates its own program, but with some coordination with the mental health center program.

Morrill (1975) avers that experience shows only the Joint Endeavor and Autonomous models to be maximally effective in providing mental health services. These integrative arrangements seem to result in a higher utilization rate by patients who would not otherwise reach the mental health facility. Mental health staff members who belong to the health center and have a commitment to it operate more effectively through its system. At the same time, ties to the mental health center can be maintained for coordination purposes. It is a solution that combines the best of both worlds—giving access to consumers and families through the health agency and carrying out the mental health agency responsibility for the mental health care for all the catchment area.

There is a bit of irony in this move to mandate the linkages between health and mental health services. In a great many states, the beginnings of the community mental health programs were in local health departments. State health departments administered both their own monies and the federal mental health funding formula grants to states. State health officials, however were often not diligent enough nor sufficiently receptive to these new categorical mental health programs to be able to continue them. In state after state, the forces for setting up separate mental health programs combining the community and institutional components, were great enough to produce statutorial mental health departments. So what in many states had been a good beginning for integrated health/mental health programs gave way to health and mental health becoming separate territories. As newcomers in the community, the mental health program leaders at both the national and state levels were convinced that the only opportunity for appropriate program growth lay in going the separate way. The changes in a number of states were accompanied by considerably less than a happy response on the part of persons who had worked hard at starting integrated community programs.

The present writer began his public mental health service in a semi-rural county health department in Florida in the early 1950s. The position was funded by a grant from the county school system to provide clinical services primarily for school children, and consultation and education services for parents and teachers. Public health nurses were integral to the service, receiving most of the school referrals, doing the home visiting, and frequently participating in remedial efforts. There was access to the health department clinics, through which preventive and educational activities were conducted with parents and families. Such clnics as the well-baby, the prenatal and maternity, and the tumor clinic are examples of ready collaborative opportunities.

Some Rural Linkages

While most of the analyses of linkage arrangements have so far come from urban settings, there are already a variety of relationships in operation between grantees under the Rural Health Initiative–Health Underserved Rural Areas (RHI-HURA) programs and community mental health centers (Ozarin, Samuels, & Biedenkapp, 1977; Ozarin, Sharfstein, & Albert, 1979; Ozarin, 1982). Sometimes the RHIs contract for mental health services; sometimes RHIs and community mental health centers make referrals to each other, with mental health staff providing consultation to RHI staff. The RHI physicians sometimes provide medical back-up for mental health satellite staff. In a great many instances the health agency may budget for social workers, psychologists, psychiatrists, or mental health coordinators. Such staff members serve as links with the mental health center, evaluate patients referred from primary care practitioners, provide consultation to the practitioners, carry a case load for brief individual or group treatment, do in-service training with health center staff, and make referrals to the mental health center. Staff functions will vary with the characteristics of the site, the respective staff philosophies, the determined needs, and the resources.

In a migrant health center in North Carolina the linkage is spelled out in an agreement with the mental health center (Gates, 1980). The purposes include: improving access to mental health services for migrant and seasonal farm workers through the portal of the health service; providing treatment for mental health problems at the health center in order to provide more comprehensive health services; improving continuity of care, especially of patients discharged from the mental health center; and increasing the competence of the health center clinic staff with in-service training in mental health. The primary staff person is a master's level mental health-psychiatric nurse; a social worker is also employed. The nurse was hired with the concurrence of the mental health center.

The mental health center agreed to provide the comprehensive spectrum of treatment services, including 24-hour emergency services, plus consultation and education for health center staff, weekly case consultation and supervision for the health clinic nurse, and psychiatrist back-up for the health clinic physician. The directors or key liaison staff of each center attend the other center's board meetings, joint board meetings are held quarterly, and the directors of the two centers meet quarterly. The health center provides transportation for patients. Necessary records are transferred with patient referral both ways. The two agencies agree to participate in evaluating the effectiveness of the linkage program. There is an advisory board to the health agency administrator comprised of a representative from each of the three county mental health center staffs and/or boards whose catchment areas overlap with the service area of the migrant health center.

One other example of an integrated service model in a rural area is the development of an interagency human resources center (Kagarise, 1979). Staff from participating agencies serve in a multipurpose center in a key location. This common portal of entry from consumers needing multiple services increases accessibility and acceptability, decreases transportation problems, raises awareness of other services, eases referral, and reduces unit costs of services. One full-time staff person from each agency, with backup as needed, contributes to a program of health, mental health, social services, aging, vocational rehabilitation, and technical instruction. Space that houses a mental health day-care program in the day is available for an evening class or a meeting of senior citizens.

Association with Private Medical Practitioners

In 1973 a group of university psychologists worked out an agreement with a private group of pediatricians to provide preventive education services to parents of preschool children (Schroeder, 1979; Schroeder, Goolsby, & Stangler, 1975; Schroeder, Mesibov, Eastman, & Goolsby, 1981). Services are provided on a regular basis, and students from psychology, nursing, medicine and social work are trained.

The services include parent-education groups, a call-in hour, and a come-in appointment time. Parent education takes place in three consecutive weekly sessions a month for one of six age groups, covering a total range of three months to eight years, and occurring twice each year. Normal child development is reviewed and principles of child management are introduced, followed by group problem-solving.

Call-ins are scheduled twice weekly for parents to call the psychologists in the pediatric office. A parent with a problem judged too complex to be handled by the call-in is invited to come in for an appointment. Parents may make a come-in appointment outside the call-in arrangement. If treatment is indicated, then appropriate referrals are made.

Techniques generally include behavior management, education, and emotional support. These are clearly preventive activities, and some are crisis-intervention services, but they stress the strengths of parents and children rather than their deficiencies or pathologies.

A somewhat similar service was organized in the early 1960s by a pediatrician and a psychologist in Kalamazoo, Michigan. The parents of the pediatrician's patients could come to his office at specified times for consultation or counseling on developmental, management, or family problems (Margolis, 1963).

Although none of these services is strictly rural, any parents can avail themselves of the service, and some of the clientele of these primary care physicians are rural citizens from the surrounding area.

Services in General Hospitals and Other Health Care Settings

In only the past 10 years there has been a tremendous burgeoning in the functions of psychologists in health-care settings (Schofield, 1969; Matarazzo, 1980; Budman & Wertlieb, 1979). In every major medical center and teaching hospital, and in a high percentage of major general hospitals, psychologists provide evaluation and participate in treatment processes for patients who suffer a variety of physical illnesses. This is especially true for the so-called psychosomatic disorders, but it is also true of the developmental diseases that occur from childhood through senescence. It is increasingly accepted that personality and emotional factors, as well as the environmental setting, affect the onset, as well as the treatment of a great many diseases.

The model of service delivery prevalent in medical care settings is most frequently a variant of behavioral training. Persons are taught to manage those situations or those bodily processes that are contributory to the disease in question. An example is to learn how to avoid or manage stressful situations, or to control blood pressure in cardiovascular disorders. Perusal of the August, 1979, special issue of *Professional Psychology* (devoted to psychologists in health-care settings) will confirm the variety of settings and foci of activity for psychologists (Budman & Wertlieb, 1979). Included are family practice, pediatric oncology, geropsychology, cardiology, pain management, multiple sclerosis, rehabilitation, dentistry, and asthma.

While most of these activities of psychologists do not now take place in rural areas, it seems very likely that as more physicians are trained in sensitivity to psychosocial factors and deployed in rural areas, that these behavioral management techniques will find their way there also. Psychologists will be working with rural medical practitioners and in the small hospitals that serve rural areas.

The Model of Alternatives to Clinical Care

A feasibility study conducted by this writer and his colleagues (Hollister, Edgerton, Bentz, Miller, & Aponte, 1973), which focused on the development and implementation of a rural mental health service, attempted to muster all the appropriate community resources to meet the mental health needs of the people from two experimental counties. The baseline epidemiological survey of mental or emotional disorder in that rural population showed that 10% of the people had "psychiatric" disorder, that another 14% were "borderline" or of "probable psychiatric disorder," and that the remaining 76% were "normal" or lacked significant stress reactions or emotional disorder. The program strategies for meeting the needs of these three groups included various clinical and nonclinical interventions. For the most disturbed persons it was necessary to provide either direct clinical care or referral to a clinical resource. The strategy for the more moderate level of disability was to provide case consultation, supervision, and education to enable the indigenous helpers to meet the needs. For the normal group there was a range of educational activities through which emotional growth and self-help could be effected. These and other experiences in rural mental health programming (Bakker & Armstrong, 1976; Gottesfeld, 1977; Huey, 1976; Lamb, 1979; Miller, Mazade, Muller, & Andrulis, 1978; President's Commission, 1978a, 1978b) have led to a model of alternatives to clinical care.

Alternative services have been developed for the chronically mentally ill, alienated and/or drug-abusing youths, the developmentally disabled, the adult substance abuser, the aging, and children. The rural mental health center may have some members of all of these groups in its case load and thus would be justified in developing an organized network of alternative services. Justification also derives from the expense of psychotherapy, hospitalization, detoxification, or counseling usually prescribed for the disorders of schizophrenia, depression, or substance abuse, as well as from the scarcity of qualified professional personnel in rural areas. Further justification resides in the changing character of the disorders being diagnosed in mental health centers. Bass and Ozarin (1977) reported an almost fivefold increase from 1970 to 1975 (4.6% to 21.8%) in "social maladjustments" diagnosed in the federally funded mental health centers. In addition, in 1975 38.6% of admissions were diagnosed as "other" disorders, making a total of 60.4% of admissions not of the traditional diagnoses. Alternatives to clinical care may well be the most appropriate, effective, and economical approach to this majority of admissions.

The Characteristics of Alternative Care Contrasted with the Characteristics of Clinical Care

The modes of alternative care intervention as contrasted with the modes of clinical area, have been described as follows (Hollister, 1980):

1. The care focuses on the interpersonal and social problems or aspects of one's behavior.
2. The focus is on the development and augmentation of existing ego strengths, competencies, interpersonal skills, coping, and problem-solving abilities.
3. The focus is on dealing with environmental, group, or interpersonal stressors(frustrations, conflicts, demands) and one's stress reactions to them.
4. The major modes of intervention are mediated through generalized culturally syntonic group, interpersonal, living, work, recreational and other socialization experiences, and not targeted exclusively on the person.

5. Persons are helped to utilize sources of help, support, and protection other than meeting with a therapist.

Clinical interventions as contrasted with alternative care have been characterized as follows (Hollister, 1980):

1. Care may involve patient bed care.
2. Care may be individual or group outpatient therapy where the focus could be on identification of disease or pathological process, uncovering genetic roots of the behavior, analyzing psychological economics and transferences, setting up behavioral modification regimes, uncovering intraphysic causes, and achieving insights into personality dynamics.
3. The interventions are individualized for the person in an intense interpersonal relationship, a relationship structured so that a staff person assumes a primary therapeutic responsibility and the person seeking help assumes the patient role and focuses on difficulties of personality and behavior.
4. Biological forces are an expectable target of the intervention (i.e., concurrent related physical illness that may require the use of drugs, or a crisis necessitating medical intervention).

From these two characterizations it can be readily seen that alternative care involves a broader spectrum of resources that may be less specialized, less pathology-oriented and perhaps more normalizing, which may be in place in the average rural community through its social, educational, health, religious, recreational, and other service institutions. Clinical services are very specialized, are more pathology-oriented, must be organized particularly, and are more expensive to establish and maintain than are alternative services.

The Categories of Alternative Care

One conception of an alternative-to-clinical-care program categorizes the activities into six nonexclusive groupings (Hollister, 1980). They are as follows, with examples of each.

1. *Group Educational Experiences:*
   (A) Education programs for alcoholics, drunken drivers, and other offenders
   (B) Education groups for parents of emotionally and mentally handicapped
   (C) Daily classes for emotionally disturbed children
   (D) Parent, education, behavioral guidance, and family–life education groups through Agricultural Extension Service

2. *Group Support Networks:*
   (A) Support network for persons discharged from the state mental hospital
   (B) Support groups for senior citizens
   (C) Single parents' groups
   (D) Alcoholics Anonymous
3. *Supportive Home Care:*
   (A) Home-centered work with the parents of mentally and emotionally handicapped
   (B) Homes visits to provide learning experiences for retarded or epileptic children
4. *Non-Clinical Personal Services:*
   (A) Supplemental chore services—cooking, shopping, and cleaning services
   (B) Transportation for handicapped and overwhelmed individuals
5. *Resocialization and Rehabilitation:*
   (A) Therapeutic day activity programs for adults
   (B) Sheltered rehabilitation workshops
   (C) Vocational, basic education, survival, social and work skills workshops
   (D) Developmental group learning experiences for developmentally disabled unsocialized multiply handicapped children
6. *Sheltered Living:*
   (A) Halfway houses for former hospital patients
   (B) Group homes for emotionally disturbed adolescents
   (C) Group homes for adolescent drug abusers

This alternative services model is especially appropriate for rural areas, and psychologists may be associated through evaluating clients, developing programs, administering programs, doing program evaluation, or other appropriate activity. Its efficacy as a model is being tested, in whole or in part in a project which will compare outcomes with those from a parallel clinical services model (Hollister, 1980). Most of the guiding principles, and the program elements which spring from them, have already won considerable acceptance in rural programs.

INDIVIDUAL AND COMMUNITY CHANGE

All of the foregoing models of service delivery represent efforts by mental health, or other community personnel to facilitate change in individuals who live in rural areas. These efforts have been directed at mental or emotional strain or distress brought about through intrapersonal, interpersonal or environmental pressures. Some have been notably successful for some rural people, and some have seemed not to work at all, even when rural citizens could avail themselves of the services. Certainly the ingenuity, creativity, and innovativeness of those professionals, and of the rural community leaders who recruit and support them, will continue to be felt in assuring that needed clinical services will be accessible geographically, psychologically, and culturally to a diverse rural population. This will include appropriate inpatient services as provided now by contract with the general hospitals that serve rural areas, by independent mental health centers, or by regionalized state hospitals.

What seems even more certain is that preventive and educational efforts, as represented particularly in the alternative services model and in the model of the psychologist teaming with the medical practitioner, will become not only more effective, but also more accepted. Already the educational programs aimed at certain stress factors have had some effect, as witnessed by the decline in prevalence of smoking in adults and the decline in consumption of high-cholesterol diets in some segments of the population. Rural people will continue to have access to education programs for their own mental health through the popular media, whether or not exposure is provided through organized agency programs. Hollister (1976) tells us that mental health education exists both for clinical purposes and for personal growth, and that its prevalence is of such an order that it is not possible to conceive of its absence. It is pervasive through the various media.

It does seem clear that there is a greater awareness of the strategies designed to prevent the effects of stressful events through avoiding the stressful force or strengthening the person to withstand it. Organized stress-management learning experiences are available through a host of rural agencies and individual practitioners. There is now a clearer understanding of the role of social supports in the development and amelioration of emotional difficulties, and even in the reduction of mortality rates, (which helps to validate earlier rural values). Also, the building of coping skills is a legitimate preventive activity for any group, and not only a survival strategy for the chronic mental patient who returns to the community from the hospital (Bloom, 1980). The burgeoning self-help movement is very compatible with the rural values of "taking care of our own," and in the future it can be expected to be even more prominent in rural communities.

But what of community change? Are we able to promote the development of a competent rural community, one that is aware of its needs and has an ability to plan to meet those needs? Community psychologists are focusing on community change, and dreaming of interventions that will help change to come about. Rural psychologists must also focus on interventions at the community level.

Their job will be both easier and more difficult than for their urban counterparts. It will be easier because of the ease in feeling "community" in rural and small town and village places. Countless rural communities have organized themselves to provide a needed service, particularly the recent rural and small town and village places. Countless rural communities have organized themselves to provide a needed service, particularly the recent rural health services with their mental health linkages. The job of the rural psychologist will be more difficult for all those reasons stated at the beginning of this chapter, especially if the methods for change are attempted from without, by persons not identified with the dominant rural culture. If the community change that is necessary to permit the development of more viable and adequate models of service delivery is dependent upon changes in the political, economic, and social systems, then changing the community will continue to be a very formidable task indeed.

But rural psychologists who possess the philosophy, the wisdom, the skill, the understanding, and the perserverance described in Chapter 12 should attempt it.

REFERENCES

Bakker, C. B., & Armstrong, H. E. The adult development program: An educational approach to the delivery of mental health services. *Hospital and Community Psychiatry*, 1976, 27, 330–334.

Bass, R., & Ozarin, L. D. *The community mental health center program: What is past is prologue.* Paper presented at the Annual Meeting of the American Psychiatric Association, Toronto, May 1977.

Bloom, B. L. Social and community interventions. *Annual Review of Psychology*, 1980, 31, 111–142.

Borus, J. F., Janowitch, L. A., & Kieffer, F. The coordination of mental health services at the neighborhood level. *American Journal of Psychiatry*, 1975, 32, 1177–1181.

Borus, J. F., Burns, B. J., Jacobson, H. M., Morrill, R. G., & Wilson, B. A. *Neighborhood health centers as providers of coordinated mental health care: A report for the President's Commission on Mental Health.* Washington, D.C.: Institute of Medicine, National Academy of Science, 1978.

Budman, S. H., & Wertlieb, D. (Guest Eds.). Special Issue: Psychologists in health care settings. *Professional Psychology*, 1979, 10(4), 397–644.

Coffey, J. A. *Child and youth program.* Dillsboro, N.C.: Smoky Mountain Area Mental Health, 1979.

Flax, J. W., Wagenfeld, M. O., Ivens, R. E., & Weiss, R. J. *Mental health and rural America: An overview and annotated bibliography* (DHEW Publication No. ADM-78-753). Washington, D.C.: U.S. Government Printing Office, 1979.

Gates, C. Personal communication, March 1980.

Gottesfeld, H. *Alternatives to psychiatric hospitalization.* New York: Gardner Press, 1977.

Griffin, C. R., & Libo, L. M. *Mental health consultants: Agents of community change.* San Francisco: Jossey-Bass, 1968.

Hollister, W. G. The service guide. *American Journal of Public Health,* 1970, *60,* 428–429.

Hollister, W. G. Programming consultation, education, and prevention: Unfulfilled strategies. In B. H. Kaplan, R. N. Wilson, & A. H. Leighton (Eds.), *Further Explorations in social psychiatry.* New York: Basic Books, 1976.

Hollister, W. G. Personal communication, January 1980.

Hollister, W. G., Edgerton, J. W., Bentz, W. K., Miller, F. T., & Aponte, J. F.*Experiences in rural mental health.* Chapel Hill: Division of Community Psychiatry, Department of Psychiatry, School of Medicine, University of North Carolina, 1973.

Huey, K. (Ed.). Special report: Alternatives to mental hospital treatment. *Hospital and Community Psychiatry,* 1976, *27,* 186–192.

Kagarise, M. J. *The interface between primary mental health care and primary medical services.* Paper prepared for the North Carolina Division of Mental Health, Mental Retardation, and Substance Abuse Services, Raleigh, N.C., July 1979.

Kilburn, M. Personal communication, April 15, 1980.

Lamb, H. R. (Ed.). *Alternatives to acute hospitalization.* San Francisco: Jossey-Bass, 1979.

LeCompte, M. *Chesapeake emergency intervention service.* Chesapeake, Va.: Mental Health and Mental Retardation Services Board, 1978.

LeCompte, M. Personal communication, November 1980.

Mannino, F. V., & Shore, M. F. Evaluation of consultation: Problems and prospects. In A. S. Rogawski (Guest Ed.), *Mental health consultations in community settings.* San Francisco: Jossey-Bass, 1979.

Margolis, F. Personal communication, July 1963.

Matarazzo, J. D. Behavioral health and behavioral medicine: Frontiers for a new health psychology. *American Psychologist,* 1980, *35,* 807–817.

McCarty, C. L., & Rosen, B. Mental health and mental health services in rural communities. In L. G. Burchinal (Ed.), *Rural youth in crisis: Facts, myths, and social change* (U.S. DHEW Publication No. JD-3001-1965). Washington, D.C.: U.S. Government Printing Office, 1965.

McGee, R. K. *Crisis intervention in the community.* Baltimore: University Park Press, 1974.

Miller, F. T. Emergency-crisis services in rural mental health centers. In P. A. Keller & J. D. Murray (Eds.), *Handbook of rural community mental health.* New York: Human Sciences Press, 1982.

Miller, F. T., Mazade, N. A., Muller, S., & Andrulis, D. Trends in mental health center programming. *American Journal of Community Psychology,* 1978, *6,* 191–198.

Monroe, B. D. *Therapeutic home program.* Dillsboro, N.C.: Smoky Mountain Area Mental Health, 1979.

Monroe, B. D. *Crisis intervention program.* Dillsboro, N.C.: Smoky Mountain Area Mental Health, 1980.

Morrill, R. G. A new mental health services model for the comprehensive neighborhood health center. *American Journal of Public Health,* 1972, *68,* 1108–1111.

Morrill, R. G. Comprehensive mental health through a neighborhood health center. In E. J. Lieberman (Ed.), *Mental health: The public health challenge.* Washington, D.C.: American Public Health Association, 1975.

Ozarin, L. D. The activities of the National Institute of Mental Health in relation to rural mental health services. In P. A. Keller & J. D. Murray (Eds.), *Handbook of rural community mental health.* New York: Human Sciences Press, 1982.

Ozarin, L. D., Samuels M. E., & Biedenkapp, J. *Mental health services and primary care*. Paper presented at the Annual Meeting of the American Psychiatric Association, Toronto, May 1977.

Ozarin, L. D., Sharfstein, S. S., & Albert, M. *Mainstreaming mental health into health*. Paper presented at the Annual Meeting of the American Psychiatric Association, Chicago, May 1979.

President's Commission on Mental Health. *Report to the President* (Vol. 1). Washington, D.C.: U.S. Government Printing Office, 1978. (a)

President's Commission on Mental Health. *Report to the President* (Vol. 2). Washington, D.C.: U.S. Government Printing Office, 1978. (b)

President's Commission on Mental Health. *Report to the President* (Vol. 3). Washington, D.C.: U.S. Government Printing Office, 1978. (c)

Public Law 88-164. 88th Congress, S. 1576, October 31, 1963. Mental Retardation Facilities and Community Mental Health Centers Construction Act of 1963.

Public Law 93-641. 93rd Congress. Health Planning and Resources Development Act of 1974.

Public Law 94-63. 94th Congress, S. 66, July 29, 1975. Title III Community Mental Health Centers Amendments of 1975.

Public Law 95-626. 95th Congress. Health Services and Centers Amendments of 1978.

Schofield, W. The role of psychology in the delivery of health services. *American Psychologist*, 1969, *24*, 565–584.

Schroeder, C. S. Psychologists in a private pediatric practice. *Journal of Pediatric Psychology*, 1979, *4*, 5–18.

Schroeder, C. S., Goolsby, E., & Stangler, S. Preventive services in private pediatric practice. *Journal of Clinical Child Psychology*, 1975, *Fall*, 32–33.

Schroeder, C. S., Mesibov, G. B., Eastman, J., & Goolsby, E. A prevention service model for children. In A. W. Burgess & B. A. Baldwin (Eds.), *Crisis theory and practice: A clinical handbook*. New York: Prentice-Hall, 1981.

Segal, J. (Ed.). *The mental health of rural America* (DHEW Publication No. HSM 73-9035). Washington, D.C.: U.S. Government Printing Office, 1973.

Stai, R., & Atkinson, T. M., Jr. Decentralized outpatient services in a rural setting. In A. Beigel & A. Levinson (Eds.), *The community mental health center*. New York: Basic Books, 1972.

Tranel, N. Rural program development. In H. Grunebaum, *The practice of community mental health*. Boston: Little, Brown, 1970.

Wagenfeld, M. O. *Cultural barriers to the delivery of mental health services in rural areas: A conceptual overview*. Paper prepared for Conference on Rural Community Mental Health, National Institute of Mental Health, Rockville, Md., May 1977.

14

Child Abuse

A Review with Special Focus on an Ecological Approach in Rural Communities

MINDY S. ROSENBERG AND N. DICKON REPPUCCI

Over the course of centuries, people have justified physical and emotional abuse of children to "expel evil spirits, please certain gods, transmit educational ideas, or maintain discipline" (Radbill, 1968, p. 3). Only in the last 20 years have scholars, professionals, and the public labeled the parental abuse of children as a problem. With the application of roentgenological procedures to detect fractures and the highly publicized article by Kempe and his colleagues (Kempe, Silverman, Steele, Droegemueller, & Silver, 1962), which introduced the term "the battered child syndrome," concern for the welfare of children has steadily increased. By the end of the 1960s, every state in the union had passed laws that required, or at least recommended, that incidents of suspected abuse be reported to specified authorities (Gil, 1970). Studies of abusive families began to fill journals across a variety of disciplines as people sought to understand this sad phenomenon.

Several theoretical models have been advanced to explain child abuse, including the psychiatric, sociological, and ecological models (Garbarino, 1977b; Parke & Collmer, 1975). Each model posits a different set of assumptions about the etiology of child abuse, with the psychiatric and sociological positions at extreme ends of a spectrum. The psychiatric perspective assumes that the parent is the primary cause of the problem.

MINDY S. ROSENBERG AND N. DICKON REPPUCCI • Department of Psychology, University of Virginia, Charlottesville, Virginia 22901.

Research is focused on identifying personality characteristics that distinguish abusive from nonabusive parents. Reconstructing the child-rearing histories of abusive parents is a second emphasis of this approach. Sociologists, on the other hand, explain child abuse by shifting the locus of blame from parent to society. They are primarily concerned with societal attitudes towards violence and social stresses that are thought to contribute to the phenomenon. An ecological model assumes that the causes of child abuse are multiply determined. Abuse is viewed as a pathological adaptation between caregiver, child, and the immediate environment (Garbarino, 1977b). The focus of research is to identify environmental conditions that undermine rather than support healthy parent–child relationships and to examine those transactions between environments, individuals, and groups that yield a context for abuse.

Which of these three models is chosen as an explanatory conceptual framework is of concern for more than academic debate. The basic assumptions that underlie the definition of any "social problem" have inherent within them approaches to its solution (Caplan & Nelson, 1973). Since the basic goal is to alleviate the incidence of child abuse (in fact, to eradicate it completely, if possible), the theoretical model chosen to explain the phenomenon will have implications for the sorts of actions taken by both policymakers and service providers in their attempts to deal with it.

The purpose of this chapter is twofold: (1) to summarize the basic information gleaned from research that has utilized psychiatric, sociological and ecological perspectives; and (2) to examine child abuse in rural communities from an ecological perspective. Two problems immediately arise with these ostensibly straightforward goals. First, although Lewin (1935) was one of the primary theorists to define behavior as the interaction of person and environment, the systematic application of this principle in psychological research is relatively recent (Barker, 1965; Bronfenbrenner, 1977, 1979; Kelly, 1966; Trickett, Kelly, & Todd, 1972). Moreover, ecological research on child abuse *per se* is in its early stages of development (Garbarino, 1976, 1977b, 1979; Garbarino & Crouter, 1978; Sattin & Miller, 1970). Consequently, our knowledge of the ecology of child abuse is limited. Secondly, while sociologists have studied the changes in rural America and contemplated the rural-urban distinction for decades, psychologists have focused primarily on urban populations. Both psychological and sociological research on abusive families in rural settings is simply nonexistent. Whether or not to study a rural ecology of child abuse as a separate entity from an urban ecology of abuse is an unanswered empirical question. Basically, one is attempting to determine whether there are overarching processes related to child abuse, regardless of environment, or whether the processes that contribute to abusive behavior are elicited differentially by rural and urban contexts.

In light of these limitations, the portion of the chapter on processes that contribute to rural abuse will, by necessity, be somewhat speculative. The theoretical basis of these speculations will be extrapolated from research on urban abusive families. The unique contribution of rural environmental conditions that impinge on family life will be considered. Before pursuing the two goals, a brief review of definitions of child abuse is presented.

DEFINITIONS OF CHILD ABUSE

Child abuse is defined in a number of different ways, and each definition has its shortcomings. The simplest conceptualization of abuse is in terms of *outcome;* specifically, any behavior that results in the injury of another individual is considered abuse (Elmer, 1966). According to this definition, a parent or caretaker can be labeled as a child abuser on the basis of objective evidence of the injury. Several difficulties arise with this definition. First, physical signs of abuse usually disappear over time, and without these visible signs there is often no way to prove that abuse occurred. Second, the definition does not acknowledge the possibility of emotional abuse unless it also has physical manifestations. Martin (1976) emphasizes that physical attack is perhaps the most noticeable component of child abuse, but should be considered as only one of a series of indications pointing to unhealthy parent–child interactions. Third, as Parke and Collmer (1975) note, it would be impossible to differentiate accident from intentionally inflicted injuries by employing this definition.

Kempe and Helfer (1972) define the "battered child" by excluding accidental occurances and including the concept of *intentionality.* Thus, "any child who received nonaccidental physical injury (or injuries) as a result of acts (or omissions) on the part of his parents or guardians" (p. xi) will be labeled abused (Kempe & Helfer, 1972). The provision for emotional abuse is again overlooked, and although adding the concept of intentionality does eliminate accidental injury, it now raises the issue of whether one can make an accurate judgment by inferring another's intentions (Gil, 1970).

According to Parke and Collmer (1975), "child abuse is a community-defined phenomenon" and as such, "the definition of child abuse will vary with social class and the cultural background of the defining individual" (pp. 512–513). Variations in caregiver–child interactions will become apparent when rural and urban families of the same social class are contrasted. Any definition of abuse that fails to consider community norms that govern interactions between adults and children will be of limited use in distinguishing abusive from culturally accepted behavior.

Gil's (1970) definition of abuse incorporates the element of intentionality but disregards the cultural and personal relativity of child-rearing procedures. According to Gil (1970),

> physical abuse of children is the intentional, nonaccidental use of physical force, or intentional, nonaccidental acts of omission, on the part of a parent or caretaker interacting with a child in his care, aimed at hurting, injuring, or destroying that child. (p. 6)

Although Gil argues that his definition "reduces ambiguity by including all use of physical force and all acts of omission . . . irrespective of the degree of seriousness of the act, the omission, and/or the outcome" (Gil, 1970, p. 6), in actuality he increases ambiguity by blurring the boundaries between parents who raise their children using physical force and those who abuse their children. These boundaries are further obscured by evidence that suggests a national sanctioning of physical punishment as a child-rearing technique. In his national survey of public attitudes and opinions regarding abuse, Gil (1970) found that 6 out of 10 Americans thought anyone could injure a child in his care at some time. Stark and McEvoy (1970) reported that physical punishment was used by 93% of parents in their survey. Thus, by including all forms of physical force, regardless of the act's seriousness or outcome, Gil's definition covers the vast majority of American parents and therefore does not appropriately delimit the phenomenon.

A more adequate definition of child abuse might include Kempe and Helfer's (1972) concept of intentionality, acknowledgement of emotional abuse as included in the *Code of the Commonwealth of Virginia* (1975), and Parke and Collmer's (1975) contribution of community norms. Thus, a child would be considered abused if she or he receives nonaccidental physical or emotional injury as a result of acts (or omissions) on the part of his or her parents or guardians that violate the community standards concerning the treatment of children. This definition will be employed here.

CHILD ABUSE AS A PSYCHIATRIC PROBLEM

A psychiatric approach to understanding child abuse labels the parent as the principal cause of abuse, and assumes the problem to be a function of personality deficits and child-rearing history. Early efforts to comprehend the dynamics of abuse classified the parents as psychotic, and explained the abusive behavior as an indication of a broader form of mental illness (Parke & Collmer, 1975). However, Spinetta and Rigler's (1972) review of the literature on personality characteristics found few abusive parents to be psychotic. Kempe (1973) estimates that approximately 10% of abusive parents can be diagnosed as mentally ill. Therefore, although some psychotic individuals are child abusers, the vast majority are not.

Current research is concerned with uncovering personality characteristics that distinguish child abusers from the general population. Studies in this area have been largely unsuccessful in finding a consistent pattern of traits to describe abusive parents. Gelles (1973) found that at least two or more authors agreed on only 4 out of 19 personality traits suggested in the literature. Spinetta and Rigler (1972) concluded from their review that

> while the authors generally agree that there is a defect in the abusive parent's personality that allows aggressive impulses to be expressed too freely, . . . disagreement comes in describing the source of the aggressive impulses. (p. 299)

Not only is there disagreement as to which traits adequately describe abusive parents, but even when there is some consensus, the traits do not sufficiently capture the differences between abusers and nonabusers. As Steele and Pollock (1968) remark:

> Child abusers have been described as immature, impulse-ridden, dependent, egocentric, demanding, and narcissistic. Such adjectives are essentially appropriate to those who abuse children, yet these qualities are so prevalent among people in general that they add little to specific understanding. (p. 109)

Several methodological problems with the research tend to obscure what little knowledge there is. The primary criticism voiced by many authors (e.g., Gelles, 1974; Jayaratne, 1977; Parke & Collmer, 1975) is the lack of an appropriate comparison group of nonabusers that would allow researchers to determine whether these personality characteristics are unique to abusive parents or whether they are found in other clinical populations or in normal populations from the same culture. An exception to this criticism is a controlled study conducted by Melnick and Hurley (1969) that looked at 20 lower-class, black, abusive and nonabusive mothers on 18 personality variables. Abusive mothers showed greater difficulty in parenting, especially concerning their ability to empathize and provide nurturance to their children. The small, select sample greatly limits the generalizability of the results.

Since the research on psychiatric explanations of abuse has been predominantly ex post facto, serious problems arise with regard to this

approach. As Parke and Collmer (1975) observe, "descriptive characterization should be the starting point in attempting to understand the
behavior and is not, in any sense, an explanation" (p. 520). Thus, we can
learn relatively little about the phenomenon of child abuse from describing the parents' deficits in personality, after they have committed one or
more acts of abuse and are already labeled as child abusers.

In addition to the research on personality characteristics, a psychiatric approach examines the abusive parent's child-rearing history to
ascertain whether "abusive" child-rearing patterns are passed through
generations. This theme has received mixed reactions in the literature.
While several investigators express the view that abusive parents were
very frequently abused and neglected as children (Baken, 1971; Kempe
et al., 1962; Spinetta & Rigler, 1972), there is actually little empirical
evidence to support this statement (NIMH, 1978). Gil's (1970) national
survey found 14% of mothers and 7% of fathers in the abusive sample
report having been abused as children. Jayaratne (1977) believes that the
generational hypothesis of abuse is one of the most commonly held
misconceptions in the literature.

Steele and Pollock (1968) argue that abusive parents are exposed to
a particular pattern of child-rearing that becomes an important determinant of future abuse, regardless of whether they were physically abused
as children. They believe that abusive parents are deprived of "basic
mothering," defined as "a lack of the deep sense of being cared for and
cared about from the beginning of one's life" (Steele & Pollock, 1968, p.
112), and differing from the mechanical aspects of mothering such as
feeding and cleaning.

Abusive parents also report having experienced continual demands
from their parents in the form of "expectations of good, submissive
behavior, prompt obedience, never to make mistakes, to be sympathetic
and comforting of parental distress, and to show approval and help
from parental actions" (Steele & Pollock, 1968, p. 111); demands that
were unrealistic to meet. As a result, abusive parents feel helpless, inferior, unlovable, and unable to find empathy from others (Steele, 1970).
Because of their own unmet dependencey needs (unable to be satisfied
due to a lack of basic mothering), the parent turns to the infant or small
child for nurturance and protection. Morris and Gould (1963) refer to
this process as "role reversal." When this occurs, the parent subsequently places the same high expectations and demands for performance on the child, coupled with a disregard for the child's own needs;
physical punishment is applied when these expectations are not met.

The basis for Steele and Pollock's psychiatric theory is derived from
clinical interviews where abusive parents provide retrospective accounts
of their childhood, some interviews with the abusive parent's own parents, and some ovservation of parent–child interaction. Again, the chief

objection to this methodology is that without appropriate comparison groups, one does not know whether these child-rearing patterns are unique to abusive parents, and/or characteristic of particular cultures. Because of this obstacle, it is difficult to draw conclusions about the generational hypothesis of child abuse.

In summary, the psychiatric approach to child abuse offers descriptive information but little empirical support for the assumption that the parent's intrapsychic deficits are the sole determinants of abusive behaviors. Psychiatric data would be more valuable if appropriate comparison groups were utilized, but even then, the problem of abuse is too complex to be explained comprehensively by one approach. The psychiatric approach may provide some indication of an individual's personal coping resources (i.e., the ability to trust, cope with change, or feel empathy), which partially derives from childhood experiences with significant adults. However, the traditional psychiatric approach does not acknowledge the dynamic interplay between individual and environmental factors. Individuals help to shape and modify the contexts in which they live, while the immediate and larger contexts, in turn, alter individual behavior. Thus, to know that abusive parents may be impulsive and aggressive is only part of the story. These qualities may be enhanced or mitigated by particular life circumstances. Lack of money, limited or no access to child-care facilities, and frequent mobility that results in high turnover of friends and neighbors are stressful situational factors that may elicit "impulsive" and "aggressive" behavior, particularly if individuals are accustomed to responding in such a manner when under stress. The propensity to act "impulsively" and "aggressively" may also be minimized when sufficient environmental supports are present, such as close friends or family members who are willing to share child-care responsibility and help relieve the financial strain. Thus, the usefulness of a purely psychiatric approach to explain abuse is questionable, at best.

CHILD ABUSE AS A SOCIOLOGICAL PROBLEM

The sociological perspective of child abuse focuses on the social values, attitudes, and economic conditions in society as a way to understand abuse. According to this viewpoint, sociocultural variables are assumed to maintain conditions under which abuse is likely to occur. Specifically, the literature is concerned with attitudes that support societal, institutional, and familial maltreatment of children, demographic factors, the effects of stress, and the relationship of social isolation to abuse.

An obstacle to thinking along sociological lines is suggested by

Ryan (1971) in his book, *Blaming the Victim*. Ryan discusses the tendency in our society to interpret social problems such as crime, poverty, or child abuse in terms of individual factors, rather than studying those aspects of society that may have given rise to and/or continue to support the social problems. Positing individual solutions to social problems diverts attention from other likely sources and absolves society from responsibility to change (Ryan, 1971). Sociologists argue that child abuse is a result of social, not psychological, forces and that to study the psychology of abuse is what Watzlawick, Weakland, and Fisch (1974) would refer to as an "error of logical typing."

Societal, Institutional, and Familial Abuse

Gil (1974) argues that the manifestation of child abuse occurs on three levels: societal, institutional, and familial. Societal abuse results from

> social policies which sanction, or cause, severe deficits between the actual circumstances of children and conditions needed for their optimal development. As direct or indirect consequences of such social policies, millions of children live in poverty and are inadequately nourished, clothed, housed, and educated; their health is not assured because of substandard medical care; their neighborhoods decay; meaningful occupational opportunities are not available to them, and alienation is widespread among them. (pp. 115–116)

In supporting this position, Garbarino (1977b) acknowledges that child abuse can only be understood as "part and parcel of the overall society's commitment to the welfare of children and families" (p. 722).

In addition to having serious ramifications by itself, the societal manifestations of abuse also affect the institutional and familial levels. The definition of abusive acts or conditions on the institutional level parallels that of societal abuse, but the settings in which it occurs are different: "day-care centers, schools, courts, child-care agencies, welfare departments, correctional and other residential child-care settings" (Gil, 1974, p. 114).

Familial abuse is the most visible form of child maltreatment and receives the majority of attention from researchers, professionals, and the public. From Gil's (1970) perspective, abuse in the home is a manifestation of the culturally sanctioned use of physical punishment as a child-rearing technique.

In a survey of maternal disciplinary methods given to 100 low- and low–middle-income mothers, one quarter of these mothers reported that they were spanking their infants within the first six months, and almost half were spanking their infants by the end of the first year

(Korsch, Christian, Gozzi, & Carlson, 1965). In fact, spanking ranked first as the preferred method of punishment. However, many of these mothers recognized that spanking did not always work. Although the research did not specify further, perhaps one reason why these mothers continued spanking is they might not have consistently tried other options to "make babies mind."

Gelles (1977) surveyed 2,143 intact families in an attempt to further define the type of physical force children of varying ages received from their parents. A national probability sample was used, stratified by geographic region, type of community, and other demographic characteristics such as socioeconomic status, occupation, and age. Although the survey excluded parents with children under three years of age, the results indicate that younger children are more likely to be subjected to physical force. During the year previous to the survey, 83% of 3- and 4-year-olds had some form of force used on them, 82% of children aged 5 through 9, 66% of children 10 to 15, and 34% of children 15 to 17. As might be expected, milder forms of force (i.e., slaps, spankings, pushes, and shoves) are the more frequently used disciplinary techniques, but at least 8% of the sample reported that at some point in raising their child, they had either kicked, bit, or hit the child with a fist, and nearly 3 in 100 parents either used or threatened to use a gun or knife on their child.

The studies of physical punishment of children tend to support Gil's (1970) stance that physical force as a child-rearing technique is a sanctioned phenomenon in our society. However, with the exception of Gelles's (1977) study, investigators have grouped together all types of physical force used against children in one category, without considering the existence of a continuum between mild punishment and abuse. There is little information about which behaviors precipitate physical punishment, so one does not know whether there is a pattern of behaviors (within age groups and cultures) that is considered dangerous or irritating for parents and is most often solved by physical force.

Demographic Variables

Child abuse is not restricted to one particular socioeconomic class; it is reported to occur in lower-, middle-, and upper-class families (Elmer, 1967; Gil, 1974; Helfer & Kempe, 1968; Steele & Pollock, 1968; Terr, 1970). Although middle- and upper-class abusers are said to exist, it is the lower socioeconomic levels that are supposedly "overrepresented" among reported cases (Gil, 1970; NIMH, 1978). Several reasons are offered for this overrepresentation. Low-income groups are more likely to use emergency rooms, public agencies, and clinics in the event of abuse, while middle- and upper-income families are abe to afford private physicians, who may not report the abuse to protect the family's reputation. Middle- and upper-income families are more likely to have detached homes, thus decreasing the possibility for detection by neighbors and relatives. Middle- and upper-income families may be more deceptive and better able to cover up their behavior (cf. Parke & Collmer, 1975).

Pelton (1978) challenges the belief that child abuse would be more or less proportionately distributed throughout all socioeconomic classes if all abuse cases in middle- and upper-class families were reported. He does not deny that lower-class families are more often subjected to "public scrutiny," but argues that there is no evidence to suggest that if middle- and upper-class families were also scrutinized, a proportionate number of abuse cases would emerge. Three arguments are cited in support of his position: (1) although a substantial increase in numbers of abuse cases have resulted from the implementation of new reporting laws, the socioeconomic pattern of reported cases has not changed significantly; (2) child abuse and neglect appear to be related to the degree of poverty within the lower class such that maltreating families are typically those living in extreme poverty; and (3) the most severe injuries seem to occur within families experiencing extreme poverty. Clearly, the relationship between socioeconomic class and abuse remains unsolved and warrants further investigation.

Because low-income groups may be overrepresented, there are a number of confounding variables related to low income which may also be overrepresented; examples are low education (Gil, 1970; NIMH, 1978), low level of occupation (NIMH, 1978), large family size (Elmer, 1967; Gil, 1970; Light, 1973), and unemployment.

Unemployment is noted by a number of investiagors as a probable contributer to abuse. Gil (1970) reported that nearly 12% of the fathers in his sample were unemployed at the time of the abusive incident. Unemployment rates were higher for nonwhite, abusive fathers. With regard to working mothers, only 30.1% were employed during the year. Light (1973) indicates that

> the variable that shows up most frequently as somehow related to child abuse is father's unemployment. This finding confirms a widely held theory that family stress, both emotional and financial, related to unemployment, ties in to incidence of abuse. (p. 588)

Job satisfaction is another work-related variable that appears to contribute to abusive behavior. The extent of a father's job satisfaction was found to be related to the degree of physical punishment imposed on his children. Fathers who were less satisfied with their jobs, across social class, tended to use harsh physical punishment (McKinley, 1964).

In their work on the relationship between life-stress events and abuse, Justice and Duncan (1977) found that work-related pressures are important contributors to abuse. Four types of situations were identified:

> unemployed fathers caring for children at home; working mothers with job and domestic obligation overloads; husbands, especially professionals working so long and hard that they neglect their wives; and traumatic experiences on the job resulting in undischarged tension. (p. 54)

Unemployment, *per se*, is probably not the variable that directly elicits abusive behavior. It appears to be the concommitant stresses, or functions of unemployment, which lead to abusive acts. Several reasons are proposed in the literature: (1) unemployment may be associated with financial strain; (2) an unemployed father is home for longer periods of time, thereby increasing the possibility for conflict between father and child; and (3) if the father views his loss of job as a decrease in status, then one way of reestablishing status is to assume greater authority in the family (Parke & Collmer, 1975).

Further study of demographic variables reveals that factors such as ethnic status, single-parent status, age at time of marriage, and age at time of first birth are also confounded with low income. As a result, no firm conclusions can be drawn regarding the extent to which any of these variables contribute to abuse. The literature is methodologically misleading when abusive families are compared to national averages rather than to appropriate comparison groups that are similar in demographic composition.

Both demographic and personality characteristics serve a similar function: description. Both attempt to explain the phenomenon of abuse from an ex post facto position and thus fail to recognize the previous processes and interactions that contributed to the final result (e.g., an abusive family with six children close in age, with a mother described as low in aggression control and an unemployed father).

Effects of Stress

One underlying assumption of a sociological approach to child abuse is that stress and frustration elicit abusive behavior (Parke & Collmer, 1975). Unemployment and insufficient income may be more predominant in the lower class, but many stresses said to contribute to abuse cut across socioeconomic classes, such as job-related tensions (Justice & Duncan, 1977), degree of job satisfaction (Parke & Collmer, 1975), single-parent families (Gil, 1970), and marital conflict (National Center on Child Abuse and Neglect, 1977).

Justice and Duncan (1977) compared abusive and nonabusive parents on the Social Readjustment Rating Scale, an instrument that measures life stress. Scores over 150 are indicative of "life stress" and are said to predict the onset of illness (Holmes & Rhae, 1967). The mean stress score of abusive parents was 234, compared to 124 for nonabusive parents. Thus, in this sample, abusive parents had experienced an excess of change and stress in their lives during the year previous to the abusive incident. However, there is no indication whether the families had one incident and were identified by it, or whether the abuse had been occurring unnoticed for some time. Moreover, information on socioeconomic status (SES) and whether the groups were matched for SES is not provided.

Newberger, Reed, Daniel, Hyde, and Kotelchuck (1977) interviewed 560 families matched for age, SES, and ethnic group whose children were diagnosed as abused, neglected, failure-to-thrive, accident, and poisoning cases, to look at the association of family stress and the occurrence of these pediatric social illnesses. Children with acute medical problems were used as a comparsion group. Three *a priori* stress scales were developed: stress in the mother's childhood, stress in the current household, and lack of social support. All pediatric social illnesses were positively correlated with stress. Abusive families were distinguished from the other diagnoses by their high scores on all three stress scales, particularly the category of current household stress, which was based on questions involving mobility and stability of household composition.

Although stress appears to be an extremely important variable, the presence of stress alone does not seem to elicit abusive behavior. As Elmer (1967) indicates, stressful conditions may precipitate abuse, but only when they occur in families that already have a number of other problems. Stress appears to be a contributing, rather than a sufficient condition for abuse. However, a large amount of stress in conjunction with isolation from supports could be a strong enough combination to place a family at a high-risk level for abuse.

Relationship between Social Isolation and Abuse

Abusive families are reported to be socially isolated from community supports and natural support systems such as extended family and friends, (Garbarino, 1976, 1977a, 1977b). According to Caplan (1974) a support system can

> provide individuals with opportunities for feedback about themselves and for validation for their expectations about others, which may offset deficiencies in these communications within the larger community context. . . . People have a variety of specific needs that demand satisfaction through endur-

> ing interpersonal relationships, such as for love and affection, for intimacy that provides the freedom to express feelings easily and unselfconsciously, for validation of personal identity and worth, for satisfaction of nurturance and dependence, for help with tasks, and for support in handling and controlling impulses. (pp. 4–5)

It seems as though the use of support systems would be particularly helpful for abusive families. Garbarino (1977b) states that it is the "unmanageability of the stress which is the most important factor" (in the relationship between stress and abuse) and that "unmanageability is a product of a mismatch between the level of stress and the availability and potency of support systems" (p. 727).

A number of studies show that abusive families fail to use available supports. Young (1964) found that 95% of the severely abusive families in her sample and 83% of the moderately abusive families had limited or no continuing relationships outside the family. Not only did these parents socially isolate themselves, but they were more likely to prevent their children from developing friendships or participating in extracurricular activities. Elmer (1967) found a difference between abusive and nonabusive parents on her anomie scale, which measured distrust, retreat, and isolation from society. Lenoski (1974) noted that of the abusive parents who have telephones, 89% have unlisted numbers, compared with 12% of nonabusive parents. In addition, 81% of the abusive parents preferred to resolve crises alone while 43% of the nonabusive parents chose to handle crises in that manner. The abusive mothers in Melnick and Hurley's (1969) sample reported feelings of being unable to cope with life responsibilities in conjunction with a perceived lack of supports.

With the exception of a few studies (cf. Parke & Collmer, 1975), investigators have only explored the hypothesis of self-imposed isolation. Few attempts are made to examine the reasons why abusive families appear to remain isolated and whether community resources are accessible and receptive to the needs of these families. Although there is much evidence to suggest that social isolation is characteristic of abusive families, it is not clear whether they initiate the isolation themselves to escape detection, lack the social skills needed to maintain social relationships, or are avoided by others because of the way they treat their children (Parke & Collmer, 1975). No information has been gathered regarding the history of isolation (e.g., whether these adults were always socially isolated). In addition, the concept of "isolation" needs to be sufficiently defined to specify whether it refers to the use of supports, a perception of availability of supports, the lack of feedback to parents from outside their neighborhood or culture, an unlisted phone number, parents who do not read newspapers, etc.

In summary, the sociological perspective identifies societal attitudes, values, and life circumstances that may contribute to and/or maintain abusive behavior. However, the fact remains that not all people who are subject to excessive stress and other environmental conditions that undermine healthy family relationships become abusive towards their children. A sociological analysis of abuse, similar to the psychiatric approach, does not by itself sufficiently explain the phenomenon.

CHILD ABUSE AS AN ECOLOGICAL PROBLEM

Child abuse appears to be multiply determined. The ecological perspective acknowledges that behavior is a function of both person and environment. It does not disregard the contributions of individual, environment, or societal analyses, nor does it consider the data from these sources to be conflictual. An ecological approach to behavior focuses on the mutual adaptations of child and family in the context of their neighborhood, community, and culture. Emphasis is placed on the dynamic nature of the individual–environment interaction, as opposed to studying one or the other variable in isolation. Child abuse is conceived as a maladaptive response between family and child to an environment that does not provide the resources and supports necessary to offset the stress and abusive behavior. According to Garbarino (1979), the basic premise of an ecological analysis is to "identify situations in which the conditions of life conspire to compound rather than counteract the deficiencies and vulnerabilities of parents" (pp. 5–6).

Bronfenbrenner (1977, 1979), the foremost advocate of the ecological approach, emphasizes the contexts in which human development takes place. He divides the ecological environment into four interdependent systems, the micro-, meso-, exo-, and macrosystems, and suggests that interactions within and between these systems shape behavior. The *microsystem* is the immediate setting that contains the developing child (e.g., family, school, day-care center). The *mesosystem* encompasses the interrelations between two or more settings that contain the child (e.g., the connections among family, school, and peer group). "An exosystem refers to one or more settings that do not involve the developing person as an active participant, but in which events occur that affect, or are affected by what happens in the setting containing the developing person" (Bronfenbrenner, 1979, p. 25). *Exosystem* structures include "the world of work, the neighborhood ... the distribution of goods and services, communication and transportation facilities, and informal social networks" (Bronfenbrenner, 1977, p. 515). The *macrosystem* contains the cultural and subcultural values that influence the micro-, meso-, and exosystems.

Belsky (1980) integrates Bronfenbrenner's (1977, 1979) model of human development with the concepts of ontogenic development, originally proposed by Tinbergen (1951) and recently modified by Burgess (1978), to produce an ecological conceptualization of child maltreatment. He defines four levels of analysis, "which subsume almost all of the factors and explanations that have been posited in efforts to account for the etiology of child abuse and neglect" (Belsky, 1980, p. 321). These levels include: (1) ontogenic development, which appears to correspond to the psychiatric approach as it "represents what individual parents who mistreat their offspring bring with them to the family setting and to the parenting role" (Belsky, 1980, p. 321), and three of Bronfenbrenner's systems, (2) the microsystem, (3) exosystem, and (4) macrosystem.

In the remainder of this chapter, the ecological conditions that may foster child abuse in rural communities are discussed. Attention is focused on rural conditions that enhance and undermine healthy parent–child relationships, specifically, such exosystem factors as informal support networks, the effects of work and other stressors, physical and social isolation, the arrangement of neighborhoods, and the distribution of resources. The emphasis on rural exosystem factors was chosen for several reasons. First, much (if not all) of the empirical, ecological research conducted with abusive families has utilized exosystem factors; this research has begun to isolate several important factors, out of the myriad of possible relationships, that contribute to abusive behavior. Second, based on the largely descriptive psychological literature on rural family life, the exosystem factors mentioned above appear to be the most likely environmental factors that would affect individual behavior, and thus may discriminate processes that contribute to rural and urban abuse.

The Rural Context

Historically, "the term 'rural' referred to areas of low population density, small absolute size, and relative isolation, where the major economic base was agricultural production and where the way of life of the people was reasonably homogeneous and differentiated from that of other sectors of society, most notably the 'city'" (Bealer, Wittits, & Kuvlesky, 1965, p. 255). No longer is this description accurate. Rural-urban differences are gradually diminishing as a result of "mass cultural diffusion" (VanEs & Brown, 1974), which refers to improvements in mass communication (e.g., television, radio, magazines, newspapers); transportation (e.g., paved roads and highways, cars); education (e.g., change from a one-room school to a consolidated school, statewide curriculum standardization); and employment opportunities (e.g., access to employment in urban centers, provision of options other than farming) (Photiadis, 1970; VanEs & Brown, 1974). This trend toward the increasing urbanization of rural life has, to some extent, penetrated the isolation that was previously a large part of rural existence.

However, the physical distribution of people in space is still a salient and contrasting feature of a rural versus urban ecology. Each geographic region is characterized by a distinct arrangement of its inhabitants, which encourages different potentials for social interaction, social and physical isolation, specific family relationships, and types of social problems (Heller & Quesada, 1977; Huessy, 1972).

Huessy (1972) gives several examples of the range in distribution of people in rural areas and the types of social problems encountered. For instance, farm communities in the rural Midwest and New England are typically three miles apart and individual farms are usually within walking distance of each other. Social interaction may be encouraged by this arrangement. Poverty is dispersed widely in these regions, so that it is not as noticeable as, for example, in the rural South, where dense "pockets of poverty" exist. Problems in the Rocky Mountain area are primarily those of extreme social isolation that stem from the physical isolation of villages, which may be as far as 30 to 40 miles apart. A very different ecology is found in the Indian reservations of Arizona and New Mexico, where the problems of poverty, and social and physical isolation are compounded by conflicts in culture (Huessy, 1972). Because rural communities differ markedly in their ecologies, it is important to specify which rural area is being studied. One cannot make blanket statements about "rural life" and think that they will apply equally to each geographic region. Likewise, the experience of urban living would be expected to differ in various cities across the country and between neighborhoods within a single city.

For purposes of this chapter, the rural South and Appalachia will serve as guides for discussion. Ecologically, these regions present an interesting mixture of conditions that both fosters effective parenting (e.g., close family ties, shared responsibility for child care among extended family members) and undermines the quality of family life (e.g., extreme poverty, limited education and resources). The South is reported to have the greatest proportion of the nation's low-income and subsistence farmers (Taylor, 1968), and within this region, Appalachia is considered to be the most concentrated "pocket of poverty" (Photiadis, 1970). Since the most severe abuse is said to occur in families experiencing extreme poverty (cf. Pelton, 1978), the focus on Appalachia and the rural South seems appropriate.

Linkages between Abusive Families and the Community

An ecological perspective is concerned with relationships between people within a setting and the nature of linkages between settings (Bronfenbrenner, 1979). Thus, behavior is determined by events that occur in a person's immediate environment and circumstances that are present in settings which do not necessarily contain the individual but influence his or her immediate situation. With regard to parenting, Bronfenbrenner (1979) suggests that

> whether parents can perform effectively in their child-rearing roles within the family depends on role demands, stresses, and supports emanating from other settings . . . parents' evaluations of their own capacity to function, as well as their view of the child, are related to such external factors as flexibility of job schedules, adequacy of child care arrangements, the presence of friends and neighbors who can help out in large and small emergencies, the quality of health and social services, and neighborhood safety. The availability of supportive settings is, in turn, a function of their existence and frequency in a given culture or subculture. (p. 7)

As previously stated in the review of sociological literature, stress has emerged consistently as a factor related to abuse (Justice & Duncan, 1977; National Center for the Prevention and Treatment of Child Abuse and Neglect, 1977; Newberger *et al.*, 1977; Parke & Collmer, 1975; Rosenberg & Reppucci, 1980). In keeping with a multiply determined model of behavior, the occurrence of stress alone does not automatically lead to abuse. The presence or absence of both personal and environmental resources seems to mediate stressful life conditions, in that a highly supportive environment may be able to offset the personal vulnerabilities of parents and the deleterious effects of stress.

Research with abusive families has revealed an association between stress, isolation from supports, and abuse. Garbarino (1976) investigated the relationship between these three factors in 58 rural and urban New York State counties. Rates of reported child abuse and maltreatment were analyzed in relation to 12 indices of socioeconomic and demographic characteristics. The extent to which mothers experienced socioeconomic stress without the buffering effects of supports accounted for 36% of the variance in rates of child abuse, while general economic conditions alone accounted for 16% of the variance. Garbarino describes the scenario of child abuse and maltreatment as "economically depressed mothers, often alone in the role of parent, attempting to cope in isolation without adequate facilities and resources for their children" (p. 183).

Garbarino's (1976) results were replicated and refined by Garbarino and Crouter (1978). Child maltreatment rates in 20 subareas and 93 census tracts in urban, industrial Douglas County, Nebraska, were related to economic, socioeconomic, and demographic variables (specifically, low income, geographical mobility, and stress due to work and the pressures of being a single parent).

Giovannoni and Billingsley (1970) examined the relationship between environmental factors and child neglect in three ethnic groups residing in San Francisco. Documented cases of neglect were obtained from protective service caseloads. Public health nurses divided the sample that they submitted for the research into three categories of parenting—adequate, potentially neglectful, and neglectful mothers—on the basis of ratings given to families on six problem areas of child rearing. Black, Caucasian, and Spanish-speaking families constituted the three ethnic groups, which yielded a total of 9 cells. Of the black mothers, 24 were rated adequate, 20 potentially neglectful, and 22 neglectful; of the Caucasians, 21 were adequate, 15 potentially neglectful, and 18 neglectful; and of the Spanish-speaking mothers, 24 were adequate, 20 potentially neglectful, and 18 neglectful. Variables that were associated with neglect were number of children, single-parent status, extreme poverty, inadequate housing and sleeping arrangements, and absence of a wristwatch and telephone. Assessments of informal and formal support systems revealed that "neglectful" mothers had little or no ongoing relationships with their kin, in contrast to a positive kin attachment with "adequate" mothers. Church attendance was the only formal community activity that was significantly related to maternal adequacy. Adequate mothers were more often involved with the church than less adequate and neglectful mothers. The authors' conclusion is reminiscent of the findings of Garbarino and his colleague (Garbarino, 1976; Garbarino & Crouter, 1978): "The low-income neglectful parent is under greater environmental and situational stress and has fewer resources and supports in coping with these stresses than does the adequate mother" (Giovannoni & Billingsley, 1970, p. 203). Thus, "among low-income people, 'neglect' would seem to be a social problem that is as much a manifestation of social and community conditions as it is of any individual parent's pathology" (Giovannoni & Billingsley, 1970, p. 204).

Stress in the Rural Environment

Rural living has been romanticized as a peaceful, harmonious existence with nature, where stresses that commonly lead to psychological disorders and social problems are nonexistent (Huessy, 1972). The city life, by contrast, is considered to be inherently stressful. These are misperceptions. Webb and Collette (1977) studied rural-urban differences in the use of stress-alleviative drugs and found that the consumption of tranquilizers, antacids, and hypnotics increased as size of community decreased. These authors cited the lack of stimulation, the routinization of an isolated lifestyle, the limited access to resources where one can escape and be distracted for short periods of time, and the social pressures of small-town living as possible explanations for the increased drug usage. Another uninvestigated explanation was the possibility that rural physicians rely on drug therapy because of the scarcity of therapists and general mental health services. An alternative interpretation is that the quantity of stress is not actually greater in rural as compared with urban settings, but the symptom expression varies between these settings.

Work-related stresses may vary as a function of occupation. In the rural South, the major occupations open to low-income people include mining, farming, factory work, carpentry and other crafts, secretarial work, and sales. Of these, mining probably exerts the most stress on family life. Erikson (1976) describes mining in Appalachia as "more dangerous than service in wartime" (p. 113), and suggests that "the coal camps placed an enormous burden on the men and women who went into them" (p. 114). Psychosomatic disorders are the behavioral manifestations of the stress and anxiety that accompanies this line of work. Myers, Lindenthal, and Pepper (1974) indicate that the high rate of psychological distress frequently reported to be experienced by the lower class may be a function of stressful life events.

Job dissatisfaction, which has been related to abuse (McKinley, 1964) may be an important factor in rural areas, in light of the limited range of job options available for the rural poor who cannot travel to urban centers for employment. In addition to the dissatisfaction they might feel with their present work situation, the rural poor may have less opportunity to get together socially with their co-workers because of the distance and time involved in travel, the scarcity of social gathering places, and the likelihood that rural people may work in relative isolation (e.g., farming). Thus if the work environment is perceived as unfulfilling, not only does it produce a significant amount of stress, but also it fails to provide the social avenues for the constructive release of stress.

There is some evidence to suggest that stressful life events are perceived differently by rural and urban people. Miller, Bentz, Aponte, and Brogan (1974) presented the Social Readjustment Rating Scale (SRRS) to an urban, Northeastern population and a rural, Southeastern population, using a random area sampling technique that represented the range of race and socioeconomic status that was characteristic of the particular area. The SRRS is composed of 43 life-crisis events, both positive (e.g., getting married) and negative (e.g., being fired from a job), which are likely to be experienced by adults sometime in their lives and are assumed to require a certain amount of readjustment (Holmes & Rhae, 1967). People were asked to rank order the events from those that would cause the most to those that would cause the least stress and readjustment. Four events received the most disparate ratings from the two populations; "getting married" and "change in number of arguments with spouse" were more stressful for urbanites, while "taking out a mortgage greater than $10,000" and "minor law violations" were more stressful for the rural population. Thus, whereas rural and urban populations may be subjected to many of the same stresses, the perceived amount of readjustment required for certain life crises was different. One problem with this study was that the investigators may have confounded the rural-urban differences with regional differences. These results should be taken into account if further research is conducted with the SRRS on rural populations, since the typical method is to assign standardized "life crisis units" for each event experienced. Other research utilizing this method with more urban populations has found an association between degree of life stress and onset of physical illness (Holmes & Rhae, 1967) and between life stress and abuse (Justice & Duncan, 1977; Rosenberg & Reppucci, 1980).

Thus stress is not foreign to a rural lifestyle. The types of stress experienced by rural people may originate from different sources than the stresses of urban life, and may be perceived as requiring different degrees of adjustment in comparison to the perceptions of urbanities. Life stress is implicated as a critical variable for understanding abusive behavior in urban families (Elmer, 1979; Garbarino, 1976; 1977b, Garbarino & Crouter, 1978; Justice & Duncan, 1977; Newberger et al., 1977; Rosenberg & Reppucci, 1980), and it should also be considered with regard to rural families. However, according to Garbarino (1977b), it is the unmanageability of stress that is the most important factor in the relationship between stress and abuse. "Unmanageability is a product of a mismatch between the level of stress and the availability and potency of support systems" (Garbarino, 1977b, p. 727).

The Role of Family Support in the Rural South

Reliance on the nuclear family and extended kin was, and continues to be, an essential component of the rural lifestyle (Brown & Schwarzeller, 1970; Erikson, 1976; Landis, 1940; Taylor, 1968). Particularly in the rural South, the strength of family ties evolved from a process of mutual adaptation between individual and environment. The mountainous geography in much of the region encouraged the clustering of families in hollows, which are "mountain pockets usually carved by streams winding down from mountain tops" to the valleys below

(Heller & Quesada, 1977, p. 226). Families and extended kin became the main sources of economic, social, and emotional sustenance. Individual behavior was governed by the family group, which was the most effective mechanism of social control (Brown & Schwarzweller, 1970). Erikson (1976) describes the Appalachian family of yesterday in these terms:

> For all practical purposes, the family was a community unto itself: it was an industry, a school, a church, a hospital. It was the only real shelter a person had. The bonds that were fashioned in this enclave were very close, and legends coming out of the mountains emphasizing the fierce loyalty of people not only to their immediate family but to the wider tracings of kin are not at all exaggerated. The clanlike society of the mountains may owe something to the Scottish highlands and to the tribal organization of ancient Britian, but it was perfectly adapted to local conditions. In a country with no public institutions, no townships, no systems of social control, few stable congregations, and no other associations of any kind, membership in a family unit was the only source of identification and support one had. (pp. 58–59)

Family support continues to be a prominent factor in modern rural life. The physical arrangement of families, which is partially a function of regional geography, seems to influence the type of family support structure. Heller and Quesada (1977) contrasted two disparate rural populations—families residing in the Virginia Blue Ridge Mountain hollows and on ranches in Elko County, Nevada—to assess the impact of diverse "socioecological" conditions on family organization. They found two distinct types of family associations. "Extended-kin-oriented familism" was prevalent in Virginia, where the extended kin relationships were utilized heavily for support; in fact, they took priority over the nuclear family itself. In this type of network arrangement, the outside community has minimal influence and may be perceived as antagonistic to extended-family cohesion (Heller & Quesada, 1977). The hollows seem to function as a natural boundary line, both physically and psychologically, where family cohesion is maintained within and "outsiders" are not welcome.

In contrast, the ranchers of Nevada were characterized by "primary-kin-oriented familism," which developed as an adaptation to extreme physical and social isolation. In this region, families live great distances from neighbors and in some areas, they are as much as 100 miles from the nearest town or urban center. Consequently, individuals rely on their nuclear families for support, and the larger community tends to be viewed as a positive source of social activities (Heller & Quesada, 1977).

The extent to which rural families are able to rely on other family members for support has direct implications for the quality of child care and the management of stress. In extended-kin-oriented families such as those characteristic of Appalachia, the responsibility for child care is shared among parents, siblings, and extended kin (Brown & Schwarzweller, 1970). Children do not depend on parents and siblings alone for attention and fulfillment of their emotional needs as they would in primary-kin-oriented families. The fact that extended-kin-oriented networks typically have more family members who can interchange roles suggests that this type of family organization may be able to absorb more stress, while continuing to maintain family cohesion, than would be expected in primary-kin-oriented families. Thus, if a parent is faced with considerable stress so that she or he is physically or mentally unable to provide adequate child care, other family members in the extended-kin network would be expected to compensate for the "dysfunctional" member, either temporarily or perhaps even permanently. Heller and Quesada (1977) found that members of extended-kin networks were more likely to consider mutual aid in times of need and daily emotional support for both nuclear and extended family members as "obligatory role commitments." Commitments and interactions of this type in primary-kin-oriented families were evident in the nuclear family, but were "no more likely to be obligatory for extended family members than . . . for nonmembers" (Heller & Quesada, 1977, p. 224). Therefore, not only are there practical reasons for members of an extended-kin-oriented network to "pick up the slack" (e.g., more family members available in terms of sheer number and physical proximity), but the ethos that stems from this type of family organization defines these obligations as mandatory.

Strong ties to an extended family has its advantages. In instances of child abuse, the extended family can serve several important functions. The physical act of abuse is considered to be the most noticeable outcome of unhealthy parent–child interactions (Martin, 1976), but there are other signs to indicate that parents and children are relating poorly (e.g., loud arguments, constant shouting, breaking objects, and frequent crying). If the extended family recognizes that a problem exists, they may try to solve it internally, before it reaches the point of needing outside intervention. In the rural South, where the nuclear and extended kin are physically clustered together, it is likely that family members are in close proximity to witness the escalation of negative parent–child interactions. Whether these negative interactions culminate in violent behavior is, in part, affected by the presence of an "audience" (Hepburn, 1973). Family members can actively intervene by providing alternative ways to settle the problem by giving the parent a "time-out" to regain composure and judge the appropriateness of his or her behavior, and by holding the person accountable for his or her actions. However, if the audience gives implicit or explicit support for the use of violent means to solve problems, then the violent behavior is more likely to occur (Hepburn, 1973). The latter dynamic is present in families where one or more members watch passively and do nothing to stop the physical attack (implicit support) or actively reinforce the use of violent behavior to discipline the child (explicit support).

The problem may escalate to the point where it cannot be contained within the family and a formal complaint of abuse is made. In extended-kin-oriented families, the expectation is that the extended family would relieve the stressed parent(s) by assuming the greater responsibility for child care. This would be another attempt to solve the problem internally with family cohesion maintained and outside intervention kept to a minimum. Perhaps in primary-kin-oriented networks finding extended kin to assume the added responsibility for childcare would be difficult, and some form of community intervention might be more welcome.

One problem with the literature on family life and child care in rural areas is that it is largely impressionistic and descriptive in nature. The authors were unable to locate empirical studies on the differences, if any, between rural and urban child rearing practices, particularly with regard to corporal punishment. Perhaps the rurality–urbanism distinction is not as significant in the realm of child care as the differences between social classes (cf. Hess, 1970, for a comprehensive review of class and ethnic differences in children's socialization).

Polansky, Borgman, and DeSaix (1972) compared the perceptions of social workers and public health nurses from rural and urban areas to determine whether professionals from rural communities viewed child neglect differently from their urban counterparts. They found that the dimensions of "inadequate parenting" were just as salient for rural professionals as they were for urban workers. Ninety-five per cent of rural workers cited at least one incident of inadequate parenting that fell under the category of "insufficient physical care, protection, or health care" in comparison to ninety-four percent of urban professionals. Significantly more rural than urban workers mentioned inadequate housing as a salient characteristic of neglect, while urban workers were more concerned about emotional neglect. Thus, it appears that rural and urban professionals tend to agree when it comes to behavioral indices of child neglect. Whether the same is true for child abuse is yet to be studied.

Rural Isolation

The extent to which families are connected to informal and formal sources of support in their community has been shown to have a profound effect on caregiver-child relations (Garbarino, 1976; Giovannoni & Billingsley, 1970). For rural families, isolation from informal and formal means of support can occur on two levels: physical and social. Research literature on urban abusive families has documented the association between social isolation and abuse (Elmer, 1967; Lenoski, 1974; Parke & Collmer, 1975; Young, 1964), but physical isolation may be even more of a critical factor in rural abuse. Physical isolation can compound the effects of social isolation, and thereby create conditions that seriously undermine healthy parent–child relationships.

Physical isolation from supports can be discussed in terms of vehicular inaccessibility and actual physical distance from resources. Vehicular inaccessibility implies that access to and from resources is limited by the absence of roads. An example of this type of physical isolation can be found in rural Virginia, where some homes are located a few miles past the last accessible dirt road and the only means of reaching the home is to hike the few miles on foot. Situations such as these are difficult for residents as well as visitors, particularly when weather conditions are bad. It would seem that only the most dedicated professionals would make frequent home visits in these cases, and ironically, these families are probably the ones that have the greatest need for outside contacts.

Rural families that are physically distant from supports and resources encounter the problem of transportation. If cars are available to these families, the problem is minimized. Social services and churches usually have their own vehicles to transport people, although the fact that families are scattered widely across counties causes dificulties in terms of systematic routing, time, and money.

The distribution of resources in rural areas differs markedly from the density of resources typically available in urban centers and is yet another problem caused by physical isolation. Families that need specialized services for their children, such as a physically handicapped child who requires extensive physical therapy, may be forced to travel to the nearest city in order to get the appropriate service. Since travel to urban services may demand significant amounts of time and money, poor rural people may decide that the service is not worth the trouble. Service providers may interpret the family's broken appointments as medical neglect, while glossing over the possibility of service inaccessibility.

The processes that result in the social isolation of abusive families are not clearly understood, primarily due to the lack of longitudinal studies that investigate the unfolding process of isolation. Thus far, research has largely focused on self-imposed isolation, or to be more precise, what looks like self-imposed isolation. When data are generated from people who have been already labeled abusive, caution must be taken when making interpretations about cause and effect relationships;

for example, does the community alienate abusive parents or do the parents purposefully alienate themselves? At least two etiologies of social isolation have been proposed (Garbarino, 1977b). Type 1 families form a "deviant subculture" and may remain isolated from traditional supports for generations. Type 2 families become isolated through the occurrence of one or several events that severs their relationship with community supports (e.g., geographic mobility).

Kin and community supports may be severed when a family's behavior is severely abusive. In an unpublishd pilot study by the first author, protective service supervisors from four welfare departments (a city, suburban-rural, and two rural departments) were interviewed about their perceptions of factors that contribute to child abuse in their respective settings. Supervisors from the suburban-rural and rural areas noted that in cases of mild abuse and neglect, the extended families were cooperative with regard to child placement (when necessary) and support for the nuclear family. However, in cases of severe abuse and chronic neglect, the extended family offered little or no assistance and sometimes joined the rest of the community in ostracizing the family. In general, these supervisors perceived their respective rural communities (i.e., neighbors) as unsupportive when it came to helping abusive families. Folklore and rumors would typically develop about certain families and people would refuse to help them if crises occurred (e.g., a home catching on fire). In the rural South, where individuals and families evaluate each other on the basis of family generations (Brown & Schwarzweller, 1970), a bad reputation can plague a family for years by severing their linkages to neighbors and community supports.

There are additional reasons why families become isolated from support systems:

> They include the developmental history of parents, social stresses which cut families off from potential and actual supports, mobility patterns which disrupt social networks, characteristics of the families which alienate others, the inclination and ability of neighborhoods to provide the observation and resources essential to the feedback function, and social service systems inadequate to the task of identifying and "monitoring" high-risk families. (Garbarino, 1977b, p. 728)

The end result of social isolation can be detrimental to family relationships whether or not it is self- or community-imposed, or whether it is exacerbated by physical isolation. First, the flow of information between the family and outside world is blocked so that parents do not have the opportunity to learn different methods of child rearing by observing other parents, nor do they receive feedback about their own behavior from people outside their nuclear family. Second, the experience of growing up in an isolated environment may begin a vicious cycle that might be difficult to break: socially isolated families may produce children who lack the social skills necessary to maintain intimate friendships; these children may develop into adults who act on their environment in such a way as to maintain their socially isolated circumstances.

CONCLUSION

Child abuse has been studied from a number of different perspectives, predominantly in urban populations. As Parke and Collmer (1975) and others (Garbarino, 1977a, 1977b; Light, 1973) have noted, the phenomenon requires a multidimensional approach to capture its true complexity. An ecological model of abuse provides such an approach by studying the mutual adaptation between the caregiver, child, and successively larger environmental levels that affects the caregiver-child relationship. This chapter focused primarily on one environmental level, the exosystem, and identified several factors that may undermine effective family functioning in rural communities.

Whether the ecologies of rural and urban abuse differ significantly remains an unanswered empirical question. It is highly likely that many of the same factors that contribute to urban abuse also comprise the rural ecology of abuse. Nevertheless, although the end result may be the same (e.g., isolated, highly stressed families with inadequate resources to cope effectively), it is conceivable that the underlying processes that foster rural abuse may produce slightly different patterns than those found in urban areas, and the "weight" or power of each factor may vary as a function of place of residence. In addition, there may be specific pattern differences across rival geographic regions, so that the factors that contribute to abuse in a rural southern family may be missing, modified, or substituted for other factors in a rural western family.

An ecological researcher concerned with rural abuse would not only be focusing on rural-urban differences or comparing rural abusive and nonabusive families, but she or he would be studying simultaneously the various meso- or exosystem factors that interact with the rural/urban individual and/or family characteristics. It is this interaction between person and environment that is of concern in the ecological approach. One of the problems in applying an ecological perspective to rural abuse is that the lack of an empirical base of knowledge about rural individuals and families makes it possible only to suggest ways that the previously discussed exosystem factors may influence rural family life.

The ecological approach provides an organization framework for the understanding and investigation of the multitude of factors that influence behavior. Nevertheless, it is a complex and often confusing task to formulate an integrated and executable research project on a social problem such as child abuse, particularly when the goal is to compare ecologies for different populations. Therefore, a research model will be presented in an attempt to specify concretely some of the questions that could be generated concerning rural child abuse, and how it may, or may not, differ from urban abuse.

One of the essential components to child abuse appears to be excessive stress, which can result from a variety of sources. The source of stress will probably vary with place of residence so that urban and rural stresses may be quite different. For example, the stress of crowding is typical of life in urban centers while the stress of physical isolation is characteristic of rural life, particularly in the West. Stress resulting from social isolation, however, may be found in both rural and urban communities, regardless of whether one is living in a crowded, high-rise apartment building in New York City or on a ranch in southern Utah. Since some form of stress is present in everyday life, it is the manner in which individuals, families, and environments combat, or fail to combat stress that will ultimately affect the caregiver–child relationship. "Vulnerability" can exist at each level—whether it be a parent's child rearing history (individual level or ontogenic development), the pathological relationship between husband and wife (microsystem), limited neighborhood or community child-care facilities (exosystem), and/or national sanctioning of physical punishment as a child-rearing practice (macrosystem). Ecological research needs to address at least the following two questions:

1. What resources at one level or combination of levels are necessary to offset the particular vulnerabilities at another level(s)? For example, can the positive effects of family support of various kinds override such negative stresses as limited financial resources, job dissatisfaction, and a difficult child?
2. Are there any factors that are specific to either a rural or urban life-style that are particularly "lethal" or "beneficial" to the caregiver–child relationship?

The potential for extended families to provide feedback about child-rearing practices and general support may vary in rural and urban communities. Dependence on kin and family loyalty is a strong component of rural life, particularly in the rural South, and family life is vulnerable to the scrutiny and support of extended kin. If the scrutiny, support, and feedback is appropriate and constructive, then strong family ties may be a deterrent to the escalation of negative parent–child interactions.

Extended kinship networks are present in urban environments as well (cf. Nye & Berardo, 1973), but there seem to be variations in the type of urban kin contact that may have some implications for child abuse. Litwak (1960a, 1960b) suggests that the modern urban family is involved in a "modified extended family system." Traditional extended family systems, such as those characteristic of Appalachia and the rural South, encourage geographic proximity and "occupational nepotism," while the modified extended family system allows geographic and occupational mobility but maintains communication and provides support and guidance. Family support by telephone, letter, and/or infrequent face-to-face contacts may not be sufficient for families undergoing considerable stress and socially isolated from other sources of support.

Physical isolation, a factor unique to some rural communities, may be crucial in fostering abuse. The relationship between physical isolation, social isolation, and stress needs clarification. First, is there a positive relationship between physical isolation and abuse? Is the degree of physical isolation (e.g., physical distance and/or vehicular inaccessibility) related to increases in stress and severity of abuse? When physical isolation is present, what other factors are necessary to elicit abuse? What types of families choose to live in vehicularly inaccessible areas, which is the extreme of both physical and socially isolated circumstances?

The comparison of rural abusive populations in different geographic regions is another promising avenue of ecological research. Whereas physical isolation may be a critical factor in the Rocky Mountain areas, it may be less powerful for New England rural families and perhaps some other factor or factors will emerge as characteristics of this region.

The importance of undertaking these investigations should not be minimized. If, as was stated in the beginning of this chapter, the goal of understanding child abuse is to eradicate it, then a comprehensive knowledge of the various interacting factors that contribute to it is a necessity. Such knowledge is the only base that may eventually lead to intervention strategies for primary prevention. Social scientists have usually investigated social problems from disciplinary perspectives that tend not to view these problems in their complexity. An ecological approach, as advocated here, is a clear plea for the elimination of disciplinary myopia. Garbarino has been the leader in initiating inquiry into child abuse from this perspective. The near total neglect of rural communities must cease. The problem of child abuse is too important not to push forward as expeditiously, and yet thoroughly, as possible.

REFERENCES

Bakan, D. *Slaughter of the innocents*. San Francisco: Jossey-Bass, 1971.

Barker, R. G. Explorations in ecological psychology. *American Psychologist*, 1965, *20*, 1–14.

Bealer, R. C., Willits, F. K., & Kuvlesky, W. The meaning of rurality in American society: Some implications of alternative definitions. *Rural Sociology*, 1965, *30*, 255–266.

Belsky, J. Child maltreatment: An ecological integration. *American Psychologist*, 1980, *35*, 321–335.

Bronfenbrenner, U. Toward an experimental ecology of human development. *American Psychologist*, 1977, *32*, 513–531.

Bronfenbrenner, U. *The ecology of human development*. Cambridge: Harvard University Press, 1979.

Brown, J. S., & Schwarzeller, H. K. The Applachian family. In John D. Photiadis & Harry K. Schwarzeller (Eds.), *Change in rural Appalachia: Implications for action programs*. Philadelphia: University of Pennsylvania Press, 1970.

Burgess, R. *Project Interact: A study of patterns of interaction in abusive, neglectful, and control families*. Final Report to the National Center on Child Abuse and Neglect, U.S. Department of Health, Education, and Welfare, August 1978. Cited in Jay Belsky, Child maltreatment: An ecological integration. *American Psychologist*, 1980, *35*, 320–335.

Caplan, G. *Support systems and community mental health: Lectures on concept development*. New York: Behavioral Publications, 1974.

Caplan, G., & Nelson, S. On being useful: The nature and consequences of psychological research on social problems. *American Psychologist*, 1973, *28*, 199–211.

Coles, R. *Migrants, sharecroppers, mountaineers. Children of Crisis* (Vol. 2). Boston: Little, Brown, 1967.

Code of the Commonwealth of Virginia. Child abuse and neglect: Persons required to report (Sections 63.1–248.17). Amended March 1975.

Elmer, E. Hazards in determining child abuse. *Child Welfare*, 1966, *45*, 28–33.

Elmer, E. *Children in jeopardy: A study of abused minors and their families*. Pittsburg: University of Pittsburgh Press, 1967.

Elmer, E. Child abuse and family stress. *Journal of Social Issues*, 1979, *35*, 60–71.

Erikson, K. T. *Everything in its path: Destruction of community in the Buffalo Creek flood*. New York: Simon & Schuster, 1976.

Garbarino, J. A preliminary study of some ecological correlates of child abuse: The impact of socioeconomic stress on mothers. *Child Development*, 1976, *47*, 178–185.

Garbarino, J. The price of privacy in the social dynamics of child abuse. *Child Welfare*, 1977, *56*, 565–575. (a)

Garbarino, J. The human ecology of child maltreatment: A conceptual model of research. *Journal of Marriage and the Family*, November 1977, 721–235. (b)

Garbarino, J. An ecological approach to child maltreatment. In L. Pelton (Ed.), *The social context of child abuse and neglect*. New York: Human Sciences Press, 1979.

Garbarino, J., & Crouter, A. Defining the community context of parent–child relations. *Child Development*, 1978, *49*, 604–616.

Garbarino, J., & Stocking, S. H. (Eds.). *Supporting families and protecting children*. Boys Town, Nebr.: Center for the Study of Youth Development, 1978.

Gelles, R. J. Child abuse as psychopathology: A sociological critique and reformulation. *American Journal of Orthospychiatry*, 1973, *43*, 611–621.

Gelles, R. J. A psychosocial approach in child abuse. *Nursing Digest*, April 1974, 53–59.

Gelles, R. J. Violence toward children in the United States. Paper presented in a symposium on *Violence at home and at school* at the meeting of the American Association for the Advancement of Science, Denver, February 1977.

Gil, D. G. *Violence against children: Physical abuse in the United States.* Cambridge: Harvard University Press, 1970.

Gil, D. G. A holistic perspective on child abuse and its prevention. *Journal of Sociology and Social Welfare*, 1974, *2*, 110–125.

Giovannoni, J. M., & Billingsley, A. Child neglect among the poor: A study of parental adequacy in families of three ethnic groups. *Child Welfare*, 1970, *49*, 196–204.

Helfer, R. E., & Kempe, C. H. *The battered child.* Chicago: The University of Chicago Press, 1968.

Heller, P. L., & Quesada, G. Rural familism: An interregional analysis. *Rural Sociology*, 1977, *42*, 220–240.

Hepburn, J. R. Violent behavior in interpersonal relationships. *Sociological Quarterly*, 1973, *14*, 419–429.

Hess, R. D. Class and ethnic influences upon socialization. In P. H. Mussen (Ed.), *Carmichael's manual of child psychology* (Vol. 2, 3rd ed.). New York: Wiley, 1970.

Holmes, T. H. & Rhae, R. H. The social readjustment rating scale. *Journal of Psychosomatic Research*, 1967, *11*, 213–218.

Huessy, H. R. Tactics and targets in the rural setting. In S. E. Golann & C. Eisdorfer (Eds.), *Handbook of community mental health.* New York: Appleton-Century-Crofts, 1972.

Jayaratne, S. Child abusers as parents and children: A review. *Social Work*, January 1977, 5–9.

Justice, G., & Duncan, D. Child abuse as a work-related problem. *Corrective and Social Psychiatry and Journal of Behavior Technology, Methods, and Therapy*, 1977, *23*, 53–55.

Kelly, J. G. Ecological constrains on mental health services. *American Psychologist*, 1966, *21*, 535–539.

Kempe, C. H. A practical approach to the protection of the abused child and rehabilitation of the abusing parent. *Pediatrics*, 1973, *51*, 804–812.

Kempe, C. H., & Helfer, R. E. (Eds) *Helping the battered child and his family.* Philadelphia: J. B. Lippincott, 1972.

Kempe, C. H., Silverman, F. N., Steele, B., Droegemueller, W., & Silver, H. The battered child syndrome. *Journal of the American Medical Association*, 1962, *181*, 17–24.

Korsch, B. M., Christian, J. B., Gozzi, E. K., & Carlson, P. V. Infant care and punishment: A pilot study. *American Journal of Public Health*, 1965, *55*, 1880–1888.

Landis, P. H. *Rural life in process.* New York: McGraw-Hill, 1940.

Lenoski, E. F. *Translating inquiry data into preventive and health care services—physical child abuse.* Unpublished manuscript, University of Southern California School of Medicine, Los Angeles, 1974. Cited in R. D. Parke & W. C. Collmer, Child abuse: An interdisciplinary analysis. In E. M. Hetherington (Ed.), *Child development research* (Vol. 5). Chicago: University of Chicago Press, 1975.

Lewin, K. *A dynamic theory of personality.* New York: McGraw-Hill, 1935.

Light, R. Abused and neglected children in America: A study of alternative policies. *Harvard Educational Review*, 1973, *44*, 556–598.

Litwak, E. Geographical mobility and extended-family cohesion. *American Sociological Review*, 1960, *25*, 9–21. (a)

Litwak, E. Geographical mobility and extended family cohesion. *American Sociological Review*, 1960, *25*, 385–394. (b)

Martin, H. (Ed.). *The abused child: A multidisciplinary approach to developmental issues and treatment.* Cambridge, Mass.: Ballinger, 1976.

McKinley, D. G. *Social class and family life.* New York: Free Press, 1964.

Melnick, B., & Hurley, J. R. Distinctive personality attributes of child abusing mothers. *Journal of Consulting and Clinical Psychology*, 1969, *33*, 746–479.

Miller, F. T., Bentz, W. K., Aponte, J. F., & Brogan, D. R. Perception of life crisis events: A comparative study of rural and urban samples. In B. S. Dohrenwend & B. P. Dohrenwend (Eds.), *Stressful life events: Their nature and effects*. New York: Wiley, 1974.

Morris, M. G., & Gould, R. W. Role reversal: A necessary concept in dealing with the "Battered Child Syndrome." *American Journal of Orthopsychiatry*, 1963, *33*, 298–299.

Myers, J. K., Lindenthal, J. J., & Pepper, M. P. Social class, life events, and psychiatric symptoms: A longitudinal study. In B. S. Dohrenwend & B. P. Dohrenwend (Eds.), *Stressful life events: Their nature and effects*. New York: Wiley, 1974.

National Center for the Prevention and Treatment of Child Abuse and Neglect. *1977 analysis of child abuse and neglect research*. Washington, D.C.: United States Children's Bureau, Department of Health, Education, and Welfare, 1977.

National Institute of Mental Health. *Child abuse and neglect programs: Practice and theory*. Washington, D.C.: United States Department of Health, Education, and Welfare, 1978.

Newberger, E. H., Reed, R. B., Daniel, J. H., Hyde, J. N., & Kotelchuck, M. Pediatric social illness: Toward an etiologic classification. *Pediatrics*, 1977, *60*, 178–185.

Nye, F. I., & Berardo, F. M. *The family: Its structure and interaction*. New York: Macmillan, 1973.

Parke, R. D., & Collmer, W. C. Child abuse: An interdisciplinary analysis. In E. M. Hetherington (Ed.), *Child development research* (Vol. 5). Chicago: University of Chicago Press, 1975.

Pelton, L. H. Child abuse and neglect: The myth of classlessness. *American Journal of Orthospychiatry*, 1978, *48*, 608–617.

Photiadis, J. D. Rural southern Appalachia and mass society. In J. D. Photiadis & H. K. Schwarzweller (Eds.), *Change in rural Appalachia: Implications for action programs*. Philadelphia: University of Pennsylvania Press, 1970.

Photiadis, J. D., & Schwarzweller, H. K. *Change in rural Appalachia: Implications for action programs*. Philadelphia: University of Pennsylvania Press, 1970.

Polansky, N. A., Borgman, R. D., & DeSaix, D. *Roots of futility*. San Francisco: Jossey-Bass, 1972.

Radbill, S. Y. A history of child abuse and infanticide. In R. E. Helfer & C. H. Kempe (Eds.), *The battered child*. Chicago: University of Chicago Press, 1968.

Rosenberg, M., & Reppucci, N. D. *Abusive mothers: Perceptions of their own and their children's behavior*. Paper presented at the meeting of the American Psychological Association, Montreal, September 1980.

Ryan, W. *Blaming the victim*. New York: Vintage Books, 1971.

Sattin, D. B., & Miller, J. K. The ecology of child abuse within a military community. *American Journal of Orthopsychiatry*, 1971, *41*, 675–678.

Spinetta, J., & Rigler, D. The child abusing parent: A psychological review. *Psychological Bulletin*, 1972, *77*, 296–304.

Stark, R., and McEvoy, J. Middle class violence. *Psychology Today*, 1970, *4*, 52–65.

Steele, B. F. Parental abuse of infants and small children. In E. J. Anthony & T. Benedek (Eds.), *Parenthood, its psychology and psychopathology*. Boston: Little, Brown, 1970.

Steele, B. F., & Pollock, C. B. A psychiatric study of parents who abuse infants and small children. In R. E. Helfer & C. H. Kempe (Eds.), *The battered child*. Chicago: University of Chicago Press, 1968.

Taylor, L. *Urban-rural problems*. Belmont, Calif.: Dickenson, 1968.

Terr, L. C. A family study of child abuse. *American Journal of Psychiatry*, 1970, *127*, 665–671.

Tinbergen, N. *The study of instinct*. London: Oxford University Press, 1951.

Trickett, E. J., Kelly, J. G., & Todd, D. M. The social environment of the high school: Guidelines for individual change and organization redevelopment. In S. E. Golann & C. Eisdorfer (Eds.), *Handbook of community mental health*. New York: Appleton-Century-Crofts, 1972.

VanEs, J. C. & Brown, J. E. The rural-urban variable once more: Some individual level observations. *Rural Sociology, 1974, 39,* 373–391.

Warren, D. Support systems in different types of neighborhoods. In J. Garbarino & S. H. Stocking (Eds.), *Supporting families and protecting children*. Boys Town, Nebr.: Center for the Study of Youth Development, 1978.

Watzlawick, P., Weakland, J., & Fisch, R. *Change: Principles of problem formulation and problem-resolution*. New York: W. W. Norton, 1974.

Webb, S. D., & Collette, J. Rural-urban differences in the use of stress-alleviative drugs. *American Journal of Sociology, 1977, 83,* 700–707.

Young, L. *Wednesday's children: A study of child neglect and abuse*. New York: McGraw-Hill, 1964.

15

Home-Based Early Intervention

Edward E. Gotts

The problems of delivering human services in rural areas are multiple: physical isolation, poor roads, and nonexistent public transportation; scarcity of resources and services; remoteness from institutions of higher education and medical centers. In addition, apathy, indifference, and opposition—products of rural people's perception that new ideas and procedures may disturb or destroy traditional values and patterns of living—are pervasive. Finally, there is a history of neglect of rural needs by state and federal officials who have been decidedly more responsive to the needs of urban communities. These problems, described in detail in Chapter 12, are magnified in much of rural Appalachia because of its mountainous topography, sparse population, severe poverty, and traditional culture.

RATIONALE

When the Appalachia Educational Laboratory (AEL) was created in 1966, its initial challenge was to analyze and document the exact nature of regional needs. A major needs study confirmed the described pattern of regional characteristics. The Lab's response was to design a plan

EDWARD E. GOTTS • Appalachia Educational Laboratory, Charleston, West Virginia 25325. The work reported herein was performed pursuant to one or more grants from the National Institute of Education. However, the opinions expressed herein do not necessarily reflect the position or policy of the National Institute of Education or the Appalachia Educational Laboratory, and no official endorsement by the National Institute of Education or the Appalachia Educational Laboratory should be inferred.

through 1968 for regional interventions that might be carried out by local education agencies, after they had been bonded together into multicounty cooperatives. Such cooperatives would increase the availability of scarce resources and focus them upon specific needs. The first step was to create a climate to encourage such multicounty efforts.

Preschool children were identified as requiring special attention; these children's needs often went unmet. As a result, they were not prepared to participate in school. Manifestations included extreme shyness when they entered school, reduced verbal interaction in the classroom, and a high incidence of early school failure (i.e., retention in grade) and poor performance on standardized achievement tests. The Lab, accordingly, decided to focus one of its main efforts on preschool program development.

Geographic isolation was to be overcome by the use of: (a) television to reach all homes; (b) mobile instructional facilities that could travel into small communities over almost impassable roads; and (c) selection, training, and use of local paraprofessionals who could visit homes relatively near their own places of residence. The home-oriented approach would draw on the strength of the Appalachian rural family as a support system. By relying on the children's families, the families became collaborators, rather than "outsiders," in the service delivery process. These approaches were also selected as cost-effective in view of the scarce resources. Once produced, the television signal could be broadcast at virtually no cost to the local preschool program; a teacher in a mobile classroom could travel during a normal week to as many as eight sites to provide once-a-week half-day group experience sessions; and paraprofessionals could extend services in a highly individualized manner to families at a relatively modest cost.

THE AEL EXPERIMENT

Home-based early intervention is by no means a new idea (Gotts, Spriggs, & Sattes, 1979). Nor is its application in rural settings unique or without precedent (Klaus & Gray, 1968). The intervention reported here was, nevertheless, the first to use as its strategy a particular combination of treatment components: daily television lessons in the home, weekly printed support materials and home visitation to parent and child by a carefully trained paraprofessional, and weekly group experiences for children in a mobile classroom van capable of serving isolated rural settings. Moreover, the intervention was carried out as a well-designed experiment. The study qualifies, in addition, as a clear instance of a primary prevention experiment.

Nearly ten years have passed since the initial three-year experiment (1968–1971) was concluded in West Virginia. It has since been essentially and successfully replicated in rural settings in four other states, ranging from Ohio through Alabama (1971–1973). Two of its replication sites were subsequently integrated into the national demonstration known as *Home Start,* which has been a variant and option within Head Start since 1975. From 1974–1977, the AEL developed and validated materials to support widespread operation of home-based interventions of this type for families of preschool and early primary age children. These materials collectively are called "Aids to Early Learning" (Gotts, 1979). From 1978–1980, AEL staff have been gathering and analyzing extensive follow-up data on children and parents from the original experiment. This current work seeks to examine the persistence and pervasiveness of the intervention's effects.

Characteristics of Rural Appalachians

A thorough analysis was made by AEL of regional and sample site demography to determine the extent to which its findings could be generalized to other nonurban[1] settings in the Northeast and Southeast.

Demographics: Then and Now

The original AEL experiment in Home-Oriented Preschool Education (HOPE) was operated in four counties of southern West Virginia. The mining of metallurgical coal was and continues to be the major source of employment in these counties. In 1968 the largest urbanized center in the site area had a population of less than 20,000. The least rural of the counties had a nonurban population of 63.3% at the time of the 1970 census; the most rural had a nonurban population of 86.8% (Bertram & MacDonald, 1971).

In 1974/1975 AEL, in cooperation with the United States Bureau of the Census, performed a reanalysis of 1970 census individual data records for the nonurban portions of a thirteen-state region of northeastern and southeastern states, including West Virginia, to determine further the characteristics of families of preschool children (Bertram, 1975). Previous census data had not been compiled to examine this particular demographic subgroup. At the same time (1974), AEL interviewed a seven-state sample of nonurban families, who were matched

---

[1]*Nonurban* and *rural* are used interchangeably to refer to unincorporated areas and to incorporated areas having a population of less than 2,500.

to represent the 1970 census for their respective counties. The interviews sought to clarify additional issues that had not been addressed in the census data collection of 1970 (Shively, Bertram, & Hines, 1975).

These efforts confirmed that the four-county site of the HOPE experiment was slightly more rural and had somewhat lower parental education and per capita income levels than West Virginia as a whole (Bertram & MacDonald, 1971; Bertram, 1975). Moreover, the West Virginia percentage of nonurban population was 5.5% higher (i.e., more rural) than the Northeast and Southeast average; West Virginia's median years of parental education matched those for the region; and West Virginia had about 5% more families below the poverty level than the regional nonurban average. Together, these facts suggest that the HOPE sample was drawn from an area generally resembling the nonurban portions of the region as a whole, but differing by being somewhat more rural and by having lower per capita income and lower median parental education. Although the 1980 census had not been performed at the time of this writing, there appear to have been no major population shifts over the past decade which would have altered the basic demographic similarities and contrasts between the HOPE site and West Virginia or the overall nonurban region.

It appears from other comparisons that the isolated rural populations of the thirteen-state region studied (Alabama, Georgia, Kentucky, Maryland, Mississippi, New York, North Carolina, Ohio, Pennsylvania, South Carolina, Tennessee, Virginia, and West Virginia) experience conditions similar to those faced by isolated rural dwellers elsewhere in the United States (Tamblyn, 1973). The HOPE experience and its replications thus provide findings that are suggestive for other isolated rural communities in the United States. The sampling methods used in the HOPE experiment have been described as follows by the original evaluation team:

> The initial [HOPE] sample was selected in 1968 by randomly assigning treatments to 3-, 4-, and 5-year-old children and their parents who were living within randomly selected geographic grids in the rural areas. Additional children were added each year [in 1969 and 1970, by these methods] as some of the sample became old enough to enter public schools [or were otherwise lost to attrition]. (Bertram, Hines, & MacDonald, 1971)

These methods of selection and assignment were used to assure that the HOPE sample would represent the nonurban homes of these counties in both the community control and treatment groups. It should, nevertheless, be recognized that subsequent busing to consolidated schools brought many of these rural children into contact with children from somewhat urbanized areas.

Inferred Child-Rearing Practices

Nearly all of the regional literature has identified a core mythology regarding mountain families and their probable child-rearing practices. There is not at present a data base sufficient to define clearly what these families are like, although the *HOPE Follow-Up Study* will eventually do much to increase our understanding of these families' methods of child rearing. These problems of the literature have been discussed in more detail elsewhere (Gotts & Higginbotham, 1980).

Although it is clear that there is considerable diversity of family types in the Appalachian rural population (Hansen & Stevic, 1971), some generalizations can be made. Unfortunately, these are based on relatively soft data. For example, according to Brown and Schwarzweller (1970) characteristics on which Appalachian families differ from other American families are that they: (a) place greater emphasis on family traditions; (b) tend to have larger families, although these differences are declining; (c) more sharply differentiate the role activities of the sexes; (d) are less child centered (i.e., are less permissive, more directive, and more apt to use physical punishment); (e) exert tighter controls over adolescents, resulting in low rates of juvenile delinquency, particularly in the more remote rural areas; and (f) are more likely, especially in rural areas having longtime residential stability, to restrict informally the free choice of mates.

These same authors have also commented on characteristics of these families that do not differ from other American families (Brown & Schwarzweller, 1970): (a) the fertility rates are declining; (b) the family of residence is the conjugal or nuclear family (i.e., parents and immature children), although the extended family continues to be important; (c) the conjugal family maintains contact with both sets of in-laws; and (d) male dominance is prevalent.

The foregoing observations suggest some of the more general parameters that influence child rearing. These general parameters have not, however, been rigorously studied; they should, consequently, be viewed as anecdotal inferences more than adequately researched population characteristics.

The Psychosocial Interior of the Family

Even less is known empirically of interaction in rural families (see Chapter 3). Although it has been a major focus of AEL's HOPE follow-up study, these portions of the findings will not be ready for presentation for another year. We will, for these reasons, find it useful to examine the soft and nonrepresentative but suggestive findings of Looff (1971) from Eastern Kentucky.

Looff's (1971) own review of literature did not uncover any adequate epidemiologic studies for the region. He found, moreover, that there were no in-depth studies of representative samples of mountain families. Whereas his own most in-depth data came from a rural child mental health sample, his intensive look at the families themselves did provide considerable insight into family dynamics. He also compared the incidence of disorders he encountered and those that he seldom saw with their rates of occurrence in an urban Kentucky mental health sample—thereby providing further support for some of his hypotheses regarding the impact of family life on child development and psychopathology.

The major family environment themes that he could elaborate from his data were: (a) an emphasis on family interdependence and an overemphasis on infancy; (b) family-engendered conflict over physical maturation and a subsequent increased incidence of pathology among children related to sexual maturation; and (c) in a sizeable subgroup of families, high conflict over verbal communication, leading to what Looff has termed "consolidated school syndrome" (i.e., children who become immobile and nonverbal when moved from one-room schools to consolidated schools). Based on the clarity of the raw data, we can already anticipate that the HOPE follow-up study findings on a representative sample of non-clinic children will corroborate strongly Looff's first two themes as being important focal points of Appalachian family life. It remains to be seen, on the basis of more refined analyses, whether the HOPE findings will support the validity of his third thematic emphasis. Such a possibility is not now evident from the raw data, even among the most isolated rural families.

Generalizability to the Region

The preceding discussion has already touched upon the issue of how generalizable the findings of the HOPE experiment are to the region. In summary, the HOPE findings appear to be of potential value for understanding the experience of growing up rural and isolated, in the context of close, extended-family kinship ties, even when there has been considerable exposure to the broader culture through experience in consolidated schools and via television. Although our studies suggest, from a demographic perspective, that the HOPE results may be generally applicable to nonurban families in a thirteen-state region, this inference cannot yet be made with a high degree of certainty.

As some of us have reasoned elsewhere, it is not only possible but frequently the rule that social science mythologies and stereotypes about groups of people are generated by a well-meaning overapplication of the method of generalization (Gotts & Higginbotham, 1980). With Photiadis, we are inclined to believe that neighborhood and locale exert a more substantial influence upon the ethos of groups of people than is generally appreciated in our science (Photiadis, 1980). It seems to us that current research trends toward performing community case studies and toward relying more upon qualitative methodologies are serving as correctives to psychology's obsession with quantification and generalization in the face of its long-standing lack of commitment to replication and cross-validation of findings. Thus, it may be possible to generalize with greater integrity when there is less compulsion to generalize at all.

HOPE: AN EARLY INTERVENTION STRATEGY

The overall approach of the HOPE intervention will first be examined; then its individual treatment components will be considered in detail; finally, its status as a primary prevention will be reviewed.

Overview of Program Rationale and Strategy

Background information on HOPE's operation is available from many scattered sources. The most satisfactory single source is an overview manual prepared by Alford (1972). This is one of seven HOPE program manuals, all of which may now be obtained from the ERIC Document Reproduction Service.

HOPE originally consisted of three components: (1) daily television lessons in the home for the preschool child (3–5 years old) and printed parent guides to help parents to understand what the child was learning on television and to follow up with related activities at home; (2) weekly visits to the home from a local, trained paraprofessional who demonstrated to the parents how to teach their children, and who listened, helped "problem-solve," and put parents in contact with community resources relative to family health and social issues; and (3) a weekly half-day group experience for the child with other children in a mobile classroom under the supervision of a qualified teacher and an aide. A fourth component, parent discussion groups, was added later.

Contribution of Daily Television Series

The television series and printed support materials were together called "Around the Bend." A permanent archive of these materials is now being organized at Marshall University, Huntington, West Virginia. The archive will contain complete documentation on the series' curriculum structure and on the formative evaluation studies that were conducted by AEL during the development of the series.

Originally the television component was conceptualized as imparting information and providing experiences to foster preschoolers' cognitive development. AEL was the first television producer to observe preschool viewers in their own homes at broadcast time in order to determine how they responded to each show. These observations by home visitors were scheduled to provide an age-by-sex cross section of viewers each day. The observations focused on features (segments) that held the children's attention and on the program's capacity to produce active responding (e.g., verbalizing answers, performing actions, going after suggested materials). This information was immediately fed back from the field site to the production team in Charleston, West Virginia, to enable them to emphasize those program elements that produced an active response and held the children's attention (Miller, 1970). By the end of the first year of production (1968/1969), much progress had been made in achieving a balance of program features. Over 500 half-hour shows were produced in the years 1968–1971. The careful formative evaluation paid off: the series was highly effective both in promoting active attending and responding by three-, four- and five-year old children and in stimulating their cognitive development.

Home visitors eventually began to encourage parents to look in on the show with their children. Parents did this much more than the series' developers had expected, with questionnaire results suggesting that approximately 80% of the parents looked at the program with great regularity (Bertram, Hines, & MacDonald, 1971). It is essential to realize that over 85% of these rural children were cared for at home by their mothers in the daytime, and that an additional 11% were cared for by another family member, most often a grandmother. The main character on the program, Miss Patty, consequently provided a regular role model. Her potential impact as a role model can be more fully understood by examining parents' attitudes toward her and the program. These attitudes were found to be highly positive in terms of which available children's programs the parents considered "best" (Bertram, 1970).

The television component served an additional, unanticipated function. It served as a daily reminder to parents to carry out at home some simple developmental activities that were printed in the weekly parent guides. The reminder function likely brought about a more continuous treatment effect for children than do home-oriented programs that lack a television component.

The Home-Visitor Role

AEL recruited only local people to serve as home visitors. Because nearly all of the persons being visited in their homes were females, all home visitors selected were females, in conformity with community folkways and mores. Home visitors had all completed high school or earned a high school equivalency certificate; some had completed college work. All were judged in their communities to be trustworthy, reliable, able to keep confidences, effective communicators, and persons capable of relating to young children and their parents. They were recommended by local school principals.

They were trained in the special role functions that they would perform, given instruction in how to access community resources, provided more general instruction in child development, teaching, and early learning, and taught how to handle various problematic situations which might arise (e.g., sexual advances, aggression, involvement in family quarrels, etc.). Continuous in-service training and supervision were used to maintain skills and to resolve problems.

During the weekly home visits, the visitor delivered the printed materials, discussed simple developmental learning activities for the child, adapted activities to the child's skills and interest, and completed records on program compliance and reactions. In addition, the home visitor sometimes, at the parent's instigation, became involved with the parent in any of a variety of areas with which the parent may have requested help (e.g., child-care routines, nutrition, personal health problem, etc.). The visitor handled as many of these matters as she could and referred others. Over time the home visitor became a trusted friend and, in many instances, a confidante.

In all that the home visitor did, the central purpose was to facilitate the parent's functioning as the child's first teacher. The home visitor was, therefore, trained not to usurp the parent's role or to displace the parent. That this distinction was sometimes blurred was evident from the fact that the home visitors were often referred to by parents as "teacher." Despite this conception of the visitor, an acceptable degree of parental compliance was achieved, as will be discussed later under "Parent Participation and Reactions."

The Classroom or Group Experience

During one half-day session a week, approximately 15 children were assembled for the arrival of the mobile classroom van. This fully equipped and self-contained unit needed only a power hook-up to be totally operational. It was staffed by the teacher and an aide. Working four days a week, with one day for planning and preparation, they could provide educational services for eight groups of 15 children—at a great economic advantage over other half-day or full-day preschool programs. Moreover, as a fully portable operation, the van provided age-appropriate facilities and materials in communities that offered no comparable learning environments.

The instruction that occurred in the mobile classroom was correlated with that provided by the television and materials. It provided some direct hands-on experiences for children with learning materials not readily available in homes. Perhaps as important as any of the foregoing, however, was the social milieu of the classroom. The children could engage in social interaction with small groups of their peers. Such opportunities are usually scarce and difficult to arrange for children in isolated rural settings because there are too few age-mates living near one another to sustain such experiences. The social milieu also differed from the home by exposing these young children to a weekly experience of being cared for, guided, and supervised by adults outside the family. Such experiences were viewed as having the potential for reducing later separation anxiety when the children reached school age in a population known to manifest a high incidence of separation anxiety (e.g., Looff, 1971).

Parent Participation and Reactions

Many parent reactions and patterns of participation were observed during the home visits. Most typically, parents generally carried out their part of the contract by being available for the home visit, observing their child watching the television program, and carrying out activities suggested by the home visitor. Such behavior may be indicative only of social compliance, although the impressions of home visitors and field evaluators was that parents generally felt some personal commitment to the HOPE program. At one extreme, a few parents thought up extra things to do, carried them out, and then related their experiences to the home visitor. At the other extreme, a few parents always managed to be busy in the kitchen, for example, during the home visit, thereby leaving the home visitor in the role of a direct teacher of the child rather than as an instructor and model for the parent. The parents' reactions to the television series became more positive during the second and third years of the experiment, apparently because of the production team's increasing success in implementing what they learned through the formative evaluation process.

Much less attention was devoted by the staff to studying changes in the parents themselves than to learning how the children had been affected by the experience. Thus, an opportunity was missed to gain what might have been some of the most valuable data in the entire experiment. It has been possible, nevertheless, to design into the HOPE follow-up study a fairly rigorous test of how parents of the experimental and control groups differed after about 10 years had elapsed. This could be accomplished because experimental and control parents had been randomly assigned in the beginning. Yet the follow-up study cannot address certain vital process questions about the critical events that brought about any differences between the two parent groups.

HOPE as Primary Prevention

Although the child population served by the HOPE experiment had an elevated rate of risk for the subsequent development of certain conditions (e.g., Looff, 1971), they were not a specifically at-risk group. Many of them could have been expected to turn out as reasonably well-coping, adaptive children in the school population without any intervention. Intervention under these specific circumstances—where risk has not been identified or assessed and no labeling has occurred—may be viewed as a primary prevention. Children who may have been at special risk were as likely to be assigned to experimental or control conditions as were children who may not have been at special risk. Results of the HOPE experiment are, therefore, of particular importance for what they may have to say about this home-oriented primary prevention strategy as a means of averting certain unfavorable outcomes. The long-term follow-up study now in progress was designed to examine this question.

IMMEDIATE PROGRAM EFFECTS

During the time that the HOPE experiment was conducted (1968–1971), the staff took an unusually comprehensive approach to the assessment of the program's effects on children, while only minimally examining its effects on parents.

Parent Involvement in Children's Early Learning and Development

The study's results document a high rate of concurrent parent involvement in their children's learning and development. There was, unfortunately, no attempt to obtain correlated records on parents and children in order to determine how differing degrees or rates of parents' involvement may have related to differential outcomes in children. The HOPE follow-up study is unable to remedy this information gap.

Children's Performance on Cognitive Measures

An individually administered criterion-outcome test was developed: the Appalachia Preschool Test (APT). This is now available to qualified users with supporting documentation from the Educational Testing Service's Test Collection, Princeton, New Jersey. The APT went through various editions, as the curriculum was refined. Throughout the process and the various versions, however, it is appropriate to think of the APT as a measure of early conceptual development.

The program's effects on children's APT scores, as well as on all other measures, were documented systematically in a series of technical reports. A representative summary report from this series provides the essential highlights of the final program year 1970–1971 (Bertram, Hines, & MacDonald, 1971). It also reports on program effects on the Peabody Picture Vocabulary Test (PPVT), the Illinois Test of Psycholinguistic Abilities (ITPA)-Revised, and the Frostig Developmental Test of Visual Perception, as well as on some noncognitive measures. A preliminary study established the acceptability of these measures with this population in the sense that their performance approximated the tests' norms.

The effects upon participants may be summarized with reference to four groups of children:

1. An outside-of-community control group that received no treatment (C)
2. A within-community control group that could receive the television signal but was provided with no other treatment (TV-only)
3. Those who received the television program, the printed support materials, and weekly home visitation (TV-HV)
4. Those who received the television program, home visitation, and the weekly group experience (TV-HV-GE or Package)

Cognitive effects for the various individual measures were as follows: (a) on the APT, Package and TV-HV were equal, both significantly outperforming TV-only, and TV-only significantly exceeded the outside control group; (b) on the PPVT, Package and TV-HV were about equal, both significantly exceeding TV-only and outside control (which were not different from each other); (c) on the ITPA, the groups differed on three subtests only, with the patterns of differences not clearly interpretable, since they varied for each subtest; and (d) on the Frostig test, the groups differed on four of the subtests and on total score (they were not different on figure-ground discrimination), with the four groups always ordered from highest to lowest as Package, TV-HV, TV-only, and outside control (Bertram, Hines, & MacDonald, 1971).

The overall set of results was similar for each year of the program, lending support to the overall conclusion that participation in more components of the program resulted in greater immediate effects upon the children's cognitive development. The importance of having within-community (TV-only) and outside control groups was also evident, showing that exposure to TV alone resulted in a wide range of immediate cognitive gains.

Children's Curiosity and Social Development

To measure children's gains in other areas, special situations were arranged in which their behavior could be observed directly. In the first of these, a small room was furnished with familiar children's toys, along with an unusual device that the children could manipulate to produce varied lighting and sound effects. A random sample of children from the three within-community groups (Package, TV-HV, and TV-only) was selected for observation. Each child, accompanied by his or her parent, entered the room; no one else was present. The amount of time spent interacting with the various objects was recorded for 15 minutes, and the percentage of time spent with the unfamiliar device was used to estimate the child's curiosity or urge to learn. The Package children, by this index, showed the greatest curiosity; the TV-HV children manifested more curiosity than the TV-only group. A sex difference also appeared, with boys displaying significantly more curiosity (Bertram, Hines, & MacDonald, 1971).

Immediate program effects upon social interaction were analyzed for a random sample of children from the same three groups by systematically coding their social behavior from videotaped recordings. Recordings were made of groups of from two to four children manipulating a battery-operated train and other play materials. The Package group initiated more constructive statements than TV-HV, who in turn surpassed TV-only. The Package group showed the most enthusiasm and was the least inclined to withdraw from the task or to become distracted, whereas the TV-HV children were least inclined to stop working but were most likely to become distracted; TV-only children tended to withdraw from the group, either to work alone and/or for security. TV-only children met antagonism with antagonism and often initiated antagonistic behavior. The TV-HV children appeared to be more helpful than the Package children.

The preceding group differences tended in general to follow the pattern, from greatest to least social skills: Package, TV-HV, TV-only (Bertram, Hines, & MacDonald, 1971). These findings generally support the expectation that the group experience would facilitate social skills development in these children. Contact with the home visitor also had a clear effect on social skill development.

Effects on "At-Risk" Children

Some recent reanalyses have been made of the original HOPE data by dividing children into groups of differing ability level, based on their average PPVT scores from two separate administrations. The sample was partitioned into three groups, according to the following ability ranges: below average (BA), IQ 91.5 and below; lower average (LA), IQ 92–102.5; and higher average (HA), IQ 103 and above. The first of these groups, BA, was considered an "at-risk" group for later poor school performance. Therefore, the general question raised in the following analyses was how these at-risk children did in the HOPE experiment in comparison to the LA and HA groups (Gotts, 1981).

The comparisons were made for the three ability levels (G), the measurement occasions (T) (pre-test scores versus post-test scores), and their interactions (G × T). To make the results applicable to the entire experiment, the BA, LA, and HA groups were drawn at random in balanced proportions from the Package, TV-HV and TV-only groups. That is, the BA, LA, and HA groups contained proportionalized numbers of children from all three treatments. The resultant findings were required to hold up, therefore, for a composite of all treatments. In this type of analysis, the interaction term (G × T) is of special interest, because it reveals the extent to which the at-risk group's (BA) performance from pre-test to post-test parallels that of the other groups (LA and HA).

For the Frostig test total scores, the (G × T) interaction was nonsignificant ($F = .110$, $p = .89$, $df = 2,104$); for the ITPA, (G × T) was nonsignificant ($F = .740$, $p = .51$, $df = 2,104$); for the PPVT, (G × T) was nonsignificant ($F = .420$, $p = .66$, $df = 2,104$); and for the APT, (G × T) was significant ($F = 3.290$, $p = .04$, $df = 2,104$). The findings for the Frostig test, ITPA, and PPVT all suggest that the at-risk BA group of children made pre-test to post-test gains that paralleled those of the LA and HA groups. The HOPE experiment seems, therefore, to have stabilized the BA children relative to their more mentally favored agemates, thereby reducing their at-risk status. Only on the APT was this pattern of findings not supported. For the APT, the BA and LA groups had completely parallel gain lines, but the HA group gained at a significantly more rapid rate in conceptual skills than did either of the other groups (Gotts, 1981).

ENDURING PROGRAM EFFECTS: LONG-TERM FOLLOW-UP

As was noted earlier, AEL is now in the process of performing a comprehensive follow-up study of children and parents from the original HOPE experiment. The results will be reported over the next several years; it will take that long because of the study's scope and the amount of data to be analyzed. Only the most initial findings are available at this time.

Effect on Families

AEL has developed a measure of parental "generativity" (Gotts & Paul, 1979) based on the theory of Erik Erikson (1963) as one procedure for examining possible enduring effects of the HOPE treatment. The measure's internal consistency has been checked with a validation sample (Gotts, 1980) and found to be acceptable (alpha = .83). Its validity appears to be high, in terms of its ability to differentiate between the parents of coping and noncoping children whose status was determined from judgments made by their teachers (Gotts, 1976). That is, within the validation sample, low-generativity parents had 10 noncoping and 6 coping children and high-generativity parents had 3 noncoping and 11 coping children. The chi-square value associated with this distribution is 5.129 ($p < .05$). Parental generativity, measured when the children were in secondary school, was correlated with their grade point averages for grades 1 through 4. All these correlations were significant and positive. Parents higher in generativity also expressed greater current satisfaction ($r = .51$, $p < .01$) in their children's school performance (Gotts, 1980).

A very preliminary analysis suggested that parents who received home visitation (Package and TV-HV) are higher in generativity than those whose children received TV only. This portion of the follow-up study, however, is not sufficiently complete to permit us to report these findings with confidence; they must await a later report.

Effects on Children's School Performance

These results also are preliminary ones, based on single data points only (e.g., grades in grade 1 or grade 2). Subsequent analyses of children's school performance will be accomplished by comparing, for example, slopes and mean levels that summarize each child's school record for grades 1 through 5, inclusive.

In the preliminary findings, student grade point averages of home-visited children (Package and TV-HV) were compared with those of children who did not receive home visitation (TV-only). These groups differed significantly at grade 1 ($F = 5.097$, $p = .025$) and grade 2 ($F = 5.831$, $p = .017$), with the former group receiving higher grades. For grades 3 and following, school grades were not significantly different between these comparison groups.

In another comparison of the home-visited children with the TV-only group, matched samples of 80 of the former group and 40 of the latter group were included. Between grades 1 and 9, only 4 of the former group of children repeated a grade, whereas 10 of the TV-only children were retained in grade. The chi-square value associated with this difference is 10.350 ($p < .01$). Home visitation seems, thus, to have reduced the rate of retention in grade from about 25% (TV-only) to 5% by the addition of home visitation. It is worth noting that there was a very low use of special education in these rural schools in the early 1970s. Retention in grade appears to have been used in place of special education.

Effects on Children's Social and Emotional Adjustment

Findings from the *School Behavior Checklist* (Gotts, 1976), unlike those mentioned in the two preceding sections, have reached a final stage of analysis. The following results can, accordingly, be viewed with considerable confidence as reflecting some of the ultimate conclusions of the HOPE follow-up study.

Home-visited children were significantly lower ($M = 1.66$) on personal disorganization than TV-only children ($M = 3.28$) ($F = 4.580$, $p = .034$). TV-only children had more symptoms of depression ($M = 1.21$) than home-visited children ($M = .104$) ($F = 6.104$, $p = .016$).

An epidemiological model of analysis can be used when considering the frequencies of coping (i.e., those who are identified by teachers as cooperative, responsible, etc.) and noncoping children in these groups. Using this approach, 62 (28%) of the home-visited and 33 (40%) of the TV-only children would be classified as noncoping, while 159 (72%) and 50 (60%), respectively, would be classified as coping. This overall distribution has a chi-square value of 3.847 ($p = .05$), suggesting that the home-oriented portion of the treatment resulted in an absolute reduction of mild behavior disorders of about 12%. This represents a reduction in the incidence rate of 12/40 or about 30% (Gotts, 1980).

Unanswered Questions

Other questions remain to be explored using measures that are still being coded from the HOPE follow-up study. For example, the Tasks of Emotional Development (TED) Test (Cohen & Weil, 1975) has been administered to all the children in the sample. The TED Test will permit us to make comparisons of home-visited and TV-only groups on several important dimensions of social and emotional development. The TED scores will, also, provide sensitive comparisons between parents who are high and low in generativity. It will be evident, then, that the HOPE follow-up study will eventually yield additional answers to vital questions regarding the long-term effects of this home-based intervention with rural families.

REPLICATION PHASE AND KINDERGARTEN COMPARISON

The question of how generalizable the HOPE approach is to other community settings can be examined by reviewing some additional studies performed from 1970 to 1973.

Selection of Sites

A kindergarten comparison study was performed concurrently with the final year (1970/1971) of the HOPE experiment. Two half-day kindergartens were in operation that year within the "Around the Bend" viewing area. A comparison was made between them and the other HOPE experiment groups (Bertram, Hines, & MacDonald, 1971).

For the replication studies, rural sites were selected in the mountainous areas of Virginia, Alabama, Tennessee, Ohio, and another part of West Virginia between 1971 and 1973. One of the reports of this work is available from ERIC (Alford & Hines, 1972). All of these sites were selected because they appeared to represent field conditions similar to those that had prompted AEL to design HOPE. They were physically isolated communities without facilities to support preschool programs and they were communities in which most daytime child care took place in nuclear or extended families.

Implementation Requirements and Process

The kindergarten comparison study was implemented by simply selecting already operating kindergartens (i.e., both located in more urbanized areas of the HOPE experiment site) and comparing them to the HOPE experiment groups.

For the HOPE replication phase, implementation requirements and processes were described in the first of the seven HOPE manuals (Alford, 1972), which provided the *Program Overview and Requirements*. The reader is referred to that document for details. Suffice it here to say that "Around the Bend" served as the television series; home visitors were trained locally to function under a field director at each site; and either mobile classrooms were purchased and used or suitable facilities were otherwise located. AEL continued to be the major curriculum resource center and source of training and technical assistance.

Results

Evaluation data gathered for the kindergarten comparison study focused on the APT. The socioeconomic status of the kindergarten group was somewhat higher than that of the HOPE groups, probably because of the more urbanized settings in which the two kindergartens were located. It will also be recalled that, like the TV-only group, the kindergarten children had access to the "Around the Bend" broadcast. Since the kindergarten children were all five-year-olds, comparisons with HOPE children were limited to those of the same chronological age.

The Package group in HOPE outperformed the outside control group on all three parts of the APT, whereas the kindergarten group outperformed the control group on only one part of the APT. The Package children also excelled over the kindergarten children on the two remaining parts of the APT. The TV-HV group performed slightly above the kindergarten group (nonsignificant) on the same two APT subtests on which the Package group exceeded the kindergarten group; on the third APT subtest, the TV-HV outperformed the kindergarten group. The TV-only group did not differ from the kindergarten group (Bertram, 1971).

In the several initial replication sites, generally only the APT was used as an outcome measure. Comparisons were, therefore, limited to conceptual development. In these sites children were provided the Package version of HOPE. Based on an operational test in 1971/1972 at seven sites in four states, HOPE was found to be replicable in quite varied rural locations, with program results similar (i.e., on the APT) to those obtained in the original experiment (Alford & Hines, 1972). Three new demonstration sites were added in 1972/1973, including the first site in Alabama. Each evaluation was conducted independently and differently at this stage, and in each instance the inference was drawn that HOPE was a workable program. Thus, HOPE was replicated successfully in 10 sites in five states from 1971 to 1973.

Summary of Study's Scope and Effects

The HOPE experiment was and remains a landmark study of home-oriented preschool intervention as primary prevention. The study's unique character consisted of: (a) a well-defined intervention directed toward serving (b) rural families of preschool children (c) without regard to family income level or restriction to particular segments of the rural population and with (d) families being representatively included and randomly assigned to conditions and (e) the children's progress being comprehensively evaluated in terms of the intervention's objectives. The experiment was, moreover, subsequently replicated in additional rural communities in five states.

As befits the original experiment, an unusually comprehensive long-term follow-up study is now being completed. Ultimately, enduring effects of the intervention will be analyzed for parents, child participants, and their younger siblings. Many of the data remain to be examined. It is clear nonetheless, from the varied effects studied thus far, that this relatively circumscribed intervention has had far-reaching effects upon the HOPE children.

The HOPE process of early intervention has been made widely available by the commercial publication of the materials required to operate each program component. Collectively these materials are called "Aids to Early Learning." Their usability and effectiveness were evaluated in typical early-childhood program settings in 14 Atlantic, Appalachian, midwestern, and western states in 1976/1977 (Gotts, 1979).

Implications for Working with Rural Parents

The first group of implications concerning the interaction between psychologists and rural parents relates to the ecology of rural communities. As was indicated earlier, although these communities have limited funds and facilities, they have the asset of the extended family. Not only has the AEL's experience attested to the efficacy of its multicomponents approach; the entire experience of the national Home Start option, within Head Start, is reassuring regarding the appropriateness of some combinations of these intervention methods. The special contribution of daily television to this mix can be inferred, however, only from the HOPE experiment and its replications. These methods represent cost-effective ways of intervening in rural areas.

A second group of implications relates to the danger of creating damaging social mythologies about people. Unlike HOPE, Head Start and nearly all other early interventions have singled out only the children of low-income families for services. This approach is based on the 1960's "cultural disadvantage" myth that only the children of poor families need or benefit from such services and that all poor children do need special services. The economic cutting points typically used for admission to such programs exclude from participation many children of the working poor, as well as lower middle-class and middle-class children. Moreover, such programs and their participants become strongly associated in the public's mind with poverty—thus serving to reinforce label-ing and to further the process of stigmatizing both program and partici-pant with an aura of incompetence and inferiority. This process ulti-mately results in the segregation of those who deserve the opportunity to become socially integrated before they tackle their transition into formal schooling.

HOPE, on the other hand, sought to include together all rural chil-dren who would subsequently enter the same local school—this was done irrespective of family socioeconomic status. In this manner the process of social integration was encouraged; children did not need to be labeled as poor in order to receive services; and the process of stigmatiz-ing those served was avoided. Judging from the results discussed earlier (Gotts, 1981), this approach furthered the competence of children of all ability levels and was especially effective in preventing the usually ob-served progressive erosion of tested competence in children who were initially at low levels of ability. It may further be assumed—which our observation suggests is the case—that the self-esteem needs of rural children and parents do not differ from those of others from different life circumstances. Thus, though they may be poor, they would prefer not to be related to as "poor." They value self-respect and want to be known and related to as individuals. In this connection, the use of trained, local paraprofessionals as home visitors has much to commend it. Our experi-ence suggests that local paraprofessionals can readily establish relation-ships with parents that focus on the individual needs of their children and of themselves. When, on the other hand, an outside professional enters a rural home, a host of other issues is likely to be introduced, some of which require both the client and the professional to work through the issue of their differential social status.

A third group of implications arises from the scarcity of services in rural areas. The needs of nonurban communities are not only different, they are greater than those of urban areas, judging by a number of indicators (Tamblyn, 1973). Median income is lower, participation in any kind of preschool education is lower, education level of adults is lower, substandard housing is more prevalent, and the incidence of disable-ment among heads of household is higher. Poor transportation is an endemic problem that hinders reception of services of all kinds. Poor health care, high infant-mortality rates, and chronic disability are harsh realities that directly affect both access to and effectiveness of any part of parenting services. All of this reminds one of the familiar complaint about "going out to drain the swamp, only to find you're up to your elbows in alligators." From these facts it is evident that large quantities of traditional services can be poured into a rural slum with little notice-able impact. It is only by learning to build upon the "hidden" resources there that one can make headway. The resources that HOPE sought to develop were family strengths, community cohesiveness fostered by parent and paraprofessional working together, and the capacities of rural people to recognize and appreciate the significance of small tokens of progress evidenced in their children's development. HOPE was delivered administratively on a multicounty basis and was tied to what is the strongest local resource in most rural communities—the local school system. In this manner, existing resources were brought to bear and no major new infusion of resources was attempted.

ACKNOWLEDGMENTS

I am grateful to Elizabeth Marzo for her assistance in copyediting.

REFERENCES

Alford, R. W. *Home-oriented preschool education. Program overview and requirements.* Charleston, W.Va.: Appalachia Educational Laboratory, 1972. (ERIC Document Reproduction Service No. ED 072 843)

Alford, R. W., & Hines, B. W. *Demonstration of home-oriented preschool education program. Final Report.* Charleston, W.Va.: Appalachia Educational Laboratory, 1972. (ERIC Document Reproduction Service No. ED 069 391)

Bertram, C. L. *A comparison of parents' attitudes toward AEL's AROUND THE BEND and other children's television programs.* Charleston, W.Va.: Appalachia Educational Laboratory, 1970. (ERIC Document Reproduction Service No. ED 052 842)

Bertram, C. L. *A comparison of AEL's preschool education program with standard kindergarten programs.* Charleston, W.Va.: Appalachia Educational Laboratory, 1971. (ERIC Document Reproduction Service No. ED 062 023)

Bertram, C. L. *Social and educational characteristics of rural Appalachian preschool children* (Technical Report No. 57). Charleston, W.Va.: Appalachia Educational Laboratory, 1975. (ERIC Document Reproduction No. ED 127 028)

Bertram, C., & MacDonald, R. *Demographic and socioeconomic data of the Beckley, W.Va., area and 1968–1971 development costs of AEL's preschool education field study.* Charleston, W.Va.: Appalachia Educational Laboratory, 1971. (ERIC Document Reproduction Service No. ED 062 049)

Bertram, C. L., Hines, B. W., & MacDonald, R. *Summative evaluation of the Appalachia preschool education program.* Charleston, W.Va.: Appalachia Educational Laboratory, 1971. (ERIC Document Reproduction Service No. ED 062 024)

Brown, J. S., & Schwarzweller, H. K. The Appalachian family. In J. D. Photiadis & H. K. Schwarzweller (Eds.), *Change in rural Appalachia.* Philadelphia: University of Pennsylvania, 1970.

Cohen, H., & Weil, G. R. *Tasks of emotional development test manual.* Brookline, Mass.: TED Associates, 1975.

Erikson, E. H. *Childhood and society* (2nd ed.). New York: Norton, 1963.

Gotts, E. E. *School behavior checklist (individual).* In O. G. Johnson, *Tests and measurements in child development: Handbook II* (Vol. 1). San Francisco: Jossey-Bass, 1976.

Gotts, E. E. *"Aids to early learning" technical manual. Design, development and validation of an empirically-based curriculum.* Miami, Fla.: Educational Communications, 1979.

Gotts, E. E. Long-term effects of a home-oriented preschool program. *Childhood Education*, 1980, *56*, 228–234.

Gotts, E. E. The training of intelligence as a component of early interventions: Past, present and future. *Journal of Special Education*, 1981, *15*, 257–268.

Gotts, E. E., & Higginbotham, L. A. The Appalachian child. *Children in Comtemporary Society*, 1980, *13*(2), 43–48.

Gotts, E. E., & Paul, K. *Manual for rating indirect parent interview*. Charleston, W.Va.: Appalachia Educational Laboratory, 1979.

Gotts, E. E., Spriggs, A. M., & Sattes, B. D. *Review of major programs and activities in parenting*. Charleston, W.Va.: Appalachia Educational Laboratory, 1979.

Hansen, J. C., & Stevic, R. R. *Appalachian students and guidance*. Boston: Houghton Mifflin, 1971.

Klaus, R. A., & Gray, S. W. The early training project for disadvantaged children: A report after five years. *Monographs of the Society for Research in Child Development*, 1968, *33* (4, Serial No. 120).

Looff, D. H. *Appalachia's children: The challenge of mental health*. Lexington: University of Kentucky Press, 1971.

Miller, G. L. *Analysis of children's reactions to AEL's preschool television program*. Charleston, W.Va.: Appalachia Educational Laboratory, 1970. (ERIC Document Reproduction Service No. ED 052 841)

Photiadis, J. D. *The changing rural Appalachian community and low income family: Implications for community development*. Morgantown: Office of Research and Development, Center for Extension and Continuing Education, West Virginia University, 1980.

Shively, J. E., Bertram, C. L., & Hines, B. W. *Four field studies of Appalachian parents of young children*. Charleston, W.Va.: Appalachia Educational Laboratory, 1975. (ERIC Document Reproduction Service No. ED 127 027)

Tamblyn, L. R. *Inequality: A portrait of rural America*. Washington, D.C.: Rural Education Association, 1973.

16

Community Psychology and Rural Legal Systems

GARY B. MELTON

In recent years increasing attention has been given to the potential contributions of psychology to the legal system. In addition to traditional problems of forensic evaluations (Bonnie & Slobogin, 1980; Poythress, 1979) and of delivery of clinical services in the correctional system (Brodsky, 1972), psychologists have become more involved in research and consultation on general questions of legal policy (Loftus & Monahan, 1980; Tanke & Tanke, 1979). Psychologists have been involved in the study of such diverse problems as: bail reform (Nietzel & Dade, 1973); children's competency to consent to various procedures (Melton, 1981; Melton, Koocher, & Saks, in press; Saks, 1978); reliability of eyewitness testimony (Loftus, 1979); prediction of dangerousness (Monahan, 1976b), and effects of jury size (Saks, 1977).

Additionally, community psychologists have recognized a number of ways in which nontraditional services can be delivered to legal systems. Among the topics of consultation and intervention reported in the literature have been: police personnel selection (Cohen & Chaiken, 1975; McDonough & Monahan, 1975); police crisis intervention, especially in response to calls concerning domestic violence (Bard, 1969, 1971; Bard & Berkowitz, 1967; Driscoll, Meyer, & Schanie, 1973; Liebman & Schwartz, 1973); juvenile diversion and advocacy (Davidson, 1975, 1982; Davidson & Rapp, 1976), and restructuring of juvenile correctional facilities (Cohen & Filipczak, 1971; Reppucci, 1973).

GARY B. MELTON • Department of Psychology, University of Nebraska, Lincoln, Nebraska 68588.

One commonality of these model projects is that they have been undertaken almost exclusively in large urban areas (see, e.g., projects reported in Monahan, 1976a). For example, Bard's (Bard, 1969, 1971; Bard & Berkowitz, 1967) work in New York City has served as the model for police consultation and for training in mediation and dispute resolution (Bard, Cohen, & Touster, 1979). However, community psychologists may actually have more opportunity to use police consultation to affect the quality of life substantially in rural communities, where law-enforcement officers typically have less training but broader and more informal responsibilities. The purpose of this chapter is to review particular needs of rural legal systems and their implications for community-psychology research and practice.

PROBLEMS OF RURAL JUDICIAL ADMINISTRATION

As described by Edgerton (Chapter 13) and Heyman (Chapter 12) elsewhere in this volume, there are numerous obstacles to effective and efficient delivery of human services in rural communities. Legal systems are not immune to these problems but they take on particular significance in the context of the unique demands of legal systems.

Familiarity

For example, the familiarity common in small communities where "everyone knows everyone else," may generally affect traditional professional roles based on some measure of social distance. As Heyman (Chapter 12) noted, mental health professionals may be uncomfortable when professional relationships inevitably overlap with social acquaintances. In the legal system, however, this familiarity has particularly striking consequences. The issue is not just one of professional role-strain, but one of a violation of the usual assumptions of judicial disinterest as a basis for equitable decision making:

> Community familiarity may . . . require a judge to tread a fine line between individualized treatment and conflict of interest. Urban judges automatically disqualify themselves when a litigant or criminal defendant whom they know appears before them. For rural judges to follow such practice would create significant problems of judicial assignment. One rural judge remembers disqualifying himself only once during his thirteen years on the bench— when the defendant was accused of hitting the judge's car. (Stott, Fetter, & Crites, 1977, p. 5)

Similarly, selection of an unbiased jury may be difficult, although community knowledge may at least make the biases clear:

> As in the case of judges, jurors are normally disqualified when they are personally acquainted with one of the litigants. Following this practice in rural areas where everyone knows everyone else would be highly impractical. Consequently, voir dire and the attorney's personal acquaintance with the community often simplify the identification of philosophical or religious biases which could adversely affect the case. For example, religious conservatism in some rural areas may prohibit drinking alcohol; in a drunkenness case, attorneys may disqualify a prospective juror who is known to have such beliefs. (Stott *et al.*, 1977, p. 5)

There are other more subtle effects of familiarity on legal-system functioning. As will be discussed in detail later in this chapter, there is some reason to believe that dispute processing tends to be more informal in small, relatively homogeneous communities. Citizens may be less likely to define disputes as legal problems if the conflicts are with neighbors with whom they have to interact regularly.

Professional Recruitment and Training

The difficulties in recruitment, retention, and continuing education and training of professionals in isolated areas are well known. These problems are again not unique to the legal system, but they do have particular ramifications in rural courts. Justice requires that individuals approaching the bar with the same fact situations receive essentially the same resolutions (Rawls, 1971). Such equality is unlikely to occur if the attorneys and the judge lack up-to-date knowledge of the law or if attorneys are in fact often unavailable.

Several factors make this lack of legal expertise more common in rural areas. First, in part because attorneys are often less available in rural areas (see, e.g., Note, 1970), lower-court judgeships are often filled by nonlawyers. According to the Supreme Court,[1] lay judges may constitutionally hear and decide cases, provided that the right to a trial *de novo* before a law-trained judge is preserved. This practice is endemic to rural courts, as indicated by a study by the National Center for State Courts (Stott *et al.*, 1977):

> Statutes in six states require all judges to be attorneys, but most other states have lay judges. In many rural states, it is very difficult to recruit lawyers for the lower court judgeships. In Montana, for example, only about five of over 200 justices of the peace and city judges are lawyers, and they are generally in the larger cities of Billings and Great Falls. In the neighboring state of Wyoming, the statutes encourage filling the justice of the peace and municipal judge positions with lawyers. For these elective offices, only lawyers may run. If no lawyer files, however, the city or county government can appoint a

---

[1] *North v. Russell*, 427 U.S. 378 (1975).

nonlawyer from those who apply. This system allows any lawyer, no matter
how inexperienced, to fill the position over any lay person. In spite of the
system, only about half of the 104 judges are lawyers. (p. 15)

Furthermore, provision of counsel in misdemeanor cases is still far
from routine in many courts (Alfini & Doan, 1977; see Table 1). Thus, the
probability of the proceeding being held and decided according to law is
still further reduced. These differences between urban and rural courts
are not trivial ones. Compared to law-trained judges, lay judges are
more likely to perceive police as better witnesses and better investigators
and the prosecution as better prepared, more efficient, and more experienced (Ryan & Guterman, 1977). Thus, lay judges are more likely to rely
on the prosecution's evidence. Also, presumably because of the relative
absence of attorneys, rural misdemeanor courts are much more likely
than more urban courts to dispose of cases at the initial appearance
(Alfini & Doan, 1977). There is strong evidence that the lack of attorneys
in rural areas has a marked effect on the administration of justice.

Second, because rural courts tend to be "low volume," salaries of
judges are lower for nonmetropolitan courts in 13 states (Stott *et al.*,
1977). Even if monetary reward is equal to metropolitan courts, other
expected trappings of the office are more likely to be lacking in rural
areas. Frequently rural judges have no secretary or other assistants, and
physical facilities may be poor. Consequently, even the prestige that
often attracts qualified judges may be absent.

Third, even if qualified candidates are attracted, they may have
problems remaining acquainted with changes in the law. Besides the
relative lack of informal means of dissemination through professional
networks, formal dissemination of case law may be impaired by the lack
of legal library materials. A description of legal practice in a rural are of
southeastern Colorado included an observation that there was no copy
of the *Federal Supplement* or the *Federal Reporter* in the county (Pearson,

TABLE 1. FREQUENCY OF ATTORNEY PRESENCE AT DISPOSITION
BY COMMUNITY SIZE[a]

Presence of attorney (always or frequently)	Big city	Suburban & medium-sized city	Small city & rural
Prosecuting attorney	100%	95%	81%
Defense attorney (at trial)	97%	96%	83%
Defense attorney (upon plea of guilty)	94%	69%	45%

[a]From "A New Perspective on State Misdemeanor Courts" by J. J. Alfini and R. Doan, *Judicature*, 1977,
60, p. 430. Copyright 1977 by Judicature. Reprinted by permission.

1977). It has been estimated that the *Supreme Court Reports* is available only in Cooper, Laramie, and Cheyenne in Wyoming and in Fargo, Bismarck, Minot, and Dickinson in North Dakota (Wasby, 1976). Specialized materials, such as the *Criminal Law Reporter*, are also frequently relatively inaccessible to the rural bar and law enforcement personnel.

Furthermore, opportunities for learning through practice are often limited in rural communities. Both police and trial lawyers often are motivated to learn new developments in criminal law because of the need to be clear about the law relevant to a major case (Wasby, 1976). Such cases are uncommon in rural areas. Furthermore, there is rarely specialization of practice, so opportunities for acquisition of knowledge through repeated experience with a particular area of the law may be unavailable. In short, except for relatively cosmopolitan rural areas (like western Massachusetts) which are near metropolitan areas, new law is often slow to filter down to rural legal systems.

Lack of Social Services

Court-related social services, such as probation, substance abuse, victim assistance, and diversion programs, are frequently missing in rural communities. The typically low tax base and diseconomies of scale combine to make such services seem fiscally unrealistic to many rural governments, even if professionals could be recruited to provide them. Furthermore, practical issues aside, such services conflict with the political and social conservatism common in many rural areas. Findings of a survey of judges and other court personnel in Montana, North Dakota, South Dakota, and Wyoming are exemplary:

> The surveys of judges and other court personnel in this project showed an appreciation of the importance of social services, but frequently acceptance was mixed with a reluctance to implement the programs too quickly or too widely. Judges in North Dakota and South Dakota, for example, overwhelmingly declared that adequate probation services, juvenile care, alcohol and drug programs, and mental health programs were very important; yet with the exception of alcohol treatment programs, they consistently rated their current services in these areas as adequate or better. They did so despite the facts that separate juvenile holding facilities exist in only a few counties and that not every jurisdiction has fully established programs for diversion, counseling, and several other services. (Stott *et al.*, 1977, pp. 53–54)

Wasby's (1976) account of community resistance to professionalization of police departments in southern Illinois is similar:

> While a 1973 article in an area newspaper carried the headline "Mayberry RFD is gone forever," shortly afterwards an area police chief was fired partly for attending junior college law enforcement classes four nights a week and thus not being available to the town although other officers were on duty,

and another chief was asked to resign because, in the words of the town mayor, "He's just got too many ideas. This is a little town. We feel like we can't do these things"— which included hiring an additional full-time patrolman and a clerk-typist, purchasing an additional patrol car, and establishing a formal training program for the department's officers. (p. 16)

It should be noted that while presenting obvious problems, this dearth of established services in rural areas may have some elements of a blessing in disguise as well (see Heyman, Chapter 12). Because social-services bureaucracies are less likely to be entrenched, there may be more opportunities for using community resources in innovative service delivery than in urban areas where services are more likely to be professional, circumscribed, and discipline- rather than problem-centered. An example of this innovative use of resources is Libertoff's (1979) development of a network of indigenous helpers in rural Vermont to provide temporary shelter and assistance to runaway youth. Similarly, a rural judge in Idaho enlisted old people in the community to serve as volunteer probation officers for local juvenile offenders (Tate, 1971). Several similar rural court programs are described, without evaluation, in a Law Enforcement Assistance Administration booklet (Office of Juvenile Justice and Delinquency Prevention, 1979).

Summary

In summary, there are formidable obstacles to effective judicial and police administration in many rural areas. Many of these obstacles, such as problems of professional recruitment and retention and of the dearth of social-service supports, are not specific to legal systems. However, these obstacles are particularly acute in the legal system because fairness mandates a reasonably uniform system of justice. Consequently, attention might well be placed on ways in which the legal system can be shaped to match the rural ecology without sacrificing due process. The remainder of this chapter will be focused on this topic with attention to the potential contributions of psychologists. Discussion will be centered first on criminal issues and then on primarily civil problems.

PATTERNS OF RURAL CRIME

The stereotypical image of rural America is that it is practically crime-free, the part of our country where people are unafraid to leave doors unlocked and the most serious crime is an occasional shoplifting by a wayward youngster of a piece of candy from the general store.

While there is still a grain of truth in this stereotype, the image is becoming increasingly invalid. Crime in rural areas is still less violent and less prevalent than in more urbanized areas, but this discrepancy is narrowing rapidly. According to FBI statistics, reported crime is three times higher in Standard Metropolitan Statistical Areas than in rural areas. However, violent crime is increasing at a much faster rate in rural than in urban areas (Fischer, 1980; Smith & Donnermeyer, 1979).

At least part of this increase is attributable to increased accessibility of rural areas. For example, 60% of the persons arrested in rural areas of Ohio were actually urban residents (Phillips, 1976). Similarly, in Botetourt County, a rural, mountainous county of Virginia, 43% of the persons arrested for felonies were residents of the urban areas of the Roanoke Valley, easily accessible by interstate highways. The sheriff of rural Franklin County, near Roanoke, reported that over half of the county's solved crimes were committed by Roanoke residents (Associated Press, 1980). The ease of access to rural counties means that offenders can enter an area in which law-enforcement personnel are likely to be very dispersed and then make a quick getaway. The increased ease of access also works to make rural residents more vulnerable to urban crime. Smith and Donnermeyer (1979) found that about 40% of victimizations reported by residents of a rural county in Indiana happened outside the county, generally in a medium-sized city that serves as a trading center for the county.

Several recent studies of victimization rates (as opposed to rates of reported crime) have shed some light on the character of rural crime. Surveys have been conducted in rural areas of Illinois (Burdge, Kelly, Schweitzer, Keasler, & Russelmann, 1978), Indiana (Smith & Donnermeyer, 1979), Ohio (Phillips & Wurschmidt, 1979), and the nation as a whole (Gibbs, 1979). Data from the rural victimization studies are laregly supportive of police statistics and are consistent across jurisdictions, at least within the Midwest where most of the research has been conducted. Rural people report fewer instances of victimization than either urban or suburban residents. These differences are particularly striking for violent crimes. Crimes against the person are much less common in rural areas, and those violent crimes that do occur are more likely to be simple assaults.

According to victim surveys, the crime that does occur consists largely of minor property offenses: most commonly, vandalism and secondarily, theft. (The order is reversed in reported crimes.) Not surprisingly, therefore, offenders in rural areas tend to be juvenile males (Phillips, 1976). Juveniles accounted for about 60% of arrests for rural vandalism, and the ratio of males to females arrested for rural vandalism was 14:1, according to 1973 FBI statistics (Phillips & Bartlett, 1976). Indicative of the relatively petty, unorganized nature of most rural crime was the lack of *any* auto theft reported by Smith and Donnermeyer's (1979) Benton County, Indiana, sample.[2]

Phillips and Bartlett (1976) administered a questionnaire to high-school sophomores in three rural areas of Ohio to ascertain more specifically the circumstances under which vandalism occurs. Fifty-two percent (37% of girls and 68% of boys) reported that they have committed one or more acts of vandalism. Most of these students were repeat offenders. The vandalism was almost always committed in groups (93%) as a leisure-time activity. Acts of vandalism commonly occurred on the weekends (59%) and were often accompanied by drinking alcoholic beverages (39% of group offenses). Nearly three-fourths of the students admitting a history of vandalism reported that they did not perceive their destructive behavior as criminal. They most commonly reported that they engaged in vandalism for fun, as a part of a game, or as a part of a contest of skills (60%).

While giving a good indication of the character of rural vandalism, Phillips and Bartlett's data provide little suggestion as to reasons *why* the large increase of reported incidents has occurred. Phillips and Bartlett speculated that a number of social factors have contributed to this increase. First, greater affluence may have resulted in decreased subjective value of property. Second, there may have been a shift from a "community of customs" to a "community of laws." Citizens may be more prone to report "a 'customary prank' of putting corn shocks in the road at Halloween" (p. 3). More generally,

> modern transportation, consolidation of schools, an increasing number of one spouse households [a good predictor of whether a given youngster will engage in vandalism], the declining sense of belonging to a community, and less defined roles for adolescents, perhaps in part, explain the rising phenomenon of vandalism in rural areas. (p. 3)

These hypotheses are worthy of empirical tests through, for example, ecological investigations of the effects of community integration (cf. Garbarino & Sherman, 1980) on vandalism rates. Such data would be helpful in determining foci for preventive interventions.

In addition to studying the circumstances of rural crime through the self-reports of offenders, victim surveys can also illuminate correlates of offenses. In a study of factors in burglary, theft, and vandalism in rural

---

[2]Automobile theft is often considered to be a "professional" crime, particularly when the rate of automobile theft is very high.

Ohio, Phillips, Kreps, and Moody (1976) found only two demographic variables to differentiate victims from nonvictims at a statistically significant level. Higher income families (> $12,000 in 1975) were twice as prone to having been victims of vandalism, although not burglary or theft. Presumably they simply have more property to be destroyed. It is also conceivable that the higher income families reside in more densely populated "suburban-type" developments within rural areas. The other variable that was correlated with victimization (specifically, having property vandalized) was church membership. There were notable differences among denominations in number of property crimes, but church members generally were more subject to vandalsim than nonmembers. There is no intuitive explanation for this finding. Phillips and his associates suggested two possibilities: "it may be due to the fact that church members leave their properties unattended for longer periods of time or that the property of church members may attract acts of vandalism as an expression of vandals' frustration with community norms" (Phillips et al., 1976, p. 11).

Probably of more import for planning of interventions were environmental variables. The concept of "defensible space" (Newman, 1972) has attracted attention from urban planners and environmental psychologists. Essentially, it was derived from Newman's attempts to design urban housing projects so that territoriality and community surveillance would be enhanced. "Safe" areas would thus be created. While Newman's observations are compelling and consonant with theory and research in environmental psychology (Sommer, 1969), it is not clear how the principles that he has postulated apply specifically to areas in which there are a few people living on hundreds of acres, rather than the converse.

Phillips and his colleagues (1976) did find, however, that the physical environment appears to have some effect on the probability of victimization in rural areas. Property crimes occur less frequently when the dwelling house is the building closest to the road and when nonresidential buildings are more than 100 feet from a public road. Vandalism is also less common for residents living on rolling terrain than for those residing on flat or hilly terrain, where buildings are more likely to be easily visible. The latter finding should be viewed with caution because it may reflect regional differences within Ohio (i.e., more crime in Appalachia) rather than effects of terrain itself.

Additionally, the neighborliness and the low crime rate prevalent in rural areas may result in residents' not taking steps to prevent the crime that does occur. A survey of Farm Bureau members in Indiana found that:

(a) only 60% always locked their doors to their home at night or
    when they are away from the home for any period of time,
(b) nearly one-third left their keys in the ignition of their car, truck,
    or tractor when not in use because it was "convenient," and
(c) less than 10% of the farm operators marked or engraved their
    heavy farm machinery. (Donnermeyer, 1979, p. 5)

The impact of such laxity may not be very strong, however. Phillips and
his associates (1976) found, in fact, that always locking the doors when
one left the house was *positively* correlated with having the house bur-
glarized. Presumably people who locked their houses had some reason
to believe that their homes were at risk, perhaps because of their location or the presence of valuables. In any case, this finding is worthy of
more investigation in order to attempt to pinpoint the factors that are
significant.

To summarize, rural crime is less prevalent and less serious than in
more densely populated areas, but the crime rate is rising rapidly. Most
rural crime consists of minor property offenses committed by juveniles.
A large proportion of reported crimes, which tend to include more thefts
than simple vandalism, are committed by nonresidents of rural areas.

Implications for Community Psychology

The available research on patterns of rural crime suggests that the
content of the community psychologist's consultation to the police and
the bar probably needs to be different than in urban areas, where such
programs have typically been conducted. First, perhaps because of the
lack of "real" crime in rural areas, belief in public service is negatively
correlated with level of role conflict among rural police but not among
urban police (Regoli & Poole, 1980). Thus, consultants may be helpful in
supporting police in their "public-service" and "peace-keeping" (dispute resolution) functions, a point that will be explored further in the
next section of this chapter. Second, psychologists may be able to assist
in projects to reduce the property crime that does occur. Such prevention projects could be focused on modifying potential offenders' behavior or on community education and environmental design to reduce the
opportunities for theft and vandalism.

Given that rural crime is for the most part petty juvenile crime,
initial efforts might be focused on interventions aimed at preventing
youngsters' participation in vandalism. The prevalent notion among
rural adolescents that such behavior is recreational and noncriminal
(Phillips & Bartlett, 1976) is particularly disturbing. Perhaps the most
obvious way of attempting to change these attitudes is through educa-

tion. One such effort has been undertaken at the National Rural Crime Prevention Center at Ohio State University, where a curriculum in rural crime prevention for middle-school students was developed (Wurschmidt & Phillips, 1978). While this curriculum resulted in changes in knowledge about the law and rural crime, it did not result in changes of behavior, according to questionnaire data.[3]

Given that changes in knowledge or even attitudes may have little effect on behavior, community psychologists may be more successful in altering situations in which crime might occur. This might be attempted through consultation with architects on environmental design, although more research is necessary on the particular aspects of the rural physical environment that increase security and vulnerability.

Behavioral interventions might also be helpful. There have been several projects in urban and university communities in which shoplifting has been reduced through behavioral prompts. In ABA-design studies performed in Murfreesboro, Tennessee (McNees, Egli, Marshall, Schnelle, & Risley, 1976), reductions in shoplifting in a young women's apparel store were achieved through the use of warning signs and a procedure designed to increase the threat of detection. In the first study, five general antishoplifting signs (e.g., "shoplifting is not uplifting") resulted in a shoplifting reduction of about one-third. In the second study, warning signs on specific merchandise marked with a red star resulted in a 90% reduction in shoplifting of those items but no change in shoplifting of control merchandise.

In a third study, aimed at schoolchildren in a Nashville neighborhood (McNees, Kennon, Schnelle, Kirchner, & Thomas, 1980), visual and verbal prompts and reinforcement were used to decrease shoplifting in a convenience store. A poster was placed in the store which said:

KIDS!!! CAN YOU HELP STOP "JAWS" THE SHOPLIFTING SHARK?

When children came to the cash register, they were asked, "Have you remembered to pay for everything?" Children who answered in the affirmative were rewarded with a shark's tooth, and when children accumulated five shark's teeth they could draw a prize from a Treasure Chest. There was also a group contingency; when theft fell below a predetermined level each day, Jaws was "hooked," and children were rewarded with two shark's teeth instead of one. The overall project resulted in a shoplifting reduction of more than 50% over baseline.

Similar multiple-baseline studies of the effects of prompts in reducing theft were undertaken by Geller (1980; Geller, Koltuniak, & Shilling, in press). In one such study, theft from newspaper racks was monitored

[3]Personal communication, August 1980.

under three conditions: no sign, sign with a conscience appeal, and sign with a threat of prosecution. Both types of signs resulted in a decrease of theft. Of particular interest is the finding that these effects appear to persist as long as the signs are in place (see Figure 1).

The investigations by McNees *et al.* and Geller and his students suggest that behavioral techniques can result in significant decreases in petty theft. Furthermore, the methodology of behavior analysis can be a useful way of determining the effects of crime-prevention interventions.

Although there has been no parallel research on behavioral approaches to the prevention of vandalism, presumably the same technology would be applicable. It would be expected that prompts would have an effect in reducing vandalism. However, such interventions may be impractical in rural areas where targets of vandals may be widely dispersed and rather unpredictable. Behavioral technology might best be used in "favorite" spots, as determined by local needs assessments. Geller's newspaper-rack interventions are of particular import here be-

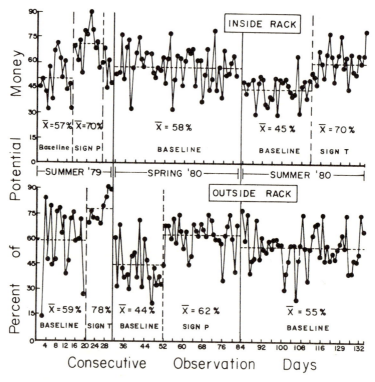

FIGURE 1. Changes in theft from newspaper racks as a result of signs involving threat of prosecution (Sign T) or appeal to conscience (Sign P). (Acknowledgment is due to E. Scott Geller for providing these data.)

cause they have involved settings without the surveillance potential of the retail stores where the other studies have been undertaken. Thus, prompts placed at relatively isolated targets of thieves and vandals may still be effective. Special reminders could also be posted or disseminated through mass media at times of the year (Halloween and early spring) when rural vandalism is most likely to occur (Phillips & Bartlett, 1976). A caveat that should be added, though, is that, because vandalism is typically a group crime, some alteration of group contingencies may also be necessary.

Behavioral technology is also potentially applicable to attempts to increase residents' use of security devices. The literature on behavioral technology in conservation of natural resources is analogous (see Geller, Chapter 18).

Finally, as discussed previously, psychological consultation may be useful in creating defensible space through environmental design and increasing or sustaining the monitoring of property through involvement with neighbors. However, the literature on these factors in rural areas is extremely sparse, and additional basic research is needed before consultation can be based on much more than intuition.

DISPUTE PROCESSING IN RURAL COMMUNITIES

The relatively low crime rate in rural areas may result from a higher level of community involvement and closer relationships with neighbors (Phillips *et al.*, 1976). This intensity and personalism of relationships may also affect the ways in which disputes are most commonly resolved. Accordingly, the range of problems encountered in the civil law in rural communities may differ in quantity and quality from urban civil disputes.

Although psychologists have given little attention to processes of resolution of disputes in rural areas, sociologists and anthropologists of law have been particularly interested in the organization of dispute processing in various cultures and settings, many of them rural. The most influential explanatory model has been Black's (1976) theory of "the behavior of law." Briefly, Black defined the law as governmental social control, which he conceptualized as a quantitative variable that varies inversely with other forms of social control. That is, the law is likely to be invoked when informal means of social control are unavailable. While there are a large number of postulates subsumed within Black's theory, two postulates are of particular importance here:

1. The relationship between law and differentiation is curvilinear.
2. Law varies directly with organization.

Thus, in Black's theory, one would expect more informal means of dispute resolution in homogeneous, relatively undeveloped, unbureaucratized societies. Furthermore, according to Black, when the law is invoked, it is likely to be invoked "centrifugally" rather than "centripetally" (i.e., toward the marginals or outsiders of the society).

Other social theoreticians have developed similar positions. Felstiner (1974) argued that the formality of methods of dispute processing could be expected to vary with level of social organization. Of particular interest here is Felstiner's observation that mediation (as opposed to adjudication) is most likely to be used widely in relatively homogeneous societies where there are shared values and experiences:

> Since successful mediation requires an outcome acceptable to the parties, the mediator cannot rely primarily on rules but must construct an outcome in the light of the social and cultural context of the dispute, the full scope of the relations between the disputants and the perspectives from which they view the dispute. Mediation then flourishes where mediators share the social and cultural experience of the disputants they serve, and where they bring to the processing of disputes an intimate and detailed knowledge of the perspectives of the disputants. (pp. 73–74)

Moreover, as Sarat and Grossman (1975) have noted, informal means of dispute processing allow a resolution of problems without the necessity of acknowledging that the relationship is in trouble, an important advantage when the disputants have frequent contact. Members of distinct subcultural groups may also prefer dispute resolution by someone with shared values and background.

Similar views have been expressed by Nader and Todd (1978) in their analysis of dispute processing in isolated societies. They noted that the interdependence and familiarity present in small, homogeneous societies results in community-based social control and a relative lack of need for formal law.

There is ample evidence from ethnographic studies for the general positions described here. In general, less complex and more isolated societies tend to use more informal means of dispute processing (Schwartz & Miller, 1964). Furthermore, when litigation is brought, it tends to be among "marginals" or against outsiders (Caudill, 1962; Todd, 1978). In such instances, the social risk of open conflict is small. Exceptions to this general principle tend to result from a breakdown of community control mechanisms, such as a disruption of the extended family (Nader & Metzger, 1963), or from the necessity of resolving disputes over control of scarce resources (Starr & Yngvesson, 1965).

Yngvesson (1978) has given a clear description of these processes in her discussion of disputes in an isolated Nova Scotian fishing village of about 300 people. Her summary of her observations is consistent with the dominant theoretical positions:

On Rock Island, disputes are focused less on *acts* than on *people. What was done* is less important than *who did it.* An act considered normal when done by a kinsman or fellow community member may generate an entirely different response when done by an "outsider." (p. 59)

Disputes with outsiders were observed to be resolved quickly and formally, often with an outside remedy agent. Disputes within the community tended to be characterized by "nonaction."

Yngvesson's observations in Nova Scotia were very similar to Caudill's (1962) findings in Appalachia, as well as to those of other ethnographers in other isolated areas (see Schwartz & Miller, 1964). However, it should be noted that the processes described thus far are probably not very applicable to rural areas that are not homogeneous (see Felstiner, 1974) and that are close to metropolitan areas. For example, in a study of court records, Friedman and Percival (1976) found little discernible difference between Alameda (urban) and San Benito (rural) counties in northern California in types, procedures, and dispositions of civil cases. Furthermore, mediation does not necessarily require homogeneity of experience (Danzig & Lowy, 1975). Nonetheless, it does appear that more informal means of dispute resolution are particularly congruent with the rural ecology, especially in relatively isolated communities where there is a high level of interdependence.

Implications for Community Psychology

To the extent to which rural communities rely particularly strongly on informal means of dispute processing, there may be considerable opportunity for psychologists to assist rural police in mediation. While the training of urban police that specializes in mediating interpersonal disputes has met with some success from the points of view of both police and citizens (Liebman & Schwartz, 1973), there has also typically been resistance by urban police to taking on such a helping role, which they perceive as detracting from their principal job of apprehending criminals (Danzig & Lowy, 1975). However, as noted previously, rural police who are satisfied with their roles *already* perceive themselves as public servants in the broadest sense (Regoli & Poole, 1980).

There may also be opportunities for similar consultation with the rural bar. Family cases are obvious ones in which some clinical skills are helpful. There are more subtle areas of potential consultation as well. For example, discussion with lawyers in a legal-aid society in Appalachia revealed that a particularly large and difficult client-group for them were middle-aged adults who were seeking disability determinations because they were simply tired of confronting a depressed economy. Rather than becoming involved in disputes with employers, these clients just ignored the points of conflict and somatized their distress.

Such a passive coping style is ubiquitous within Appalachia but less common in other rural areas (Gotts, 1980). Psychological consultation might have been useful to the attorneys in helping their clients to focus their concerns and to make use of the adversary system. Hill (1979) described one such program in which a community-psychology intern assisted a legal-aid office.

There are obvious psychological research questions suggested by the sociological/anthropological literature. It would be useful to explore rural-urban differences in interpersonal problem-solving and perception of alternative means of resolution of disputes, for both family members and nonrelatives. Baseline data on the responses of rural police to interpersonal disputes, especially family strife, would also be helpful in planning consultations.

Carefully evaluated demonstration projects in mediation in rural communities are also needed. In addition to police programs, consideration should be given to using other indigenous helpers as mediators. The Neighborhood Justice Centers that have been adopted on an experimental basis in some urban communities (Sheppard, Roehl, & Cook, 1979) might be at least as applicable to rural communities, although the impetus for such programs is less because of more manageable caseloads. In rural communities, such programs would be based on two broad substantive considerations, rather than on the practical need to reduce the courts' backlog of cases. First, the apparent amenability of rural communities to mediation suggests that adaptations of the legal system may be useful alternatives to traditional mental health services. Second, mediation techniques may be particularly helpful to rural police in dealing with interpersonal conflict. Thus, community psychologists may deliver services in rural communities both *through* and *to* the legal system by training police and others in mediation skills.

LEGAL SOCIALIZATION IN RURAL COMMUNITIES

Finally and most broadly, rural community psychologists may be interested in the law as a mobility belt, a means of empowerment of disadvantaged communities (Tapp & Levine, 1974). In that regard, it is important to socialize an understanding of one's potential as both a creator and a consumer of law and of rights as *entitlements* rather than as privileges that may be revoked by authority. A truly democratic society requires that its citizens perceive an opportunity—indeed a *right*—to be full participants in the society. However, there is ample evidence that poor people are relatively unlikely to be aware of specific civil rights or to conceptualize these rights as applicable to themselves (Melton, 1980,

1982), although the poor are arguably the segment of our society most in need of such knowledge and concepts.

There is not much direct evidence on rural-urban differences in legal knowledge and assertion of rights. Law-review studies that have shown infrequent perceptions by the rural poor of disputes as having legal dimensions (Note, 1970; Project, 1969) have not included comparison groups. Consequently, it is not clear if ruralness, independent of social class, exerts a negative influence on rights consciousness. This question is worthy of research, particularly since the literature on attitudes toward civil rights gives reason to hypothesize such an effect.

While Americans generally espouse civil liberties in the abstract (e.g., free speech), this favorable attitude often does not extend to assertion of these rights by unpopular groups (Montero, 1975; Prothro & Grigg, 1960; Wilson, 1975; Zellman, 1975) and hence does not include an understanding of rights as *universal* entitlements (Friedman, 1977). This inconsistency in attitudes is strongest in rural areas, even when education and region are held constant (see Stouffer's classic study of attitudes toward civil liberties, 1955). There are at least three possible explanations for this discrepancy. First and most simply, it may just be a correlate of a general political conservatism in rural areas that may reflect delays in the dissemination of new ideas (Rogers, 1962). Second, at least in isolated homogeneous areas, there may not be much opportunity for participation in diverse role-taking. Principled moral and legal reasoning requires exposure to conflicting ideas and experience in participation in decision making (Melton, 1982; Tapp & Levine, 1974; Zellman, 1975). Third, it is likely that deviants would "stick out" more in small communities. Minimal nonconformity to authority may provoke intolerance by the community.

Implications for Community Psychology

Regardless of the specific psychosocial dynamics underlying antilibertarian attitudes in rural communities, the existence of such attitudes suggests that disadvantaged groups in rural communities may be particularly unlikely to perceive themselves as having the right to challenge authority. This specific hypothesis and the general topic of rural-urban differences in rights consciousness are worthy of research.

If the hypothesis were confirmed, the implication would be that broad legal-educational efforts would be useful in increasing both legal knowledge and sense of efficacy (Koocher, 1979; Melton, 1982). Research on community views of civil rights might also be useful in planning community organization efforts. The literature on community organization in rural communities is virtually nil, but the task may be to

integrate a sense of efficacy with the prevailing neighborliness and cohesiveness, as has been done historically by some rural labor unions,
such as the United Farm Workers (Hoffman, 1978) and the United Mine
Workers. In any case, research on both community characteristics and
individual differences in participation in community organizations
would be useful to community psychologists (see Wandersman and
Giamartino's study in urban neighborhoods, 1980). Thus, the interaction between individual rights consciousness and community norms in
use of the legal system might be interesting to examine.

SUMMARY

Many of the obstacles to efficient and effective delivery of services
in rural legal systems are similar to other rural service-delivery problems. However, because of the impact of legal decisions on the lives of
individuals, these impediments assume particular significance in the
legal system, especially when they result in aberrations in legal procedures and standards.

In designing psychological consultation to rural legal systems, it is
important to consider that the form and content of such consultations
need to be matched to the rural ecology. For example, rural communities
may find mediation to be a particularly useful way of resolving interpersonal disputes. As noted throughout this chapter, however, the research on the psychological aspects of rural legal problems is sparse.
There are needs for both applied and basic research. Thus, there is
sufficient evidence on rural dispute processing from legal anthropology
to warrant investment in rural demonstration centers for mediation of
minor disputes, which could be the foci for careful evaluation studies.
At the same time, to enrich our understanding, we need basic research
on rural-urban differences in the use of helpers and the perception of
alternatives in resolution of disputes. Similarly, in terms of criminal
issues, enough is known about patterns of rural crime to suggest foci for
programs of prevention and police consultation, which might then be
evaluated. At the same time, though, more information is needed about
the relationship of environmental design to rural crime and about general factors leading to the striking increase in rural crime. Thus, there are
considerable opportunities for research that would enhance psychologists' contributions to delivery of services by rural legal systems.

ACKNOWLEDGMENTS

I am grateful to John Monahan and Edward Mulvey for their helpful
comments on an earlier version of this chapter.

REFERENCES

Alfini, J. J., & Doan, R. A new perspective on state misdemeanor courts. *Judicature*, 1977, *60*, 425–434.

Associated Press. Roanoke overflow crime, lack of funding burns sheriffs. *The Charlottesville Daily Progress*, April 15, 1980, p. B8.

Bard, M. Extending psychology's impact through existing community interventions. *American Psychologist*, 1969, *24*, 610–612.

Bard, M. The role of law enforcement in the helping system. *Community Mental Health Journal*, 1971, *7*, 151–160.

Bard, M., & Berkowitz, B. Training police as specialists in family crisis intervention: A community psychology action program. *Community Mental Health Journal*, 1967, *3*, 315–317.

Bard, M., Cohen, S. P., & Touster, S. *A novel training program in conflict resolution for doctoral students in law and social psychology*. Paper presented at the meeting of the American Psychology-Law Society, Baltimore, October 1979.

Black, D. *The behavior of law*. New York: Academic Press, 1976.

Bonnie, R. J., & Slobogin, C. The role of mental health professionals in the criminal process: The case for informed speculation. *Virginia Law Review*, 1980, *66*, 427–524.

Brodsky, S. L. *Psychologists in the criminal justice system*. University, Ala.: American Association of Correctional Psychologists, 1972.

Burdge, R. J., Kelly, R. M., Schweitzer, H. J., Keasler, L., & Russelmann, A. *Crime victimization in Illinois: The citizens' perspective*. Urbana-Champaign: University of Illinois, 1978.

Caudill, H. M. *Night comes to the Cumberlands*. Boston: Little, Brown, 1962.

Cohen, B., & Chaiken, J. M. *Police background characteristics and performance*. Lexington, Mass.: D. C. Heath, 1975.

Cohen, H. L., & Filipczak, J. *A new learning environment*. San Francisco: Jossey-Bass, 1971.

Danzig, R., & Lowy, M. J. Everyday disputes and mediation in the United States: A reply to Professor Felstiner. *Law and Society Review*, 1975, *10*, 675–694.

Davidson, W. S. *The diversion of juvenile delinquents: An examination of the processes and relative efficacy of child advocacy and behavioral contracting*. Unpublished doctoral dissertation, University of Illinois at Urbana-Champaign, 1975.

Davidson, W. S. Child advocacy in the juvenile court. In G. B. Melton (Ed.), *Legal reforms affecting child and youth services*. New York: Haworth Press, 1982.

Davidson, W. S., & Rapp, C. Child advocacy in the justice system. *Social Work*, 1976, *21*, 225–232.

Donnermeyer, J. G. *Community development and crime prevention for rural areas*. Paper presented at the meeting of the Community Development Society, Kansas City, Mo., August 1979.

Driscoll, J. M., Meyer, R. G., & Schanie, C. F. Training in family crisis intervention. *Journal of Applied Behavioral Science*, 1973, *9*, 62–82.

Felstiner, W. L. F. Influences of social organization on dispute processing. *Law and Society Review*, 1974, *9*, 63–94.

Fischer, C. S. The spread of violent crime from city to countryside, 1955 to 1975. *Rural Sociology*, 1980, *45*, 416–434.

Friedman, L. M. The idea of right as a social and legal concept. In J. L. Tapp & F. J. Levine (Eds.), *Law, justice, and the individual in society: Psychological and legal issues*. New York: Holt, Rinehart & Winston, 1977.

Friedman, L. M., & Percival, R. V. A tale of two courts: Litigation in Alameda and San Benito counties. *Law and Society Review*, 1976, *11*, 267–301.

Garbarino, J., & Sherman, D. Hign-risk neighborhoods and high-risk families: The human ecology of child maltreatment. *Child Development*, 1980, *51*, 188–198.

Geller, E. S. *Promoting compliance in the community: Are words enough?* Paper presented at the meeting of the Association for Behavior Analysis, Dearborn, Mich., 1980.

Geller, E. S., Koltuniak, T. A., & Shilling, J. S. Response avoidance prompting: A cost-effective strategy for theft deterrence. *Behavioral Counseling Quarterly*, in press.

Gibbs, J. J. *Crime against persons in urban, suburban, and rural areas: A comparative analysis of victimization rates.* Washington, D.C.: Law Enforcement Assistance Administration, 1979.

Gotts, E. E. *Distinguishing characteristics of Appalachian children and families: Some findings and needs for further study.* Paper presented at the First Annual Conference on Appalachian Children and Families, Institute, West Virginia, June 1980.

Hill, G. W. Interdisciplinary field training for social change: A case study for psychology and law. *American Journal of Community Psychology*, 1979, *7*, 223–230.

Hoffman, C. Empowerment movements and mental health: Locus of control and commitment to the United Farm Workers. *Journal of Community Psychology*, 1978, *6*, 216–221.

Koocher, G. P. Child advocacy and mental health professionals. In P. A. Vardin & I. N. Brody (Eds.), *Children's rights: Contemporary perspectives.* New York: Teachers College Press, 1979.

Libertoff, K. *Natural helping networks in rural youth and families.* Paper presented at the meeting of the American Psychological Association, New York, September 1979.

Liebman, D. A., & Schwartz, J. Police programs in crisis intervention: A review. In J. R. Snibbe & H. M. Snibbe (Eds.), *The urban policeman in transition: A psychological and sociological review.* Springfield, Ill.: Charles C Thomas, 1973.

Loftus, E. *Eyewitness testimony.* Cambridge: Harvard University Press, 1979.

Loftus, E., & Monahan, J. Trial by data: Psychological research as legal evidence. *American Psychologist*, 1980, *35*, 270–283.

McDonough, L. B., & Monahan, J. The quality of community care-takers: A study of mental health screening in a sheriff's department. *Community Mental Health Journal*, 1975, *11*, 33–43.

McNees, M. P., Egli, D. S., Marshall, R. S., Schnelle, J. F., & Risley, T. R. Shoplifting prevention: Providing information through signs. *Journal of Applied Behavior Analysis*, 1976, *9*, 399–405.

McNees, M. P., Kennon, M., Schnelle, J. F., Kirchner, R. E., & Thomas, M. M. An experimental analysis of a program to reduce retail theft. *American Journal of Community Psychology*, 1980, *8*, 379–385.

Melton, G. B. Children's concepts of their rights. *Journal of Clinical Child Psychology*, 1980, *9*, 186–190.

Melton, G. B. Children's participation in treatment planning: Psychological and legal issues. *Professional Psychology*, 1981, *12*, 647–654.

Melton, G. B. Teaching children about their rights. In J. S. Henning (Ed.), *The rights of children: Legal and psychological perspectives.* Springfield, Ill.: Charles C Thomas, 1982.

Melton, G. B., Koocher, G. P., & Saks, M. J. (Eds.). *Children's competence to consent.* New York: Plenum Press, in press.

Monahan, J. (Ed.). *Community mental health and the criminal justice system.* New York: Pergamon, 1976. (a)

Monahan, J. The prediction of violence. In J. Monahan (Ed.), *Community mental health and the criminal justice system.* New York: Pergamon, 1976. (b)

Montero, D. Support for civil liberties among a cohort of high school graduates and college students. *Journal of Social Issues*, 1975, *31*(2), 123–136.

Nader, L., & Metzger, D. Conflict resolution in two Mexican communities. *American Anthropologist*, 1963, *65*, 584–592.

Nader, L., & Todd, H. F., Jr. Introduction. In L. Nader & H. T. Todd, Jr. (Eds.), *The disputing process: Law in 10 societies*. New York: Columbia University Press, 1978.

Newman, O. *Defensible space: Crime prevention through urban design*. New York: Macmillan, 1972.

Nietzel, M. T., & Dade, J. T. Bail reform as an example of a community psychology intervention in the criminal justice system. *American Journal of Community Psychology*, 1973, *1*, 238–247.

Note. Rural poverty and the law in southern Colorado. *Denver Law Journal*, 1970, *47*, 82–176.

Office of Juvenile Justice and Delinquency Prevention. *Rural programs*. Washington, D.C.: Law Enforcement Assistance Administration, 1979.

Pearson, J. Rural society and its view of the legal system. In E. K. Stott, Jr., T. J. Fetter, & L. L. Crites (Eds.), *Rural courts: The effect of space and distance on the administration of justice*. Denver: National Center for State Courts, 1977.

Phillips, G. H. *Rural crimes and rural offenders*. Columbus: Ohio Cooperative Extension Service, 1976.

Phillips, G. H., & Bartlett, K. *Vandals and vandalism in rural Ohio* (Research Circular 222). Wooster: Ohio Agricultural Research and Development Center, 1976.

Phillips, G. H., & Wurschmidt, T. N. *The Ohio rural victimization study*. Paper presented at the meeting of the Rural Sociological Society, Burlington, Vermont, August 1979.

Phillips, G. H., Kreps, G. M., & Moody, C. W. *Environmental factors in rural crime* (Research Circular 224). Wooster: Ohio Agricultural Research and Development Center, 1976.

Poythress, N. G., Jr. A proposal for training in forensic psychology. *American Psychologist*, 1979, *34*, 612–621.

Project. The legal problems of the rural poor. *Duke Law Journal*, 1969, 495–621.

Prothro, J. W., & Grigg, C. W. Fundamental principles of democracy: Bases of agreement and disagreement. *Journal of Politics*, 1960, *22*, 276–294.

Rawls, J. W. *A theory of justice*. Cambridge: Harvard University Press, 1971.

Regoli, R. M., & Poole, E. D. Police professionalism and role conflict: A comparison of rural and urban departments. *Human Relations*, 1980, *33*, 241–252.

Reppucci, N. D. The social psychology of institutional change: General principles for intervention. *American Journal of Community Psychology*, 1973, *1*, 330–341.

Rogers, E. M. *Diffusion of innovations*. New York: Free Press of Glencoe, 1962.

Ryan, J. P., & Guterman, J. H. Lawyer versus nonlawyer town justices: An empirical footnote to *North* v. *Russell*. *Judicature*, 1977, *60*, 272–280.

Saks, M. J. *Jury verdicts*. Lexington, Mass.: Lexington Books, 1977.

Saks, M. J. Social psychological contributions to a legislative subcommittee on organ and tissue transplants. *American Psychologist*, 1978, *33*, 680–690.

Sarat, A., & Grossman, J. B. Courts and conflict resolution: Problems in the mobilization of adjudication. *American Political Science Review*, 1975, *69*, 1200–1217.

Schwartz, R. D., & Miller, J. C. Legal evolution and societal complexity. *American Journal of Sociology*, 1964, *20*, 159–169.

Sheppard, D. I., Roehl, J. A., & Cook, R. F. *Neighborhood Justice Centers field test: Interim evaluation report*. Washington, D.C.: Law Enforcement Assistance Administration, 1979.

Smith, B. L., & Donnermeyer, J. F. *Victimization in rural and urban areas: A comparative analysis*. Paper presented at the meeting of the Rural Sociological Society, Burlington, Vermont, August 1979.

Sommer, R. *Personal space*. Englewood Cliffs, N.J.: Prentice-Hall, 1969.

Starr, J., & Yngvesson, B. B. Scarity and disputing: Zeroing-in on compromise decisions. *American Ethnologist*, 1965, *2*, 553–556.

Stott, E. K., Jr., Fetter, T. J., & Crites, L. L. *Rural courts: The effect of space and distance on the administration of justice*. Denver: National Center for State Courts, 1977.

Stouffer, S. A. *Communism, conformity, and civil liberties: A cross-section of the nation speaks its mind*. Garden City, N.Y.: Doubleday, 1955.

Tanke, E. D., & Tanke, T. J. Getting off a slippery slope: Social science in the judicial process. *American Psychologist*, 1979, *34*, 1130–1138.

Tapp, J. L., & Levine, F. J. Legal socialization: Strategies for an ethical legality. *Stanford Law Review*, 1974, *27*, 1–72.

Tate, S. D. Youth and senior citizens in creative rural courts. *Juvenile Court Journal*, 1971, *22*, 52–54.

Todd, H. F., Jr. Litigious marginals: Character and disputing in a Bavarian village. In L. Nader & H. F. Todd, Jr. (Eds.), *The disputing process: Law in 10 societies*. New York: Columbia University Press, 1978.

Wandersman, A., & Giamartino, G. A. Community and individual difference characteristics as influences on initial participation. *American Journal of Community Psychology*, 1980, *8*, 217–228.

Wasby, S. L. *Small town police and the Supreme Court: Hearing the word*. Lexington, Mass.: Lexington Books, 1976.

Wilson, W. C. Belief in freedom of speech and press. *Journal of Social Issues*, 1975, *31*(2), 69–76.

Wurschmidt, T. N., & Phillips, G. H. *Teachers' guide: Rural crime prevention guide for young people*. Columbus: Ohio Cooperative Extension Service, 1978.

Yngvesson, B. B. The Atlantic fisherman. In L. Nader & H. F. Todd, Jr. (Eds.), *The disputing process: Law in 10 societies*. New York: Columbia University Press, 1978.

Zellman, G. L. Antidemocratic beliefs. A survey and some explanations. *Journal of Social Issues*, 1975, *31*(2), 31–54.

17

The Energy Crisis and Behavioral Science

A Conceptual Framework for Large-Scale Intervention

E. SCOTT GELLER

The United States occupies the unenviable position in the world today of being the preeminent energy glutton. We are using up the world's fossil fuel reserves at a rate which is out of proportion with our population, our economy, and our own natural resources. Most experienced observers suggest that the countries currently supplying petroleum to our economy will, in the next ten years, cut back significantly on their exports and increase the use of petroleum resources in their own countries. Predicted shortages and interruptions in the supply of petroleum will probably have at least the following negative consequences: (a) a general increase in energy fuel prices; (b) a squeeze on family budgets, with families sacrificing "nonessential" budget items like educational materials, recreation, preventive medical care, and cultural activities; (c) extra tensions of economic pressures affecting poor interpersonal relationships within the family (e.g., marital discord, child abuse), and increased individual suffering of those who are poor and older; (d) a reappearance of the relative isolation of the rural population; (e) a general shrinkage of the available living space per person in the cold months; and (f) reduced comfort for everyone during hot and cold weather.

E. SCOTT GELLER • Department of Psychology, Virginia Polytechnic Institute and State University, Blacksburg, Virginia 24061.

The anticipated danger to our society and its needs over the next 6 to 12 years is quite awesome and hopefully, overly pessimistic. However, much of the society is quite apathetic with regard to energy use and discounts the possibility of many of the prospects outlined above. Communities must raise the consciousness of their people to the expectations of our energy futures and organize facilities to promote communitywide action toward energy conservation. In other words, communities must help their citizens adopt new life-styles that are more energy efficient and, therefore, more stable to the energy-supply future.

Hence, there is a national need for community sources of applicable energy information and for teaching/learning models that can organize appropriate community services and consumer education for helping householders cope with energy-supply problems. A primary objective of the present chapter is to provide a conceptual framework for organizing large-scale action toward energy conservation and environmental protection that is appropriate for rural communities. Our discussion begins with the specification of the role of applied behavioral science in solving environmental problems and ends with the presentation of a comprehensive model for coordinating behavioral and engineering technology for communitywide energy conservation. Recent behavioral research that contributes to a definition of cost-effective strategies for encouraging energy conservation will be summarized, but not discussed in detail. Many comprehensive reviews of this literature are already available (e.g., Cone & Hayes, 1978; Kazdin, 1977; Tuso & Geller, 1976).

Why is Energy a Topic for Rural Psychology?

Given the recent literature reviews cited above, general texts in contemporary applied psychology should certainly include discussions of psychology-based approaches to solving energy/environment problems. But why is such a topic particularly relevant for a specialized study of rural psychology? In general it could be argued that current environmental problems related to energy should be covered in all applied psychology texts, whatever the milieu of focus (e.g., institutions, businesses, communities, urban or rural settings). On an intuitive level, it seems that a text in rural psychology ought to cover energy/environment issues because energy shortages and environmental degradation may be particularly debilitating to rural residents who are relatively isolated from each other. Indeed, the dissemination of strategies for coping with energy shortages (from information and materials to actual home visitation) is less readily accomplished in rural than urban areas, where media, communication, and transportation systems are more effective, community services are more plentiful and accessible, and volunteer groups are more easily available for public assistance.

On an empirical level, there is also reason to believe that coping with severe energy/environment problems will be most difficult in relatively isolated rural settings. Specifically, attitude surveys of individuals' environmental concern have suggested that the rural resident is generally less concerned about (or aware of) environmental problems than the urban resident (Buttel & Flinn, 1976; Tremblay & Dunlap, 1978; Van Liere & Dunlap, 1980); thus, one should expect more difficulty in implementing and maintaining energy conservation or environmental protection programs among rural populations. This statement is consistent with a frequently cited survey accomplished for Keep America Beautiful, Inc. (Public Opinion Surveys, Inc., 1968), which found farmers and residents of relatively small communities (populations under 2,500) to be more likely to litter than residents of larger cities. However, it is important to realize that this conclusion was based on personal interviews rather than actual observations and may simply mean that rural residents were more apt than urban residents to admit to having littered.

The behavioral results of a three-year effort by the present author and his colleagues to promote energy conservation in both rural and urban communities were highly supportive of the notion that rural dwellers are less responsive to energy/environment issues than city dwellers. Our rather comprehensive attempt to disseminate energy-conservation strategies began with the presentation of energy-conservation workshops in rural and urban communities in Virginia. The workshop materials and presentations were interdisciplinary (resulting from the contributions of students and professors in architecture, education, engineering, physics, and psychology); as detailed elsewhere (Geller, 1981a; Geller, Brasted, & Augustine, 1978; Geller, Ferguson, & Brasted, 1978), this program increased significantly the awareness, concern, and personal commitment toward conserving energy of those who attended each workshop. However, equivalent promotion of the workshops in rural and urban areas resulted in much better attendance at the urban workshops, and many more urban than rural participants showed involvement in individual follow-up projects to the workshops (Ferguson, Bowen, Carlyle, & Geller, 1979; Geller, 1978; Geller, Bowen, & Chiang, 1978). Furthermore, home visits to 40 participants of the rural workshops and 40 rural residents who had not attended a conservation workshop showed no substantial behavioral effects of the rural workshops, even though (six weeks earlier) these same workshop attendants had indicated a strong verbal commitment to implementing the specific conservation practices that were assessed (Geller, 1981a; Geller, Ferguson,

& Brasted, 1978). On the other hand, home visits to the urban homes of
workshop participants (near Richmond, Virginia) showed prominently
more applications of energy/conservation strategies than the rural visits,
although it could not be determined whether the urban applications
were a direct result of the workshops (Geller, 1978).

Following the development, implementation, and evaluation of community energy-conservation workshops, the interdisciplinary team of professors and students at Virginia Polytechnic Institute and State University
attempted to implement a communitywide energy-conservation program in
an urban environment (Fairfax County, Virginia) and a rural setting (Dublin,
Virginia). These programs were preliminary to the community action
model presented at the end of this chapter and were designed: (a) to
locate members of existing community structures who were willing to
dedicate time and effort for conservation projects, and (b) to train and
assist community volunteers in organizing, supervising, and evaluating
these projects. The university team provided workshop materials and
project ideas for the local community and helped to establish a local
Energy Advisory Committee from lists of potential volunteers obtained
from extension agents and government officials. This advisory board
was responsible for coordinating energy-education services with local
governmental agencies, for finding individuals who would be capable
and willing to serve as neighborhood energy advisors and workshop
presentors, and for helping the neighborhood advisors locate residents
who needed (and wanted) assistance regarding the application of energy-conservation strategies (Ferguson et al., 1979; Geller, 1978). These
efforts were quite successful in the urban setting but were a dismal
failure in Dublin, Virginia (the rural setting). More specifically, in Fairfax
County, Virginia, a local Energy Advisory Committee was established in
September of 1978 which located members of the League of Women
Voters who were trained as neighborhood advisors and who within two
months assisted more than 200 individuals with a specific energy-retrofit
strategy in their homes. Today, the essence of this community plan for
promoting energy conservation has been incorporated into the Fairfax
County Energy Conservation Task Force. In sharp contrast, we were
unable to obtain enough support from the local government or citizens
in Dublin, Virginia to organize a single community-service committee
for energy conservation (Geller, 1978).

An Interdisciplinary Large-Scale Framework

The consumption of environmental resources occurs constantly
during the various roles of daily existence, and most often this consumption is controllable by the role player. Whether relaxing at home,

working at an occupation, or traveling between locations, we are usually using energy resources and are often in a position to vary the amount of energy consumed. Thus, a comprehensive approach toward promoting energy conservation and saving environmental resources must consider several points of intervention, as well as a variety of intervention strategies. For example, consider a $2 \times 3 \times 4$ factorial array, with the following variables:

1. Two basic intervention *approaches* (i.e., physical vs. psychological technology)
2. Three community *sectors* requiring direct intervention (i.e., the residential/consumer, governmental/institutional, and commercial/industrial sectors)
3. Four *targets* or domains for intervention within each sector (i.e., heating/cooling, solid waste management, transportation, and equipment efficiency)[1]

Each cell of the three-dimensional, 24-cell matrix resulting from this factorial represents an area of expertise required in a comprehensive energy-conservation program. Basically, the physical approach involves the application of physical technology (e.g., architecture, engineering, physics) to conserve energy and is often manifested in altering or adding to the structure of a building, purchasing or modifying equipment, using certain energy-saving devices, and separating solid waste for resource recycling and/or energy fuel. It is quite obvious that the type of recommended physical intervention (and necessary technical expertise) is dependent upon both the general target area (i.e., heating/cooling, solid-waste management, transportation, or equipment efficiency) and the community sector in which the intervention is applied (i.e., residences, institutions, or industrial complexes).

The application of physical interventions for energy conservation

---

[1] A fifth target demanding special attention in a comprehensive program for energy conservation and environmental protection is water consumption. Water is obviously a vital environmental resource; water usage consumes much energy during processes of delivery, heating, and disposal; and water pollution is the result of inappropriate management of the environment. Due to space limitations, however, water conservation is not considered as a separate target area in this chapter, although approaches to water conservation are considered as they overlap with other topics, and many of the behavioral strategies discussed in other contexts can be readily refined to target water consumption. Actually, a comprehensive literature search revealed very little behavioral research that targeted water conservation (except for recent work in Australia by Robin C. Winkler and his students). Indeed, none of the recent convention papers, technical reports, journal articles or book chapters in behavioral science that the author reviewed to write this chapter gave serious attention to water usage as an important aspect of energy conservation or environmental protection, except for two recent texts (Cone & Hayes, 1980; and Geller, Winett, & Everett, 1982).

usually requires human intervention, and therefore psychological approaches are necessary to teach and motivate appropriate human action. Such human action (in residential, commercial/industrial or governmental/institutional settings) may involve the purchase of particular devices or equipment (for heating or cooling, transportation, waste management, or time-saving operations), or the application of certain devices or equipment in certain energy-efficient ways. For example, action in the consumer/transportation cell of the factorial includes both the purchase of an energy-efficient vehicle and the adoption of energy-efficient driving habits. Physical technology is required in this case to prescribe the most energy-efficient vehicle and its optional use, whereas psychology is needed to recommend strategies for disseminating information regarding energy-efficient vehicles and driving behaviors and for motivating desired public reaction. The situation is certainly complex, requiring much challenging research and development for just the consumer/transportation aspect of energy conservation. The fact that each of the 24 cells of the $2 \times 3 \times 4$ energy array presented above requires the design, implementation, and evaluation of special conservation strategies is mind-boggling. At the very least, energy research efforts are needed which combine the expertise of both physical and psychological technology.

Practically all of the psychologists who reviewed recent behavioral science approaches toward energy conservation and/or environmental protection advocated interdisciplinary research as an urgent need and future challenge for energy researchers (e.g., Geller, 1980b; Lloyd, 1980; Reichel & Geller, 1981; Stern & Gardner, 1980, 1981; Winett, 1980). For example, Stern and Gardner (1981) stressed that almost all of the energy issues for which psychology is relevant are interdisciplinary and thus "psychologists must learn to understand and work with economists, engineers, marketers, building contractors, and/or members of other disciplines or professions" (p. 22). Johnson and Geller (1980) discussed a conceptual model for research collaboration between engineering and behavior analysis, illustrating the positive gains that could result from behavioral science's input into engineering technology under four situational categories: (a) when the appropriate engineering technology has been developed and is available for widespread dissemination, (b) while the engineering technology is being researched and developed, (c) when available engineering strategies are not working or being applied as planned, and (d) when no engineering technology is available.

Several psychologists researching energy problems have recently attested to the extreme lack of valuation of the behavioral and social sciences among professionals from other disciplines (e.g., Becker & Seligman, 1981; Geller, 1980b, 1981b; Shippee, 1980; Zerega, 1981). Most of the behavioral and social science research related to energy conservation and environmental protection has been accomplished without grant support from state or federal agencies, and interdisciplinary advisory panels for energy conservation or environmental protection do not regularly consider input from social and behavioral scientists (cf. Geller, 1980b). Perhaps after behavioral and social scientists demonstrate the patience to learn the jargon of other disciplines and their approaches to problem solving, then the experts from these other disciplines may be more apt to develop an understanding and appreciation for the potential of psychological information in the development, dissemination, and evaluation of energy-saving technologies. A significant approximation toward large-scale collaboration between the physical and psychological sciences will occur when reviewers of the energy literature outside of the behavioral and social sciences emphasize the need for interdisciplinary research with psychologists to the same extent that the reviewers of energy research in the psychological literature have stressed the need for interdisciplinary research with architects, engineers, economists, etc.

Why Behavioral Science?

By now the slogan disseminated by Keep America Beautiful, Inc. (KAB), "People Start Pollution—People Can Stop It," is familiar to most Americans; most people understand that much of the litter problem is a behavioral problem and thus appreciate the validity of the KAB motto. Indeed, the communitywide litter-control program of KAB (termed the Clean Community System) is publicized as "the nation's first local-level waste-control program to be based on behavioral change techniques" (KAB, 1977b, p. 1). Now consider an energy slogan, "People Consume Energy—People Can Conserve It!" This statement is as valid as the KAB litter-control motto, and behavioral change techniques are as appropriate for facilitating energy conservation as litter control. Thus, behaviors that contribute to energy waste can be decreased on a large scale and behaviors that conserve energy can be increased on communitywide levels. Furthermore, it is often possible to influence energy-related behaviors through simple manipulations of environmental stimuli and response contingencies, and it is usually most cost-effective to apply interventions directly at the target behaviors, rather than attempting to change attitudes and values, hoping for subsequent, indirect influence on behaviors. Of course, behavioral scientists are hopeful that attitudes, values, and even norms will change in desirable directions after consistent, long-term behavior change.

It is noteworthy that there have been numerous psychology-based studies that focused on correlating individuals actions, demographic characteristics, personality traits, or value systems with awareness or concern for environmental protection (e.g., see recent review by Van Liere & Dunlap, 1980). Although the number of such attitude–behavior, correlational studies are probably more numerous than those aimed at finding strategies for directly influencing environment-related behaviors (e.g., see annotated bibliographies by Frankena, Buttel, & Morrison, 1977; and Weigel, Woolston, & Gendelman, 1977), this author seriously questions whether this correlational research will ever have any practical significance for energy conservation or environmental protection. The attitude/value measurement scales are not consistent across studies and their reliability and validity may be questioned (cf. Hendee, 1971; Van Liere & Dunlap, 1981). Furthermore, it has often been shown that what people indicate on a questionnaire is often inconsistent with their actual behaviors (e.g., Bickman, 1972; Deutscher, 1966, 1973; Wicker, 1969, 1971). Finally, even if significant (and valid) relationships are found between individual characteristics and environment-related attitudes or behaviors, it is not clear how such results could be used to alleviate energy/environment problems. Thus, in this author's opinion the psychology factor of the 2 × 3 × 4 energy array represents the direct application of sociobehavioral principles to influence behaviors related to energy consumption.

Target Behaviors

The variety of human responses related to energy conservation are numerous. Each cell of the 2 × 3 × 4 energy array suggests several behaviors of people in particular situations (e.g., at home, at work, at school, at a business location, or in transition) that imply energy consumption (directly or indirectly), and which can be altered so as to be more energy efficient. Of course, defining these energy-related responses and making specific recommendations regarding desirable change often requires interdisciplinary input. For example, engineering data are required to advise which appliance or vehicle is most energy efficient, architectural data are often helpful in defining optimal insulation techniques and landscape designs for the conservation of energy for home heating and cooling, biological data are necessary for prescribing optional composting procedures, and information from physics and human-factors engineering is relevant for defining energy-efficient ways of using appliances, vehicles, industrial machinery, conservation devices, and heating or cooling systems.

Some energy-saving strategies imply repetitive action, whereas others do not. In other words, one class of conservation behaviors require repeated occurrences in order to effect significant energy savings (such as setting back room thermostats each night, riding in a car pool and driving 55 m.p.h. or less, taking shorter showers, turning off lights when not needed, using separate containers for recyclable paper, metal, glass and biodegradable trash, opening window shades during the day and closing them at night, and wearing more clothes in order to withstand lower room temperatures). On the other hand, a particular conservation strategy may require only one occurrence of the target behavior (e.g., installing a thermostat that automatically changes room-temperature settings at preprogrammed levels, purchasing an energy-efficient vehicle, wrapping insulation around the water heater and inserting a shower-flow restrictor in the showerhead, changing light bulbs from incandescent to fluorescent, operating a high-technology waste-separation system, installing a solar heating system, and adding insulation to an attic).

Notice that each of the examples given for the *repeated-response* category has a concomitant behavior listed in the *one-shot* category and that for one-shot behaviors the user usually pays an initial high cost in time and money for the subsequent convenience of not having to make continued response input. Selecting one target behavior over another may often be a complex decision process, requiring a careful examination of the long-term costs and benefits of each alternative. Indeed, a complete cost-effectiveness analysis often requires interdisciplinary input, including physical and psychological data that may not be available. For example, just deciding whether to install a shower-flow restrictor requires much field data that are currently not available. In fact, valid information regarding the amount of hot water and energy conserved with a shower-flow restrictor cannot be estimated until human reaction to this low-cost device is field tested. Will people take longer or more showers (or switch to baths) if their shower flow is limited? To what extent does a flow restrictor lessen perceived (or real) shower comfort? Does the flow restrictor promote increased adjustments in water temperature (perhaps due to surges of hot or cold water), with concomitant increases in water usage, inconvenience, and discomfort? It is unfortunate that the United States Department of Energy (DOE) did not undertake an adequate field test and cost-effective analysis of shower-flow restrictors before distributing them to 4.5 million New England households in a recent $2.6 million DOE program (U.S. DOE, 1980).

Stern and Gardner (1981) indicated that "frequently repeated behaviors usually involve curtailment while one-shot actions usually involve efficiency" (p. 10). This statement cannot be accurate, given the dictionary meaning of "curtail"—"to cut off or cut short; abbreviate; lessen; reduce" (*Funk & Wagnalls Standard College Dictionary*, 1977, p.

330). Indeed, while most of the conservation behaviors that require re-peated occurrence do involve a cut-back (or curtailment) on energy con-sumption, numerous "one-shot" behaviors also imply curtailment. Thus, insulating walls, ceilings, and water heaters, inserting water con-servation devices, installing thermostat controls, tuning up engines, and putting air in underinflated tires all involve changing existing facilities or equipment so that less energy is consumed (i.e., a curtailment). More-over, several conservation strategies involve both a one-time investment and repeated actions. Thus, one can purchase a window fan to sub-stitute for an air conditioner, or a moped to substitute for an automobile, but energy conservation does not occur unless the individual makes repeated decisions to use the more energy-efficient machine. Likewise, energy-saving settings on new energy-efficient appliances (e.g., dish-washers, air conditioners, clothes dryers and washing machines, and industrial equipment) are not worth much unless they are continuously used. Special receptacles for separating trash do not conserve energy unless they are used appropriately each day and the contents are trans-ported to a recycling center.

Stern and Gardner also concluded "that behaviors involving adop-tion of energy-efficient technology generally offer more potential for conservation than behaviors involving curtailed use of existing energy systems" (1981, p. 9). Such an assertion is quite risky (given the lack of appropriate engineering and human-factors data) and could actually be detrimental to the energy situation if taken seriously. One could take this statement to mean that individuals should go out and purchase new energy-efficient appliances, vehicles, machinery, and even heating and cooling systems, rather than modifying existing equipment or structures and/or changing usage habits with respect to their present situation. Not only is such a recommendation impractical with regard to large-scale conservation, but the purchase of new equipment rather than the repair of existing equipment implicates increased energy consumption to pro-duce the new and dispose of the old. An evaluation of energy-efficiency technology requires a comprehensive analysis of energy costs and sav-ings throughout the production, use, and eventual disposal of the com-modities involved; such long-term, interdisciplinary information is sore-ly needed.

Regarding the presumed low conservation potential of repeated curtailment behaviors, it is noteworthy that Winett and his students recently showed that residents (N = 49 households) saved a mean of 15% of their winter electric bill by setting back their thermostats from an average of 65° to 59° F. when not at home or asleep, and a different sample (N = 35 households) saved a mean of 16% of their summer electric costs by increasing their thermostats from an average of 75° to

79° F. when not at home or asleep (Geller, Winett, & Everett, 1982; Winett *et al.*, 1981). These savings from actual field observation are significantly higher than the 4% estimated savings in winter reported by Stern and Gardner (1981) for setting back room thermostats from 72° to 68° F. daily and to 65° F. nightly.

The winter baseline and set-back temperatures observed by Winett and his colleagues were quite low and suggest another set of behaviors which ought to be considered in a comprehensive energy conservation program. Specifically, the insulation value of the clothing worn by the residents in the Winett *et al.* study (as assessed by weekly self-reports) correlated significantly with the temperature setting of the room thermostats. Those who set lower temperatures in the winter wore more clothing, and those who set higher temperatures in the summer wore less clothing. Thus, the amount of clothing worn in the home was a coping strategy for helping people adapt to temperature changes. Therefore, another target for an energy-conservation program is the attire worn by men and women at home and at work. It is often the case that dress codes actually conflict with energy conservation. For example, Winett and Neale (1979) offer the scenario of businessmen and politicians wearing three-piece suits in Washington, D.C., during the hot summer. Such attire is feasible only because of the energy-wasteful use of air conditioning in cars, homes, offices, and most other indoor settings.

Besides repeated and one-shot curtailment behaviors, one-shot efficiency behaviors, and coping behaviors (discussed above), there is one additional set of potential target behaviors for energy conservation. These have been termed "peak shift behaviors," referring to changing the time when individuals emit energy-consumption behaviors. Reducing peak demands for energy decreases the need for power companies to build or borrow supplementary generators or other energy sources (i.e., nuclear). Indeed, electricity suppliers have been willing to vary their rates according to peak demand (i.e., peak-load pricing), although residents have found it difficult to shift various energy-consuming tasks (Kohlenberg, Phillips, & Proctor, 1976).

Peak shifting is usually associated with residential energy use (e.g., changing cooking, showering, and sleeping times), but it may be even more feasible as a large-scale conservation strategy for other community sectors. Consider, for example, the peak-shift advantages of altering the scheduling and/or length of work shifts at industrial complexes and government agencies (e.g., through the adoption of flexible work schedules or a four-day work week). Certain large-scale changes in work schedules could result in peak shifts (and energy savings) at the work setting, at home, and during commuting. For example, the major function of urban transit systems is to serve people going to and from work, and since most of such commuting occurs during two short rush-periods a day, numerous bus drivers make nonproductive runs or actually sit idle most of the day (Zerega, 1981). Note that before instituting large-scale shifts in work schedules it is necessary to do comprehensive, multifaceted pilot testing in order to define the most energy-efficient plan without disrupting family life, leisure activity, and other functions of a "healthy" community.

Behavioral Strategies: Antecedents

Behavioral interventions for energy conservation and environmental protection can be generally categorized as antecedent or consequence strategies, as in the first published review of the research in this area (Tuso & Geller, 1976). Antecedent strategies (sometimes referred to as prompting or response-priming procedures) are stimulus events occurring before the target behavior and are designed to increase the probability of the target if the response is desirable or to decrease the likelihood of the target response if it is undesirable. Prompts for environmental protection have been displayed through television commercials, verbal statements (e.g., from parents, teachers, public officials, and peers), and through environmental manipulations (e.g., such as beautified waste receptacles, containers with separate bins labeled for different types of recyclable trash, parked police cars along a highway, and thermostats and appliance controls with special settings for energy conservation). Furthermore, the nature or format of the prompting procedure implies different types of control. Some prompts for environmental protection have been *general* exhortations or appeals with no specification of the target response (e.g., Use energy wisely; Help keep our community clean; Please dispose of properly; Don't be a litterbug), whereas other prompting has taken the form of *specific* instructions which indicate the target behavior to emit or avoid (e.g., Drive 55 m.p.h. to conserve energy; Deposit for recycling in green trash receptacle; Turn off lights when leaving room; Don't litter here; Don't trample the grass). Education information (disseminated through books, magazines, newspapers, pamphlets, or workshops) represents general prompting if facts are given with no specification of desirable or undesirable behaviors, although much environmental information has occurred as *specific* prompts, with particular recommendations for action accompanying the facts and figures.

Some prompts announce incentive conditions by specifying pleasant or unpleasant consequences which will follow occurrences of the target response (e.g., a $50 fine for littering; one raffle coupon per pound of recyclable paper; persons depositing litter in this container will sometimes be rewarded; $2 for a 10% decrease in electricity use; $1 per week for each 5% reduction in miles driven with automobile). Some announcement prompts signal when the pleasant or unpleasant event is available and thus serve as discriminative stimuli for the target response (such as a sign displayed intermittently to indicate that reinforcement is available for a particular response); other prompts do not specify a contingency but do signal that reinforcement is available if the response is emitted (i.e., a discriminative stimulus). In this latter case, it is presumed that the public has become aware of the contingency. Thus, a police car signals the availability of a negative reinforcer if speeding occurs (without defining the particular contingency); and in the transportation-conservation experiments by Peter B. Everett and his students (Everett, 1973; Everett, Hayward, & Meyers, 1974; Deslauriers & Everett, 1977) only the special campus bus with three large red stars signaled the availability of a positive reinforcer (a quarter or token) for boarding. The reinforcement contingencies for the Everett et al. studies were announced in the campus newspaper (i.e., an announcement prompt which did not serve as a discriminative stimulus for bus riding).

Prompting procedures without concomitant reinforcement procedures are relatively cheap and easy to administer; but as shown in earlier reviews of the literature, the efficacy of prompting strategies for energy conservation and environmental protection has been limited (e.g., Geller, 1980a, 1980b, 1981; Shippee, 1980; Winett, 1980). In summary, prompts (without accompanying reinforcement) were successful in promoting a significant degree of compliance related to environmental protection when the prompt: (a) was administered in close proximity with the opportunity to emit the requested response, (b) specified what behavior was desired, (c) requested a response that was relatively convenient to emit, and (d) was given in polite, nondemanding language. For example, Delprata (1977) and Winett (1978) were successful in prompting occupants of public buildings to turn off room lights when they placed messages at light switches which specified that the lights should be turned out when leaving the room; Geller, Witmer, and Orebaugh (1976) and Geller, Witmer, and Tuso (1977) found 20% to 30% compliance with antilitter messages on handbills when the prompt politely requested that the handbill be deposited for recycling in a conveniently located (and obtrusive) trash receptacle. On the other hand, educational programs and informational packages (without special incentive provisions) have been quite unsuccessful in motivating the occurrence of relatively inconvenient and/or time-consuming energy conservation strategies (e.g., Geller, Ferguson, & Brasted, 1978; Hayes & Cone, 1977; Heberlein, 1975; Kohlenberg et al., 1976; Palmer, Lloyd, & Lloyd, 1978;

Winett, Kagel, Battalio, & Winkler, 1978). Handbills with a general plea and specific instructions regarding a campus paper recycling program were not sufficient to get residents of university dormitories to bring recyclable paper to a particular collection room (Geller, Chaffee, & Ingram, 1975; Witmer & Geller, 1976), even when the specific prompts were given personally to dorm residents via verbal exhortation and a flier (Ingram & Geller, 1975).

One additional antecedent strategy for influencing behavior is labeled modeling (cf. Bandura, 1977), which refers to the demonstration of specific behaviors and which sometimes includes the explicit presentation of pleasant or unpleasant events following the behavior. Modeling can occur via live demonstrations or on a movie screen (e.g., television, film, or videotape), and implies the presentation of a specific prompt with the announcement of a reinforcement contingency (i.e., the model receives an extrinsic reward following a specific response) or a specific prompt without the specification of a reinforcement contingency (i.e., no response consequences are shown). Energy studies and environmental protection programs have essentially ignored modeling strategies, yet modeling (through television or video cassette) has the potential of reaching and influencing millions of residents. Indeed, in two recent studies by Winett and his students (detailed in Geller et al., 1982; and Winett et al., 1981), a 21-minute videotape program (showing specific conservation practices) was found to reduce the heating bill of 33 households an average of 27% and the cooling bill of 23 households an average of 30%.

It is noteworthy that prompts which are perceived as demands (rather than polite requests) may elicit psychological reactance and actually motivate behaviors contrary to those desired (Brehm, 1966, 1972). In other words, individuals may perceive verbal or written prompts as a threat to their personal freedom and may not only disregard the request, but may in fact emit a response contrary to the instructions in order to assert their freedom. This notion was supported in a field study by Reich and Robertson (1979), who distributed antilitter flyers at a public swimming pool and found significantly more littering of fliers with the message "Don't litter" than fliers with the message "Help keep your pool clean" (Experiment 1); and fliers with the antilitter message "Don't you *dare* litter" were littered significantly more often than fliers with the message "Keeping the pool clean depends on you" or "Help keep your pool clean" (Experiment 2). Likewise, Geller and his students (detailed in reviews by Brasted, Mann, & Geller, 1979; and Geller, 1980a) found that significantly more patrons of a shopping center complied with a specific, *polite* prompt at the bottom of distributed handbills (i.e., "Please dispose of in trash can in front of Woolco") than with a specific, *demand* prompt (i.e., "You must dispose of in trash can in front of Woolco").

Behavioral Strategies: Consequences

Antecedent strategies alone have rarely been effective in influencing the occurrence of environmental protection responses that require more effort than adjusting a room thermostat (Winett *et al.*, 1981), flicking a light switch (Delprata, 1977; Winett, 1978), purchasing drinks in one container over another (Geller, Wylie, & Farris, 1971; Geller, Farris, & Post, 1973), or dropping a handbill in a conveniently located trash receptacle (Geller, 1975; Geller *et al.*, 1976, 1977). However, the frequency of inconvenient environmental protection behaviors has been increased with the addition of reinforcing consequences. Behavioral consequences can be pleasant (technically termed positive reinforcers if the frequency of the preceding behavior increases) or they can be unpleasant (technically termed negative reinforcers or punishers if the preceding behavior decreases in frequency). Punishment and negative reinforcement procedures to protect the environment usually take the form of laws or ordinances (e.g., fines for speeding, littering, watering lawns, strip mining, and polluting air or water), and require extensive enforcement and legal personnel to make an impact. A beneficial behavioral impact occurs via punishment when individuals make the undesirable response, receive an unpleasant consequence, and are subsequently less likely to repeat the punished response. A behavioral impact occurs via negative reinforcement when individuals emit environment-protecting behaviors in order to avoid the aversive consequence for a particular environment-damaging response.

Applied behavioral scientists have demonstrated empirically a variety of reasons for preferring positive reinforcement over punishment and negative reinforcement, including the fact that positive reinforcement is usually most acceptable, easiest to administer, and most cost-effective. Therefore, behaviorists working for energy conservation and environmental protection have avoided the use of negative reinforcement and punishment procedures. However, to protect our environment, governments and communities have applied positive reinforcement much less often than punishment and negative reinforcement (as manifested through bills, laws and ordinances). Indeed, the "Bottle Bill" of eight states, which specifies monetary remuneration for the return of certain drink containers for recycling, is the only large-scale, positive reinforcement procedure attempted by government, and has probably caused more widespread controversy than any of the negative reinforcement and punishment procedures established by federal and/or state governments for environmental protection (see Geller, 1980b, 1981b; and Osborne & Powers, 1980, for reviews of the issues and ramifications of bottle bills).

The positive consequences applied for environmental protection have varied widely. Some consequences have been given contingent upon the performance of a particular response, whereas other consequence strategies have not specified a desired behavior but were contingent upon a given outcome (e.g., on the basis of energy consumption or environmental cleanliness). The following *response*-contingent consequences were successful in increasing the frequency of the target behavior significantly above baseline levels: (a) raffle tickets for specified amounts of paper brought to a recycling center (Couch, Garber, & Karpus, 1978–79; Ingram & Geller, 1975; Witmer & Geller, 1976); (b) a $5 payment if room thermostat is set at 74° F. in summer and all doors and windows are closed when the air conditioner is on (Walker, 1977); (c) a merchandise token (redeemable for goods and services at local businesses) for riding a particular bus (Deslauriers & Everett, 1977; Everett, Hayward, & Meyers, 1974); (d) a coupon redeemable for a soft drink following litter deposits in a particular trash receptacle (Kohlenberg & Phillips, 1973); (e) a $1 payment and a self-photograph for collecting a specially marked item of litter (Bacon-Prue, Blount, Pickering, & Drabman, 1980); and (f) points exchangeable for family outings and special favors for reduced use of certain home equipment, including the television, music system, oven and furnace (Wodarski, 1976). Examples of cost-effective, *outcome*-contingent consequences are: (a) a payment of 10¢ for cleaning a littered yard to criterion (Chapman & Risley, 1974); (b) a tour of a mental health facility for a 20% or greater reduction in vehicular miles of travel (Foxx & Hake, 1977); (c) the payment of $5 for averaging a 10% reduction in miles of travel over 28 days and $2.50 for each additional 10% reduction up to 30% (Hake & Foxx, 1978); (d) a payment of $2 per week for a 5% to 10% reduction in home-heating energy, $3 for an 11% to 20% reduction, and $5 per week for reductions greater than 20% (Winett & Nietzel, 1975); and (e) the return of 75% of energy savings from expected costs to the residents of a master-metered apartment complex (Slavin & Wodarski, 1977; Slavin, Wodarski, & Blackburn, 1981).

The variety of energy-conservation studies that showed beneficial effects of giving residents frequent and specific feedback regarding energy consumption may also be considered outcome consequences (see reviews by Shippee, 1980; Winett, 1980; and Winett & Neale, 1979). The consequence is an indication of energy consumption in terms of kilowatt hours, cubic feet of gas, and/or monetary cost, and such a consequence can be positive (if the feedback implies a savings in energy costs) or it can be unpleasant or negative (if the feedback indicates an increase in consumption and costs). Most of the feedback studies of environmental protection have targeted residential energy consumption, and for most of these studies the feedback was given individually to target residences. Methods of giving such consumption feedback have included: (a) a special feedback card delivered to the home monthly (Seaver & Patterson, 1976), weekly (Kohlenberg et al., 1976; Winett et al., 1978), or daily (Becker, 1978; Hayes & Cone, 1977; Palmer et al., 1978; Seligman & Darley, 1977; Winett, Kaiser, & Haberkorn, 1977); (b) a mechanical apparatus which illuminated a light whenever current levels exceeded 90% of the peak-use level for the household (Blakely, Lloyd, & Alferink, 1977; Kohlenberg et al., 1976); (c) an electronic feedback meter with digital display of electricity cost per hour (Becker & Seligman, 1978a; McClelland & Cook, 1979–80); and (d) training packages for teaching and motivating residents to read their own electric meters regularly and to record energy consumption (Winett, Neale, & Grier, 1979). A few feedback studies have targeted transportation conservation, showing that vehicular miles of travel (vmt) can be reduced with public display of vmt per individual (Reichel & Geller, 1980); and vehicular miles per gallon (mpg) can be increased with a fuel-flow meter indicating continuous mpg or gallons-per-hour consumption (Lauridsen, 1977) or public display of mpg for short-run and long-haul truck drivers (Runnion, Watson, & McWhorter, 1978). In addition, one feedback intervention targeted litter control, demonstrating a 35% average reduction in ground litter following daily displays of litter counts on the front page of a community newspaper (Schnelle, Gendrich, Beegle, Thomas, & McNees, 1980).

Whereas *response* consequences provide specific information regarding the appropriateness or inappropriateness of a particular behavior, most *outcome* consequences (including consumption feedback) do not prescribe changes in particular responses. In other words, a specific consequence of a response serves to prompt the occurrence of a similar response (if the consequence was pleasant) or the occurrence of an alternative response (if the consequence was unpleasant); outcome consequences that are not associated with specific behaviors (such as consumption feedback) may not necessarily prompt specific behavioral changes. Thus, outcome consequences should be less influential than response consequences, although this author is not aware of a field study that has made this important comparison.

Two consumption-feedback studies did target specific conservation responses. Seligman and Darley (1977) advised residents of a townhouse development to decrease the use of their air conditioner in order to conserve electricity, and subsequently provided residents with daily feedback regarding relative usage of electricity for home cooling. Another consumption feedback intervention with a specific response prescription involved the application of a simple apparatus consisting of a blue light connected to the central air-conditioning system and to a thermostat located on the outside of the house (Becker & Seligman, 1978b). The blue light, obtrusively located in the kitchen, flashed repeatedly when the air conditioning was on and the outside temperature was below 68° F. and stopped flashing when the air conditioning was turned off. Homes with this response-specific feedback device consumed an average of 15.7% less electricity than control homes without this device. In this study periodic feedback regarding overall residential consumption (i.e., outcome consequence) did not add to the electricity savings prompted by the response-consequence device (Becker & Seligman, 1978b).

Behavioral Applications

The behavioral strategies for energy conservation have almost always been applied and tested in the residential sector (rather than industrial/commercial or governmental/institutional sectors), and have targeted home heating or cooling more often than transportation, solid-waste management, or equipment efficiency. This section offers an overview of specific behavior applications for energy conservation, with an emphasis on issues and outcome rather than research design and methodology. Several recent publications have critically reviewed in detail the paradigms and procedures of the behavioral studies which targeted residential heating and cooling (Carlyle & Geller, 1979; Shippee, 1980; Winett, 1980; Winett & Neale, 1979), transportation-energy management (Everett, 1980, 1981; Reichel & Geller, 1981), and solid-waste management, with waste reduction and resource recovery (Geller, 1980b, 1981b) treated separately from litter control (Brasted, Mann, & Geller, 1979; Geller, 1980a; Osborne & Powers, 1980). This section also considers unique aspects of rural settings with regard to the application of strategies for energy conservation.

Heating and Cooling

Daily operations in homes account for approximately 20% of all the energy consumed in the United States; of this residential energy, 30% is used for home heating and about 3% is used for home cooling, including the operation of air conditioners and fans (cf. Large, 1973; Stern & Gardner, 1981). The industrial and commercial sectors actually account for as much as 56% of the nation's energy, with a large portion of this being applied to heating and cooling (Large, 1973). Thus, it may indeed be unfortunate that most of the psychological research on energy conservation has been done in the residential sector and with home heating and cooling (cf. Stern & Gardner, 1981). In fact, the most productive behavioral scientists in this research area have recently made pleas for increased research in other community sectors (i.e., industrial/commercial and governmental) and with target areas other than heating and cooling (e.g., Winett, 1980; Seligman, Becker, & Darley, 1981). On the other hand, it has been estimated that residential heating alone accounted for 44% of the *increase* in electricity consumption from 1960 to 1970 (Large, 1973); furthermore, strategies that are cost-effective in conserving energy used for home heating and cooling may be quite applicable in other settings (e.g., schools, industrial complexes, office buildings, and commercial establishments).

Monetary rebates have been consistently effective in reducing residential energy consumption (primarily for heating and cooling), whether used as individual contingencies (wherein monetary rewards are contingent upon savings by individual households) or as group contingencies (wherein a group of residencies share a monetary reward which is contingent upon savings by the whole group or upon showing the most conservation in a contest between groups). Group contingencies for energy conservation have not been studied nearly as frequently as individual contingencies, yet group contingencies may be more critical for large-scale community applications. This may be the case, not only because there are large numbers of apartments in the United States that have utility bills determined by master-meters (which record only the total energy usage of groups of families), but also because group contingencies can foster mutual collaboration toward desirable goals. Actually, a social effort toward conserving energy for heating and cooling can lead to a realization of conservation as a social norm and to other group behaviors which save energy and protect the environment. In fact, the beneficial effects of many environmental protection strategies are only visible, cost-effective, and reinforcing when large numbers of individuals contribute to a group effort. Thus, car pools, recycling programs, and litter-cleanup campaigns require an initial organizational effort among several individuals. The successful application of group contingencies may be one important way of prompting such collaboration.

Whereas rebate systems have perhaps been the most successful strategy for motivating high levels of conservation in home heating and cooling (i.e., reduction ranging from 12% to over 30%), they have not been the most cost-effective. Frequent consumption feedback has resulted in savings of residential electricity as high as 30%, and these feedback procedures have been much less costly to implement than monetary rebates. Moreover, recent studies of feedback effects showed maintenance of the energy savings achieved during feedback for 6 to 12 weeks after the feedback was abruptly ended (Winett, Neale, & Grier, 1979; Winett, Neale, Williams, Yokley, & Kauder, 1979).

Feedback programs can be expected to be most effective when homeowners are initially committed to saving energy, when residents pick difficult but achievable consumption reduction goals, such as a 20% reduction (Becker, 1978), when the consumption information is provided for individual households rather than for groups of households (Winett et al., 1979), and when the feedback is frequent and credible (Becker & Seligman, 1978b). Regarding the credibility issue, Seligman et al. (1981) warn that reporting actual fluctuations in energy consumption (e.g., from a 20% decrease on one day to a 20% increase on the next day) might actually be detrimental to a feedback program because residents may not believe the consumption feedback or the calculations used to determine comparison percentages. One way to avoid this problem may be to teach residents to read their own electric meters and calculate comparisons between expected and actual usage. Such a feedback system could be readily implemented on a large scale. The resulting self-monitoring behavior would be an excellent way to initiate family interest in energy conservation, and daily charting (or graphing) of the meter readings would provide consumption feedback capable of making residents cognizant of their own consumption and of prompting conservation behaviors. In fact, it would be worthwhile if power companies gave residents the option of calling in their own meter readings each month for billing. Monetary rebates (or special deductions) might even be feasible for accurately self-reporting one's electricity consumption, since such a procedure would eliminate many travel and salary expenses of professional meter readers (except for annual or biannual reliability checks). The resultant savings in transportation energy would be especially substantial in rural areas.

Both the feasibility and the conservation potential of having residents call in monthly meter readings were supported by a provocative study by Winett, Neale, and Grier (1979). These investigations implemented a program to promote self-monitoring of electric meters (including 10 minutes of personal instruction, a training package, special data-recording sheets, and weekly reminders), and found that residents did in fact read their meters daily on more than 90% of the possible occasions, even during periods of rain, sleet, and snow. Daily reliability checks by research assistants resulted in matched readings for 96% of the comparisons. Furthermore, during the self-monitoring period, residents reduced their electricity usage by 7% to 8%, saving an average of 9 kilowatt-hours per day and $11 a month.

The electricity savings in the Winett et al. (1979) study correlated highly with reported reductions in thermostat settings. This is consistent with the notion that "thermostat-setting is the conservation activity with the single greatest potential for influencing energy consumption in buildings" (Becker & Seligman, 1981, p. 8). Indeed, recent field studies by Winett and his students showed that residents could save as much as 27% of their winter heating bill and 42% of their summer cooling bill by appropriately adjusting thermostat settings 3–4 degrees (Geller et al., 1982; Winett et al., 1981). Actually, Winett et al. found that residents could adapt to colder (about 61° F.) and warmer (about 80° F.) temperatures than had been expected from prior laboratory findings on comfort, with changes in indoor clothing ensembles being the primary strategy for dealing with residential temperature extremes. Indeed, strategies for coping with temperature change following efforts to conserve heating and cooling energy should play an important role in a comprehensive energy-conservation program. The problem is that field research in this area is minimal, although recent findings from laboratory research in thermal comfort are certainly worth considering in this regard (see review by Rohles, 1981).

Although clothing is the most economical and influential factor determining thermal comfort, Rohles discusses several additional strategies for saving heating and cooling energy in buildings, including the use of dehumidifiers, window fans, radiant heaters, electric blankets, and even particular room decor, including room size, lighting, color, and furnishings.

Transportation Energy

Transportation consumes 55% of the petroleum used in the United States; half of this amount is used by passenger cars and taxis, 25% by trucks, 8% by airplanes, buses, and transit vehicles (Zerega, 1981). Furthermore, it has been estimated that 32% of all trips by automobiles are made for commuting back and forth to work; these trips are the least energy-efficient, because 75% of these commuting vehicles carry only the driver (U.S. Department of Transportation, 1973). For example, during the summer of 1980 the present author conducted a field study that included the daily observation of vehicles entering the Virginia Tech parking lots during morning arrival times, and only 17% of 13,709 vehicles included one or more passengers. Thus, passenger cars should be the prime target for transportation conservation, and the work trip offers much potential for energy savings. Curtailment strategies for conserving transportation energy include ride sharing (e.g., car and van pools), the use of mass transit (e.g., buses, trains, and subways), and the adoption of driving and car-maintenance habits which increase vehicular miles per gallon (e.g., by not exceeding 55 m.p.h., but avoiding rapid acceleration, and by keeping vehicle engines properly tuned and tires properly inflated). Of course, the important efficiency strategy for conserving transportation energy is to purchase and use energy-efficient vehicles (including mopeds and bicycles). When considering strategies for conserving transportation energy, it is important to realize that the automobile is the most significant contributor to air pollution, and urban noise and congestion (cf. Dorf, 1974; Everett, 1981). Thus, strategies that reduce use of gas-driven vehicles (e.g., ride sharing, mass transit, bicycling, and walking) are usually more beneficial to the environment than are those which increase miles per gallon (e.g., through driving habits, vehicular maintenance, or purchase decisions).

As reviewed by Everett (1980, 1981) and Reichel and Geller (1981), a rather large number of communities have applied positive reinforcement contingencies to manage transportation for conservation goals. Most of these programs have been designed to increase bus ridership (e.g., by reinforcing bus usage with such rewards as food coupons, zoo passes, novelty items, and raffle tickets) although there have been communitywide attempts to promote car pooling (e.g., by offering priority "fast" traffic lanes, reductions in fares on toll roads, or preferential parking to vehicles with at least a certain number of passengers). Unfortunately, these incentive programs were not systematically evaluated with regard to cost-effectiveness or behavioral and attitudinal impact; therefore they provide only minimal instructive information for the development and refinement of transportation programs.

The research by Everett and his students stands as the seminal work in the behavioral analysis of transportation programs (Deslauriers & Everett, 1977; Everett, Deslauriers, Newson, & Anderson, 1978; Everett & Hayward, 1974; Everett et al., 1974). Their work demonstrates: (a) the cost effectiveness of using incentives for promoting bus usage (e.g., coupons exchangeable for discounts at community businesses), (b) the critical problems associated with some interventions (e.g., the incentive conditions influenced people who would normally walk to ride the bus rather than people who drive automobiles), and (c) a model for a systematic behavioral analysis of potential solutions to a community problem. However, bus ridership as a target for energy conservation may have limited large-scale benefit in many situations, given that there are only a few peak usage times during the day and that meeting an increased demand at these times can result in an increase in nonproductive bus runs and idle bus drivers during a greater part of the work day (Zerega, 1981). Furthermore, mass-transit considerations are only appropriate for urban environments; private vehicles are essentially the only source of transportation in semiurban and rural environments.

Thus, programs to conserve transportation energy in rural environments must target the use of personal cars and trucks, in order to decrease their usage and increase the efficiency of their usage.

Actually, only a few behavioral studies have targeted the private automobile and implemented strategies applicable in rural settings. Foxx and Hake (1977) and Hake and Foxx (1978) developed and field tested incentive programs for reducing the use of personal vehicles. In both studies, college students significantly reduced the use of their automobiles when financial remuneration and other rewards (e.g., a university parking sticker, an oil change and lubrication, or a tour of a mental health facility) were contingent upon certain percentage reductions in odometer readings from baseline levels. A cost–benefit analysis of the particular interventions in these studies revealed more costs than savings, thus indicating that contingencies sufficient to reduce vehicular miles of travel may be impractical for communitywide application. However, large-scale applications of reinforcement procedures can often provide for more benefits than costs. For example, the reinforcers can be lottery tickets for a community drawing at which prizes donated by local merchants are raffled off, and an increase in numbers of participants (with no change in reward costs) obviously increases potential benefits without raising costs. Furthermore, in some situations (e.g., work or school settings) public display of vehicular miles traveled per individual and commendation from group leaders for reductions might be sufficient for motivating decreased usage of private automobiles. Indeed, Reichel and Geller (1980) found college students to reduce significantly the mileage on their odometer for chances to win prizes which were donated by community merchants. Further reductions in vehicular miles were realized when the group leader (i.e., the present author) offered special encouragement and commendation for significant reduction shown by daily public displays of individual mileage and percent change from baseline.

Reinforcement contingencies, similar to those designed to promote reduced use of private automobiles, have been successfully applied in programs to encourage fuel-saving driving among truck drivers of a textile company (Runnion, Watson, & McWhorter, 1978), and to promote car pooling among employees at a gas pipeline company (Letzkus & Scharfe, 1975) and among students at a university (Jacobs, Fairbanks, Poche, & Bailey, 1979). Furthermore, miles per gallon have been increased through feedback (Lauridsen, 1977), and ride sharing has been facilitated significantly by such environmental interventions as priority lanes (MacCalden & Davis, 1972; Rose & Hinds, 1976), preferential parking (Hirst, 1976; Pratsch, 1975), and organizational matching efforts (Jones & Derby, 1976). These and other programs for encouraging conservation in transportation energy are critically reviewed elsewhere (Reichel & Geller, 1981); here it is useful to consider a few additional strategies which may be particularly appropriate for rural settings.

Employer-sponsored van pools, which have increased markedly in recent years (cf. Forstater & Twomey, 1976), have excellent potential for saving transportation energy. For example, Pratsch (1977) estimated that a typical eight-passenger van pool saves about 5,000 gallons of gasoline a year. As reported by Owens and Sever (1977), the 3M Commute-A-Van (CAV) program provides an excellent model for a cost-effective van pool (which was originally developed by the company to eliminate employee parking problems rather than to conserve gas). The CAV essentially involves the use of company-owned vans to transport employees to and from work. Employees volunteer to be van coordinators who are responsible for picking up and returning passengers, arranging for service, maintaining the van, training backup drivers, keeping records, parking overnight, and billing riders (e.g., from $19.50 to $29.50 per month in 1974, depending upon commuting distance). In return for these services, the van coordinator receives a free ride to and from work, personal use of the van at seven cents per mile, convenient parking at 3M, and the receipt of all passenger fares over some minimum (based on fixed and operating costs). As reviewed by Owens and Sever (1977) the benefits of the CAV for 3M far outweighed the costs, and the average occupancy per community vehicle at the 3M Company increased 25% (from 1.24 to 1.55) after implementation of the van pool.

Besides car pooling and van pooling, a third type of ride sharing may have special significance for small-town, rural transportation needs. This ride-sharing concept, referred to as *ad hoc pooling* (cf. Barkow, 1974), requires three basic components: (a) a central dispatcher who matches the travel demands of individuals without an automobile to the trip-making intentions of people with an automobile; (b) a social system to efficiently acquaint people (perhaps via church or community gatherings) so that drivers and riders feel comfortable with one another; and (c) positive reinforcement contingencies to promote and maintain the system. Then the individual in need of a ride simply calls into the central dispatcher in order to be matched with individuals who will be driving to the same area. To this author's knowledge, such a system has not been formally implemented, although programs to formalize hitchhiking do represent an extension of this notion of ad hoc pooling. For example, Cone and Hayes (1978) summarized a government-sponsored project in Poland, whereby hitchhiking is made more acceptable. More specifically, potential hitchhikers apply for an identification card from the government which certifies them as safe riders, and they purchase tickets which they present to certified drivers who offer them rides. The tickets are subsequently turned in by the driver for remuneration and for chances in a national lottery.

A program to encourage legalized hitchhiking was also attempted in the United States. Specifically, the city of Eugene, Oregon, initiated the "Eugene Ride Stop" program in 1972, which provided a voluntary system of registration for hitchhikers and designated special "pull-over and pick-up" points. The pick-up points were located away from intersections and provided pull-over space that did not obstruct traffic. The program was canceled after approximately one year, because of neighborhood complaints and increased crimes (e.g., muggings). (See Dallmeyer, 1975, for a more detailed account of the issues and problems involved in regulating hitchhiking.) It is certainly possible that appropriate environmental conditions and social contingencies can be developed to make the concepts of ad hoc pooling and formalized hitchhiking feasible in rural environments. This is certainly a ripe area for valuable community research. One point worth noting is that the typical hitchhiker does not own an automobile and thus the energy savings that could be realized from regulated hitchhiking programs is questionable, unless automobile drivers become hitchhikers. However, most automobile drivers could not be expected to forego their reliable vehicle for the possibility of obtaining a free ride through hitchhiking, unless the system provides for safe and rapid pickup and/or purchase of gasoline becomes a debilitating hardship for car owners.

One final approach to conserving transportation energy that is quite applicable to rural environments is to decrease the perceived need for mobility by making the home environment more rewarding and efficient in meeting family pleasures (cf. Skinner, 1975). For example, Gurin (1976) considered several strategies for decreasing mobility from home, including the following: (a) substituting phone calls for trips; (b) reducing personal and household stress; (c) improving dwelling designs to lessen family conflicts, thereby reducing the need to "get away from it all"; (d) increasing home-centered recreational activities; (e) facilitating home delivery of goals and services; (f) locating desired destination activities nearer to home; and (g) reducing peak-hour travel.

From a review of the social science literature and from his survey of male high school students, Gurin estimated substantial institutional, cultural, and psychosocial barriers to implementing these strategies. For example, just to substitute telephone calls for travel among teenagers, the following factors would have to be considered: (a) some parents are reluctant to install telephones in rooms where teenagers can hold private phone conversations, (b) teenagers value face-to-face interactions when developing friendships, (c) teenage social exchanges often take place in groups, and (d) teenage panelists expressed distrust of the telephone company. These potential barriers do not preclude the application of incentive techniques to encourage phone calls instead of travel, but do provide guidelines for developing appropriate contingencies. This is a domain of energy conservation and community research that is in much need of empirical study.

Solid Waste Management

The communitywide management of solid waste consumes enormous amounts of energy; and there are a variety of approaches to solid waste management, each determining a significant change (increase or decrease) in energy consumption and environmental degradation. Three domains are relevant here, namely, waste reduction, resource recovery, and litter control, and each includes a variety of approaches for conserving environmental resources and alleviating energy shortages. Furthermore, each of these components of solid waste management requires human intervention and can therefore benefit from applied behavioral analysis. Indeed, it is this author's opinion that input from the behavioral and social sciences is critical for the success of more conservation strategies in solid waste management than in the other general target areas (i.e., heating/cooling, transportation, and equipment efficiency). However, solid waste management is barely mentioned in recent reviews of the role of behavioral science in energy conservation (e.g., Lloyd, 1980; McClelland & Carter, 1981; Shippee, 1980; Stern & Gardner, 1981; Winett, 1980; Winett & Neale, 1979); nor are issues of solid waste management considered in any of the articles comprising a special edition (1981) of *Journal of Social Issues* (edited by Clive Seligman and Lawrence Becker) which was devoted entirely to energy conservation.

Strategies for resource recovery are considered either *high-technology* or *low-technology* approaches. A high-technology recovery system (involving maximum use of engineering science) is quite expensive but most convenient for the consumer. Under such a system, garbage is collected as usual and transported to a "resource recovery" plant, which mechanically separates paper, glass, aluminum, and metal for reuse in manufacturing. The remaining refuse is burned with coal and oil to produce steam for electricity generation or oil through a process called *pyrolysis* (cf. Seldman, 1975; 1976b; 1977). In contrast, the low-technology approach to resource recovery refers to the more economical but less consumer-convenient system of separating garbage into reusable materials at the place where the waste was produced (e.g., the residence, institution, or factory) and then transporting separated waste to appropriate manufacturers (e.g., paper to a paper mill, glass to a glass factory, and aluminum to a can company). The low-technology approach to resource recovery usually requires a mechanism for initiating and maintaining appropriate human input during the first link of the system (i.e., the separation component), and here input from the behavioral sciences is invaluable.

It is noteworthy that high- versus low-technology approaches to resource recovery are quite incompatible and implicate a conflict between physical and psychological strategies for energy conservation. For example, an expensive resource recovery plant requires a minimum quota of trash each year to be profitable, and thus serves as a disincentive for waste reduction and low-technology resource recovery (cf. Seldman, 1977). The purported advantages and disadvantages of high- versus low-technology recycling and reclamation are reviewed elsewhere (Geller, 1980b; 1981b), but are relatively unimportant here because only low-technology systems are feasible for rural settings. High-technology systems require large amounts of concentrated and convenient sources of trash, as well as substantial capital investments for system development and maintenance (cf. LaBreque, 1977; Seldman, 1976a, 1976b), and thus are only practical for densely populated urban environments. Indeed, some experts have argued convincingly that the high-technology approach to resource recovery is even less desirable than low-technology systems in big cities (e.g., see reviews by Geller, 1980b, 1981b, and the recent attempt to develop a national recycling policy by the Institute for Local Self-Reliance, 1980). For example, "design shortcomings and technological bugs" in New York City's resource-recovery plants have prompted serious consideration of "instituting low-technology recycling on a citywide basis"; and a large-scale, low-technology program was initiated in East Harlem in 1979, and its fantastic success has been attributed to a "coupon-incentive idea" which provides coupons per specified amounts of recyclables and "people save the coupons like green stamps and redeem them for movie, play, or sports event tickets that have been donated" (McDermott, 1980, p. 9).

Litter is typically considered a behavioral problem and has been advertised as such by Keep America Beautiful, Inc. (KAB), a highly publicized, nonprofit agency whose primary goal is to combat environmental litter (cf. KAB, 1977a, 1977b). In fact, litter control is the aspect of environmental protection which was targeted first by behavioral scientists and has been the focus of a substantial number of applied environmental studies (e.g., see reviews by Brasted et al., 1979; Geller, 1980a; Kazdin, 1977; Osborne & Powers, 1980; Tuso & Geller, 1976). Although litter control is clearly recognized as a necessary component for environmental protection, it is typically not included in discussions of energy conservation. However, litter can be considered wasted energy, in the sense that most discarded solid waste can be (a) used as raw material for the production of new commodities, (b) modified or repaired for reuse, (c) added to a compost pile for improved gardening, or (d) burned to produce energy (cf. Geller, 1980b; 1981b; Osborne & Powers, 1980). The behavioral strategies that prevent littering (e.g., by promoting trash-can disposals) or improve a littered environment (e.g., by motivating litter pickup) make it possible for the discarded items to be rechanneled in energy conserving ways. Alternatively, strategies that encourage waste reduction or resource recovery and have a direct impact on energy conservation indirectly reduce potential for environmental litter.

Durable Waste. Municipal waste can be categorized into five types: durable waste, nondurable waste, packaging waste, food waste, and yard waste (Wahl & Allison, 1975); each trash category is a potential target for particular waste reduction and/or recovery strategies. The variety of strategies are reviewed by Geller (1980b, 1981b) and will not be presented here; instead, certain strategies based on behavioral principles and especially relevant for rural settings are highlighted as they relate to particular waste categories. For example, the "marked item technique" demonstrated by behavioral scientists as a cost-effective strategy for litter control (Bacon-Prue *et al.*, 1980; Hayes, Johnson, & Cone, 1975; LeHart & Bailey, 1975) may be quite appropriate for encouraging the redistribution of large discarded durables (such as televisions, refrigerators, lawn mowers, furniture, and automobiles) to repair shops, recycling centers, or scrap yards. That is, certain durables could be specifically marked unobtrusively by officials from redemption centers; subsequently, the reporting and/or the appropriate relocation of these marked items would result in a large financial reward and/or public recognition through the news media. Another feasible reward strategy would be to offer a lottery ticket for each recyclable durable. Tickets for weekly raffles were quite cost-effective in encouraging newspaper recycling at universities (Couch, Garber, & Karpus, 1978–79; Geller *et al.*, 1975; Ingram & Geller, 1975; Witmer & Geller, 1976).

A recently introduced strategy for recovering durables that is particularly cost-effective and especially applicable for rural settings has been termed *highgrading* by the few individuals who have practiced the technique of retrieving reusable materials from garbage bins and dumping areas (Appelhof, 1980a; Knapp, 1979). For example, in Lane County, Oregon, highgrade recyclers were located at the local landfill to recover and clean recyclable metals, including aluminum, copper, brass, cast iron, and heavy steel. Cards distributed to landfill users which explained the metal recovery program were effective in prompting most individuals to keep metals separate from the rest of their trash and to drop them off in the "metals recovery area" adjacent to the landfill dump. During one 10-week period, two highgraders (each working an average of 24 hours a week) processed 15 tons of metals which met market requirements (Knapp, 1979). Another highgrading program (i.e., at the landfill in Berkeley, California) employs three to six full-time workers doing metal salvage, metal processing and direct sales, and as of July, 1980, was producing from 100 to 150 tons of recyclable metal per month at values ranging from $5,000 to $7,000 (Appelhof, 1980a).

Nondurable Wastes.   A majority of the nondurable wastes are paper-based (e.g., newspapers, magazines, tissues, towels, paper cups and plates) which can be used as a raw material for paper manufacturing (i.e., recycling). However, nondurables are also prime candidates for waste-reduction programs since so many nondurable commodities can be replaced with reusables (e.g., returnable bottles, plastic cups and plates, and cloth napkins, diapers, and tissues). Behavioral scientists have studied techniques for encouraging the recycling of newspapers and aluminum cans and for influencing consumers to make waste-reduction decisions (i.e., to purchase drinks in returnable rather than nonreturnable containers). These studies demonstrated the utility of applied behavioral analysis in establishing and evaluating low-technology, recycling and waste-reduction programs, and further showed that to maintain such programs it is necessary to implement incentive strategies when the desired participant behaviors are relatively inconvenient. For example, antecedent strategies (i.e., prompting) were sufficient to influence about 20% of a store's drink customers to make the convenient response of selecting their drinks in returnable rather than throwaway containers (Geller *et al.*, 1971, 1973); but prompting alone was not effective in increasing participation in newspaper-recycling programs when participant behaviors were relatively inconvenient, such as transporting newspapers to a collection center (e.g., Geller *et al.*, 1975; Hamad, Bettinger, Cooper, & Semb, 1978; Witmer & Geller, 1976). However, when the response cost for participants in a recycling program was minimized (e.g., by the convenient location of special recycling containers), prompting alone (without consequence strategies) resulted in the collection of substantial amounts of recyclable newspapers and aluminum cans in both institutions (e.g., Humphrey, Bord, Hammond, & Mann, 1977; Luyben, Warren, & Randall, 1979–80) and residential settings (e.g., Jacobs & Bailey, 1979; Luyben & Bailey, 1979; Reid, Luyben, Rawers, & Bailey, 1976). As reviewed by Geller (1980b, 1981b) these studies also demonstrated the need to perform a comprehensive analysis of both the energy costs and benefits of a recycling program. For example, elementary schools and institutional offices can tap a larger source of recyclable newspapers than college dormitories, but such programs should be set up so that extra transportation energy is not used to transport the recyclables. Recycling programs should use convenience and/or incentive strategies to encourage the delivery of recyclables as a part of another trip. Thus, schools and churches have excellent potential as "recycling centers" because participants can make deliveries as a supplement to their normal transportation to the facility and because announcements and reminders about the programs can be given to a "captive" audience.

Packaging Waste. The major portion of municipal waste includes the cans, bottles, cartons, boxes, and wrappings in which consumer goods are transported and sold. In 1971 packaging and containerization consumed approximately 75% of all glass production, 50% of all paper, 29% of all plastics, 14% of all aluminum, and 8% of all steel production (Wahl & Allison, 1975; Wendt, 1975). In fact, if the amount of per capita packaging in the United States would have been controlled at the 1958 level (the year that marked the beginning of the "packaging explosion"), it was estimated that the nation "would have saved more than 566 trillion BTUs, the equivalent of 267,000 barrels of oil each day" (Wahl & Allison, 1975, p. 24).

Governmental controls offer potential for the greatest impact toward decreasing waste due to unnecessary packaging, but such regulatory legislation is usually difficult to get past the lobbying and political pressures of special interest groups. For example, even though a bottle bill which mandates a deposit on all drink containers has clear benefits for litter control, waste reduction, and energy conservation, lobbying by bottle manufacturers and distributors (and confusion and misunderstanding by the public) has prevented passage of a bottle bill in all but eight states. (For more details on the issues regarding bottle bill legislation see reviews by Geller, 1980b, 1981b; Osborne & Powers, 1980.) Actually, public understanding and support for packaging regulations may depend upon the development of community resource-conservation projects. Cooperating in one waste-reduction or resource-recovery program may not only result in positive attitudes toward that particular program, but may in fact increase the probability of attitudinal and behavioral support for additional efforts toward energy conservation and environmental protection. Thus, it is perhaps no coincidence that Oregon was the first state to ban the nonreturnable drink container (in 1971) and subsequently has led all states in the implementation of large-scale, energy-efficient programs for managing solid waste (e.g., Buel, 1977; Duncan, 1976a, 1976b; Seldman, 1975).

Food and Yard Waste. Taken together, food and yard waste comprise the largest proportion of municipal waste, e.g., about 36% in 1973 (Wahl & Allison, 1975). However, it is also the case that a low-technology procedure is available for disposing of these wastes which is particularly suitable for rural settings and "has the highest 'net energy' yield of all recycling processes" (Duncan, 1976b, p. 32). This procedure is *composting*, which essentially consists of stockpiling food and yard wastes and intermittently turning the compost pile to allow for oxygenation. Then, if the pile is turned at least biweekly, compost will be available in about three weeks for upgrading the soil characteristics of a flower or vegetable garden. Compost improves soil workability for plowing and planting, increases water-holding capacity and resistance to erosion, provides trace minerals and some nutrients, decreases soil compactibility for better aeration and gas exchange around plant roots, and increases the quantity and nutritional quality of yields (Institute for Local Self-Reliance, 1975; Tietjen & Hart, 1969).

Soil can be further improved for gardening with the addition of another low-technology procedure which has just recently been receiving serious attention. This procedure is termed *vermicomposting* and involves the maintenance of a worm bin (e.g., a 2' × 2' × 8" plywood box containing from three to four pounds of worms) in which residents dispose of their food wastes and from which they obtain humus-rich nutrient-laden vermicompost. Combining vermicompost with soil or adding it to a compost pile of yard waste (grass, leaves, twigs, etc.) results in an almost optimal medium for plant growth. Details of building and maintaining bins for vermicomposting are presented elsewhere, and research is currently underway to make these procedures more convenient, efficient, and acceptable to the householder (e.g., Appelhof, 1974, 1979, 1980b). At any rate, the procedures recommended for successful vermicomposting are extremely cost-effective, requiring: (a) a small initial financial investment for bin materials, worms, and worm bedding; (b) a few hours to prepare the household compost bin; (c) ten minutes each week to bury food waste in the bin; and (d) two hours every four months to collect the vermicompost from the bin and apply fresh bedding (Appelhof, 1980b). As the worms multiply they can be added to the household garden or compost pile, but in rural settings there is a high probability that a local fisherman will claim to have an even better use for these extra worms.

Composting and vermicomposting require relatively minimal response cost—not much more effort than bagging food and yard waste weekly for the garbage collector or piling and burning leaves. However, before composting will occur to any great extent, education programs are necessary to teach and promote the appropriate procedures for meeting health standards (e.g., keeping compost relatively free of odors, seepage, rodents, and insects) and for minimizing financial costs, energy consumption, and individual effort. Household vermicomposting will require the application of special tactics to overcome initial negative reactions to bringing earthworms into one's home. One approach might be to introduce vermicomposting in school science classes and include the building and maintenance of vermicomposting bins as individual or group activity projects. Such a project would be educational and contribute to the development of a waste reduction and resource recovery ethic.

Equipment Efficiency

Stern and Gardner (1981) suggested that purchasing the most energy-efficient equipment available offers the most potential for large-scale energy conservation. For example, these authors compiled data from ten reputable sources (i.e., journal articles, energy manuals and technical reports) and presented the following percentages of current total household energy consumption that could be saved if all consumers were to purchase the most energy-efficient equipment available when old equipment wears out and would normally be replaced: (a) more efficient automobile (27.5 miles per gallon)—a 20% savings; (b) more efficient heating equipment—a 8% savings; (c) more efficient water heater—a 2% savings; (d) more efficient refrigerator/freezer—a 1.6% savings; (e) more efficient stove—a 0.9% savings; and (f) more efficient air conditioner—a 0.7% savings. As reported by Stern and Gardner, each of these estimates is higher than the estimated energy savings that would result from nationwide adoption of the usage or curtailment behaviors related to the particular equipment item, that is: car pooling to work—a 4.6% savings; setting back thermostat from 72° to 68° F. during day and to 65° F. at night—a 4% savings; setting back thermostat of water heater by 20° F.—a 1% savings; opening and closing refrigerator door quickly, thawing frozen foods in refrigerator before cooking and cleaning refrigerator coils frequently—a 0.7% savings; avoiding the use of self-cleaning feature on oven, using appropriate-sized cooking pots, and avoiding opening oven door to check food—a 0.2% savings; and increasing thermostat setting of air conditioner from 73° to 78° F.—a 0.6% savings. Thus, replacing the six equipment items when necessary with the most energy-efficient alternative amounts to a total 33.2% estimated savings of current total household energy consumption, compared with an estimated total maximum savings of 12.5% for using automobiles, appliances, and heating units in more energy-efficient ways.

Since these estimated energy savings of equipment purchase versus equipment usage were based on laboratory tests and mathematical forecasting that included many unknown factors, extreme caution is advised when considering this information. Indeed, as discussed earlier, actual field tests of electricity savings following thermostat adjustments indicated that the estimate reported by Stern and Gardner was a gross underestimation. Furthermore, repairing and reusing equipment rather than purchasing new equipment saves both disposal and manufacturing energy, as well as landfill space. At any rate, the estimates reported by Stern and Gardner do support the importance of considering equipment efficiency (including both purchase and usage strategies) when planning energy-conservation programs. Such considerations are perhaps more important in the industrial and government sectors than in the residential sector, where the equipment is a much higher consumer of energy; small improvements in residential efficiency can result in large reductions of energy consumption and such savings can occur with only one decision regarding equipment purchase or usage policy.

Within the context of equipment efficiency, people can purchase and use appropriately equipment designed specifically to reduce energy consumption. The *Fitch energy monitor* is an example of this, as is the *psychostat*—a clock-driven thermostat that can be automatically set to raise and lower residential temperatures at specific times during the day, with a special override feature that enables the resident to select a temperature setting not originally programmed (Darley, 1978). There are numerous other devices on the market that are designed to help consumers conserve energy (ranging from low-cost, simple gadgets to reduce the flow of water or electricity to more expensive and complex systems for using solar energy to heat air and/or water). Psychologists can certainly contribute information relevant to persuading the public to buy and apply energy-efficient equipment, but interdisciplinary input is drastically needed in this area. For example, before large-scale dissemination and promotion of equipment efficiency strategies can occur, technical manuals should be developed that list the variety of equipment items available in a particular application category (such as water-flow restriction, solar water heating, solar air heating, etc.); for each item, the manual should specify the expected energy savings, the financial payback period, and the response costs for the consumer (including installation, daily usage, and repair or replacement costs). Actually, equipment efficiency manuals are also needed to advise homeowners, businessmen, building managers and community managers when and how to replace old inefficient equipment and how to use both old and new equipment efficiently. Such information requires both laboratory and field investigation, each with intensive and extended collaboration between architects, engineers, economists, policy planners, and psychologists.

A Framework for Organizing Community Action

At the end of a lengthy discussion of components in a comprehensive approach to promoting large-scale energy conservation, the following points are evident:

1. The energy crisis is multifaceted and demanding of inter-disciplinary attention.
2. A large number of conservation strategies are currently available in each of the target areas (i.e., heating and cooling, transportation, solid waste management, and equipment efficiency).
3. Many of these strategies involve human intervention and/or impact on quality of human life, and therefore require input from the behavioral and social sciences.
4. Much information is lacking (especially field data) regarding the relative cost-effectiveness of the large variety of conservation strategies.
5. There are sufficient data regarding some conservation strategies to strongly recommend communitywide adoption.
6. Dissemination techniques and action plans are urgently needed for motivating large-scale application of the various cost-effective, conservation strategies currently available.

The remainder of this chapter outlines a plan for disseminating conservation strategies throughout a community and for encouraging their adoption. The plan, termed an *Energy Conserving Community* (ECC) *System,* is not presented as a specific recommendation based on empirical tests, but rather as a general guideline requiring refinement for particular situations and needing systematic evaluation regarding: (a) its acceptability to community leaders and consumers, (b) the amount of actual community involvement stimulated, (c) the cost-effectiveness of the various operations, and (d) the degree of actual (and potential) energy conservation per community sector, target, and strategy.

First, it should be noted that the ECC system was influenced by the organizational scheme of the Clean Community System (CCS) of Keep America Beautiful, Inc. (KAB), which has been very successful in promoting practical relationships between local government, businesses, and civic organizations for cooperative community action toward solving waste-management problems (cf. KAB, 1977a). As of this writing, the CCS has been initiated in more than 166 United States communities (many of them rural), and has influenced significantly the litter-control programming in six other countries: Australia, Bermuda, Canada, Great Britain, New Zealand, and South Africa ("Canada Seventh Country," 1979). Thus, the CCS program is probably the most appropriate *working* model for organizing, motivating, and evaluating community action toward the large-scale solution of environmental problems. The CCS has been critically reviewed elsewhere, including its specific weaknesses (i.e., see Geller, 1980a; Geller *et al.*, 1982) and will not be described here. Actually, the ECC plan represents an adaptation of the CCS for energy conservation, incorporating the framework around which this chapter was organized; that is, a $2 \times 3 \times 4$ factorial of two general approaches (Physical and Psychological), three community sectors that must be reached (Residential/Consumer, Commercial/Industrial, and Governmental/Institutional), and four basic targets for conservation intervention (Heating/Cooling, Transportation, Solid Waste Management, and Equipment Efficiency).

Procedures for motivating individual and group action are critical aspects of both the CCS and ECC plans and are largely based on principles of positive reinforcement (rather than negative reinforcement and punishment), with social approval and public recognition being primary rewarding consequences. Indeed, anticipated local and national commendation are major potential motivators for becoming a "certified clean community" under the CCS. The proposed ECC plan is a two-stage system, whereby communities first initiate conservation action in order to earn eligibility as a "certified energy *conserving* community" (ECC), and then specific criteria are developed for qualification as a "certified energy *efficient* community" (EEC). Completing each stage of the ECC plan results in state and national acknowledgment and special financial rewards through government grants. Indeed, it is proposed that certain government contingency funds (state and/or federal) would only be available for communities reaching the EEC status, and that these communities are reviewed annually with regard to their maintenance of the EEC criteria. Throughout an ECC program, local incentives must be developed in order to encourage the accomplishment of successive approximations toward reaching EEC status; and after becoming an EEC, local incentive systems are necessary to reward maintenance activities.

General procedures toward becoming an ECC and then earning certification as an EEC are outlined in Figure 1. A community initiates an ECC application with a letter of endorsement from the mayor (or similar high-ranking official), an agreement to send an eight-member work team to an ECC training conference and the allocation of sufficient funds for the first year of operation. The training conferences are organized through state extension systems and/or state energy offices, who in turn are accountable to a national coordinating agency (such as the United States Department of Energy). The eight-member ECC work team includes one representative for each cell of the 2(Approach) $\times$ 4(Target) factorial.

At the training conference, work teams from particular communities learn the ECC plan for coordinating, motivating, and evaluating a communitywide program for energy conservation. Some workshop presentations are specialized according to the four conservation targets and

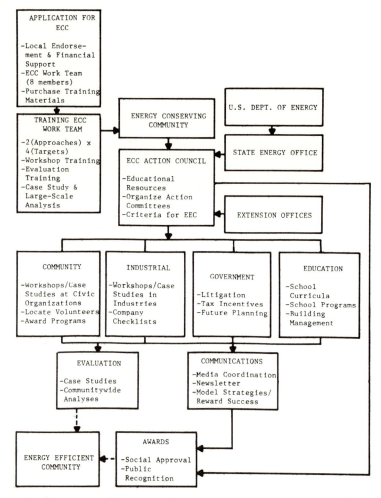

FIGURE 1. Organizational structure of an Energy Conserving Community (ECC) plan and the functional relationship between the components of an ECC.

two basic approaches, and on these occasions the work teams split up according to individual areas of expertise. As a group the teams are given the background, techniques, and materials for presenting local workshops to the three community sectors. These local workshops are designed to inform individuals of cost-effective conservation strategies for their particular situations, and to collaborate with the work teams on the design of local incentive programs for stimulating and maintaining conservation activities in four target areas of three community sectors.

After the week-long training conference, the eight-member work teams return home to initiate large-scale conservation programs under the overall 2(Approach) × 3(Sector) × 4(Target) factorial. The participating community is considered a certified ECC, and local progress toward becoming a certified EEC community is continually monitored and rewarded by local, state, and federal intervention. Major initial tasks of the ECC work team include:

1. Establishment of a local headquarters
2. Allocation of financial support
3. Administration of ECC workshops to key leaders in government institutions, commercial enterprises, industrial complexes, and community agencies
4. Implementation of an overall community analysis of energy consumption in the four target areas of the three major community sectors
5. Selection of demonstration projects, representative of each target area within each sector
6. Organization of an ECC Action Council

The ECC Action Council is the key organizational component and work force of the ECC plan. This 30-member council includes influential leaders from the three community sectors, experts in the four target areas, and professionals from disciplines related to the physical and psychological approaches to energy conservation (e.g., architecture, economics, education, engineering, physics, psychology, and sociology). Important responsibilities of this committee include:

1. Maintaining an up-to-date library of resources relevant to energy conservation
2. Maintaining communications with local extension agents and with the energy-conservation specialists who ran the ECC training conference, certified the community as an ECC, and were responsible for certifying communities as energy-efficient (i.e., an EEC)
3. Organizing and monitoring the five ECC action teams (described below) that carry out energy conservation education, promotion, and demonstration projects
4. Evaluating progress of the ECC action teams, including comparisons of baseline, treatment and follow-up data
5. Developing criteria for an energy efficient community (EEC)

The real success of a local ECC program is determined by the activities of five ECC action teams which are coordinated and monitored by the ECC Action Council. The following five components of the comprehensive ECC plan outline briefly the primary responsibilities of the five concomitant action teams.

1. The *Communications Team* is responsible for communicating the activities of an ECC, thereby publicly commending individual and group efforts toward energy conservation and showing other people strategies for reducing energy consumption. All communication media are used (television, radio, newspaper) and an in-house newsletter is developed.

2. The *Education Team* is responsible for keeping all the other teams informed about relevant techniques for conserving energy, and for promoting increases in energy education in public schools. This committee may sponsor public education programs for teaching energy concepts or special school projects that demonstrate the principles of energy use and energy savings.

3. The *Community Team* is responsible for locating and coordinating local civic organizations for energy-conservation activities. The located volunteer groups are taught to administer mini-workshops, implement neighborhood conservation projects, assist in communitywide analyses of energy use, and run special award programs among individuals and groups for motivating action toward conservation goals.

4. The *Government Team* is responsible for applying governmental policy to encourage energy conservation and for planning strategies to meet long-range energy needs. For example, such a team might be able to formulate policies, ordinances, and tax-rebate programs for motivating energy education and conservation. Government agencies and institutions could establish simple conservation programs in any of the four target areas and thus establish themselves as public examples of the appropriate application of conservation strategies. These teams also sponsor the administration of energy workshops to government personnel.

5. The *Industrial Team* is responsible for promoting energy conservation in the commercial/industrial sector of the community, and in establishing visible examples of the successful application of energy-conserving procedures in commercial and industrial enterprises. An attempt is made to demonstrate publicly the application of conservation strategies in all four target areas. This committee promotes the ECC by administering energy-conservation workshops to special work groups in commercial and industrial settings.

Obviously, this ECC proposal for coordinating community activities toward energy conservation and environmental protection is only a general framework within which specific policies and action plans must be developed, implemented, and tested. The essential contribution of this ECC plan is a scheme for coordinating the numerous facets of energy conservation among the citizens of local communities, where major program control should be focused. State energy offices, university extension services, local community agencies, and even the United States Department of Energy have been implementing and evaluating various conservation programs that relate to particular components of a comprehensive ECC plan. Now it is time to study these various conservation efforts and to coordinate the most cost-effective strategies and schemes under a nationwide program. Such a program should emphasize interdisciplinary and comprehensive input, large-scale and long-term intervention, integration of physical and psychological approaches, immediate rewards to motivate behavior change, cost-effectiveness evaluations of high- versus low-technology strategies, local participation in planning community conservation policy, and the mutual contribution of as many individuals as possible, in as many different situations as possible. The present chapter attempted to demonstrate the validity of this summary recommendation and provoke ideas relevant to the organization and implementation of programs and policy for encouraging communitywide energy conservation and environmental protection. But, action does speak louder than words!

ACKNOWLEDGMENTS

The author is grateful for the various interdisciplinary contracts over the past five years which were invaluable in formulating the concepts, ideas, and recommendations presented in this chapter. Particularly helpful were frequent communications with the following professionals: Samual P. Bowen, Robert N. S. Chiang, Jerard F. Kehoe, Robert H. Pusey, and Richard A. Winett. The author is also indebted to many dedicated students who collected field data and contributed to analyzing and interpreting research results that helped to shape the author's appreciation and critical evaluation of the subject matter; in this regard special contributions were offered by Kathy Brehony, Jamie Carlyle, John Cope, John Ferguson, and David Reichel.

REFERENCES

Appelhof, M. Worms—A safe, effective garbage disposal. *Organic Gardening and Farming Magazine*, August 1974, pp. 56–69.

Appelhof, M. *Composting your garbage with worms.* Kalamazoo Nature Center, Kalamazoo, Mich., 1979.

Appelhof, M. *Energy considerations: Resource recycling and energy recovery.* Presentation before the Resource Recovery Advisory Committee, South Central Michigan Planning Council, July 1980. (a)

Appelhof, M. Worms vs. high technology. *The Creative Woman*, 1980 (Summer), 4, 23–28. (b)

Bacon-Prue, A., Blount, R., Pickering, D., & Drabman, R. An evaluation of three litter control procedures—Trash receptacles, paid workers, and the marked item technique. *Journal of Applied Behavior Analysis*, 1980, 13, 165–170.

Bandura, A. *Social learning theory.* New York: Prentice-Hall, 1977.

Barkow, B. *The psychology of car pooling*. Ontario: Ministry of Transportation and Communications, 1974.

Becker, L. J. The joint effect of feedback and goal setting on performance: A field study of residential energy conservation. *Journal of Applied Psychology*, 1978, *63*, 228–233.

Becker, L. J., & Seligman, C. *Preliminary evaluation of an energy feedback conservation program*. Symposium presentation at the meeting of the Eastern Psychological Association, Washington, D.C., April 1978. (a)

Becker, L. J., & Seligman, C. Reducing air-conditioning waste by signalling it is cool outside. *Personality and Social Psychology Bulletin*, 1978, *4*, 412–415. (b)

Becker, L. J., & Seligman, C. Welcome to the energy crisis. *Journal of Social Issues*, 1981, *37*, 1–7.

Bickman, L. Environmental attitudes and actions. *The Journal of Social Psychology*, 1972, *87*, 323–324.

Blakely, E. Q., Lloyd, K. E., & Alferink, L. A. *The effects of feedback on residential electrical peaking and hourly kilowatt consumption*. Unpublished manuscript, Department of Psychology, Drake University, 1977.

Brasted, W., Mann, M., & Geller, E. S. Behavioral interventions for litter control: A critical review. *Cornell Journal of Social Relations*, 1979 (Summer), *14*, 75–90.

Brehm, J. W. *A theory of psychological reactance*. New York: Academic Press, 1966.

Brehm, J. *Responses to loss of freedom: A theory of psychological reactance*. New York: General Learning Press, 1972.

Buel, M. H. Local trashmen agree to collect recyclables. *Willamette Week*, August 29, 1977, pp. 1; 3.

Burgess, R. L., Clark, R. N., & Hendee, J. C. An experimental analysis of anti-littering procedures. *Journal of Applied Behavior Analysis*, 1971, *4*, 71–75.

Buttel, F. H., & Flinn, W. L. Environmental politics: The structuring of partisan and ideological cleavages in mass environmental attitudes. *Sociological Quarterly*, 1976, *17*, 477–490.

Canada seventh country to implement CCS. *CCS Bulletin*, August 1979, pp. 1–2.

Carlyle, J. J., & Geller, E. S. *Behavioral approaches to reducing residential energy consumption: a critical review*. Unpublished manuscript, Department of Psychology, Virginia Polytechnic Institute and State University, Blacksburg, Va., 1979.

Chapman, C., & Risley, T. R. Anti-litter procedures in an urban high-density area. *Journal of Applied Behavior Analysis*, 1974, *7*, 377–384.

Cone, J. D., & Hayes, S. C. Applied behavior analysis and the solution of environmental problems. In J. F. Wohlwill & I. Altman (Eds.), *Human behavior and environment: Advances in theory and research* (Vol. 2), New York: Plenum Press, 1978.

Cone, J. D., & Hayes, S. C. *Environmental problems/behavioral solutions*. Monterey, Calif.: Brooks/Cole, 1980.

Couch, J. V., Garber, T., & Karpus, L. Response maintenance and paper recycling. *Journal of Environmental Systems*, 1978–79, *8*, 127–137.

Dallmeyer, K. E. *Hitchhiking—A viable addition to a multimodel transportation system*. Boulder, Colorado: Center for Transportation Studies, University of Colorado, March 1975. (NTIS No. PB-242 203)

Darley, J. M. Energy conservation techniques as innovations, and their diffusion. *Energy and Buildings*, 1978, *1*, 339–343.

Delprata, D. J. Prompting electrical energy conservation in commercial users. *Environment and Behavior*, 1977, *9*, 433–440.

Deslauriers, B. C., & Everett, P. B. Effects of intermittent and continuous token reinforcement on bus ridership. *Journal of Applied Psychology*, 1977, *62*, 369–375.

Deutscher, I. Words and deeds: Social science and social policy. *Social Problems*, 1966, *13*, 235–254.

Deutscher, I. *What we say/what we do: Sentiments and acts.* Glenview, Ill.: Scott, Foresman, 1973.

Dorf, R. C. *Technology and society.* San Francisco: Boyd & Fraser 1974.

Duncan, R. C. An economic garbage collection and recycling service. *Compost Science,* January-February, 1976, 12–25. (a)

Duncan, R. C. The role of the ORE plan in developing a nationwide recycling network. *Compost Science,* 1976 (Summer), 25–32. (b)

Everett, P. B. The use of the reinforcement procedure to increase bus ridership. *Proceedings of the 81st Annual Convention of the American Psychological Association,* 1973, *8,* 891–892. (Summary)

Everett, P. B. A behavioral approach to transportation systems management. In D. Glenwick & L. Jason (Eds.), *Behavioral community psychology: Progress and prospects,* New York: Praeger, 1980.

Everett, P. B. Reinforcement theory strategies for modifying transit ridership. In I. Altman, J. Wohlwill, & P. Everett (Eds.), *Human behavior and environment* (Vol. 5): *Transportation and behavior,* New York: Plenum Press, 1981.

Everett, P. B., & Hayward, S. C. Behavioral technology—An essential design component of transportation systems. *High Speed Ground Transportation Journal,* 1974, *8,* 134–143.

Everett, P. B., Hayward, S. C., & Meyers, A. W. Effects of a token reinforcement procedure on bus ridership. *Journal of Applied Behavior Analysis,* 1974, *7,* 1–9.

Everett, P. B., Deslauriers, B. C., Newson, T., & Anderson, V. B. The differential effect of two free ride dissemination procedures on bus ridership. *Transportation Research,* 1978, *12,* 1–6.

Ferguson, J. F., Bowen, S. P., Carlyle, J. J., & Geller, E. S. Interdisciplinary attempts to promote community-wide energy conservation. *Proceedings of the Annual Southeastern Regional Meeting of the Society for General System Research,* Blacksburg, Va., April 1979.

Forstater, I., & Twomey, E. *Vanpooling: A summary and description of existing vanpool programs.* Washington, D.C.: U.S. Environmental Protection Agency, January 1976.

Foxx, R. M., & Hake, D. F. Gasoline conservation: A procedure for measuring and reducing the driving of college students. *Journal of Applied Behavior Analysis,* 1977, *10,* 61–74.

Frankena, F., Buttel, F. H., & Morrison, D. E. *Energy/society annotations.* Unpublished manuscript, Department of Sociology, Michigan State University, 1977.

Franz, M. This town accepts the composting challenge. *Compost Science,* 1976 (Summer), 25–32.

Funk & Wagnalls Standard College Dictionary. New York: Harper & Row, 1977.

Geller, E. S. Increasing desired waste disposals with instructions. *Man–Environment Systems,* 1975, *5,* 125–128.

Geller, E. S. Proenvironmental behavior: Policy implications of applied behavior analysis. Symposium presentation at the meeting of the American Psychological Association, Toronto, Canada, August 1978.

Geller, E. S. Applications of behavioral analysis for litter control. In D. Glenwick & L. Jason (Eds.), *Behavioral community psychology: Progress and prospects,* New York: Praeger, 1980. (a)

Geller, E. S. Saving environmental resources through waste reduction and recycling: How the behavioral community psychologist can help. In G. L. Martin & J. G. Osborne (Eds.), *Helping in the community: Behavioral applications,* New York: Plenum Press, 1980. (b)

Geller, E. S., Evaluation of energy conservation programs: Is self-report enough? *Journal of Consumer Research,* 1981, *8,* 331–335. (a)

Geller, E. S. Waste reduction and resource recovery: Strategies for energy conservation. In A. Baum & J. E. Singer (Eds.), *Advances in environmental psychology* (Vol. 3). Hillsdale, N.J.: Lawrence Erlbaum, 1981. (b)

Geller, E. S., Wylie, R. C., & Farris, J. C. An attempt at applying prompting and reinforcement toward pollution control. *Proceedings of the 79th Annual Convention of the American Psychological Association*, 1971, *6*, 701–702. (Summary)

Geller, E. S., Farris, J. C., & Post, D. S. Prompting a consumer behavior for pollution control. *Journal of Applied Behavior Analysis*, 1973, *6*, 367–376.

Geller, E. S., Chaffee, J. L., & Ingram, R. E. Promoting paper-recycling on a university campus. *Journal of Environmental Systems*, 1975, *5*, 39–57.

Geller, E. S., Witmer, J. F., & Orebaugh, A. L. Instructions as a determinant of paper-disposal behaviors. *Environment and Behavior*, 1976, *8*, 417–438.

Geller, E. S., Witmer, J. F., & Tuso, M. E. Environmental interventions for litter control. *Journal of Applied Psychology*, 1977, *62*, 344–351.

Geller, E. S., Bowen, S. P., & Chiang, R. N. S. *A community-based approach to promoting energy conservation.* Symposium presentation at the meeting of the American Psychological Association, Toronto, September 1978.

Geller, E. S., Brasted, W. S., & Augustine, M. N. *A community education model for energy conservation: Implementation, evaluation, and implication.* Symposium presentation at the meeting of the Eastern Psychological Association, Washington, D.C., 1978.

Geller, E. S., Ferguson, J. F., & Brasted, W. S. *Attempts to promote residential energy conservation: Attitudinal versus behavioral outcome.* (Technical Report for Title I Grant, 1978). Blacksburg, Va.: Department of Psychology, Virginia Polytechnic Institute and State University, 1978.

Geller, E. S., Winett, R. A., & Everett, P. B. *Preserving the environment: New strategies for behavior change.* New York: Pergamon Press, 1982.

Gurin, D. B. Pragmatic evaluation of telephones, activity scheduling, and other strategies to modify travel behavior of population subgroups. *Transportation Research Record*, 1976, No. 583, 29–35.

Hake, D. F., & Foxx, R. M. Promoting gasoline conservation: The effects of reinforcement schedules, a leader and self-recording. *Behavior Modification*, 1978, *2*, 339–369.

Hamad, C. D., Bettinger, R., Cooper, D., & Semb, G. *Using behavioral procedures to establish an elementary school paper recycling program.* Unpublished manuscript, Department of Psychology, University of Kansas, Lawrence, 1978.

Hayes, S. C., & Cone, J. D. Reducing residential electrical use: Payments, information, and feedback. *Journal of Applied Behavior Analysis*, 1977, *10*, 425–435.

Hayes, S. C., Johnson, V. S., & Cone, J. D. The marked item technique: A practical procedure for litter control. *Journal of Applied Behavior Analysis*, 1975, *8*, 381–386.

Heberlein, T. A. Conservation information: The energy crisis and electricity conservation in an apartment complex. *Energy Systems and Policy*, 1975, *1*, 105–117.

Hendee, J. C. No, to attitudes to evaluate environmental education. *The Journal of Environmental Education*, 1971, *3*, 65.

Hirst, E. Transportation energy conservation policies. *Science*, 1976, *192*, 15–20.

Humphrey, C. R., Bord, R. J., Hammond, M. M., & Mann, S. Attitudes and conditions for cooperation in a paper recycling program. *Environment and Behavior*, 1977, *9*, 107–124.

Ingram, R. E., & Geller, E. S. A community-integrated, behavior modification approach to facilitating paper recycling. *JSAS Catalog of Selected Documents in Psychology*, 1975, *5*, 327. (Ms. No. 1097)

Institute for Local Self-Reliance. *Composting in the city.* Community Self-Reliance Series, Washington, D.C., 1975.

Institute for Local Self-Reliance. *National recycling research agenda project for the National Science Foundation: Final report.* (Technical Report for Grant OPA 79-19013 from the National Science Foundation). Washington, D.C.: Waste Utilization Division, Institute for Local Self-Reliance, March 1980.

Jacobs, H. E., & Bailey, J. S. *The Leon County recycling program: The development of an empirically derived communitywide resource recovery program.* Symposium presentation at meeting of the Association for Behavior Analysis, Dearborn, Mich., 1979.

Jacobs, H., Fairbanks, D., Poche, C., & Bailey, J. S. *Behavioral community psychology: Multiple incentives in encouraging carpool formation on a university campus.* Unpublished manuscript, Department of Psychology, Florida State University, 1979.

Johnson, R. P., & Geller, E. S. Engineering technology and behavior analysis for interdisciplinary environmental protection. *Behavior Analyst*, 1980, *3*, 23–29.

Jones, B., & Derby, J. Sacramento car-pool projects: Interim evaluation report. *Transportation Research Record*, 1976, No. 619, 38–42.

Kazdin, A. E. Extensions of reinforcement techniques to socially and environmentally relevant behaviors. In M. Hersen, R. M. Eisler, & P. M. Miller (Eds.), *Progress in behavior modification.* New York: Academic Press, 1977.

Keep America Beautiful, Inc. *Clean community system: Trainer's manual.* New York: Author, 1977. (a)

Keep America Beautiful, Inc. *Initiating the clean community system.* New York: Author, 1977. (b)

Knapp, D. *Case studies in resource recovery: Highgrading in Lane County, Oregon.* Invited address at Recycling Research Agenda Conference for the National Science Foundation, Washington, D.C., December 1979.

Kohlenberg, R., & Phillips, T. Reinforcement and rate of litter depositing. *Journal of Applied Behavior Analysis*, 1973, *6*, 391–396.

Kohlenberg, R. J., Phillips, T., & Proctor, W. A behavioral analysis of peaking in residential electricity energy consumption. *Journal of Applied Behavior Analysis*, 1976, *9*, 13–18.

LaBreque, M. Garbage—Refuse or resource? *Popular Science*, June 1977, pp. 95–98; 166.

LeHart, D., & Bailey, J. S. Reducing children's littering on a nature trail. *Journal of Environmental Education*, 1975, *7*, 37–45.

Large, D. B. *Hidden waste: Potentials for energy conservation.* Washington, D.C.: The Conservation Foundation, 1973.

Lauridsen, P. K. *Decreasing gasoline consumption in fleet-owned automobiles through feedback and feedback-plus-lottery.* Unpublished manuscript, Drake University, Department of Psychology, 1977.

Letzkus, T., & Scharfe, V. Employer incentive programs. *Proceedings of the 1975 National Conference on Areawide Carpooling*, Washington, D.C.: Federal Highway Administration, Urban Planning Division, 1975.

Lloyd, K. E. Reactions to a forthcoming energy shortage: A topic in behavioral ecology. In G. L. Marten & J. G. Osborne (Eds.), *Helping in the community: Behavioral applications.* New York: Plenum Press, 1980.

Luyben, P. S., & Bailey, J. S. The effects of rewards and proximity of containers on newspaper recycling. *Environment and Behavior*, 1979, *11*, 539–557.

Luyben, P. D., Warren, S. B., & Randall, T. A. Recycling beverage containers on a college campus. *Journal of Environmental Systems*, 1979–80, *9*, 180–202.

MacCalden, M., & Davis, C. *Report on priority lane experiment on the San Francisco-Oakland Bay Bridge.* San Francisco: Department of Public Works, 1972.

McClelland, L., & Carter, R. J. Psychological research on energy conservation: Context, approaches, methods. In A. Baum & J. E. Singer (Eds.), *Advances in environmental psychology* (Vol. 3). Hillsdale, N.J.: Lawrence Erlbaum, 1981.

McClelland, L., & Cook, S. W. Energy conservation effects of continuous in-home feedback in all-electric homes. *Journal of Environmental Systems*, 1979–80, *9*, 169–173.

McDermott, J. Recycling: New answers to NYC's big problem. *Journal of Appropriate Technology*, 1980 (Spring), *1*, 9–10.

Osborne, J. G., & Powers, R. B. Controlling the litter problem. In G. L. Martin & J. G. Osborne (Eds.), *Helping in the community: Behavioral applications.* New York: Plenum Press, 1980.

Owens, R. D., & Sever, H. L. *The 3M commute-a-van program,* Progress Report II. St. Paul, Minn.: 3M Company, 1977.

Palmer, M. H., Lloyd, M. E., & Lloyd, K. E. An experimental analysis of electricity conservation procedures. *Journal of Applied Behavior Analysis,* 1978, *10,* 665–672.

Pratsch, L. *Carpool and buspool matching guide* (4th ed.). Washington, D.C.: U.S. Department of Transportation, Federal Highway Administration, January 1975.

Pratsch, L. *Vanpooling discussion paper.* Unpublished manuscript. Washington, D.C.: Federal Highway Administration, April, 1977.

Public Opinion Surveys, Inc. Who litters—and why. Prepared for Keep America Beautiful, Inc., Princeton, N.J., 1968.

Reich, J. W., & Robertson, J. L. Reactance and norm appeal in antilittering messages. *Journal of Applied Social Psychology,* 1979, *9,* 91–101.

Reichel, D. A., & Geller, E. S. *Group vs. individual contingencies to conserve transportation energy.* Paper presentation at the meeting of the Southeastern Psychological Association, Washington, D.C., 1980.

Reichel, D. A., & Geller, E. S. Attempts to modify transportation behavior for energy conservation: A critical review. In A Baum & J. E. Singer (Eds.), *Advances in environmental psychology* (Vol. 3). Hillsdale, N.J.: Erlbaum Associates, 1981.

Reid, D. H., Luyben, P. S., Rawers, R. J., & Bailey, J. S. The effects of prompting and proximity of containers on newspaper recycling behavior. *Environment and Behavior,* 1976, *8,* 471–483.

Rohles, F. H. Thermal comfort and strategies for energy conservation. *Journal of Social Issues,* 1981, *37,* 132–149.

Rose, H. S., & Hinds, D. H. South Dixie Highway contraflow bus and car-pool lane demonstration project. *Transportation Research Record,* 1976, No. 606, 18–22.

Runnion, A., Watson, J. D., & McWhorter, J. Energy savings in interstate transportation through feedback and reinforcement. *Journal of Organizational Behavior Management,* 1978, *1,* 180–191.

Schnelle, J. F., Gendrich, J. G., Beegle, G. P., Thomas, M. M., & McNees, M. P. Mass media techniques for prompting behavior change in the community. *Environment and Behavior,* 1980, *12,* 157–166.

Seaver, W. B., & Patterson, A. H. Decreasing fuel oil consumption through feedback and social commendation. *Journal of Applied Behavior Analysis.* 1976, *9,* 147–152.

Seldman, N. *Garbage in America: Approaches to recycling.* Institute for Local Self-Reliance, Washington, D.C., 1975.

Seldman, N. Collection/recycling systems challenge resource recovery. *Environmental Action Bulletin,* October 1976. (a)

Seldman, N. Waste utilization—The trouble with high technology. *Self-Reliance,* September 1976, 11–16. (b)

Seldman, N. *New directions in solid waste planning.* Washington, D.C.: Institute for Local Self-Reliance, April 1977.

Seligman, C., & Darley, J. M. Feedback as a means of decreasing residential energy consumption. *Journal of Applied Psychology,* 1977, *62,* 363–368.

Seligman, C., Becker, L. J., & Darley, J. M. Encouraging residential energy conservation through feedback. In A. Baum & J. E. Singer (Eds.), *Advances in environmental psychology* (Vol. 3). Hillsdale, N.J.: Lawrence Erlbaum, 1981.

Shippee, G. The psychology of energy consumption and conservation: A review and conceptual analysis. *Environmental Management,* 1980, *4,* 297–314.

Skinner, B. F. *Walden two revisited.* Paper presented at the meeting of the American Psychological Association, Chicago, September 1975.

Slavin, R. E., & Wodarski, J. S. *Using group contingencies to reduce natural gas consumption in master-metered apartments* (Technical Report No. 232). Center for Social Organization of Schools, Johns Hopkins University, 1977.

Slavin, R. E., Wodarski, J. S., & Blackburn, B. L. A group contingency for electricity conservation in master-metered apartments. *Journal of Applied Behavior Analysis,* 1981, *14,* 357–363.

Stern, P. C., & Gardner, G. T. *The place of behavior change in the management of environmental problems.* Unpublished manuscript, Institution for Social and Policy Studies, Yale University, 1980.

Stern, P. C., & Gardner, G. T. Psychological research and energy policy. *American Psychologist,* 1981, *1,* 329–342.

Tietjen, C., & Hart, S. S. Compost for agricultural land? *Journal of the Sanitary Engineering Division,* 1969, *95,* 269–287.

Tremblay, K. R., Jr., & Dunlap, R. E. Rural-urban residence and concern with environmental quality: A replication and extension. *Rural Sociology,* 1978, *43,* 474–491.

Tuso, M., & Geller, E. S. Behavior analysis applied to environmental/ecological problems: A review. *Journal of Applied Behavior Analysis,* 1976, *9,* 526.

U.S. Department of Energy. *The low cost/no cost energy conservation program in New England: An evaluation.* U.S. Department of Energy, Office of Buildings and Community Systems, Market Development Branch, Contract No. DE-AM0180CS21366, 1980.

U.S. Department of Transportation. *Nationwide Personal Transportation Study, Mode of Transportation and Personal Characteristics of Tripmakers* (Report No. 9). Washington, D.C.: U.S. Government Printing Office, November, 1973.

Van Liere, K. D., & Dunlap, R. E. The social bases of environmental concern: A review of hypotheses, explanations and empirical evidence. *Public Opinion Quarterly,* 1980, *44,* 181–197.

Van Liere, K. D., & Dunlap, R. E. Environmental concern: Does it make a difference how it's measured? *Environment and Behavior,* 1981, *13,* 651–676.

Wahl, D. & Allison, G. *Reduce: Targets, means and impacts of source reduction.* Washington, D.C.: League of Women Voters Education Fund, 1975.

Walker, J. M. *Reducing electricity consumption in a master-metered apartment complex.* Unpublished manuscript, Texas A & M University, Department of Economics, 1977.

Weigel, R. H., Woolston, V. L., & Gendelman, D. S. *Psychological studies of pollution control: An annotated bibliography.* Unpublished manuscript, Department of Psychology, Amherst College, 1977.

Wendt, K. A. Approaches to source reduction. *Proceedings, 1975 Conference on Waste Reduction,* U.S. Environmental Protection Agency, Washington, D.C., 1975, pp. 66–77.

Wicker, A. W. Attitudes vs. actions: The relationship of verbal and overt behavioral responses to attitude objects. *Journal of Social Issues,* 1969, *25,* 41–78.

Wicker, A. W. An examination of the "other variables" explanation of attitude–behavior inconsistency. *Journal of Personality and Social Psychology,* 1971, *19,* 18–30.

Winett, R. A. Prompting turning-out lights in unoccupied rooms. *Journal of Environmental Systems,* 1978, *6,* 237–241.

Winett, R. A. An emerging approach to energy conservation. In D. Glenwick & L. Jason (Eds.), *Behavioral community psychology: Progress and prospects,* New York: Praeger, 1980.

Winett, R. A., & Neale, M. S. Psychological framework for energy conservation in buildings: Strategies, outcomes, directions. *Energy and Buildings,* 1979, *2,* 101–116.

Winett, R. A., & Nietzel, M. Behavioral ecology: Contingency management of residential use. *American Journal of Community Psychology,* 1975, *3,* 123–133.

Winett, R. A., Kaiser, S., & Haberkorn, E. The effects of monetary rebates and daily feedback on electricity conservation. *Journal of Environmental Systems,* 1977, *5,* 327–338.

Winett, R. A., Kagel, J. H., Battalio, R. C., & Winkler, R. C. Effects of monetary rebates, feedback, and information on residential electricity conservation. *Journal of Environmental Systems,* 1978, *5,* 327–338.

Winett, R. A., Neale, M. S., & Grier, H. C. The effects of self-monitoring and feedback on residential electricity consumption. *Journal of Applied Behavior Analysis,* 1979, *12,* 173–184.

Winett, R. A., Neale, M. S., Williams, K. R., Yokley, J., & Kauder, H. The effects of individual and group feedback on residential electricity consumption: Three replications. *Journal of Environmental Systems,* 1979, *8,* 217–233.

Winett, R. A., Hatcher, J., Leckliter, I., Fort, R., Fishback, J. F., & Riley, A. Modifying perceptions of comfort and electricity used for heating by social learning strategies: Residential field experiments. *ASHRAE Transactions,* 1981, *87,* 555–565.

Witmer, J. F., & Geller, E. S. Facilitating paper recycling: Effects of prompts, raffles, and contests. *Journal of Applied Behavior Analysis,* 1976, *9,* 315–322.

Wodarski, J. S. The reduction of electrical energy consumption: The application of behavior analysis. *Behavior Therapy,* 1976, *8,* 347–353.

Zerega, A. M. Transportation energy conservation policy: Implications for social science research. *Journal of Social Issues,* 1981, *37,* 31–50.

18

Epilogue

Some Research Questions

GARY B. MELTON AND ALAN W. CHILDS

A theme throughout this book has been the general lack of attention that psychologists have paid to rural communities. Rural sociology is a well-established subdiscipline, and there is a rather large literature on the social structure of rural communities, both in the United States and in developing countries. On the other hand, most of what we know about the *experience* of living in rural communities is based on anecdotal reports, quality-of-life surveys (Chapter 10[1]), and surveys of attitudes and values by sociologists (e.g., Colliver & Warner, 1979; Ford, 1962; Nelson & Frost, 1971; Tremblay & Dunlap, 1978). Given the general dearth of research, however, it is fitting to close this volume with some suggestions for directions in attempting to learn more about rural psychology. In so doing, we have attempted to identify the key questions raised or implied by the contributors to this volume. The discussion here is by no means meant to be exhaustive.

METHODOLOGICAL AND CONCEPTUAL ISSUES

One of the major problems with available attempts to study *rural* issues has been a lack of clarity as to what is subsumed by the term and

---

[1]Chapter numbers refer to those in this volume. The ideas or data cited in this way are, of course, those of the individual chapter authors.

GARY B. MELTON • Department of Psychology, University of Nebraska, Lincoln, Nebraska 68588. ALAN W. CHILDS • Department of Psychology, Lafayette College, Easton, Pennsylvania 18042.

as to what is uniquely rural rather than the product of a confounding variable. There are obvious differences in the ecology of the exurbs of New Jersey and Connecticut, the hollows of eastern Kentucky, and the expanses of the Western deserts. Nonetheless, there have been few attempts to separate regional differences from rural-urban differences in behavior. Exceptions are Gotts's (1980) cross-regional comparisons of personality development and Heller and Quesada's (1977) cross-regional analysis of familism. Similarly, few studies have included controls for social class. Given the disproportionate prevalence of poverty in rural areas (especially those which are very isolated), it is conceivable that many of the phenomena that have been reported at least anecdotally as rural are in fact manifestations of social-class effects. Reports of interaction processes in rural families may be good examples (Chapter 3). The clear need is for systematic matching on social class in future research.

More clarity is also needed in operational definitions of "rural." As pointed out by several authors, the census definition of rural as communities with a population under 2,500 is of questionable meaningfulness. Although there is certainly some utility to a standard definition using easily accessible data, the lack of consideration of degree of physical isolation in the census definition masks differences in degree of ruralness. The use of population density as an independent variable presents such a problem generally. One solution may be to combine a population density measure with a measure of distance from a metropolitan core area in defining ruralness.

Perhaps most parsimonious from a psychological viewpoint in determining the nature and effects of ruralness would be simply to ask people whether they live in a rural area (or, more psychologically, whether they consider themselves to be rural people) and to use these self-reports as the independent variable (see Chapter 1). Besides relying on "common-sense" subjective perceptions of ruralness, such a definition would have the advantage of avoiding some of the pitfalls of aggregate data. One of the problems of such data is that, as communities grow (for example, beyond 2,500 population) or as political boundaries change, they may be dropped from analyses. Time-series data may thus be distorted (the "ecological fallacy"). Aggregate data based on population density also mask individual differences in ruralness, related, for example, to length of residence. These differences are important for psychologically conceptualizing ruralness. They may also be important to understand for political reasons, given recent conflicts in many rural communities over growth and identification with urban interests.

Other self-report definitions may also be useful. For example, the degree to which one chooses rural individuals and groups, such as fellow church members (Chapter 9), as referents for social comparisons may be a behavioral definition of ruralness. Number of visits annually to metropolitan areas may be another, as may the length of residence in rural areas, however defined. Whether an individual was reared in a rural area may be a particularly sensitive variable. Darley and Latané (1968) found, for example, that whether urban residents had been reared in nonmetropolitan areas predicted whether they would help bystanders in distress.[2] It would be interesting to measure the strength of this sort of definition of ruralness through regression analysis of cross-generational effects. How much do place of birth and length of rural residence of parents and grandparents contribute to variation in ruralness? In any case, the power of each of these definitions (geographic and psychological) is an empirical question. Research is needed comparing the effects of ruralness on behavior, using different measures of "rural" and controlling for the confounding variables discussed earlier.

In addition to a need for more conceptual clarity concerning what is rural, there is a general need for research that is based on hypotheses about ways in which *specific* aspects of specific rural environments may affect specific behaviors of specific populations. There may be environmental characteristics that are generalizable across many rural settings and that present particular stimulus demands. For example, as discussed in some detail in Chapter 1, *undermanning* may be a feature common to many rural communities. However, obviously not all rural settings are undermanned. To give an example, large consolidated schools are often grossly overmanned. The tasks for the psychologist are to identify characteristics that are particularly common in rural communities, especially those which are very rural, and to identify particular ecological characteristics of particular communities.

Attention also needs to be given to the fact that ruralness probably interacts with other psychological and demographic variables. Attention to these interactions may be most useful both conceptually and in the planning of services. As Dibner (Chapter 6) clearly showed, the impact of retirement, for example, on rural old people is likely to vary depending on such variables as length of residence within the community. Lee and Lassey (1980) made a similar argument:

> Further research on absolute differences between rural and urban elderly is not likely to be very productive. We need, instead, multivariate research strategies that are designed to explore the causal processes by which subjective well being is determined, and that incorporate residential location within

---

[2]It is important to note, however, that Darley and Latané's findings in this regard have not withstood replication (Korte, 1980). Nonetheless, the point to be made here is that early experiences in rural communities—and the family's entrenchment in a rural lifestyle—may have effects on later behavior. This possibility is still largely unexplored.

> a network of variables and explanatory models. We need to investigate and
> identify some of the specific advantages of rural life for older people, and we
> need to consider seriously the possibility that different theories are required
> to explain subjective and emotional adjustment for different elderly popula-
> tions. (p. 71)

Similar points have been made elsewhere in this volume. For example,
Hollos (Chapter 4) noted the importance of developing specific hypotheses about the way in which environment affects cognitive and social
development. A related point is that attention needs to be paid to the
meaningfulness of dependent variables used in rural-urban research.
The tendency has been to adopt overly global measures which tell us
little about the environmental demands of rural settings. To continue
with Hollos's argument, the well-established rural-urban difference in
IQ is of little meaning in identifying particular effects on information
processing, for example, of living in isolated communities. Again, these
finer distinctions are important both in the development of a rural psychology and in the identification of particular possible points of intervention. As Hollos noted, we need to begin to look at specific ecological
determinants and effects, at "patterns of 'highs' and 'lows'" in order to
develop a richer notion of the experience in particular rural communities
and cultures.

It should be noted that this more sophisticated view of rural phenomena invites collaboration across disciplines. Hollos's work is again
exemplary. In describing the conclusions from her examination of cognitive and social development in rural Norwegian communities, Hollos
noted a number of questions which were central to understanding the
data:

> The actual context in which the child grows up and learns should be
> outlined. "Norwegian" culture or even "Norwegian rural" culture would
> have been misleading designations of the environmental context of our
> study unless certain dimensions were enumerated. All three groups of chil-
> dren were "Norwegian" and two of them "rural," yet their social environ-
> ments and the pattern of the development were quite different. In order to
> understand the demands of these environments, the following questions had
> to be answered. What actually goes on in the everyday life of an isolated farm
> and what sort of stimulation do children receive from such an environment?
> Does spatial isolation imply psychological isolation as well? Does the level of
> noise in the urban environment necessarily mean stimulation? Failure to
> understand the combination of these factors can lead to a biased expectation
> and errors in the judgment of the intellectual capacities of the rural children.
> (pp. 67–68)

To reach her understanding of the children she studied, Hollos relied
heavily on her skills as an anthropologist in ethnography. She was particularly open to observing the stimuli presented by the settings that she

studied and simply examining the cultural context. At the same time, the Hollos study used specific measures of particular kinds of cognitive skills as the dependent variables. Therefore, there was a fruitful mixture of the anthropologist's attention to cultural demands and the psychologist's attention to particular kinds of effects on individual children. There are, of course, methodologies from psychology itself that are relevant to community description (e.g., Barker's counting of incidents in settings). The point is that the rural psychology would profit at this point in its development from the mixture of ethnography and "harder" methods of study. Moreover, the observations should be firmly rooted in a conceptual framework. Researchers need to think through clearly what their expectations are about particular stimulus demands of rural communities, rather than to rely solely on atheoretical operational definitions of rural and overly global and arbitrarily selected dependent variables. More attempts at truly conceptually based research should begin to address some of the basic questions about ruralness discussed in Chapter 1 and at the beginning of this epilogue.

SPECIFIC AREAS OF RESEARCH

Family Interaction

The literature on rural families is perhaps most exemplary of the general problems of much of what we "know" about rural psychology. While there has been much discussion of the strengths and weaknesses of rural families (particularly in isolated rural cultures, such as Appalachia), there has been little systematic empirical research. One particular line of possible research that seems especially needed concerns the nature and extent of familism. As Urey and Henggeler (Chapter 3) indicated, familism as a concept has been the subject of much more speculation and "clinical impression" than hard research. The one study that was an attempt to understand the concept more fully (Heller & Quesada, 1977) suggested that familism should be differentiated on the basis of the importance of extended-kin networks versus primary-kin. Their data suggested, in fact, that the nature of familism varied cross-regionally. Further research is necessary to determine whether familism is in fact ubiquitous within rural cultures and if particular kinds of rural settings are especially prone to induce specific forms of familism. In the same vein, further understanding is needed of the circumstances under which familism is adaptive and those under which it inhibits utilization of broader resources. Reiss's (1971a, 1971b) work on "consensus-sensitive" families may be a useful conceptual underpinning for future research. Beyond its theoretical elegance, the work by Reiss is useful in terms of providing methods of simulation of family processes in which the family members reject or include information relevant to problem solving from sources outside the family. Such psychological simulations might be helpful in identifying the specific processes involved in familism on an interactive level and the mechanisms by which familistic values are transmitted.

A second line of much-needed research on rural families has to do with parental disciplinary styles. Urey and Henggler's (Chapter 3) review was noteworthy for its lack of observational studies of parent–child relations. Similarly, Rosenberg and Reppucci (Chapter 14) were unable to find rural-urban comparisons of disciplinary practices. Particularly in view of the potential role of restrictive parental styles in fostering dependency, direct study of these processes is warranted. Control, of course, needs to be added to any such studies for effects of social class. Nonetheless, it is at least plausible that in relatively isolated areas there would be a tendency to maintain strict discipline within the relatively small social order. Gotts[3] in fact has preliminary data suggesting that, at least in Appalachia, there is a single factor related to encouragement of dependency or autonomy in parenting. Such a finding clashes with the classic two-factor model of parenting found in the early Fels studies of Virginia Crandell and others (cf. Shaefer, 1959). Such differences, of course, may be related primarily to social class (in view of the largely upper middle-class sample used in the Fels work) or to region (in view of Gotts's finding of a strong tendency toward dependency among Appalachian people). In any case, such hypotheses of differences in parental values and behavior need to be examined through direct and systematic studies of interaction within the family. Both simulations, as suggested in the preceding paragraph, and observations in natural settings would be useful.

Cognitive and Linguistic Development

Hollos's (Chapter 4) thorough review of cross-cultural developmental research is useful in its delineation of the need for ecologically based investigations of particular demands of rural environments. As Hollos noted in her conclusion, researchers should "search out and identify those features of each environment that foster the development of particular cognitive skills and . . . devise tasks that accurately tap those skills." Besides providing greater conceptual richness, such an approach has more potential for direct applicability to instructional strategies than

[3]Personal communication, October 1980.

more typical rural-urban comparisons of global test scores. We need to know if the variant experiences that rural children have result in variant styles of information processing. For example, does learning to read in a "second dialect" present particular tasks and problems for children from rural subcultures?

The implications for linguistic development of growing up in small, relatively closed and homogeneous communities need to be better understood. As Wolfram (Chapter 5) noted, there are significant conceptual and political problems with "deficiency" models of rural dialects. Nonetheless, there is an intuitive logic to the notion that linguistic diversity and richness would be less functional in communities with largely shared experiences and presumably less need for verbal nuances in communication. At least as schools are currently structured, this lack of verbal expressiveness (to the extent to which it exists) may penalize many rural children in school and in other contacts with the "mainstream" culture. Similar arguments may be posed concerning the breadth and quality of social-perception and role-taking skills among children growing up in communities with little diversity of models. These hypotheses are worthy of systematic investigation.

Regardless, however, Gotts's (Chapter 15) documentation of the long-term effects of a preschool program using local resources in reducing the probability of academic and personality "deficits" is indeed promising. The suggestion is that, even in very isolated mountainous communities, a brief but intensive attempt to ensure exposure to social and linguistic diversity may forestall developmental problems, provided that the program actively involves parents and matches the ecology of the community.

Environmental Perception and Aesthetics

Feimer's (Chapter 7) discussion of possible rural-urban differences in development of spatial cognition is provocative. As he pointed out, the available studies are inconsistent and need to be explored further, with more attention to controls for nature of the terrain, education, and other potentially confounding variables. This area of research might have important applied implications. As Geller (Chapter 17) discussed, there is evidence of less concern for maintenance of the environment among rural than urban residents (see also Tremblay & Dunlap, 1978). Does this lack of investment in environmentalism emanate from the experience of growing up in the midst of expanses of land where natural resources are plentiful? How does such an experience affect one's general world view and the territory that an individual or a community claims? How are the boundaries defined? Although, as Geller noted, there is not necessarily a direct link between attitudes and behavior, examination of these cognitions and attitudes may help to identify some of the potential points of intervention. For example, the immediate rewards of exploitation of the environment when resources appear abundant may mask the long-term consequences for a community economically dependent upon these resources (through farming or mining). One clear gap in the available research on rural environmental perception is that the studies have tended to focus on the perceptions of urbanities visiting rural recreational areas rather than those of the residents, who may more directly affect how the local environment is designed and managed.

Sense of Efficacy and Personal Control

Lefcourt and Martin (Chapter 8) showed that sense of personal control over the environment does not differ consistently between rural and urban residents. Nonetheless, as they further noted, there are systematic effects of particular rural environments and lifestyles. Especially worthy of further investigation are the effects of economic restructuring (such as development of agricultural conglomerates and absentee mine ownership by large corporations) and of political policies (e.g., dependency on government farm supports) on sense of personal control. Community organization efforts might be evaluated in such terms. Melton's (Chapter 16) suggestions for research on legal socialization and political intolerance in rural communities are complementary to such a framework.

Service Delivery Issues

A point made frequently in this volume is that service needs are often greater but that services are in fact fewer in rural areas. Furthermore, the nature of successful services may be different than in metropolitan areas, but there has been virtually no research on this point (Chapter 12).

Heyman (Chapter 12) suggested one line of research that might be profitable: factors in the recruitment and retention of successful professionals in rural communities. While the geographic maldistribution of professionals has been frequently noted, little systematic research is available on ways of addressing the problem or on the personal characteristics and training needs of rural professionals. It should be noted that the problem of maldistribution is not limited to the health-care professions. For example, there is a shortage of attorneys in many rural communities (Chapter 16). Research on recruitment and retention problems in the health-care professions may have some generalizability to other professions.

In the meantime, attention should be given to evaluation of models of service delivery not requiring large concentrations and a high degree of specialization of professionals. It may be that services can be delivered more effectively and efficiently in many rural communities through use of "natural" helping networks, particularly given the high levels of neighborliness and interpersonal trust in rural areas (see studies on altruism reviewed by Korte, Chapter 10). Beyond anecdotal reports, however, the quality and density of rural helping networks, including the place of professionals in them, have not been the subject of research. This phenomenon, and interventions based on it, should be investigated. Similarly, research on processes of informal dispute resolution (Chapter 16) and crisis intervention in rural communities might be useful in designing programs based on indigenous resources and in further understanding the rural experience.

Rural Psychology and Social Change

A closing caveat concerns the level of social stability in rural communities. It is true that innovations and changes in cultural norms are relatively slow to filter through rural communities (Rogers & Burdge, 1972; Rogers & Shoemaker, 1971). Indeed, much of the literature on diffusion of innovations has focused on rural communities and the role of extension agents in the dissemination of knowledge (Havelock, 1969). Consistent with this picture of general conservatism and of slow diffusion of innovations is a common perception that rural communities are essentially static. However, it is important to remember that the delay in the diffusion of innovations does not imply that change does not occur in rural communities.

Indeed, there is reason to believe that in recent years rural areas have been under *more* pressure of social change than has been true of metropolitan areas. First, the trend of migration is now toward rather than away from the rural areas of the country (Chapters 2 and 10), although there is still a tendency for young, highly educated people from rural areas to move to the cities (Lichter, Heaton, & Fuguitt, 1979). There is obvious potential for conflict between "old" and "new " residents, both politically (as in land-use policies) and interpersonally (in terms of value clashes). Second, post-World War II out-migration disrupted social networks that had existed for some time as supports for individuals in isolated, economically deprived areas (Photiadis & Schwarzweller, 1970). Third, it is reasonable to assume that the racial and class conflict and general social change that shook metropolitan areas in the sixties and early seventies may just now be directly affecting some rural areas. Recent conflicts over "old" and "new" morality in many rural communities may be exemplary. Fourth, and more generally, rural areas tend to be subject to "boom-or-bust" economies. As such, they may be more subject to rapid swings in social climate than metropolitan areas, where the economy is usually more diversified. When a rural area dependent on agriculture suffers a severe drought, the level of affluence of the community may change suddenly. Conversely, the recent revival of interest in coal as an energy source has led to the sudden prosperity of many mining communities.

One implication of this discussion is that researchers interested in rural people might consider quasi-experimental, time-series designs in order to assess changes in rural life over time.[4] Another implication is that change itself should be considered as an independent variable in future research. What are the effects on personality of facing a boom-or-bust economy? What is the social psychology of integration of in-migrants and longtime residents? As Korte (Chapter 10) noted, there is a possibility that the favorable subjective quality of life enjoyed by rural Americans is dependent upon the personality and social characteristics of people already living there and that immigrants may be frustrated in their desire for the good life. In any case, research on the psychology of social change in rural areas may help to ensure that the very quality of life attracting new migrants is not damaged by the demographic changes it has stimulated. Seen in this context, attention by researchers to rural communities is important in helping to understand life in previously neglected but increasingly vital and rapidly changing areas of our nation.

WHY A RURAL PSYCHOLOGY?

In conclusion, it may be worthwhile to consider whether the reviews by the contributors to this volume tell us anything about the need for a psychology of rural communities. While sociologists have found the concept of rurality to be a useful one (and indeed have based a

---

[4]There are other, more general methodological concerns in advocating increased use of time-series, repeated-measures designs. Epstein (1980) has persuasively argued that failure to achieve psychological trait stability has frequently been the result of reliance on single-shot laboratory experiments rather than aggregate data summed across events and across situations over time. Given that the parameters of ruralness are likely to be multidimensional and perhaps inadequately and unreliably sampled by single observations, there is particular reason to use time-series designs.

subdiscipline on it), psychologists have paid scant attention to rural-ness. Given the research reviewed in this volume, does a rural psychology (or, for that matter, an urban psychology) have value?

In our view, the answer is a qualified yes. There are objectively measured differences in social indicators between rural and metropolitan areas (Chapter 10) that might reasonably be expected to have behavioral effects. More subjectively, people can identify salient aspects of rural life that they do or do not like. On a gross level, living in Louisville or Lexington, Kentucky, is simply different from living in Crab Orchard or Beauty. Moreover, low population density and physical isolation may in and of themselves have expectable effects of particular kinds of behavior (see, e.g., Chapters 1 and 16).

At the same time, however, a theme through many of the chapters—and, indeed, this epilogue—has been the need to test hypotheses about person–environment interactions. Several of the authors (e.g., Chapters 3, 6, 8, and 14) have suggested that ruralness *per se* may be less important than correlated variables, such as social class, and that there is a need to examine effects of particular kinds of rural environments on particular populations. Obviously, ruralness also may contribute more to the variance in some kinds of behaviors than others. We noted our support for such an ecological view early in this epilogue.

Two points should be emphasized, however. First, to the extent to which there are identifiable environmental commonalities among rural communities, rural-urban comparisons are not inconsistent with an ecological view. Second, given the lack of much "hard" research using rural populations and the popularity of intuitive notions surrounding the concept of ruralness, until we have broad data indicating the contrary, it makes sense to behave as if there quite possibly *are* psychological phenomena common among rural people and to test these hypotheses actively. While there may not be *a* rural psychology, there certainly are special problems and rewards of rural living. In the face of social change, the psychological impact of these problems and rewards may be altered. With trends toward reverse migration now well established, the zeitgeist is now well suited to beginning a systematic examination of the rural experience.

References

Colliver, M. C., & Warner, P. D. *Appalachian values: A longitudinal analysis.* Paper presented at the meeting of the Rural Sociological Society, Burlington, Vermont, August 1979.

Darley, J., & Latané, B. Bystander intervention into emergencies: Diffusion of responsibility. *Journal of Personality and Social Psychology,* 1968, *8,* 377–383.

Epstein, S. The stability of behavior: II. Implications for psychological research. *American Psychologist*, 1980, *35*, 790–806.

Ford, T. R. The passing of provincialism. In T. R. Ford (Ed.), *The Southern Appalachian Region: A Survey*. Lexington: University of Kentucky Press, 1962.

Gotts, E. E. *Distinguishing characteristics of Appalachian children and families: Some findings and needs for further study*. Paper presented at the First Annual Conference on Appalachian Children and Families, Institute, West Virginia, June 1980.

Havelock, R. G. *Planning for innovation through dissemination and utilization of knowledge*. Ann Arbor, Mich.: Center for Research on Utilization of Knowledge, Institute for Social Research, 1969.

Heller, P. L., & Quesada, G. M. Rural familism: An interregional analysis. *Rurual Sociology*, 1977, *42*, 220–240.

Korte, C. Urban-nonurban differences in social behavior and social psychological models of urban impact. *Journal of Social Issues*, 1980, *36*(3), 29–51.

Lee, G. R., & Lassey, M. L. Rural-urban differences among the elderly: Economic, social, and subjective factors. *Journal of Social Issues*, 1980, *36*(2), 62–74.

Lichter, D. T., Heaton, T. B., & Fuguitt, G. V. Trends in the selectivity of migration between metropolitan and nonmetropolitan areas: 1955–1975. *Rural Sociology*, 1979, *44*, 645–666.

Nelson, H. M., & Frost, E. Residence, anomic, and receptivity to education among Southern Appalachian Presbyterians. *Rural Sociology*, 1971, *36*, 521–532.

Photiadis, J. D., & Schwarzweller, H. K. *Change in rural Appalachia: Implications for action programs*. Philadelphia: University of Pennsylvania Press, 1970.

Reiss, D. Intimacy and problem-solving: An automated procedure for testing a theory of consensual experience in families. *Archives of General Psychiatry*, 1971, *25*, 442–455. (a)

Reiss, D. Varities of consensual experience, I: A theory for relating family interaction to individual thinking. *Family Process*, 1971, *10*, 1–27. (b)

Rogers, E. M., & Burdge, R. J. *Social change in rural societies* (2nd ed.). Englewood Cliffs, N.J.: Prentice-Hall, 1972.

Rogers, E. M., & Shoemaker, F. F. *Communication of innovations* (2nd ed.). New York: Free Press, 1971.

Shaefer, E. S. A circumplex model for maternal behavior. *Journal of Abnormal and Social Psychology*, 1959, *59*, 226–235.

Tremblay, K. R., Jr., & Dunlap, R. E. Rural-urban residence and concern with environmental quality: A replication and extension. *Rural Sociology*, 1978, *43*, 474–491.

Index